Study Guide

Nick Noble
Miami University

MACROECONOMICS
Second Edition

R. Glenn Hubbard
Anthony O'Brien

PEARSON

Prentice
Hall

Upper Saddle River, New Jersey 07458

VP/Editorial Director: Natalie Anderson
Acquisitions Editor: David Alexander
Senior Development Editor: Lena Buonanno
Project Manager: Christina Volpe
Associate Managing Editor: Suzanne DeWorken
Senior Operations Specialist: Arnold Vila

Pearson Prentice Hall[TM] **is a trademark of Pearson Education, Inc.**

10 9 8 7 6 5 4 3 2 1

ISBN-13: 978-0-13-235683-1
ISBN-10:   0-13-235683-X

Contents

(The numbers in parentheses indicate the combined volume chapters.)

Preface

Why You Should Use the Study Guide

This Study Guide has been written for use with *Macroeconomics, Second Edition,* by R. Glenn Hubbard and Anthony Patrick O'Brien. The textbook and Study Guide both apply economic principles to real-world business and policy examples. The Study Guide summarizes the material covered in the main text and provides you with additional exercises to help you practice interpreting graphs, analyzing problems, and applying the economic concepts you learn to real-life situations. The Study Guide will be especially helpful to you if this is your first course in economics. You can use many of the key concepts you will learn in other economics and business courses you take.

Study Guide Contents

Each of the 18 chapters of the Study Guide contains the following components:

1. Chapter Summary

A brief summary of the material in the textbook.

2. Learning Objectives

Several learning objectives appear at the beginning of each textbook chapter. These learning objectives are listed in the Study Guide along with a brief description.

3. Chapter Review

This offers you a synopsis of each of the sections in each chapter. Reading the Chapter Reviews is a great way to reinforce your understanding of the material in the textbook and prepare for examinations.

4. Helpful Study Hints

These are found in the Chapter Review. There is at least one *Hint* for each major chapter section. The *Hints* will help you understand economic principles and their application through the use of examples that are different from those in the textbook. *Hints* also refer you to features in the textbook – for example, *Solved Problems*, *Making the Connection*, and end-of-chapter *Problems and Applications* – that relate to the topics covered in the Chapter Review.

5. Solved Problems

The textbook includes worked-out problems, usually two or three per chapter, each of which is tied to one of the learning objectives. Each of the Study Guide chapters includes one or more additional Solved Problems.

6. Key Terms

Each of the corresponding textbook chapter's bold key terms is defined.

7. Self-Test

This section of the Guide will help you prepare for quizzes and exams. There are 40 multiple-choice questions, five short answer questions and 15 true/false questions for each chapter. The answers to all questions appear at the end of the Self-Test.

More Study Resources for You

Here are two other resources you can use in addition to this Study Guide to help you understand economic concepts and build your skills solving problems and exercises

MyEconLab, located at www.myeconlab.com, puts you in control of your learning through a collection of testing, practice, and study tools tied to the online, interactive version of the textbook and other media resources.

Within MyEconLab's structured environment, you practice what you learn, test your understanding, and pursue a personalized Study Plan generated from your performance on Sample Tests and tests created by your instructor. MyEconLab has the following key features:

- Sample Tests, two per chapter
- Personal Study Plan
- Tutorial Instruction
- Graphing Tool

Sample Tests

Two Sample Tests for each chapter are pre-loaded in MyEconLab, enabling you to practice what you have learned, test your understanding, and identify areas in which you need to do further work. You can study on your own, or you can complete assignments created by your instructor.

Personal Study Plan

Based on your performance on tests, MyEconLab generates a personal Study Plan that shows where you need further study. The *Study Plan* consists of a series of additional practice exercises with detailed feedback and guided solutions and keyed to other tutorial resources.

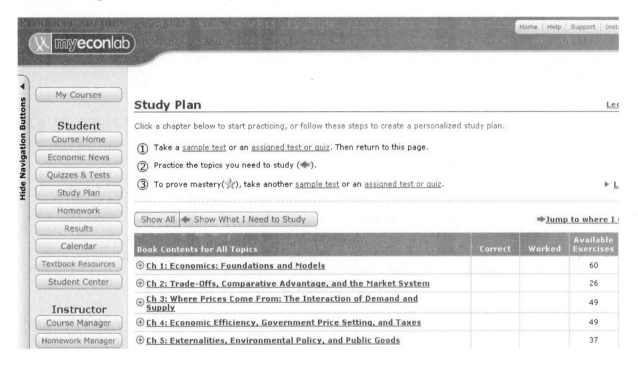

Tutorial Instruction

Launched from many of the exercises in the *Study Plan*, MyEconLab provides tutorial instruction in the form of step-by-step solutions and other media-based explanations.

Graphing Tool

A graphing tool is integrated into the Tests and Study Plan exercises to enable you to create and manipulate graphs. This feature helps you understand how concepts, numbers, and graphs connect.

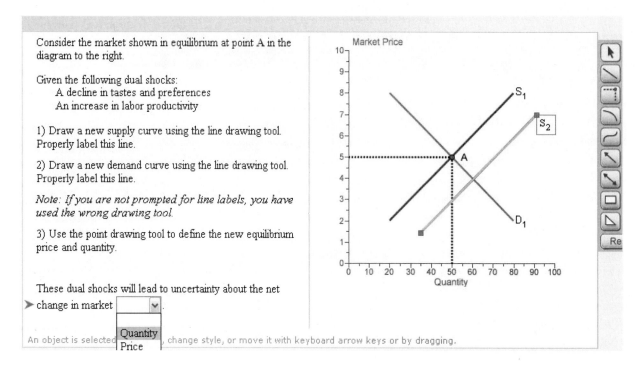

Additional MyEconLab Tools

MyEconLab also includes the following additional features:

1. **Economics in the News**—weekly news article updates during the school year of news items with links to sources for further reading and discussion questions.
2. **eText**—while working in the Study Plan or completing homework assignments, part of the tutorial resources available is a link directly to the relevant page of the text so the student can review the appropriate material to help them complete the exercise.
3. **Glossary**—a searchable version of the textbook glossary with additional examples and links to related terms.
4. **Glossary Flashcards**—every key term is available as a flashcard, allowing students to quiz themselves on vocabulary from one or more chapters at a time.
5. **Ask the Author**—email economic related questions to the author.
6. **Research Navigator (CourseCompass version only)**—extensive help on the research process and four exclusive databases of credible and reliable source material, including *The New York Times*, the *Financial Times*, and peer-reviewed journals.

Vango Notes

Study on the go with VangoNotes (**www.VangoNotes.com**), detailed chapter reviews in downloadable MP3 format. Now wherever you are and whatever you're doing, you can study on the go by listening to the following for each chapter of your textbook:

- Big Ideas: Your "need to know" for each chapter
- Practice Questions: A gut check for the Big Ideas—tells you if you need to keep studying
- Key Terms: Audio "flashcards"—help you review key concepts and terms
- Rapid Review: Quick-drill session—use it right before your test
- *VangoNotes* are **flexible**: Download all the material (or only the chapters you need) directly to your player. And *VangoNotes* are **efficient**: Use them in your car, at the gym, walking to class, wherever you go. So get yours today, and get studying.

Study Tips

1. *Read the textbook chapter – but don't just read the chapter.* To do well in your economics course, you must learn to apply what you learn and not just memorize definitions and read graphs. Both the textbook and the Study Guide have a number of features that allow you to apply and understand what you learn. Take advantage of these learning aids. Economics is a participant sport, not a spectator sport. Use your pencil. Draw graphs, don't just look at them. Try the calculations. Use your calculator.

2. *Attend class and ask questions.* Take this course as seriously as your instructor does. Taking days off will not help you do well in any course and is poor preparation for your life after graduation. Many students are hesitant to ask questions during or outside of classroom meetings because they feel they are the only ones who do not understand a topic (this is almost never true) or that their instructors feel they have better things to do (this is almost never true as well). Your instructor will appreciate the effort you make to learn what can be a challenging subject.

3. *Don't leave the subject in the classroom.* The key to doing well in your course is to understand how to apply economic concepts in real-world situations. Learning economics is similar to learning a new language. You will become fluent in the economic way of thinking only after you learn to recognize and apply concepts found in newspaper articles, magazines, and everyday conversation.

4. *Organize a study group.* If possible, study with other students in your class. Participating in a study group can help you learn economics – students will bring different insights to the group – and make learning more enjoyable. Explaining a topic to a friend will help you discover areas where you need to spend more study time.

Economics: Foundations and Models

Chapter Summary

People must make choices as they try to attain their goals. These choices usually mean that people must accept trade-offs among various competing objectives due to society's limited resources. **Economics** is the study of the choices people make to attain their goods, given their scarce resources. Economists assume that people are rational, respond to economic incentives, and make decisions at the margin. Economists construct **models**, simplified versions of some aspect of economic life, to analyze economic issues such as how buyers and sellers make decisions.

Every society faces the economic problem of limited resources. Therefore, society can produce only limited quantities of goods and services. Societies face trade-offs and must consider the opportunity costs of decisions, particularly when answering the three fundamental questions any economy must answer:

1. *What* goods and services will be produced?
2. *How* will the goods and services be produced?
3. *Who* will receive the goods and services?

Societies organize their economies in two main ways to answer these questions. A society can have a **centrally planned economy** characterized by extensive government decision making. Or, a society can have a market economy where resource allocation is determined by the decisions of households and firms interacting in markets. All high-income democracies have market economies or mixed economies. A **mixed economy** is a market-based economy with some government intervention. Market economies tend to allocate resources more efficiently than do centrally planned economies, but efficient outcomes may not be perceived as fair. Determining what is a fair or equitable outcome calls for the application of **normative analysis** – *what ought to be*. **Positive analysis** is concerned with *what is*. While most or all economists can agree on the results of positive economic analysis, their opinions often differ on *what ought to be*.

Microeconomics is the study of how individual choices are made by households, firms, and the government. **Macroeconomics** is the study of the economy as a whole.

The Appendix to Chapter 1 provides a review of basic mathematical tools and techniques that will be applied through the textbook.

Learning Objectives

When you finish this chapter, you should be able to:

1. **Explain these three important ideas: People are rational. People respond to incentives. Optimal decisions are made at the margin.** Economists use these ideas to analyze the way people make decisions. These ideas are especially important in analyzing what happens in markets, which is the primary focus of economic analysis.

2. **Discuss how an economy answers these questions: *What* goods and services will be produced? *How* will the goods and services be produced? *Who* will receive the goods and services?** Every society must answer these questions because the resources available to produce goods and services are scarce. Even nations with abundant supplies of natural resources cannot produce enough goods and services to satisfy the desires of all their citizens. Therefore, societies face trade-offs. Producing more of one good or service means producing less of another good or service.

3. **Understand the role of models in economic analysis.** Economic models are created by applying the scientific method to economic data. These models are simplified versions of reality used to analyze real-world issues. Economic models are used to explain issues such as whether or not outsourcing has been good or bad for the U.S. economy. This is a complex question that requires more than one model to explain different aspects of the issue.

4. **Distinguish between microeconomics and macroeconomics.** Economic decision-making is grouped into two areas. Microeconomics is the study of how households and firms make choices, interact in markets, and how the government attempts to influence their choices. Macroeconomics studies the economy as a whole, including topics such as inflation, unemployment, and economic growth.

5. **Become familiar with important economic terms.** This chapter includes descriptions and definitions of important terms that will be used in other chapters of the textbook.

Appendix: Review the use of graphs and formulas. Graphs simplify economic ideas and make the ideas concrete so they can be applied to real-world problems. Whether or not your instructor assigns the appendix, it is a good idea to read it because it will help you understand how to read and interpret the many graphs that appear throughout the book.

Chapter Review

Chapter Opener: What Happens When U.S. Firms Move to China? (pages 2-3)

In 2004, executives of 3Com Corporation decided to build a new network switch for corporate security systems in China. Part of the rationale for these executives was to save money: Chinese engineers receive lower salaries than engineers in the United States. 3Com is one of many U.S. firms that have established manufacturing, service, and design operations in other countries. This practice is often called *outsourcing*. An understanding of economics will help you to understand outsourcing and many other important issues that you hear in the news and in classes.

The textbook describes how economics is used to answer many important questions, including whether or not a firm should outsource. All of these questions represent a basic economic fact of life: people must make choices as they try to attain their goals. These choices occur because of scarcity, which is the most fundamental economic concept. The resources available to any society – for example, land, and labor – to produce the goods and services its citizens want are limited. Society has to choose which goods and services will be produced and who will receive them.

📖 Helpful Study Hint

At the beginning of each chapter in this textbook is a chapter opener that describes an economic issue facing one or more real-world companies. You will find other special features throughout the book. For instance *An Inside Look* appears at the end of each chapter. This feature analyzes a topic related to the chapter opener using a magazine or newspaper article. Questions are included at the end of each article to test your knowledge of the topic. In this chapter, *An Inside Look* discusses whether the United States should be concerned about competition from high-tech firms in China and India. The article argues that fear of competition from China and India is exaggerated because the United States has many advantages that should allow it retain many high-skilled, high wage jobs.

    The *Economics in YOUR Life!* feature asks whether it is likely that you will experience a job loss due to outsourcing. Think about this question as you read the chapter. The authors will answer this question at the end of the chapter.

1.1 LEARNING OBJECTIVE

1.1 Three Key Economic Ideas (pages 4-7)

Learning Objective 1 Explain these three important ideas: People are rational. People respond to incentives. Optimal decisions are made at the margin.

Economics examines how people interact in markets. A **market** refers to a group of buyers and sellers of a good or service and the institution or arrangement by which they come together to trade. Economists make three important assumptions about the way people interact in markets. First, people are rational. This means that buyers and sellers use all available information to achieve their goals. Second, people act in response to economic incentives. Third, optimal decisions are made at the margin. The terms "marginal benefit" and "marginal cost" refer to the additional benefits and costs of a decision. Economists reason that the best, or optimal, decision is to continue any activity up to the point where the marginal benefit (or *MB*) equals the marginal cost (*MC*). In symbols, we can write *MB* = *MC*.

📖 Helpful Study Hint

The image many people have of a market is a supermarket, neighborhood store, or shopping mall. But some markets do not have an easily identifiable image. Many people make online purchases with their computers. In these markets, buyers and sellers do not see each other and may be located hundreds of miles from one another. For some goods (for example, books and CDs), is it not necessary for buyers to see or test merchandise before they buy it. For other goods (clothing, food, automobiles), some personal contact is important. In many of these cases, sellers have a physical location to which buyers must travel to try out the product. There are also markets in which sellers travel to their buyers. Pharmaceutical salespersons who visit doctors' offices are one well-known example.

In the movie *Wall Street,* Gordon Gekko, a ruthless businessman played by Michael Douglas, proclaims "Greed is good." You should not assume that the phrase "people respond to economic incentives" means that people are greedy. The phrase "people respond to economic incentives" is an objective statement or a statement shown to be true rather than a belief or opinion. In contrast, Gordon Gekko's statement was subjective; he stated his opinion that "greed is good." Economists do not believe people are motivated solely by monetary incentives. Many people voluntarily devote their time and financial resources to friends, family members and charities.

See the ***Making the Connection*** "Will Women Have More Babies if the Government Pays Them To?" for a discussion of how economic incentives may alter people's behavior. Some countries have been experiencing a decline in birth rates, which will mean a decrease in population growth and future tax revenues. In some countries, the birth rate has fallen below the replacement level, which means that the population will actually begin shrinking. Some countries have begun to provide incentives to encourage women to have babies. There is evidence that this is working in Estonia, but it may be too early into the program to know if it will be successful.

The first ***Solved Problem*** is at the end of this section of the textbook. Each ***Solved Problem*** helps you understand one of the chapter's learning objectives. The authors use a step-by-step process to show how you can solve the problem. Additional Solved Problems, different from those that appear in the textbook, are included in each chapter of this Study Guide. ***Solved Problem 1-1*** in the textbook is an example of how Apple can use marginal analysis to decide whether to increase output. To make this decision, Apple must compare the additional benefit – the margin benefit – generated by producing the extra output to the additional cost – marginal cost – from the production of that output. If the additional (or marginal) benefit is greater than the marginal cost, then Apple should produce more iPods.

1.2 The Economic Problem That Every Society Must Solve (pages 8-11)

Learning Objective 2 Discuss how an economy answers these questions: *What* goods and services will be produced? *How* will the goods and services be produced? *Who* will receive the goods and services?

The basic economic problem any society faces is that it has only a limited amount of economic resources and so can produce only a limited amount of goods and services. Societies face **trade-offs** when answering the three fundamental economic questions:

1. *What* goods and services will be produced?
2. *How* will the goods and services be produced?
3. *Who* will receive the goods and services?

Societies organize their economies in two main ways. A **centrally planned economy** is an economy in which the government decides how economic resources will be allocated. From 1917 to 1991, the Soviet Union was the most important centrally planned economy. Today Cuba and North Korea are among the few remaining centrally planned economies. A **market economy** is an economy in which the decisions of households and firms interacting in markets allocate economic resources. The United States, Canada, Western Europe, and Japan all have market economies. Privately owned firms must produce and sell goods and services consumers want to stay in business. An individual's income is determined by the payments he receives for what he has to sell.

📖 Helpful Study Hint

In a planned economy, government officials or "planners" are responsible for determining how much of each good to produce, who should produce it, and where it should be produced. In contrast, in a market economy no government official determines how much corn, wheat, or potatoes should be produced. Individual producers and consumers interact in markets for these goods to determine the answers to *What*? *How*? and *Who*? The role of government in a market economy is similar to that of an umpire in a baseball game. Government officials can pass and enforce laws that allow people to act in certain ways but do not participate directly in markets as consumers or producers.

The high rates of unemployment and business bankruptcies of the Great Depression caused a dramatic increase in government intervention in the economy in the United States and other market economies. Some government intervention is designed to raise the incomes of the elderly, the sick, and people with limited skills. In recent years, government intervention has expanded to meet social goals such as protection of the environment and the promotion of civil rights. The expanded role of government in market economies has led most economists to argue that the United States and other nations have **mixed economies** rather than market economies.

Market economies tend to be more efficient than planned economies because market economies promote competition and voluntary exchange. There are two types of efficiency. **Productive efficiency** occurs when a good or service is produced at the lowest possible cost. **Allocative efficiency** is a state of the economy in which production represents consumer preferences. Specifically, every good or service is produced up to the point where the marginal benefit that the last unit produced provides to consumers is equal to the marginal cost of producing it. Inefficiencies do occur in markets for three main reasons. First, it may take time for firms to achieve productive efficiency. Second, governments may reduce efficiency by interfering with voluntary exchanges in markets. Third, production of some goods may harm the environment when firms ignore the costs of environmental damage.

Society may not find efficient economic outcomes to be the most desirable outcomes. Many people prefer economic outcomes they consider fair or equitable even if these outcomes are less efficient. Equity is the fair distribution of economic benefits.

📖 Helpful Study Hint

There are many examples of government regulation on private markets in the United States. The sale and use of cocaine and other drugs is illegal, and the sale of cigarettes is allowed only to people 18 years and older. Between 1920 and 1933, the production and sale of alcoholic beverages was also illegal in the United States.

Extra Solved Problem 1-2

Chapter 1 in the textbook includes a Solved Problem. Here is an extra Solved Problem to help you build your skills solving economic problems.

Supports Learning Objective 2: Discuss how an economy answers these questions: *What goods and services will be produced? How will the goods and services be produced? Who will receive the goods and services?*

Giving Advice to New Government Leaders

Suppose that a developing nation is experiencing a change in government leadership. Prior to this change the nation had a centrally planned economy. The new leaders are willing to try a different system if they can be convinced that it will yield better results. They hire an economist from a nation with a market economy to advise them and will order their citizens to follow this advisor's recommendations for change. The economist suggests that a market economy replace central planning to answer the nation's economic questions (*what*, *how* and *who*?).

a.   What will the economist suggest the leaders order their citizens to do?

b.   Do you believe the leaders and citizens will accept the economist's suggestions?

SOLVING THE PROBLEM

Step 1:   **Review the chapter material.**
The problem concerns the choice of economic system a nation must make, so you may want to review the section "Centrally Planned Economies versus Market Economies," which begins on page 9 in the textbook.

Step 2:   **What will the economist suggest the leaders order their citizens to do?**
Market economies allow members of households to follow their self-interest in selecting which occupation to enter and which goods and services to purchase. Market economies also allow privately owned firms to follow their self-interest in selecting which goods and services to produce. Therefore, the economist would ask the leaders of the poor country to not issue any orders. Government officials should ordinarily not attempt to influence individual decisions made in markets.

Step 3:   **Do you believe the leaders and citizens will accept the economist's suggestions?**
Even democratically elected rulers, especially those with previous experience with significant government involvement in the nation's resource allocation, will find it difficult to accept the

new system. They may wonder how self-interested individuals will produce and distribute goods and services so as to promote the welfare of the entire nation. This new system requires a significant reduction in the government's power to influence people's lives. History has shown that government officials are often reluctant to give up this power. Acceptance is most likely to occur when the rulers have some knowledge of the successful operation of a market economy in other countries. Most ordinary citizens are more likely to accept the economist's suggestions because they will have more freedom to pursue their own economic goals. However, those who benefited from the previous system will resist change.

1.3 LEARNING OBJECTIVE

1.3 Economic Models (pages 11-15)

Learning Objective 3   Understand the role of models in economic analysis.

Models are simplified versions of reality used to analyze real-world situations. To develop a model, economists generally follow five steps.

1. Decide on the assumptions to be used in developing the model.
2. Formulate a testable hypothesis.
3. Use economic data to test the hypothesis.
4. Revise the model if it fails to explain well the economic data.
5. Retain the revised model to help answer similar economic questions in the future.

Models rely on assumptions because models must be simplified to be useful. For example, models make behavioral assumptions about the motives of consumers and firms. Economists assume that consumers will buy the goods and services that will maximize their satisfaction and that firms will produce the goods and services that will maximize their profits.

An **economic variable** is something measurable that can have different values, such as the wages of software programmers. A *hypothesis* is a statement that may be correct or incorrect about an economic variable. An economic hypothesis usually states a causal relationship where a change in one variable causes a change in another variable. For example, "outsourcing leads to lower wages for software programmers" means that an increase in the amount of outsourcing will reduce the wages of software programmers. **Positive analysis** is analysis concerned with what is and involves questions that can be estimated. **Normative analysis** is analysis concerned with what ought to be and involves questions of values and basic assumptions.

📖 Helpful Study Hint

For a good explanation of what a model is and how models are used in economics, read the first section of the Appendix to Chapter 1.

A feature introduced in Chapter 1 of the text – ***Making the Connection*** – describes a debate between two prominent economists over outsourcing. ***Making the Connection*** features in other chapters relate concepts described in the text to recent business stories.

Positive economic analysis deals with statements that can be proved correct or incorrect by examining facts. If your instructor stated that "It is snowing outside," it would be easy to determine whether this statement is true or false by looking out a window. Normative analysis concerns statements of belief or opinion. If your instructor wants to go skiing that evening and states that "It *should* be snowing outside today," you could not prove the statement wrong because it is a statement of *opinion*. It is important to recognize the difference between these two types of statements. The feature *Don't Let This Happen to You!* appears in each chapter to alert you to mistakes often made by economics students. To reinforce the difference between positive and normative statements, review *Don't Let This Happen To YOU!* "Don't Confuse Positive Analysis with Normative Analysis," where the minimum wage law is discussed. Positive analysis can show us the effects of the minimum wage law on the economy, but it cannot tell us whether the policy is good or bad. Nor can positive analysis tell us whether we should increase or decrease the minimum wage. The discussion of whether a policy is good or bad will depend on an individual's values and experiences and falls under the realm of normative analysis.

1.4 LEARNING OBJECTIVE

1.4   Microeconomics and Macroeconomics (page 15)

Learning Objective 4   Distinguish between microeconomics and macroeconomics.

Microeconomics is the study of how households and firms make choices, how they interact in markets, and how the government attempts to influence their choices. **Macroeconomics** is the study of the economy as a whole, including topics such as inflation, unemployment, and economic growth.

1.5 LEARNING OBJECTIVE

1.5   A Preview of Important Economic Terms (pages 15-16)

Learning Objective 5   Become familiar with important economic terms.

This chapter introduces twelve economic terms that will each be covered in depth in future chapters. Those terms are: entrepreneur, innovation, technology, firm, goods, services, revenue, profit, household, factors of production, capital, and human capital.

📖 Helpful Study Hint

At the beginning of the chapter, you read the *Economics in YOUR Life!* question: "Are You Likely to Lose Your Job to Outsourcing?" The authors answer the question at the end of the chapter. Jobs are continuously created and eliminated in the U.S. economy. Only a small percentage of jobs are outsourced, so, even though you are likely to lose your job once or twice during your career, it will probably *not* be due to outsourcing.

Appendix

Using Graphs and Formulas (pages 24-35)

LEARNING OBJECTIVE: Review the use of graphs and formulas.

Graphs of One Variable

Bar charts, pie charts and time-series graphs are alternative ways to display data visually. Figures 1A-1 and 1A-2 illustrate how relationships are often easier to understand with graphs than with words or tables alone.

Graphs of Two Variables

Both microeconomics and macroeconomics use two-variable graphs extensively. You need to understand how to measure the slope of a straight line drawn in a graph. The slope of a straight line can be measured between any two points on a line because the slope of a straight line has a constant value, so we don't need to worry about the value of the slope changing as we move up and down the line. Slope can be measured as the change in the value measured on the vertical axis divided by the change in the value measured on the horizontal axis. In symbols, the slope formula is written as $\Delta y/\Delta x$. The formula is also described as "rise over run." The usual custom is to place the variable y on the graph's vertical axis and the variable x the horizontal axis. If the slope is negative, then the two variables are inversely related. If the slope is positive, then the two variables are positively related. We can show the effect of more than two variables in a graph by shifting the line representing the relationship between the first two variables. For example, we can draw a graph showing the effect of a change in the price of pizza on the quantity of pizza demand during a given week. We can then shift this line to show the effect of an change in the price of hamburgers on the quantity of pizza demanded.

Formulas

The formula for a percentage change of a variable over time (or growth rate) is:

$$\frac{Value_2 - Value_1}{Value_1} \times 100\%$$

The formula for the area of a rectangle is Base x Height. The formula for the area of a triangle is ½ x Base x Height.

Key Terms

Allocative efficiency. A state of the economy in which production is in accordance with consumer preferences; in particular, every good or service is produced up to the point where the last unit provides a marginal benefit to society equal to the marginal cost of producing it.

Centrally planned economy. An economy in which the government decides how economic resources will be allocated.

Economic model. A simplified version of reality used to analyze real-world economic situations.

Economic variable. Something measurable that can have different values, such as the wages of software programmers.

Economics. The study of the choices people make to attain their goals, given their scarce resources.

Equity. The fair distribution of economic benefits.

Macroeconomics.   The study of the economy as a whole, including topics such as inflation, unemployment, and economic growth.

Marginal analysis. Analysis that involves comparing marginal benefits and marginal costs.

Market. A group of buyers and sellers of a good or service and the institution or arrangement by which they come together to trade.

Market economy. An economy in which the decisions of households and firms interacting in markets allocate economic resources.

Microeconomics. The study of how households and firms make choices, how they interact in markets, and how the government attempts to influence their choices.

Mixed economy. An economy in which most economic decisions result from the interaction of buyers and sellers in markets but in which the government plays a significant role in the allocation of resources.

Opportunity cost. The highest-valued alternative that must be given up to engage in an activity.

Normative analysis. Analysis concerned with what ought to be.

Positive analysis. Analysis concerned with what is.

Productive efficiency. The situation in which a good or service is produced at the lowest possible cost.

Scarcity. The situation in which unlimited wants exceed the limited resources available to fulfill those wants.

Trade-off. The idea that because of scarcity, producing more of one good or service means producing less of another good or service.

Voluntary exchange. The situation that occurs when both the buyer and the seller of a product are made better off by the transaction.

Self-Test

(Answers are provided at the end of the Self-Test.)

Multiple-Choice Questions

1. Which of the following questions could be answered using economics?
   a. "How are the prices of goods and services determined?"
   b. "How does pollution affect the economy, and how should government policy deal with these effects?"
   c. "Why do firms engage in international trade, and how do government policies affect international trade?"
   d. All of the above are economic questions.

2. Which of the following statements best describes scarcity?
   a. Scarcity studies the choices people make to attain their goals.
   b. Scarcity is a situation where unlimited wants exceed limited resources.
   c. Scarcity is an imbalance between buyers and sellers in a specific market.
   d. Scarcity refers to a lack of tradeoffs.

3. When you think of an arrangement or institution that brings buyers and sellers of a good or service together, what are you thinking of?
   a. Marginal analysis
   b. A market
   c. Scarcity
   d. Rational behavior

4. Fill in the blanks. In economics, as well as in life, optimal decisions are made _____.
   a. once all costs have been considered
   b. only when all benefits have been considered
   c. in their totality
   d. at the margin

5. In Solved Problem 1-1: "Should Apple produce an additional 300,000 iPods?" which of the concepts below is most applicable in solving the problem?
   a. The concept of what a market is
   b. Rational behavior and how people respond to economic incentives
   c. Marginal analysis
   d. The concept of scarcity and tradeoffs

6. Which of the following is not among the fundamental economic questions that every society must solve?
   a. What goods and services will be produced?
   b. How will the goods and services be produced?
   c. What goods and services will be exchanged?
   d. Who will receive the goods and services produced?

7. What types of economies require that we answer the questions of what, how, and for whom to produce goods and services?
   a. Market economies
   b. Centrally planned economies
   c. Mixed economies
   d. All of the above

8. In what type of economy does the government decide how economic resources will be allocated?
   a. In a market economy
   b. In a mixed economy
   c. In a centrally planned economy
   d. In none of the above

9. Which of the following is the best classification for the economies of the United States, Canada, Japan, and Western Europe?
   a. Market economies
   b. Mixed economies
   c. Centrally planned economies
   d. None of the above

10. Which of the following terms best relates to a fair distribution of economic benefits?
    a. Productive efficiency
    b. Allocative efficiency
    c. Voluntary exchange
    d. Equity

11. Which of the following is achieved when a good or service is produced up to the point where the marginal benefit to consumers is equal to the marginal cost of producing it?
    a. Productive efficiency
    b. Allocative efficiency
    c. Equality
    d. Equity

12. Which of the following terms summarizes the situation in which a buyer and a seller exchange a product in a market and, as a result, both are made better off by the transaction?
    a. Productive efficiency
    b. Allocative efficiency
    c. Voluntary exchange
    d. Equity

13. What does an economy achieve by producing a good or service at the least possible cost?
    a. Productive efficiency
    b. Allocative efficiency
    c. Voluntary exchange
    d. Equity

14. Which of the following best describes the characteristics of models used in economics?
    a. Models are approximations to reality that capture as many details as possible.
    b. Models are usually complex abstractions of reality that simulate practical problems.
    c. Models are demonstrations of how economic concepts and theories accurately predict real situations.
    d. Models are simplifications of reality that include only essential elements and exclude less relevant details.

15. Which of the following is not an essential component of an economic model?
    a. Assumptions
    b. Hypotheses
    c. Variables
    d. Normative statements

16. What is the purpose of an economic hypothesis?
    a. To establish a behavioral assumption
    b. To establish a causal relationship
    c. To make a statement based on fact
    d. To determine the validity of statistical analyses used in testing a model

17. What type of economic analysis is concerned with the way things ought to be?
    a. Positive analysis
    b. Marginal analysis
    c. Normative analysis
    d. Rational behavior

18. What type of statement would "A minimum wage actually reduces employment" be considered?
    a. A positive statement
    b. A marginal statement
    c. A normative statement
    d. An irrational conclusion

19. Which of the following is an example of a positive question?
    a. Should the university offer free parking to students?
    b. Should the university provide more financial aid assistance to students?
    c. If the college increased tuition, will class sizes decline?
    d. Should the college cut tuition to stimulate enrollments?

20. Which of the following questions can be answered using normative economic reasoning?
    a. If the college offers free parking, will more students drive to campus?
    b. If the college provided more financial aid, would more students go to college?
    c. If the college hires better qualified instructors, will more students attend?
    d. Should the college cut tuition in order to stimulate enrollments?

21. Which of the following involves an estimation of the benefits and costs of a particular action?
    a. Positive economics
    b. Normative economics
    c. The market mechanism
    d. An irrational conclusion

22. What type of assessment is one where a person's values and political views form part of that assessment?
    a. A positive assessment
    b. A normative assessment
    c. A microeconomic assessment
    d. A macroeconomic assessment

23. Fill in the blank: _____ is the study of how households and businesses make choices.
    a. Microeconomics
    b. Macroeconomics
    c. A market mechanism
    d. Marginal analysis

24. Which of the following covers the study of topics such as inflation or unemployment?
    a. Microeconomics
    b. Macroeconomics
    c. Both microeconomics and macroeconomics give equal emphasis to these problems.
    d. None of the above

25. What is the name given to the development of a new good or a new process for making a good?
    a. An invention
    b. An innovation
    c. Entrepreneurship
    d. Capital

26. What is the name given to the practical application of an invention?
    a. A model
    b. An innovation
    c. Voluntary exchange
    d. Capital

27. What is the stock of computers, factory buildings, and machine tools used to produce goods better known as?
    a. Physical capital
    b. Technology
    c. Innovation
    d. Goods and services

28. Human capital is similar to physical capital because
    a. both represent the value of money as a productive resource.
    b. both are financed by the profits of firms.
    c. both are productive resources.
    d. both represent changes in technology.

29. Which of the following graphs shown below is the graph of a single variable?

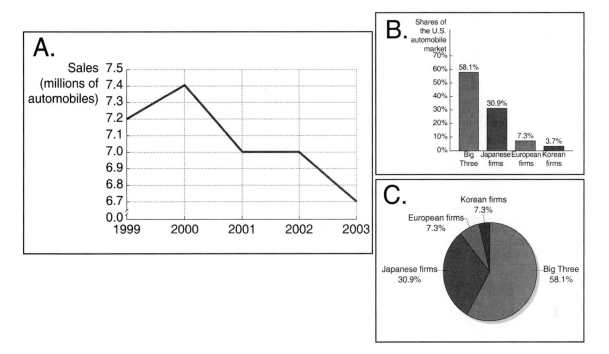

a. A
b. B
c. C
d. All of the above.

30. Which of the following is a graph of the relationship between two variables?

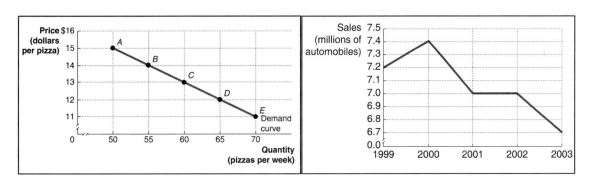

a. The graph on the left
b. The graph on the right
c. Both graphs
d. Neither graph

31. Fill in the blanks. The slope of a straight line equals the change in value on the _____ axis _____ by the change in the value of the other axis between any two points on the line.
a. horizontal; multiplied
b. horizontal; divided
c. vertical; multiplied
d. vertical; divided

32. Refer to the graph below. What is the value of the slope of this line?

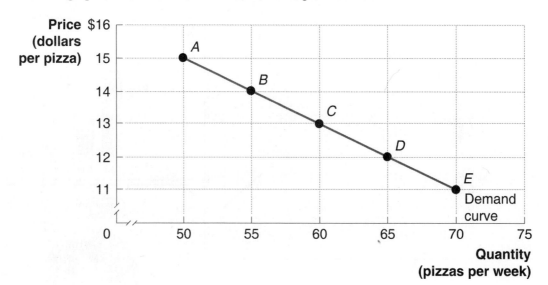

    a. −5
    b. −1/5
    c. −1
    d. There is insufficient information to compute the slope of this line.

33. Refer to the graph below. Which variable explains why the line shifts to the right?

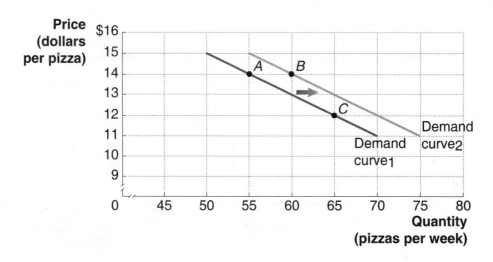

    a. The price of pizza
    b. The quantity of pizza
    c. A third variable other than the price or quantity of pizza
    d. All of the above.

34. Refer to the graph below. How many variables are involved in explaining the move from point *A* to point *C* on this graph?

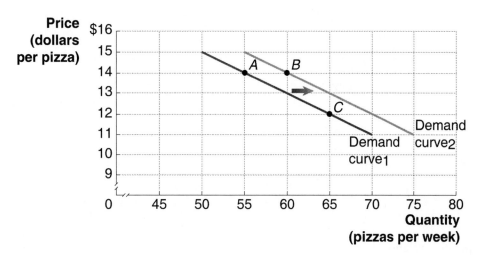

a. One
b. Two
c. Three
d. More than three, at least four.

35. Suppose that there are three variables involved in the graph below: (1) quantity, (2) price, and (3) a third variable. Which of those variables causes the move from point *A* to point *D* in the graph?

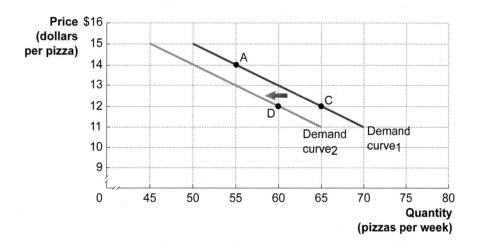

a. The first variable, quantity.
b. The second variable, price.
c. The third variable.
d. Either a. or b.

36. Refer to the graph below. What is the best descriptor of the relationship between disposable personal income and consumption spending?

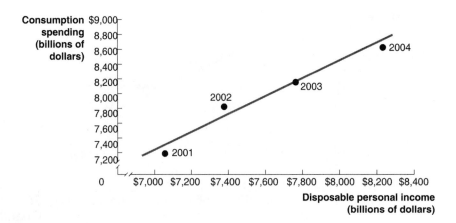

a. A positive relationship
b. A negative relationship
c. A relationship that is sometimes positive and sometimes negative
d. A relationship that may be positive and negative, but sometimes neither positive nor negative

37. Refer to the graph below. What can be said about the value of the slope of this curve?

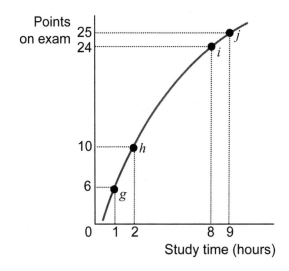

a. The value of the slope is greater between points i and j than between points g and h.
b. The value of the slope is greater between points g and h than between points i and j.
c. The value of the slope is the same between any two points along the curve.
d. It is difficult to establish the value of the slope because the relationship is not linear.

38. Let V_1 equal the value of a variable in period 1, and V_2 equal the value of the same variable in period 2. What is the rate of growth between periods 1 and 2?
a. $[(V_1 + V_2)/2] \times 100$
b. $[(V_2 - V_1)/V_1] \times 100$
c. $(V_2 - V_1)/(V_1 + V_2)$
d. $V_2 - V_1$

39. Refer to the graph below. Which of the formulas below must you apply in order to compute the grey area shown on the graph?

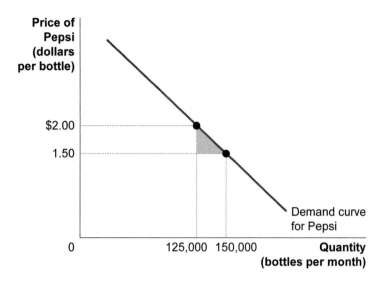

a. Base x Height
b. ½ x Base x Height
c. Both of the above
d. None of the above

40. Refer to the graph below. What is the name of the area contained in rectangle A?

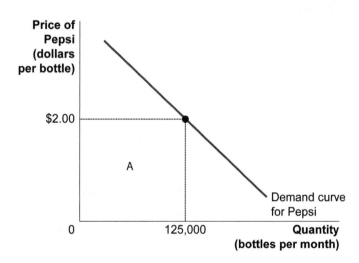

a. Total cost
b. Total revenue
c. Price
d. Average cost

41. Refer to the graph below. What is the value of the grey area shown on the graph?

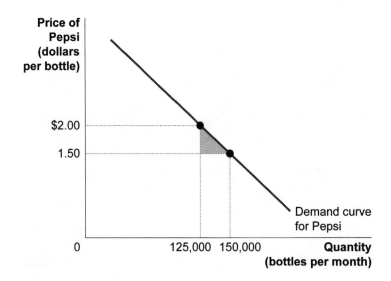

a. $300,000
b. $225,000
c. $62,500
d. $6,250

42. Refer to the graph below. What is the value of the area contained in rectangle A?

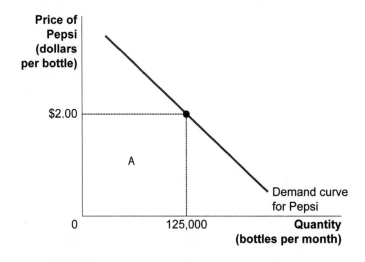

a. $2.00.
b. $125,000
c. $250,000
d. There is not enough information to determine the area.

Short Answer Questions

1. Why do economists distinguish between financial capital and physical capital?

    _____

    _____

2. Explain the difference between productive efficiency and allocative efficiency.

    _____

    _____

3. Economists rely on economic models and tests of hypotheses to analyze real-world issues. The use of models and hypothesis testing is common in the natural sciences such as physics and chemistry. Yet, economics is considered a social science, not a natural science. Why?

    _____

    _____

    _____

    _____

4. Write an example of a positive statement and an example of a normative statement.

    _____

    _____

    _____

    _____

5. Duncan Grant, a freshman economics student at John Borts University, claimed that fresh water is a necessity for all human beings. When asked by his economics instructor if he would be willing to buy a 16 ounce bottle of water for $5.00, Duncan declined. What economic principle would explain Duncan's refusal to buy something that he insists is a necessity?

    _____

    _____

True/False Questions

T F 1. Stating a hypothesis in an economic model is an example of normative analysis.

T F 2. An entrepreneur is someone who works for a government agency.

T F 3. Economists assume that human beings respond only to economic incentives.

T F 4. In a centrally planned economy the goods and services produced are always distributed equally to all citizens.

T F 5. Equity is achieved when economic benefits are equally distributed.

T F 6. A mixed economy is an economy in which the three fundamental questions (*What? How? Who?*) are answered by a mixture of consumers and producers.

T F 7. Both market economies and centrally planned economies face trade-offs when producing goods and services.

T F 8. When economists assume people are rational, this means that consumers and firms use available information in order to achieve their goals.

T F 9. Government intervention in the United States economy increased dramatically as a result of the Great Depression.

T F 10. Economists use normative analysis to argue that the minimum wage law causes unemployment.

T F 11. Microeconomics is the study of how households and firms make choices, how they interact in markets and how the government attempts to influence their choices.

T F 12. The slope of a straight line is the same at any point.

T F 13. To measure the slope of a nonlinear curve at a particular point one must draw a straight line from the origin to the point. The slope of this line is equal to the slope of the curve at that point.

T F 14. All societies face the economic problem of having a limited amount of economic resources.

T F 15. Economic models can help analyze simple real-world economic situations but are of little value in analyzing complicated economic situations.

Answers to the Self-Test

Multiple-Choice Questions

Question	Answer	Comment
1	d	In this textbook, we use economics to answer questions such as those found in all of the choices given.
2	b	This is the textbook definition of scarcity.
3	b	The question is precisely the definition of a market.
4	d	The textbook presents three important ideas: People are rational; people respond to economic incentives; optimal decisions are made at the margin.
5	c	In solving the problem, consider that optimal decisions are made at the margin. An activity should be continued to the point where the marginal benefit is equal to the marginal cost.
6	c	The three questions are: What goods and services will be produced? How will the goods and services be produced? Who will receive the goods and services?
7	d	These questions refer to the economic problem *every* society must solve.
8	c	A centrally planned economy is an economy in which the government decides how economic resources will be allocated.
9	b	A mixed economy is an economy in which most economic decisions result from the interaction of buyers and sellers in markets, but where the government plays a significant role in the allocation of resources.

10	d	Equity, or fairness, refers to the fair distribution of economic benefits.
11	b	This is a state of the economy in which production reflects consumer preferences; in particular, every good or service is produced up to the point where the last unit produced provides a marginal benefit to consumers equal to the marginal cost of producing it.
12	c	This is a situation that occurs in markets when both the buyer and the seller of a product are made better off by the transaction.
13	a	This occurs when a good or service is produced at the lowest possible cost.
14	d	Economic models are simplified versions of some aspects of economic life used to analyze an economic issue.
15	d	Normative statements are not components of an economic model.
16	b	An economic hypothesis is usually about a causal relationship, or how one thing causes another.
17	c	Normative analysis is analysis concerned with "what ought to be."
18	a	Positive statements describe "what is."
19	c	This question objectively examines a relationship between tuition and class sizes, or "what is."
20	d	This is a question of "what ought to be."
21	a	Positive analysis uses economic models to estimate gains and losses. Positive questions are questions that can be tested.
22	b	A normative statement is a matter of "what ought to be," not "what is," and this is determined by one's values and beliefs.
23	a	Microeconomics is the study of how households and businesses make choices, how they interact in markets, and how the government attempts to influence their choices.
24	b	Macroeconomics is the study of the economy as a whole, including topics such as inflation, unemployment and economic growth.
25	a	An invention is different from an innovation.
26	b	An innovation is the application of an invention.
27	a	In economics, capital refers to physical capital.
28	c	Human and physical capital are used to produce goods and services.
29	d	The bar chart, pie chart, and time series graph are all graphs of a single variable.
30	a	This graph shows the relationship between two variables: price and quantity demanded.
31	d	The slope of a line equals the value on the vertical axis divided by the value on the horizontal axis.
32	b	Along this line, the value of the slope is the same between any two points. As an example, as we move from B (55, 14) to C (60, 13), the value of rise is (13-14) = -1 and the value of the run is (55-60) = -5. Then, the value of the slope is -1/5.
33	c	Shifting a line involves taking into account more than two variables on a graph. In this case, something other than the price of pizza has changed, causing the demand curve to shift to the right, and showing the quantity of pizza demanded is greater for each of the prices shown.
34	a	The movement from A to C is explained by one and only one thing: a change in price. The (price, quantity demanded) combination at A is different from that at C, but the movement from A to C is explained by a change in only one variable: price.
35	c	A shift of the demand curve is caused by a change in something other than price, such as a change in income. For each price, quantity demanded is less than it was before.
36	a	An upward sloping line shows that the relationship between two variables is positive, i.e. the variables change in the same direction.

37	b	As you move upward along the curve, the value of the slope decreases. The slope between g and h is (10-6)/(2-1) = 4 and the slope between i and j is (25-24)/(9-8) = 1.
38	b	This is the formula for computing a percentage change.
39	b	You are computing the area of a triangle, which is ½ x Base x Height.
40	b	Total revenue equals price x quantity, which is the area of the rectangle (Base x Height).
41	d	The area of the triangle is ½ x ($2.00 - $1.50) x (150,000 – 125,000) = $6,250.
42	c	The area of the rectangle is equal to $2.00/bottle x 125,000 bottles = $250,000, which is $250,000 in total revenue.

Short Answers

1. Economists distinguish financial capital and physical capital because only physical capital (for example, machinery, tools and buildings) is a productive resource. Financial capital includes stocks, bonds, and holdings of money. Financial capital is not part of a country's capital stock, because financial capital does not produce output.

2. Productive efficiency is the situation in which a good or service is produced at the lowest possible cost. Allocative efficiency is a state of the economy in which production reflects consumer preferences. Every good or service is produced to the point at which the last unit provides a marginal benefit to consumers equal to the marginal cost of producing it.

3. Economics, unlike physics and chemistry, is a social science because it applies the use of models and hypothesis testing to the study of the interactions of people.

4. Positive statements are statements or facts, or statements that can be proven to be correct or incorrect. Example: "Abraham Lincoln was the 15ᵗʰ president of the United States." (This is a false statement – Lincoln was the 16ᵗʰ president). A normative statement is an opinion or a statement of what should or ought to be. Example: "The United States should elect a female as president of the United States."

5. The principle that best describes Duncan's refusal to pay for the bottle of water is marginal analysis. The total benefit to people from fresh water is very high but the marginal benefit of water – the benefit to Duncan from an additional 16 ounces of water – is very low. Duncan probably is not very thirsty. If Duncan had not had anything to drink for two days the benefit to him of the next 16 ounces of water he drinks will be much higher.

True/False Answers

1. F A hypothesis is a testable statement about how the world is.
2. F An entrepreneur is someone who operates a business.
3. F Economists believe people respond to incentives.
4. F The distribution of goods and services is determined by the government and that need not be equal.
5. F People differ on what they believe is equitable or fair.
6. F A mixed economy is one in which government influence on the choices of buyers and sellers is greater than in a market economy.
7. T All economies face trade-offs due to scarce resources.
8. T
9. T See the section titled "The Modern 'Mixed' Economy" on page 10.
10. F Economists would use positive economics analysis to address this issue.
11. T This is the definition of microeconomics.
12. T
13. F The slope of a point on a nonlinear curve is measured by the slope of a tangent to the curve at that point.
14. T
15. F Economic models provide a basic foundation for use in the analysis of both simplistic and complicated economic situations.

Chapter 2

Trade-offs, Comparative Advantage, and the Market System

Chapter Summary

A nation can produce only limited quantities of goods and services because it has scarce resources. Economists use the **production possibilities frontier** (*PPF*) to analyze the opportunity costs and trade-offs that nations, firms, and individuals face as a result of **scarcity**. The *PPF* is a curve that illustrates the combinations of two goods a nation can produce using all of its economic resources and a current state of technology in a given time period. The more resources that are devoted to an activity, the smaller the payoff to devoting additional resources to that activity. Production possibilities frontiers can be used to demonstrate the benefits of specialization in production and trade for two individuals or two nations.

Markets enable buyers and sellers of goods and services to come together to trade. The **circular-flow diagram** shows how buyers (households) and sellers (firms) interact in both product and factor markets. Free markets exist when governments place few restrictions on how a good or service can be produced and sold or on how a factor of production can be employed.

Entrepreneurs, those who own and operate businesses, are critical to the working of a market system. The businesses they operate produce goods and services consumers want. The entrepreneur decides how these goods and services should be produced to yield the most profit. Entrepreneurs organize factors of production and risk their own funds to start businesses. Successful entrepreneurs are rewarded for their efforts with profits, but most entrepreneurs, including many who later meet with success, suffer financial losses and business failures if they do not satisfy consumers' wants. Although government does not restrict how firms produce and sell goods and services in a free market, it is essential that government protect an individual's right to private property in order for a market system work well.

Learning Objectives

When you finish this chapter, you should be able to:

1. **Use a production possibilities frontier to analyze opportunity costs and trade-offs**. Each point on a production possibilities frontier represents a combination of two goods that can be produced by using all of a nation's available resources given the state of technology and during a specific time period. Along the frontier, an increase in production of one good requires a decrease in production of the other good. Production possibilities frontiers usually appear bowed outward because marginal opportunity costs typically increase as the production of any good or service rises.

2. **Understand comparative advantage and explain how it is the basis for trade.** Comparative advantage explains why a person is better off specializing in the production of the good or service that he or she can produce at a lower opportunity cost than another person. Each person can then trade for the good or service the other person produces.

3. **Explain the basic idea of how a market system works.** In a market system, buyers and sellers in product markets and resource markets are free to trade with few restrictions on how a good or service can be sold or how a factor of production can be employed. Individual buyers and sellers are assumed to act in rational, self-interested ways.

Chapter Review

Chapter Opener: Managers Making Choices at BMW (pages 36-37)

The managers at firms such as BMW (Bavarian Motor Works) must make decisions regarding the production and marketing of their products. These decisions include the location of manufacturing plants and the production methods used at these plants. Because BMW is a German firm, there are good reasons to locate factories in Germany. However, locating factories in other countries can reduce manufacturing costs (for example, by paying lower wages). Locating in countries where the automobiles are sold also reduces the risk that foreign governments will impose import restrictions.

📖 Helpful Study Hint

The authors use a production possibilities frontier to illustrate BMW's decision to produce Z4 roadsters and X5 sports utility vehicles. See Figure 2-1. An *Inside Look* at the end of the chapter uses the concepts explained in the chapter to analyze BMW's production decisions during 2007. BMW generated a new production possibilities frontier (*PPF*) due to technological change and is moving in the direction of producing on the new *PPF*. As production increases, BMW is substituting the production of SUVs for coupes.

 Economics in YOUR Life! "The Trade-offs When You Buy a Car" asks whether there is a relationship between gas mileage and safety and whether we can increase both safety and the mileage. Keep this question in mind as you read the chapter. The authors will answer this question at the end of the chapter.

2.1 LEARNING OBJECTIVE

2.1 Production Possibilities Frontiers and Opportunity Costs (pages 38-44)

Learning Objective 1 Use a production possibilities frontier to analyze opportunity costs and trade-offs.

A **production possibilities frontier** (*PPF*) is a curve showing the maximum alternative combinations of two products that may be produced with available resources. The slope of a *PPF* is used to measure the opportunity cost of increasing the production of one good along the frontier relative to the other good.

The slope of a linear frontier and the opportunity cost of moving along the frontier are constant. But convex or "bowed out" production possibilities frontiers represent a more likely outcome. A convex *PPF* means marginal opportunity costs rise as more and more of one good is produced. For example, starting from point *A* in Figure 2-2 and moving downward to points *B* and *C*, the slope of the frontier becomes steeper and steeper. This means that the cost of producing one more automobile (the number of tanks that must be given up as resources are transferred to automobile production) is greater at each point.

Along a production possibilities frontier, resources and technology are fixed. If there is an increase in the available resources or an improvement in the technology used to produce goods and services, the *PPF* will shift outward. The economy will be able to produce more goods and services, which means the economy has experienced economic growth. **Economic growth** is the ability of the economy to produce increasing quantities of goods and services. Growth may lead to greater increases in production of one good than another.

📖 Helpful Study Hint

Solved Problem 2-1 will help you draw a *PPF* and understand how a linear *PPF* illustrates opportunity costs incurred in production. Be sure you understand how slope is measured along the frontier and that this slope represents the opportunity cost of substituting the production of one good for the production of another.

   Making the Connection "Trade-offs: Hurricane Katrina, Tsunami Relief, and Charitable Giving" describes a sobering example of the opportunity cost of making donations to charitable organizations when aid is solicited as a result of a natural disaster. Households and firms typically have a fixed budget for charities, and contributions to one charitable cause will diminish the supply of funds available to another charitable cause. When natural disasters strike, the focus for charitable giving becomes the relief fund for that disaster and other charitable causes typically see a reduction in giving.

2.2 LEARNING OBJECTIVE

2.2 Comparative Advantage and Trade (pages 44-49)

Learning Objective 2 Understand comparative advantage and explain how it is the basis for trade.

By specializing in production and engaging in trade, individuals can enjoy a higher standard of living than would be possible if these individuals produced everything they consumed. Specialization in production is so common that most people take for granted that they must trade income earned from their own labor to buy the services of plumbers, carpenters, medical doctors, and stock brokers. Specialization makes trade necessary. **Trade** is the act of buying or selling.

Absolute advantage is the ability of an individual, firm, or country to produce more of a good or service than competitors using the same amount of resources. **Comparative advantage** is the ability of an individual, firm, or country to produce a good or service at a lower opportunity cost than other producers. An individual country should specialize in the production of the good or services in which it has a comparative advantage, and then trade this good to other countries for goods in which it does not have a comparative advantage.

📖 Helpful Study Hint

Don't Let This Happen to You! clarifies the differences between absolute and comparative advantage using the example of individuals picking apples and picking cherries. A country has the absolute advantage in the production of a good if the country can produce more of the good, while the comparative advantage in the production of a good goes to the country that can produce the good relatively inexpensively (that is, with the lower opportunity cost). In the simple case with two goods, a country can have an absolute advantage in the production of both goods, but the country will only have a comparative advantage in the production of only one of the two goods.

Solved Problem 2-2 describes the benefits realized when a nation specializes in the production of a good for which it has a comparative advantage. In the problem, the United States has a comparative advantage in producing honey, while Canada has a comparative advantage in producing maple syrup. Each country should specialize in producing the good for which it has a comparative advantage and trade some of that good for the other good. With trade, the United States and Canada can consume outside of their *PPFs*.

Most examples of absolute and comparative advantage are similar to the hypothetical examples in section 2.2 of the textbook. This is due, in part, to the difficulty of identifying people who have an absolute advantage in two different areas. But the career of Babe Ruth offers a good example of someone with an absolute advantage in two activities who was still ultimately better off specializing in the activity in which he had a comparative advantage. Before he achieved his greatest fame as a home run hitter and outfielder with the New York Yankees, Ruth was a star pitcher with the Boston Red Sox. Ruth may have been the best left-handed pitcher in the American League during his years with Boston (1914-1919), but he was used more and more as a fielder in his last two years with the team. In fact, he established a record for home runs in a season (29) in 1919 when he was still pitching. The Yankees acquired Ruth in 1920 and made him a full-time outfielder. The opportunity cost of this decision for the Yankees was the wins Ruth could have earned as a pitcher. But because New York already had skilled pitchers, the opportunity cost of replacing Ruth as a pitcher was lower than the cost of replacing him as a hitter. No one else on the Yankees could have hit 54 home runs, Ruth's total in 1920; the next highest Yankee total was 11. It can be argued that Ruth had an absolute advantage as both a hitter and pitcher in 1920 but a comparative advantage only as a hitter.

2.3   The Market System (pages 50-56)

Learning Objective 3   Explain the basic idea of how a market system works.

A **market** is a group of buyers and sellers of a good or service and the institution or arrangement by which they come together to trade. **Product markets** are markets for goods, such as computers, and services, such as medical treatment. **Factor markets** are markets for the factors of production, such as labor, capital, natural resources, and entrepreneurial ability. A **circular-flow diagram** is a model that illustrates how participants in markets are linked. The diagram demonstrates the interaction between firms and households in both product and factor markets. Households buy goods and services in the product market and provide resources for sale in the factor market, while firms provide goods and services in the product market and buy resources in the factor market. A **free market** is a market with few government restrictions on how a good or service can be produced or sold, or on how a factor of production can be employed.

Entrepreneurs are an essential part of a market economy. An **entrepreneur** is someone who operates a business, bringing together the factors of production – labor, capital, and natural resources – to produce goods and services. Entrepreneurs often risk their own funds to start businesses and organize factors of production to produce those goods and services consumers want.

The role of government in a market system is limited but essential. Although government in a market economy imposes few restrictions on the choices made by consumers, resource owners, and firms, government protection of private property rights is necessary for markets to operate efficiently.

Property rights are the rights individuals or firms have to the exclusive use of their physical and intellectual property, including the right to buy or sell it. New technology has created challenges to protection of property rights. Unauthorized copying of music and other intellectual property in cyberspace reduces the rewards to creativity and may reduce the amount of such activity in the future.

📖 Helpful Study Hint

Consumers seldom know the identity of the people who produce the products they buy. The impersonal and decentralized character of markets is illustrated very well by the discussion of the production of Apple's iPod found in *Making the Connection* "A Story of the Market System in Action: How Do You Make an iPod?" The iPod contains 451 parts. Many of the manufacturers of the components of the iPod do not know what the final product will be. No one person at Apple knows how to produce all of these components, so Apple relies heavily on its suppliers.

The role of government in a free market economy can be compared to that of an umpire or referee in a sporting event. The most vocal critics of these officials would not argue they are not needed. It would not take long for a professional football or baseball game to turn into a shouting match (or worse!) if players were allowed to enforce the rules of their own games. On the other hand, the quality of sporting events suffers when officials bar players, coaches, or managers from participating in contests for frivolous reasons. *Making the Connection*

"Property Rights in Cyberspace: YouTube and MySpace" reinforces the need for government protection of property rights and the difficulties associated with enforcing intellectual property rights. Material can easily be uploaded to and posted on the Internet. Once on the Internet, the material can be easily downloaded, reproduced, reposted, and the like. It is highly unlikely that you will get caught for piracy when reproducing the material for your personal use, so these intellectual property rights are nearly impossible to protect.

The stories of successful businesses such as Microsoft and Google can give a misleading impression about the risks of business ownership. Many businesses fail. The National Restaurant Association estimates an 80 percent failure rate for independently owned restaurants within their first two years of operation. The average work week for many small business owners is much longer than that of the average employee – 80 hours is not uncommon – and owners often borrow heavily to start and maintain their businesses.

At the start of the chapter, *Economics in YOUR Life!* "The Trade-offs When You Buy a Car" asks whether there is a relationship between gas mileage and safety and whether we can increase both safety and the mileage rate. You can analyze these questions using a *PPF*. The trade-off between safety and gas mileage can be depicted by looking at a given *PPF*. We know that bigger, heavier cars are safer, but they also have worse gas mileage. We could get a combination of safety and fuel mileage that is outside the given *PPF* by improvements in the technology used in manufacturing automobiles. This would give us a new *PPF* and an increase in both safety and gas mileage.

Extra Solved Problem 2-3

The chapter includes 2 Solved Problems. Here is an extra Solved Problem to help you build your skills solving economic problems.

Supports Learning Objective 2-3: Explain the basic idea of how a market system works.

Adam Smith's "Invisible Hand"

Alan Krueger, an economist at Princeton University, has argued that Adam Smith "…worried that if merchants and manufacturers pursued their self-interest by seeking government regulation and privilege, the invisible hand would not work its magic…"

Source: Alan B. Krueger, "Rediscovering the Wealth of Nations," *New York Times*, August 16, 2001.

a. What types of regulation and privilege might merchants and manufacturers seek from the government?

b. How might these regulations and privileges keep the invisible hand from working?

SOLVING THE PROBLEM

Step 1:   Review the chapter material.

This problem is about how goods and services are produced and sold and how factors of production are employed in a free market economic system as described by Adam Smith in *An Inquiry into the Nature and Causes of the Wealth of Nations.* You may want to review the section "The Gains from Free Markets," which begins on page 52 in the textbook.

Step 2:   Answer question (a) by noting the economic system in place in Europe in 1776.

At that time, governments gave guilds – associations of producers – the authority to control production. The production controls limited the amount of output of goods such as shoes and clothing as well as the number of producers of these items. Limiting production and competition led to higher prices and fewer choices for consumers. Instead of catering to the wants of consumers, producers sought the favor of government officials.

Step 3:   Answer question (b) by contrasting the behavior of merchants and manufacturers under a guild system and a market system.

Because governments gave producers the power to control production, producers did not have to respond to consumers' demands for better quality, more variety, and lower prices. Under a market system, producers who sell goods of poor quality at high prices suffer economic losses; producers who provide better quality goods at low prices are rewarded with profits. Therefore, in a market system it is in the self-interest of producers to address consumer wants. This is how the invisible hand works in a free market economy, but not in eighteenth century Europe.

Key Terms

Absolute advantage. The ability of an individual, firm, or country to produce more of a good or service than competitors, using the same amount of resources.

Circular-flow diagram. A model that illustrates how participants in markets are linked.

Comparative advantage. The ability of an individual, firm, or country to produce a good or service at a lower opportunity cost than competitors.

Economic growth. The ability of the economy to produce increasing quantities of goods and services.

Entrepreneur. Someone who operates a business, bringing together the factors of production – labor, capital, and natural resources – to produce goods and services.

Factor markets. Markets for the factors of production, such as labor, capital, natural resources, and entrepreneurial ability.

Factors of production. The inputs used to make goods and services.

Free market. A market with few government restrictions on how a good or service can be produced or sold or how a factor of production can be employed.

Market. A group of buyers and sellers of a good or service and the institution or arrangement by which they come together to trade.

Opportunity cost. The highest-valued alternative that must be given up to engage in an activity.

Product markets. Markets for goods – such as computers – and services – such as medical treatment.

Production possibilities frontier (*PPF*). A curve showing the maximum attainable combinations of two products that may be produced with available resources and current technology.

Property rights. The rights individuals or firms have to the exclusive use of their property, including the right to buy or sell it.

Scarcity. The situation in which unlimited wants exceed the limited resources available to fulfill those wants.

Trade. The act of buying or selling.

Self-Test

(Answers are provided at the end of the Self-Test.)

Multiple-Choice Questions

1. What is the name given to the highest-valued alternative that must be given up to engage in any activity?
    a. Scarcity
    b. The production possibilities frontier
    c. Opportunity cost
    d. A tradeoff

2. What happens if a country produces a combination of goods that uses all of the resources available in the economy?
    a. The country is operating on its production possibilities frontier.
    b. The country is maximizing its opportunity cost.
    c. The country has eliminated scarcity.
    d. All of the above

3. Refer to the graph below. Which of the following combinations is unattainable with the current resources available in this economy?

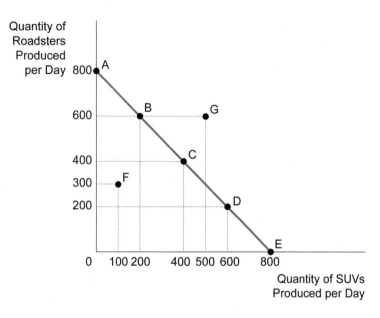

    a.   Combination G
    b.   Combination F
    c.   Combinations A or E
    d.   All of the above. None of the combinations above can be attained with current resources.

4. Refer to the graph below. Which of the following combinations is inefficient?

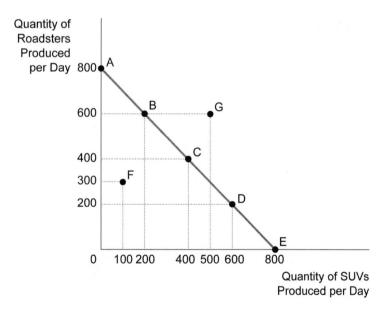

    a.   Combination G
    b.   Combination F
    c.   Combinations A or E
    d.   Both F and G

5. Refer to the graph below. Which of the following best represents the situation in which BMW *must* face a tradeoff between producing SUVs and producing roadsters?

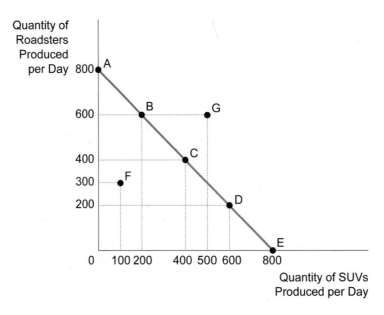

   a. Any point on the graph represents that tradeoff.
   b. Moving from B to C
   c. Moving from F to B
   d. Moving from C and G

6. Refer to the graph below. How many roadsters are produced at the point where BMW produces 800 SUVs?

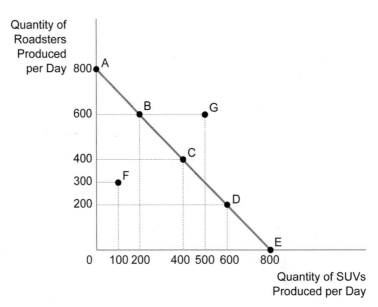

   a. Zero
   b. Any amount up to 800
   c. Exactly 800
   d. 400

7. Refer to the graph below. What is the opportunity cost of moving from point B to point C?

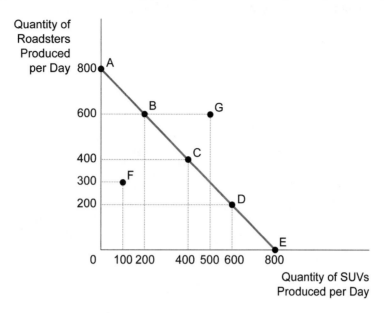

a. 200 SUVs
b. 400 SUVs
c. 200 roadsters
d. 400 roadsters

8. Refer to the graph below. The graph shows the data from Solved Problem 2-1. What is the opportunity cost of switching from Choice D to Choice E?

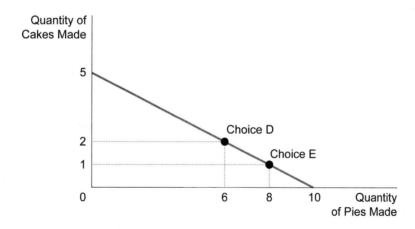

a. Two pies
b. Eight pies
c. Two cakes
d. One cake

9. Refer to the graph below. The graph is a representation of the data in Solved Problem 2-1. In this problem, what is the opportunity cost of producing five cakes?

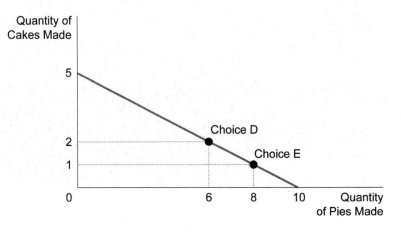

a. Zero cakes
b. Zero pies
c. Ten pies
d. There is insufficient information to answer the question.

10. Refer to the graph below. As you move from point A to point B and then to C on this graph, what happens to the marginal opportunity cost?

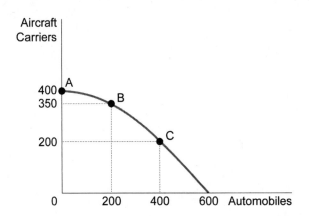

a. It increases
b. It decreases
c. It remains constant
d. It equals zero

11. Refer to the graph below. What is the opportunity cost of producing 400 aircraft carriers?

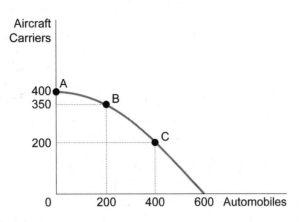

    a.   200 automobiles
    b.   50 aircraft carriers
    c.   200 automobiles
    d.   600 automobiles

12. Refer to the graph below. What is the opportunity cost of moving from point B to point C?

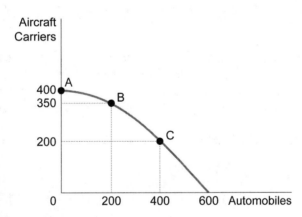

    a.   200 automobiles
    b.   400 automobiles
    c.   50 aircraft carriers
    d.   150 aircraft carriers

13. Refer to the graph below. Precisely what does the term "increasing marginal opportunity cost" mean in this graph?

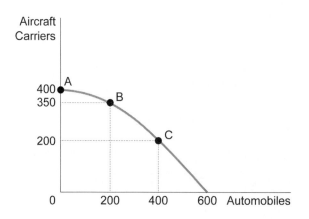

a. It means that there is a higher opportunity cost of producing either aircrafts or automobiles, so long as the quantity produced of that good is decreasing.
b. It means that there is a higher opportunity cost of producing either aircrafts or automobiles, so long as the quantity produced of that good is increasing.
c. It means that increasing the production of aircrafts results in higher automobile production costs, such as the costs of labor and capital to build automobiles.
d. It means that increasing the production of either aircrafts or automobiles creates more opportunities in the economy.

14. A production possibilities frontier will be linear instead of bowed out if
a. the tradeoff between the two goods is always constant.
b. no tradeoffs exist.
c. unemployment is zero.
d. resources are employed efficiently.

15. The principle of increasing marginal opportunity cost states that the more resources devoted to any activity, the _____ the payoff to devoting additional resources to that activity.
a. smaller
b. greater
c. proportional
d. more instant

16. Refer to the graphs below. Which graph best represents an improvement in the technology used to make automobiles?

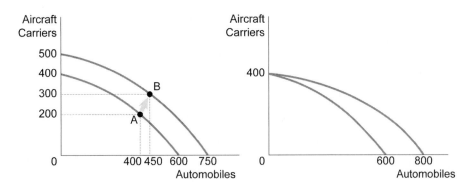

    a. The graph on the left
    b. The graph on the right
    c. Both graphs
    d. Neither graph

17. Refer to the graphs below. Which graph best represents an increase in the economy's resources?

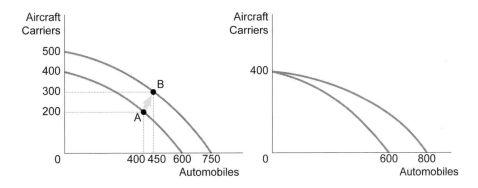

    a. The graph on the left
    b. The graph on the right
    c. Both graphs
    d. Neither graph

18. Refer to the graphs below. Which graph best represents the concept of *economic growth*?

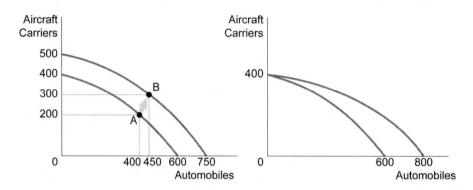

    a.   The graph on the left
    b.   The graph on the right
    c.   Both graphs
    d.   Neither graph

19. Refer to the graphs below. Which of the following could have caused the outward shift of the curve in the graph on the left side?

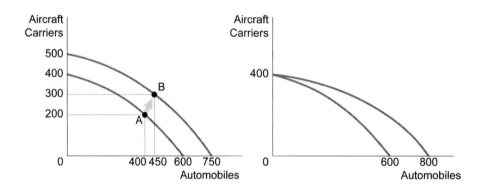

    a.   An increase in technology that affects the production of both aircraft carriers and automobiles.
    b.   Technological change that affects only the aircraft carrier industry.
    c.   Unemployment in the economy
    d.   A change in the cost of producing automobiles.

20. Which of the following would create economic growth, that is, shift the production possibilities frontier outward?
    a.   An increase in the available labor.
    b.   An increase in technology that affects the production of both goods.
    c.   An increase in the available natural resources.
    d.   All of the above

21. According to textbook section 2.2 on trade, which of the following statements is most consistent with positive economic analysis?
    a. The United States would be better off being self-sufficient, so we don't have to rely on other nations for certain goods.
    b. The United States would be better off if we specialize in the production of some goods, and then trade some of them to other countries.
    c. We should produce at home the goods that we now import—that way we can generate additional jobs here at home.
    d. We should establish trade with friendly countries and avoid trade with our enemies.

22. *Absolute advantage* is the ability of an individual, firm, or country to
    a. produce more of a good or service than competitors using the same amount of resources.
    b. produce a good or service at a lower opportunity cost than other producers.
    c. consume more goods or services than others at lower costs.
    d. reach a higher production possibilities frontier by lowering opportunity costs.

23. If a country has a *comparative advantage* in the production of a good, then that country
    a. also has an absolute advantage in producing that good.
    b. should allow another country to specialize in the production of that good.
    c. has a lower opportunity cost in the production of that good.
    d. All of the above

24. Refer to the graphs below. Each graph represents one country. Which country has a comparative advantage in the production of shirts?

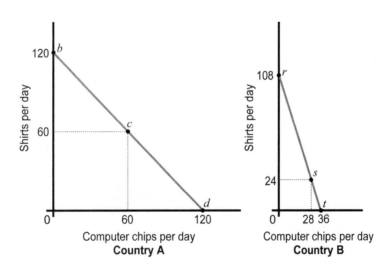

    a. Country A
    b. Country B
    c. Neither country
    d. Both countries

25. Refer to the graphs below. Each graph represents one country. Which country should specialize in the production of chips?

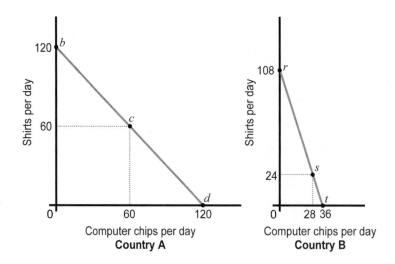

a.   Country A
b.   Country B
c.   Neither country; they both should produce some chips and some shirts.
d.   Both countries should specialize in the production of chips.

26. The table below shows the quantity of two goods that a worker can produce per day in a given country. Which country has an *absolute advantage* in the production of each good?

	Output per day of work	
	Food	Clothing
Country A	6	3
Country B	1	2

a.   Country A has an absolute advantage in the production of each good.
b.   Country B has an absolute advantage in the production of each good.
c.   Both countries have an absolute advantage in the production of each good.
d.   Neither country has an absolute advantage in the production of each good.

27. Consider the table below. Which country has a *comparative advantage* in the production of each good?

	Output per day of work	
	Food	Clothing
Country A	6	3
Country B	1	2

a.   Country A has a comparative advantage in the production of both goods.
b.   Country B has a comparative advantage in the production of both goods.
c.   Country A has a comparative advantage in the production of food.
d.   Country B has a comparative advantage in the production of food.

28. Refer to the graphs below. If you have a comparative advantage in the production of apples, what point would best represent your production with trade?

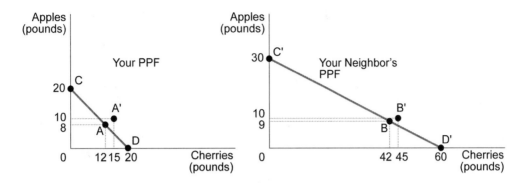

a. A
b. A'
c. C
d. D

29. Refer to the graphs below. What is point B' on your neighbor's *PPF* curve?

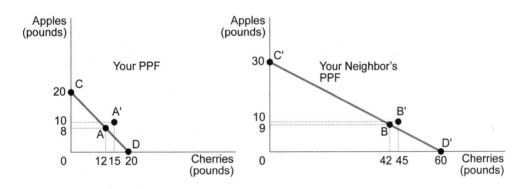

a. Point B' is your neighbor's production before trade.
b. Point B' is your neighbor's consumption before trade.
c. Point B' is your neighbor's production after trade.
d. Point B' is your neighbor's consumption after trade.

30. Which of the following refers to markets where goods such as computers or services such as medical treatment are offered?
a. Product markets
b. Essential markets
c. Factor markets
d. Competitive markets

31. In which markets are factors of production, such as labor, capital, natural resources, and entrepreneurial ability traded?
a. In product markets
b. In essential markets
c. In factor markets
d. In competitive markets

32. Which of the following comprises the two key groups of participants in the circular flow of income?
    a. Product markets and factor markets
    b. Government and the financial sector
    c. Households and firms
    d. Buyers and sellers

33. Fill in the blanks. In a simple circular flow model, there are flows of _____ and flows of _____.
    a. factors of production; goods and services
    b. funds received from the sale of factors of production; spending on final goods and services
    c. Both of the above are correct.
    d. None of the above. Actually, there are no flows in the circular flow of income.

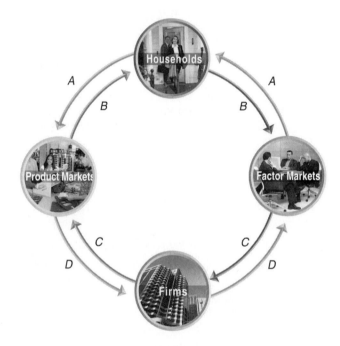

34. In the circular-flow diagram above, which arrow shows the flow of goods and services?
    a. A
    b. B
    c. C
    d. D

35. In the circular-flow diagram above, which arrow shows the flow of spending by households?
    a. A
    b. B
    c. C
    d. D

36. In the circular-flow diagram on the previous page, which arrow shows the flow of factors of production?
    a. A
    b. B
    c. C
    d. D

37. In the circular-flow diagram on the previous page, which arrow shows the flow of income paid to the factors of production?
    a. A
    b. B
    c. C
    d. D

38. According to Adam Smith, which of the following is true?
    a. Markets work because producers, aided by government, ensure that neither too many nor too few goods are produced.
    b. Market prices can come to reflect the prices desired by all consumers.
    c. Individuals usually act in a rational, self-interested way.
    d. All of the above.

39. According to Adam Smith, which of the following is the instrument the invisible hand uses to direct economic activity?
    a. Price
    b. Government regulation
    c. Financial markets
    d. Cost

40. According to Adam Smith, which of the following is necessary for the proper functioning of the market system?
    a. For markets to work, people should take into account how their decisions affect society as a whole.
    b. For markets to work, government should help citizens make the right decisions.
    c. For markets to work, people must be free to pursue their self-interest.
    d. For markets to work, people and government need to coordinate their decisions.

41. What is the role of an entrepreneur?
    a. To operate a business that produces a good or service.
    b. To bring together the factors of production—labor, capital, and natural resources.
    c. To take risks.
    d. All of the above

42. In a free market system, which of the following groups brings together the factors of production—labor, capital, and natural resources—in order to produce goods and services?
    a. The government
    b. Entrepreneurs
    c. Lobbyists
    d. Politicians

43. Which of the following is critical for the success of a market system?
    a. To allow individuals or firms to have exclusive use of their property.
    b. To prevent individuals from buying or selling their property depending on the circumstances.
    c. Either choice above.
    d. To allow the government to determine the optimal use of private property.

44. Generally speaking, for a market system to work, individuals must
    a. be very cautious in their approach to saving and investment.
    b. take risks and act in rational, self-interested ways.
    c. be able to evaluate and understand all available options.
    d. consult people who have experience.

45. What are patents and copyrights designed to do?
    a. Prevent entrepreneurs from earning excessive profits.
    b. Eliminate unnecessary duplication whenever it arises.
    c. Protect intellectual property rights.
    d. All of the above

46. What is the outcome of enforcing contracts and property rights in a market system?
    a. Increased economic activity
    b. Decreased economic activity
    c. No change or no effect on economic activity
    d. An unpredictable but definite effect on economic activity

47. If a market system functions well, which of the following is necessary for the enforcement of contracts and property rights?
    a. Powerful political connections
    b. An independent court system
    c. Action by government to prevent the exercise of certain property rights
    d. All of the above

Short Answer Questions

1. Does the story about Apple's production of the iPod imply that people must cooperate with one another in order for specialization in production and trade to occur? Explain.

_____

_____

_____

_____

_____

2. Comment briefly on the following statement: "The circular-flow diagram implies that the income household members receive is directly related to the market value of the resources they own."

_____

_____

_____

3. How has the emergence of companies such as Napster and Kazaa changed the manner in which music companies and artists market their CDs?

_____

_____

_____

_____

4. Some companies have had success selling goods and services through the Internet, but others have failed. What types of goods or services would consumers prefer to buy in stores rather than online?

_____

_____

5. In the explanation of Adam Smith's argument in favor of replacing the guild system with a market system, the textbook states that "_the key to understanding Smith's argument is the assumption that individuals usually act in a rational, self-interested way._" Did Smith believe that the success of a market system requires that people act selfishly?

_____

_____

_____

True/False Questions

T F 1. In his book _An Inquiry into the Nature and Causes of the Wealth of Nations_, Adam Smith argued that a guild system was the most efficient way for a nation to coordinate the decisions of buyers and sellers.

T F 2. The story about Apple's production of the iPod shows how production requires the coordinated activities of many people, spread around the world.

T F 3. A nation with an absolute advantage in the production of two goods will usually have a comparative advantage in only one of the goods.

T F 4. A production possibilities frontier that is bowed outward illustrates increasing marginal opportunity costs.

T F 5. Technological advances always benefit the production of all goods and services equally.

T F 6. It is possible to have an absolute advantage in producing a good without having a comparative advantage.

T F 7. Households are suppliers of the factors of production that are used by firms to produce goods and services.

T F 8. The circular-flow diagram is used to explain why the opportunity cost of increasing the production of one good is the decrease in production of another good.

T F 9. The 5th and 14th amendments to the U.S. Constitution guarantee property rights.

T F 10. Opportunity cost refers to the all of the alternatives that must be given up to engage in an activity.

T F 11. The popularity of Napster and Kazaa was due to the difficulty music companies and artists had in protecting intellectual property rights.

T F 12. Private contributions to the relief effort following the December 2004 tsunami led to an increase in donations for the homeless and poor as donors realized the need to fund other charities.

T F 13. Because the governments of Hong Kong, Estonia, and Singapore impose few restrictions on economic activity, the economies of these countries approximate free market economies.

T F 14. The Bavarian Motor Works Company has always produced its automobiles in Germany in order to supervise production and employ German workers, who have high levels of technical skills.

T F 15. The marginal opportunity cost along a linear (straight-line) production possibilities frontier is constant.

Answers to the Self-Test

Multiple-Choice Questions

Question	Answer	Comment
1	c	Opportunity cost is the highest-valued alternative that must be given up to engage in an activity. Refer to page 39 of the textbook.
2	a	The production possibilities frontier is a curve showing all the attainable combinations of two products that may be produced with available resources.
3	a	In order to produce the combination G, the economy needs more machines, more workers, or more of both.
4	b	This combination is attainable but inefficient because not all resources are being used. Refer to page 39 of the textbook.
5	b	A move along the curve shows the sacrifice associated with increasing the quantity of SUVs, or the amount by which roadsters will have to be reduced.
6	a	Point E describes this choice. Point E shows that 800 SUVs are produced when zero roadsters are produced.
7	c	Opportunity cost is what you sacrifice. As you move from point B to point C, the production of SUVs increases, and the quantity of roadsters sacrificed to do so is 200.
8	d	As you move from D to E, you increase the production of pies by 2 and sacrifice one cake. Refer to pages 40-41 of the textbook.
9	c	Opportunity cost is what you sacrifice. If Rosie produced zero cakes, Rosie could make 10 pies.

10	a	The sacrifice associated with producing more automobiles is ever greater. Refer to Figure 2-2 on page 39.
11	d	Either the economy produces 400 aircraft carriers or it produces 600 automobiles with the same amount of resources.
12	d	The economy can now produce 400 automobiles instead of 200. In order to produce these additional 200 automobiles, the economy produces 200 aircraft carriers instead of 350 (an opportunity cost of $350 - 200 = 150$ aircraft carriers).
13	b	As the economy moves down the production possibilities frontier, it experiences increasing marginal opportunity costs because increasing automobile production by a given quantity requires larger and larger decreases in aircraft carrier production.
14	a	A linear production possibilities frontier has a constant slope and, therefore, a fixed opportunity cost.
15	a	This is the principle of increasing marginal opportunity cost.
16	b	An improvement in the technology used to make automobiles causes a shift of the production possibilities frontier along the horizontal axis.
17	a	This graph shows that something affects both the production of automobiles and the production of aircraft carriers, such as an increase in resources or better technologies.
18	c	These graphs show an increase in the production of one or both goods. This increase in the productive capacity of the economy is referred to as *economic growth*.
19	a	Economic growth is the ability of the economy to produce increasing quantities of goods and services.
20	d	All of the above factors create economic growth.
21	b	If a nation produced everything it consumed, it would not depend on any other nation for its livelihood. Although self-sufficiency sounds appealing, countries are better off if they specialize in the production of some products and trade some of them to other countries. Refer to the section of the book entitled "Comparative Advantage and the Gains From Trade" on page 47.
22	a	Absolute advantage is the ability of an individual, firm, or country to produce more of a good or service than competitors using the same amount of resources.
23	c	The country with a lower opportunity cost of production has a comparative advantage in the production of that good.
24	b	The opportunity costs are as follows: The opportunity cost of shirts is: 1 chip for country A, and 1/3 chip for country B. The opportunity cost of chips is: 1 shirt for country A and 3 shirts for country B. Country B has a comparative advantage in the production of shirts because it sacrifices fewer chips to produce one shirt. Country B should therefore produce shirts.
25	a	The opportunity costs are as follows: The opportunity cost of shirts is: 1 chip for country A, and 1/3 chip for country B. The opportunity cost of chips is: 1 shirt for country A and 3 shirts for country B. Therefore, country A has a comparative advantage (or lower opportunity cost) in the production of chips because it sacrifices fewer shirts to produce one chip. Country A should therefore produce chips.
26	a	Country A can produce more food and more clothing in one day than Country B.
27	c	A worker in Country A can produce 6 times as many units of food as a worker in Country B, but only 1.5 as many units of clothing. Country A is more efficient in producing food than clothing relative to Country B.
28	c	If you have a comparative advantage in the production of apples, you would specialize entirely in the production of apples.
29	d	After trade, you and your neighbor can consume more than you can produce.
30	a	Goods and services are exchanged in product markets.

31	c	The focus here is on the types of markets where households and firms interact. Read page 50.
32	c	A household is all the individuals in a home. Firms are suppliers of goods and services.
33	c	In the circular flow of income, there are flows of funds and spending, and also flows of factors of production and goods and services.
34	b	Goods and services flow from firms to the households through the product market.
35	a	Spending on goods and services flows from households to firms through the product market.
36	c	Factors of production flow from households to the firms through the factor market.
37	d	Income flows from firms to the households through the factor market.
38	c	Individuals usually act in a rational, self-interested way. Adam Smith understood that people's motives can be complex.
39	a	Price represents both the value of the good to consumers and the cost (to producers) of making those goods.
40	c	Individuals usually act in a rational, self-interested way. When people act in their own self-interest, the right quantity of goods will be produced.
41	d	The role of an entrepreneur is to operate a business and take risks in bringing together the factors of production—labor, capital, and natural resources—in order to produce goods and services.
42	b	In a market system, entrepreneurs bring together the factors of production—labor, capital, and natural resources—in order to produce goods and services.
43	a	The legal basis for a successful market is property rights. Property rights are the rights individuals or firms have to the exclusive use of their property, including the right to buy or sell it.
44	b	Risk taking is an essential ingredient of entrepreneurship and this risk taking is essential for the market system to function well.
45	c	Property rights are very important in any modern economy.
46	a	Much business activity involves someone agreeing to carry out some action in the future. For a market to work, business and individuals have to rely on contracts.
47	b	Independence and impartiality on the part of judges are very important.

Short Answer Responses

1. Cooperation is essential for specialization and trade but it is an impersonal cooperation. It is not necessary for business owners, workers, suppliers and consumers to know or see one another. In fact, many of these individuals can be located thousands of miles away from each other, live in different countries and speak different languages. Their cooperation is due to their self-interest, not their regard for one another's welfare.

2. This is true. In order for household members to earn income to buy the goods and services they want, they must first sell their resource services to firms who purchase these services in factor markets. The market value of factor services determines the income resource owners receive.

3. Traditional music companies face competition from firms such as Napster and Kazaa that can offer downloaded music at low prices. And consumers can purchase online one or two songs rather the entire CD that contains the songs they want. Music companies must offer more attractive options for consumers and consider lowering prices on the CDs they sell. Artists can market directly to consumers through their own web sites rather than through music companies as they have done in the past.

4. Many consumers are reluctant to buy items they cannot see, touch or taste before buying. Clothing, food and automobiles are usually purchased after close inspection.

5. Smith did not believe that self-interest was the sole motive nor did he believe that self-interest was synonymous with selfishness. People are motivated by a broad range of factors, but when they buy and sell in markets, monetary rewards usually provide the most important motivation. Note that people may give to charity due to their own self-interest such as tax breaks and a good feeling about oneself.

True/False Answers

1. F Adam Smith explained the inefficiencies of the guild system and explained how markets were more efficient.
2. T See Making the Connection "A Story of the Market System in Action: How Do You Make an iPod?" on page 53.
3. T A nation can only have the comparative advantage in the production of one of the two goods being compared.
4. T As the slope of the frontier becomes steeper, the opportunity cost of obtaining one more unit of one good increases.
5. F Technological advances often affect the production of some goods (those that use the advances most) more than others.
6. T Absolute advantage is about who produces more, while comparative advantage is about who produces the good relatively inexpensively.
7. T See the section titled "The Circular Flow of Income" on page 50.
8. F A production possibilities frontier, not the circular flow diagram, illustrates opportunity cost in production.
9. T Refer to page 54 for a discussion of the U.S. Constitution.
10. F See the definition of opportunity cost on page 39 of the textbook.
11. T See a discussion of similar companies, such as YouTube and MySpace, on page 55 in the textbook.
12. F Donations to other charities were reduced as people donated to the tsunami relief effort. See Making the Connection "Trade-offs: Hurricane Katrina, Tsunami Relief, and Charitable Giving" on page 41.
13. T The countries that are mentioned in this problem are in the list of examples of free markets in the textbook.
14. F The Chapter Opener discusses the BMW plant in Spartanburg, South Carolina.
15. T The change in the opportunity cost per each additional unit of the good being produced; i.e. the marginal opportunity cost; is constant along a linear *PPF*.

Chapter 3

Where Prices Come From: The Interaction of Demand and Supply

Chapter Summary

The model of demand and supply explains how prices are determined in a market system. The main factor affecting the demand for a product is its price. A **demand schedule** is a table that lists various prices of a product and the quantities that would be demanded at those prices. A **demand curve** shows this same relationship in a graph. The **law of demand** is the negative relationship between price and **quantity demanded**, holding everything else constant. A change in the price of the product causes a movement along the demand curve and is called a change in the quantity demanded. Other factors that affect demand include prices of related goods (**substitutes** and **complements**), income, tastes, population and **demographics**, and expected future prices. A change in any of these will shift a product's demand curve and is called a change in demand.

The most important factor affecting the supply of a product is its price. A **supply schedule** is a table that lists various prices of a product and the quantities that would be supplied at those prices. A **supply curve** shows this same relationship in a graph. The **law of supply** is the positive relationship between price and **quantity supplied**, holding everything else constant. A change in the price of the product causes a movement along the supply curve and is called a change in the quantity supplied. Other factors that affect supply include prices of inputs, technological change, prices of substitutes in production, expected future prices, and the number of firms in the market. In response to a change in any one of these factors, there will be a change in supply or a shift in the supply curve.

The equilibrium price is the price that will make the quantity demanded be equal to the quantity supplied. This occurs where the supply curve and demand curve intersect. A **surplus** exists when the price charged is above the equilibrium price. A **shortage** exists when the price charged is below the equilibrium price. When the market price is not the equilibrium price, the price will adjust toward the equilibrium price. When the price charged equals the equilibrium price, both consumers and producers are willing to exchange the same quantity of the product and there is no further movement in the market price.

An increase in demand increases equilibrium price and increases the equilibrium quantity. A decrease in demand decreases equilibrium price and decreases the equilibrium quantity. An increase in supply decreases equilibrium price and increases the equilibrium quantity. A decrease in supply increases equilibrium price and decreases the equilibrium quantity.

Learning Objectives

When you finish this chapter, you should be able to:

1. **Discuss the variables that influence demand**. Many factors influence the willingness of consumers to buy a particular product. Among these factors are the income they have to spend and the effectiveness of advertising campaigns of the companies that sell products consumers want. The most important factor in consumer decisions, though, is the price of the product. It is important to note that demand refers not to what a consumer wants to buy but what the consumer is both willing and able to buy. In other words, it's not only what consumers want but also what they can afford.

2. **Discuss the variables that influence supply**. Just as many variables influence consumer demand, many variables influence the willingness and ability of firms to sell a good or service. Among these variables are the prices of inputs used in production and the number of firms in the market. The most important variable that affects firms is the price of whatever they sell.

3. **Use a graph to illustrate market equilibrium.** Economists use graphs to show how demand and supply interact in a competitive market to establish equilibrium. The graph of a competitive market shows that quantity demanded equals quantity supplied at the equilibrium price. When the price is greater than the equilibrium price, a surplus exists. In response to the surplus, the market price will fall to the equilibrium level. When the price is less than the equilibrium price, a shortage exists. In response to the shortage, the market price will rise to the equilibrium level.

4. **Use demand and supply graphs to predict changes in prices and quantities**. Demand and supply in most markets change constantly. As a result, equilibrium prices and quantities change constantly. Graphs show the impact on competitive market equilibrium of increases and decreases in demand and supply.

Chapter Review

Chapter Opener: Apple and the Demand for iPods (pages 66-67)

Apple is a leading seller of digital music players in the United States. Apple's ability to sell iPods is affected by the sales of music from Apple's iTunes website and by the competition's sales of digital music players. Apple currently sells its music on iTunes at a price significantly lower than competitors and at a very low profit margin in order to increase its sales of iPods. Many consumers are choosing to purchase music phones as these provide both a digital music player and a telephone. Apple's success depends on the ability of its executives to analyze and react to changes in the demand and supply of its products.

📖 Helpful Study Hint

Apple and the market for digital music players are used throughout the chapter to demonstrate changes in demand and supply and how they affect prices. ***Making the Connection*** "Apple Forecasts the Demand for iPhones and Other Consumer Electronics" describes Apple's efforts to forecast the demand for the new iPhone in order to determine the price to charge and the expected profit the firm will receive. Apple's projections may or may not be correct, and this could affect the success of the company. At the end of this chapter, *An Inside Look* describes how Apple and AT&T may benefit from teaming up to supply the iPhone.

Economics in YOUR Life! asks what would happen to your consumption of iPods and Zunes if the prices of these digital music players changed or if the prices of the music downloaded from iTunes and Zune Marketplace changed. Keep this question in mind as you read the chapter. The authors will answer this question at the end of the chapter.

3.1 LEARNING OBJECTIVE

3.1 The Demand Side of the Market (pages 68-75)

Learning Objective 1 Discuss the variables that influence demand.

Although many factors influence the willingness and ability of consumers to buy a particular product, the main influence on consumer decisions is the product's price. The **quantity demanded** of a good or service is the amount that a consumer is willing and able to purchase at a given price. A **demand schedule** is a table showing the relationship between the price of a product and the quantity of the product demanded. A **demand curve** shows this same relationship in a graph. Since quantity demanded always increases in response to a decrease in price, this relationship is called the **law of demand**. The law of demand is explained by the substitution and income effects. The **substitution effect** is the change in the quantity demanded of a good that results from a change in price, making the good more or less expensive relative to other goods that are substitutes. The **income effect** is the change in the quantity demanded of a good that results from the effect of a change in the good's price on consumer purchasing power.

Ceteris paribus ("all else equal") is the requirement that when analyzing the relationship between two variables – such as price and quantity demanded – other variables must be held constant. When one of the non-price factors that influence demand changes, the result is a shift in the demand curve – an increase or decrease in demand. The most important non-price factors that influence demand are prices of related goods (substitutes and complements), income, tastes, population and demographics, and expected future prices.

Substitutes are goods and services that can be used for the same purpose, while **complements** are goods that are used together. A decrease in the price of a substitute for a good, such as iPods, causes the quantity demanded of the substitute, such as Microsoft's Zune music player, to increase (a move along the demand curve for Zunes), which causes the demand for iPods to fall. A fall in demand means that the demand curve for iPods will shift to the left. An increase in the price of Zunes causes the quantity of Zunes demanded to decrease, shifting the demand curve for iPods to the right. Changes in prices of complements have the opposite effect. A decrease in the price of a complement for iPods causes the quantity demanded of the complement, say music downloads from iTunes, to increase, shifting the demand curve for iPods to the right. An increase in the price of downloads on iTunes causes the quantity of downloads demanded to decrease, shifting the demand curve for iPods to the left.

The income that consumers have available to spend affects their willingness to buy a good. A **normal good** is a good for which demand increases as income rises and decreases as income falls. An **inferior good** is a good for which demand increases as income falls and decreases as income rises. When consumers' tastes for a product increase, the demand curve for the product will shift to the right, and when consumers' tastes for a product decrease, the demand curve for the product will shift to the left.

As population increases, the demand for most products increases. **Demographics** are the characteristics of a population with respect to age, race, and gender. As demographics change, the demand for particular goods will increase or decrease because as different demographic groups become more prevalent in the population their unique preferences will become more prevalent in the market. If enough consumers become convinced that a good will be selling for a lower price in the near future, the demand for the good will decrease in the present. If enough consumers become convinced that the price of a good will be higher in the near future, the demand for the good will increase in the present.

📖 Helpful Study Hint

Students often confuse a change in quantity demanded with a change in demand. Only one variable, the price of a good or service, can cause changes in the quantity demanded of that good or service. This change is described as a movement along a demand curve. Notice that the price of the good or service is on the vertical axis. Changes in demand are caused by changes in nonprice factors. A change in any of these factors causes a shift in the demand curve. Constant repetition is essential to understand this important difference. Use **Making the Connection** "Why Supermarkets Need to Understand Substitutes and Complement" and **Making the Connection** "Companies Respond to a Growing Hispanic Population" to find examples of factors that change demand. Be sure you understand why it is demand and not quantity demanded that changes. Supermarket managers must have a clear understanding of which goods are substitutes and which are complements when deciding what to stock on the shelf. If a product is eliminated because there are other substitutes on the shelf, the demand for a complement to the eliminated product is likely to fall. Companies must also consider the changing demographics of the population and adjust their resources to meeting the needs of the growing demographic groups.

Take time to study Figure 3.3, which shows the difference between a change in demand and a change in quantity demanded. Also take time to study Table 3.1, which lists all the variables that shift market demand curves.

Extra Solved Problem 3-1

Chapter 3 of the textbook includes two Solved Problems. Here is an extra Solved Problem to help you build your skills solving economic problems.

Supports Learning Objective 3-1: Discuss the variables that influence demand.

Suppose that Bob needs to buy an automobile. Bob has decided to purchase a new Miata convertible. Bob's neighbor tells him that Mazda will be offering a $3,500 rebate on all its automobiles starting next month.

a.   Assuming that Bob can wait until next month to buy an automobile, what effect will the rebate have on Bob's demand for the Miata?

b.   Which of the variables that influence demand would explain Bob's change in demand?

SOLVING THE PROBLEM

Step 1: Review the chapter material.
This problem is about variables that shift market demand, so you may want to review the section "Variables That Shift Market Demand," which begins on page 70 in the textbook.

Step 2: Answer question (a).
Bob's demand for the Miata will decrease now and increase next month as he will wait to make his purchase in order to take advantage of the rebate.

Step 3: Answer question (b).
Other things being equal, as the expected future price of the Miata falls, the demand for Miatas will fall in the present time period.

3.2 The Supply Side of the Market (pages 75-79)

Learning Objective 2 Discuss the variables that influence supply.

Many variables influence the willingness and ability of firms to sell a good or service. The most important of these variables is the price of the good or service. **Quantity supplied** is the amount of a good or service that a firm is willing to sell at a given price. A **supply schedule** is a table that shows the relationship between the price of a product and the quantity of the product supplied. A **supply curve** shows this same relationship in a graph. The **law of supply** states that, holding everything else constant, increases in the price of the good or service cause increases in the quantity supplied and decreases in the price of the good or service cause decreases in the quantity supplied.

Variables other than the price of the product affect supply. When any of these variables change, a shift in supply – an increase or a decrease in supply – results. The following are the most important variables that shift supply: prices of inputs used in production, technological change, prices of substitutes in production, expected future prices, and the number of firms in the market.

If the price of an input (for example, labor or energy) used to produce a good rises, the supply of the good will decrease and the supply curve will shift to the left. If the price of an input decreases, the supply of the good will increase and the supply curve will shift to the right. **Technological change** is a positive or negative change in the ability of a firm to produce a given level of output with a given amount of inputs. A positive technological change will shift a firm's supply curve to the right, while a negative technological change will shift a firm's supply curve to the left.

An increase in the price of an alternative good (B) that a firm could produce instead of producing good A will shift the firm's supply curve for good A to the left. If a firm expects the price of its product will rise in the future, the firm has an incentive to decrease supply in the present and increase supply in the future. When firms enter a market, the market supply curve shifts to the right. When firms exit a market, the market supply curve shifts to the left.

📖 Helpful Study Hint

The law of supply may seem logical because producers earn more profit when the price they sell their product for rises. But consider Figure 3-4 and the following question: "If Apple can earn a profit from selling 40 million players per month at a price of $200, why not increase quantity supplied to 45 million and make even more profit?" The upward slope of the supply curve is due not only to the profit motive but the increasing marginal cost of printers. (Increasing marginal costs were discussed in Chapter 2.) Apple will increase its quantity supplied from 40 to 45 million in Figure 3-4 only if the price it will receive is $250, because the cost of producing 5 million more players is greater than the cost of the last 5 million players.

As with demand and quantity demanded, be careful not to confuse a change in quantity supplied (due only to a change in the price of a product) and a change in supply (a shift of the supply curve in response to one of the non-price factors). Constant reinforcement of this is necessary. Be careful not to refer to an increase in supply as "a downward shift" or a decrease in supply as "an upward shift." Because demand curves are downward-sloping, an increase in demand appears in a graph as an "upward shift." But because supply curves are upward-sloping, a *decrease* in supply appears in a graph as an "upward shift." You should always refer to both changes in demand and supply as being "shifts to the right" for an increase and "shifts to the left" for a decrease to avoid confusion.

Take time to study Figure 3.6, which shows the difference between a change in supply and a change in quantity supplied. Also take time to study Table 3.2, which lists all the variables that shift market supply curves.

Extra Solved Problem 3-2

Supports Learning Objective 3-2: Discuss the variables that influence supply.

To (Soy)bean or not to (Soy)bean ?

Television programming in Illinois features many commercials aimed at farmers. Ads for fertilizer, seed, and farm equipment are as common as commercials for laundry soap and soft drinks. Much of the nation's corn is grown in Illinois, but the climate and soil conditions in the state are well-suited for growing soybeans as well. Each year, a farmer must decide how many acres of land to plant with corn and how many acres to plant with soybeans.

a. If both crops can be grown on the same land, why would a farmer choose to produce corn rather than soybeans?

b. Which of the variables that influence supply would explain a farmer's choice to produce soybeans or corn?

SOLVING THE PROBLEM

Step 1: **Review the chapter material.**
This problem is about variables that shift supply, so you may want to refers to the section "Variables That Shift Supply," which begins on page 77 of the textbook.

Step 2: **Answer question (a).**
Among the factors that would influence a farmer's choice is the expected profitability of the two crops. A farmer will grow corn rather than soybeans if he expects the profits from growing corn will be greater than those earned from growing soybeans.

Step 3: **Answer question (b).**
Other things being equal, as the price of soybeans falls relative to the price of corn, the supply of corn would rise. Because corn and soybeans are substitutes in production, the variable "prices of substitutes in production" is the one that would explain the farmer's choice.

3.3 LEARNING OBJECTIVE

3.3 Market Equilibrium: Putting Demand and Supply Together (pages 79-82)

Learning Objective 3 Use a graph to illustrate market equilibrium.

The purpose of markets is to bring buyers and sellers together. The interaction of buyers and sellers in markets results in firms producing goods and services consumers both want and can afford. At **market equilibrium,** the price of the product makes quantity demanded equal quantity supplied. A **competitive market equilibrium** is a market equilibrium with many buyers and many sellers. The market price (the actual price you would pay for the product) will not always be the equilibrium price. A **surplus** is a situation in which the quantity supplied is greater than the quantity demanded, which occurs when the market price is above the equilibrium price. Firms have an incentive to increase sales by lowering price. As the market price is lowered, quantity demanded will rise and quantity supplied will fall until the market reaches equilibrium.

A **shortage** is a situation in which quantity demanded is greater than the quantity supplied, which occurs when the market price is below the equilibrium price. Some consumers will want to buy the product at a higher price to make sure they get what they want. As the market price rises, the quantity demanded will fall – not everyone will want to buy at a higher price – and quantity supplied will rise until the market reaches equilibrium. At the competitive market equilibrium, there is no reason for the price to change unless either the demand curve or the supply curve shifts.

📖 Helpful Study Hint

It's very important to understand how demand and supply interact to reach equilibrium. Remember that adjustments to a shortage or a surplus represent changes in quantity demanded (not demand) and quantity supplied (not supply). *Solved Problem 3-3* and problem 3.4 in the Problems and Applications at the end of the chapter address this topic. In *Solved Problem 3-3*, we see how the demand and supply for the letters written by Lincoln and Booth determine the price for the letters written by each author. Because the supply is low relative to the demand for Booth's letters, his letters sell for a high equilibrium price. Similarly, because the supply of Lincoln's letters is large relative to the demand, his letters sell for a lower equilibrium price. Market or actual prices are easy to understand because these are the prices consumers are charged. You know the price you paid for a CD because it is printed on the receipt. But no receipt has "equilibrium price" written on it.

To help you understand what an equilibrium price and quantity are, it may help to use an analogy. Suppose you were to push an inflated ball under the surface of a sink filled with water. If you were to release the ball it would move quickly to the surface. If you were to hold the ball above the sink and drop it, the ball would fall to the surface. The surface of the water is the equilibrium position for the ball. A market equilibrium is the position a market will move towards if there is a shortage or surplus.

3.4 LEARNING OBJECTIVE

3.4 The Effect of Demand and Supply Shifts on Equilibrium (pages 83-88)

Learning Objective 4 Use demand and supply graphs to predict changes in prices and quantities.

When the supply curve shifts, the equilibrium price and quantity change in the opposite direction. Increases in supply result from the following non-price factor changes: a decrease in an input price, positive technological change, a decrease in the price of a substitute in production, a lower expected future product price, and an increase in the number of firms in the market. A decrease in supply results in a higher equilibrium price and a lower equilibrium quantity. Decreases in supply result from the following non-price factor changes: an increase in an input price, negative technological change, an increase in the price of a substitute in production, a higher expected future product price, and a decrease in the number of firms in the market.

When the demand curve shifts, the equilibrium price and quantity shift in the same direction. Increases in demand can be caused by any change in a variable that affects demand *except price*. For example, demand will increase if the price of a substitute rises, the price of a complement falls, income rises (for a normal good), income falls (for an inferior good), population increases or the expected future price of the product rises. A decrease in demand results in a lower equilibrium price and lower equilibrium quantity. Decreases in demand can be caused by any change in a variable that affects demand *except the price of the product itself*. For example, demand will decrease if the price of a substitute falls, the price of a complement rises, income falls (for a normal good), incomes rises (for an inferior good), population decreases, or the expected future price of the product falls.

📖 Helpful Study Hint

Use the following features to conduct your own research on how changes in demand and supply affect prices:
- *Making the Connection* "The Falling Prices of LCD TVs"
- *Solved Problem 3-4* on lobsters
- Problem 4.5 on watermelons in the Problems and Applications section

Visit stores that sell these items and find out their market prices. For flat screen televisions, compare the market price you find with the expected prices as described in **Making the Connection** "The Falling Prices of LCD TVs." **Solved Problem 3-4** shows how the demand and supply for lobsters changes during different times of the year and the effect of those changes on the equilibrium price. In the spring, the demand and supply are both low and the equilibrium price is relatively high. In the summer, the demand for lobsters increases, but the supply of lobsters increases relatively more. This causes the summer price for lobsters to be lower than the equilibrium price in the spring. For lobsters and watermelon, ask sellers how current prices compare with prices at different times of the year. Draw demand and supply graphs that represent the market conditions you observe. You can ask your instructor if your analysis is correct.

In **Don't Let This Happen to YOU!** "Remember: A Change in a Good's Price Does *Not* Cause the Demand or Supply Curve to Shift," the textbook reiterates the idea that a change in the price of a good causes a movement along the curve under analysis. For example, an increase in supply will cause the equilibrium price of the good to rise. This increase in the price of the good will cause a movement up along the demand curve, or a decrease in the quantity demanded. This is not a change in demand and not a shift in the curve.

The section **Economics in YOUR Life!** in this chapter asks what would happen to your consumption of iPods and Zunes if the prices of these digital music players changed or if the prices of the music downloaded from iTunes and Zune Marketplace changed. Because the Zune and the iPod are substitutes, if the price of one of the players increased, the demand for the other music player would increase. For example, if the price of the Zune increases, the demand curve for the iPod would shift to the right. Similarly, the price of complements, such as music downloaded from iTunes or Zune Marketplace, affects the demand for the digital music players. For example, if the price of music downloads on iTunes falls, the demand for iPods would increase and the demand for Zunes would decrease.

Key Terms

Ceteris paribus ("all else equal"). The requirement that when analyzing the relationship between two variables – such as price and quantity demanded – other variables must be held constant.

Competitive market equilibrium. A market equilibrium with many buyers and sellers.

Complements. Goods and services that are used together.

Demand curve. A curve that shows the relationship between the price of a product and the quantity of the product demanded.

Demand schedule. A table showing the relationship between the price of a product and the quantity of the product demanded.

Demographics. The characteristics of a population with respect to age, race, and gender.

Income effect. The change in the quantity demanded of a good that results from the effect of a change in the good's price on consumers' purchasing power.

Inferior good. A good for which the demand increases as income falls and decreases as income rises.

Law of demand. The rule that, holding everything else constant, when the price of a product falls, the quantity demanded of the product will increase, and when the price of a product rises, the quantity demanded of the product will decrease.

Law of supply. The rule that, holding everything else constant, increases in price cause increases in the quantity supplied, and decreases in price cause decreases in the quantity supplied.

Market demand. The demand by all the consumers of a given good or service.

Market equilibrium. A situation in which quantity demanded equals quantity supplied.

Normal good. A good for which the demand increases as income rises and demand decreases as income falls.

Perfectly competitive market. A market that meets the conditions of (1) many buyers and sellers, (2) all firms selling identical products, and (3) no barriers to new firms entering the market.

Quantity demanded. The amount of a good or service that a consumer is willing and able to purchase at a given price.

Quantity supplied. The amount of a good or service that a firm is willing and able to supply at a given price.

Shortage. A situation in which the quantity demanded is greater than the quantity supplied.

Substitutes. Goods and services that can be used for the same purpose.

Substitution effect. The change in the quantity demanded of a good that results from a change in price, making the good more or less expensive relative to goods that are substitutes.

Supply curve. A curve that shows the relationship between the price of a product and the quantity of the product supplied.

Supply schedule. A table that shows the relationship between the price of a product and the quantity of the product supplied.

Surplus. A situation in which the quantity supplied is greater than the quantity demanded.

Technological change. A positive or negative change in the ability of a firm to produce a given level of output with a given amount of inputs.

Self-Test

(Answers are provided at the end of the Self-Test.)

Multiple-Choice Questions

1. Refer to the graph below. The point of $250 and 35 million players represents a point on the market demand curve for digital music players. Which of the following interpretations of this point on the graph is correct?

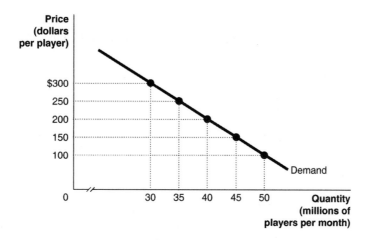

   a. The dot shows that consumers spend a total of $250 on 35 million players each month.
   b. When one player costs $250, consumers buy 35 million of them per month.
   c. When one player costs $250, suppliers sell 35 million of them per month.
   d. At $250, quantity demanded equals quantity supplied.

2. What does the term *quantity demanded* refer to?
   a. The total amount of a good that a consumer is willing to buy per month.
   b. The quantity of a good or service demanded that corresponds to the quantity supplied.
   c. The quantity of a good or service that a consumer is willing and able to purchase at a given price.
   d. None of the above.

3. Which of the following is the correct definition of *demand schedule*?
   a. The quantity of a good or service that a consumer is willing to purchase at a given price.
   b. A table showing the relationship between the price of a product and the quantity of the product demanded.
   c. A curve that shows the relationship between the price of a product and the quantity of the product demanded.
   d. The demand for a product by all the consumers in a given geographical area.

4. Which of the following is the correct definition of *demand curve*?
   a. The quantity of a good or service that a consumer is willing to purchase at a given price.
   b. A table showing the relationship between the price of a product and the quantity of the product demanded.
   c. A curve that shows the relationship between the price of a product and the quantity of the product demanded.
   d. The demand for a product by all the consumers in a given geographical area.

5. Which of the following is the correct definition of *market demand*?
   a. The quantity of a good or service that a consumer is willing to purchase at a given price.
   b. A table showing the relationship between the price of a product and the quantity of the product demanded.
   c. A curve that shows the relationship between the price of a product and the quantity of the product demanded.
   d. The demand by all the consumers for a given good or service.

6. Refer to the graph below. What happens to quantity demanded along this demand curve?

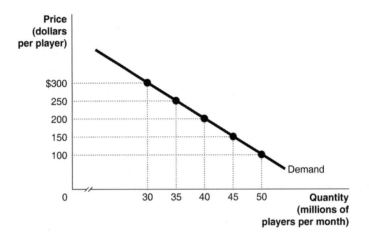

   a. It increases as the price increases.
   b. It increases as the price decreases.
   c. It may increase or decrease as the price increases.
   d. It is not related to price.

7. Refer to the graph below. Along the demand curve, what happens to the quantity demanded as the price falls from $250 to $200 per player?

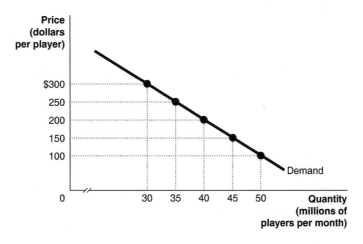

a.   The quantity demanded rises from 35 million to 40 million players per month.
b.   The quantity demanded falls from 40 million to 35 million players per month.
c.   We cannot predict the change in the quantity demanded without the supply curve.
d.   The change in the quantity demanded is not related to a change in price.

8. When the price of a digital music players rises, the quantity of digital music players demanded by consumers falls. According to this statement, what do we call the demand curve for digital music players?
a.   Unpredictable
b.   Upward sloping
c.   Downward sloping
d.   An exception to the law of demand

9. Which of the following explains why there is an inverse relationship between the price of a product and the quantity of the product demanded?
a.   The substitution effect
b.   The income effect
c.   The law of demand
d.   The price effect

10. What is the *law of demand*?
a.   The law of demand states that a change in the quantity demanded, caused by changes in price, makes the good more or less expensive relative to other goods.
b.   The law of demand states that a change in the quantity demanded, caused by changes in price, affects a consumer's purchasing power.
c.   The law of demand states that, holding everything else constant, when the price of good falls, the quantity demanded will increase, and vice versa.
d.   The law of demand is the requirement that when analyzing the relationship between price and quantity demanded, other variables must be held constant.

11. Which of the following best describes how changes in price affect a consumer's purchasing power?
    a. The law of demand
    b. The substitution effect
    c. The income effect
    d. The term *ceteris paribus*

12. Which of the following best describes how consumers consider buying other goods when the price of a good rises?
    a. The law of demand
    b. The substitution effect
    c. The income effect
    d. The term *ceteris paribus*

13. When analyzing the relationship between the price of a good and quantity demanded, other variables must be held constant. Which term best describes such an assumption?
    a. The law of demand
    b. The substitution effect
    c. The income effect
    d. *Ceteris paribus*

14. Refer to the graphs below. Each graph refers to the demand for digital music players. Which of the graphs best describes the impact of an increase in the price of a substitute good?

    a. The graph on the left
    b. The graph on the right
    c. Both graphs
    d. Neither graph

15. Refer to the graphs below. Each graph refers to the demand for digital music players. Which of the graphs best describes the impact of an increase in the price of a complementary good?

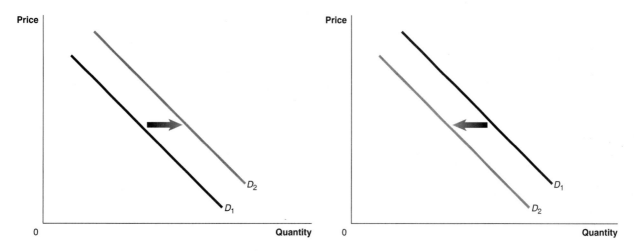

    a. The graph on the left
    b. The graph on the right
    c. Both graphs
    d. Neither graph

16. Refer to the graphs below. Each graph refers to the demand for digital music players. Which of the graphs best describes the impact of an increase in income, assuming that printers are a normal good?

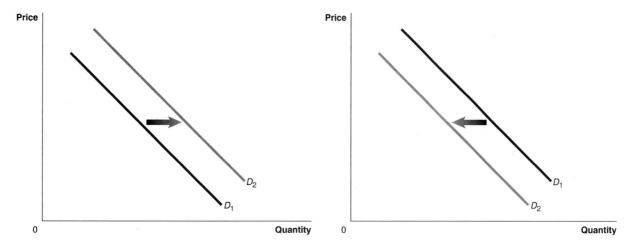

    a. The graph on the left
    b. The graph on the right
    c. Both graphs
    d. Neither graph

17. Refer to the graphs below. Each graph refers to the demand for digital music players. Which of the graphs best describes the impact of an increase in the *taste* for digital music players?

    a. The graph on the left
    b. The graph on the right
    c. Both graphs
    d. Neither graph

18. Refer to the graphs below. Each graph refers to the demand for digital music players. Which of the graphs best describes the impact of an increase in population?

    a. The graph on the left
    b. The graph on the right
    c. Both graphs
    d. Neither graph

19. Refer to the graphs below. Each graph refers to the demand for digital music players. Which of the graphs best describes the impact of an increase in the expected price of digital music players in the future?

a. The graph on the left
b. The graph on the right
c. Both graphs
d. Neither graph

20. When two goods are *complements*, which of the following occurs?
    a. The two goods can be used for the same purpose.
    b. The two goods are used together.
    c. The demand for each of these goods increases when income rises.
    d. The demand for each of these goods increases as income falls.

21. When two goods are *substitutes*, which of the following occurs?
    a. The two goods can be used for the same purpose.
    b. The two goods are used together.
    c. The demand for each of these goods increases when income rises.
    d. The demand for each of these goods increases as income falls.

22. What is an *inferior good*?
    a. A good for which demand increases as income rises.
    b. A good for which demand decreases as income rises.
    c. A good that cannot be used together with another good.
    d. A good that does not serve any real purpose.

23. What is a *normal good*?
    a. A good for which demand increases as income rises.
    b. A good for which demand decreases as income rises.
    c. A good that can be used together with another good.
    d. A good that does serves more than one purpose.

24. Refer to the graph below. Which of the following moves best describes a *change in demand*?

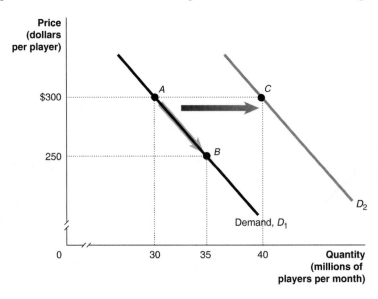

a. The move from *A* to *B*
b. The move from *A* to *C*
c. Either the move from *A* to *B* or from *A* to *C*
d. The move from *B* to *A*

25. Refer to the graph below. Which of the following moves best describes a *change in quantity demanded*?

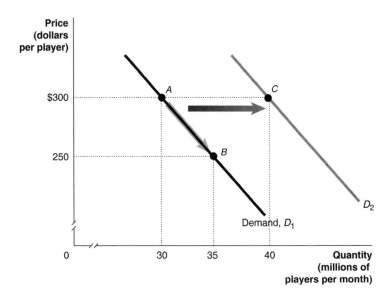

a. The move from *A* to *B*
b. The move from *A* to *C*
c. Either the move from *A* to *B* or from *A* to *C*
d. The move from *B* to *C*

26. Refer to the graph below. Which of the following moves best describes what happens when there is a change in a determinant of the demand for digital music players other than the price of players?

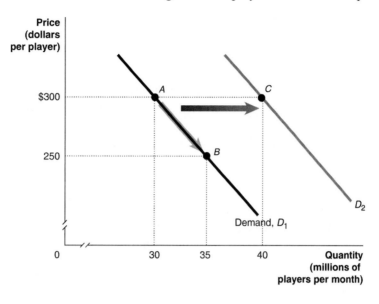

a. A move from *A* to *B*
b. A move from *A* to *C*
c. Either the move from *A* to *B* or from *A* to *C*
d. None of the above

27. Refer to the graph below. Which of the following moves best describes what happens when a change in the price of digital music players affects the market demand for players?

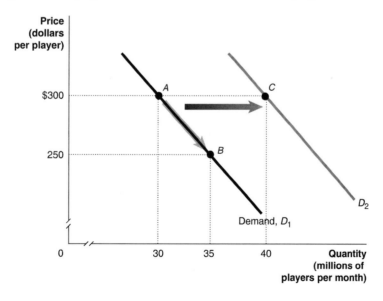

a. A move from *A* to *B*
b. A move from *A* to *C*
c. Either the move from *A* to *B* or from *A* to *C*
d. None of the above

28. Which of the following would NOT shift the demand curve for a good or service?
    a. A change in the price of a related good
    b. A change in the price of the good or service
    c. A change in expectations about the price of the good or service
    d. A change in income

29. What does the term *quantity supplied* refer to?
    a. The quantity of a good or service that a firm is willing and able to supply at a given price.
    b. A table that shows the relationship between the price of a product and the quantity of the product supplied.
    c. A curve that shows the relationship between the price of a product and the quantity of the product demanded.
    d. None of the above

30. Which of the following is the textbook's definition of *supply schedule*?
    a. The quantity of a good or service that a firm is willing to supply at a given price.
    b. A table that shows the relationship between the price of a product and the quantity of the product supplied.
    c. A curve that shows the relationship between the price of a product and the quantity of the product demanded.
    d. None of the above

31. Which of the following is the textbook's definition of *supply curve*?
    a. The quantity of a good or service that a firm is willing to supply at a given price.
    b. A table that shows the relationship between the price of a product and the quantity of the product supplied.
    c. A curve that shows the relationship between the price of a product and the quantity of the product supplied.
    d. None of the above

32. Which of the following is consistent with the law of supply?
    a. An increase in price causes an increase in the quantity supplied, and a decrease in price causes decrease in the quantity supplied.
    b. A change in price causes a shift of the supply curve.
    c. Supply shifts are caused not by a single variable but most likely by a number of different variables.
    d. All of the above

33. Refer to the graphs below. Each graph refers to the supply for digital music players. Which of the graphs best describes the impact of an increase in the price of an input?

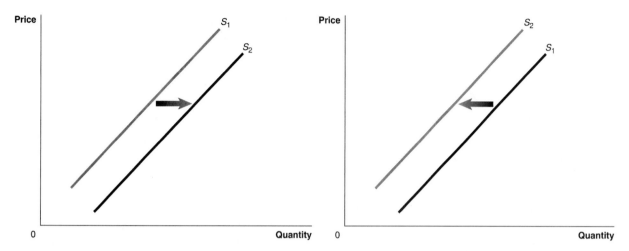

    a. The graph on the left
    b. The graph on the right
    c. Both graphs
    d. Neither graph

34. Refer to the graphs below. Each graph refers to the supply for digital music players. Which of the graphs best describes the impact of an increase in productivity?

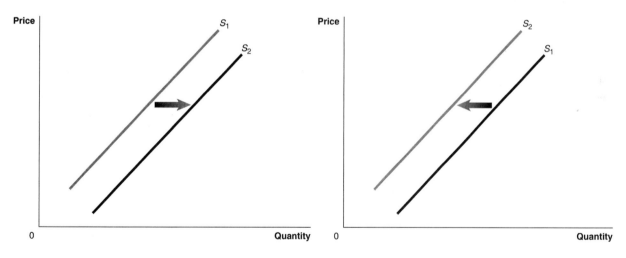

    a. The graph on the left
    b. The graph on the right
    c. Both graphs
    d. Neither graph

35. Refer to the graphs below. Each graph refers to the supply for digital music players. Which of the graphs best describes the impact of an increase in the price of a substitute in production?

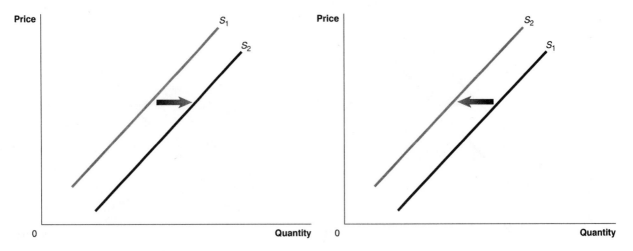

 a. The graph on the left
 b. The graph on the right
 c. Both graphs
 d. Neither graph

36. Refer to the graphs below. Each graph refers to the supply for digital music players. Which of the graphs best describes the impact of an increase in the expected future price of the product?

 a. The graph on the left
 b. The graph on the right
 c. Both graphs
 d. Neither graph

37. Refer to the graphs below. Each graph refers to the supply for digital music players. Which of the graphs best describes the impact of an increase in the number of firms in the market?

   a. The graph on the left
   b. The graph on the right
   c. Both graphs
   d. Neither graph

38. Refer to the graph below. Which of the following moves best describes what happens when there is a change in a determinant of the supply for digital music players other than the price of players?

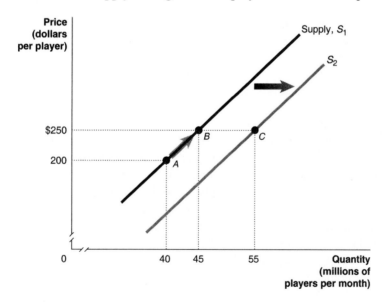

   a. A move from *A* to *B*
   b. A move from *A* to *C*
   c. Either the move from *A* to *B* or from *A* to *C*
   d. None of the above

39. Refer to the graph below. Which of the following moves best describes what happens when a change in the price of digital music players affects the market supply for players?

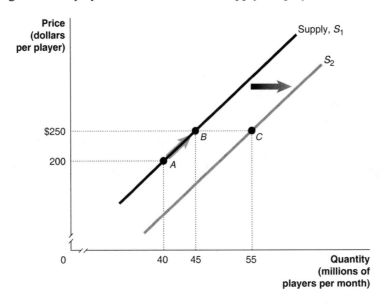

    a. A move from A to B
    b. A move from A to C
    c. Either the move from A to B or from A to C
    d. None of the above

40. A surplus exists in a market if the actual price is
    a. equal to equilibrium price.
    b. below equilibrium price.
    c. above equilibrium price.
    d. either above or below the equilibrium price.

41. If a shortage exists in a market we know that the actual price is
    a. below equilibrium price and quantity demanded is greater than quantity supplied.
    b. above equilibrium price and quantity demanded is greater than quantity supplied.
    c. above equilibrium price and quantity supplied is greater than quantity demanded.
    d. below equilibrium price and quantity supplied is greater than quantity demanded.

42. An early frost in the apple orchards of Washington State would cause
    a. an increase in the demand for apple juice, increasing price.
    b. an increase in the supply of apple juice, decreasing price.
    c. a decrease in the demand for apple juice, decreasing price.
    d. a decrease in the supply of apple juice, increasing price.

43. Which of the following would definitely result in a higher price in the market for tennis shoes?
    a. demand increases and supply decreases
    b. demand and supply both decrease
    c. demand decreases and supply increases
    d. demand and supply both increase

44. Suppose that the income of buyers in a market increases and a technological advancement also occurs. What would we expect to happen in the market for a normal good?
    a. The equilibrium price would increase, but the impact on the amount sold in the market would be ambiguous.
    b. The equilibrium price would decrease, but the impact on the amount sold in the market would be ambiguous.
    c. Equilibrium quantity would increase, but the impact on equilibrium price would be ambiguous.
    d. Both equilibrium price and equilibrium quantity would increase.

Short Answer Questions

1. What evidence can be used to support the following statement? "Tickets to the World Series and the Super Bowl do not sell at their equilibrium prices."

   _____

   _____

   _____

   _____

   _____

2. In response to a surplus, a firm will lower a product's price until the quantity supplied equals quantity demanded. But prices of some goods will fall more quickly than others. What type of good would a firm lower the price of quickly in response to a surplus?

   _____

   _____

   _____

   _____

3. Explain the difference between a shortage and scarcity.

   _____

   _____

   _____

   _____

4. During 2007 there were over 80,000 people on waiting lists for kidney, lung, and other organ transplant operations. By law, organ donors and their families in the United States may not be paid for the donated organs. If payments for organ donations were made legal in the United States, would this affect the demand or the quantity demanded for organ transplants demanded?

_____

_____

_____

_____

5. The demand for health care in the United States is expected to rise throughout the first part of the twenty-first century. Which of the variables that influence market demand is most responsible for this expected increase?

_____

_____

_____

True/False Questions

T F 1. A market demand curve demonstrates the quantity that each consumer is willing to buy at each possible price.

T F 2. The law of demand states that, holding everything else constant, increases in price cause decreases in demand.

T F 3. The price of lobsters is higher in the spring than in the summer, even though demand is greater in summer. The lower summer price results from increases in the supply of lobsters in the summer.

T F 4. As a result of a surplus, the price in a market will fall; quantity supplied falls and quantity demanded rises until the new equilibrium is reached.

T F 5. An increase in income causes demand for a normal good to increase.

T F 6. It is better for a supermarket to remove a slow-selling good from its shelves if it is a substitute for another good than if it is a complement with another good.

T F 7. Inferior goods are goods that are of lesser quality than other similar goods.

T F 8. Substitution and income effects are used to explain the law of supply.

T F 9. A negative technological change will shift the supply curve for a product to the left.

T F 10. Increases in the supply of flat-screen televisions led to lower prices and increased quantity demanded for these televisions.

T F 11. An increase in the price of a complement for good A will decrease the demand for good A.

T F 12. When Microsoft decided to start producing the Zune music player, the market supply curve for players shifted to the left.

T F 13. An increase in the demand for digital music players will cause an increase in the price of digital music players and an increase in the supply of digital music players.

T F 14. A change in price will not cause a change in demand or supply.

T F 15. Competitive markets have many buyers and many sellers.

Answers to the Self-Test

Multiple-Choice Questions

Question	Answer	Comment
1	b	In this example, the quantity of players demanded per month is 35 million when the price per player is $250.
2	c	Quantity demanded is the quantity purchased per period of time for a given price.
3	b	The demand schedule is a table, not a curve or a single amount of quantity demanded at a given price.
4	c	This is the definition of *demand curve*.
5	d	This is the definition of *market demand*.
6	b	The demand curve is downward sloping. There is an inverse relationship between price and quantity demanded. Price and quantity demanded move in opposite directions.
7	a	The demand curve is downward sloping, so as the price falls the quantity demanded rises.
8	c	The consumers' demand curve is downward sloping. There is an inverse relationship between price and quantity demanded. Price and quantity demanded move in opposite directions.
9	c	The law of demand states that there is an inverse relationship between the price of a product and the quantity of the product demanded.
10	c	According to the law of demand, there is an inverse relationship between the price of a product and the quantity of the product demanded.
11	c	Along with the substitution effect, the income effect helps to explain why a demand curve is downward sloping. (Note that the income effect only works in this direction for normal goods.)
12	b	The substitution effect, along with the income effect, helps to explain why a demand curve is downward sloping. (Note that the income effect only works in this direction for normal goods.)
13	d	The term *ceteris paribus* means controlling variables during an analysis.
14	a	This graph shows an increase in demand. When the price of a substitute good rises, the demand for the good in question also rises.
15	b	Demand decreases when the price of a complementary good increases.
16	a	This graph shows an increase in demand. When income rises, the demand for any normal good also rises.
17	a	This graph shows an increase in demand. When tastes for a product rise, the demand for the good in question also rises.
18	a	This graph shows an increase in demand. When population rises, the demand for the good in question also rises.
19	a	This graph shows an increase in demand. When the expected future price of a product rises, the demand for the good in question today also rises.
20	b	Complementary goods work together.
21	a	The two goods can be used in place of each other.
22	b	The term inferior good means consumers will buy less of a good as income rises.

23	a	The term normal good means consumers will buy more of a good as income rises.
24	b	By definition, anything that causes a demand curve to shift also causes a change in demand.
25	a	By definition, anything that causes movement along a single demand curve also causes a change in quantity demanded. And the only factor that can change quantity demanded is a change in the price of the product.
26	b	When any variable that affects demand changes, demand shifts. (The sole exception to this rule is changes in the price of the product.)
27	a	By definition anything that causes movement along a single demand curve also causes a change in quantity demanded. And the only factor that can change quantity demanded is a change in the price of the product.
28	b	A change in the price of a good or service does not cause a shift in the demand curve. It would cause a movement along the demand curve.
29	a	*Quantity supplied* is the quantity of a good or service that a firm is willing to supply at a given price. When any variable that affects demand changes, demand shifts. (The sole exception to this rule is changes in the price of the product.)
30	b	A table that shows the relationship between the price of a product and the quantity of the product supplied is called the *supply schedule*. By definition anything that causes movement along a single demand curve also causes a change in quantity demanded. And the only factor that can change quantity demanded is a change in the price of the product.
31	c	A curve that shows the relationship between the price of a product and the quantity of the product supplied is called a supply curve. *Quantity supplied* is the quantity of a good or service that a firm is willing to supply at a given price.
32	a	This is the law of supply. A table that shows the relationship between the price of a product and the quantity of the product supplied is called the *supply schedule*.
33	a	This graph shows a decrease in supply. When the price of an input increases, supply decreases.
34	b	This graph shows an increase in supply. When productivity increases, supply increases.
35	a	This graph shows a decrease in supply. When the price of a substitute in production increases, supply for the good in question decreases because more of the substitute is produced and less of the good in question is produced.
36	a	This graph shows a decrease in supply. When the expected future price of a product increases, supply for the good in question decreases today because less of the good will be produced today and more will be produced in the future in order to take advantage of the higher price in the future.
37	b	This graph shows an increase in supply. When the number of firms in the market increases, market supply increases.
38	b	A determinant of supply other than price will cause a shift in the supply curve. In this case, the supply increases or the supply curve shifts to the right.
39	a	If the price of a good changes that will cause a movement along the supply curve. This movement from *A* to *B* is an increase the quantity supplied.
40	c	If the actual price is above the equilibrium price, the quantity supplied is greater than the quantity demanded, so there is a surplus.
41	a	If the actual price is below the equilibrium price, the quantity demanded is greater than the quantity supplied, so there is a shortage.
42	d	If there is a frost, it will destroy the apples, which will cause the price of apples to rise. Since apples are an input in the production of apple juice, the supply of apple juice will decrease.
43	a	The price will rise when the demand increases and the supply decreases, though the effect on the equilibrium quantity will be ambiguous.

44   c   Both the demand and supply shift right, which will cause an increase in the equilibrium quantity and an ambiguous effect on the price.

Short Answer Responses

1. Tickets for these events typically sell out soon after they are offered to the public. Many of these tickets are later resold at prices higher than the original prices buyers paid for them. This implies that the quantity demanded for the tickets is greater than the quantity supplied at the original prices. The prices the tickets are first sold at are below their equilibrium levels. (Event promoters often price tickets this way to create additional publicity about the event.)

2. Prices of perishable goods such as fresh fish, baked goods, milk, and fruit are likely to be lowered quickly. A key factor is the product's durability. Services are the most perishable products, but a head of lettuce is not much more durable. On the other hand, cars and home appliances can be stored as inventories for quite some time without spoiling.

3. A shortage exists when the price for a product is less than the equilibrium price. If the price is allowed to rise to its equilibrium level, the shortage will be eliminated. But the product will be scarce whether the market price is above, below, or equal to its equilibrium value. Every economic product is scarce because unlimited human wants exceed society's limited productive resources.

4. Because the price of organs and transplant operations would rise, this would affect quantity demanded rather than demand. An increase in the price of organs and transplant operations would typically decrease the quantity demanded. But it is unlikely that the quantity demanded would change very much, if at all, because there are no good substitutes for the operations. And it's unusual for the transplant recipient to pay for the operation since surgery is usually covered by health insurance. This makes demand even less responsive to changes in price.

5. Demographics are most responsible for this change. As more members of the so-called "baby boomer" generation reach retirement age, their demand for health care will increase. (Most health care spending is for care of those over age 60.)

True/False Answers

1. F   The demand curve shows the quantity that all consumers would collectively demand at each possible price.
2. F   Increases in price cause decreases in quantity demanded, not demand.
3. T   Even though demand increases in the summer, the supply increases even more.
4. T   A surplus would cause firms to want to decrease their supply to reduce their inventories. As the price falls the quantity demanded increases and the quantity supplied decreases.
5. T   A normal good is one for which as income rises the demand increases.
6. T   If the good is a substitute, consumers will buy the related good instead. If it is a complement and you remove it from the shelf they will no longer buy the complement.
7. F   Inferior goods are ones that you buy less of as your inferior rises.
8. F   Substitution and income effects explain the law of demand.
9. T   If something causes technology to decrease, the supply will decrease.
10. T   As the supply increases, the market price will fall, which will cause a movement down the demand curve, i.e. there will be an increase in the quantity demanded.

11. T Complements are consumed together, such as coffee and creamer. If the price of one increases, consumers will buy less of the related good.
12. F An increase in the number of suppliers for digital music players will cause an increase in supply.
13. F An increase in demand for digital music players will cause an increase in the supply of digital music players, but it will not increase the supply. It will increase the quantity supplied.
14. T A change in price causes a change in the quantity demanded or quantity supplied, not demand or supply.
15. T A competitive market must have many buyers and many sellers.

Chapter 4

Economic Efficiency, Government Price Setting, and Taxes

Chapter Summary

Governments of over 200 cities in the United States have placed ceilings on the maximum rent some landlords can charge for their apartments. Governments also impose taxes in some markets. To understand the economic impact of government in markets, it is necessary to understand consumer surplus and producer surplus.

Consumer surplus is the dollar benefit consumers receive from buying goods and services at market prices that are less than the maximum prices they would be willing to pay. **Producer surplus** is the dollar benefit producers receive from selling goods and services at prices greater than the minimum prices they would be willing to accept. **Economic surplus** is the sum of consumer surplus and producer surplus. In a competitive market with no externalities, the equilibrium price for a good or service occurs where the marginal cost of the last unit produced and sold is equal to the marginal benefit consumers receive from the last unit bought. Therefore the equilibrium quantity produced in a competitive market is economically efficient. At this equilibrium level of output, economic surplus is maximized.

In some markets, producers lobby for government action to set a legal price greater than the equilibrium price – a **price floor**. Some consumers lobby the government to force firms to charge a price lower than the equilibrium price – a **price ceiling**. Price floors were established in agricultural markets in the United States during the Great Depression. The minimum wage is another example of a price floor. For most occupations, it is illegal for an employer to pay less than the minimum wage established by Congress. Price ceilings are most often found in the markets for apartments in various cities. You're probably more familiar with these ceilings under their usual name: *rent control*. Compared to the competitive equilibrium, price ceilings and price floors reduce economic efficiency.

A tax on the sale of a good or service also reduces economic efficiency. **Tax incidence** is the actual division of the burden of a tax between buyers and sellers. The incidence of a tax depends on how responsive producers and consumers are to the price change caused by the tax.

Learning Objectives

When you finish this chapter, you should be able to:

1. **Distinguish between the concepts of consumer surplus and producer surplus**. Consumer surplus is the benefit consumers receive from paying a price lower than the maximum price they would be willing to pay. Producer surplus is the benefit a firm receives from selling a good or a service at a price higher than the minimum the firm would be willing to accept. Economic surplus is the consumer surplus plus producer surplus.

2. **Understand the concept of economic efficiency.** Maximum economic efficiency results when the marginal benefit received by consumers from the last unit bought equals the marginal cost to producers from selling the unit. An economically efficient outcome occurs when a competitive market equilibrium is reached.

3. **Explain the economic effect of government-imposed price ceilings and price floors.** Though total economic surplus is maximized when a competitive market equilibrium is reached, individual consumers would rather pay a price lower than the equilibrium price and individual producers would rather charge a higher price. Producers or consumers who are dissatisfied with the equilibrium price can lobby government to legally require a different price. When the government intervenes it can aid sellers by requiring a price above equilibrium, a price floor, or it can aid consumers by requiring a price below equilibrium, a price ceiling. Price floors and ceilings reduce economic efficiency, causing a deadweight loss.

4. **Analyze the economic impact of taxes.** Whenever a government places a tax on a good or service, economic efficiency is reduced. Some of the reduction in economic surplus due to the tax becomes revenue for the government while the rest of the reduction is a deadweight loss, that is, a net reduction in economic surplus that is not transferred to government or anyone.

Appendix: Use quantitative demand and supply analysis. Your instructor may assign this appendix.

Chapter Review

Chapter Opener: Should the Government Control Apartment Rents? (pages 98-99)

Rent control is an example of a price ceiling. Rent controls exist in about 200 cities in the United States. Although the rules that govern rent control are complex and vary by city, rent control drives up the demand and price for apartments not subject to the controls. Like any price control, rent control also has many unintended consequences including lower quality of rent-controlled units, black markets, and unwanted, inefficient side conditions.

📖 Helpful Study Hint

Read *Solved Problem 4-3* and *An Inside Look* from this chapter to reinforce your understanding of the impact of rent control on the demand and supply of apartments.

Economics in YOUR Life! asks if rent control makes it easier for you to find an affordable apartment. Keep this question in mind as you read the chapter. The authors will answer this question at the end of the chapter.

4.1 Consumer Surplus and Producer Surplus (pages 100-105)

Learning Objective 1 Distinguish between the concepts of consumer surplus and producer surplus.

Consumer surplus is the difference between the highest price a consumer is willing to pay and the price the consumer actually pays. **Producer surplus** is the difference between the lowest price a firm would be willing to accept and the price it actually receives. Consumer and producer surplus represent the net benefits consumers and producers receive from buying and selling a good or service in a market.

Marginal benefit is the additional benefit to a consumer from consuming one more unit of a good or service. The height of a market demand curve at a given quantity measures the marginal benefit to someone from consuming that quantity. Consumer surplus refers to the difference between this marginal benefit and the market price the consumer pays. Total consumer surplus is the difference between marginal benefit and price for all quantities bought by consumers. Total consumer surplus is equal to the area below the demand curve and above the market price for the number of units consumed.

Marginal cost is the additional cost to a firm of producing one more unit of a good or service. The height of a market supply curve at a given quantity measures the marginal cost of this quantity. Producer surplus refers to the difference between this marginal cost and the market price the producer receives. Total producer surplus equals the area above the supply curve and below price for all quantities sold.

📖 Helpful Study Hint

You probably have bought something you thought was a bargain. If you did, the difference between what you would have been willing to pay and what you did pay was your consumer surplus. Consumers differ in the value they place on the same item but typically pay the same price for the item. Those who value an item the most receive the most consumer surplus. Because the marginal cost of producing a good rises as more is produced, and price will equal marginal cost only for the last unit of output sold, price must be greater than the marginal cost of producing all but the last unit of output. Therefore, firms will earn producer surplus on all but the last unit sold. Be sure you understand Figure 4-5 and Figure 4-6 and the explanation of these figures in the textbook.

Extra Solved Problem 4-1

Chapter 4 of the textbook includes two Solved Problems. Here is an extra Solved Problem to help you build your skills solving economic problems.

Consumer and Producer Surplus for the NFL Sunday Ticket

Supports Learning Objective 4-1: Distinguish between the concepts of consumer surplus and producer surplus.

Making the Connection "The Consumer Surplus from Satellite Television" explained consumer surplus using the example of customers of DirecTV and the DISH Network, both providers of satellite television. But only DirecTV offers its customers the option of subscribing to the NFL Sunday Ticket. In 2007, subscribers to this service paid $229 for the right to watch every regular season NFL Sunday game broadcast except for those games played on Sunday evenings. For fans that have moved to cities that don't broadcast their favorite team's games, this option is very attractive. Local television stations offer games played by teams with the most local interest. A long-time fan of the New York Giants or Denver Broncos who moved to Illinois would likely have to settle for watching the Chicago Bears most Sunday afternoons – unless he had signed up for the DirecTV NFL Sunday Ticket.

Team Marketing Report estimated that the 2005 average ticket price for NFL games for all teams was $58.95 and the per-game average Fan Cost was about $330 (this amount includes four average price tickets, four small soft drinks, two small beers, four hot dogs, two game programs, parking and two adult size caps). Each NFL team plays eight regular-season games in their home stadium.

a. Estimate the value of consumer surplus for the NFL Sunday Ticket for a representative fan.

b. Estimate the value of producer surplus for the NFL Sunday Ticket.

Source: www.teammarketing.com

SOLVING THE PROBLEM

Step 1:   Review the chapter material.
This problem is about consumer and producer surplus, so you may want to review the section "Consumer Surplus and Producer Surplus," which begins on page 100 in the textbook.

Step 2:   Identify the maximum price a consumer would pay for the NFL Sunday Ticket.
The consumers who benefit most from the NFL Sunday Ticket are those who have the strongest demand to watch their favorite team play on Sundays. Assume that an average season ticket holder found out prior to fall 2005 that he was being transferred by his employer to a location that required him to forego season tickets for himself and three other family members. Using the Team Marketing estimate, he would save $330 for each home game that he and his family would no longer attend. Therefore, his total saving would be $330 x 8 = $2,640. This is an estimate of the maximum price he would pay for the NFL Sunday Ticket. (Note that he would also be able to watch his team's away games but would probably be able to view these games from his home at no additional cost if he had not moved).

Step 3:   Estimate the value of consumer surplus.
For the average season ticket holder and his family, an estimate of the consumer surplus is: $2,640 − $229 = $2,411. Note that each family member who no longer attended home games can watch these games at home.

Step 4:   Identify the minimum price DirecTV would accept for the NFL Sunday Ticket.
The NFL Package is offered to existing DirecTV customers as an additional viewing option. Therefore, only trivial additional costs are incurred by DirecTV. The customer's billing must be adjusted to include this option, and the service must be "switched on" for this customer. Assume that these costs and an economic profit sufficient to compensate DirecTV for offering this service is $30. Assume that the marginal cost is zero so that the minimum price DirecTV would accept for the NFL Sunday Ticket is $0.

Step 5: **Estimate the value of producer surplus.**
Because DirecTV receives $229 for the NFL Sunday Ticket its producer surplus for this customer is $229 − $0 = $229.

4.2 The Efficiency of Competitive Markets (pages 105-107)

Learning Objective 2 Understand the concept of economic efficiency.

Economic surplus is the sum of consumer and producer surplus. When equilibrium is reached in a competitive market, the marginal benefit equals the marginal cost of the last unit sold. This is an economically efficient outcome. If less than the equilibrium output were produced, the marginal benefit of the last unit bought would exceed its marginal cost. If more than the equilibrium quantity were produced, the marginal benefit of this last unit would be less than its marginal cost. We can also think of the concept of economic efficiency in terms of economic surplus. When in equilibrium, the willingness of the consumer to pay for the last unit is equal to the lowest price a firm will be willing to accept. If less than the equilibrium output were produced, the willingness to pay for the last unit bought would exceed the minimum price that firms would be willing to accept. If more than equilibrium quantity were produced, the willingness to pay of this last unit would be less than the minimum price that producers would accept.

Economic efficiency is a market outcome in which the marginal benefit to consumers of the last unit produced is equal to its marginal cost of production and where the sum of consumer and producer surplus is at a maximum. A **deadweight loss** is the reduction in economic surplus that results when a market is not in competitive equilibrium.

📖 Helpful Study Hint

Figure 4-7 illustrates the deadweight loss from production at a nonequilibrium point in a competitive market. You should understand that when the quantity of chai tea cups sold is 14,000 instead of 15,000, there is a loss of both producer surplus and consumer surplus.

Extra Solved Problem 4-2

Chapter 4 of the textbook includes two Solved Problems. Here is an extra Solved Problem to help you build your skills solving economic problems.

Supports Learning Objective 4-2: Understand the concept of economic efficiency.

Suppose that the tickets for a Kelly Clarkson concert just went on sale in your local area. The tickets are selling for $25 each, the equilibrium price. Suppose that the willingness to pay of the last consumer to buy a ticket was $50 and the minimum that the producer was willing to accept was $10.

a.   Is this market outcome economically efficient?

b.   If not, what would need to occur for this market to become economically efficient?

SOLVING THE PROBLEM

Step 1:   Review the chapter material.
This problem is about economic efficiency, so you may want to review the section "The Efficiency of Competitive Markets," which begins on page 105 in the textbook.

Step 2:   Compare the minimum price that the concert producer is willing to accept to the price the consumer is willing to pay.
Because the value to the consumer of the last ticker sold is higher than the minimum price that the producer is willing to accept, the market is not efficient. The willingness to pay by the consumer must be equal to the minimum price that the producer is willing to accept in order for efficiency to be maximized.

Step 3:   Determine what needs to occur in the market for the market to become efficient.
Because the willingness to pay is greater than the minimum the firm is willing to accept, there is additional consumer and producer surplus that could be gained by increasing the number of tickets sold. The number of tickets sold should increase until the willingness to pay of last consumer is equal to the minimum that the producer is willing to accept.

4.3 LEARNING OBJECTIVE

4.3   Government Intervention in the Market: Price Floors and Price Ceilings (pages 107-115)

Learning Objective 3 Explain the economic effect of government-imposed price ceilings and price floors.

Though the net benefit to society is maximized at a competitive market equilibrium, individual consumers would be better off if they could pay a lower than equilibrium price and individual producers would be better off if they could sell at a higher than equilibrium price. Consumers and producers sometimes lobby government to legally require a market price different from the equilibrium price. These lobbying efforts are sometimes successful. During the Great Depression of the 1930s, farm prices fell to very low levels. Farmers were able to convince the federal government to raise prices by setting price floors for many agricultural prices.

A **price floor** is a legally determined minimum price that sellers may receive. A price floor encourages producers to produce more output than consumers want to buy at the floor price. The government often buys the surplus, which is equal to the quantity supplied minus the quantity demanded, at the floor price. The government may also pay farmers to take some land out of cultivation, which would decrease supply. The marginal cost of production exceeds the marginal benefit, and there is a deadweight loss, which represents a decline in efficiency due to the price floor.

A **price ceiling** is a legally determined maximum price that sellers may charge. Price ceilings are meant to help consumers who lobby for lower prices. Consumers typically lobby for price ceilings after a sharp increase in the price of an item on which they spend a significant amount of their budgets (for example, rent or gasoline). At the ceiling price, the quantity demanded is greater than the quantity supplied so that the marginal benefit of the last item sold (the quantity supplied) exceeds the marginal cost of producing it. Price ceilings result in a deadweight loss and a reduction of economic efficiency. Price ceilings create incentives for black markets. A **black market** refers to buying and selling at prices that violate government price regulations.

With any price floor or price ceiling, there are winners and losers from the policy. The deadweight loss associated with a given policy tells us that the gains to the winners are outweighed by the losses to the losers.

📖 Helpful Study Hint

An interesting question to consider is why politicians maintain agricultural price supports despite the significant costs their constituents pay for these programs. Part of the explanation is that because each individual incurs a small fraction of the total cost, it is hardly worth the trouble to register a complaint to lawmakers. But the benefits of price floors are concentrated among a few producers who have a strong incentive to lobby for the continuation of the price supports. Politicians act quite rationally by ignoring the interests of those who pay for these programs.

You may be swayed by the argument that a price ceiling is justified because its intent is to help low-income consumers afford a price-controlled product. Though some low-income consumers may be among those who buy the product, there is no guarantee of this. Suppose you were a landlord who owned an apartment subject to rent control. As a result, there are 5 potential tenants for one apartment you have to rent. The potential tenants include a male college student, a single female school teacher with a pet dog, a low-income retail worker with a spouse and two children, a medical doctor, and a lawyer. Assume that you can select any one of these as your tenant. Would you select the retail worker? What about the college student?

4.4 LEARNING OBJECTIVE

4.4 The Economic Impact of Taxes (pages 115-120)

Learning Objective 4 Analyze the economic impact of taxes.

Government taxes on goods and services reduce the quantity produced. A tax imposed on producers of a product will shift the supply curve up by the amount of the tax. Consumers pay a higher price for the product, and there will be a loss of consumer surplus. Because the price producers receive after paying the tax falls, there is also a loss of producer surplus. The imposition of a tax will also cause a deadweight loss. **Tax incidence** is the actual division of the burden of the tax between buyers and sellers. The incidence of a tax is not dependent on who is legally required to collect and pay the tax. Tax incidence is determined by the degree to which the market price rises as a result of a tax. This rise, in turn, is determined by the willingness of suppliers to change the quantity of the good or service they offer and the willingness of consumers to change their quantity demanded as a result of the tax.

📖 Helpful Study Hint

Estimating the impact of cigarette taxes is more complicated than it appears from Figure 4-10. This is because state excise taxes on cigarettes vary widely. In 2007, the tax per pack ranged from 17 cents in Missouri to $2.58 in New Jersey. In addition, some counties and cities impose their own taxes. The variation in taxes creates a black market that reduces legal sales of cigarettes and tax revenue in states with the highest tax rates. Bootleggers can earn illegal profits by buying cigarettes in states with low tax rates and selling them to retail stores in states with the highest taxes. A disturbing example of cigarette bootlegging was reported in 2002 when a suspected terrorist was found guilty by a federal court of buying cigarettes in North Carolina and selling them in Michigan where the per-pack tax differential was about 70 cents. Revenue from the illegal cigarette sales was allegedly used to fund Hezbollah, a terrorist organization with headquarters in the Middle East.

📖 Helpful Study Hint

Economics in YOUR Life! asked if you are more likely to find an affordable apartment in the city with rent control? Although rent control can keep rents lower than they might otherwise be, it can also lead to a permanent shortage of apartments. You may have to search for a long time to find a suitable apartment, and landlords may even ask you to give them payments "under the table," which would make your actual rent higher than the controlled rent. Finding an apartment in a city without rent control should be much easier, although the rent may be higher.

Key Terms

Black market. A market in which buying and selling take place at prices that violate government price regulations.

Consumer surplus. The difference between the highest price a consumer is willing to pay and the price the consumer actually pays.

Deadweight loss. The reduction in economic surplus resulting from a market not being in competitive equilibrium.

Economic efficiency. A market outcome in which the marginal benefit to consumers of the last unit produced is equal to its marginal cost of production and in which the sum of consumer surplus and producer surplus is at a maximum.

Economic surplus. The sum of consumer surplus and producer surplus.

Marginal benefit. The additional benefit to a consumer from consuming one more unit of a good or service.

Marginal cost. The additional cost to a firm of producing one more unit of a good or service.

Price ceiling. A legally determined maximum price that sellers may charge.

Price floor. A legally determined minimum price that sellers may receive.

Producer surplus. The difference between the lowest price a firm would be willing to accept and the price it actually receives.

Tax incidence. The actual division of the burden of a tax between buyers and sellers in a market.

Appendix

Quantitative Demand and Supply Analysis (pages 131-135)

LEARNING OBJECTIVE: Use quantitative demand and supply analysis.

Quantitative analysis supplements the use of demand and supply curves with equations. An example of the demand and supply for apartments in New York City is

$$Q^S = -450{,}000 + 1{,}300P$$

$$Q^D = 3{,}000{,}000 - 1{,}000P$$

Q^D and Q^S are the quantity demanded and quantity supplied of apartments per month, respectively. The coefficient of P in the first equation equals the change in quantity supplied for a one dollar per month change in price.

$$\frac{\Delta Q^S}{\Delta P} = 1{,}300$$

The coefficient of the price term in the second equation equals the change in quantity demanded for a one dollar per month change in price.

$$\frac{\Delta Q^S}{\Delta P} = -1{,}000$$

At the competitive market equilibrium quantity demanded equals quantity supplied

$$Q^D = Q^S \text{ or}$$

$$3{,}000{,}000 - 1{,}000P = -450{,}000 + 1{,}300P$$

Rearranging terms and solving for P yields the price at which quantity demanded equals the quantity supplied. This is the equilibrium price.

$$3{,}000{,}000 + 450{,}000 = 1{,}300P + 1{,}000P$$

$$3{,}450{,}000 = 2{,}300P$$

$$P = \$1{,}500$$

Substituting the equilibrium price into the equation for either demand or supply yields the equilibrium quantity.

$$Q^D = 3{,}000{,}000 - 1{,}000(1{,}500)$$

$$Q^D = 3{,}000{,}000 - 1{,}500{,}000$$

$$Q^D = 1{,}500{,}000$$

$$Q^S = -450{,}000 + 1{,}300P$$

$$Q^S = -450{,}000 + 1{,}300\,(1{,}500)$$

$$Q^S = 1{,}500{,}000$$

The demand equation can be used to determine the price at which the quantity demanded is zero.

$$Q^D = 3{,}000{,}000 - 1{,}000P$$

$$0 = 3{,}000{,}000 - 1{,}000P$$

$$-3{,}000{,}000 = -1{,}000P$$

$$P = (-3{,}000{,}000)/(-1{,}000)$$

$$P = \$3{,}000$$

The supply equation can be used to determine the price at which the quantity supplied equals zero.

$$Q^S = -450{,}000 + 1{,}300P$$

$$0 = -450{,}000 + 1{,}300P$$

$$450{,}000 = 1{,}300P$$

$$P = \$346.15$$

📖 Helpful Study Hint

The equations highlight an oddity of demand and supply analysis. The dependent variable in most graphs is the Y variable, or the variable measured along the vertical axis, while the independent or X variable is measured along the horizontal axis. Economists assume that price changes cause changes in quantity, so the dependent variable appears on

> the left hand side of the demand and supply equations. In turn, the coefficient of the price terms in these equations equals the change in quantity divided by a one unit change in price ($\Delta Q/\Delta P$). Unfortunately, for historical reasons, our demand and supply graphs have it backwards, with price on the vertical axis and quantity on the horizontal axis.

Calculating Consumer Surplus and Producer Surplus

Demand and supply equations can be used to measure consumer and producer surplus. Figure 4A-1 uses a graph to illustrate demand and supply. Because the demand curve is linear, consumer surplus is equal to the area of the blue triangle in Figure 4A-1. The area of a triangle is ½ multiplied by the base of the triangle multiplied by the height of the triangle, or

$$½ \times (1,500,000) \times (3000 - 1,500) = \$1,125,000,000.$$

Producer surplus is calculated in a similar way. Producer surplus is equal to the area above the supply curve and below the line representing market price. The supply curve is a straight line, so producer surplus equals the area of the right triangle:

$$½ \times (1,500,000) \times (1,500 - 346) = \$865,500,000$$

Producer surplus in the market for rental apartments in New York City is about $865 million.

Economic surplus is the sum of the consumer surplus and the producer surplus, so economic surplus is as follows:

$$\$1,125,000,000 + \$865,500,000 = \$1,990,500,000$$

Self-Test

(Answers are provided at the end of the Self-Test.)

Multiple-Choice Questions

1. What is the name of a legally determined minimum price that sellers may receive?
   a. A price ceiling
   b. A price floor
   c. Marginal benefit
   d. Consumer surplus

2. What is the name of a legally determined maximum price that sellers may charge?
   a. A price ceiling
   b. A price floor
   c. Marginal benefit
   d. Consumer surplus

3. Which of the following is the definition of *consumer surplus*?
    a. The additional benefit to a consumer from consuming one more unit of a good or service.
    b. The additional cost to a firm of producing one more unit of a good or service.
    c. The difference between the highest price a consumer is willing to pay and the price the consumer actually pays.
    d. The difference between the lowest price a firm would have been willing to accept and the price it actually receives.

4. Which of the following is the definition of *producer surplus*?
    a. The additional benefit to a consumer from consuming one more unit of a good or service.
    b. The additional cost to a firm of producing one more unit of a good or service.
    c. The difference between the highest price a consumer is willing to pay and the price the consumer actually pays.
    d. The difference between the lowest price a firm would have been willing to accept and the price it actually receives.

5. Which of the following is the definition of *marginal benefit*?
    a. The additional benefit to a consumer from consuming one more unit of a good or service.
    b. The additional cost to a firm of producing one more unit of a good or service.
    c. The difference between the highest price a consumer is willing to pay and the price the consumer actually pays.
    d. The difference between the lowest price a firm would have been willing to accept and the price it actually receives.

6. Which of the following is the definition of *marginal cost*?
    a. The additional benefit to a consumer from consuming one more unit of a good or service.
    b. The difference between the highest price a consumer is willing to pay and the price the consumer actually pays.
    c. The additional cost to a firm of producing one more unit of a good or service.
    d. The difference between the lowest price a firm would have been willing to accept and the price it actually receives.

7. Refer to the graph below. What name other than *demand curve* can you give this curve?

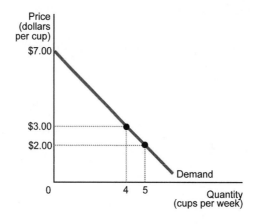

    a. The marginal cost curve
    b. The marginal benefit curve
    c. Consumer surplus
    d. The price-equilibrium curve

8. Refer to the graph below. The graph shows an individual's demand curve for tea. At a price of two dollars, the consumer is willing to buy five cups of tea per week. More precisely, what does this mean?

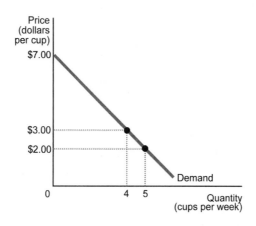

a. It means that marginal benefit equals marginal cost when five cups are consumed.
b. It means that the total cost of consuming five cups is $2.00.
c. It means that the marginal cost of producing five cups is $2.00.
d. It means that the marginal benefit of consuming the fifth cup is $2.00.

9. If the average price that cable subscribers are willing to pay for cable television is $208, but the actual price they pay is $81, how much is *consumer surplus* per subscriber?
   a. $208 + $81
   b. $208 – $81
   c. $81 + $127
   d. $81

10. Refer to the graph below. The graph shows the market demand for satellite TV service. If the market price is $81, which consumers receive consumer surplus in this market?

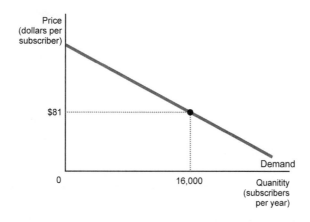

a. Those willing to pay something less than $81
b. Those willing to pay exactly $81
c. Those willing to pay more than $81
d. All of the above

11. Refer to the graph below. When market price is $2.00, how much is the *producer surplus* obtained from selling the 40th cup?

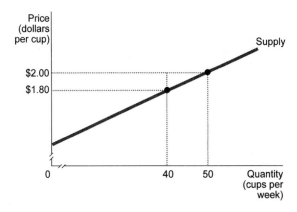

 a. $72.00
 b. $1.80
 c. $0.20
 d. $36.00

12. Refer to the graph below. How much is the marginal cost of producing the 50th cup?

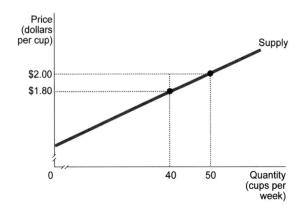

 a. $100.00
 b. $0.20
 c. $2.00
 d. None of the above; there is insufficient information to answer the question.

13. Precisely what does *consumer surplus* measure?
 a. The *total* benefit to consumers from participating in the market
 b. The *net* benefit to consumers from participating in the market
 c. The marginal cost of consumption
 d. The efficiency of competitive markets

14. Precisely what does *producer surplus* measure?
 a. The *total* benefit to producers from participating in the market
 b. The *net* benefit to producers from participating in the market
 c. The marginal cost of production
 d. The efficiency of competitive markets

15. Refer to the graph below. To achieve economic efficiency, which output level should be produced?

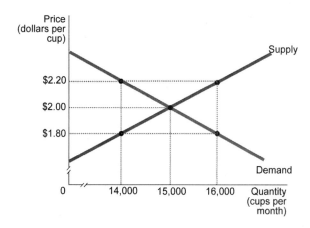

   a. 14,000 cups per month, because at this level of output, marginal benefit is greater than marginal cost.

   b. 15,000 cups per month, because at this level of output, marginal benefit is equal to marginal cost.

   c. 16,000 cups per month, because at this level of output, marginal benefit is less than marginal cost.

   d. Any of the output levels above is efficient.

16. Refer to the graph below. When should the level of output be reduced in order to increase economic efficiency?

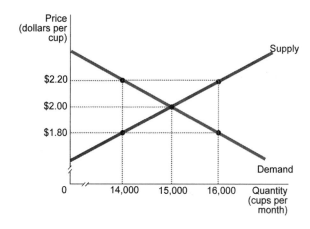

   a. If 14,000 cups were produced

   b. If 15,000 cups were produced

   c. If 16,000 cups were produced

   d. Never; output should always increase in order to increase economic efficiency.

17. When is output inefficiently low?

   a. When marginal benefit is greater than marginal cost.

   b. When marginal cost is greater than marginal benefit.

   c. When marginal cost is equal to marginal benefit.

   d. Any of the above; output can be inefficiently low at any time.

18. When a competitive market is in equilibrium, what is the economically efficient level of output?
    a. Any output level where marginal benefit is greater than marginal cost.
    b. Any output level where marginal cost is greater than marginal benefit.
    c. The output level where marginal cost is equal to marginal benefit.
    d. Any of the above; any output level can be efficient or inefficient.

19. What does the sum of consumer surplus and producer surplus equal?
    a. Economic efficiency
    b. Economic surplus
    c. A deadweight loss
    d. Competitive equilibrium

20. Refer to the graph below. Assume this is a competitive market. Which of the following *does not* exist when the price is $2.00?

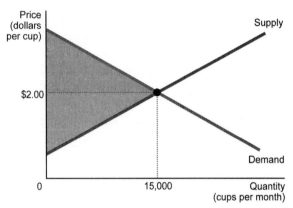

    a. Economic efficiency
    b. Economic surplus
    c. A deadweight loss
    d. Competitive equilibrium

21. Refer to the graph below. How much producer surplus is lost when the price is $2.20?

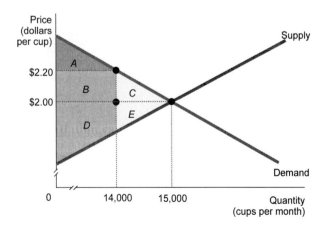

    a. Area *E*
    b. Area *C* + *E*
    c. Area *D*
    d. Area *B* + *D*

22. Refer to the graph below. Which area equals producer surplus when price is $2.20?

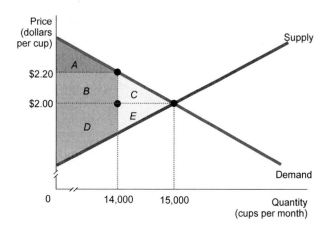

a. Area *E*
b. Area *C* + *E*
c. Area *D* + *E*
d. Area *B* + *D*

23. Refer to the graph below. Which area equals consumer surplus when price is $2.00?

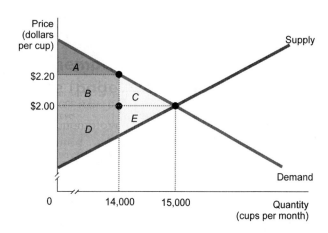

a. Area *A*
b. Area *B* + *C*
c. Area *A* + *B* + *C*
d. Area *B* + *C* + *D*

24. Refer to the graph below. Which area equals consumer surplus when price is $2.20?

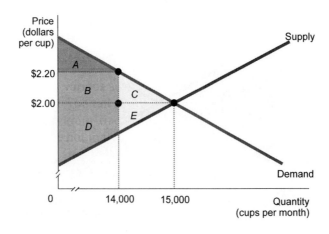

    a. Area *A*
    b. Area *B*
    c. Area *C*
    d. Area *D*

25. Refer to the graph below. After a price of $3.50 is imposed by the government in this market, what meaning do we give to area *A*?

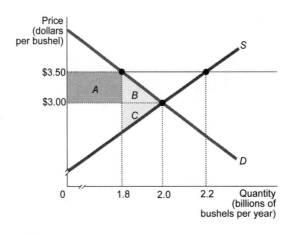

    a. Area *A* is consumer surplus transferred to producers.
    b. Area *A* is additional consumer surplus that goes to existing consumers in the market.
    c. Area *A* is a deadweight loss.
    d. Area *A* is a surplus of wheat.

26. Refer to the graph below. After a price of $3.50 is imposed by the government in this market, what meaning do we give to area $B + C$?

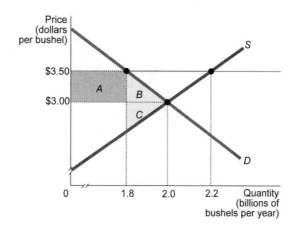

   a.   Producer surplus transferred to consumers
   b.   Additional consumer surplus to existing consumers in the market
   c.   Deadweight loss
   d.   A surplus of wheat

27. Refer to the graph below. According to this graph, the existence of a minimum wage in the market for low-skilled workers results in:

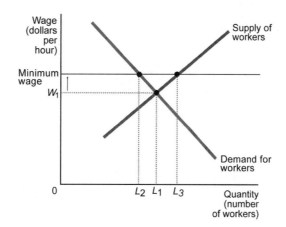

   a.   An increase in wages and employment
   b.   An increase in wages but lower employment
   c.   A decrease in wages but higher employment
   d.   A decrease in wages and employment

28. Refer to the graph below. According to this graph, the existence of a minimum wage in the market for low-skilled workers results in:

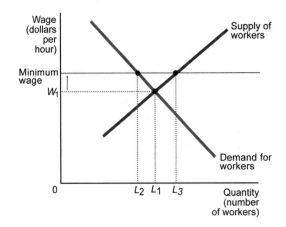

a. A shortage of workers
b. A surplus of workers
c. Neither a shortage nor a surplus of workers
d. A scarcity of workers

29. Refer to the graph below. After the rent control is imposed, area *A* represents:

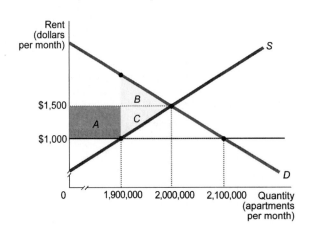

a. Consumer surplus transferred from renters to landlords
b. Producer surplus transferred from landlords to renters
c. A deadweight loss
d. A shortage of apartments

30. Refer to the graph below. After the rent control is imposed, which area represents a deadweight loss?

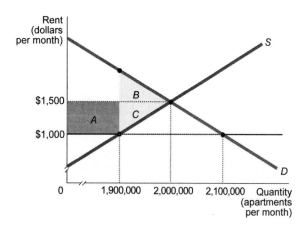

a. *A*
b. *A + B + C*
c. *B + C*
d. An area other than *A, B,* or *C*

31. Which of the following statements is correct?
    a. There is a shortage of every good that is scarce.
    b. There is no shortage of most scarce goods.
    c. Scarcity and shortage mean pretty much the same thing to economists.
    d. None of the above statements are correct.

32. Which of the following terms corresponds to a market in which buying and selling takes place at prices that violate government price regulations?
    a. Price conspiracy
    b. Scalping
    c. Competitive market
    d. Black market

33. Refer to the graph below. Suppose that this market is operating under the established rent control of $1,000 per month. Then, a black market for rent-controlled apartments develops, and the apartments then rent for $2,000 per month. What meaning does the sum of areas *A* + *E* have in this situation?

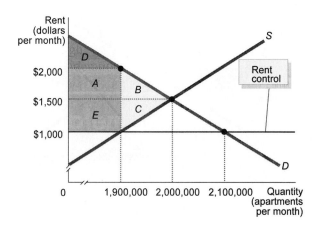

a. Consumer surplus transferred from renters to landlords
b. Producer surplus transferred from renters to landlords
c. Deadweight loss
d. A surplus of apartments

34. Refer to the graph below. When a black market for rent-controlled apartments develops, what is the area of deadweight loss?

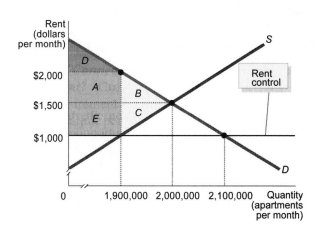

a. None; the deadweight loss disappears.
b. *B* + *C*
c. *A* + *E*
d. *D*

35. When the government imposes price floors or price ceilings, which of the following occurs?
a. Some people win
b. Some people lose
c. There is a loss of economic efficiency
d. All of the above

36. The term *tax incidence* refers to
    a. the type of product the tax is levied on.
    b. the amount of revenue collected by the government from a tax.
    c. the actual division of the burden of a tax.
    d. the actual versus the desired impact of a tax burden.

37. Refer to the graph below. What price do producers receive after this tax is imposed?

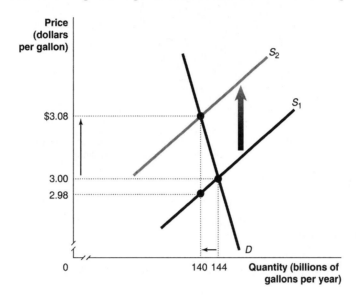

    a. $1.98
    b. $2.98
    c. $3.08
    d. None of the above

38. Refer to the graph below. What area corresponds to the *excess burden* from the tax?

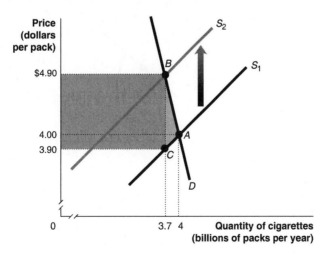

    a. The dark grey area
    b. The light grey area
    c. The sum of the dark grey and light grey areas
    d. An area not shown on this graph

39. Refer to the graph below. What area corresponds to the revenue collected by the government from the tax?

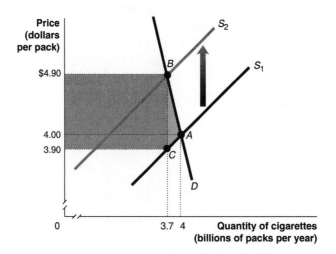

a. The dark grey area
b. The light grey area
c. The sum of the dark grey and light grey areas
d. An area not shown on this graph

40. Refer to the graph below. In this graph, how much of the gas tax do consumers pay?

a. 2 cents per gallon
b. 8 cents per gallon
c. 10 cents per gallon
d. $1.50 per gallon

41. Refer to the graphs below. In each of the graphs below, a curve has shifted as a result of a new social security tax. In which graph does the employer pay the social security tax?

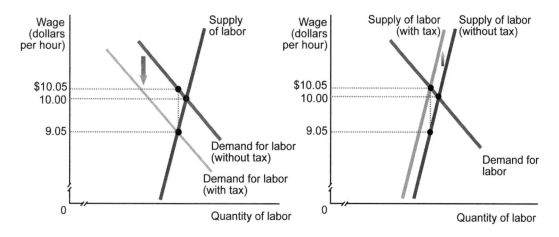

   a. In the graph on the left
   b. In the graph on the right
   c. In both cases
   d. In neither case

42. Refer to the graphs below. In each of the graphs below, a curve has shifted as a result of a new social security tax. In which graph do the workers pay the social security tax?

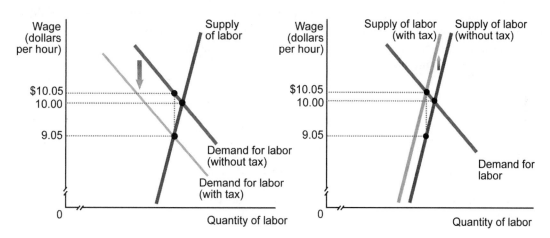

   a. In the graph on the left
   b. In the graph on the right
   c. In both cases
   d. In neither case

43. Refer to the graphs below. In each of the graphs below, a curve has shifted as a result of a new social security tax. In which graph is the tax incidence larger on workers?

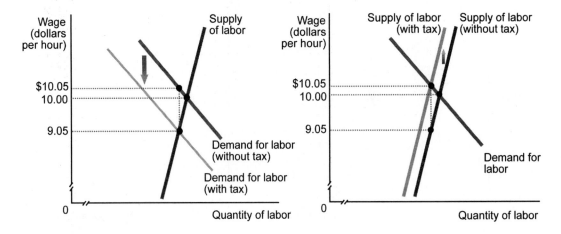

a. In the graph on the left
b. In the graph on the right
c. In neither case because the workers are not affected by the tax
d. In both cases the tax incidence is the same

Short Answer Questions

1. Some economists oppose raising the minimum wage because they believe this would lead to a significant increase in unemployment among low-skilled workers. Is there an alternative to a higher minimum wage to raise the incomes of the working poor? Why do some economists favor raising the minimum wage?

_____

_____

_____

2. Federal and state governments periodically raise excise taxes on cigarettes. Politicians often argue that these tax increases discourage smoking. What other motive is there for raising taxes on cigarettes?

_____

_____

_____

3. One effect of rent control in New York City is a reduction in the number of apartment buildings. If rent control were eliminated, would this result in an increase in the number of apartment buildings and, therefore, lower rents for apartment dwellers?

_____

_____

4. Price floors have been imposed in markets for dairy products such as milk and cheese. Surplus dairy products are bought by the government to maintain the floor price. These surplus products must be stored in some location. As an alternative to storage, suppose a program was established to distribute surplus dairy products freely to the elderly and poor. Would this eliminate the government's storage problem?

_____

_____

_____

5. The federal government has made several attempts to reduce agricultural surpluses that result from price floors. One such attempt was a program that paid farmers to reduce the amount of land they devoted to planting crops subject to price floors. What was the reason for the failure of this program? (Hint: Use one of the "three important ideas" from Chapter 1 to answer this question.)

_____

_____

_____

True False Questions

T F 1. The total amount of consumer surplus in a market is equal to the area under the demand curve.

T F 2. Government intervention in agriculture in the United States increased significantly as a result of the Great Depression.

T F 3. A study of fast food restaurants in New Jersey and Pennsylvania found that increases in the minimum wage caused larges increases in unemployment.

T F 4. Those people who lose because of rent control include landlords who abide by the law.

T F 5. It was Oliver Wendell Holmes who once said "Taxes are what we pay for a civilized society."

T F 6. The deadweight loss from a tax is equal to the revenue collected by government from the tax.

T F 7. Consumers will pay all of an increase in a sales tax only if the demand curve is a horizontal line at the market price.

T F 8. Economists who have studied the incidence of the social security tax have found that the tax burden is shared equally by employers and their employees.

T F 9. A tax is efficient if it imposes a small excess burden relative to the tax revenue it raises.

T   F   10.   One effect of rent control in New York City and London has been a large reduction in the number of apartment buildings.

T   F   11.   The Freedom to Farm Act was passed in Congress in 1996 to phase out price floors and government purchases of agricultural surpluses.

T   F   12.   Producer surplus refers to the surplus goods that result from price floors.

T   F   13.   Positive economic analysis is used to determine the economic results of price ceilings and price floors. Whether these price controls are desirable or not is a normative question.

T   F   14.   The earned income tax credit reduces the amount of tax lower income wage earners pay to the federal government.

T   F   15.   Economic efficiency results when the total benefit to consumers is equal to the total cost of production.

Answers to the Self-Test

Multiple-Choice Questions

Question	Answer	Comment
1	b	A price floor is a legally determined minimum price that sellers may receive.
2	a	A price ceiling is a legally determined maximum price that sellers may charge.
3	c	Consumer surplus is the area under the demand curve and above the established price level.
4	d	Producer surplus is the area above the supply curve and below the established price level.
5	a	See the definition of marginal benefit on page 100 of the textbook.
6	c	See the definition of marginal cost on page 103 of the textbook.
7	b	Marginal benefit is the additional benefit to a consumer from consuming one more unit of a good or service, and price is a measure of that additional benefit, so the demand curve is also the marginal benefit curve.
8	d	The willingness of a consumer to pay $2 for five cups of tea per week means that the fifth cup consumed is worth exactly $2.00 to the consumer.
9	b	Consumer surplus is the difference between the price a consumer is willing to pay and the price actually paid.
10	c	These consumers participate in the market and receive consumer surplus equal to the difference between the highest price the consumers are willing to pay and the price they actually paid.
11	c	Producer surplus is the difference between the lowest price a firm would have been willing to accept ($1.80) and the price it actually receives ($2.00).
12	c	Price equals marginal cost, or the additional cost to a firm of producing one more unit of a good or service.
13	b	Consumer surplus measures the *net* benefit to consumers from participating in the market, not the total benefit.
14	b	Producer surplus measures the *net* benefit to producers from participating in the market, not the total benefit.
15	b	To achieve maximum efficiency, output should be produced up until the marginal benefit to consumers is equal to the marginal cost to producers.
16	c	In this case, decreasing the level of output would increase efficiency. As output decreases, the gap between marginal cost and marginal benefit decreases, until the two are equal at 15,000 units of output.
17	a	This occurs when output is less than equilibrium output.

18	c	In this case, the current output level yields maximum economic efficiency; the market is in equilibrium, and the sum of consumer surplus and producer surplus yields the largest possible value.
19	b	The sum of consumer surplus and producer surplus is equal to the sum of the areas above the supply curve and below the demand curve up to a certain quantity of output produced.
20	c	In this case, the equilibrium output level yields maximum economic efficiency; the market is in equilibrium, and the sum of consumer surplus and producer surplus yields the largest possible value. There is no deadweight loss.
21	a	Area E is the producer portion of the deadweight loss.
22	d	Producers capture some of the consumer surplus after market price increases to $2.20.
23	c	Consumer surplus is the area below the demand curve and above the price out to the number of units sold.
24	a	Consumer surplus is the area below the demand curve and above the price out to the number of units sold.
25	a	Producers capture some of the consumer surplus after market price increases to $3.50.
26	c	After the price of $3.50 is imposed by government, some producers and consumers no longer participate in the market, so a deadweight loss is created.
27	b	The minimum wage causes an excess of quantity supplied over quantity demanded, which corresponds to additional unemployment.
28	b	The minimum wage causes an excess of quantity supplied over quantity demanded, or a surplus of workers.
29	b	The lower price at which the first 1,900,000 apartments are rented benefits consumers who would have paid more in the absence of the rent control. So producer surplus is transferred from landlords to renters.
30	c	In the absence of the rent control, more landlords and renters would have participated in the market. This area shows that loss.
31	b	Scarcity and shortage are not the same thing. A shortage is the difference between quantity demanded and quantity supplied of a good. Scarcity exists as long as the resources used to produce one thing could be used to produce another. There is no shortage of most scarce goods.
32	d	A market where buying and selling takes place at prices that violate government price regulations is the textbook definition of *black market*. Price scalping (b) is not always illegal.
33	a	Renters would have paid $1,000 but now pay more. When price rises, consumer surplus decreases and producer surplus increases.
34	b	The black market does not change the deadweight loss.
35	d	Price controls have the consequences mentioned in all of these answers.
36	c	Tax incidence in the division of the responsibility of a tax between buyers and sellers.
37	b	Producers charge a price of $3.08 and give the government $0.10, leaving them effectively with $2.98 per gallon sold.
38	b	The *excess burden* from the tax is equivalent to the deadweight loss created by the tax.
39	a	That amount of revenue equals ($4.90 – $3.90) x 3.7 = $3.7 billion.
40	b	Consumers pay a price of $3.08, which is an 8-cent increase in price from the $3.00 equilibrium price. Producers receive $3.08 from consumers, pay 10 cents to the government, and keep $2.98 per pack.
41	a	The demand curve represents employers.

| 42 | b | Supply represents workers. When workers are assessed a tax, the supply curve shifts to the left. |
| 43 | d | It does not matter who pays the tax to the government, the tax incidence will remain the same. |

Short Answer Responses

1. Opponents of the minimum wage argue that raising the minimum wage will reduce employment, especially among workers with the least skills. An alternative policy is the earned income tax credit. Workers who do not owe any federal taxes receive payments from the federal government. This program increases the incomes of low-skilled workers without the risk of increasing unemployment. Despite these arguments against the minimum wage and the clear evidence from positive economic analysis that a higher minimum wage reduces employment, a few economists still favor raising the minimum wage. They base their argument on normative economics. First, they believe the benefits of higher wages to those still employed outweigh the costs to those thrown into unemployment. This is a value judgment; you are free to agree or disagree. Second, they argue that many low-income workers miss the earned income tax credit because they don't file tax returns.

2. Because cigarettes are addictive many smokers will pay higher prices for cigarettes rather than reduce the quantity they purchase. This results in greater government revenue from the cigarette taxes. Taxes on cigarettes and alcohol (often called "sin taxes") do not affect as many people as a sales tax or income tax. Therefore, politicians do not face as much public opposition to tax increases on these products.

3. Although this result is likely to occur eventually, it will take time for the elimination of rent controls to affect the quantity of apartments in New York City. The immediate effect would likely be an increase in rents on existing apartments. This is one reason why many New Yorkers oppose the elimination of rent control.

4. In fact, such as program was initiated in the 1980s. Although the storage problem is partially alleviated, some of the dairy products that are given away freely replace purchases made by the elderly and poor.

5. The "important idea" that can be used to answer this question is: people respond to economic incentives. Given the opportunity to reduce the amount of land they used to grow crops, many farmers removed their least productive land from production and planted more on the land they did use. This program resulted in greater money payments to farmers – for the land they did not cultivate – and a smaller than expected reduction in crops harvested and sold.

True/False Answers

1. F   The total amount of consumer surplus in a market is equal to the area under the demand curve above the market price.
2. T   The government supported prices for the farmers because of the extremely low recession prices on agricultural goods.
3. F   This study found only small increases in unemployment as a result of minimum wage increases.
4. T   Producer surplus is typically reduced by rent control.
5. T

6. F   Government revenue is not a deadweight loss. This revenue will be used to provide goods and services to the economy.
7. F   Consumers will pay all of an increase in a sales tax if the demand curve is a vertical line.
8. F   Economists have found that the burden falls almost entirely on workers.
9. T   The tax revenue will be used for the provision of goods and services.
10. T   Landlords often sell or convert their buildings to other uses in order to avoid rent control regulations.
11. T
12. F   Producer surplus is the net benefit producers receive from participating in the market.
13. T   Positive analysis tells us the cost and benefits associated with particular policy measures.
14. T   The earned income credit is seen by some as a good alternative to the minimum wage.
15. F   Economic efficiency results when the marginal benefit to consumers of the last unit produced equals the marginal cost of production.

Chapter 5 (7)

Firms, the Stock Market, and Corporate Governance

Chapter Summary

This chapter examines the organization of business firms, how these firms raise funds to finance their operations, and how they provide information to their owners (both actual and prospective). In the United States, there are three legal types of firms: (1) **sole proprietorships,** (2) **partnerships,** and (3) **corporations**.

Owners of sole proprietorships and partnerships have **unlimited liability**, which means that if the firm goes bankrupt, the owners' personal assets can be seized by anyone the firm owes money to. In the early nineteenth century, state legislatures recognized that unlimited liability interfered with the ability of firms to raise money and passed laws allowing firms to be organized as corporations. Corporations limit the financial liability of firm owners to the amount of their investment in the firm. Limited liability and the ability to raise funds through the sale of corporate stock are key advantages of the corporate form of organization. Corporations are, on average, larger than the other types of businesses. Their size contributes to the difficulty of organizing and managing them.

Corporations are owned by shareholders who elect a board of directors to represent their interests. The directors appoint managers to run the day-to-day operations of the firm. The separation of ownership from control creates an incentive for managers to pursue their own interests, rather than the interests of shareholders. This conflict of interest is referred to as the principal-agent problem.

Stock refers to a financial security that represents partial ownership of a firm. Investors who buy shares of stocks buy part ownership of the firm. Corporations usually choose to keep some part of their profits as retained earnings and pay the remainder as dividends to shareholders. When a corporation's future profits are expected to rise, its stock's share price will rise, providing shareholders with a capital gain. A bond is a financial security that represents a promise to make one or more future payments that are fixed in money terms. Corporations that sell bonds must make promised payments to their bondholders before paying any dividends. Stockholders make an open-ended commitment of funds to the corporations they own so the firm is not obligated to return their funds at any particular date.

Daily buying and selling of stocks and bonds mostly involves existing rather then new issues. Trading takes place in "exchanges" and does not generate new funds for companies whose stocks are being bought and sold. To raise funds through the sale of stocks and bonds, a firm's managers must persuade potential buyers that the firm is profitable. The Securities and Exchange Commission requires U.S. firms that sell stocks and bonds to report their performance in financial statements using generally accepted accounting principles. The firm's income statement and balance sheet provide the public with information regarding the firm's profits or losses, and its assets and liabilities.

The importance of accurate financial statements was highlighted by a series of financial scandals that came to light in 2001 and 2002. Executives of Enron, WorldCom, and other firms falsified financial statements to make their firms appear more profitable than they were. In response to these scandals, the Sarbanes-Oxley Act was passed in 2002 to increase the accountability of corporate officers for the accuracy of their firm's financial statements.

Learning Objectives

When you finish this chapter, you should be able to:

1. **Categorize the major types of firms in the United States.** There are three legal categories of firms in the United States. A sole proprietorship is owned by a single individual. Partnerships are firms owned jointly by two or more persons. A corporation can have any number of owners. The main point of creating a corporation is to construct a legal form of business that provides owners with limited liability.

2. **Describe the typical management structure of corporations and understand the concepts of separation of ownership from control and the principal-agent problem.** Corporations are owned by their shareholders, the owners of the corporation's stock. Shareholders elect a board of directors who represent their interests and appoint managers who run the day-to-day operations of the firms. Since top management usually does not own a large share of their firm's stock, they may have an incentive to decrease profits in order to pursue their own interests.

3. **Explain how firms obtain the funds they need to operate and expand.** Firms can raise funds from profits earned from their operations by taking on partners or new owners who invest in the firms and by borrowing. Firms raise external funds directly through financial markets or indirectly through banks and other financial intermediaries.

4. **Understand the information provided in corporations' financial statements.** A firm's income statement summarizes its revenues, costs, and profit over a period of time. A firm's balance sheet summarizes its financial position on a particular day. A balance sheet lists a firm's assets and its liabilities. The value of a firm's assets minus its liabilities equals its net worth.

5. **Understand the role of government in corporate governance.** Several firms including Enron and WorldCom were caught falsifying their financial statements and engaging in deceptive accounting practices. In response to these accounting scandals, new legislation – the Sarbanes-Oxley Act – was enacted. The Act mandates that chief executive officers of corporations personally certify the accuracy of their financial statements and requires financial analysts and auditors to disclose any conflicts of interest that would limit their independence in evaluating a firm's financial condition.

Appendix: Understand the concept of present value and the information contained on a firm's income statement and balance sheet. Your instructor may assign this appendix.

Chapter Review

Chapter Opener: Google: From Dorm Room to Wall Street (pages 136-137)

In 2004, the founders of Internet search engine Google sold part of their firm to outside investors by offering stock to the public. This decision gave the firm a much needed infusion of cash to allow for future growth, and growth for Google has increased the challenges in managing a large firm. Other firms made news in

2001 and 2002 due not to their success but through their involvement in accounting scandals that resulted in the passage of federal legislation intended to improve the accuracy of corporations' financial statements.

📖 Helpful Study Hint

The popularity of Google's stock offering resulted in rich rewards for Google's founders and a huge inflow of funds that the firm can use for future growth. *An Inside Look* at the end of this chapter describes the compensation that the owners and the CEO receive and shows the movement in Google's stock price in from 2004 to 2007. Growth has meant that Google's ownership no longer rests solely in the hands of its founders, Larry Page and Sergey Brin. CEO Eric Schmidt is responsible for the operation of the business. To decrease the principal-agent problem, Schmidt receives only a small salary; most of his compensation comes from increases in Google's stock price because Schmidt owns many shares of Google.

Economics in YOUR Life! asks if it is too risky to own the stock of a firm like Google. Keep this question in mind as you read the chapter. The authors will answer this question at the end of the chapter.

5.1 LEARNING OBJECTIVE

5.1   Types of Firms (pages 138-140)

Learning Objective 1   Categorize the major types of firms in the United States.

In the United States, there are three basic legal structures a firm can assume. A **sole proprietorship** is a firm owned by a single individual and not organized as a corporation. A **partnership** is a firm owned by two or more persons and not organized as a corporation. Owners of sole proprietorships and partnerships have control of their day-to-day operations but they are subject to unlimited liability. There is no legal distinction between the owners' personal assets and those of the firms they own. As a result, employees or suppliers have a legal right to sue if they are owed money by these firms, even if this requires the owners to sell their personal assets.

A **corporation** is a legal form of business that provides owners with limited liability. **Limited liability** is the legal provision that shields owners of a corporation from losing more than they have invested in the firm. The profits of corporations are taxed twice in the United States, and corporations are more difficult to organize and run than sole proprietorships and partnerships. Despite these disadvantages, limited liability and the possibility of raising funds by issuing stock make corporations an attractive form of business.

📖 Helpful Study Hint

Corporations are often described as "publicly owned." This phrase means that corporations are owned by members of the general public, not that they are owned by the government.

Making the Connection "What's in a 'Name'? Lloyd's of London Learns about Unlimited Liability the Hard Way" explains that the shareholders of Lloyd's of London did not have the limited liability that is enjoyed by corporate shareholders. The "Names," or owners of

Lloyd's, learned they were not protected by corporate status when the company experienced significant losses and the Names were required to pay this money out of their own pockets. Many Names went bankrupt, while others committed suicide.

Extra Solved Problem 5-1

Chapter 5 in the textbook includes two Solved Problems. Here is another Solved Problem to help you build your skills solving economic problems.

Supports Learning Objective 1: Categorize the major types of firms in the United States.

The Risks of Private Enterprise: Lloyd's of London's "Names" and Enron's Shareholders

The first *Making the Connection* of chapter 5 describes the sad fate that befell investors ("Names") in the Lloyd's of London insurance company in the late 1980s and 1990s. Another section of the chapter described the scandal that drove Enron into bankruptcy in 2002 and caused billions of dollars in shareholder losses.

a. What characteristics of each firm's form of business organization were responsible for the financial losses suffered by the owners of these two firms?

b. How did the nature of these losses differ for each firm?

SOLVING THE PROBLEM

Step 1: Review the chapter material.
This problem is about firms and corporate governance, so you may want to review "Types of Firms," which begins on page 138 in the textbook, and the section "Corporate Structure and Corporate Governance Policy," which begins on page 141.

Step 2: Evaluate the losses suffered by investors in Lloyd's of London and the characteristic of the firm's form of business organization that was responsible for the size of these losses.
Making the Connection "What's in a "Name"? Lloyd's of London Learns about Unlimited Liability the Hard Way" describes Lloyd's of London as a partnership. A disadvantage of a partnership, as well as sole proprietorships, is the unlimited personal liability of the owners of the firm. The liability Lloyd's partners, or Names, incurred went beyond the amount of funds they invested in the company. Therefore, when the insurance company was hit with a series of financial losses, some of the Names suffered severe personal financial losses.

Step 3: Evaluate the losses suffered by Enron shareholders and the characteristic of the firm's form of business organization that was responsible for these losses.
Although Enron eventually became bankrupt, its shareholders' losses were limited to the amount of funds they had invested in the firm. But the management of Enron was able to engage in highly questionable business practices, the consequences of which were hidden through misleading financial statements. This is a manifestation of the principal-agent problem. The separation of management and ownership inherent in a corporate form of organization allowed Enron's managers to pursue strategies contrary to the interests of the firm's shareholders.

5.2 The Structure of Corporations and the Principal-Agent Problem (pages 140-142)

Learning Objective 2 Describe the typical management structure of corporations and understand the concepts of separation of ownership from control and the principal-agent problem.

Corporate governance is the way corporations are structured and the effect that structure has on the firm's behavior. Shareholders in a corporation elect a board of directors to represent their interests. The board of directors appoints a chief executive officer (CEO) to run day-to-day operations and may appoint other top managers. Managers may serve on the board of directors (they are referred to as inside directors). Outside directors are directors who do not have a management role in the firm. In corporations, there is a **separation of ownership from control.** In most large corporations the top management, rather than the shareholders, control day-to-day operations. The separation of ownership from control is an example of a **principal-agent problem**, a problem caused by an agent pursuing his own interests rather than the interests of the principal who hired him.

📖 Helpful Study Hint

Although the principal-agent problem is a serious one, managers who pursue their own goals at the expense of the firm's best interests risk the scrutiny of institutional investors (for example, mutual funds and pension funds). Unlike many shareholders who have modest stock holdings, institutional investors may hold a significant percentage of a firm's outstanding shares. These large investors can (and sometimes do) demand that a board of directors make strategic or personnel changes if the firm's performance is unsatisfactory, and they may cause a drop in share prices by selling some or all of their stock holdings.

Read *Solved Problem 5-2* in the main text to strengthen your understanding of the principal-agent problem. This Solved Problem explains how the principal-agent problem is easily extended to the relationship between management and workers. Managers would like workers to work as hard as possible, while workers would sometimes prefer to shirk. It may be difficult for management to determine whether a worker is working sufficiently hard or not.

5.3 How Firms Raise Funds (pages 142-146)

Learning Objective 3 Explain how firms obtain the funds they need to operate and expand.

To finance expansion, firms can use some of their profits, called retained earnings, rather than pay the profits to owners as dividends. Firms may obtain external funds in two ways. **Indirect finance** is the flow of funds from savers to borrowers through financial intermediaries such as banks. Intermediaries raise funds from savers to lend to firms and other borrowers. **Direct finance** is the flow of funds from savers to firms through financial markets. Direct finance usually takes the form of the borrower selling a financial security to a lender.

A financial security is a document that states the terms under which the funds have passed from the buyer of the security to the borrower. There are two main types of financial securities. A **bond** is a financial security that represents a promise to repay a fixed amount of funds. When a firm sells a bond to raise funds, it promises to pay the purchaser of the bond an interest payment each year for the term of the loan as well as the final payment (or principal) of the loan. The interest payments on a bond are referred to as **coupon payments**. The **interest rate** is the cost of borrowing funds, usually expressed as a percentage of the amount borrowed. If the coupon is expressed as a percentage of the face value of the bond, we have the coupon rate of the bond.

If the face value of a bond is $1,000 and the annual interest payment on the bond is $60, then the coupon rate is

$$\frac{\$60}{\$1,000} = 0.06 \text{ or } 10 \text{ percent}$$

A **stock** is a financial security that represents partial ownership of a firm. As an owner of the firm, a shareholder is entitled to a share of the corporation's profits. Management decides how much profit to reinvest in the firm (retained earnings). The remaining profits are paid to stockholders as **dividends**. Owners receive **capital gains** when there are increases in the price of a firm's shares.

There is a broad market for previously owned stocks and bonds. Changes in the prices of these financial instruments represent future expectations of the profits likely to be earned by the firms that issued them. Changes in the prices of bonds issued by a corporation reflect investors' perceptions of the firm's ability to make interest payments as well as the prices of newly issued bonds. A previously issued bond with a coupon payment of $80 and a principal of $1,000 is less attractive than a newly issued bond with a coupon payment of $100 and a principal of $1,000. The price of the previously issued bond must fall, and its interest rate must rise, to induce investors to buy it.

📖 Helpful Study Hint

The double taxation of corporate profits—once via the corporate profits tax and again via the income tax on shareholders' dividends—gives corporations an incentive to raise funds more through debt (bonds) than equity (stocks). Some economists have criticized the corporation profits tax because it gives corporations an incentive to incur debt solely to reduce taxes.

Don't Let This Happen to YOU! "When Google Shares Change Hands, Google Doesn't Get the Money" explains the difference between primary and secondary markets for stocks and bonds. In the primary market, stocks and bonds are sold by the issuing companies and the issuing company receives the funds. In the secondary market, stocks and bonds are resold by investors and the investors receive the funds from the sales.

Making the Connection "Following Abercrombie and Fitch's Stock Price in the Financial Pages" provides a thorough explanation of how to read the stock pages in the newspaper using Abercrombie and Fitch as an example.

Extra Solved Problem 5-3

Chapter 5 in the textbook includes two Solved Problems. Here is an extra Solved Problem to help you build your skills solving economic problems.

Supports Learning Objective 3: Explain how firms obtain the funds they need to operate and expand.

Google's Stocks

On October 25, 2007, Google's stock closed at a price of $668.51 per share and the trading volume for the day was 5,789,704. The trading volume is the number of shares that traded on the secondary market for that day.

a. How much financial capital did the trading of these stocks raise for Google to use for expansion?

b. How could Google raise additional funds for growth?

SOLVING THE PROBLEM

Step 1: **Review the chapter material.**
This problem is about how firms raise funds, so you may want to review the section "How Firms Raise Funds," which begins on page 142 in the textbook.

Step 2: **Discuss the secondary market for stocks and the impact on funds available for Google to expand.**
In the feature *Don't Let This Happen to YOU!* entitled "When Google Shares Change Hands, Google Doesn't Get the Money" you will find a description of secondary markets. The majority of stocks that are bought and sold on a daily basis are being traded in the secondary market. Trading in the secondary market does not raise additional funds for Google.

Step 3: **Consider the options that Google has to raise funds for growth.**
There are three main options for a firm to obtain funds for growth. A firm can save some of its profits, called retained earnings. They can borrow money from a bank. Or they can issue more stocks or bonds and sell them directly to the public. All of these options are available to Google.

Source: http://quotes.nasdaq.com/asp/summaryquote.asp?symbol=GOOG%60&selected=GOOG%60

5.4   Using Financial Statements to Evaluate a Corporation (pages 147-149)

Learning Objective 4   Understand the information provided in corporations' financial statements.

A firm must accurately disclose its financial condition to enable potential investors to make informed decisions about the firm's stock and bond offerings. The Securities and Exchange Commission (SEC) requires publicly owned firms to report their performance according to generally accepted accounting principles.

There are two main types of financial statements. An **income statement** is a financial statement that sums up a firm's revenues, costs, and profit over a period of time. The income statement is used to compute the firm's **accounting profit**, which is the firm's net income measured by revenue minus operating expenses and taxes paid. A **balance sheet** is a financial statement that sums up a firm's financial position on a particular day, usually the end of a quarter or year. The balance sheet summarizes a firm's assets and liabilities. An **asset** is anything of value owned by a person or a firm. A **liability** is anything owed by a person or a firm. The difference between the value of assets and liabilities is the firm's net worth.

📖 Helpful Study Hint

Making the Connection "A Bull in China's Financial Shop" explains that although China is experiencing economic growth, its financial markets are still struggling to perform efficiently. Loans for investment and future growth are typically being made to those with political connections, rather than those firms that would receive the funds in a well-functioning financial market. There are a significant number of loans going unpaid being funds are being allocated on the basis of political connections rather than economic efficiency. Many economists doubt whether the Chinese economy can continue its rapid growth without efficient financial markets.

Extra Solved Problem 5-4

Chapter 5 in the textbook includes two Solved Problems. Here is an extra Solved Problem to help you build your skills solving economic problems.

Supports Learning Objective 4: Understand the information provided in corporations' financial statements.

Accounting Profit versus Economic Profit

Suppose that Sally decides to open a business. Opening Sally's Sassy Salon will cost $200,000 for the necessary capital equipment. Sally is considering two options for financing her new beauty salon. The first option she is considering is to borrow $100,000 and take $100,000 from her savings. The second option is to take $200,000 from her savings to start the business. Suppose that her savings account is earning 5 percent interest and the loan that her bank offered her also has a 5 percent interest rate.

a. What is the explicit cost of opening Sally's Sassy Salon is she chooses the first option? If she chooses the second option? What is the implicit cost of opening Sally's Sassy Salon using the first option? The second option?

b. Which option will give Sally the higher economic profit? The higher accounting profit?

SOLVING THE PROBLEM

Step 1: **Review the chapter material.**
This problem is about financial statements, so you may want to review the section "Using Financial Statements to Evaluate a Corporation," which begins on page beginning on page 147 in the textbook.

Step 2: **Determine the implicit and explicit costs of each option.**
The explicit costs would be costs that require an outlay of money, for example, the interest on the loan, and the implicit costs would be the foregone interest on her savings. The first option has an explicit cost of 0.05 x $100,000 = $5,000 and an implicit cost of 0.05 x $100,000 = $5,000. The second option has no explicit cost and has 0.05 x $200,000 = $10,000 in implicit costs.

Step 3: **Evaluate the economic and accounting profit for Sally's Sassy Salon.**
Assuming that her revenue will be unaffected by her choice of how she finances her new firm, we can see that the explicit cost of the second option is lower than the first option. This means that the second option would have a higher accounting profit. If we consider all of the costs, both explicit and implicit, then we are calculating the economic profit. In this case, the explicit cost plus implicit cost is the same for both options, so the economic profit would be the same for either option.

5.5 LEARNING OBJECTIVE

5.5 Corporate Governance Policy (pages 149-152)

Learning Objective 5 Understand the role of government in corporate governance.

During 2001 and 2002, the importance of providing accurate financial information through financial statements was illustrated by several major financial scandals. The Sarbanes-Oxley Act of 2002 was passed in response to these scandals. The act requires corporate directors and chief executive officers to have greater accountability for the accuracy of their firms' financial statements. The Sarbanes-Oxley Act created a Public Company Accounting Oversight Board to oversee the auditing of public companies' financial reports.

📖 Helpful Study Hint

One result, likely an unintended one, of the Sarbanes-Oxley Act was to increase the demand for newly hired accountants. For example, the accounting firm Ernst and Young hired 4,500 undergraduate accounting students in 2005, an increase of 30 percent from the previous year.

Source: "Jobs: Accountants are kings among grads," *CNNMoney*, June 5, 2005. http://money.cnn.com/2005/06/pf/accountant.jobs.reut/index.htm?ccc=yes

Solved Problem 5-5 describes the characteristics of a good board of directors. The majority of the board should be independent outsiders who have no business connections with the firm. The auditing and compensation committees should be made up entirely of outsiders in order to protect the best interest of the shareholders. The directors who are affiliated with the firm should own stock because, as stockholders, they will share the same goal as other stockholders to maximize profits.

📖 Helpful Study Hint

Economics in YOUR Life! asked if owning stock in a company such as Google is risky. The principal-agent problem adds to your risk. But the rewards to owning stock can also be substantial because you are likely to earn a higher return on your investment over the long run than if you had put your money in a bank account. Buying stock of well-known companies, such as Google, that are closely followed by Wall Street investment analysts helps to reduce the principal-agent problem.

Key Terms

Accounting profit. A firm's net income measured by revenue less operating expenses and taxes paid.

Asset. Anything of value owned by a person or a firm.

Balance sheet. A financial statement that sums up a firm's financial position on a particular day, usually the end of a quarter or a year.

Bond. A financial security that represents a promise to repay a fixed amount of funds.

Corporate governance. The way in which a corporation is structured and the effect a corporation's structure has on the firm's behavior.

Corporation. A legal form of business that provides the owners with limited liability.

Coupon payment. An interest payment on a bond.

Direct finance. A flow of funds from savers to firms through financial markets, such as the New York Stock Exchange.

Dividends. Payments by a corporation to its shareholders.

Economic profit. A firm's revenues minus all of its costs, implicit and explicit.

Explicit cost. A cost that involves spending money.

Implicit cost. A nonmonetary opportunity cost.

Income statement. A financial statement that sums up a firm's revenues, costs, and profit over a period of time.

Indirect finance. A flow of funds from savers to borrowers through financial intermediaries such as banks. Intermediaries raise funds from savers to lend to firms (and other borrowers).

Interest rate. The cost of borrowing funds, usually expressed as a percentage of the amount borrowed.

Liability. Anything owed by a person or a firm.

Limited liability. The legal provision that shields owners of a corporation from losing more than they have invested in the firm.

Opportunity cost. The highest-valued alternative that must be given up to engage in an activity.

Partnership. A firm owned jointly by two or more persons and not organized as a corporation.

Present value. The value in today's dollars of funds to be paid or received in the future.

Principal-agent problem. A problem caused by an agent pursuing his own interests rather than the interests of the principal who hired him.

Separation of ownership from control. A situation in a corporation in which the top management, rather than the shareholders, control day-to-day operations.

Sole proprietorship. A firm owned by a single individual and not organized as a corporation.

Stock. A financial security that represents partial ownership of a firm.

Stockholders' equity. The difference between the value of a corporation's assets and the value of its liabilities; also known as net worth.

Appendix

Tools to Analyze Firms' Financial Information (pages 161-169)

LEARNING OBJECTIVE: Understand the concept of present value and the information contained on a firm's income statement and balance sheet.

Using Present Value to Make Investment Decisions

Most people value funds they have today more highly than funds they will receive in the future. **Present value** is the value in today's dollars of funds to be paid or received in the future. Someone who lends money expects to be paid back the amount of the loan and some additional interest. If someone lends $1,000 for one year at 10 percent interest, the value of money received in the future is:

$$\$1,000 \times (1 + 0.10) = \$1,100$$

Dividing this expression by $(1 + 0.10)$ and adjusting terms:

$$\$1,000 = \frac{\$1,000}{(1.10)}$$

Writing this more generally:

$$\text{Present Value} = \frac{\text{Future Value}}{(1 + i)}$$

The present value formula for funds received any number of years in the future (n represents the number of years) is:

$$\text{Present Value} = \frac{\text{Future Value}}{(1 + i)^n}$$

The present value formula can be used to calculate the price of a financial asset. The price of a financial asset should be equal to the present value of the payments to be received from owning that asset. The general formula for the price of a bond is:

$$\text{Bond Price} = \frac{\text{Coupon}_1}{(1 + i)^1} + \frac{\text{Coupon}_2}{(1 + i)^2} + \ldots + \frac{\text{Coupon}_n}{(1 + i)^n} + \frac{\text{Face Value}_n}{(1 + i)^n}$$

In this formula,

Coupon$_1$ is the coupon payment, or interest payment, to be received after one year.
Coupon$_2$ is the coupon payment after two years.

Coupon$_n$ is the coupon payment in the year the bond matures.
Face Value is the face value of the bond to be received when the bond matures.
The interest rate on comparable newly issued bonds is i.

The price of a share of stock should be equal to the present value of the dividends, or the profits paid to shareholders, investors expect to receive as a result of owning the stock. The general formula for the price of a stock is:

$$\text{Stock Price} = \frac{\text{Dividend}_1}{(1+i)} + \frac{\text{Dividend}_2}{(1+i)^2} + \dots$$

Unlike a bond, a stock has no maturity date, so the stock price is the present value of an infinite number of dividend payments. Unlike coupon payments which are written on the bond and can't be changed, dividend payments are uncertain. If dividends grow at a constant rate, the formula for determining the price of a stock is:

$$\text{Stock Price} = \frac{\text{Dividend}}{(i\text{-Growth Rate})}$$

Dividend refers to the dividend currently received and Growth Rate is the rate at which dividends are expected to grow.

Going Deeper Into Financial Statements

Corporations disclose substantial information about their business operations and financial position to investors. This information is provided for two reasons. First, participants in financial markets demand the information. Second, some of this information meets the requirements of the U.S. Securities and Exchange Commission. The key sources of information about a corporation's profitability and financial position are its income statement and balance sheet. Income statements summarize a firm's revenues, costs and profit over a time period (for example, one year). These statements list the firm's revenues and its cost of revenue (also called its costs of sales or cost of goods sold). The difference between a firm's revenues and costs is its profit. Operating income is the difference between revenue and operating expenses. Investment income is income earned on holdings of investments such as government and corporate bonds. The net income firms report on income statements is referred to as their after-tax accounting profit.

A balance sheet summarizes a firm's financial position on a particular day. An asset is anything of value owned by the firm. A liability is a debt or obligation owed by the firm. **Stockholders' equity** is the difference between the value of a corporation's assets and the value of its liabilities, also known as net worth. Balance sheets list assets on the left side and liabilities and new worth or stockholders' equity on the right side. The value on the left side of the balance sheet must equal the value on the right side. Current assets are assets the firm could convert into cash quickly. Goodwill represents the difference between the purchase price of a company and the market value of its assets. Current liabilities are short-term debts. Long-term liabilities include long-term bank loans and outstanding corporate bonds.

Key Terms – Appendix

Present value. The value in today's dollars of funds to be paid or received in the future.

Stockholders' equity. The difference between the value of a corporation's assets and the value of its liabilities; also known as net worth.

Self-Test

(Answers are provided at the end of the Self-Test.)

Multiple-Choice Questions

1. Which of the following statements is true?
   a. In the United States most firms are organized as corporations.
   b. In the United States there are more partnerships than sole proprietorships.
   c. In the United States corporations account for the majority of total revenue and profits earned by all firms.
   d. All of the above

2. Which of the following types of firms have limited liability?
   a. A corporation
   b. A sole proprietorship
   c. A partnership
   d. All of the above

3. Which of the following sets of firms are likely to be partnerships?
   a. Technology and telecommunications firms
   b. Law and accounting firms
   c. Public utilities, such as the power company and the gas company
   d. All of the above

4. Which of the following is true about liability for a corporation?
   a. The owners of a corporation have limited liability.
   b. The owners of a corporation have unlimited liability.
   c. The owners of a corporation may or may not be subject to unlimited liability.
   d. The owners of a corporation do not face any constraints with regard to liability issues.

5. In which of the following cases is there a legal distinction between the personal assets of the owners of the firm and the assets of the firm?
   a. Sole proprietorships
   b. Partnerships
   c. Corporations
   d. In both the case of sole proprietorships and the case of partnerships

6. When a corporation fails, which of the following is true?
   a. The owners can always lose more than the amount they invested in the firm.
   b. The owners can never lose more than the amount they had invested in the firm.
   c. The owners will always lose less than the amount they had invested in the firm.
   d. What the owners lose is unrelated to liability laws.

7. In the United States, how many times are corporate profits taxed?
   a. Once
   b. Twice
   c. Three times
   d. Often more than three times

8. Refer to the Figure 5-1 in the textbook. Which type of firms account for the majority of revenue earned in the United States in 2007?
   a. Sole proprietorships
   b. Corporations
   c. Partnerships
   d. None of the above

9. Refer to the Figure 5-1 in the textbook. Which type of firm accounts for the majority of the profits earned by different business organizations in the United States in 2007?
   a. Sole proprietorships
   b. Partnerships
   c. Corporations
   d. None of the above

10. Fill in the blanks. According to the textbook, there are more than _____ corporations in the United States, but only _____ have annual revenues of more than $50 million.
    a. 20 million; 1.2 million
    b. 18 million; 2 million
    c. 8 million; 10,000
    d. 5 million; 26,000

11. How much of the total corporate profits in the United States is earned by large firms?
    a. About 10 percent of all U.S. corporate profits
    b. One-half of all U.S. corporate profits
    c. Almost 85 percent of all U.S. corporate profits
    d. 99 percent of all U.S. corporate profits

12. What is *corporate governance*?
    a. Corporate governance is a structure imposed on all corporations by the Securities and Exchange Commission.
    b. Corporate governance is the way in which corporations are structured and the impact a corporation's structure has on the firm's behavior.
    c. Corporate governance is the division of business firms between proprietorships, partnerships, and corporations.
    d. Corporate governance is the relationship between corporations and the government officials in the states in which firms operate.

13. What term do economists use to refer to the conflict between the interests of shareholders and the interests of top management?
    a. Corporate governance
    b. A principal-agent problem
    c. Gold plating
    d. Capture theory

14. How can a firm obtain the funds for an expansion?
    a. By reinvesting profits
    b. By taking on one or more partners who would invest in the firm
    c. By borrowing funds from relatives, friends, or a bank
    d. All of the above

15. Which of the following refers to a flow of funds from savers to firms through financial markets?
    a. Indirect finance
    b. Direct finance
    c. Business finance
    d. Financial borrowing

16. What is the name given to the interest payments on a bond?
    a. Coupon payments
    b. The cost of borrowing funds
    c. The face value of the bond
    d. Capital gains

17. What are the payments by a corporation to its shareholders?
    a. Stocks
    b. Dividends
    c. Retained earnings
    d. Interest

18. Which instruments account for most of the funds raised by borrowers in the United States?
    a. Equity instruments
    b. Debt instruments
    c. Capital instruments
    d. Secondary-market instruments

19. According to the textbook, which of the following are valuable sources of information for corporations that are considering raising funds?
    a. Primary markets
    b. Secondary markets
    c. Tertiary markets
    d. All markets equally

20. What are markets in which newly issued claims are sold to initial buyers by the borrower called?
    a. Primary markets
    b. Secondary markets
    c. Tertiary markets
    d. Initial public offerings

21. In the United States, what market trades the stocks and bonds of the largest corporations?
    a.   The Nasdaq
    b.   The New York Stock Exchange
    c.   The American Stock Exchange
    d.   The Chicago Board of Trade

22. Which of the following is the most important of the over-the-counter markets?
    a.   The New York Stock Exchange
    b.   The American Stock Exchange
    c.   The Nasdaq
    d.   The S & P 500

23. In the United States the Securities and Exchange Commission requires publicly owned firms to report their performance in financial statements using standard methods. What are these methods called?
    a.   Standard and Poor's Accounting Standards
    b.   Generally accepted accounting principles
    c.   Moody's Investors Service Standards
    d.   U.S. Standard Financial Practices

24. If investors are more optimistic about the firm's profit prospects, and the firm's managers want to expand the firm's operations as a result, what will happen to the price of the company's stock?
    a.   It will rise.
    b.   It will fall.
    c.   It will remain constant.
    d.   It may rise for a while, then fall.

25. If a bond has a face value of $1,000 and pays a coupon of $70 per year, what is the coupon rate?
    a.   70
    b. $7
    c.   7%
    d.   70%

26. To answer the three basic questions: what to produce, how to produce it, and what price to charge, what does a firm's management need to know?
    a.   The firm's revenues and costs
    b.   The value of the property and other assets the firm owns
    c.   The firm's debts, or other liabilities, that it owes to another person or business
    d.   All of the above

27. Which of the following sums up a firm's revenues, costs, and profit over a period of time?
    a.   The balance sheet
    b.   The income statement
    c.   The firm's accounting profit
    d.   The firm's economic profit

28. An *income statement* starts with the firm's revenue and subtracts its expenses and taxes paid. What is the remainder called?
    a.   Net income, which is the accounting profit of the firm
    b.   Gross income, which is the economic profit of the firm
    c.   Implicit cost
    d.   Explicit cost

29. Which of the following is considered an *explicit cost*?
    a. The cost of labor
    b. The cost of materials
    c. The cost of electricity
    d. All of the above

30. What term do economists use to refer to the minimum amount that investors must earn on the funds they invest in a firm, expressed as a percentage of the amount invested?
    a. Opportunity cost
    b. The normal rate of return
    c. Explicit cost
    d. Economic profit

31. Accounting profit is equal to which of the following?
    (i)   Total revenue – explicit costs
    (ii) Total revenue – opportunity costs
    (iii) Economic profit + implicit costs
    a. (i) only
    b. (ii) only
    c. (iiii) only
    d. (i) and (iii) only

32. In which of the following industries do investors require a higher rate of return?
    a. In more risky industries
    b. In less risky industries
    c. In more established industries, such as electric utilities
    d. In any industry; investors always need to receive high rates of return regardless of the type of investment or the risk involved.

33. Which of the following statements is correct?
    a. Economic profit equals the firm's revenues minus its explicit costs.
    b. Accounting profit equals the firm's revenues minus all of its costs, implicit and explicit.
    c. Accounting profit is larger than economic profit.
    d. All of the above

34. What is a balance sheet?
    a. A summary of a firm's financial position on a particular day
    b. A summary of revenues, costs, and profit over a particular period of time
    c. A firm's net income measured by revenue less operating expenses and taxes paid
    d. A list of anything owed by a person or business

35. What do you obtain by subtracting the value of a firm's liabilities from the value of its assets?
    a. Income
    b. Net worth
    c. Economic profit
    d. Accounting profit

36. Which set of incentives does the top management of a corporation have?
    a. An incentive to attract investors and to keep the firm's stock price high
    b. An incentive to attract investors and to keep the firm's stock price low
    c. An incentive to discourage investors and to keep the firm's stock price high
    d. An incentive to discourage investors and to keep the firm's stock price low

37. Which of the following is true? Top managers who are determined to cheat and hide the true financial condition of their firms can
    a. easily deceive investors, but never outside auditors.
    b. deceive outside auditors, but never investors.
    c. deceive investors, and sometimes also deceive outside auditors.
    d. deceive other managers, but never the company's investors or its outside auditors.

38. The landmark Sarbanes-Oxley Act of 2002 strengthened the expertise with financial information required of corporate directors and mandated that
    a. chief executive officers personally certify the accuracy of financial statements.
    b. financial analysts and auditors shall disclose whether any conflicts of interest might exist that could limit their independence in evaluating a firm's financial condition.
    c. managers shall be held accountable and face stiff penalties (including long jail sentences) for not meeting their responsibilities.
    d. All of the above

39. The creation of the Public Company Accounting Oversight Board is the most noticeable corporate governance reform under the Sarbanes-Oxley Act. What is the mission of this special national board?
    a. To oversee the auditing of public companies' financial reports
    b. To oversee the writing of financial reports
    c. To oversee the behavior of corporate officers
    d. All of the above

40. What does the term "insiders" refer to in the realm of corporate management?
    a. Insiders are auditors who have access to the corporation's financial statements.
    b. Insiders are members of top management who also serve on the board of directors.
    c. Insiders are managers who have connections with people on independent auditing boards.
    d. An insider is anyone who is not part of a public corporation but who knows something that the public at large does not know.

Short Answer Questions

1. Owners of successful sole proprietorships may choose to become corporations in order to raise money to finance expansion and limit the owner's liability. But this will also subject the firm to the principal-agent problem. Why don't sole proprietorships face the principal-agent problem?

_____

_____

_____

2. Why did the passage of the Sarbanes-Oxley Act lead to an increase in the demand for accountants?

_____

_____

_____

_____

_____

3. In addition to salary and benefits, the compensation of the top managers of many corporations often includes of shares of company stock or options to buy the stock at a favorable price. Why?

_____

_____

_____

_____

_____

4. Explain why a firm that reports a profit on its income statement may suffer an economic loss.

_____

_____

_____

_____

_____

5. Publicly owned firms in the United States are required to report their performance in financial statements using generally accepted accounting principles. These statements are examined closely by private firms and investors. Why did the public disclosure of the statements of Enron and WorldCom fail to provide investors with advance warning of serious financial problems that resulted in billions of dollars of shareholders' losses?

_____

_____

_____

_____

True/False Questions

T F 1. In the United States, Standard and Poor's requires publicly owned firms to report their performance in financial statements.

T F 2. If investors expect a firm to earn economic profits, the firm's share price will rise, providing a dividend for shareholders.

T F 3. Indirect finance refers to raising funds through financial intermediaries such as banks.

T F 4. A disadvantage of organizing a firm as a sole proprietorship or a partnership is that owners have limited liability.

T F 5. A disadvantage of organizing a firm as a corporation is that the firm is subject to the principal-agent problem.

T F 6. Profits that are reinvested in a firm rather than paid to the firm's owners are called retained earnings.

T F 7. The most important of the so-called "over-the-counter" stock markets is the New York Stock Exchange.

T F 8. The value someone gives today to money she will receive in the future is called the future payment's present value.

T F 9. The price of a bond is equal to the present value of dividends, or the profits paid out by the firm that issues the bond.

T F 10. The unexpected rise in the price of Google stock in 2004 led to the passage of the Sarbanes-Oxley Act.

T F 11. Over 70 percent of firms in the United States are sole proprietorships.

T F 12. The day-to-day operations of a corporation are run by the firm's board of directors.

T F 13. An advantage of organizing a firm as a partnership is that the partners share the risks of owning the firm.

T F 14. The legal and financial problems incurred by Enron, WorldCom, and other well-known firms were due to the unlimited liability of the firms' owners.

T F 15. Economic profit is equal to a firm's revenue minus its operating expenses and taxes paid for a given time period.

Answers to the Self-Test

Multiple-Choice Questions

Question	Answer	Explanation
1	c	Based on data for 2007, corporations accounted for 84 percent of revenue and 59 percent of the profits earned by all firms in the United States. See Figure 5-1.
2	a	The owners of corporations have limited liability, while sole proprietorships and partnerships have unlimited liability. Read page 138 in the textbook.
3	b	Partnerships are firms owned jointly by two or more—sometimes many— persons. Most law and accounting firms are partnerships.
4	a	Most large firms are organized as corporations. A corporation is a legal form of business that provides the owners with limited liability.
5	c	Unlimited liability means there is no legal distinction between the personal assets of the owners of the firm and the assets of the firm. In sole proprietorships and partnerships, the owners are not legally distinct from the firms they own.
6	b	Limited liability is the legal provision that shields owners of a corporation from losing more than they have invested in the firm.

7	b	Corporate profits are taxed twice—once at the corporate level and again when investors receive a share of corporate profits, or (revenues less expenses).
8	b	Although only 20 percent of all firms are corporations, corporations account for the majority of revenue and profits earned by all firms.
9	c	Corporations account for a majority of the total revenue and profits earned by businesses.
10	d	There are more than 5 million corporations in the United States, but only 26,000 have annual revenues of more than $50 million. We can think of these 26,000 firms—including Microsoft, General Electric, and Exxon-Mobil—as representing "big business."
11	c	There are more than 5 million corporations in the United States, but only 26,000 have annual revenues of more than $50 million. We can think of these 26,000 firms—including Microsoft, General Electric, and Exxon-Mobil—as representing "big business." These large firms account for almost 85 percent of all U.S. corporate profits.
12	b	The way in which corporations are structured and the impact a corporation's structure has on the firm's behavior is referred to as corporate governance.
13	b	The fact that top managers do not own the entire firm means they may have an incentive to decrease the firm's profits by spending money to purchase private jets or schedule management meetings at luxurious resorts. This problem occurs when agents—in this case, a firm's top management—pursue their own interests rather than the interests of the principal who hired them—in this case, the shareholders of the corporation.
14	d	All of the above are ways in which firms raise the funds they need to expand operations.
15	b	A flow of funds from savers to firms through financial markets is known as direct finance. Direct finance usually takes the form of the borrower selling the lender a financial security.
16	a	A coupon payment is the interest payment on a bond, usually expressed as a percentage of the amount borrowed.
17	b	Dividends are payments by a corporation to its shareholders.
18	b	Although you hear about the stock market fluctuations each night on the evening news, debt instruments actually account for more of the funds raised by borrowers. In mid-2004, the value of debt instruments in the United States was about $20 trillion compared to $12 trillion for equities.
19	b	According to the textbook, secondary markets are valuable sources of information for corporations that are considering raising funds.
20	a	Primary markets are those in which newly issued claims are sold to initial buyers by the borrower.
21	b	In the United States, the stocks and bonds of the largest corporations are traded on the New York Stock Exchange.
22	c	The stocks of many computer and other high-technology firms—including Microsoft and Intel—are traded on the Nasdaq.
23	b	In most high-income countries, government agencies establish standard requirements for information that is disclosed in order for publicly owned firms to sell stocks and bonds. In the United States this government agency is the Securities and Exchange Commission. To maintain consistency, all firms are required to use generally accepted accounting principles.

24	a	Changes in the value of a firm's stocks and bonds offer important information for a firm's managers, as well as for investors. An increase in the stock price means that investors are more optimistic about the firm's profit prospects, and the firm's managers may wish to expand the firm's operations as a result.
25	c	The coupon rate is always expressed as a percentage of the face value. If the face value is $1,000 and this corporate bond pays a coupon of $70.00 per year, then the coupon rate is 7.00 percent.
26	d	To answer these questions, a firm's management needs the following information: The firm's revenues and costs, the value of the property and other assets the firm owns, and the firm's debts, or other liabilities that it owes to another person or business.
27	b	A firm's income statement sums up the firm's revenues, costs, and profits over a period of time.
28	a	A firm's net income is revenue less expenses and taxes paid in a given time period.
29	d	Firms pay explicit labor costs to employees. They have many other explicit costs as well, such as the cost of the electricity used to light their office buildings.
30	b	Economists refer to the minimum amount that investors must earn on the funds they invest in a firm, expressed as a percentage of the amount invested, as a normal rate of return.
31	d	You can calculate accounting profit by taking the revenue and subtracting out the explicit costs. This is equivalent to taking economic profit and adding back in the implicit costs.
32	a	The necessary rate of return that investors must receive to continue investing in a firm varies from firm to firm. If the investment is risky, investors will require a high rate of return to compensate them for the risk.
33	c	Because accounting profit excludes some implicit costs, it will be larger than economic profit.
34	a	A firm's balance sheet sums up its financial position on a particular day, usually the end of a quarter or a year.
35	b	We can think of the net worth as what the firm's owners would be left with if the firm were closed, its assets were sold, and its liabilities were paid off. Investors can determine a firm's net worth by inspecting its balance sheet.
36	a	The top management of a firm has at least two reasons to attract investors and keep the firm's stock price high. First, a higher stock price increases the funds the firm can raise when it sells a given amount of stock. Second, to reduce the principal-agent problem, boards of directors will often tie the salaries of top managers to the firm's stock price or to the profitability of the firm.
37	c	This is what the textbook argues in "Corporate Governance Policy," beginning on page 141 in the textbook.
38	d	Each of the responses is a provision of the Sarbanes-Oxley Act.
39	a	The board's mission is to promote the independence of auditors to ensure they disclose accurate information.
40	b	"Insiders" are members of top management who also serve on the board of directors.

Short Answer Responses

1. The principal-agent problem is used to describe the consequence of separating ownership and management. There is no such division with a sole proprietorship and no principal-agent problem because the principal is also the agent!

2. The Act requires senior executives of publicly owned firms to have greater accountability for the accuracy of their firms' reporting and created a board to oversee the auditing of companies' financial reports. Because of the financial scandals of 2001 and 2002, there is a demand on the part of government officials and analysts for transparent and accurate financial information.

3. Tying the compensation of managers to the stock price of the firms they manage provides a greater incentive to pursue strategies that enhance profitability. Members of corporate boards of directors choose this form of compensation, in part, in response to the principal-agent problem.

4. An income statement reports a firm's accounting profit, which is net income measured by revenue minus explicit costs—operating expenses and taxes paid—over a period of time. Since the income statement does not account for the implicit costs incurred by the firm, accounting profit will be greater than economic profit. Remember, economic profit is computed by subtracting both explicit and implicit costs from total revenue.

5. Ultimately the accuracy of a firm's statements is dependent on the integrity of corporate officials and the accountants who audit these statements. There is strong evidence that some corporate officials deliberately chose to provide incomplete and misleading information in their financial statements in order to persuade analysts that their firms were more profitable than the actually were.

True/False Answers

1.   F   This is the responsibility of the Securities and Exchange Commission.
2.   F   An increase in the share price results in a capital gain.
3.   T   This is the definition of indirect finance.
4.   F   These firms have unlimited liability.
5.   T   The managers of a corporation are typically not the owners, so the principal-agent problem is likely to arise.
6.   T   This is the definition of retained earnings.
7.   F   The most important "over-the-counter" market is the National Association of Securities Dealers' Automated Quotation System (NASDAQ).
8.   T   See the definition of present values in the Appendix to Chapter 5.
9.   F   This statement confuses stocks with bonds.
10. F   The Sarbanes-Oxley Act came about to prevent future accounting scandals like those of Enron and WorldCom in 2001.
11. T   See Figure 5-1 on page 140.
12. F   The Chief Executive Officer of a corporation is appointed by the Board of Directors to conduct the day-to-day operations.
13. T   See pages 138 and 139.
14. F   The legal problems resulted due to the stock incentive system associated with top management's pay. The capital gains and dividends that these managers received on their own units of stock were higher due to their manipulation of the accounting information.
15. F   This is the definition of accounting profit.

Chapter 6 (8)

Comparative Advantage and the Gains from International Trade

Chapter Summary

Over the past 50 years, international trade has grown significantly as many governments reached agreements to reduce tariffs and other trade barriers. In Chapter 2, you learned about comparative advantage. **Comparative advantage** shows that individuals, firms, and countries will be made better off by producing goods and services for which they have a lower opportunity cost than competitors and trading for those goods and services for which they have a higher opportunity cost. Absolute advantage is the ability of an individual, firm, or country to produce more of a good or service than competitors when using the same amount of resources. Nations develop comparative advantages for different reasons including a favorable climate, the availability of natural resources, an abundance of labor or capital, and access to superior production technologies.

On average, countries benefit from trade, but while some firms and workers benefit from international trade, others do not. When a country becomes more open to trade, the profits of firms that produce the same goods that are imported will fall and some of the firms' workers may lose their jobs. Those harmed by trade often lobby their governments to impose import restrictions. Despite the gains that exist from **free trade**, nations still sometimes impose trade restrictions that result in higher prices for traded goods. Trade restrictions usually are in the form of **tariffs, quotas, voluntary export restraints,** and other non-tariff barriers. Although tariffs and quotas save jobs in the countries that impose them, the employment gains often are achieved at a high cost.

After World War II, the United States and Europe negotiated treaties to reduce the high tariff rates imposed during the Great Depression. Recent discussions have focused on expanding trade in services and products that incorporate intellectual property, rather than trade in goods. The **World Trade Organization** (WTO) was established in 1995 to facilitate these negotiations. Opposition to liberalization of international trade and investment, also known as **globalization**, grew in the 1990s. Supporters of the anti-globalization movement want to protect domestic industries from competition and believe globalization unfairly favors the interests of high-income countries.

The United States government has extended protection to some domestic industries due to allegations of dumping by foreign companies. **Dumping** refers to selling a product for a price below its cost of production.

Multinational enterprises conduct operations in more than one nation. They may open offices in a foreign country to avoid tariffs on exports; to gain access to raw materials available in other nations; to gain access to low-cost labor; to minimize foreign exchange risk; and/or to respond to competition from other firms in their industry.

Learning Objectives

When you finish this chapter, you should be able to:

1. **Discuss the role of international trade in the U.S. economy.** From 1950 to 2007, both exports and imports have steadily increased as a fraction of U.S. gross domestic product. Each year, the United States exports about 50 percent of its wheat crop, 40 percent of its rice crop and 20 percent of its corn crop. About 20 percent of U.S. manufacturing jobs depend directly or indirectly on exports.

2. **Understand the difference between comparative advantage and absolute advantage in international trade.** Absolute advantage is the ability of a country to produce more of a good than other countries using the same amount of resources. However, comparative advantage is the key to determining specialization and trade. Countries have a comparative advantage in production when they can produce a good or service at a lower opportunity cost than other producers. Countries are better off if they specialize in producing the goods for which they have a comparative advantage. They can then trade for the goods for which other countries have a comparative advantage.

3. **Explain how countries gain from international trade.** By trading, nations are able to consume more than they could without trade. This is possible because total world production of traded goods increases after trade. Shifting production to the more efficient country – the one with the comparative advantage – increases total production. (Remember, every country has a comparative advantage in producing at least one good or service.) The sources of comparative advantage include a favorable climate or supplies of natural resources; relatively abundant supplies of labor and capital; access to technology; and external economies.

4. **Analyze the economic effects of government policies that restrict international trade.** Government restrictions on international trade, such as tariffs and quotas, reduce the foreign competition faced by domestic firms. By limiting competition, trade restrictions raise the domestic price of a good above the world price. Trade restrictions help domestic producers but harm domestic consumers and reduce economic efficiency. Costs imposed by the high prices paid by consumers almost always exceed the value of the jobs saved by trade barriers.

5. **Evaluate the arguments over trade policy and globalization.** Advocates for policies that restrict trade (protectionism) argue that free trade reduces employment by driving domestic firms out of business and forces firms to pay lower wages to compete with firms in other industries. However, no economic study has found a connection in the long run between the total number of available jobs and the level of protection for domestic industries. Rather than lowering wages, free trade raises living standards by increasing economic efficiency.

Appendix: Understand why firms operate in more than one country. Your instructor may assign this appendix.

Chapter Review

Chapter Opener: Is Using Trade Policy to Help U.S. Industries a Good Idea? (pages 170-171)

Although trading between states in the United States is not controversial, trading between countries meets with a significant amount of opposition. The United States Congress enacted a tariff on Brazilian ethanol, so that this cheaper alternative fuel becomes unaffordable in the United States. There is also a quota on the importation of sugar into the United States in order to preserve jobs in the domestic sugar industry. The quota resulted in higher sugar prices for consumers, including firms, such as candy manufacturers, that use sugar as an input to produce other products. As a result, Life Savers and other candy products are no longer produced in the United States but in other countries where the costs of production are lower.

📖 Helpful Study Hint

Advocates for quotas stress how quotas will increase employment in the protected industry, but minimize their impact on prices and on employment in other industries. Tables 6-5 and 6-6 compare the number of jobs saved and the cost to consumers per year for each of these jobs in different markets as a result of tariffs and quotas. At the end of this chapter, *An Inside Look* examines the impact of reducing trade restrictions between the United States and South Korea. If the bilateral agreement is ratified by the governments of both countries, U.S. car consumers and Korean car producers will gain. Likewise, U.S. producers of food and Korean consumers of food will gain. The domestic producers of the goods that will be imported will lose.

Economics in YOUR Life! asks how sugar companies have convinced Congress to enact the sugar quota and why very few people who buy and use sugar have ever heard of the quota. Keep this question in mind as you read the chapter. The authors will answer this question at the end of the chapter.

6.1 LEARNING OBJECTIVE

6.1 The United States in the International Economy (pages 172-175)

Learning Objective 1 Discuss the role of international trade in the U. S. economy.

Imports are goods and services bought domestically but produced in other countries. A **tariff** is a tax imposed by a government on imports. **Exports** are goods and services produced domestically but sold to other countries. Tariff rates in the United States have fallen, and international trade has increased significantly since 1930. The United States is the world's largest exporter, although exports and imports are a smaller fraction of GDP in the United States than in most other countries.

📖 Helpful Study Hint

International trade is a controversial topic among politicians and the general public. You may have formed opinions about trade based on comments made through newspaper and magazine articles and conversations with family and friends. In every country there are winners and losers from international trade. Read *Making the Connection* "How Expanding International Trade Has Helped Boeing" for a discussion of how one U.S. firm has benefited from trade. The increase in trade around the world has helped Boeing because the Boeing 747 can be used for long-range freight transportation.

Extra Solved Problem 6-1

Chapter 6 in the textbook includes two Solved Problems. Here is an extra Solved Problem to help you build your skills solving economic problems.

Supports Learning Objective 1: Discuss the role of international trade in the U. S. economy.

Paper Tariffs Canceled

U.S. manufacturers of glossy paper requested tariffs on glossy paper imported from Chinese firms. This request was made because U.S. firms feel that the subsidies paid by the Chinese government to Chinese paper manufacturers has given them an unfair advantage over U.S. firms. The Bush Administration responded to the concerns of the U.S. producers by imposing tariffs on the imported glossy paper. The U.S. International Trade Commission canceled the tariffs, saying that there was not significant evidence that the U.S. manufacturers had been harmed by the Chinese subsidies.

Source: Steven R. Weisman, "U.S. Trade Panel Rejects Tariff on Chinese Paper," *The International Herald Tribune*, November 22, 2007.

Explain the impact that the tariff on glossy paper would have had on U.S. imports and exports.

Step 1: **Review the chapter material.**
This problem asks you to interpret the effect of trade on the United States., so you may want to review section "The United States in the International Economy," which begins on page 172 of the textbook.

Step 2: **Explain the impact on imports and exports if the tariff were to remain in place.**
A tariff will cause Chinese glossy paper to become more expensive in the United States. This makes it more difficult for Chinese firms to compete with U.S. firms. The tariff would cause imports to fall and U.S. firms would be able to sell more paper at a higher price. However, U.S. firms that use glossy paper in producing catalogs, calendars, and other products would find their costs rising, which might lead them to raise prices and reduce production and employment.

6.2 Comparative Advantage in International Trade (pages 175-176)

Learning Objective 2 Understand the difference between comparative advantage and absolute advantage in international trade.

Comparative advantage is the ability of an individual, firm or country to produce a good or service at a lower opportunity cost than another individual, firm, or country. Mutually beneficial trade between two parties is possible when they specialize in the production of the goods and services for which they have a comparative advantage and trade for the goods and services for which they have comparative disadvantage in production. Comparative advantage is the basic argument in favor of free domestic as well as free international trade.

📖 Helpful Study Hint

Absolute advantage and comparative advantage were explained in chapter 2 on pages 46-47. Review **Solved Problem 2-2** on page 48 from that chapter as well as the example of comparative advantage illustrated in Tables 6-1 and 6-2 on page 176 to ensure you understand these two concepts.

Extra Solved Problem 6-2

Chapter 6 in the textbook includes two Solved Problems. Here is an extra Solved Problem to help you build your skills solving economic problems.

Supports Learning Objective 2: Understand the difference between comparative advantage and absolute advantage in international trade.

Suppose that the United States and China each produce only two goods, wheat and shirts. Further assume that these two countries use only labor to produce the two goods. Use the productivity information in this table to answer the questions below.

	Output per hour of work	
	Wheat	**Shirts**
United States	2 bushels	10 shirts
China	1 bushel	8 shirts

a. Who has the absolute advantage in the production of wheat? Shirts?

b. Who has the comparative advantage in the production of wheat? Shirts? What good should the United States specialize in? What good should China specialize in?

Step 1:   Review the chapter material.
This problem is about comparative advantage, so you may want to review the section "Comparative Advantage in International Trade," which begins on page 175 in the textbook.

Step 2:   **Determine who has the absolute advantage in the production of each good.**
To determine absolute advantage, you should begin by looking at each good individually and ask yourself the question "Who can produce more of the good?" The United States can produce more wheat than China, so the United States has the absolute advantage in the production of wheat. The United States can also produce more shirts, so the United States also has the absolute advantage in the production of shirts.

Step 3:   **Determine who has the comparative advantage in the production of each good by calculating opportunity costs.**
In order for the United States to produce 1 bushel of wheat, it must give up 5 shirts, while China has to give up 8 shirts for the same bushel of wheat. The United States gives up less to produce wheat, so it has the comparative advantage in the production of wheat. To produce 1 shirt, the United States must give up 1/5 of a bushel of wheat, while China only gives up 1/8 bushel of wheat. Therefore, China has the comparative advantage in the production of shirts.

Step 4:   **Determine specialization by looking at the comparative advantage.**
To receive gains from trade, countries should specialize in the good in which they have a comparative advantage and then trade that good for goods from other countries. In this case, the United States should specialize in the production of wheat and China should specialize in the production of shirts.

6.3 LEARNING OBJECTIVE

6.3   How Countries Gain From International Trade (pages 177-183)

Learning Objective 3   Explain how countries gain from international trade.

The gains from trade can be illustrated with an example of two countries that produce the same two goods under conditions of autarky. **Autarky** is a situation where a country does not trade with other countries. When each country specializes in the production of the good for which it has a comparative advantage and trades some of this good for some of the good produced by the other country, (a) total production of both goods can be greater than it would be under conditions of autarky and (b) total consumption of both goods in both countries can be greater with trade than under conditions of autarky.

The **terms of trade** is the ratio at which a country can trade its exports for imports from other countries. Although countries as a whole are made better off from trade, trade can harm firms and workers in industries that produce goods at a higher cost than foreign competitors.

📖 Helpful Study Hint

Read *Solved Problem 6-3* "The Gains From Trade," which describes the gains from trade in David Ricardo's famous cloth and wine example. In this example, Portugal and England each gain from trade. Portugal can specialize in wine, while England specializes in the production of cloth. The two countries can make themselves better off through trade Be sure you understand the example in the textbook where Japan and the United States are both able to consume more cell phones and MP3 players after trade than under autarky.

In reality, countries do not specialize completely in the goods in which they have the comparative advantage. This lack of complete specialization is because some goods are not traded internationally, opportunity costs increase as production increases, and consumers in different countries have different preferences for products. There are several reasons why a country may have a comparative advantage in producing a particular good. A firm in one country may have a relatively low opportunity cost in the production of a good because of favorable climate, abundant supplies of certain natural resources, or relatively abundant supplies of labor or capital. Another source of comparative advantage is superior technology in one country. Comparative advantage may also result from external economies. **External economies** are reductions in a firm's costs that result from an expansion in the size of an industry.

📖 Helpful Study Hint

Raymond Vernon provided a classic example of the importance of external economies. Anyone who lives in or has visited New York City, Manhattan in particular, knows that prices for most goods and services are higher there than in most other cities. Real estate and transportation are expensive, streets are crowded, and firms must pay employees a premium to compensate for the high cost of living. Yet, the garment and financial industries located in Manhattan continue to thrive despite these disadvantages. For both of these industries, ready access to suppliers, customers, and competitors are important assets. Personal contacts and face-to-face meetings are critical to the success of doing business. The large market size and concentration of related businesses offered by New York City are more important assets than the lower cost of real estate and transportation offered by locations outside of Manhattan. See *Making the Connection* "Why is Dalton, Georgia, the Carpet-Making Capital of the World?" for another example of external economies.

The carpet industry has clustered in Dalton, Georgia, to take advantage of skilled workers and suppliers who specialize in servicing the carpet industry.

Don't Let This Happen to YOU! "Remember That Trade Creates Both Winners and Losers" explains that international trade may be a win-win situation for countries, but that not all individual consumers and producers are winners. Because there is a net gain to society from international trade, some of the gains to the winners could be used to compensate the losers.

6.4 LEARNING OBJECTIVE

6.4 Government Policies that Restrict International Trade (pages 183-190)

Learning Objective 4 Analyze the economic effects of government policies that restrict international trade.

Free trade refers to trade between countries that is free from government restrictions. Free trade policies offer benefits to consumers of imported goods and allow for a more efficient allocation of resources than is possible when international trade is restricted by tariffs or other trade barriers. But free trade also harms domestic firms that are less efficient than their foreign competitors.

A **tariff** is a tax on imports imposed by the government. A **quota** is a numerical limit imposed by the government on the quantity of a good that can be imported into a country. A **voluntary export restraint** is an agreement negotiated between two countries that places a numerical limit on the quantity of a good that can be imported by one country from the other country. A *non-tariff barrier* is a government restriction on international trade other than a quota, voluntary export restraint, or tariff. The imposition of these barriers to free trade create a deadweight loss for the domestic economy.

📖 Helpful Study Hint

Figures 6-6 and 6-7 illustrate the deadweight losses that result from the imposition of a tariff or quota. Tables 6-5 and 6-6 describe the costs of trade restrictions in a different but compelling manner. The tables list estimates of the per-job cost to consumers of saving jobs in industries protected by trade restrictions. Those who favor restrictions on international trade must be willing to argue that these high costs of preserving jobs in domestic industries are justified. See **Solved Problem 6-4**, "Measuring the Economic Effect of a Quota," for additional practice with analyzing the deadweight losses associated with a quota. If the United States imposes a quota on the number of apples that can be imported into the country, the price of apples will increase and the quantity of apples that can be purchased will decrease. This causes a decrease in consumer surplus and a deadweight loss to the economy.

6.5 LEARNING OBJECTIVE

6.5   The Argument over Trade Policies and Globalization (pages 190-195)

Learning Objective 5   Evaluate the arguments over trade policy and globalization.

Debates over the merits of free trade and policies to restrict trade date back to the beginning of the United States. After World War II, government officials from the United States and Europe negotiated an international agreement to reduce trade barriers and promote free trade. Some interest groups began to oppose free trade policies in the 1990s. You have probably heard the term globalization. **Globalization** refers to the process of countries becoming more open to foreign trade and investment. Opposition to globalization is based on the fear that low-income countries are at risk of losing their cultural identity as multinational countries sell Western goods in their markets and relocate factories in their countries to take advantage of low-cost labor.

Protectionism is demanded by those who wish to preserve domestic jobs in certain industries or who believe that certain domestic industries should be protected from foreign competition for reasons of national security. **Dumping** refers to selling a product for a price below the cost of production. If a country is able to establish that foreign firms have dumped products on the domestic market, then they are allowed under international agreements to impose tariffs on these products. The **World Trade Organization (WTO)** is an international organization that oversees international trade agreements.

📖 Helpful Study Hint

Arguments for and against free trade and globalization offer you an opportunity to analyze important policy issues in an objective manner.

You may have formed opinions about these issues after reading or seeing reports of low wages and poor working conditions offered by multinational corporations in developing countries. *Making the Connection* "The Unintended Consequences of Banning Goods Made with Child Labor" explains how in some developing countries the alternative to working in a multinational firm is begging or illegal activity. As incomes rise in countries, families rely less on child labor...

Making the Connection "Has NAFTA Helped or Hurt the U.S. Economy?" discusses the effects of NAFTA on the U.S. economy. Even though in the United States there were both winners and losers from NAFTA, there was an overall gain to the economy. U.S. firms have become more efficient and consumers have been able to buy greater quantities of goods at lower prices.

Extra Solved Problem 6-5

Chapter 6 in the textbook includes two Solved Problems. Here is an extra Solved Problem to help you build your skills solving economic problems.

Supports Learning Objective 5: Evaluate the arguments over trade policy and globalization.

Sunlight! Bah, Humbug!

Arguments over international trade are nothing new. Alexander Hamilton called for the protection of so-called "infant industries" in the United States, and farming interests have long lobbied for trade restrictions to prevent consumers from buying cheaper food products from abroad. Although the countries and industries change over time, the arguments over trade restrictions have not. The 19th century French economist, Frédéric Bastiat, satirized French opponents of free trade in writing a petition to the French government supposedly from the manufacturers of "candles, waxlights, lamps, candlesticks, street lamps...generally of everything connected with lighting": Bastiat's "petition of the candlemakers" has been reprinted many times and often appears in textbooks because of its clever theme as well as its applicability to the arguments of 21st century "petitioners."

> We are suffering from the intolerable competition of a foreign rival, placed, it would seem, in a condition so superior to ours for the production of light that he absolutely inundates our national market with it at a price fabulously reduced. The moment he shows himself, our trade leaves us – all consumers apply to him; and a branch of native industry, having countless ramifications, is all at once rendered completely stagnant. This rival...is no other than the sun...

> What we pray for is, that it may please you to pass a law ordering the shutting up of all windows, skylights, dormer-windows, outside and inside shutters, curtains, blinds...all openings, holes, chinks, clefts, and fissures by or through which the light of the sun has been in use to enter houses, to the prejudice of the meritorious manufacturers with which we flatter ourselves we have accommodated our country – a country which, in gratitude, ought not to abandon us now to strife so unequal.

Source: Frédèric Bastiat, *Social Fallacies*, translated by Patrick James Stirling, Santa Anna, CA: Register Publishing, 1944, pp. 60-61.

Cite arguments from chapter 6 that are similar to those raised in Bastiat's petition.

Step 1: Review the chapter material.
This problem is about arguments over trade policies, so you may want to review the section "The Argument over Trade Policies and Globalization," which begins on page 190 of the textbook.

Step 2: Cite arguments from chapter 6 that are similar to those raised in Bastiat's petition.
In describing protectionism the textbook notes that:

> For as long as international trade has existed, governments have attempted to restrict it to protect domestic firms...protectionism causes losses to consumers and eliminates jobs in domestic industries that use the protected product...Supporters of protectionism argue that free trade reduces employment by driving domestic firms out of business...jobs are lost, but jobs are also lost when more-efficient domestic firms drive less-efficient domestic firms out of business...No economic study has ever found a connection in the long run between the total number of jobs available and the level of tariff protection for domestic industries.

Source: page 192.

As Bastiat might have said: "plus ça change, plus c'est la même chose." ("The more things change, the more they stay the same.")

📖 Helpful Study Hint

Economics in YOUR Life! "Why Haven't You Heard of the Sugar Quota?" explains why individual citizens and politicians don't care much about the sugar quota. The sugar quota costs U.S. consumers about $2 billion per year, which works out to be about $7.50 per person. The individual citizen is not likely to be informed about the quota and its effects; and, even if he was informed, it is unlikely that he would take much action for $7.50 per year. Politicians have no incentive to alter the policy as voters are unlikely to protest and the sugar industry continues to press for the quota to stay in place.

Key Terms

Absolute advantage. The ability to produce more of a good or service than competitors when using the same amount of resources.

Autarky. A situation in which a country does not trade with other countries.

Comparative advantage. The ability of an individual, a firm, or a country to produce a good or service at a lower opportunity cost than competitors.

Dumping. Selling a product for a price below its cost of production.

Exports. Goods and services produced domestically but sold to other countries.

External economies. Reductions in a firm's costs that result from an increase in the size of an industry.

Foreign direct investment. The purchase or building by a domestic firm of a facility in a foreign country.

Foregin portfolio investment. The purchase by an individual or firm of stocks or bonds issued in another country.

Free trade. Trade between countries that is without government restrictions.

Globalization. The process of countries becoming more open to foreign trade and investment.

Imports. Goods and services bought domestically but produced in other countries.

Multinational enterprise. A firm that conducts operations in more than one country.

Opportunity cost. The highest-valued alternative that must be given up to engage in an activity.

Protectionism. The use of trade barriers to shield domestic firms from foreign competition.

Quota. A numerical limit imposed by a government on the quantity of a good that can be imported into the country.

Tariff. A tax imposed by a government on imports.

Terms of trade. The ratio at which a country can trade its exports for its imports from other countries.

Voluntary export restraint (VER). An agreement negotiated between two countries that places a numerical limit on the quantity of a good that can be imported by one country from the other country.

World Trade Organization (WTO). An international organization that enforces international trade agreements.

Appendix

Multinational Firms (pages 205-210)

LEARNING OBJECTIVE: Understand why firms operate in more than one country.

Multinational Firms

Multinational enterprises are firms that conduct operations in more than one country. Two innovations made it possible for firms to coordinate operations on several continents. The first was the completion of the transatlantic cable in 1866, which made possible instant communication by telegraph between the United States and Europe. The second was the development of more efficient steam engines, which reduced the cost and increased the speed of long ocean voyages.

Foreign direct investment is the purchase or building by a domestic firm of a facility in a foreign country. **Foreign portfolio investment** is the purchase by an individual or firm of stocks or bonds issued in another country. In the early 20th century, most U.S. firms expanded abroad through foreign direct investment because the stock and bond markets in other countries were often too poorly developed to make foreign portfolio investment practical.

Today, most large U.S. corporations have established facilities overseas because they expect to increase their profitability by doing so. Firms might expect to increase their profits though overseas operations for five reasons:

1. To avoid tariffs or the threat of tariffs.
2. To gain access to raw materials.
3. To gain access to low-cost labor.
4. To minimize exchange-rate risk.
5. To respond to industry competition.

Most newly established U.S. firms begin by selling only in the United States. If successful, they will begin to export, using foreign firms to market and distribute their products. If firms' exporting efforts are successful, they may establish their own overseas marketing and distribution networks. Finally, the firms will establish their own production facilities in foreign countries.

Firms face costs from expanding into foreign markets that differ from the costs of operating in domestic markets. One problem is that tastes differ between consumers in foreign and domestic markets. Products that are popular in one country may not be as popular in another country because of cultural differences or foreign government restrictions.

U.S. firms possess certain competitive advantages when operating in foreign countries. Some firms, such as Coca-Cola and McDonald's, have strong name recognition. Some firms possess a significant technological edge over foreign rivals and other firms have developed efficient, low-cost production methods. Some firms have proven to be better at designing and rapidly bringing to market new products than their foreign competitors.

📖 Helpful Study Hint

Many people believe that when U.S. firms locate production facilities in other countries the level of employment and wages in the U.S. decline. *Making the Connection* "Have Multinational Corporations Reduced Employment and Lowered Wages in the United States?" explains that wages of U.S. workers are determined by their productivity. Competition from low-wage workers in other countries has little impact on the wages of U.S. workers. Because in the U.S. economy about 31 million jobs are created and 29 million jobs disappear every year, workers who lose jobs at one firm, whether due to foreign competition or some other factor, can eventually find jobs at other firms with, on average, little effect on the workers' wages.

Key Terms – Appendix

Foreign direct investment.   The purchase or building by a domestic firm of a facility in a foreign country.

Foreign portfolio investment.   The purchase by an individual or firm of stocks or bonds issued in another country.

Multinational enterprises.   Firms that conduct operations in more than one country.

Self-Test

(Answers are provided at the end of the Self-Test.)

Multiple-Choice Questions

1. The sugar quota in the United States creates winners and losers. Which of these groups end up being a winner?
    a.   U.S. producers of sugar
    b.   U.S. companies that use sugar
    c.   U.S. consumers
    d.   All of the above

2. Which of the following has contributed to forming a global marketplace?
    a.   The falling costs of shipping
    b.   Cheaper and more reliable communications and the Internet
    c.   Fast, cheap, and reliable air transportation
    d.   All of the above

3. Over the past 50 years, what has happened to tariff rates?
    a.   Tariff rates have risen
    b.   Tariff rates have fallen
    c.   Tariff rates have remained the same
    d.   Tariffs rates have fluctuated up and down

4. Goods and services produced domestically, but sold to other countries are called
    a. imports.
    b. exports.
    c. tariffs.
    d. net exports.

5. Which of the following is true about the importance of trade in the U.S. economy?
    a. Exports and imports have steadily declined as a fraction of U.S. GDP.
    b. While exports and imports have been steadily rising as a fraction of GDP, not all sectors of the U.S. economy have been affected equally by international trade.
    c. Only a few U.S. manufacturing industries depend on trade.
    d. All of the above

6. Refer to the graph below. The figure is a representation of the pattern of U.S. international trade. Which trend line shows exports?

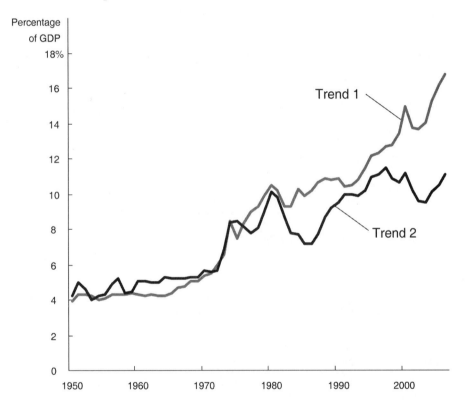

    a. Trend 1
    b. Trend 2
    c. Both lines show exports.
    d. Both lines show imports.

7. Refer to the bar graph below. The graph shows the eight leading exporting countries. The values are the shares of total world exports of merchandise and commercial services. In which of the four positions does the United States come in?

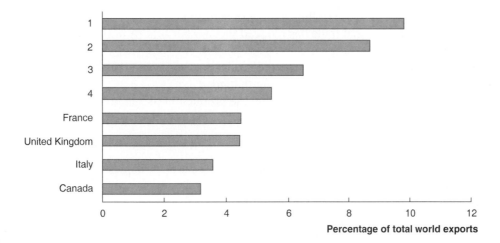

a. 1
b. 2
c. 3
d. 4

8. Refer to the bar graph below. The graph shows the importance of international trade to several countries. In which position does the United States come in?

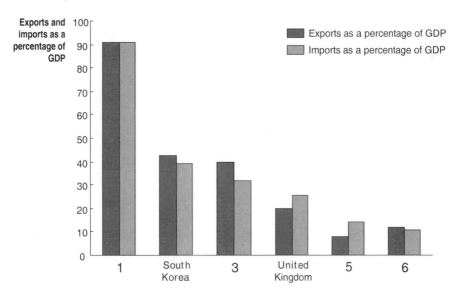

a. Position 1
b. Position 3
c. Position 5
d. Position 6

9. Select the answer that best fits the story in "Making the Connection: How Expanding International Trade Has Helped Boeing."
   a. Outsourcing has played a significant role in the slow employment growth in the United States.
   b. The production and use of the Boeing 747 has increased due to international trade.
   c. Boeing has moved production of the 747 to Korea to reduce costs.
   d. The increase in international trade has reduced the number of jobs in Boeing factories.

10. If a country has a *comparative advantage* in the production of a good, then that country
    a. also has an absolute advantage in producing that good.
    b. should allow another country to specialize in the production of that good.
    c. has a lower opportunity cost in the production of that good.
    d. All of the above

11. You and your neighbor pick apples and cherries. If you can pick apples at a lower opportunity cost than your neighbor can, which of the following is true?
    a. You have a comparative advantage in picking apples.
    b. Your neighbor is better off specializing in picking cherries.
    c. You can then trade some of your apples for some of your neighbor's cherries and both of you will end up with more of both fruit.
    d. All of the above

12. What is *absolute advantage*?
    a. The ability of an individual, firm, or country to produce more of a good or service than competitors using the same amount of resources.
    b. The ability of an individual, firm, or country to produce a good or service at a lower opportunity cost than other producers.
    c. The ability of an individual, firm, or country to consume more goods or services than others at lower costs.
    d. The ability of an individual, firm, or country to reach a higher production possibilities frontier by lowering opportunity costs.

13. Fill in the blanks. Countries gain from specializing in producing goods in which they have a(n) _____ advantage and trading for goods in which other countries have a(n) _____ advantage.
    a. absolute; absolute
    b. absolute; comparative
    c. comparative; absolute
    d. comparative; comparative

14. This case is similar to the one in Solved Problem 6-3. Consider the table below. The table shows the quantity of two goods that a worker can produce per day in a given country. Which country has an *absolute advantage*?

Output per day of work		
	Food	Clothing
Country A	6	3
Country B	1	2

   a. Country A has an absolute advantage in the production of both goods.
   b. Country B has an absolute advantage in the production of both goods.
   c. Both countries have an absolute advantage in the production of both goods.
   d. Neither country has an absolute advantage in the production of either good.

15. This case is similar to the one in Solved Problem 6-3. Consider the table below. Which country has a *comparative advantage*?

Output per day of work		
	Food	Clothing
Country A	6	3
Country B	1	2

   a. Country A has a comparative advantage in the production of both goods.
   b. Country B has a comparative advantage in the production of both goods.
   c. Country A has a comparative advantage in the production of food.
   d. Country B has a comparative advantage in the production of food.

16. In the real world, specialization is not complete. Why do countries not completely specialize?
   a. Because not all goods are traded internationally
   b. Because production of most goods involves increasing opportunity costs
   c. Because tastes for products differ
   d. All of the above

17. Which of the following is a source of comparative advantage?
   a. Autarky
   b. Absolute advantage
   c. The relative abundance of capital and labor
   d. All of the above

18. The term *external economies* refers to
   a. the process of turning inputs into goods and services.
   b. the reduction of production costs due to increased capacity utilization.
   c. the reduction of costs resulting from increases in the size of an industry in a given area.
   d. the benefits an industry derives from other industries located nearby.

19. Refer to the graph below. What does the light grey area represent?

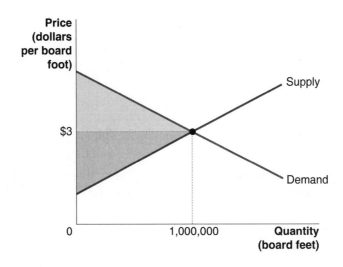

a. Autarky
b. Consumer surplus
c. Producer surplus
d. Economic surplus

20. Refer to the graph below. Under autarky, which area represents consumer surplus?

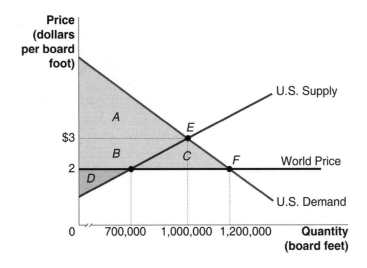

a. *A*
b. *A + B*
c. *A + B + C*
d. *C* only

21. Refer to the graph below. Under autarky, which area represents the total economic surplus?

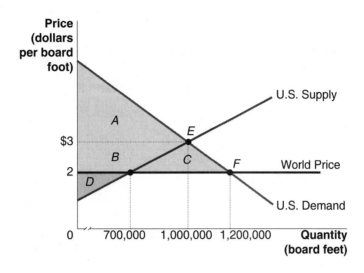

a. A
b. $A + B$
c. $A + B + C$
d. $A + B + D$

22. Refer to the graph below. How many board feet of lumber are imported when imports are allowed into the United States?

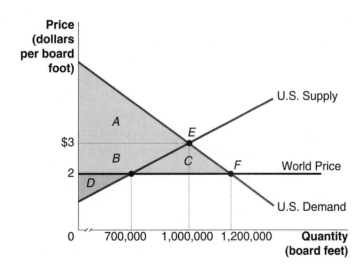

a. 1,000,000
b. 500,000
c. 700,000
d. 1,200,000

23. Refer to the graph below. Which situation results in higher domestic producer surplus?

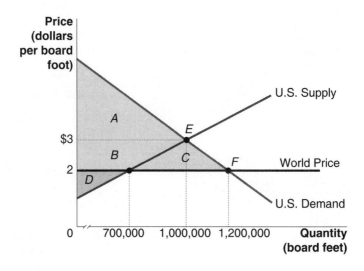

    a.   Autarky
    b.   The economy with imports
    c.   Both autarky and the economy with imports result in the same amount of producer surplus.
    d.   Any situation other than autarky or imports

24. Refer to the graph below. Which area represents the net benefit from opening the economy to imports?

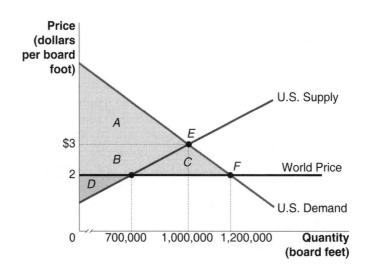

    a.   Area *A*
    b.   Area *B* + *C*
    c.   Area *C*
    d.   Area *D*

25. Refer to the graph below. The figure shows the effect of a $0.50 per board foot tariff on lumber. Which area represents the deadweight loss from this tariff?

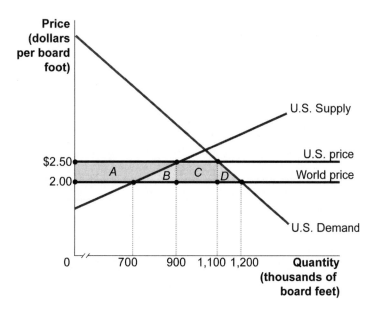

   a.   *A*
   b.   *C*
   c.   *B* + *D*
   d.   *B* + *C* + *D*

26. Refer to the graph below. The graph shows the effect of a $0.50 per board foot tariff on lumber. What is the quantity of lumber supplied (in thousands of board feet) by domestic producers after the tariff?

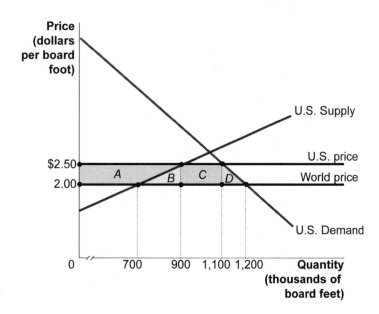

   a.   700
   b.   900
   c.   1,100
   d.   1,200

27. Refer to the graph below. The graph shows the effect of a $0.50 per board foot tariff on lumber. What is the reduction in U.S. lumber consumption (in thousands of board feet) as a result of the tariff?

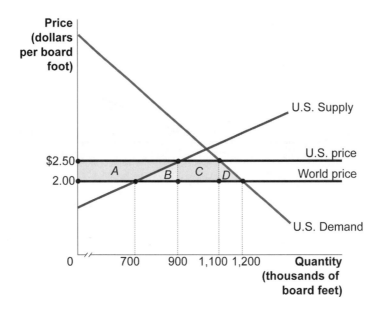

    a. 100
    b. 200
    c. 300
    d. 500

28. Refer to the graph below. The graph shows the effect of a $0.50 per board foot tariff on lumber. Which area represents the revenue collected by government from the tariff?

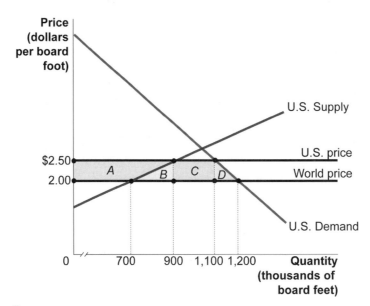

    a. $A + B + C + D$
    b. $B + D$
    c. C
    d. A

29. What is a *quota*?
    a. A quota is a numerical limit on the quantity of a good that can be imported.
    b. A quota is an agreement negotiated between two countries that places a numerical limit on the quantity of a good that can be imported by one country from the other country.
    c. A quota is the same thing as a voluntary export restraint.
    d. All of the above

30. What is a *voluntary export restraint*?
    a. A numerical limit on the quantity of a good that can be imported
    b. An agreement negotiated between two countries that places a numerical limit on the quantity of a good that can be imported by one country from the other country
    c. A quota imposed by the WTO
    d. The same as a tariff

31. In countries like the United States and Japan, the cost of saving jobs through trade barriers such as tariffs and quotas is
    a. very low in both countries.
    b. very high in both countries.
    c. high for the United States but small for Japan.
    d. low for the United States but high for Japan.

32. Which of the following acronyms applies to the international trade agreement that covers services and intellectual property as well as goods?
    a. GATT
    b. WTO
    c. NTB
    d. NAFTA

33. Which of the following are characteristics of the process of globalization that began in the 1980s?
    a. An increase in tariffs and restrictions on foreign trade and investment
    b. An increase in tariffs and elimination of restrictions on foreign trade and investment
    c. A decrease in tariffs and opening to foreign trade and investment
    d. A decrease in tariffs and restrictions on foreign trade and investment

34. Which of the following groups of people are significant sources of opposition to the WTO?
    a. People who want to protect domestic firms
    b. People who believe that low-income countries gain at the expense of high-income countries
    c. People who favor globalization
    d. All of the above

35. The opponents of globalization contend that
    a. globalization destroys cultures.
    b. globalization causes factories to relocate from low-income to high-income countries.
    c. globalization means that workers in poor countries lose jobs.
    d. All of the above

36. The use of trade barriers to shield domestic companies from foreign competition is called
    a. protectionism.
    b. dumping.
    c. dlobalization.
    d. patriotism.

37. Which of the following arguments is used to justify protectionism?
    a. Tariffs and quotas save jobs.
    b. Tariffs and quotas protect national security.
    c. Tariffs and quotas protect infant industries.
    d. All of the above

38. Which of the following statements about NAFTA is correct?
    a. NAFTA resulted in reduced consumption for the countries involved.
    b. NAFTA led to an overall loss of jobs.
    c. NAFTA reduced wages for both U.S. and Mexican workers.
    d. None of the above

39. What is the name given to the sale of a product for a price below its cost of production?
    a. Bargain pricing
    b. Cut-throat pricing
    c. Grim-trigger pricing
    d. Dumping

40. Which of the following is an example of positive economic analysis?
    a. Measuring the impact of the sugar quota on the U.S. economy.
    b. Asserting that the sugar quota is bad public policy and should be eliminated.
    c. Justifying the profits of U.S. sugar companies based on the number of workers they employ.
    d. All of the above

Short Answer Questions

1. The textbook notes that: "The effect of a quota is very similar to the effect of a tariff." If the effects are similar, why would a nation impose a quota rather than a tariff on an imported good?

   _____

   _____

   _____

2. Tables 6-5 and 6-6 list the high cost of trade restrictions to consumers in the United States and Japan for each job saved in several product markets. Because the number of jobs saved is much smaller than the number of consumers who must pay high prices to save these jobs, why do the governments of the United States and Japan maintain these trade restrictions?

   _____

   _____

   _____

3. Comparative advantage is used to explain why nations export products that they can produce at a lower opportunity cost than other nations. How, then, can one explain why the United States both exports and imports automobiles?

_____

_____

_____

_____

_____

4. David Ricardo's explanation of comparative advantage is considered to be one of the most important contributions to the history of economic thought. Why is comparative advantage so important?

_____

_____

_____

_____

_____

_____

5. The World Trade Organization (WTO) allows member nations to impose tariffs on imported products if dumping can be demonstrated. Why is it difficult to prove accusations of dumping?

_____

_____

_____

True/False Questions

T F 1.   As a percentage of GDP, U.S. imports and exports have both decreased during the past 20 years.

T F 2.   Demand for the Boeing 747 has increased due to international trade.

T F 3.   Although imports and exports are a small fraction of GDP in the United States, they are a much larger fraction of the GDP for smaller nations such as Japan.

T F 4.   One reason why countries do not specialize completely in production is that not all goods and services are traded internationally.

T   F   5.   Although United States firms were able to produce consumer electronics goods more cheaply and with higher quality than Japanese firms in the 1970s and 1980s, Japanese firms used superior process technology to move ahead of U.S. firms by 2005.

T   F   6.   Firms in Dalton, Georgia developed a comparative advantage in carpet-making because of external economies.

T   F   7.   Between 1994, when the North American Free Trade Agreement (NAFTA) went into effect, and 2007, the number of jobs in the U.S. declined by 21 million. Some of this decrease was due to NAFTA.

T   F   8.   Barriers to international trade include health and safety requirements that are more strictly imposed on imported goods than goods produced by domestic firms.

T   F   9.   The Smoot-Hawley Tariff of 1930 lowered average tariff rates in the U.S. by about 50 percent.

T   F   10.   One reason why countries do not specialize completely in production is that complete specialization requires countries to have an absolute advantage in the products they produce.

T   F   11.   Although countries gain from international trade, some individuals are harmed, including some workers who lose their jobs.

T   F   12.   The terms of trade refers to the length of trade agreements (for example, NAFTA) signed by officials from countries that are parties to these agreements.

T   F   13.   Each year the United States exports about 50 percent of its wheat crop.

T   F   14.   Germany is the leading exporting country, accounting for about 10 percent of total world exports.

T   F   15.   A tariff imposed on imports of textiles will raise the price of textiles in the importing country and create a deadweight loss in the domestic textile market.

Answers to the Self-Test

Multiple-Choice Questions

Question	Answer	Explanation
1	a	The sugar quota creates winners—U.S. sugar companies and their employees—and losers—U.S. companies that use sugar, their employees, and U.S. consumers who must pay higher prices for goods that contain sugar.
2	d	Improvements in transportation and communications have created a global marketplace.
3	b	Tariff rates have fallen. In the 1930s, the United States charged an average tariff rate above 50 percent. Today, the rate is less than 2 percent.
4	b	Imports are goods and services bought domestically but produced in other countries. Exports are goods and services produced domestically, but sold to other countries.
5	b	Not all sectors of the U.S. economy have been affected equally by international trade.
6	b	Exports have been less than imports since 1982.
7	a	The United States is the leading exporting country, accounting for about 10 percent of total world exports.
8	c	International trade is less important to the United States than to most other countries, with the significant exception of Japan.
9	b	Boeing received a significant increase in demand for the 747 to transport air freight.
10	c	The country with a lower opportunity cost of production has a comparative advantage in the production of that good.
11	d	If you can pick apples at a lower opportunity cost than your neighbor can, you have a comparative advantage in picking apples. Your neighbor is better off specializing

in picking cherries, and you are better off specializing in picking apples. You can then trade some of your apples for some of your neighbor's cherries and both of you will end up with more of both fruit.

12	a	Absolute advantage is the ability of an individual, firm, or country to produce more of a good or service than competitors using the same amount of resources.
13	d	Countries gain from specializing in producing goods in which they have a comparative advantage and trading for goods in which other countries have a comparative advantage.
14	a	Country A can produce more food and more clothing in one day than Country B.
15	c	A worker in Country A can produce 6 times as many units of food as a worker in Country B, but only 1.5 as many units of clothing. Country A is more efficient in producing food than clothing relative to Country B.
16	d	The three reasons above are the explanations given in the textbook.
17	c	The main sources are: climate and natural resources, the relative abundance of labor and capital, technology, and external economies.
18	c	The advantages include the availability of skilled workers, the opportunity to interact with other companies in the same industry, and being close to suppliers. These advantages result in lower costs to firms located in the area. Because these lower costs result from increases in the size of the industry in an area, economists refer to them as external economies.
19	b	The light grey area represents consumer surplus and the dark grey area represents producer surplus.
20	a	Autarky refers to equilibrium without trade. Area A is consumer surplus when price equals domestic price, or $3 per board foot.
21	d	The total economic surplus is the area between the demand and supply curves out to the domestic equilibrium.
22	b	Imports will equal 500,000 board feet, which is the difference between U.S. consumption and U.S. production at the world price.
23	a	The area of surplus under autarky is B + D.
24	c	Area C is additional consumer surplus that did not exist under autarky.
25	c	The areas B and D represent deadweight loss.
26	b	After the tariff is imposed, the quantity supplied domestically is 900 board feet, at a price of $2.50.
27	a	At a price (before tariff) of $2.00, U.S. consumption is 1,200. After the tariff is imposed, U.S. consumption falls to 1,100, so the decrease is 100.
28	c	Government revenue equals the tariff multiplied by the number of board feet imported, or $0.50 x (1,100,000 − 900,000) = $0.50 x 200,000 = $100,000.
29	a	A quota is a numerical limit on the quantity of a good that can be imported, and it has an effect similar to a tariff. Government revenue equals the tariff multiplied by the number of board feet imported, or $0.50 x (1,100,000 − 900,000 = $0.50 x 200,000 = $100,000).
30	b	That is a voluntary export restraint.
31	b	Tables 6-5 and 6-6 show how expensive it is to save jobs in each country.
32	b	In the 1940s, most international trade was in goods, and the GATT agreement covered only goods. In the following decades, trade in services and in products incorporating intellectual property, such as software programs and movies grew in importance. Many GATT members pressed for a new agreement that would cover services and intellectual property, as well as goods. A new agreement was negotiated, and in January 1995, the World Trade Organization (WTO), headquartered in Geneva, Switzerland, replaced the GATT.

33	c	During the years immediately after World War II, many developing countries erected high tariffs and restricted investment by foreign companies. When these policies failed to produce much economic growth, many of these countries decided during the 1980s to become more open to foreign trade and investment. This process became known as globalization.
34	a	The WTO favors the opening of trade and opposes most trade restrictions.
35	a	Some believe that free trade and foreign investment destroy the distinctive cultures of many countries.
36	a	Protectionism is the use of trade barriers to shield domestic companies from foreign competition.
37	d	According to the textbook, all of the reasons above, in addition to protecting high wages, are in support of protectionism.
38	d	The results of NAFTA were the precise opposite of those listed.
39	d	Dumping is selling a product for a price below its cost of production. The results of NAFTA were the precise opposite of those listed.
40	a	Positive economics concerns "what is." Measuring the impact of the sugar quota on the U.S. economy is an example of positive analysis.

Short Answer Responses

1. Quotas may be used to restrict trade when there are legal and political obstacles to raising tariffs. Quotas may also be used when there is a desire to limit imports by a specified amount. It is difficult to know the impact of a tariff rate on the amount of imports before the tariff is imposed.

2. Because the benefits are concentrated among relatively few workers, these workers and their employers have strong incentives to lobby for trade restrictions. Although many consumers are negatively affected, the impact is widely spread so that no individual has a strong incentive to lobby for the removal of the trade restrictions.

3. Real markets are more complex than the simple models used to explain comparative advantage. Automobiles are not standardized products that all look and perform in exactly the same way. One reason why the United States imports automobiles from some nations (for example, Japan) is that these nations specialize in producing the types of automobiles that appeal to certain consumers (consumers who desired relatively small fuel-efficient cars). The United States exports different types of automobiles that may appeal to consumers with different tastes in automobiles (for example, SUVs).

4. Comparative advantage explains why domestic and international trade is mutually beneficial under very general conditions, even when one of the parties to a trade has an absolute advantage in both traded goods. Nobel Laureate Paul Samuelson commented on a conversation he had with a mathematician who asked him to "name me one proposition in all of the social sciences which is both true and non-trivial." After much thought, Samuelson provided this response: comparative advantage. "That it is logically true need not be argued before a mathematician; that it is not trivial is attested by the thousands of important intelligent men who have never been able to grasp the doctrine for themselves or to believe it after it was explained to them."

Source: P.A. Samuelson, "The Way of an Economist," in *International Economic Relations: Proceedings of the Third Congress of the International Economic Association.* Macmillan: London, pp. 1-11.

5. Dumping (selling a good below its cost of production) is difficult to prove for two main reasons. First, it can be difficult to measure the true cost of production for firms from countries different from the country where the dumping allegedly occurred. Second, what is dumping to a firm harmed by the practice may be normal business practice to the firm that does the selling.

True/False Answers

1. F U.S. imports and exports have both increases as a fraction of GDP.
2. T See Making the Connection "How Expanding International Trade Has Helped Boeing."
3. F Although the ratio of exports and imports to GDP is greater in some nations that are smaller than the U.S., the ratio for Japan is smaller.
4. T Since not all goods are traded internationally, countries will have to produce some goods domestically to satisfy the demands of the domestic consumers.
5. F Japanese firms were producing consumer electronics goods more cheaply and with higher quality than U.S. firms in the 1970s and 1980s. U.S. firms used superior process technology to move ahead of Japanese firms by 2005.
6. T See Making the Connection "Why is Dalton, Georgia, the Carpet-Making Capital of the World?"
7. F The number of jobs *increased* by about 21 million during this time period.
8. T
9. F The Smoot-Hawley Tariff raised average tariffs rates to more than 50 percent.
10. F You need not have an absolute advantage in any good in order to specialize and gain from trade.
11. T There are winners and losers in international trade and the workers who work in the industry that competes with the imported goods often lose their jobs.
12. F Terms of trade refers to the ratio at which goods trade between two countries.
13. T See page 172.
14. F The United States is the leading export country.
15. T

GDP: Measuring Total Production and Income

Chapter Summary

While **microeconomics** is the study of how households and firms make choices, how they interact in markets, and how the government attempts to influence their choices, **macroeconomics** is the study of the economy as a whole. This includes such topics as **economic growth**, **business cycles**, the inflation rate, employment, unemployment, and trade with other nations. In order to talk about these topics, it is necessary to be able to measure how the economy is performing and make comparisons between time periods and countries.

To measure the performance of the economy, economists use a measure of economic activity called **gross domestic product** (GDP). In this chapter, you will learn about GDP: how it is constructed, what its components are, and its strengths and weaknesses as a measure of production. Also covered in the chapter is the concept of real and nominal variables and a price index referred to as the **GDP deflator**.

Learning Objectives

When you finish this chapter, you should be able to:

1. **Explain how total production is measured.** Total production is measured by **gross domestic product (GDP)**, which is the value of all **final goods and services** produced in an economy during a period of time. When we measure the value of total production in the economy by calculating GDP, we are simultaneously measuring the value of total income. GDP is divided into four major categories of expenditures: consumption, investment, government purchases, and net exports. We can also calculate GDP by adding up the **value added** of every firm involved in producing final goods and services.

2. **Discuss whether GDP is a good measure of well-being.** GDP does not include household production, which refers to goods and services people produce for themselves, or production in the **underground economy**, which consists of concealed buying and selling. The underground economy in some poorer countries may be more than half of measured GDP. GDP is a flawed measure of well-being because it does not include the value of leisure, it is not adjusted for pollution or other negative effects of production, and it is not adjusted for changes in crime and other social problems.

3. **Discuss the difference between real GDP and nominal GDP. Nominal GDP** is the value of goods and services evaluated at current year prices. **Real GDP** is the value of goods and services evaluated at **base year** prices. By keeping prices constant, we know that changes in real GDP represent changes in the quantity of goods and services produced in the economy. Real GDP is greater than nominal

GDP in years before the base year and less than nominal GDP for years after the base year. The **GDP deflator** is a measure of the price index and is calculated as (Nominal GDP/Real GDP) x 100.

4.   **Become familiar with other measures of total production and total income. Gross domestic product (GDP)** is the most important measure of total production and total income. As we will see in later chapters, for some purposes, other measures of total production and total income turn out to be more useful than GDP. These other measures are: gross national product (GNP), net national product (NNP), national income, personal income, and disposable personal income.

Chapter Review

Chapter Opener: Increases in GDP Help Revive American Airlines (pages 212–213)

Why is GDP important to you? Economic expansions and contractions have a dramatic impact on business outcomes. American Airlines, for example, flies more passengers than any airline in the world. In 2006 they earned a profit and continued to earn a profit during the first three months of 2007, unlike their large losses of 2005. This led to a decision by American Airlines to purchase 47 new jets from Boeing. The increase in profits and the subsequent purchase of additional jets were due to an increase in demand for air travel. American Airlines' situation is an effect of economic expansion or of the business cycle, known as the periodic expansion and contraction in the level of production in the United States.

📖 Helpful Study Hint

Read *An Inside Look* at the end of the chapter for an example of how another segment of the transportation business has experienced an economic slowdown in 2006. Pay attention to how this contrasts with the profits that American Airlines was experiencing.

   Would you rather work in China, which has a GDP of over 10 percent, or in Canada, which has a GDP of over only 2 percent? *Economics in YOUR Life!* at the start of this chapter poses this question. Keep the question in mind as you read the chapter. The authors will answer the question at the end of the chapter.

7.1 LEARNING OBJECTIVE

7.1   Gross Domestic Product Measures Total Production (pages 215–222)

Learning Objective 1   Explain how total production is measured.

An economy that produces a large quantity of goods and services creates an interesting measurement problem. How do we add together the production of different goods and services to arrive at an aggregate measure of total production?

Economists have developed a method of aggregating the wide variety of production by calculating a measure called **gross domestic product** or **GDP**. GDP is defined as the market value of all **final goods and services** produced in a country during a period of time. We aggregate goods by adding their value, and we determine their value by their price. We count only newly-produced goods and services, not all transactions, and we count only transactions that have a market price. **Transfer payments**, such as Social Security and unemployment insurance, are not counted in GDP because they are payments by the government for which the government does not receive a new good or service in return. **Intermediate goods** are not counted because they are an input into a final good. For example, General Motors produces cars, but it does not produce the tires that go on the car. General Motors buys tires from Goodyear and Michelin. The tires are an intermediate good. In calculating GDP, we include the value of the General Motors truck but not the value of the tire. If we included the value of the tire, we would be *double counting*: The value of the tire would be counted once when the tire company sold it to General Motors, and a second time when General Motors sold the truck, with the tire installed, to a consumer. GDP is the sum of price multiplied by quantity for all final goods and services produced.

📖 Helpful Study Hint

Work through **Solved Problem 7-1** to practice calculating GDP. Understanding these calculations and how GDP is measured is important in mastering macroeconomics.

When we calculate GDP as the value of production in a country, we are also measuring the value of income in that country. This is because $100 spent on a good will ultimately result in $100 worth of income for the various factors of production that produced that good. The measurement of GDP is often referred to as national income accounting. GDP measures both production and income.

We can also look at GDP from the point of view of expenditures. From the expenditure point of view, we divide GDP into four components:

1. **Consumption** expenditures are expenditures made by households (excluding the purchase of new houses, which we count in investment expenditures).
2. **Investment** expenditures are final goods and services purchased by business firms (equipment for production and new buildings), changes in inventories (which is the difference between production and sales), and residential construction purchased by households. Look at the **Don't Let This Happen to You!** in this chapter in the textbook for more discussion of the definition of investment.
3. **Government purchases** are spending by the federal, state, and local governments.
4. **Net exports** are exports minus imports.

📖 Helpful Study Hint

The feature **Don't Let This Happen to YOU!** appears in this and other chapters to show you how to avoid mistakes often made by economics students. A primary component of investment is the purchase of final goods by business firms. These purchases include equipment used in production and buildings used for production, such as factories and office buildings. Investment in the sense we are using it in this chapter does not include buying stocks, bonds, and other types of financial assets.

The components of GDP can be expressed in an equation as:

$$Y = C + I + G + NX$$

The equation tells us that GDP (Y) equals consumption (C) plus investment (I) plus government purchases (G) plus net exports (NX).

Value added refers to the additional market value a firm gives to a product and is equal to the difference between the price the firm sells a good for and the price it paid other firms for intermediate goods. The value-added method is an alternative way of calculating GDP that also avoids the problem of double counting intermediate goods.

📖 Helpful Study Hint

For a good example of government purchases, look at the *Making the Connection: Spending on Homeland Security.* The Department of Homeland Security was established to guard against future terrorist attacks within the United States after the terrorist attacks of September 11, 2001. Spending by this department of the Federal Government is a part of the government spending component of GDP. The Department of Homeland Security provides grants to state and local government agencies to help cover security expenses for state and local needs.

7.2 LEARNING OBJECTIVE

7.2 Does GDP Measure What We Want it to Measure? (pages 222-225)

Learning Objective 2 Discuss whether GDP is a good measure of well-being.

Economists use GDP to measure the total production in the economy. As a measure of production, GDP calculations exclude two types of production: production in the home and production in the underground economy. Household production refers to goods and services that people produce for themselves, such as the services that a homemaker provides for his or her family. The **underground economy** refers to the buying and selling of goods and services that are concealed from the government to avoid taxes or regulations because the goods or services are illegal, such as drugs or prostitution. For the United States, these omissions do not cause a serious distortion in the measurement of total production because the underground economy is relatively small and does not change in size very much from year to year. For some lesser developed countries, these values may be very large.

📖 Helpful Study Hint

For a good example of how the underground economy contributes to measured GDP, look at the *Making the Connection: How the Underground Economy Hurts Developing Countries.* While the underground economy in the United States is about 10 percent of GDP, in some developing countries, the underground economy may be more than 50 percent of GDP. The underground economy in developing countries, known as the informal sector, can be a sign that government polices are retarding economic growth because they represent activities that we do not measure and include in GDP.

In addition to measuring a country's total production, GDP is also frequently used as a measure of well-being. Although increases in GDP lead to increases in the well-being of a population, it is not a perfect measure for several reasons. GDP does not measure leisure, unless leisure results in a market transaction, such as spending on vacations. GDP also does not subtract the costs of negative non-market effects of production, such as pollution and crime. On the other hand, GDP will increase as households make expenditures to offset the impact of these negative non-market effects of production. Examples of these expenditures include health care costs due to poor air quality or spending on burglar alarms.

GDP also does not say anything about the distribution of income. Is income distributed equally among the people in the economy, or is the income distribution very unequal, so that a few get a lot of the income?

📖 Helpful Study Hint

For a good example of how the GDP relates to periods of prosperity, look at the ***Making the Connection: Did World War II Bring Prosperity?*** During the Great Depression of the 1930s, the unemployment rate in the United States reached the very high level of 10 percent *or more* and did not fall until the United States entered into World War II. Due to increases in production and the military during the years of 1941-1945, the unemployment rate fell to below 2 percent and ushered in what was believed to be a period of prosperity. However, many historians argue that this was not the case for the typical person. Although the war increased production for military goods, the typical person did not prosper during this time due to the low production and subsequent availability of consumption goods available to the public.

Extra Solved Problem 7-2

Chapter 7 of the textbook includes two Solved Problems. Here is an extra Solved Problem to help you build your skills solving economic problems:

The Relationship Between Real GDP Growth and Per-capita Real GDP Growth

Supports Learning Objective 2: Discuss whether GDP is a good measure of well-being.

The table below gives real GDP (in billions of 2000 dollars) and U.S. population (in thousands) for the years 1990-2006. For each year, calculate the growth rate in real GDP and the growth rate in per-capita real GDP. Are the growth rates the same?

Year	Real GDP (billions of 2000 dollars)	Population (in thousands)
1990	$7,112.5	250,132
1991	7,100.5	253,493
1992	7,336.6	256,894
1993	7,532.7	260,255
1994	7,835.5	263,436
1995	8,031.7	266,557
1996	8,328.9	269,667
1997	8,703.5	272,912
1998	9,066.9	276,115
1999	9,470.3	279,295
2000	9,817.0	282,403
2001	9,890.7	285,335
2002	10,048.8	288,216
2003	10,301.0	291,089
2004	10,675.8	293,908
2005	11,003.4	296,639
2006	11,319.4	299,801

SOLVING THE PROBLEM

Step 1: **Review the chapter material.**

This problem is about calculating per capita real GDP, so you may want to review the section "Shortcomings of GDP as a Measure of Well-Being," which begins on page 224 of the textbook.

Step 2: **Calculate per-capita real GDP and the growth rates.**

Per-capita real GDP is the amount of real GDP per person. This is calculated as real GDP/Population. Because real GDP is measured in billions and population is measured in thousands, you need to multiply the value of real GDP/Population by 1,000,000. Then calculate the growth rates. Remember, the growth rate between two years is calculated by subtracting the second year from the first year, dividing by the first year, and multiplying by 100. For example, the growth in real GDP for 2006 equals [($11,319.4 − $11,003.4)/ $11,003.4] x 100 = 2.9%. (Question: Why can't we calculate growth rates for 1990? Answer: Because we would need the real GDP and per capita real GDP values for 1989.)

Results:

Year	Real GDP	Real GDP growth rate	Population	Per capita real GDP	Per capita real GDP growth rate
1990	7,112.5		250,132	28,435	
1991	7,100.5	−0.2%	253,493	28,011	−1.5%
1992	7,336.6	3.3	256,894	28,559	2.0
1993	7,532.7	2.7	260,255	28,944	1.3
1994	7,835.5	4.0	263,436	29,743	2.8
1995	8,031.7	2.5	266,557	30,131	1.3
1996	8,328.9	3.7	269,667	30,886	2.5
1997	8,703.5	4.5	272,912	31,891	3.3
1998	9,066.9	4.2	276,115	32,837	3.0
1999	9,470.3	4.4	279,295	33,908	3.3
2000	9,817.0	3.7	282,403	34,762	2.5
2001	9,890.7	0.8	285,335	34,663	−0.3
2002	10,048.8	1.6	288,216	34,866	0.6
2003	10,301.0	2.5	291,089	35,388	1.5
2004	10,675.8	3.6	293,908	36,324	2.6
2005	11,003.4	3.1	296,639	37,094	2.1
2006	11,319.4	2.9	299,801	37,756	1.8

Using these numbers, we can calculate the average annual growth rate in real GDP and per capita real GDP for this time period by adding up the 16 annual growth rates listed in the table and dividing by 16. Performing these calculations, we find that the average annual growth rate for real GDP is 3.0%, while for the same period, per-capita real GDP grew at an average annual rate of 1.8%. This would suggest that the real GDP growth rate for the U.S. during this period overstates the amount of growth experienced by individuals and families.

7.3 LEARNING OBJECTIVE

7. 3 Real GDP versus Nominal GDP (pages 225-228)

Learning Objective 3   Discuss the difference between real GDP and nominal GDP.

Since GDP is calculated using the quantities of final goods and services produced at current market prices, GDP can change because (1) production changes or (2) the prices of goods and services change. If the price of a product increases from one year to the next and we produce the same quantity of the product in both years, GDP will be higher in the year with the higher price even though production has not increased.

To remedy this problem, economists have developed an alternative measure called real GDP. **Real GDP** is calculated by designating a particular year as the *base year*. The prices of goods and services in the base year are used to calculate the value of goods and services in all other years. GDP is often referred to as either **nominal GDP** or current dollar GDP, and real GDP is often called constant dollar GDP.

In an economy with rising prices, nominal GDP will be smaller than real GDP in years before the base year, and nominal GDP will be larger than real GDP in years after the base year. In the base year, nominal GDP and real GDP will have the same value.

We can use the values of nominal and real GDP to calculate a measure of **prices levels** in the economy. The **GDP deflator** is a measure of the average prices of goods and services compared to the base year. The GDP deflator is calculated as:

$$\text{GDP deflator} = \frac{\text{Nominal GDP}}{\text{Real GDP}} \times 100$$

📖 Helpful Study Hint

A value of the GDP deflator of 116 tells us that the average price of goods and services is 16 percent higher than the average price in the base year. This is not the inflation rate.

7.4   Other Measures of Total Production and Total Income (pages 228–231)

Learning Objective 4   Become familiar with other measures of total production and total income.

The Bureau of Economic Analysis (BEA) calculates several other measures of production and income in addition to GDP. These are Gross National Product (GNP), Net National Product (NNP), National Income, Personal Income, and Disposable Personal Income. Each of these gives a slightly different measure of production and income in a country. No one measure is better than another – they just measure things in a different way.

📖 Helpful Study Hint

For an example of how economic growth influences our lives, read the *Economics in YOUR Life!* feature at the end of the chapter. While a country that has a higher growth rate, such as China, is increasing the production of goods and services faster than a country with a lower growth rate, such as Canada, it is not necessarily true that the higher growth rate country is a "better" place to live. The growth rate measures the rate of change of production of goods and services. It does not measure the amount of goods and services (just the rate of change) and the well-being of people in that country

Extra Solved Problem 7-4

Chapter 7 of the textbook includes two Solved Problems. Here is an extra Solved Problem to help you build your skills solving economic problems:

GDP and GNP

Supports Learning Objective 4: Become familiar with other measures of total production and total income.

In 2006, nominal Gross Domestic Product (GDP) was $13,247 billion and nominal Gross National Product (GNP) was $13,277 billion. Explain the differences between these two measures of total production.

SOLVING THE PROBLEM

Step 1: **Review the chapter material.**
This problem is about two different measures of production, gross domestic product and gross national product, so you may want to review the definitions of these terms on pages 215 and 229 of the textbook.

Step 2: **Explain the differences.**
GDP measures final goods and services produced within the United States, and GNP is the value of final goods and services produced by the residents of the United States, even if that production takes place outside the United States.

Because in 2006, GNP was larger than GDP, income earned from the rest of the world (by U.S. firms and individuals outside the United States) must have been larger than income payments for production in the United States made to the foreign firms and foreign households. In this case, the difference was $30 billion—an amount that is only about one-quarter of one percent of GDP.

Key Terms

Business cycle. Alternating periods of economic expansion and economic recession.

Consumption. Spending by households on goods and services, not including spending on new houses.

Economic growth. The ability of an economy to produce increasing quantities of goods and services.

Expansion. The period of a business cycle during which total production and total employment are increasing.

Final good or service. A good or service purchased by a final user.

GDP deflator. A measure of the price level, calculated by dividing nominal GDP by real GDP, and multiplying by 100.

Government purchases. Spending by federal, state, and local governments on goods and services.

Gross domestic product (GDP). The market value of all final goods and services produced in a country during a period of time.

Inflation rate. The percentage increase in the price level from one year to the next.

Intermediate good or service. A good or service that is an input into another good or service, such as a tire on a truck.

Investment. Spending by firms on new factories, office buildings, machinery, and inventories, and spending by households on new houses.

Macroeconomics. The study of the economy as a whole, including topics such as inflation, unemployment, and economic growth.

Microeconomics. The study of how households and firms make choices, how they interact in markets, and how the government attempts to influence their choices.

Net exports. Exports minus imports.

Nominal GDP. The value of final goods and services evaluated at current year prices.

Price level. A measure of the average prices of goods and services in the economy.

Real GDP. The value of final goods and services evaluated at base year prices.

Recession. The period of a business cycle during which total production and total employment are decreasing.

Transfer payments. Payments by the government to individuals for which the government does not receive a good or service in return.

Underground economy. Buying and selling of goods and services that is concealed from the government to avoid taxes or regulations or because the goods and services are illegal.

Value added. The market value a firm adds to a product.

Self-Test

(Answers are provided at the end of the Self-Test.)

Multiple-Choice Questions

1. Which of the following is a macroeconomic study?
   a. the study of how households and businesses make choices
   b. the study of how households and businesses interact in markets
   c. the study of how the government attempts to influence the choices of households and businesses
   d. the study of how fast prices in general are increasing

2. The use of macroeconomic analysis to help the federal government design policies that help the economy run more efficiently is
   a. an absolute necessity, according to economists.
   b. a practice suggested by politicians but not by economists.
   c. a controversial question among economists.
   d. ideal in theory but nonexistent in practice because our knowledge of the economy as a whole is in fact very limited.

3. How does the Bureau of Economic Analysis of the U.S. Department of Commerce measure GDP?
   a. by adding the quantities produced of every good and service in the economy
   b. by adding the *value* in dollar terms of all of the final goods and services produced domestically
   c. by ascribing a historic *value* to all of the quantities produced in the economy
   d. in some cases, by adding quantities, and in others by adding the *value* of goods and services produced

4. Which is the largest component of GDP?
   a. consumption
   b. investment
   c. government purchases
   d. exports

5. Which of the following are not part of "final goods," as used in the definition of GDP?
   a. consumption goods
   b. investment goods
   c. exports
   d. intermediate goods

6. Which of the following is *not* true of GDP?
   a. GDP is measured by adding up the market values of goods produced, not the quantities of goods produced.
   b. GDP includes both intermediate and final goods.
   c. GDP includes only current production.
   d. GDP is calculated by the Bureau of Economic Analysis (BEA).

7. When a consumer purchases a new computer, how is that purchase counted in GDP?
    a. by adding the value of the various components of the computer to the final price paid for the computer by the consumer
    b. by subtracting the value of the components from the price paid by the consumer
    c. by counting only the value of the computer and ignoring the value of the components
    d. None of the above. The production and sale of the computer would not be counted in GDP.

8. Which of the following is counted in this year's GDP?
    a. only this year's production of goods and services
    b. only goods that are both produced and sold within the United States
    c. new goods produced and sold this year plus the value of used goods resold this year
    d. this year's production of goods and services added to the value of GDP last year

9. If we add up the value of every good and service produced in the economy, we get a total that is
    a. larger than GDP.
    b. smaller than GDP.
    c. equal to GDP.
    d. larger or smaller than GDP depending on whether the economy experiences inflation during the year.

10. If we add up the value of every final good and service produced in the economy, we must get a total that is exactly equal to the value of
    a. investment.
    b. net national product.
    c. disposable personal income.
    d. all of the income in the economy.

11. Which of the following would be considered a *factor of production*?
    a. capital
    b. natural resources
    c. entrepreneurship
    d. all of the above

12. In the circular-flow diagram, who supplies factors of production in exchange for income?
    a. households
    b. firms
    c. the government
    d. all of the above

13. Complete the following sentence: Total income in the economy equals the sum of wages, interest, _____ and _____.
    a. dividends; transfer payments
    b. rent; profit
    c. taxes; transfer payments
    d. disposable income; net exports

14. Fill in the blank. The flow of funds from _____ into the financial system makes it possible for government and firms to borrow.
    a. government and firms
    b. households
    c. investment banks
    d. exports

15. An important conclusion to draw from the circular-flow diagram is that
    a. personal consumption expenditures are equal to the value of GDP.
    b. only the value of total income equals the value of GDP, not the value of expenditures.
    c. only the total value of expenditures equals the value of GDP, not the value of income.
    d. we can measure GDP by calculating the total value of expenditures on final goods and services, or we can measure GDP by calculating the value of total income.

16. Which of the following goods and services would be excluded from *personal consumption expenditures* in the Bureau of Economic Analysis (BEA) statistics?
    a. medical care
    b. education
    c. a haircut
    d. a new house

17. Which of the following is counted in the *gross private domestic investment* category used by the Bureau of Economic Analysis when measuring GDP?
    a. business fixed investment
    b. residential investment
    c. changes in business inventories
    d. all of the above

18. Which of the following is included in the economist's definition of *investment*?
    a. the purchase of new machines, factories, or houses
    b. the purchase of a share of stock
    c. the purchase of a rare coin or deposit in a savings account
    d. all of the above

19. In calculating GDP, which levels of government spending are included in *government purchases*?
    a. spending by the federal government only
    b. spending by federal, state, and local governments
    c. spending by the federal government and some state governments, but not local governments
    d. spending by governments only as they relate to national security, social welfare, and other national programs

20. When accounting for exports and imports in GDP, which of the following is correct?
    a. Exports are added to the other categories of expenditures.
    b. Imports are added to the other categories of expenditures.
    c. Both exports and imports are added to the other categories of expenditures.
    d. Both exports and imports are subtracted from the other categories of expenditures.

21. In the equation that sums up the information on the components of GDP, $Y = C + I + G + NX$, which component has the largest dollar value?
    a. C
    b. I
    c. G
    d. NX

22. Which of the following is true about the *consumption* component of U.S. GDP in 2007?
    a. Consumer spending on durable and nondurable goods was greater than consumption on services.
    b. Consumer spending on durable goods was greater than the sum of spending on nondurable goods and on services.
    c. Consumer spending on nondurable goods was greater than the sum of spending on nondurable goods and on services.
    d. Consumer spending on services was greater than the sum of spending on durable and nondurable goods.

23. Which of the following is true about the *government purchases* component of U.S. GDP in 2007?
    a. The entire amount was composed of federal government purchases because state and local governments are not included.
    b. Most of the spending on education and law enforcement occurs at the federal level.
    c. Purchases by the federal government are greater than purchases by state and local governments.
    d. Purchases by state and local governments are greater than purchases by the federal government.

24. The difference between the price the firm sells a good for and the price it paid other firms for intermediate goods is called
    a. producer surplus.
    b. fixed investment.
    c. value added.
    d. profit.

25. Household production and the underground economy
    a. are fully accounted for in GDP figures gathered by the Commerce Department.
    b. are not considered formal production of goods and services and, therefore, are not included when calculating GDP.
    c. are important but unaccounted for in the Commerce Department's estimate of GDP.
    d. are irrelevant because they constitute only a very small fraction of GDP for most countries.

26. Which of the following is *not* a shortcoming of GDP as a measure of welfare?
    a. It does not include the value of leisure.
    b. It is not adjusted for the effects of pollution caused by the production of goods and services.
    c. It only counts final goods and services and not intermediate goods.
    d. It is not adjusted for crime and other social problems.

27. According to most economists, is not counting household production or production in the underground economy a serious shortcoming of GDP?
    a. Most economists would answer "no" because these types of production do not affect the most important use of the GDP measure, which is to see how the economy is performing over short periods of time.
    b. Most economists would answer "yes" because these types of production are likely to grow significantly from one year to the next.
    c. Most economists would answer "no" because the purpose of measuring GDP is to see how the economy performs over fairly long periods of a decade or more.
    d. Most economists would answer "yes" because these types of production are likely to be a large component of the economy (or large percentage of measured GDP), especially in countries like the United States.

28. In many developing countries, the informal sector is _____ because taxes are _____ and government regulations are _____.
    a. large; low; minimal
    b. large; high; extensive
    c. small; low; minimal
    d. small; low; extensive

29. If Americans still worked 60 hour weeks, as they did in 1890,
    a. both GDP and the well-being of the typical person would be much higher than they are.
    b. both GDP and the well-being of the typical person would be lower than they are.
    c. GDP would be much higher than it is, but the well-being of the typical person would not necessarily be higher.
    d. GDP would be lower than it is, but the well-being of the typical person would be higher.

30. As the value of a country's GDP increases, the country is likely to
    a. devote more resources to pollution reduction.
    b. devote fewer resources to pollution reduction.
    c. include the value of pollution in calculating GDP.
    d. exclude the value of pollution in calculating GDP.

31. Real GDP is
    a. the value of goods and services evaluated at current year prices.
    b. the value of goods and services evaluated at base year prices.
    c. equal to the value of nominal GDP in every year except for the base year.
    d. a measure of output that was replaced by nominal GDP some time ago.

32. Which measure of GDP represents changes in the quantity of goods and services produced in the economy, holding prices constant?
    a. Nominal GDP
    b. Real GDP
    c. Net national product
    d. None of the above. All GDP measures represent changes in both prices and quantities.

33. Suppose that the base year is 2000 and we want to calculate real GDP for 2007. Which procedure would you use?
    a. Multiply the quantities in 2000 by the prices in 2007, and add up the results.
    b. Multiply the quantities in 2007 by the prices in 2007, and add up the results.
    c. Multiply the quantities in 2007 by the prices in 2000, and add up the results.
    d. Multiply the quantities in 2007 by the prices in 2007, and subtract them from nominal GDP in 2000.

34. In an economy with rising prices, compared to the base year,
    a. nominal GDP is larger than real GDP in years after the base year.
    b. nominal GDP is equal to real GDP in years after the base year.
    c. nominal GDP is larger than real GDP in years before the base year.
    d. nominal GDP is equal to real GDP in years before the base year.

35. Growth in the economy is almost always measured as
    a. growth in nominal GDP.
    b. growth in real GDP.
    c. growth in net national product.
    d. the growth of personal disposable income.

36. Using the year 2000 as the base year, and assuming that prices during the 1990s were lower on average than prices in 2000, we can conclude that
    a. nominal GDP was lower than real GDP in the 1990s.
    b. nominal GDP was higher than real GDP in the 1990s.
    c. nominal GDP was equal to real GDP during all these years.
    d. neither nominal GDP nor real GDP were good measures of GDP.

37. Over time, prices may change relative to each other. To allow for this, the Bureau of Economic Analysis calculates
    a. nominal GDP using chain weights.
    b. real GDP and the price deflator using chain weights.
    c. real GDP and nominal GDP using only base-year prices.
    d. real GDP using the prices in the current year.

38. If the GDP deflator has a value of 105.0, then
    a. the inflation rate is 1.05%.
    b. the inflation rate is 0.05%.
    c. the inflation rate is 5%.
    d. prices have risen 5% since the base year.

39. When a significant fraction of domestic production takes place in foreign-owned facilities, a country's difference between GDP and GNP is as follows:
    a. GNP will be a more accurate measure of the level of production within the country's borders.
    b. GDP will be much larger than GNP.
    c. GNP will be almost identical to GDP.
    d. GNP will be closer to zero.

40. Which of the following do we subtract from GNP to obtain NNP?
    a. the production of fixed capital
    b. consumption
    c. investment
    d. depreciation

41. In the National Income and Product Accounts (NIPA), *sales taxes* are referred to as
    a. subsidies.
    b. excise taxes.
    c. indirect business taxes.
    d. government revenue.

42. The total income actually received by a country's residents is
    a. larger than the value of GDP.
    b. smaller than the value of GDP.
    c. exactly equal to the value of GDP.
    d. smaller or larger than the value of GDP depending on the year.

43. To calculate *personal income* from national income, which of the following must be done by the BEA?
    a. add corporate retained earnings
    b. add profits
    c. add government transfer payments
    d. all of the above

44. *Disposable personal income* is equal to
    a. personal income minus personal tax payments plus government transfer payments.
    b. personal income minus government transfer payments plus personal tax payments.
    c. personal income minus Social Security payments.
    d. the income households have to consume, save, and pay taxes.

45. The best measure of the income households actually have available to spend is
    a. national income.
    b. disposable personal income.
    c. net national product.
    d. gross domestic product.

Short Answer Questions

1. GDP is a measurement of the market value of final goods and services produced in an economy in one year. What is the difference between a final good and an intermediate good? Why do we only count final goods in GDP and not intermediate goods?

   _____

   _____

   _____

2. Suppose that an economy produces only baseballs and footballs. The prices and quantities of these goods for years 2000 and 2007 are given below.

Year	Baseballs		Footballs	
	P	*Q*	*P*	*Q*
2000	$4.00	75	$6.00	45
2007	$5.00	100	$9.00	60

   Calculate nominal GDP and real GDP assuming that the year 2000 is the base year. Explain why nominal GDP increased more than real GDP. Also calculate the GDP deflator.

   _____

   _____

   _____

3. If prices are rising (as they have in the U.S. economy during every year since 1939), in years before the base year, real GDP will be larger than nominal GDP. In years after the base year, nominal GDP will be larger than real GDP. Explain why this is true.

_____

_____

_____

4. You just bought a 100 year-old house. How does that transaction influence GDP? If the house is purchased with the assistance of a real estate agent, is this payment included in GDP? You then hired a local contractor to re-do the wiring. You paid the contractor $10,000. The contractor had to buy new wire. How does the purchase of wire by the contractor influence GDP? What if you had done the wiring yourself? In this case, you bought $2,000 in wire to complete the task. How would this influence GDP? Why do the two methods of wiring the house have different implications for calculating GDP when the actual production (a house rewired) is the same?

_____

_____

_____

_____

5. What is the difference between GDP and GNP? Is one always larger than the other?

_____

_____

_____

6. For the years 2005 and 2006, Nominal and Real GDP are given in the table below:

Year	Nominal GDP	Real GDP
2005	$12,433.9 billion	$11,003.4 billion
2006	13,194.7 billion	11,319.4 billion

What is the inflation rate for 2006?

_____

_____

_____

True/False Questions

T F 1. Macroeconomics is the study of the economy as a whole.

T F 2. GDP is the value of all goods and services produced in a country during a time period.

T F 3. GDP measures the value of final goods and services in an economy or the value of the income earned in producing those goods and services in that economy, for a specific time period.

T F 4. Consumption spending is divided into two parts, durable goods and non-durable goods.

T F 5. The purchase of 100 shares of Apple computer stock is an example of investment spending.

T F 6. Net exports (*NX*) are defined as imports minus exports.

T F 7. Value added is the price at which a firm sells its output minus the outlay paid to obtain the inputs to produce its output.

T F 8. Over a given time period, the sum of the value added by all firms is equal to a country's GDP.

T F 9. In the United States, household production and the underground economy is about 50 percent of GDP.

T F 10. The value of GDP is reduced to reflect the impact of pollution generated by production.

T F 11. Real GDP is a better measure of output than nominal GDP.

T F 12. For every year, nominal GDP is always greater than real GDP.

T F 13. GNP is the value of final goods and services produced by labor and capital supplied by U.S. residents, even if the production occurs outside the United States.

T F 14. NNP is GNP plus the amount of depreciation in that time period.

T F 15. Personal income is the best measure of the income households have available for spending.

Answers to the Self-Test

Multiple-Choice Questions

Question	Answer	Comment
1	d	Macroeconomics looks at what determines the total level of production of goods and services and the total levels of employment and unemployment. It also looks at what determines the inflation rate, or how fast prices in general are increasing.
2	c	It remains a controversial question among economists as to whether such policies are really needed or whether the economy might in fact work better without them.
3	b	When we measure total production in the economy, we can't just add together the quantities of every good and service because the result would be a meaningless jumble. Instead, we measure production by taking the value in dollar terms of all the goods and services produced, since this approach allows for the use of a common unit of measure: dollars.
4	a	Consumption is about 70 percent of GDP.
5	d	A distinction is made between *final* goods and services, which are purchased by final users and are not included in the production of any other goods or services, and *intermediate* goods and services, which are used as inputs into the production of other goods and services.

6	b	GDP includes only the market value of final goods. If we included the value of the inputs used in making the computer, we would be *double counting*!
7	c	To avoid double counting, GDP only counts final goods and services.
8	a	GDP includes only production that takes place during the indicated time period. GDP does not include the value of used goods. If you buy a DVD and six months later you resell that DVD, the purchase is not included in GDP.
9	a	Adding up the value of every good and service would include the values of many intermediate goods that are not counted in GDP.
10	d	When we measure the value of total production in the economy by calculating GDP, we are simultaneously measuring the value of total income.
11	d	Firms use the *factors of production* – entrepreneurship, labor, capital, and raw materials – to produce goods and services. (For brief definitions of *entrepreneur* and *capital*, see the glossary at the end of Chapter 1.)
12	a	Firms use the *factors of production* to produce goods and services. Households supply the factors of production to firms in exchange for income.
13	b	The sum of wages, interest, rent, and profit is total income in the economy.
14	b	The flow of funds from households into the financial system makes it possible for government and firms to borrow.
15	d	An important conclusion to draw from the circular flow diagram is that we can measure GDP by calculating the total value of expenditures on final goods and services, or we can measure GDP by calculating the value of total income.
16	d	Personal consumption expenditures are made by households and are divided into expenditures on *services*, such as medical care, education, and haircuts; expenditures on *nondurable goods*, such as food and clothing; and expenditures on *durable goods*, such as automobiles and furniture. The spending by households that is not included in consumption is spending on new houses. Spending on new houses is included in investment expenditures.
17	d	Gross private domestic investment (or simply "investment") is divided into three categories: *Business fixed investment* is spending by firms on new factories, office buildings, and machinery, which are used by firms in producing other goods. *Residential investment* is spending by households on new housing. *Changes in business inventories* are also included in investment.
18	a	Economists reserve the word *investment* for purchases of machinery, factories, and houses. Why don't economists include purchases of stock or rare coins or deposits in savings accounts in the definition of investment? The reason is that these other activities don't result in the production of new goods.
19	b	That is the definition of government purchases.
20	a	Exports are goods and services produced in the United States, but purchased by foreign businesses, households, and governments. We need to add exports to our other categories of expenditures because otherwise we would not be including all new goods and services produced in the United States. Imports are goods and services produced in foreign countries, but purchased by U.S. businesses, households, and governments. We need to subtract imports from total expenditures, because otherwise we would be including spending that does not result in production of new goods and services in the United States.
21	a	Figure 7-2 shows the values of the components of GDP for the year 2006. The graph in the figure highlights the fact that consumption is by far the largest component of GDP.

22	d	Consumer spending on services is greater than the sum of spending on durable and nondurable goods. In the United States and other industrial countries there has been a continuing trend away from the production of goods and towards the production of services.
23	d	Purchases by state and local governments are greater than purchases by the federal government. In the United States, state and local government purchases are greater than federal government purchases because basic government activities, such as education and law enforcement, occur largely at the state and local levels.
24	c	Value added refers to the additional market value a firm gives to a product and is equal to the difference between the price the firm sells a good for and the price it paid other firms for intermediate goods.
25	c	The Commerce Department does not attempt to estimate the value of goods and services that are not bought and sold in markets. Individuals and firms sometimes conceal the buying and selling of goods and services, so they will not have to pay taxes on the income received.
26	c	The omission of intermediate goods in the calculation of GDP is to avoid counting goods and services twice – or double counting.
27	a	The most important use of GDP is to measure how the economy is performing over short periods of time, such as from one year to the next. For this purpose, omitting household production and production in the underground economy won't have much effect, because these types of production are not likely to be significantly larger or smaller fractions of total production from one year to the next.
28	b	The informal sector is large in developing countries because taxes are high and government regulations are extensive. Many economists believe taxes in developing countries are so high because these countries are attempting to pay for government sectors that are as large relative to their economies as the government sectors of industrial economies.
29	c	GDP does not include the value of leisure, but we may value leisure as much as the income we sacrifice in order to obtain it. Output growth also comes with social problems attached, as described in the section of this chapter titled "*GDP Is Not Adjusted for Pollution or Other Negative Effects of Production.*"
30	a	Increasing GDP often leads countries to devote more resources to pollution reduction.
31	b	Real GDP is the value of goods and services evaluated at base year prices. Real GDP is calculated by designating a particular year as the base year. The prices of goods and services in the base year are used to calculate the value of goods and services in all other years.
32	b	By keeping prices constant, we know that changes in real GDP represent changes in the quantity of goods and services produced in the economy. Holding prices constant means that the purchasing power of a dollar remains the same from one year to the next.
33	c	Real GDP is the value of all final goods and services, evaluated at base year prices.
34	a	Because nominal GDP uses current prices and real GDP uses bases year prices, in an economy with rising prices current prices will be above base year prices and nominal GDP will be larger than real GDP.
35	b	Growth in the economy is almost always measured as growth in real GDP.

36	a	As prices rise, nominal GDP rises above real GDP. In the 1990s, prices were on average lower than in 2000, so nominal GDP was lower than real GDP. Since 2000, prices have been on average higher than in 2000, so nominal GDP is higher than real GDP.
37	b	Because changes in relative prices are not reflected in the fixed prices from the base year, the estimate of real GDP is somewhat distorted. In order to make the calculation of real GDP more accurate, in 1996, the BEA switched to a method that uses "chain-weighted" prices.
38	d	A GDP Deflator of 105 (or 1.05 before multiplying by 100) indicates that the current level of prices is 1.05 times the base year, not the last year, or prices have risen 5 percent from the base year.
39	b	When a significant fraction of domestic production takes place in foreign-owned facilities, GDP will be much larger than GNP, and will be a more accurate measure of the level of production within the country's borders.
40	d	If we subtract this value from GNP, we are left with net national product or NNP. In the NIPA tables, depreciation is referred to as the *consumption of fixed capital,* or the *capital consumption allowance.*
41	c	In order to calculate the total income actually received by a country's residents, the BEA has to subtract the value of sales taxes from net national product. In the NIPA tables, sales taxes are referred to as *indirect business taxes.*
42	b	The BEA has to subtract the value of sales taxes (indirect business taxes) and depreciation from gross domestic product in order to arrive at national income. A country's residents do not receive either depreciation or the taxes paid on purchases, so neither should be included in a measure of total income received.
43	c	Personal income is income received by households. To calculate personal income, we need to subtract the earnings that corporations retain rather than pay to shareholders in the form of dividends. We also need to add in the payments received by households from the government in the form of transfer payments or interest on government bonds. Transfer payments, such as Social Security payments or payments to retired government workers, are payments the government makes for which it does not receive a good or service in return.
44	a	Disposable personal income is equal to personal income minus personal tax payments, such as the federal personal income tax, plus government transfer payments, such as Social Security payments.
45	b	Disposable personal income is the best measure of the income households actually have available to spend.

Short Answer Responses

1. A final good is one that is sold to the ultimate user of the product. It is not being purchased with the plan to transform the good and resell it. The alternative to a final good, an intermediate good, is purchased with the intent of using that good in the process of producing another good or service that is resold. Intermediate goods are inputs in a production process. Intermediate goods are excluded because the value of the final goods *includes* the value of the intermediate goods employed in the production of the final good.

2. GDP and Real GDP for 2000 and 2007 are:

Year	Nominal GDP	Real GDP	GDP Deflator
2000	$570	$570	100.0
2007	$1040	$760	136.8

Nominal GDP has increased for two reasons: Output has increased and the prices of baseballs and footballs have increased.

3. Real GDP uses base year prices. Rising prices imply that in the years prior to the base year, the price used to calculate nominal GDP would be *less* than the price used to calculate real GDP (which is the price in the base year). So in the earlier years, real GDP is greater than nominal GDP. In time periods after the base year, with rising prices, the price level would be larger than the base year price level, so nominal GDP is larger than real GDP. See Figure 7-3 in Chapter 7.

4. Because the house is 100 years old, its purchase will not be included in GDP. It was counted in GDP 100 years ago when it was built. If a real estate agent is employed, the agent's fee should be counted in GDP. The agent produced a service in the current time period, bringing together the buyer and the seller of the house. All of the contractor's wiring fee is included in GDP. The contractor's purchase of wire does not count in GDP, because the wire is included in the contractor's fee. The wire in this case is an intermediate good. If the new homeowner did the wiring, then only the purchase of the wire would count in GDP. In this case, the wire is a final good. The difference in the two approaches to wiring the house is that household production that does not enter a market is not counted in GDP.

5. Gross domestic product is the value of final goods and services produced by labor and capital within the United States. The gross national product, or GNP, is the value of final goods and services produced by labor and capital supplied by residents of the United States, even if the production takes place *outside* of the United States. U.S. firms have facilities in foreign countries, and foreign firms have facilities in the United States. GNP includes foreign production by U.S. companies, but excludes U.S. production by foreign companies. For the United States, they are about the same. One is not necessarily larger than the other.

6. The GDP deflator in 2005 was 113.0 (remember that the GDP deflator is the ratio of Nominal GDP to Real GDP multiplied by 100 or = (Nominal GDP/Real GDP) x 100). The GDP deflator in 2006 was 116.6. As measured by the percentage change in the GDP deflator, the inflation rate in 2005 (which is equal to:100 x [(GDP deflator in 2006 – GDP deflator in 2005)/GDP deflator in 2005]) was 3.2 percent (= 100 x [(116.6 −113.0)/113.0]).

True/False Answers

1. T
2. F   GDP measures only final goods and services, in an economy, over a well-defined period.
3. T
4. F   durables, non-durables and services
5. F   This is a financial transaction, not investment.
6. F   exports minus imports
7. T
8. T
9. F   about 10%

10. F   GDP does not subtract "bads" generated by production.
11. T
12. F   This is true only for years where prices are greater than base year prices.
13. T
14. F   NNP = GNP – depreciation
15. F   Disposable personal income is better because it subtracts taxes.

Chapter 8 (20)

Unemployment and Inflation

Chapter Summary

Unemployment and inflation are two of the most important macroeconomic issues. This chapter explores some of the fundamental facts about these economic variables.

The **unemployment rate** is the percentage of the labor force that does not have a job, but is actively looking for one. The chapter looks at how the unemployment rate and labor force are measured. It also examines current trends in labor force participation, unemployment by demographic characteristics (gender, race, and age), and different types of unemployment. There are three types of unemployment:

1. **frictional unemployment** is short-term unemployment.
2. **structural unemployment** arises when there is a mismatch between the skills workers have and the skills employers are looking for.
3. **cyclical unemployment** arises during a recession.

The **inflation rate** is the rate of change in the price level. There are three price indexes economists use to measure the price level: the **consumer price index** (*CPI*), the **GDP deflator**, and the **producer price index** (*PPI*). Price indexes are used to adjust nominal variables for the effects of inflation.

Learning Objectives

When you finish this chapter, you should be able to:

1. **Define unemployment rate and labor force participation rate and understand how they are computed.** The U.S. Bureau of Labor Statistics uses the results of the monthly household survey to calculate the unemployment rate and the labor force participation rate. The **labor force** is the total number of people who have jobs plus the number of people who do not have jobs, but who are actively looking. The **labor force participation rate** is the percentage of the working-age population in the labor force. Since 1950, the labor force participation rate of women has been rising, while the labor force participation rate of men has been falling. White men and women have below average unemployment rates. Teenagers and black men and women have above average unemployment rates. The typical unemployed person finds a new job or returns to his or her previous job within a few months. Each year, millions of jobs are created and destroyed in the United States.

2. **Identify the three types of unemployment.** There are three types of unemployment: frictional, structural, and cyclical. **Frictional unemployment** is short-term unemployment arising from the process of matching workers with jobs. **Structural unemployment** arises from a persistent mismatch between the job skills or attributes of workers and the requirements of jobs. **Cyclical unemployment** is caused by a business cycle recession. The **natural rate of unemployment** is the normal rate of

unemployment, consisting of structural unemployment and frictional unemployment. The natural rate of unemployment is also sometimes called the *full-employment rate of unemployment*.

3. **Explain what factors determine the unemployment rate.** Government policies can reduce the level of frictional and structural unemployment by aiding job search and worker retraining. Some government policies, however, can add to the level of frictional and structural unemployment. Unemployment insurance payments can raise the unemployment rate by extending the time that unemployed workers search for jobs. Government policies have caused the unemployment rates in most other industrial countries to be higher than in the United States. Wages above market levels can also increase unemployment. Wages may be above market levels because of the minimum wage, labor unions, and **efficiency wages**.

4. **Define price level and inflation rate and understand how they are computed.** The **price level** measures the average prices of goods and services. The **inflation rate** is equal to the percentage change in the price level from one year to the next. The federal government compiles statistics on three different measures of the price level:

   - the consumer price index (*CPI*)
   - the GDP price deflator
   - the producer price index (*PPI*)

   The **consumer price index** is an average of the prices of goods and services purchased by the typical urban family of four. Changes in the consumer price index are the best measure of changes in the cost of living as experienced by the typical household. Biases in the construction of the CPI cause changes in it to overstate the true inflation rate by about one-half of a percentage point. The **producer price index** is an average of prices received by producers of goods and services at all stages of production.

5. **Use price indexes to adjust for the effects of inflation.** Price indexes are designed to measure changes in the price level over time, not the absolute level of prices. To correct for the effects of inflation, we can divide a nominal variable by a price index and then multiply the result by 100 to obtain a real variable. The real variables will be measured in dollars of the base year for the price index.

6. **Distinguish between the nominal interest rate and the real interest rate.** The stated interest rate on a loan is the **nominal interest rate**. The **real interest rate** is the nominal interest rate minus the inflation rate. Because it is corrected for the effects of inflation, the real interest rate provides a better measure of the true cost of borrowing and the true return to lending than does the nominal interest rate.

7. **Discuss the problems that inflation causes.** Inflation does not reduce the affordability of goods and services to the average consumer. When inflation is anticipated, its main costs are that paper money loses some of its value and firms incur menu costs. **Menu costs** include the costs of changing prices on products and printing new catalogs. When inflation is unanticipated, the actual inflation rate can turn out to be different from the expected inflation rate. As a result, some people gain and some people lose.

Chapter Review

Chapter Opener: Alcatel-Lucent Contributes to Unemployment (pages 238-239)

In 2001, total employment in the United States declined. One company that contributed to this decline was Lucent Technologies, a leading technology firm. By 2005, Lucent employed 31,500 workers in contrast to the 175,000 workers that they employed in 2001. Lucent merged with the French firm Alcatel to become Alcatel-Lucent. Disappointing earnings, due to strong competition from other firms such as Ericsson (of Sweden) and Huawei (of China) and shifts in spending from some North American customers, led Alcatel-Lucent to eliminate an additional 12,500 jobs.

📖 Helpful Study Hint

Read *An Inside Look* at the end of the chapter for more information on how to make sense of 2007 employment data from the U.S. Department of Labor.

If you graduate during a recession, will that affect which jobs you apply for? *Economics in YOUR Life!* at the start of this chapter poses this question. Keep the question in mind as you read the chapter. The authors will answer the question at the end of the chapter.

8.1 LEARNING OBJECTIVE

8.1 Measuring the Unemployment Rate and the Labor Force Participation Rate (pages 240–247)

Learning Objective 1 Define unemployment rate and labor force participation rate and understand how they are computed.

Our measures of unemployment come from a survey conducted each month by the U.S. Bureau of the Census. The *Current Population Survey,* often referred to as the household survey, collects the data needed to compute the unemployment rate. The survey asks questions about the employment status of people in the household and attempts to determine if a worker is employed, out of the work force (not employed nor looking for a job), or unemployed. The sum of employed and unemployed persons in the economy is known as the **labor force**. The **unemployment rate** is the percentage of the labor force that cannot find work. People who are not actively looking for a job are not considered to be a part of the labor force. This includes **discouraged workers** as well as retirees, homemakers, full-time students, and people on active military service, in prison, or in mental hospitals. The **labor force participation rate** is the percentage of the working age population that is in the labor force. Working age is defined as 16 years or older.

The results of the Current Population Survey provide the data to calculate unemployment rates and labor force participation rates. These two statistics are more precisely defined as:

$$\text{Unemployment rate} = \frac{\text{Number of Unemployed}}{\text{Labor Force}} \times 100$$

$$\text{Labor Force Participation Rate} = \frac{\text{Labor Force}}{\text{Working Age Population}} \times 100$$

📖 Helpful Study Hint

Figure 8-1 shows various segments of the population and labor force. In which category do you fall at this stage of your life?

- If you are a traditional college student who does not work, you are not in the labor force and not available for work.
- If you attend college and also work part-time, you are in the labor force.
- If you attend college and want to work but can't find a job and have stopped looking, you are not in the labor force and you are considered a discouraged worker.

The unemployment and labor force data provide a useful picture of employment, but the measures are not perfect due to sampling and reporting errors in the survey. For instance, there some people who are not counted in the labor force who might still be considered unemployed. Discouraged workers, for example, are workers who have dropped out of the labor force because they believe no jobs are available for them. These workers are not included in the measured unemployment rate, and if included would raise the measured unemployment rate.

Helpful Study Hint

Figure 8-2 and Figure 8-3 show trends in the labor force participation rate of men, women, and other demographic groups in the United States. In Figure 8-2, notice that the participation rate of women increased rapidly in the 1960s and 1970s before leveling off in recent years. The participation rate of men has steadily declined over the years. A gap still exists between male and female labor force participation rates, although it is much smaller today than it was 60 years ago. In Figure 8-3, notice that the average unemployment rate is 4.5 percent. White adults fall slightly below that rate, while white teenagers, Hispanic teenagers, and black teenagers have much higher unemployment rates.

📖 Helpful Study Hint

For an additional discussion of nonworking men, look at the ***Making the Connection: What Explains the Increase in "Kramers"?*** How do men such as the character Cosmo Kramer on Seinfeld support themselves without ever holding a job? In recent years, there has been an increase in the number of men between ages 22 and 54 who are not in school and do not have a paid job. About half of these individuals receive Social Security Disability Insurance, and many rely on other household members for food, clothing, and spending money. Recent studies have shown these men are not substituting nonmarket work, such as childcare, but are instead engaged in leisure activities.

In addition to the Current Population Survey, the establishment survey, or the payroll survey, is another way for the Department of Labor to measure total employment in the economy. The establishment survey provides information on the total number of people who are employed and on a company payroll by surveying about 300,000 business establishments. The establishment survey has the following drawbacks:

1. Does not provide information on the number of self-employed persons.
2. Fails to count people employed at newly opened businesses.
3. Does not provide information on the unemployed.

8.2 Types of Unemployment (pages 248–250)

Learning Objective 2 Identify the three types of unemployment.

It is useful to divide unemployment into three types: frictional, structural, and cyclical. **Frictional unemployment** includes unemployed workers who have left one job and are looking for another job or are out of a job due to seasonal factors. Frictionally unemployed people usually find new jobs quickly. **Structural unemployment** includes workers who have lost their jobs because their skills do not match those employers want. Structurally unemployed workers are usually out of work longer than those who are frictionally unemployed because they must learn new job skills, which takes time. **Cyclical unemployment** occurs when workers lose jobs due to a recession. As the economy begins to recover, these workers are sometimes rehired by the same firms that laid them off.

When the only types of unemployment are structural and frictional, the economy is said to be at full employment. Sometimes this is also referred to as the **natural rate of unemployment**.

📖 Helpful Study Hint

For an additional discussion of the three types of unemployment and company layoffs, read *Making the Connection: How Should We Categorize the Unemployment at Alcatel-Lucent?* The lost jobs at Alcatel-Lucent can be attributed to three reasons:
1. The recession in 2001, which caused cyclical unemployment.
2. The reduction in the demand for telecommunication products, which caused optical engineers to have a difficult time finding new jobs. This is a form of structural unemployment.
3. The trouble that Alcatel-Lucent had competing with other telecommunication firms. These job losers are frictionally unemployed. The distinction between the three types of unemployment is not always clear.

Extra Solved Problem 8-2

Chapter 8 of the textbook includes two Solved Problems. Here is an extra Solved Problem to help you build your skills solving economic problems:

The Reason for Unemployment

Supports Learning Objective 2: Identify the three types of unemployment.

The BLS collects data about the reasons people are unemployed. Some of this data is in the table below (the numbers are in thousands).

	Unemployment		Reason for unemployment					
			Job losers					
				On		Job		New
Year	Rate	Number	Total	layoff	Other	leavers	Reentrants	entrants
2000	4.0	5,692	2,517	852	1,664	780	1,961	434
2001	4.7	6,801	3,476	1,067	2,409	835	2,031	459
2002	5.8	8,377	4,607	1,124	3,483	866	2,368	536
2003	6.0	8,774	4,838	1,121	3,717	818	2,477	641
2004	5.5	8,149	4,197	998	3,199	858	2,408	686
2005	5.1	7,591	3,667	933	2,734	872	2,386	666
2006	4.6	7,001	3,321	921	2,400	827	2,237	616

a. Calculate the percentage of the unemployed who have just lost their jobs and the percentage who have left their jobs.

b. Calculate the percentage of the unemployed who are unemployed as the result of entering the labor force, either for the first time or as a reentrant.

SOLVING THE PROBLEM

Step 1: **Review the chapter material.**
This problem is about definitions of unemployment, so you may want to review the section "Types of Unemployment," which begins on page 248 in the textbook.

Step 2: **Answer question (a) by calculating the percentages of unemployed.**
For example, the percentage of job losers in 2002 can be calculated as: (4,607/8,377) x 100 = 55.0%. The percentage of reentrants and new entrants in 2002 is: [(2,368 + 536)/8,377] x 100 = 34.7%. The percentages for the three categories in each year are:

	Percentages of those unemployed due to		
Year	Job losers	Job leavers	Reentrants and new entrants
2000	44.2%	13.7%	42.1%
2001	51.1	12.3	36.6
2002	55.0	10.3	34.7
2003	55.1	9.3	35.5
2004	51.5	10.5	38.0
2005	48.3	11.5	40.2
2006	47.4	11.8	40.8

Step 3:   **Answer part (b) by comparing the different sources of unemployment.**

Notice that the major source of unemployment is job losers, followed by reentrants and new entrants. The majority of the reentrants and new entrants group is reentrants, which are people who lost or quit jobs in the past, dropped out of the labor force for some reason, and are now looking for jobs.

8.3   Explaining Unemployment (pages 250–254)

Learning Objective 3   Explain what factors determine the unemployment rate.

The business cycle is the cause of cyclical unemployment. Frictional and structural unemployment are influenced by government policies, such as unemployment insurance. This insurance program provides payments of about half the average wage to provide unemployed workers with some income while they search for a new job. Unemployment insurance helps workers take sufficient time to find a job that is a good match for their skills. Unfortunately, as workers spend more time searching, they are also unemployed longer, increasing the unemployment rate. Unemployment insurance also helps the unemployed maintain their income and lessens the severity of a recession. The minimum wage also has an impact on the unemployment rate, particularly for teenage workers. By forcing employers to pay some workers a wage above the market equilibrium wage, the minimum wage contributes to increased unemployment among those with few job skills. Firms may also pay a wage above the market level, called an **efficiency wage**, which is designed to increase worker productivity. This higher wage may result in the quantity demanded of labor being less than the quantity supplied. The result can be unemployment, even when cyclical employment is zero. Labor unions can also temporarily increase unemployment by bargaining for wages that are higher than the equilibrium level. Workers who are unable to find employment in the unionized sector can generally find employment—possibly for lower wages—in the non-unionized sector. Unions have a relatively small impact on labor markets in the United States because only about 9 percent of non-government workers are members of unions.

📖 Helpful Study Hint

For an additional discussion of efficiency wages, read *Making the Connection: Why Does Costco Pay Its Workers So Much More Than Wal-Mart Does?* In 2007, the average wage of a Wal-Mart hourly employee was about $10.50 per hour, while the average wage of a Costco hourly employee was $17.00 per hour. Costco's benefits are also more generous, with about 90 percent of employees covered by medical insurance, as opposed to about 50 percent at Wal-Mart. The difference in wages is attributed to Costco paying an efficiency wage. Costco argues that paying a higher wage reduces employee turnover and raises morale and productivity. However, some economists argue that because Costco carries higher priced goods, it "requires higher-skilled workers to sell higher-end products to its more affluent customers." If this view is correct, then the high wages at Costco may not be entirely due to efficiency wage considerations.

Extra Solved Problem 8-3

Chapter 8 of the textbook includes two Solved Problems. Here is an extra Solved Problem to help you build your skills solving economic problems:

Unemployment Insurance

Supports Learning Objective 3: Explain what factors determine the unemployment rate.

Suppose the U.S. government increases the length of time that an unemployed worker can receive unemployment insurance benefits. Predict how this will influence the unemployment rate.

SOLVING THE PROBLEM

Step 1: **Review the chapter material.**
This problem is about the effects of government policy on unemployment rates, so you may want to review the section "Government Policies and the Unemployment Rate," which begins on page 250 in the textbook.

Step 2. **Predict the effects.**
If the government extends the period for receiving unemployment insurance payments, the extension will reduce the opportunity cost of unemployment. This may cause some workers to continue their search for employment, increasing the duration of unemployment, the level of unemployment, and the unemployment rate.

8.4 LEARNING OBJECTIVE

8.4 Measuring Inflation (pages 254-258)

Learning Objective 4 Define price level and inflation rate and understand how they are computed.

The **price level** measures the average prices of goods and services in the economy, while the **inflation rate** is the percentage increase in the price level from one year to the next. There are several price indexes. The GDP deflator measures the average price of all goods and services included in GDP. The **consumer price index (CPI)** measures the average price of the goods and services purchased by a typical urban household. The **producer price index (PPI)** measures the average price paid by firms for intermediate goods. Any price index is the average price of a set of goods and services. These price indexes differ in terms of which goods are included in them and in terms of how the index is calculated. The GDP deflator is the ratio of nominal GDP to real GDP multiplied by 100:

$$\text{GDP Deflator} = \frac{\text{Nominal GDP}}{\text{Real GDP}} \times 100$$

The GDP deflator is an average of the prices of all final goods and services produced during a year. The CPI includes goods and services purchased by consumers. Every two years, the BLS does a large-scale survey to determine the goods and services a typical urban household purchases. The CPI is the ratio of the current value of that market basket of goods and services to the value of that basket in the base year multiplied by 100:

$$\text{CPI} = \frac{\text{Expenditures in the current year}}{\text{Expenditures in the base year}} \times 100$$

___

📖 Helpful Study Hint

Remember that a value of the CPI of 201 (the value for 2006), means that in that year, the average price of the market basket has increased 101 percent from the base year (the average of 1982-84). What additional information would you need to calculate the inflation rate for that year compared to the previous year? (Answer: You would need the value of the CPI for 2005.) Suppose the CPI was 82 (the value for 1980). What does that number tell us about the price level relative to the base year? (Answer: It tells us that the price level in 1980 was 18 percent lower than in the base year.)

The PPI is a measure of the average prices received by producers at all stages of production. The PPI includes intermediate goods and may sometimes give an early warning of possible future movements in the CPI.

Regardless of which price index you use, the inflation rate is the rate of change in the index from one year to the next. In the following formula, t refers to the current year and $t-1$ refers to the previous year:

$$\text{Inflation Rate}_t = \frac{\text{Price Index}_t - \text{Price Index}_{t-1}}{\text{Price Index}_{t-1}} \times 100$$

___

📖 Helpful Study Hint

The feature ***Don't Let This Happen to YOU!*** appears in this and other chapters to show you how to avoid mistakes often made by economics students. In this chapter, remember that the CPI number by itself provides a comparison to the base year and is not the inflation rate. A CPI value in 2006 of 202 implies that prices have risen 102 percent from the *base year*. The inflation rate compares the price level in one year to the price level in the previous year. For example, because the CPI in 2005 was 198, the 2006 CPI inflation rate was 2.0 percent: [(202 − 198)/198] x 100 = 2.0 percent.

📖 Helpful Study Hint

Remember that if the inflation rate falls between two years, (for example, if it is 5 percent one year and 4 percent the next year), then prices are still rising, but at a smaller rate of increase. Economists call a decline in the inflation rate *disinflation*.

Because the CPI is the most widely used measure of inflation, it is important that the CPI be as accurate as possible. There are however, four reasons why the CPI inflation rate overstates the true inflation rate:

1. The CPI has a substitution bias because it is constructed with the assumption that people buy the same goods and services and do not substitute to lower price goods and services as relative prices change.
2. The CPI does not fully take into account increases in the quality of products over time. For example, the price of a particular car model might increase from one year to the next, but part of that increase may be due to improvements in the car's safety and gas mileage. Because of increases in quality, increases in prices overstate the true rate of inflation.
3. Sometimes older products are replaced with new less expensive products. If these newer products, such as HD-DVD players, are not properly included in the CPI market basket, then decreases in their prices will be reflected in the inflation rate.
4. The CPI collects data from traditional stores, and does not sample prices at less expensive outlet stores such as Sam's Club, creating an outlet bias.

Extra Solved Problem 8-4

Chapter 8 of the textbook includes two Solved Problems. Here are two extra Solved Problems to help you build your skills solving economic problems:

Calculating the CPI

Supports Learning Objective 4: Define price level and inflation rate and understand how they are computed.

The CPI compares the cost of a market basket of goods with the cost of the same quantities of goods and services in the base year. Suppose that the basket includes (1) admission for two to the local theatre for a Friday evening movie, (2) a large popcorn at the theatre, (3) a large pepperoni pizza (carry-out from the local pizza place), and (4) a two-liter bottle of diet Coke.

Year	Theatre Admission for One Person	Popcorn	Pizza	Diet Coke
1	$5.00	$2.00	$12.00	$1.25
2	6.00	2.50	12.50	1.40
3	6.50	3.00	13.00	1.50

Calculate the value of the market basket in each year.

SOLVING THE PROBLEM

Step 1: **Review the chapter material.**
This problem is about using a price index to measure inflation, so you may want to review the section "Measuring Inflation," which begins on page 254 of the textbook.

Step 2: **Determine the value of the market basket.**
The value of the market basket is the sum of the prices of each good or service multiplied by the quantity of that good or service in the basket. (The basket above has two theater admissions but one of each of the other goods.) The value of the market basket in year 2 will be (2 x $6.00) + (1 x $2.50) + (1 x $12.50) + (1 x $1.40) = $28.40. The table below also gives the value of the market basket for years 1 and 3.

Step 3: **Calculate the CPI and CPI inflation rates for each year.**
The CPI is the ratio of the value of the market basket in a given year to the value of the market basket in the base year. Once we have calculated the CPI, we can also calculate the CPI inflation rate. These values are in the table below.

Year	Value of the Basket	CPI	Inflation
1	$25.25	100.0	–
2	28.40	112.5	12.5%
3	30.50	120.8	7.4

Comparing Inflation Rates

Supports Learning Objective 4: Define price level and inflation rate and understand how they are computed.

Below are price level data for the GDP deflator, the consumer price index (CPI), and the producer price index (PPI) for the period 2000-2006. Calculate the inflation rates for each of these price indexes for each time period. Do the different price indexes give the same inflation rate? The data are from the *Economic Report of the President*, found online at: http://www.gpoaccess.gov/eop/.

Year	GDP Deflator	CPI	PPI
2000	100.0	172.2	138.0
2001	102.4	177.1	140.7
2002	104.1	179.9	138.9
2003	106.4	184.0	143.3
2004	109.4	188.9	148.5
2005	112.7	195.3	155.7
2006	116.0	201.6	160.3

SOLVING THE PROBLEM

Step 1: **Review the chapter material.**

This problem is about using a price index to measure inflation, so you may want to review the section "Measuring Inflation," which begins on page 254 of the textbook.

Step 2: **Use the inflation formula.**

$$\text{Inflation Rate}_t = \frac{\text{Price Index}_t - \text{Price Index}_{t-1}}{\text{Price Index}_{t-1}} \times 100$$

	GDP Deflator Inflation Rate	CPI Inflation Rate	PPI Inflation Rate
2001	2.4%	2.8%	2.0%
2002	1.7	1.6	−1.3
2003	2.2	2.3	3.2
2004	2.8	2.7	3.6
2005	3.0	3.4	4.8
2006	2.9	3.2	3.0

Notice that while the numbers are different, because each price index measures the price level differently, they show a similar pattern. So which is the correct inflation rate? The answer is all are the correct inflation rate. The inflation rate measures a rate of change in prices. There are many ways to measure prices. Each measurement implies a different inflation rate.

8.5 LEARNING OBJECTIVE

8.5 Using Price Indexes to Adjust for the Effects of Inflation (pages 258–260)

Learning Objective 5 Use price indexes to adjust for the effects of inflation.

Price indexes, such as the CPI, give us a way of adjusting for the effects of inflation so that we can compare the purchasing power of dollar values in different years. The formula we would use to calculate the value in 2006 dollars of a good or service in the year 2000 would be:

$$\text{Value in 2006 dollars} = \text{Value in 2000 dollars} \times \frac{\text{CPI in 2006}}{\text{CPI in 2000}}$$

For example, suppose a pizza and two drinks from the local pizza place cost $7.99 in 2000. If the CPI in 2006 is 201 and the CPI in 2000 is 172, then the value of the pizza and two drinks in 2006 dollars is

$$\text{Value in 2006 dollars} = \$7.99 \times \frac{201}{172} = \$9.34$$

📖 Helpful Study Hint

Read *Solved Problem 8-5* in the textbook for more details on how to calculate changes in real wages.

8.6 Real versus Nominal Interest Rates (pages 260-262)

Learning Objective 6 Distinguish between the nominal interest rate and the real interest rate.

The interest rate is the return to lending or the cost of borrowing. If you lend $100 at a 5 percent interest rate, you will receive $5.00 in interest one year from now. If there is inflation over that year, the $5.00 will not buy the same amount of goods and services at the end of the year as at the beginning of the year. The **nominal interest rate** is the stated interest rate on a loan. The **real interest rate** adjusts the nominal interest rate for inflation. The real interest rate is defined as:

$$\text{Real Interest Rate} = \text{Nominal Interest Rate} - \text{Inflation Rate}$$

The real interest rate provides a better measure of the true cost of borrowing and the true rate of return to lending than does the nominal interest rate. In a period of **deflation**, where the inflation rate is negative (the price level is falling), the real interest rate will be larger than the nominal interest rate.

Extra Solved Problem 8-6

Chapter 8 of the textbook includes two Solved Problems. Here is an extra Solved Problem to help you build your skills solving economic problems:

Nominal and Real Interest Rates

Supports Learning Objective 6: Distinguish between the nominal interest rate and the real interest rate.

The table below contains interest rate data on bonds issued by large corporations. In this case, the bonds have received a "AAA" rating, which means that the corporations that issued the bonds are not likely to go out of business. The table also shows the inflation rate calculated using the CPI. Calculate the real interest rate and compare changes in the nominal and real interest rates.

Year	AAA bond interest rate (nominal interest rate)	CPI inflation rate
2001	7.1%	2.9%
2002	6.5	1.6
2003	5.7	2.3
2004	5.6	2.7
2005	5.2	3.4
2006	5.6	3.2

SOLVING THE PROBLEM

Step 1:   Review the chapter material.

This problem is about calculating the real interest rate, so you may want to review the section "Real versus Nominal Interest Rates," which begins on page 260 of the textbook.

Step 2:   Use the real interest rate formula.

$$\text{Real Interest Rate} = \text{Nominal Interest Rate} - \text{Inflation Rate}$$

The resulting real interest rates are:

Year	AAA bond interest rate (nominal rate)	CPI inflation rate	AAA bond Interest Rate (real rate)
2001	7.1%	2.9%	4.2%
2002	6.5	1.6	4.9
2003	5.7	2.3	3.4
2004	5.6	2.7	2.9
2005	5.2	3.4	1.8
2006	5.6	3.2	2.4

Notice that because the inflation rate is positive during each year, the real interest rate is always smaller than the nominal interest rate. Also notice that the patterns are sometimes different. For instance, from 2001-2002, the nominal interest rate fell from 7.1% to 6.5%, while the real interest rate increased from 4.2% to 4.9%. But, if we examine 2005-2006 changes, both the nominal and the real interest rates increased (though by different amounts).

8.7 LEARNING OBJECTIVE

8.7   Does Inflation Impose Costs on the Economy? (pages 262-265)

Learning Objective 7   Discuss the problems that inflation causes.

Inflation affects the distribution of income and can, in turn, hurt some people. For example, people on fixed nominal incomes—such as retired people who rely on company pensions that pay them a fixed amount each month—are hurt by inflation. As prices rise, their incomes do not rise, so they are able to buy fewer goods and services. Inflation can be characterized as anticipated or unanticipated. Anticipated inflation imposes costs by reducing the purchasing power of assets, such as money in a checking account. Anticipated inflation can also create additional costs to firms from raising prices—these costs are called **menu costs**. Unanticipated inflation can affect the distribution of income, causing some people to gain and some people to lose.

📖 Helpful Study Hint

For an additional discussion of the effects of inflation, read *Making the Connection: Why a Lower Inflation Rate is Like a Tax Cut for Alcatel-Lucent's Bondholders*. To keep the same real rate of interest, if the inflation rate is higher, the nominal interest rate must also be higher.

These higher nominal interest rates result in higher tax payments, so that when adjusted for inflation, real after-tax interest payments will be larger at a lower inflation rate. Inflation influences the cost of issuing a bond and the return received by the buyer of the bond.

📖 Helpful Study Hint

Economics in YOUR Life! at the end of the chapter answers the question posed at the start of the chapter: If you graduate during a recession, how will it affect your job search? Should you change careers? What we have seen in the chapter is that recessions generally are short and are followed after a year or so by expansions. This would suggest that it is not worth a major change in life plans because of a temporary event. A possible action is to wait out the recession and perhaps consider this as a time to pursue a master's degree.

Key Terms

Consumer Price Index (CPI). An average of the prices of the goods and services purchased by the typical urban family of four.

Cyclical unemployment. Unemployment caused by a business cycle recession.

Deflation. A decline in the price level.

Discouraged workers. People who are available for work, but who have not looked for a job during the previous four weeks because they believe no jobs are available for them.

Efficiency wage. A wage higher than the market wage paid by a firm in order to increase worker productivity.

Frictional unemployment. Short-term unemployment arising from the process of matching workers with jobs.

Inflation rate. The percentage increase in the price level from one year to the next.

Labor force. The sum of employed and unemployed workers in the economy.

Labor force participation rate. The percentage of the working-age population in the labor force.

Menu costs. The costs to firms of changing prices.

Natural rate of unemployment. The normal rate of unemployment, consisting of structural unemployment plus frictional unemployment.

Nominal interest rate. The stated interest rate on a loan.

Price level. A measure of the average prices of goods and services in the economy.

Producer Price Index (PPI). An average of the prices received by producers of goods and services at all stages of the production process.

Real interest rate. The nominal interest rate minus the inflation rate.

Structural unemployment. Unemployment arising from a persistent mismatch between the skills and characteristics of workers and the requirements of jobs.

Unemployment rate. The percentage of the labor force that is unemployed.

Self-Test

(Answers are provided at the end of the Self-Test.)

Multiple-Choice Questions

1. The "misery index" gives a rough measure of the state of the economy by
   a. establishing the success or failure of government spending on social programs.
   b. determining why the economy is unable to generate a higher level of real GDP per person.
   c. adding together the inflation and unemployment rates.
   d. monitoring changes in the number of people on the welfare rolls.

2. The *Current Population Survey*, conducted by the U.S. Bureau of the Census and often referred to as the household survey, is a sample of _____ households, and asks about the employment status of everyone in the household _____ and older.
   a. 1,000; 18 years of age
   b. 5,000; 21 years of age
   c. 60,000; 16 years of age
   d. 80,000; 19 years of age

3. Which of the following groups is included in the *labor force*?
   a. the unemployed
   b. retirees, homemakers, and full-time students
   c. people who could have a civilian job but are on active military service, in prison, or in mental hospitals
   d. none of the above

4. With respect to statistics on the labor market, we can say that
   a. the labor force is the sum of the employed and unemployed.
   b. the unemployment rate is calculated as: (number of unemployed/number of employed) x 100.
   c. the number unemployed includes discouraged workers.
   d. the number of unemployed includes people who are not employed and not actively looking for jobs.

5. If you are available for work and have looked for a job at some point during the previous twelve months, but have not actively looked during the previous four weeks, you are considered
   a. in the labor force, but structurally unemployed.
   b. not in the labor force.
   c. in the labor force, but frictionally unemployed.
   d. none of the above

6. Suppose that you are available for work but have not looked for a job for at least the last four weeks because you believe that no jobs are available. You would then be counted as
   a. part of the labor force.
   b. unemployed.
   c. a discouraged worker.
   d. underemployed.

7. At full employment
   a. cyclical unemployment is zero.
   b. frictional unemployment is zero.
   c. structural unemployment is zero.
   d. no one is unemployed.

8. In April 2007, the working-age population of the United States was
   a. 78.7 million.
   b. 152.6 million.
   c. 231.3 million.
   d. 303.7 million.

9. In April 2007, which of the following groups was smallest?
   a. the unemployed
   b. people who were not in the labor force and not available for work
   c. discouraged workers and those who were not working for other reasons
   d. the number of people in the labor force

10. Which of the following is the correct formula for calculating the *unemployment rate*?

    a. $\dfrac{\text{Number of unemployed}}{\text{Labor force}} \times 100$

    b. $\dfrac{\text{Labor force}}{\text{Working-age population}} \times 100$

    c. Both of the formulas above are used to calculate the unemployment rate.
    d. Neither of the formulas above are used to calculate the unemployment rate.

11. How would employment statistics be affected if they included people in the military?
    a. The unemployment rate would decrease.
    b. The working-age population would remain the same.
    c. The labor force participation rate would remain the same.
    d. all of the above

12. What would be the impact of counting as unemployed both discouraged workers and those who work part-time but would prefer to work full-time?
    a. The unemployment rate would remain the same because those people are already counted as unemployed.
    b. The unemployment rate would increase.
    c. The unemployment rate would decrease.
    d. The annual unemployment rate would have been close to 40% in the last decade.

13. Two important trends in the labor force participation rates of adults aged 20 and over in the United States since 1950 are the _____ labor force participation rate of adult women and the _____ labor force participation rate of adult men.
    a. falling; rising
    b. falling; falling
    c. rising; falling
    d. rising; rising

14. The ability of some men to survive without apparently ever holding a job
    a. has remained virtually the same since the 1960s.
    b. has all but disappeared in recent years.
    c. has been rising in recent years.
    d. is nearly impossible in today's society.

15. In April 2007, which of the following demographic groups had a higher rate of unemployment than the unemployment rate for the total population?
    a. white adults
    b. black adults
    c. Hispanic adults
    d. None of the above. The unemployment rates for these groups were all lower than the overall unemployment rate.

16. In the U.S. economy today, how long does the typical unemployed person stay unemployed?
    a. less than 5 weeks
    b. 5 to 14 weeks
    c. 15 to 26 weeks
    d. 27 weeks or more

17. Relative to the household survey, which of the following is a strength of the *establishment survey*?
    a. It provides better information on the number of persons self-employed than the household survey.
    b. It provides information on unemployment, which the household survey does not provide.
    c. It is determined by actual payrolls, rather than by the unverified answers of the household survey.
    d. all of the above

18. The extent of job creation and job destruction is
    a. a serious shortcoming of our economic system.
    b. what we would expect in a vibrant market system.
    c. an ideal feature of our economy, because very few jobs are ever destroyed while many new ones are created all the time.
    d. the main reason why the U.S. unemployment rate is persistently high.

19. From 1950 until 2007, the behavior of the annual unemployment rate in the United States demonstrated that
    a. the unemployment rate rises during both recessions and expansions.
    b. the unemployment rate falls during both recessions and expansions.
    c. the unemployment rate falls during recessions and rises during expansions.
    d. the unemployment rate rises during recessions and falls during expansions.

20. The short-term unemployment that arises from the process of matching workers with jobs is called
    a. frictional unemployment.
    b. structural unemployment.
    c. cyclical unemployment.
    d. seasonal unemployment.

21. Unemployment arising from a persistent mismatch between the skills and characteristics of workers and the requirements of jobs is called
    a. frictional unemployment.
    b. structural unemployment.
    c. cyclical unemployment.
    d. seasonal unemployment.

22. When the economy is at *full employment*, which types of unemployment remain?
    a. cyclical and structural
    b. frictional and structural
    c. frictional and cyclical
    d. None of the above. Full employment means that there is no unemployment, so the unemployment rate would be zero.

23. The "normal" underlying level of unemployment in the economy is
    a. the sum of structural unemployment and frictional unemployment.
    b. the full-employment rate of unemployment.
    c. the natural rate of unemployment.
    d. all of the above

24. Government policies can help to reduce the levels of frictional and structural unemployment, but they can also help to increase them. Which of the following policies can cause an increase in the levels of frictional or structural unemployment?
    a. increasing the length of time that the unemployed can receive payments from the government
    b. passing legislation that makes it more difficult for firms to fire workers
    c. increasing the minimum wage
    d. all of the above

25. Increases in the minimum wage will
    a. increase unemployment among workers whose market wage is higher than the new minimum wage.
    b. increase teenage unemployment.
    c. increase the level of unemployment for all groups of workers.
    d. have a large effect on the unemployment rate in the United States.

26. Which of the following is the prevailing view of economists about the unemployment insurance program in the United States?
    a. Unemployment insurance is a bad idea because the unemployed spend more time searching for jobs after they receive these payments.
    b. Unemployment insurance is a bad idea because it promotes laziness among the unemployed.
    c. Unemployment insurance is a good idea because it helps the unemployed maintain their income and spending, which helps reduce the severity of recessions.
    d. Most economists are against unemployment insurance but they don't explain why.

27. The unemployment rate in the United States is usually _____ than the unemployment rates in most other high-income countries, partly because the United States has _____ requirements for the unemployed to receive government payments.
    a. higher; less stringent
    b. higher; more stringent
    c. lower; less stringent
    d. lower; more stringent

28. If the minimum wage is set above the market-determined clearing wage
    a. the quantity of labor demanded will be greater than the quantity of labor supplied.
    b. the unemployment rate will be higher than it would be without a minimum wage.
    c. the minimum wage generates a shortage of unskilled workers.
    d. all of the above

29. A wage higher than the market wage paid by a firm in order to increase worker productivity is
    a. the idea behind the minimum wage.
    b. a burden on production costs and profits.
    c. an efficiency wage.
    d. a compensating differential.

30. To obtain prices of a representative group of goods and services, the Bureau of Labor Statistics (BLS) conducts a monthly survey of _____ households nationwide on their spending habits. The results of this survey are used to construct a market basket of _____ goods and services purchased by the typical urban family of four.
    a. 1,000; 80,000
    b. 10,000; 525
    c. 30,000; 211
    d. 5,000; 75

31. In calculating the CPI
    a. the largest group of items in the market basket is Food and Beverages.
    b. the BLS varies the quantity of a good in the market basket in response to changes in current sales of the good.
    c. the market basket of goods and services is updated monthly.
    d. the market basket does not include large equipment purchased by business firms.

32. Of the eight categories in the CPI market basket, which three categories make up more than 75 percent of the basket?
    a. medical care, recreation, and education
    b. food and beverages, apparel, and other goods and services
    c. housing, transportation, and food
    d. None of the above. Each category in the basket comprises the same percentage of the basket as the others.

33. Computation of the CPI assumes that households buy the same market basket of products each month. For this reason, one of the following is irrelevant in calculating the CPI. Which one?
    a. the prices of the products purchased in the base year
    b. the prices of the products purchased in the current year
    c. the quantities of the products purchased in the base year
    d. the quantities of the products purchased in the current year

34. If the CPI in 2002 was 180 and the CPI in 2003 was 184, what was the inflation rate between 2002 and 2003?
    a. 4%
    b. 2.22%
    c. 2.17%
    d. 97.8%

35. Changes in the CPI overstate the true inflation rate due to four "biases." If apple prices rise rapidly during the month while orange prices fall, consumers will reduce their apple purchases and increase their orange purchases. Which of the four biases is concerned with this tendency?
    a. the substitution bias
    b. the increase in quality bias
    c. the new product bias
    d. the outlet bias

36. Which of the following is a better measure of the average prices of all goods and services included in GDP?
    a. the consumer price index
    b. the producer price index
    c. the GDP deflator
    d. the inflation rate

37. If nominal GDP in a given year is $11,000 billion and real GDP is $10,000 billion, then the GDP price deflator in that year equals
    a. 1.1%.
    b. 110.
    c. 10%.
    d. 0.90, or 90%.

38. If the inflation rate is 4 percent and the nominal interest rate is 6 percent, then the real interest rate is
    a. 10 percent, which is the sum of the nominal interest rate and the inflation rate.
    b. 2 percent, which is the difference between the nominal interest rate and the inflation rate.
    c. 1.5 percent, which is the ratio of the nominal interest rate to the inflation rate.
    d. 6 percent, which is the same as the nominal interest rate.

39. The inflation rate is
    a. the percentage change in nominal GDP from one year to the next.
    b. the percentage change in real GDP from one year to the next.
    c. the percentage difference between nominal GDP and real GDP in any given year.
    d. the percentage change in the GDP deflator from one year to the next.

40. Which market basket below specifically targets *intermediate goods*?
    a. the basket used by the consumer price index
    b. the basket used by the GDP deflator
    c. the basket used by the producer price index
    d. all of the above

41. If the consumer price index was 80 in 1979 and 160 in 1999, then average prices in 1999 were
    a. half of what they were in 1979.
    b. twice as high in 1999 as in 1979.
    c. 80 times higher than in 1979.
    d. the same as they were in 1979 in real terms.

42. If the CPI was 190 in 2004 and 185 in 2003, what pay raise would someone who earned $40,000 income in 2003 have to earn in order to keep her purchasing power constant?
    a. $1,052
    b. $1,081
    c. $2,000
    d. none of the above

43. Economic variables that are calculated in current year prices are referred to as _____ variables, while variables that have been corrected to account for the effects of inflation are _____ variables.
    a. nominal; real
    b. real; nominal
    c. updated; deflated
    d. deflated; updated

44. The stated interest rate on a loan is
    a. the nominal interest rate.
    b. the real interest rate.
    c. the rate of inflation.
    d. the credit rate.

45. The real interest rate equals
    a. the inflation rate minus the nominal interest rate.
    b. the nominal interest rate minus the inflation rate.
    c. the nominal interest rate plus the inflation rate.
    d. the nominal interest rate divided by the CPI for a given year.

Short Answer Questions

1. Suppose that the working age population of a country is 500. Currently 300 are in the labor force. In addition, 275 people are currently employed. For this country, what are the labor force participation rate and the unemployment rate?

    _____

    _____

    _____

    _____

2. Suppose that because of improvements in health care, people postpone their retirement and continue working until they are 68 instead of 63. How would this influence the labor force participation rate?

_____

_____

3. Why would we expect there to be some frictional and structural unemployment but no cyclical unemployment at full employment?

_____

_____

4. Suppose that to calculate the CPI we use three goods: coffee, tea, and diet cola. A typical consumer buys 2 pounds of coffee, 3 boxes of tea, and 1 can of diet cola. Prices of these goods are given in the table below for each of three years:

Year	Price of Coffee	Price of Tea	Price of Diet Cola	Value of Market Basket	CPI	CPI Inflation Rate
1	$3.25	$2.00	$1.10			
2	$3.75	$2.22	$1.20			
3	$4.05	$2.50	$1.25			

Assume year 1 is the base year. Calculate the value of the market basket for each year. Remember the market basket of goods is the same from year to year. Then calculate the CPI and the CPI inflation rate. How would your answer differ if year 3 were the base year? (Remember, as with the CPI, use the same market basket of goods for each time period.)

_____

_____

_____

_____

5. Joe borrowed $300 from his friend Mike to buy a $300 bike. Joe agreed to pay Mike a 5% interest rate to compensate him for not having use of his $300 for that year and to adjust for the 2% inflation in the past. That nominal interest rate would imply a 3% real interest rate on the loan. Suppose that over the year the inflation rate was 3%, rather than the 2% rate Joe and Mike had expected. Who gains and who loses? How would your answer differ if the actual inflation rate over the year was 1%?

_____

_____

_____

6. Suppose an economy has a population of 5,000 people (ages 16 and up). Of that number, 2,000 people are not in the labor force, and 150 people are unemployed. Use these numbers to calculate the labor force participation rate and the unemployment rate.

_____

_____

_____

True/False Questions

T F 1. The unemployment rate is the percentage of the population that is unemployed.

T F 2. A discouraged worker is someone who has dropped out of the labor force because he believes there are no jobs available for him.

T F 3. Over the last 50 years, changes in the labor force participation rate of men and women have shown similar patterns.

T F 4. Teenage unemployment rates are about the same as adult unemployment rates.

T F 5. The household survey gives a higher total for people employed than the establishment survey because the household survey includes self-employment.

T F 6. Frictional unemployment includes people who quit their jobs to look for different jobs.

T F 7. Structural unemployment includes people who lost jobs because their job skills were no longer needed by their employer.

T F 8. Cyclical unemployment is caused by firms reducing employment due to decreased demand for their products during a recession.

T F 9. At full employment, the unemployment rate will be zero.

T F 10. The CPI is the average price of all goods and services in the economy.

T F 11. The market basket for the CPI changes every month.

T F 12. The CPI in 2004 is 189. This indicates that prices have increased 89% from the base year.

T F 13. The GDP deflator is defined as the ratio of nominal GDP to real GDP multiplied by 100.

T F 14. The real interest rate is the nominal interest rate plus the inflation rate.

T F 15. If inflation is unexpectedly high, this will benefit borrowers more than lenders.

Answers to the Self-Test

Multiple-Choice Questions

Question	Answer	Comment
1	c	In the 1960s, Arthur Okun, who was chairman of the Council of Economic Advisers during Lyndon Johnson's administration, coined the term "misery index," which adds together the inflation rate and the unemployment rate to give a rough measure of the state of the economy.
2	c	The Current Population Survey, often referred to as the household survey, is a sample of 60,000 households, chosen to represent the U.S. population, and asks about the employment status of everyone in the household 16 years of age or older.
3	a	The labor force is the sum of the employed and the unemployed.

4	a	The unemployment rate is the ratio of the number of people unemployed to the labor force, where the labor force is the sum of the employed and the unemployed. People are counted as unemployed if they are without a job, but are actively seeking a new job.
5	b	People who are available for work and who have actively looked for a job at some point during the previous twelve months, but who have not looked during the previous four weeks, are not in the labor force.
6	c	Discouraged workers are available for work, but have not looked for a job during the previous four weeks, because they believe no jobs are available for them.
7	a	Frictional and structural unemployment will exist at full employment. At full employment there is no unemployment due to the business cycle, or, in other words, no cyclical unemployment.
8	c	In April 2007, the working-age population of the United States was 231.3 million. The working-age population is divided into those in the labor force (152.6 million) and those not in the labor force (78.7 million).
9	c	The smallest group consisted of people who could possibly work but were not in the labor force, such as discouraged workers (400 thousand) and those not working for other reasons (1.0 million).
10	a	The unemployment rate measures the percentage of the labor force that is unemployed.
11	a	Including people in the military would increase the number of people counted as being in the labor force, but would leave unchanged the number of people counted as unemployed. Therefore, the unemployment rate would decrease.
12	b	For example, in April 2007, if the BLS counted as unemployed all the people who were available for work but not actively looking for a job, and all the people who were in part-time jobs but wanted full-time jobs, the unemployment rate would have increased from 4.5 percent to 8.2 percent.
13	c	Figure 8-2 highlights two important trends in labor force participation rates of adults aged 20 and over in the United States since 1950: the rising labor force participation rate of adult women and the falling labor force participation rate of adult men.
14	c	In recent years there has been an increase in the number of men who do not work and who are not receiving disability payments. In 1967, only 2.2 percent of men between the ages of 25 and 54 who were not in school did no paid work at all during the year. By 2006, 9.4 percent of men in this age category did not work.
15	b	Figure 8-3 shows that different groups in the population can have very different unemployment rates.
16	a	In April 2007, the percentage of total unemployed was as follows: less than 5 weeks: 35.6%; 5 to 14 weeks: 31.3%; 15 to 26 weeks: 15.7%, and 27 weeks or more: 17.5%.
17	c	The establishment survey has the strength of being determined by actual payrolls, rather than by unverified answers, as is the case with the household survey. In recent years, some economists have come to rely more on establishment survey data than on household survey data in analyzing current labor market conditions.

18	b	In 2005, for example, about 31.4 million jobs were created and about 29.4 million jobs were also destroyed. This degree of job creation and destruction is what we would expect in a vibrant market system where new firms are constantly being started, some existing firms are expanding, some existing firms are contracting, and some firms are going out of business.
19	d	Figure 8-4 illustrates that the unemployment rate follows the business cycle, rising during recessions and falling during expansions.
20	a	Frictional unemployment is the short-term unemployment that arises from the process of matching workers with jobs.
21	b	Structural unemployment arises from a persistent mismatch between the job skills or attributes of workers and the requirements of jobs.
22	b	When the only remaining unemployment is structural and frictional unemployment, the economy is said to be at full employment.
23	d	Economists often think of frictional and structural unemployment as being the "normal" underlying level of unemployment in the economy. This normal level of unemployment, which is the sum of frictional and structural unemployment, is referred to as the natural rate of unemployment. The natural rate of unemployment is also sometimes called the full-employment rate of unemployment.
24	d	Some government policies can add to the level of frictional and structural unemployment by either increasing the time workers devote to searching for jobs, by providing disincentives to firms to hire workers, or by keeping wages above their market level.
25	b	Increases in the minimum wage mostly affect teenage unemployment rates.
26	c	The unemployed spend more time searching for jobs because they receive these payments. This additional time spent searching raises the unemployment rate. Does this mean that the unemployment insurance program is a bad idea? Most economists would say no. Reduced spending contributes to the severity of recessions. Unemployment insurance helps the unemployed maintain their income and spending, which helps reduce the severity of recessions.
27	d	The unemployment rate in the United States is usually lower than the unemployment rates in most other high-income countries, partly because the United States has tougher requirements for the unemployed to receive government payments. This raises the costs of searching for a better job and lowers the unemployment rate.
28	b	If the minimum wage is set above the market wage determined by the demand and supply of labor, then the quantity of labor supplied will be greater than the quantity of labor demanded. As a result, the unemployment rate will be higher than it would be without a minimum wage.
29	c	An efficiency wage is a wage higher than the market wage paid by a firm in order to increase worker productivity. An efficiency wage also helps to retain and motivate workers.
30	c	To obtain prices of a representative group of goods and services, the Bureau of Labor Statistics (BLS) surveys 30,000 households nationwide on their spending habits. They use the results of this survey to construct a market basket of 211 goods and services purchased by the typical urban family of four.
31	d	In calculating the CPI, the market basket is updated only every few years.
32	c	Almost three-quarters of the market basket is in the categories of housing, transportation, and food.

33	d	The quantities of the products purchased in the current year are irrelevant in calculating the CPI because we are assuming that households buy the same market basket of products each month.
34	b	The CPI is computed as follows: [(184 – 180)/180] x 100 = 2.22%.
35	a	In constructing the CPI, the Bureau of Labor Statistics assumes that each month consumers purchase the same amount of each product in the market basket. In fact, consumers are likely to buy fewer of those products that increase most in price and more of those products that increase least in price.
36	c	The GDP deflator provides the broadest measure we have of the price level because it includes the price of every final good and service. It is an average of the prices of all goods and services included in GDP.
37	b	We can calculate the value of the GDP deflator for any year by dividing the value of nominal GDP for that year by the value of real GDP and multiplying by 100. In this case, ($11,000/$10,000) x 100 = 110.
38	b	The real interest rate is the nominal interest rate minus the inflation rate, or 6% − 4% = 2%.
39	d	We can calculate the inflation rate as the percentage change from one year to the next.
40	c	Like the consumer price index, the producer price index tracks the prices of a market basket of goods. But whereas the consumer price index tracks the prices of goods and services purchased by the typical household, the producer price index tracks the prices firms receive for goods and services at all stages of production.
41	b	On average, prices were twice as high in 1999 as in 1979, because 160/80 = 2.0.
42	b	Value in 2004 dollars = Value in 2003 dollars x (CPI in 2004/CPI in 2003). Then, 40,000 x (190/185) = 40,000 x 1.027 = $41,081. $41,081 − $40,000 = $1,081, the pay raise required.
43	a	Economic variables that are calculated in current year prices are referred to as nominal variables. When we are interested in tracking changes in an economic variable over time, rather than in seeing what its value would be in today's dollars, or to correct for the effects of inflation, we can divide the nominal variable by a price index and multiply by 100 to obtain a real variable.
44	a	The stated interest rate on a loan is the nominal interest rate. The real interest rate corrects the nominal interest rate for the impact of inflation.
45	b	The real interest rate corrects the nominal interest rate for the impact of inflation and is equal to the nominal interest rate minus the inflation rate.

Short Answer Responses

1. Using the equations:

$$\text{Labor force participation rate} = \frac{\text{Labor force}}{\text{Working-age population}} \times 100 = \left(\frac{300}{500}\right) \times 100 = 60.0\%$$

$$\text{Unemployment rate} = \frac{\text{Number of unemployed}}{\text{Labor force}} \times 100$$

$$= \left(\frac{300 - 275}{300}\right) \times 100 = 8.3\%$$

2. If workers stayed in the labor force longer, we would expect to see labor force levels increase. Given levels of the population, we would expect to see the labor force participation rate increase.

3. At full employment the economy cannot be in a recession. Therefore by definition there can be no cyclical unemployment. Frictional and structural unemployment are not due to the business cycle and can exist at any time, including at full employment.

4. With year 1 as the base year, the results are:

Year	Price of Coffee	Price of Tea	Price of Diet Coke	Value of Market Basket	CPI	CPI Inflation Rate
1	$3.25	$2.00	$1.10	$13.60	100.0	–
2	$3.75	$2.22	$1.20	$15.36	112.9	12.9%
3	$4.05	$2.50	$1.25	$16.85	123.9	9.7%

With year 3 as the base year, the results are:

Year	Price of Coffee	Price of Tea	Price of Diet Coke	Value of Market Basket	CPI	CPI Inflation Rate
1	$3.25	$2.00	$1.10	$13.60	80.7	–
2	$3.75	$2.22	$1.20	$15.36	91.2	12.9%
3	$4.05	$2.50	$1.25	$16.85	100.0	9.7%

Notice that the values for the CPI in each year are different, but the inflation rates are the same.

5. Joe and Mike agreed on a 5 percent interest rate, expecting 2 percent inflation. They implicitly agreed on a 3 percent real interest rate on the loan. If the actual inflation rate was 3 percent, the real interest rate on the loan would have been 2 percent. Mike's real return would be lower than he wanted. Mike loses. Joe, on the other hand, only pays a real cost of 2 percent instead of 3 percent. Joe gains from the higher inflation. If the inflation rate were 1 percent, the opposite would happen: Mike gains and Joe loses.

6. The labor force participation rate is the ratio of the number in the labor force to the working age population multiplied by 100. In this economy, the working age population is 5,000, and because 2,000 people are not in the labor force, the labor force will be 3,000 (= 5,000 − 2,000 = 3000), so the labor force participation rate is 60 percent = (100 x (3,000/5,000) = 60 percent). The unemployment rate is 100 multiplied by the percentage of the labor force that is unemployed, or 100 x (number unemployed/number in the labor force), so the unemployment rate is 5 percent (= 100 x (150/3,000) = 5.0 percent).

True/False Answers

1.	F	The unemployment rate is the percentage of the labor force that is unemployed.
2.	T	
3.	F	Female participation rates have risen while male rates have fallen.
4.	F	Teenage unemployment rates are much higher than adult rates.
5.	T	
6.	T	
7.	T	
8.	T	
9.	F	There will always be some structural and frictional unemployment. The natural rate of unemployment is always positive.
10.	F	The CPI includes only those goods that are in the BLS market basket.
11.	F	The market basket is updated every two years.
12.	T	
13.	T	
14.	F	The real interest rate equals the nominal interest rate minus the inflation rate.
15.	T	

Economic Growth, the Financial System, and Business Cycles

Chapter Summary

In this chapter, you learn about three topics: long-term economic growth, the financial markets that channel funds from savers to borrowers, and the properties of business cycles. The **business cycle** refers to alternating periods of economic expansion and economic recession. Financial markets (like the stock and bond markets) and financial intermediaries (like banks, credit unions, pension funds, and insurance companies) together comprise the **financial system**. **Long-run economic growth** is the process by which rising productivity increases the standard of living of the typical person. Because of economic growth, the typical American today can buy almost eight times as much as the typical American of 1900. Long-run growth is measured by increases in real GDP per capita. Increases in real GDP per capita depend on increases in labor productivity. **Labor productivity** is the quantity of goods and services that can be produced by one worker or by one hour of work. Economists believe two key factors determine labor productivity—the quantity of capital per hour worked and the level of technology. Economists often discuss economic growth in terms of growth in **potential GDP**, which is the level of GDP attained when all firms are producing at capacity.

Learning Objectives

When you finish this chapter, you should be able to:

1. **Discuss the importance of long-run economic growth.** The **business cycle** is a period of economic expansion followed by a period of economic recession. The expansion phase of a business cycle ends with a business cycle peak, followed by a period of contraction or recession. **Long-run economic growth** is the process by which rising productivity increases the standard of living of the typical person. Because of economic growth, the typical American today can buy more than eight times as much as the typical American of 1900. Long-run growth is measured by increases in real GDP per capita (or per person). Increases in real GDP per capita depend on increases in labor productivity. **Labor productivity** is the quantity of goods and services that can be produced by one worker or by one hour of work. Economists believe two key factors determine labor productivity: the quantity of capital per hour worked and the level of technology. Therefore, economic growth occurs if the quantity of capital per hour worked increases and if technological change occurs.

2. **Discuss the role of the financial system in facilitating long-run economic growth.** Firms acquire funds from households, either directly through financial markets—such as the stock and bond

markets—or indirectly through financial intermediaries such as banks. Financial markets and financial intermediaries together comprise the **financial system**. The funds available to firms come from saving. There are two categories of saving in the economy: private saving by households and public saving by the government. In the model of the **market for loanable funds**, the interaction of borrowers and lenders determines the market interest rate and the quantity of loanable funds exchanged.

3. **Explain what happens during a business cycle.** A business cycle consists of alternating periods of economic expansion and contraction. During the expansion phase of a business cycle, production, employment, and income are increasing. The period of expansion ends with a business cycle peak. Following the business cycle peak, production, employment, and income decline during the recession phase of the cycle. The recession comes to an end with a business cycle trough, after which another period of expansion begins. The inflation rate usually rises near the end of a business cycle expansion and then falls during a recession. The unemployment rate declines during the latter part of expansion and increases during a recession. The unemployment rate often continues to increase even after an expansion has begun. Economists have so far not been successful in discovering a method to predict when recessions will begin and end. Recessions are difficult to predict because they do not have only one cause.

Chapter Review

Chapter Opener: Growth and the Business Cycle at Boeing (pages 274-275)

Established in 1916, Boeing has grown into one of the world's largest designers and manufacturers of commercial jetliners, military aircraft, satellites, missiles, and defense systems. Like many other companies, Boeing's experiences have mirrored that of the U.S. economy. Because they are a producer of durable goods, their sales have been vulnerable to the business cycle. When looking at output over longer periods of time, both real GDP and real GDP per capita rise. However, over shorter periods of time, real GDP and real GDP per capita do not grow smoothly and the economy will experience the periodic increases and decreases in production called **business cycles**. During the recession of 2001, Boeing experienced a decline in business due to a fall in the demand for travel. Five years later in 2006, Boeing experienced quite the opposite: a record-breaking year with orders for airliners soaring as a result of economic growth in the United States, Europe, and Asia. Boeing is just one of many examples of a company affected by the business cycle.

📖 Helpful Study Hint

Read *An Inside Look* at the end of the chapter to learn how China's domestic aviation market is struggling to earn a profit for three reasons associated with long-run growth:
1. The Chinese airline industry's recent large investment in new planes.
2. The Chinese government's failure to liberalize markets for air travel.
3. A shortage of human capital, including pilots.

   The *Economics in YOUR Life!* feature asks you to consider what helps the economy more: when you spend money on goods and services, or when you save money instead? Keep the question in mind as you read the chapter. The authors will answer the question at the end of the chapter.

9.1   Long-Run Economic Growth (pages 276-283)

Learning Objective 1   Discuss the importance of long-run economic growth.

Long-term economic growth increases living standards. It is the reason why the standard of living for the average American today is so different from that of the 1900's. The best measure for the standard of living is real GDP per person or real GDP per capita. Real per capita GDP (in 2000 dollars) has grown from $4,900 in 1900 to $38,000 in 2006. Today, the average American can purchase about eight times as many goods and services compared to 1900. Economists use growth in real GDP per capita over time as a key measure of the long term performance of the economy.

In the following formula for calculating the growth rate in real GDP (or real GDP per capita), t refers to the current year and $t-1$ refers to the previous year:

$$\text{Real GDP growth rate}_t = \frac{\text{Real GDP}_t - \text{Real GDP}_{t-1}}{\text{Real GDP}_{t-1}} \times 100$$

Real GDP was $11,049 billion in 2005 and $11,415 billion in 2006. So the growth rate in real GDP for 2006 was:

$$\text{Real GDP growth rate } 2006 = \frac{\text{Real GDP } 2006 - \text{Real GDP } 2005}{\text{Real GDP } 2005} \times 100$$

$$= \frac{\$11,415 \text{ billion} - \$11,049 \text{ billion}}{\$11,048 \text{ billion}} \times 100 = 3.3\%$$

To find real GDP growth rates over longer periods of time, such as 10 years, we can average the growth rates for each year.

📖 Helpful Study Hint

For a discussion of the correlation between economic prosperity and national health, read *Making the Connection: The Connection Between Economic Prosperity and Health*. As noted by Nobel-Prize winner Robert Fogel, there is a close connection between economic conditions and a society's health. Economic growth fosters better nutrition and improvements in health care, as well as improving the quality of life through the introduction of technological improvements that allow workers to have more leisure time.

Increases in real GDP and real GDP per capita are caused by increases in **labor productivity** (output per hours worked). Economists believe that there are two key factors that determine labor productivity: the quantity of the capital per hour worked and the level of technology. Recall that **capital** refers to manufactured goods that are used to produce other goods or services. As the capital stock per hour increases, so does worker productivity.

Technological change has similar effects on labor productivity. Technological change refers to an increase in the quantity of output that firms can produce using the same level of inputs. This means an economy can produce more output (real GDP) with the same quantities of workers and capital. However, it is important to point out that accumulating more workers and capital does not ensure that an economy will experience economic growth unless technological change also occurs. Most technological change is embodied in new machinery, equipment, or software.

Helpful Study Hint

For a discussion of economic growth in developing countries, read *Making the Connection: What Explains Rapid Economic Growth in Botswana?* Economic growth in the majority of sub-Saharan Africa has been very slow. Botswana is an exception. Botswana has seen the largest growth rate of the six most populous sub-Saharan countries between 1960 and 2004. There are several factors that contribute to Botswana's rapid growth:
1. a lack of civil wars.
2. large diamond exports.
3. government pro-growth policies, such as protecting private property.

The concept of **potential GDP** is very useful to economists when discussing long-run economic growth. Potential GDP refers to the level of output that could be produced if all firms are producing at capacity using normal working hours and their normal work force. Potential GDP grows over time as the labor force increases, as new machinery is installed, and as technological change takes place. In the United States, potential GDP increases about 3.5 percent per year.

9.2 LEARNING OBJECTIVE

9.2   Saving, Investment, and the Financial System (pages 283-292)

Learning Objective 2   Discuss the role of the financial system in facilitating long-run economic growth.

Economic growth depends on firms purchasing capital goods. However, before a firm can acquire new buildings and machines, it must find financing. This requires access to the **financial system**. The U.S. financial system includes **financial markets** (like the stock and bond markets) and **financial intermediaries** (like banks, credit unions, pension funds, and insurance companies). The financial system channels funds from savers (lenders) to borrowers, who pay savers interest for use of the funds. Financial intermediaries pool the savings of many small savers and make large loans from the pooled funds.

A fundamental macroeconomic identity is that the total value of saving should equal the total value of investment. We can show why this identity holds: First, remember that the relationship between GDP (Y) and its components, consumption (C), investment (I), government purchases (G), and net exports (NX) can be expressed in terms of the following equation:

$$Y = C + I + G + NX.$$

In a closed economy where exports and imports (and therefore, net exports) are zero, we know that:

$$Y = C + I + G,$$

or

$$I = Y - C - G.$$

Private saving ($S_{private}$) is equal to what households retain of their income after purchasing goods and services (C) and paying taxes (T). In addition to receiving income for supplying factors of production to firms (Y), households also receive income from the government in the form of transfer payments (TR). Private saving can be expressed in the following equation:

$$S_{private} = Y + TR - C - T.$$

Public saving occurs when the government engages in saving (S_{public}). It is the difference between the government's revenue and the government's spending and can be expressed in the following equation:

$$S_{public} = T - G - TR.$$

📖 Helpful Study Hint

If S_{public} is positive, there is a budget surplus, and if S_{public} is negative, there is a budget deficit.

Total saving in the economy (S) is $S_{private} + S_{public}$. It can also be expressed through the following equations:

$$S = S_{private} + S_{public} = (Y + TR - C - T) + (T - G - TR),$$

or

$$S = Y - C - G,$$

or

$$S = I.$$

The above equations have demonstrated that total saving must equal total investment. The financial system brings about the equality of total saving and total investment through the **market for loanable funds**. Borrowers and savers interact in the market for loanable funds, which determines the quantity of loanable funds and the interest rate on these funds. The demand for loanable funds is determined by the willingness of firms to borrow funds to finance new investment projects. These projects can range from building new factories to engaging in research and development. When determining whether to borrow funds, firms compare the return they expect to receive on an investment with the interest rate they must pay to borrow the necessary funds. The demand for loanable funds is downward sloping because the lower the interest rate, the larger the number of profitable investment projects there are, and the larger the quantity of loanable funds firms want to borrow. The supply of loanable funds is determined by the willingness of households to save, and by the extent of government saving or dissaving. The government saves when it runs a budget surplus, and dissaves when it runs a deficit. The supply curve for loanable funds is upward-sloping because the higher the interest rate, the greater the quantity of loanable funds supplied by savers. Because both borrowers and lenders are interested in the real interest rate they will receive or pay, equilibrium in the market for loanable funds determines the real interest rate, not the nominal interest rate.

📖 Helpful Study Hint

For a discussion of promoting economic growth, read the *Making the Connection: Ebenezer Scrooge: Accidental Promoter of Economic Growth*. Before encountering the ghosts of Christmases past, present, and future, Ebenezer Scrooge, the well-known character from Charles Dickens's *A Christmas Carol,* was a saver and not a spender. Although Scrooge was very wealthy, he refused to heat or light his home and ate meager meals. At the end of the novel however, Scrooge begins to spend his money lavishly on himself and on others. Because the funds that he saved were available for firms to borrow to finance the purchase of new capital and because new capital helps contribute to economic growth, Steve Landsburg of the University of Rochester argues that the "old Scrooge" deserved more praise than the "reformed Scrooge." Savers provide the funds that are necessary for investment spending in order to fuel economic growth.

Equilibrium in the market for loanable funds determines the quantity of loanable funds that will flow from lenders to borrowers each period and determines the real interest rate that lenders will receive and that borrowers must pay. The demand for loanable funds is determined by the willingness of firms to borrow money and engage in new investment projects, while the supply of loanable funds is determined by the willingness of households to save. The following graph shows equilibrium in the market for loanable funds:

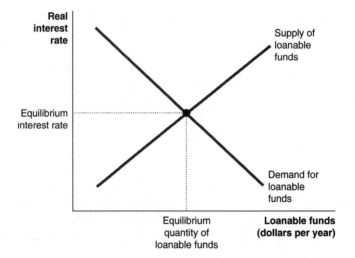

Helpful Study Hint

Draw a loanable funds market graph and show what will happen to the equilibrium real interest rate and equilibrium quantity of loanable funds if demand increases. What about if supply increases?

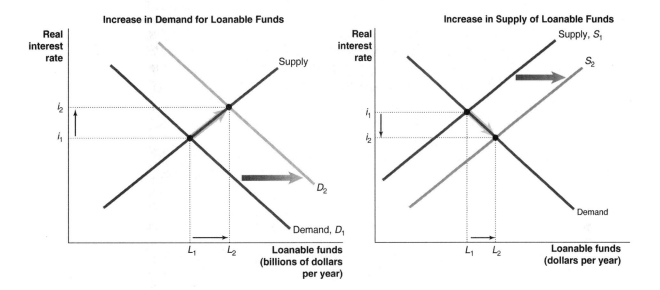

An increase in demand will increase both the real interest rate and the quantity of loanable funds.

An increase in supply will reduce the real interest rate and increase the quantity of loanable funds.

Helpful Study Hint

Don't forget the difference between a movement along a curve and a shift in the curve. A shift is caused by a change in a variable that is held constant when we draw a particular curve. For instance, a budget deficit causes a shift in the supply of loanable funds, and an increase in income causes an increase in demand for loanable funds. A change in the real interest rate will cause a movement along both the supply curve of loanable funds and the demand curve for loanable funds.

When the government runs a budget deficit, it causes the supply curve for loanable funds to shift to the left. When the supply curve for loanable funds shifts to the left, the real interest rate will rise and private investment spending will fall because there will be fewer profitable private investment projects at the new, higher interest rate. This reduction in investment is referred to as **crowding out**. A budget surplus would have the opposite effects: increasing the total amount of saving in the economy, which would shift the supply of loanable funds to the right. As a result, a government budget surplus will lead to a lower real interest rate, a larger quantity of loanable funds and higher saving and investment.

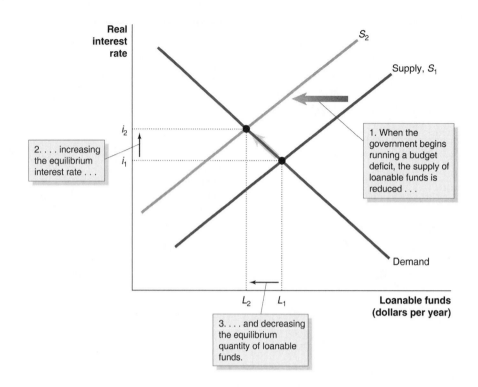

9.3 LEARNING OBJECTIVE

9.3   The Business Cycle (pages 292-301)

Learning Objective 3   Explain what happens during a business cycle.

The **business cycle** is a period of economic expansion followed by a period of economic recession. The expansion phase of a business cycle ends with a business cycle peak, followed by a period of contraction or recession. The recession phase of a business cycle ends with a business cycle trough, which is followed by another expansion. Textbook Figure 9-6 (b) shows the phases of the business cycle:

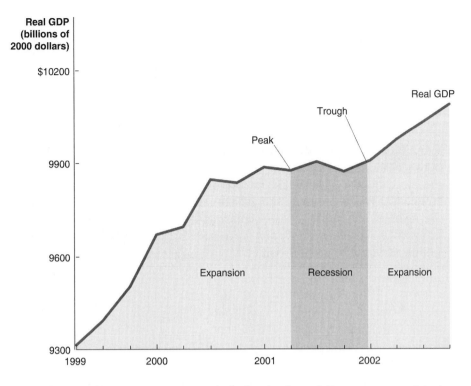

Recessions tend to reduce inflation. On average, inflation is about 2.5 percentage points lower in the year after a recession than in the year before a recession. Recessions almost always increase unemployment. The unemployment rate tends to be about 1.2 percentage points higher in the year after a recession than in the year before a recession. Since the end of World War II, expansions have gotten progressively longer and recessions have become shorter. This means recessions have become milder over the last 50 years.

Economists believe that there are three reasons behind the reduced severity of recessions and a generally more stable economy:

1. Services have been an increasing fraction of GDP over the last 50 years. Because goods are a smaller fraction of GDP, problems caused by uneven movements in business inventories have been reduced. A shift in the economy from producing durable goods, whose demand is more responsive to income changes, to services has had a damping effect on recessions in the United States. (Almost by definition, services cannot be held as inventories.)
2. Unemployment insurance provides some income for families to continue to buy goods and services during a recession.
3. Many economists believe that active government policies to combat recessions have had the effect of reducing the severity of recessions.

📖 Helpful Study Hint

For an additional discussion of the business cycle, read ***Making the Connection: Who Decides if the Economy Is in a Recession?*** The federal government does not officially decide when a recession begins and when it ends. Instead economists turn to the Business Cycle Dating Committee of the National Bureau of Economics Research (NBER). The NBER defines a recession as "a significant decline in activity across the economy, lasting more than a few months, visible in industrial production, employment, real income, and wholesale retail trade." The NBER is slow in announcing when the country is in a recession because they need time to gather and analyze economic statistics and normally are not able to do so until the recession has already begun.

📖 Helpful Study Hint

Read ***Don't Let This Happen to YOU!***, which reinforces the difference between the price level and the inflation rate. Economic growth is measured by the growth rate in real GDP, not the level of real GDP. Notice that it is possible for the growth rate in real GDP to decline while the level of real GDP is still increasing. Likewise, the price level and inflation are different. Inflation is a rate of change. Inflation can be falling while prices are still rising.

Extra Solved Problem 9-3

Chapter 9 of the textbook includes two Solved Problems. Here is an extra Solved Problem to help you build your skills solving economic problems:

Interest Rates and Recession

Supports Learning Objective 3: Explain what happens during a business cycle.

Using a graph of the market for loanable funds, predict what will happen to real interest rates as the economy enters a recession.

SOLVING THE PROBLEM

Step 1: **Review the chapter material.**
This problem is about using the market for loanable funds model, so you may want to review the section "The Market for Loanable Funds," which begins on page 287 of the textbook.

Step 2: **Draw a graph illustrating the effect of a reduction in saving.**
The equilibrium real interest rate depends on the demand and supply of loanable funds. As the economy enters a recession, we would expect income to fall, reducing both consumption (and, therefore, investment) and saving. This reduction in saving should reduce the supply of loanable funds, shifting the supply curve to the left. The reduction in the supply of loanable funds is shown in the following graph:

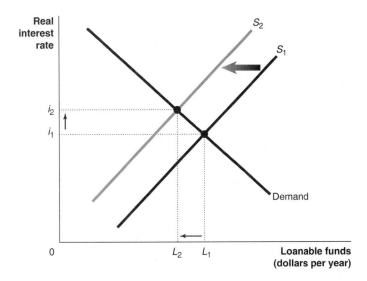

As a result of this reduction in supply, we would expect the equilibrium real interest rate to increase from i_1 to i_2.

Step 3: **Draw a graph illustrating the reduction in the demand for loanable funds.**

At the same time that the supply of loanable funds is falling, we would expect the recession to reduce business investment opportunities. If firms do not expect output to grow, they may be unwilling to commit to new investment purchases. Firms will not need to expand their capital if they are laying off employees due to reduced demand. This should have the effect of reducing the demand for loanable funds, shifting the demand curve to the left. This is seen in the graph below:

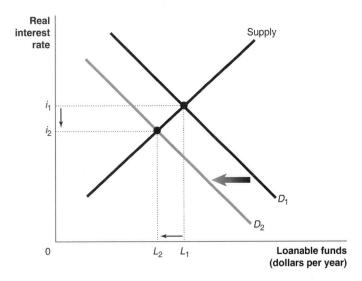

Step 4: **Predict what will happen to real interest rates.**

As a result of this reduction in demand, we would expect the equilibrium real interest rate to decrease from i_1 to i_2. As the economy enters the recession, both the demand curve and the supply curve shift. Because both curves are shifting, the effect of the recession on the equilibrium real interest rate is uncertain. This is because the shift in the supply curve causes the real interest rate to increase at the same time the shift in the demand curve causes the real interest rate to decrease.

If the effect of the shift in demand is greater than the effect of the shift in supply, then we would expect to see the equilibrium real interest rate fall as a result of the recession. This is seen in the graph below:

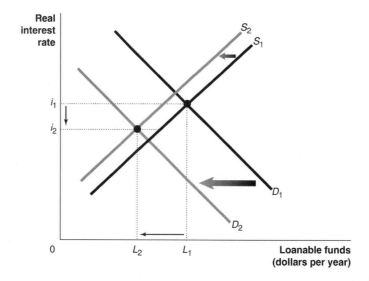

If the effect of the shift in supply is greater than the effect of the shift in demand, then we would expect to see the equilibrium real interest rate rise as a result of the recession. This is seen in the graph below:

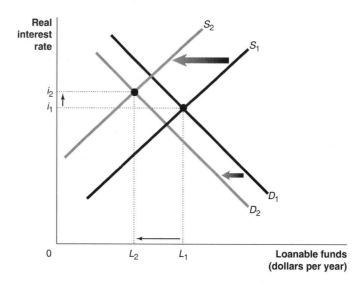

Our conclusion is that, based upon the market for loanable funds, we cannot predict what will happen to the equilibrium real interest rate as the economy enters a recession. The rate could either rise or fall. (It is possible that the rate will not change. If this happens, the shift in supply and the shift in demand have the same effect on the interest rate. Draw a graph to illustrate that situation.) In practice, we normally see the real interest rate fall during a recession, which means that the shift in the demand for loanable funds must typically be greater than the shift in supply.

📖 Helpful Study Hint

For an example of how spending influences economic growth, look at the *Economics in YOUR Life!* feature at the end of the chapter. If you decide to not purchase a product and to save the money instead, will this reduce economic growth by reducing consumption (because consumption is about 2/3 of GDP)? Consumption spending promotes the production of more consumption goods and fewer investment goods (remember the economic definition of investment). Saving is necessary to fund investment expenditures. Thus, not buying a product today and saving instead will promote economic growth.

Key Terms

Business cycle. The business cycle is the periodic alternation of economic expansion and economic recession in an economy.

Capital. Manufactured goods that are used to produce other goods and services; examples of capital are computers, factory buildings, and trucks.

Crowding out. A decline in private expenditures as a result of an increase in government purchases.

Financial intermediaries. Firms, such as banks, mutual funds, and insurance companies, that borrow funds from savers and lend them to borrowers.

Financial markets. Markets where financial securities, such as stocks and bonds, are bought and sold.

Financial system. The system of financial markets and financial intermediaries through which firms acquire funds from households.

Labor productivity. The quantity of goods and services that can be produced by one worker or by one hour of work.

Long-run economic growth. The process by which rising productivity increases the average standard of living.

Market for loanable funds. The interaction of borrowers and lenders that determines the market interest rate and the quantity of loanable funds exchanged.

Potential GDP. The level of GDP attained when all firms are producing at capacity.

Self-Test

(Answers are provided at the end of the Self-Test.)

Multiple-Choice Questions

1. The only way that the standard of living of the average person in a country can increase is by
    a. increasing population growth so output can increase.
    b. increasing production faster than population growth.
    c. ensuring that the country's economic growth is faster than economic growth in other countries.
    d. producing the amount of output necessary for subsistence.

2. A defining characteristic of the business cycle is
    a. periods of extremely slow growth followed by periods of very fast growth.
    b. frequent economic recessions followed by severe depressions.
    c. alternating periods of expansion and recession.
    d. periods of stable growth but with frequent downturns.

3. The defining characteristic of long-run economic growth is
    a. the business cycle.
    b. rising productivity.
    c. steady increases in living standards for everyone each year.
    d. high rates of inflation.

4. Because the focus of long-run economic growth is on the standard of living of the average person, we measure the standard of living in terms of
    a. real GDP.
    b. nominal GDP.
    c. nominal GDP per capita.
    d. real GDP per capita.

5. In measuring changes in the standard of living in a country, economists rely heavily on comparisons over time of real GDP per capita because
    a. it is a very precise, almost perfect measure of well-being.
    b. it is an effective means of accounting for things like the level of pollution, the level of crime, spiritual well-being, and many factors that other measures can't count.
    c. it includes the value of all production in the economy.
    d. despite its well-known flaws, it is the best means we have of comparing the performance of an economy over time.

6. The computation of the average annual growth rate of real GDP
    a. is the same for shorter periods of time as for longer periods of time.
    b. is computed by simply averaging the growth rate for each year, but only if we use a lot of years.
    c. is more complex when a long period of time is involved than when only a few years are included.
    d. involves computing the percentage change in real GDP between the first year and the last year for the period we are interested in.

7. What is the best use of the rule of 70 among those listed below?
    a. to forecast the duration of recessions
    b. to find the average annual growth rate of real GDP
    c. to judge how rapidly real GDP per capita is growing over long time periods
    d. to calculate the difference between the growth rate in real GDP and the growth rate in real GDP per capita

8. When it comes to raising the standard of living in a country, how important is the growth rate of real GDP?
    a. Growth rates in real GDP are very important. Small differences in growth rates can have large effects over long time periods.
    b. The difference in growth rates must be substantial before we notice any rise in living standards.
    c. The standard of living can increase in the long run without any growth in real GDP.
    d. When explaining changes in the standard of living, economists focus more on social factors than on growth rates of GDP.

9. Which of the following *does not* cause the quantity of goods and services that can be produced by one worker, or in one hour of work, to increase?
   a. an increase in the quantity of capital per hour worked
   b. technological change
   c. an increase in the number of workers
   d. an increase in the size of the economy

10. Which of the following terms refers to the accumulated knowledge and skills that workers acquire from education and training, or from their life experiences?
    a. capital
    b. financial capital
    c. human capital
    d. physical capital

11. Which of the following will ensure that an economy experiences sustained economic growth?
    a. increasing the amount of labor
    b. increasing the amount of capital
    c. increasing the amount of raw materials
    d. technological change

12. Which of the following government policies can help economic growth?
    a. ensuring relative political stability and relatively little corruption
    b. promoting the existence of an efficient financial system
    c. protecting private property rights, allowing for freedom of the press, and having a democratic form of government
    d. all of the above

13. Which of the following will *not* cause an economy to grow?
    a. a more productive labor force
    b. increases in capital per hour worked
    c. a low minimum wage rate
    d. technological change

14. Potential GDP is
    a. always greater than actual real GDP.
    b. always less than actual real GDP.
    c. sometimes greater, sometimes less, and sometimes equal to actual real GDP.
    d. the level of GDP that would be produced when firms are operating at maximum capacity.

15. How do firms acquire funds by using *indirect finance* rather than *direct finance*?
    a. by issuing stocks or bonds
    b. by borrowing from households
    c. by borrowing from a bank
    d. by borrowing from other firms

16. Which of the following are financial securities that represent promises to repay a fixed amount of funds?
    a. stocks
    b. bonds
    c. both stocks and bonds
    d. neither stocks nor bonds

17. Allowing savers to spread their money among many financial instruments is one of the key services offered by financial intermediaries. What is the name of this service?
    a. risk sharing
    b. liquidity
    c. information
    d. matching

18. If you read a newspaper headline announcing that an automobile has been subject to a recall to fix a seatbelt problem, how would you determine the effect of this recall on the automobile firm's profits?
    a. The recall would lead to an expectation of higher future profits and would boost the prices of the firm's stock and bonds.
    b. The recall would not have any impact on the value of the firm's stock or bonds.
    c. The recall would lead to an expectation of lower future profits and would put downward pressure on the prices of the firm's stock and bonds.
    d. Financial markets may or may not incorporate this information into the prices of stocks, bonds, and other financial securities of the firm, so the impact is indeterminate.

19. A government that collects more in taxes than it spends experiences
    a. a budget surplus.
    b. a budget deficit.
    c. a budget balance.
    d. an increase in the national debt.

20. What happens when government spending is greater than government tax revenues?
    a. There is negative public saving.
    b. There is dissaving by government and the national debt rises.
    c. The government issues more new bonds than the old bonds it pays off.
    d. all of the above

21. In determining whether or not to borrow funds, firms compare the return they expect to make on an investment with
    a. the revenue expected from the investment.
    b. the interest rate they must pay to borrow the necessary funds.
    c. the initial cost of the investment.
    d. the total amount of profit they expect to make from the investment.

22. The _____ the interest rate is, the more investment projects firms can profitably undertake, and the _____ the quantity of loanable funds they will demand.
    a. lower; greater
    b. lower; smaller
    c. higher; greater
    d. higher; smaller

23. An increase in the real interest rate will
    a. shift the demand curve for loanable funds to the left.
    b. shift the supply curve of loanable funds to the right.
    c. cause a movement along the demand curve for loanable funds.
    d. result from the supply curve for loanable funds shifting to the left.

24. Which of the following determines the *supply of loanable funds*?
    a. the willingness of households and governments to save
    b. the number of financial intermediaries available
    c. changes in the interest rate, which cause business firms to undertake more or less profitable investment projects
    d. the quantity of stocks and bonds issued by business firms

25. If technological change increases the profitability of new investment to firms, which of the following will occur?
    a. The demand for loanable funds will increase.
    b. The supply of loanable funds will increase.
    c. The demand for loanable funds will decrease.
    d. The supply of loanable funds will decrease.

26. A federal government budget deficit will
    a. increase the demand for loanable funds and increase the equilibrium real interest rate.
    b. increase the supply of loanable funds and decrease the equilibrium real interest rate.
    c. decrease the supply of loanable funds and increase the equilibrium real interest rate.
    d. decrease the supply of loanable funds and decrease the equilibrium real interest rate.

27. If the government begins running a budget deficit, what impact will the deficit have on the loanable funds market?
    a. The demand for loanable funds will increase.
    b. The supply of loanable funds will increase.
    c. The demand for loanable funds will decrease.
    d. The supply of loanable funds will decrease.

28. The impact of government budget deficits and surpluses on the equilibrium interest rate is
    a. relatively small.
    b. very large.
    c. zero.
    d. dependent on how large a shift in the demand for loanable funds is caused by the deficit or surplus.

29. How would a *consumption tax* affect the loanable funds market?
    a. The demand for loanable funds would increase.
    b. The supply of loanable funds would increase.
    c. The demand for loanable funds would decrease.
    d. The supply of loanable funds would decrease.

30. From a trough to a peak, the economy goes through
    a. the recessionary phase of the business cycle.
    b. the expansionary phase of the business cycle.
    c. falling real GDP.
    d. rising real GDP, but falling real GDP per capita.

31. Typically, when will the National Bureau of Economic Research (NBER) announce that the economy is in a recession?
    a. about six months prior to the recession
    b. on the precise date that the recession starts
    c. only well after the recession has begun
    d. exactly one year after the recession starts

32. As the economy nears the end of an expansion, which of the following occurs?
    a. Interest rates are usually rising.
    b. Wages are usually rising faster than prices.
    c. The profits of firms will be falling.
    d. all of the above

33. When do households and firms typically increase their debts substantially?
    a. toward the end of a recession
    b. toward the end of an expansion
    c. at the beginning of both recessions and expansions
    d. in the middle of a recession

34. In business cycles,
    a. expansions are usually the same length as recessions.
    b. the peak is the end of the expansion.
    c. the trough is always 6 months after the previous peak.
    d. the dates of the peak and trough are determined by Congress.

35. Which types of goods are most likely to be affected by the business cycle?
    a. durable goods
    b. nondurable goods
    c. services
    d. goods purchased by the government

36. How does the inflation rate behave during the business cycle?
    a. During expansions, the inflation rate usually increases.
    b. During recessions, the inflation rate usually increases.
    c. The inflation rate is unpredictable; it may increase or decrease during recessions or expansions.
    d. The inflation rate usually decreases during both recessions and expansions.

37. Recessions cause the inflation rate to _____, and they cause the unemployment rate to
    _____.
    a. increase; increase
    b. increase; decrease
    c. decrease; decrease
    d. decrease; increase

38. During the early stages of a recovery
    a. firms usually rush to hire new employees before other firms employ them.
    b. firms are usually reluctant to hire new employees.
    c. the rate of unemployment increases dramatically.
    d. the rate of unemployment decreases dramatically.

39. Comparing the period after 1950 with the period before 1950, how would you describe the business cycle?
    a. Recessions have been milder and the economy has been more stable.
    b. Recessions have been deeper and longer lasting and the economy has been more unstable.
    c. There have been no periods of recession since 1950, and the economy has been very stable.
    d. There have been expansions and recessions since 1950, but the recessions have been longer than the expansions.

40. Which of the following is *not* a reason that the economy is considered to be more stable now than in the past?
    a. the increasing importance of services and the declining importance of goods
    b. the establishment of unemployment insurance programs
    c. the use of active government policies to stabilize the economy
    d. the introduction of a minimum wage rate

41. During the last half of the twentieth century, the U.S. economy experienced
    a. long expansions, interrupted by relatively short recessions.
    b. long recessions, interrupted by relatively short expansions.
    c. much more severe swings in real GDP than in the first half of the twentieth century.
    d. an inflation rate that increased during both recessions and expansions.

42. Changes in the stability of the economy since 1950 have been attributed to
    a. the steady rise of manufacturing production as a percentage of GDP.
    b. the fact that the production of services fluctuates more than the production of durable goods such as automobiles.
    c. the increasing importance of services and the declining importance of goods.
    d. the fact that households will cut back on their purchases of durable goods more than they will on their purchases of nondurable goods during recessions.

43. How have the establishment of unemployment insurance and the creation of other transfer programs that provide funds to the unemployed contributed to business cycle stability?
    a. They have not contributed; in fact, they have worsened the stability of the economy.
    b. They have made it possible for workers who lose their jobs to have higher incomes and, therefore, to spend more than they would otherwise.
    c. They have limited the ability of the government to spend on other, more effective programs to bring about stability.
    d. It is difficult to establish the impact of these programs on economic stability.

44. Attempts by the government to stabilize the economy were favored by public opinion
    a. beginning in the 1990s.
    b. beginning in the 1930s.
    c. beginning in 2001.
    d. beginning in the 1950s.

45. Which of the following statements best characterizes the views of economists with respect to government stabilization policies?
    a. All economists are in favor of government policies intended to stabilize the economy.
    b. Hardly any economists are in favor of government policies intended to stabilize the economy.
    c. Some economists believe that government policies have played a key role in stabilizing the economy, but other economists disagree.
    d. Most economists agree that government policies intended to stabilize the economy policies have been very effective, while only a few disagree.

Short Answer Questions

1. If real GDP grows more slowly than the rate at which population is growing, what will happen to real GDP per capita? What will happen to the standard of living?

2. Growth in the capital stock is an important factor in economic growth. What is the link between growth in the capital stock and investment spending?

3. Suppose that households decide to save a greater fraction of their income even though the current interest rate has not changed. Use the loanable funds model to predict how the equilibrium real interest rate will change.

4. What effect does the business cycle typically have on the unemployment rate and the inflation rate? On average, how much difference is there between each rate in the year before a recession begins and the year after a recession ends?

5. Explain how unemployment insurance may cause a recession to be shorter and milder, while at the same time keeping unemployment higher for a longer time.

_____

_____

_____

6. The table below gives real GDP for Canada for the period 2002-2006:

Year	Real GDP (millions of 2002 Canadian dollars)
2002	$1,152,905
2003	1,174,592
2004	1,210,656
2005	1,247,780
2006	1,282,204

Using this data, calculate the growth rate in real GDP for each year from 2003 to 2006, and the average growth rate in real GDP for this period. If Canadian real GDP grew at this average rate, how many years would it take for real GDP to double?

_____

_____

_____

True/False Questions

T F 1. Since 1900, real GDP per capita has increased every year.

T F 2. If real GDP grows at a rate of 4.4 percent per year, it will take about 16 years for real GDP to double.

T F 3. Labor productivity is the quantity of goods and services that can be produced by one hour of work.

T F 4. Labor productivity is now about the same as it was in 1900.

T F 5. Technological change lets the economy produce more goods and services with the same quantities of resources.

T F 6. In an economy with no imports or exports, $S = I$.

T F 7. Government saving is always positive.

T F 8. An increase in the real interest rate caused by a decrease in the supply of loanable funds will reduce the demand for loanable funds and shift the loanable funds demand curve to the left.

T F 9. An increase in the demand for loanable funds will shift the demand curve to the right and result in an increase in the real interest rate.

T F 10. An increase in the equilibrium quantity of loanable funds will result in an increase in both saving and investment.

T F 11. The dates for business cycle peaks and troughs are determined by the Business Cycle Committee of Congress (BCCC).

T F 12. A business cycle is (in this order) an expansion, a peak, a recession, a trough, and then another expansion.

T F 13. Recessions usually last more than two years.

T F 14. Inflation is usually lower and unemployment is usually higher after a recession than before a recession.

T F 15. Unemployment insurance is one of the reasons that recessions have become shorter and less severe.

Answers to the Self-Test

Multiple-Choice Questions

Question	Answer	Comment
1	b	Increasing production faster than population growth is the only way that the standard of living of the average person in a country can increase.
2	c	Dating back to at least the early nineteenth century, the U.S. economy has experienced periods of expanding production and employment followed by periods of recession, during which production and employment decline. These alternating periods of expansion and recession are called the *business cycle*.
3	b	*Long-run economic growth* is the process by which rising productivity increases the standard of living of the typical person.
4	d	Because the focus of long-run economic growth is on the standard of living of the average person, we measure it by real GDP per capita. We use real GDP rather than nominal GDP to eliminate the effect of price changes.
5	d	The quantity of goods and services that a person can buy, as measured by real GDP, is not a perfect measure of how happy or contented that person may be. The level of pollution, the level of crime, spiritual well-being, and many other factors ignored in calculating GDP, contribute to a person's happiness. Nevertheless, economists rely heavily on comparisons of real GDP per capita because—flawed though the measure is—it is the best means we have of comparing the performance of an economy over time or the performance of different economies at any particular time. (Economists who have studied the issue of happiness have found a high correlation between per capita real GDP and per capita happiness.)
6	c	For example, real GDP in the United States was $1,777 billion in 1950 and $11,415 billion in 2006. To find the average annual growth rate during this 56-year period, we need to compute the growth rate that would result in $1,777 billion growing to $11,415 billion over 56 years. In this case, the growth rate is 3.4%. That is, if $1,777 billion grows at an average rate of 3.4% per year, then after 56 years it will have grown to $11,415 billion. For shorter periods of time, we get approximately the same answer by averaging the growth rate for each year.
7	c	One way to judge how rapidly real GDP per capita is growing is to calculate the number of years it would take to double. If real GDP per capita in a country doubles, say every 20 years, then most people in the country will experience significant increases in their standard of living over the course of their lives. If real GDP per capita doubles only every 100 years, then increases in the standard of living will be too slow to notice.
8	a	Small differences in growth rates can have large effects on how rapidly the standard of living in a country increases.

9	c	Increasing the number of hours of work is not sufficient to increase productivity. Economists believe two key factors determine labor productivity: the quantity of capital per hour worked and the level of technology.
10	c	*Human capital* refers to the accumulated knowledge and skills that workers acquire from education and training, or from their life experiences.
11	d	A very important point is that just accumulating more inputs—such as labor, capital, and raw materials—will not ensure that an economy experiences economic growth unless technological change also occurs.
12	d	Protecting private property, avoiding political instability and corruption, and allowing press freedom and democracy are a straightforward recipe for providing an environment in which economic growth can occur.
13	c	A low minimum wage may increase teenage employment but would not influence economic growth.
14	c	Potential real GDP increases every year as the labor force and the capital stock grow and technological change occurs. Actual real GDP has sometimes been greater than potential real GDP and sometimes less, because of the effects of the business cycle. Note that potential real GDP results from firms producing at normal capacity, rather than at maximum capacity.
15	c	Firms acquire funds from households, either directly through financial markets—such as the stock and bond markets—or indirectly through financial intermediaries, such as banks. In *financial markets* firms raise funds by selling financial securities directly to savers.
16	b	Stocks are financial securities that represent partial ownership of a firm. If you buy one share of stock in General Electric, then you become one of millions of owners of that firm. Bonds are financial securities that represent promises to repay a fixed amount of funds.
17	a	In addition to matching households that have excess funds with firms who want to borrow funds, the financial system provides three key services for savers and borrowers: risk sharing, liquidity, and information. The financial system provides risk sharing by allowing savers to spread their money among many financial instruments. In the field of finance this is called *diversification*.
18	c	Financial markets do that job for you by incorporating information into the prices of stocks, bonds, and other financial securities.
19	a	A government that collects more in taxes than it spends experiences a *budget surplus*. A government that spends more than it collects in taxes experiences a *budget deficit*.
20	d	When government spending is greater than government tax revenues, there is negative public saving. Negative saving is also referred to as *dissaving*. Only when the government runs a budget surplus does it provide funds to financial markets by paying off more old bonds than it issues new bonds.
21	b	In determining whether or not to borrow funds, firms compare the return they expect to make on an investment with the interest rate they must pay to borrow the necessary funds.
22	a	The demand for loanable funds is downward sloping because the lower the interest rate is, the more investment projects firms can profitably undertake, and the greater the quantity of loanable funds they will demand.
23	c	Because the real interest rate is plotted on the vertical axis, a change in that rate will cause a movement along the graph, not a shift.
24	a	The supply of loanable funds is determined by the willingness of households to save, and by the extent of government saving or dissaving.

25	a	The demand for loanable funds is determined by the willingness of firms to borrow money to engage in new investment projects. A technological change that increases profitability will increase that willingness for every level of the real interest rate.
26	c	A federal budget deficit takes funds out of the economy, which will shift the supply of loanable funds to the left, resulting in a higher equilibrium real interest rate.
27	d	When the government runs a budget surplus it provides funds to financial markets by paying off more old bonds than it issues new bonds—there is positive public saving. When government spending is greater than government tax revenues, there is negative public saving. Negative saving is also referred to as dissaving. Therefore, the deficit reduces the total amount of savings in the economy.
28	a	A recent study found that increasing government borrowing by an amount equal to one percent of GDP would increase the equilibrium real interest rate by only about three one-hundredths of a percentage point. However, this small effect on interest rates does not imply that we can ignore the effect of deficits on economic growth. The paying of government debt in the future may require higher taxes, which can depress economic growth.
29	b	For example, consider someone who puts her savings in a certificate of deposit at an interest rate of 4 percent and whose tax rate is 25 percent. Under an income tax, this person's after-tax return to saving is 3 percent ($4 \times (1 - 0.25)$). Under a consumption tax where savings are not taxed, the return rises to 4 percent. We can conclude that moving from an income tax to a consumption tax would increase the return to saving, causing the supply of loanable funds to increase.
30	b	The period of expansion ends with a business cycle peak. Following the business cycle peak, production, employment, and income decline as the economy enters the recession phase of the cycle.
31	c	The NBER is fairly slow in announcing business cycle dates because it takes time to gather and analyze economic statistics. Typically, the NBER will announce that the economy is in a recession only well after the recession has begun. (Sometimes the NBER Business Cycles Committee continues to debate the exact dates on which a recession began and ended for several years after the recession is over. For example, the debate about when the 2001 recession ended continued well into 2004.)
32	d	As the economy nears the end of an expansion, interest rates are usually rising, and the wages of workers are usually rising faster than prices. As a result of rising interest rates and rising wages, the profits of firms will be falling. Typically, toward the end of an expansion, both households and firms will have substantially increased their debts.
33	b	Typically, toward the end of an expansion, both households and firms will have substantially increased their debts.
34	b	The phases of the business cycle are the trough, the expansion, the peak, and the contraction followed by a trough and another cycle.
35	a	Consumer durables are affected more by the business cycle than are nondurables—such as food and clothing—or services—such haircuts or medical care. Because people can often continue to use their existing furniture, appliances, or automobiles, they are more likely to postpone spending on durables than on other goods.

36	a	During economic expansions, the inflation rate usually increases, particularly near the end of the expansion, and during recessions, the inflation rate usually decreases. In every recession since 1950, the inflation rate has been lower during the 12 months after the recession ended than it was during the 12 months before the recession began.
37	d	Recessions cause the inflation rate to fall, but they cause the unemployment rate to increase.
38	b	The reluctance of firms to hire new employees during the early stages of a recovery means that the unemployment rate usually continues to rise even after the recession has ended.
39	a	Before 1950, real GDP went through much greater year-to-year fluctuations than it has since that time. During the past 50 years, the American economy has not experienced anything similar to the sharp fluctuations in real GDP that occurred during the early 1930s.
40	d	The minimum wage has nothing to do with the stability of the economy.
41	a	During the last half of the twentieth century, the U.S. economy experienced long expansions, interrupted by relatively short recessions.
42	c	As services, such as medical care or investment advice, have become a much larger fraction of GDP, there has been a corresponding decline in the production of goods.
43	b	These and other government programs make it possible for workers who lose their jobs during recessions to have higher incomes and, therefore, to spend more than they would otherwise. This additional spending may have helped to shorten recessions.
44	b	Because the Great Depression was so severe, with the unemployment rate rising to more than 25 percent of the labor force and real GDP declining by almost 30 percent, public opinion changed towards favoring attempts by the government to stabilize the economy. In the Employment Act of 1946, the federal government committed itself to "foster and promote…conditions under which there will be afforded useful employment to those able, willing, and seeking to work; and to promote maximum employment, production, and purchasing power."
45	c	Many economists believe that these government policies have played a key role in stabilizing the economy in the years since 1950, but other economists disagree. These economists argue that far from helping to stabilize the economy, active policy has kept the economy from becoming even more stable.

Short Answer Responses

1. If the rate of growth of population is greater than the rate of growth of real GDP, then real GDP per capita will decrease and the standard of living is likely to decline.

2. Investment spending includes (1) the purchase of capital goods by firms, including new factories, office buildings, and machinery used to produced other goods, (2) changes in business inventories, and (3) new residential construction. If the purchase of new capital goods exceeds the level of depreciation (the amount of capital worn out by current production), the capital stock will increase.

3.

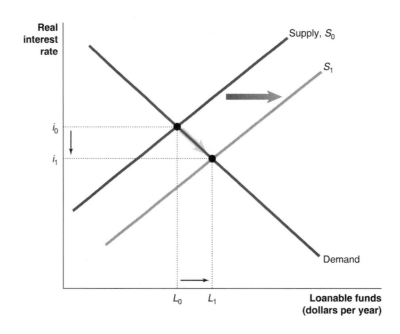

The increased desire to save by the public will shift the supply of loanable funds to the right, from $Supply_0$ to $Supply_1$. This will cause the real interest rate to fall from i_0 to i_1. The equilibrium quantity of loanable funds will increase from L_0 to L_1.

4. During expansion, the unemployment rate usually falls and the inflation rate usually rises. During recession, the unemployment rate usually rises and the inflation rate usually falls. On average, inflation is about 2.5 percentage points lower in the year after a recession than for the year before the recession. Also, on average, unemployment is about 1.5 percentage points higher the year after a recession than the year before a recession.

5. Unemployment insurance is an economic cushion. When the economy slips into a recession, some individuals will lose jobs. Unemployment insurance replaces some of the lost income and allows families to continue to buy goods and services. This makes the recession milder because spending does not fall as much as it would have if these families had no funds to spend. At the same time, unemployment insurance payments may reduce the incentive for those unemployed to take a new job quickly.

6. Based on the given information, the growth rates for the years are as given in the table (for example, the growth rate in 2003 is calculated as $100 \times [(1,174,592 - 1,152,905)/1,152,905] = 1.9$ percent). Note that because data for 2001 are not given, we cannot calculate the 2002 growth rate.

Year	Real GDP (millions of 2002 Canadian dollars)	Growth Rates
2002	$1,152,905	-
2003	1,174,592	1.9%
2004	1,210,656	3.1
2005	1,247,780	3.1
2006	1,282,204	2.8

The average growth rate for this period was 2.725 (or 2.7%) (=1.9 + 3.1 + 3.1 + 2.8)/4). According to the Rule of 70, the number of years for the economy to double is 25.7 (=70/2.725).

True/False Answers

1.	F	Because of the business cycle, GDP per capita does not always rise.
2.	T	
3.	T	
4.	F	Growing labor productivity is the major source of economic growth.
5.	T	
6.	T	
7.	F	Government saving is only positive if there is a budget surplus.
8.	F	An increase in the real interest rate caused by a decrease in the supply of loanable funds will reduce quantity demanded and cause a movement along the demand curve.
9.	T	
10.	T	
11.	F	The dates are determined by the National Bureau of Economic Research (which is not a government agency).
12.	T	
13.	F	Recessions have gotten shorter in the last 50 years. Today, a recession usually lasts less than a year.
14.	T	
15.	T	

Chapter 10 (22)

Long-Run Economic Growth: Sources and Policies

Chapter Summary

In the long run, a country will experience an increasing standard of living only if it experiences continuing technological change. This chapter looks at differences in economic growth rates over time and between countries. Because of diminishing returns to capital, sustained growth can only occur with technological change, which allows the economy to produce more output with the same quantities of inputs.

Until around the year 1300 A.D., most people survived with barely enough food. Living standards began to rise significantly only after the **Industrial Revolution** began in England in the 1700s with the application of mechanical power to the production of goods. The best measure of a country's standard of living is its level of real GDP per capita.

An **economic growth model** explains changes in real GDP per capita in the long run. **Labor productivity** is the quantity of goods and services that can be produced by one worker or by one hour of work. Economic growth depends on increases in labor productivity. **Technological change** is a change in the ability of a firm to produce a given level of output with a given quantity of inputs. There are three main sources of technological change: better machinery and equipment, increases in human capital, and better means of organizing and managing production. **Human capital** is the accumulated knowledge and skills that workers acquire from education and training or from their life experiences. **The per-worker production function** shows the relationship between capital per hour worked and output per hour worked, holding technology constant. *Diminishing returns to capital* means that increases in the quantity of capital per hour worked will result in diminishing increases in output per hour worked.

Technological change shifts up the per-worker production function, resulting in more output per hour worked at every level of capital per hour worked. The economic growth model stresses the importance of changes in capital per hour worked and technological change in explaining growth in output per hour worked. *New growth theory* is a model of long-run economic growth that emphasizes that technological change is influenced by how individuals and firms respond to economic incentives. One way governments can promote technological change is by granting **patents**, which are exclusive rights to a product for a period of 20 years from the date the product is invented.

The economic growth model predicts that poor countries will grow faster than rich countries, resulting in **catch-up**. In recent decades, some poor countries have grown faster than rich countries, but many have not. Some poor countries do not experience rapid growth for four main reasons: wars and revolutions, poor public education and health, failure to enforce the rule of law, and low rates of saving and investment. The **rule of law** refers to the ability of a government to enforce the laws of the country, particularly with respect to protecting private property and enforcing contracts. **Globalization** has aided countries that have opened their economies to foreign trade and investment. **Foreign direct investment (FDI)** is the purchase or building by a corporation of a facility in a foreign country. **Foreign portfolio investment** is the purchase by an individual or firm of stock or bonds issued in another country.

Learning Objectives

When you finish this chapter, you should be able to:

1. **Define economic growth, calculate economic growth rates, and describe global trends in economic growth.** Until 1300 A.D. most people survived with barely enough to eat. Living standards began to rise significantly only after the **Industrial Revolution** began in England in the 1700s. The best measure of a country's standard of living is its level of real GDP per capita (real GDP per capita means the same thing as real GDP per person). Economic growth occurs when real GDP per capita increases, thereby increasing the country's standard of living.

2. **Use the economic growth model to explain why growth rates differ across countries. Labor productivity** is the quantity of goods and services that can be produced by one worker or by one hour of work. Economic growth depends on increases in labor productivity. Labor productivity will increase if there is an increase in the amount of capital available to each worker and if there is a change in technology. There are three main sources of change in technology:

   - better machinery and equipment,
   - increases in **human capital** (accumulated knowledge and skills), and
   - better means of organizing and managing production.

   To sum up, we can say: An economy will have a higher standard of living the more capital it has per hour worked, the more human capital its workers have, the better its capital, and the better the job its business managers do in organizing production. The **per-worker production function** shows the relationship between capital per hour worked and output per hour worked, holding technology constant. Diminishing returns to capital mean that increases in the quantity of capital per hour worked will result in diminishing increases in output per hour worked. Technological change shifts up the per-worker production function, resulting in more output per hour worked at every level of capital per hour worked. The economic growth model stresses the importance of changes in capital per hour worked and technological change in explaining growth in output per hour worked. New growth theory, as first developed by Paul Romer, is a model of long-run economic growth that emphasizes the way technological change is influenced by economic incentives, and so is determined by the working of the market system. To Joseph Schumpeter, the entrepreneur is central to the "creative destruction" by which the standard of living increases as qualitatively better products replace existing products.

3. **Discuss fluctuations in productivity growth in the United States.** Productivity in the United States grew rapidly from the end of World War II until the mid 1970s. Growth then slowed down for 20 years before increasing again after 1995. Economists continue to debate the reasons for the growth slowdown of the mid-1970s to mid-1990s. Possible explanations for the productivity slowdown are: measurement problems, high oil prices, and a decline in labor quality. Because Western Europe and Japan experienced a productivity slowdown at the same time as the United States, explanations that focus on factors affecting only the United States are unlikely to be correct. Some economists argue that the faster growth in productivity beginning in the mid-1990s reflects the development of a New Economy based on information technology. In the period since the mid-1990's, growth in the United States has been significantly higher than in other leading industrial nations. Many economists believe

that this is due to the greater flexibility in U.S. labor markets and the greater efficiency of the U.S. financial system.

4. **Explain economic catch-up and discuss why many poor countries have not experienced rapid economic growth.** The economic growth model predicts that poor countries will grow faster than rich countries, resulting in **catch-up**. In recent decades, some poor countries have grown faster than rich countries, but many have not. Four main reasons have been offered to explain why some poor countries do not experience rapid growth:

- wars and revolutions,
- poor public education and health,
- failure to enforce the rule of law, and
- low rates of saving and investment.

Globalization has aided countries that have opened their economies to foreign trade and investment.

5. **Discuss government policies that foster economic growth.** Governments can attempt to increase economic growth through policies that enhance property rights and the rule of law, improve health and education, subsidize research and development, and provide incentives for saving and investment. Whether continued economic growth is desirable is a normative question that cannot be settled by economic analysis.

Chapter Review

Chapter Opener: MySpace Meets the Chinese Economic Miracle (pages 308-309)

MySpace.com has been expanding rapidly into international markets, including China. To protect its investment and to maintain the legality of its operations in China, MySpace has had to search for a Chinese partner to deal with the government regulation of the internet in China. China is not a democracy and the Chinese government still intervenes in the economy in sometimes arbitrary ways. China's lack of a well-established rule of law may make it difficult for the country to sustain the high levels of entrepreneurial activity that have been the key to its recent rapid growth.

> 📖 Helpful Study Hint
>
> Read *An Inside Look* at the end of the chapter for a news article from *The Economist* on why Europe's economy has been unable to grow at rates similar to those of the United States. The article cites lack of innovation as the key reason.
>
> Would you be better off without China? *Economics in YOUR Life!* at the start of this chapter poses this question. Keep the question in mind as you read the chapter. The authors will answer the question at the end of the chapter.

10.1 Economic Growth Over Time and Around the World (pages 310–314)

Learning Objective 1 Define economic growth, calculate growth rates, and describe global trends in economic growth.

There was not any significant economic growth in the world until the Industrial Revolution, which started in England around the year 1750. Estimates suggest that growth averaged about 0.2 percent per year in the 500 years before the Industrial Revolution and averaged about 1.3 percent per year in the 100 years after the Industrial Revolution. The Industrial Revolution probably started in England because of political changes that gave entrepreneurs the incentive to invest in the important technological inventions of the time, such as the steam engine.

The rate of economic growth is important because increasing growth rates allow for higher standards of living, which bring not only larger selections of goods but also health and education. Over long periods of time, small differences in economic growth rates have large effects, because compounding magnifies the effects of even slightly higher economic growth rates.

We can divide the world's countries into two groups, higher income countries, sometimes called industrial countries and poorer countries, sometimes called developing countries. In 2006, per capita GDP ranged from $68,000 in Luxembourg to only $600 in Somalia.

📖 Helpful Study Hint

You have probably read about the Industrial Revolution in some of your other classes. Read *Making the Connection: Why Did the Industrial Revolution Begin in England?* For an economic perspective on the reasons the revolution took root in England rather than in another country, such as China or India.

As a result of the Glorious Revolution of 1668, the British Parliament, rather than the king, controlled the British government. The British court system was also independent of the king. As a result, the British government was able to credibly commit to upholding private property rights, protecting wealth, and eliminating arbitrary increases in taxes. These institutional changes gave entrepreneurs the incentive to make the investments necessary to use the important technological developments of the second half of the eighteenth century—particularly the spinning jenny and the water frame, which were used in the production of cotton textiles, and the steam engine, which was used in mining and in the manufacture of textiles and other products.

You probably own many items that are stamped with "Made in China." So, you may be surprised to learn that the standard of living in China has not kept pace with that of Japan. Why not? For an answer, read *Making the Connection: The Benefits of an Earlier Start: Standards of Living in China and Japan.* During the time period 1950-1978, the economic growth rate in Japan was large compared to the economic growth rate in China. More recently, in the 1996-2006 time period, the growth rate pattern has reversed with China growing at an average annual rate of 9.1 percent, while the growth rate for Japan has been 2.1 percent. Despite China's stronger growth rate, China has still not caught up with Japan. Japanese real GDP per capita is four times the amount in China, and Japan has longer life expectancy, lower infant mortality rate, and higher percentages of the population with access to treated water and improved sanitation.

When economists talk about growth rates over periods of more than one year, they are talking about *average* annual growth rates, not total percentage changes. Read ***Don't Let This Happen To You: Don't Confuse the Average Annual Percentage Change with the Total Percentage Change***. Between 1950 and 2006, real GDP per capita in the United States increased by a total of 224 percent, but the average increase per year was 2.1 percent.

Extra Solved Problem 10-1

Chapter 10 of the textbook includes two Solved Problems. Here is an extra Solved Problem to help you build your skills solving economic problems:

Economic Growth Rates

Supports Learning Objective 1: Define economic growth, calculate economic growth rates, and describe global trends in economic growth.

The table below has data on per capita real GDP for three Western European countries (in U.S. Dollars):

Year	France	Spain	United Kingdom
2000	$27,522	$22,599	$27,946
2001	27,835	23,045	28,494
2002	27,922	23,221	28,978
2003	28,032	23,549	29,634
2004	28,539	23,925	30,458
2005	28,855	24,349	30,853
2006	29,253	24,948	31,618

For each of these countries, calculate the average growth rate over this time period.

SOLVING THE PROBLEM

Step 1:   Review the chapter material.
This problem is about computing economic growth rates, so you may want to review the section "Economic Growth Over Time and Around the World," which begins on page 310 in the textbook.

Step 2: **Calculate average growth rate.**

The total growth rates for the whole period from 2000 to 2006 would be computed as:

$$\text{Growth rate} = \frac{\text{Per capita GDP in 2006} - \text{Per capita GDP in 2000}}{\text{Per capita GDP in 2000}} \times 100$$

But we are interested in the average annual growth rate, which means we have to compute the growth each year and then average the values we obtain. For instance, to compute the average growth rate for the year 2001, we need to compute the percentage change in per capita GDP from 2000 to 2001:

$$\text{Growth rate in 2001} = \frac{\text{Per capita GDP in 2001} - \text{Per capita GDP in 2000}}{\text{Per capita GDP in 2000}} \times 100$$

For France, this value is:

$$\text{Growth rate in 2001} = \left(\frac{\$27,835 - \$27,522}{\$27,522} \right) \times 100 = 1.14\%.$$

The values for each country and each year are in the table below. The average annual growth rates are the averages of the growth rates for these years. For instance, for Spain the average annual growth rate is:

$$\frac{1.97\% + 0.76\% + 1.41\% + 1.60\% + 1.77\% + 2.46\%}{6} = 1.66\%.$$

Year	France		Spain		United Kingdom	
	GDP per capita	Growth rate	GDP per capita	Growth rate	GDP per capita	Growth rate
2000	$27,522	–	$22,599	–	$27,946	-
2001	27,835	1.14%	23,045	1.97%	28,494	1.96%
2002	27,922	0.31	23,221	0.76	28,978	1.70
2003	28,032	0.39	23,549	1.41	29,634	2.26
2004	28,539	1.81	23,925	1.60	30,458	2.78
2005	28,855	1.11	24,349	1.77	30,853	1.30
2006	29,253	1.38	24,948	2.46	31,618	2.48
Average annual growth rate		1.02%		1.66%		2.08%

10.2 What Determines How Fast Economies Grow? (pages 315–321)

Learning Objective 2   Use the economic growth model to explain why growth rates differ across countries.

An **economic growth model** explains growth rates in real GDP per capita. Growth requires that the average worker produce more goods per time period. By definition, this means **labor productivity** increases over time. Labor productivity grows with increases in the quantity of capital per worker and with **technological change.** Technological change occurs through better machinery and equipment, increases in human capital, and better means of organizing production. The **per-worker production function** exhibits diminishing returns to capital as long as technology does not change. Diminishing returns to capital are illustrated in textbook Figure 10-3.

Increases in the capital-labor ratio, given the level of technology, will result in increases in output per worker. However, because of diminishing returns to capital, as the capital-labor ratio grows, the size of the increases in output per worker will get smaller. Long-term economic growth requires more than just growth in capital. It also needs technological change. Technological change shifts up the per-worker production function, resulting in more output with the same level of resources. Shifts in the per-worker production function are due to technological changes, as shown in Figure 10-4 in the textbook.

📖 Helpful Study Hint

Changes in capita per worker cause movements along a single per-worker production function, while changes in technology cause shifts in the per-worker production function. An upward shift in the production function means that the economy can produce more with the same level of capital per worker.

Over time, living standards can increase only if a country experiences continual technological change. Paul Romer, an economist at Stanford University, argues that technological change is influenced by economic incentives. Romer's approach is referred to as the **new growth theory**. In this theory, the accumulation of knowledge capital is a key determinant of economic growth because knowledge capital is subject to increasing returns. This is true because once discovered, knowledge becomes available to everyone. Government policy can help increase the accumulation of knowledge capital by protecting intellectual property rights with patents and copyrights, subsidizing research and development, and subsidizing education.

📖 Helpful Study Hint

From 1917-1991, the Soviet Union was a centrally planned economy. The government decided what goods to produce, how to produce them, and who would receive them. To learn the details of why that country's system failed, read *Making the Connection: Why did the Soviet Union's Economy Fail?* A crucial requirement for growth is implementing new technologies. In a centrally planned economy, the people in charge of running most businesses are government employees and not entrepreneurs or independent business people, as is the case in market economies. Soviet managers had little incentive to adopt new ways of doing things. Their pay depended on producing the quantity of output specified in the government's economic plan, not on discovering new, better, and lower-cost ways to produce goods.

10.3 Economic Growth in the United States (pages 322–326)

Learning Objective 3 Discuss fluctuations in productivity growth in the United States.

Economic growth rates in the United States have varied over time. From 1950 to 1973, real GDP per hour worked grew at an annual rate of 2.6 percent. Growth then slowed to 1.3 percent per year during the period from 1973 until 1995. This slowdown in productivity growth is usually linked to measurement problems caused by the increase in the service sector of the economy and difficulties measuring increases in safety and environmental improvements, the rapid increase in oil prices, and the mismatch of worker skills with the increase in the number of jobs requiring greater technical training. Growth rates since 1995 have increased, partly due to the use of computers and information technology in the workplace. Growth rates in the United States have been faster than in other countries since 1995 probably because of the flexibility of U.S. labor markets and the greater efficiency of the U.S. financial system.

📖 Helpful Study Hint

Remember, as we saw in Chapter 9, the financial system is where the funds of savers are loaned to borrowers. This process allows loanable funds to flow from households to firms that use the funds for new investment projects.

Extra Solved Problem 10-3

Chapter 10 of the textbook includes two Solved Problems. Here is an extra Solved Problem to help you build your skills solving economic problems:

Output and Productivity Growth Rates

Supports Learning Objective 3: Discuss fluctuations in productivity growth in the United States.

The Bureau of Labor Statistics collects data on U.S. productivity. The table below lists an index of total manufacturing output and an index of manufacturing output per hour worked, which is a measure of productivity in the manufacturing sector. The base year for both indexes is 1992 (in other words, the level of manufacturing output and manufacturing output per hour worked for 1992 are both set equal to 100). Consequently, a value of 128.6 (as in manufacturing output for 1997) indicates that the value of output in 1997 was 1.286 times the value of output in 1992, or that output has increased by 28.6 percent since 1992. Calculate the average annual growth rate in output and in output per hour worked for this period from 1998 to 2006. Are the growth rates for the two indexes the same? If they are different, what are the implications of the difference?

Year	Index of manufacturing output	Index of manufacturing output per hour worked
1997	128.6	121.3
1998	135.2	127.9
1999	140.3	133.5
2000	144.2	138.9
2001	136.8	141.1
2002	135.9	150.8
2003	137.3	160.1
2004	139.7	163.5
2005	144.6	171.3
2006	151.7	178.2

SOLVING THE PROBLEM

Step 1: **Review the chapter material.**

This problem is about growth in productivity, so you may want to review the section "Economic Growth in the United States," which begins on page 322.

Step 2: **Calculate the growth rates.**

You can calculate the growth rates using the following equation:

$$\text{Growth rate in 1998} = \left(\frac{\text{Value in 1998} - \text{Value in 1997}}{\text{Value in 1997}} \right) \times 100.$$

Using this formula for both columns of data gives us:

Year	Index of manufacturing output	Growth rate of manufacturing output	Index of manufacturing output per hour worked	Growth rate of manufacturing output per hour worked
1997	128.6	–	121.3	–
1998	135.2	5.1%	127.9	5.4%
1999	140.3	3.8	133.5	4.4
2000	144.2	2.8	138.9	4.0
2001	136.8	−5.1	141.1	1.6
2002	135.9	−0.7	150.8	6.9
2003	137.3	1.0	160.1	6.2
2004	139.7	1.7	163.5	2.1
2005	144.6	3.5	171.3	4.8
2006	151.7	4.9	178.2	4.0
Average annual growth rate, 1998-2006		1.9%		4.4%

Step 3: **Discuss why the growth rates are different.**

The average annual growth rate in manufacturing output is 1.9%, while the average annual growth in manufacturing output per worker is 4.4%. How is it possible for output per hour worked to increase at a faster rate than total output? This can only happen if the number of hours worked in manufacturing has decreased during this period.

10.4 LEARNING OBJECTIVE

10.4 Why Isn't the Whole World Rich? (pages 327–334)

Learning Objective 4 Explain economic catch-up and discuss why many poor countries have not experienced rapid economic growth.

The economic growth model tells us that economies grow when the quantity of capital per hour worked increases and when technological change takes place. Growth in capital and technology will have their biggest payoffs in poorer economies. This suggests that poorer countries should grow faster than rich countries. The prediction that poorer countries should grow faster than rich countries is called **catch-up** or **convergence**. The growth data suggests that convergence applies to some, but not all, countries. Economists have suggested several reasons why a number of low income countries have not experienced rapid growth:

- A legal system that does not enforce contracts and protect property rights. In other words, some countries have failed to establish the "rule of law."
- Wars and revolutions.

- Poor public education and health.
- Low levels of saving and investment.

Globalization, the process of countries becoming more open to foreign trade and investment, can help poorer countries that have low levels of domestic saving and investment and that lack access to the latest technologies. Foreign direct investment (FDI) occurs when firms build or purchase facilities in foreign countries. This inflow of capital can help speed development. Foreign portfolio investment occurs when individuals buy stock or bonds issued in other countries. This access to new capital can also speed growth. The process of globalization can help countries deal with the problem of low saving and investment.

10.5 Growth Policies (pages 334–336)

Learning Objective 5   Discuss government policies that foster economic growth.

Governments can do many things to help promote long-run economic growth. Policies that help enforce property rights and reduce corruption will encourage investment and contribute to economic growth. Policies that support health and education lead to increases in productivity and higher levels of growth. Policies that encourage technological innovation, such as subsidizing research and development or encouraging direct foreign investment, will also increase growth. Policies that encourage saving generate more funds for financing investment and will also encourage growth.

Extra Solved Problem 10-5

Chapter 10 of the textbook includes two Solved Problems. Here is an extra Solved Problem to help you build your skills solving economic problems:

Investment Tax Credits

Supports Learning Objective 5: Discuss government policies that foster economic growth.

The government can increase the incentive for firms to acquire physical capital through investment tax credits. An investment tax credit allows firms to deduct from their taxes some fraction of the funds they have spent on investment goods. The reduction in the taxes that firms pay increases their after-tax profits, thereby increasing their incentive to invest in new factories, offices, and machines. There are two ways that an investment tax credit can affect growth in the economy. Use separate per-worker production function graphs to illustrate each way the investment tax credit can affect economic growth.

Step 1:   **Review the chapter material.**
This problem is about government policies to foster economic growth, so you may want to review the section "Policies with Respect to Saving and Investment," which begins on page 336 in the textbook.

Step 2:   **Draw two per-worker production function graphs to illustrate the effects of the investment tax credit.**
As firms increase investment spending as a result of the investment tax credit, the capital stock will also increase. If the new capital has the same technology as the existing capital

stock, then the level of technology will not change. In this case, the new capital will increase the ratio of capital to labor and cause a movement along the per-worker production function. You can illustrate this with the graph below as a movement from point A to point B.

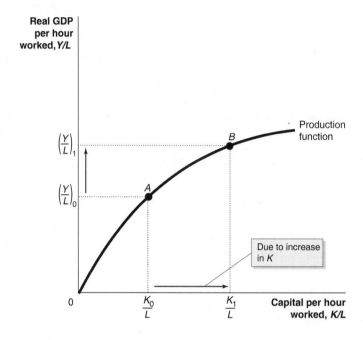

Notice that at point B, the increases in capital as a result of the new investment will result in more production as real GDP per hour worked increases.

If the new capital causes a change in the level of technology, then the new capital will also cause the production function to shift upward. So, the investment tax credit will cause both a movement along the per-worker production function and an upward shift as the level of technology changes. You can illustrate this with the graph below as a movement from point A to point B:

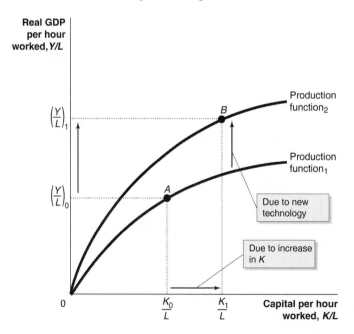

📖 Helpful Study Hint

You have probably read news stories or had class discussions about globalization. Read *Making the Connection: Globalization and the Spread of Technology in Bangladesh*. Clothing manufacturing began in Bangladesh in 1980 when Noorul Quader started Desh Garments. To obtain critical training for his employees, Quader reached an agreement with Daewoo Corporation in South Korea. Under their agreement, Quader was responsible for running the Bangladesh clothing factory, while Daewoo would train 130 workers in the Daewoo plants in Korea. As a result of this training, shirt production rose from 43,000 shirts in 1980 to 2.3 million shirts by 1987.

📖 Helpful Study Hint

At the start of the chapter, the *Economics in YOUR Life!* feature asked if you would choose to live in a world with the Chinese economy very poor and growing slowly (as it was before 1978) or a world where the Chinese economy is growing very rapidly (as it is today). The rapid economic growth that has enabled Chinese firms to be competitive with firms in the United States has been a benefit to you as a consumer; you have lower-priced goods and better goods available to buy than you would if China had remained very poor.

Key Terms

Catch-up. The prediction that the level of GDP per capita (or income per capita) in poor countries will grow faster than in rich countries.

Economic growth model. A model that explains changes in real GDP per capita in the long run.

Foreign direct investment (FDI). The purchase or construction of a facility by a corporation in a foreign country.

Foreign portfolio investment. The purchase by an individual or firm of stock or bonds issued in another country.

Globalization. The process of countries becoming more open to foreign trade and investment.

Human capital. The accumulated knowledge and skills that workers acquire from education and training or from their life experiences.

Industrial Revolution. The application of mechanical power to the production of goods, beginning in England around 1750.

Labor productivity. The quantity of goods and services that can be produced by one worker or by one hour of work.

New growth theory.   A model of long-run economic growth that emphasizes that technological change is influenced by economic incentives, and so is determined by the working of the market system.

Patent.   The exclusive right to a product for a period of 20 years from the date the product was invented.

Per-worker production function.   The relationship between real GDP, or output, per hour worked and capital per hour worked, holding the level of technology constant.

Property rights. The rights individuals or firms have to the exclusive use of their property, including the right to buy or sell it.

Rule of law. The ability of a government to enforce the laws of the country, particularly with respect to protecting private property and enforcing contracts.

Technological change. Change in the quantity of output that a firm can produce from a given quantity of inputs.

Self-Test

(Answers are provided at the end of the Self-Test.)

Multiple-Choice Questions

1. What is the best measure we have of a country's standard of living?
    a.   the unemployment rate
    b.   nominal GDP per capita
    c.   real GDP per capita
    d.   the inflation rate

2. Which of the following marks the beginning of significant economic growth in the world economy?
    a.   the victory of Mao Zedong and the Communist Party in China in 1949
    b.   the American Revolution of 1776
    c.   the Industrial Revolution in England
    d.   the Bolshevik Revolution

3. Which of these institutional changes gave entrepreneurs the incentive to make the investments necessary for technological development in the second half of the eighteenth century in England?
    a.   upholding private property rights
    b.   protecting wealth
    c.   eliminating arbitrary increases in taxes
    d.   all of the above

4. The process known as *compounding* does which of the following?
    a.   It minimizes the differences in interest rates or growth rates over short periods of time.
    b.   It magnifies even small differences in interest rates or growth rates over long periods of time.
    c.   It highlights the social characteristics necessary for economic growth to occur.
    d.   It magnifies the importance of the effect of inflation on increases in the standard of living of the typical person.

5. In the 1980s and 1990s, a small group of countries experienced high rates of growth. These countries are sometimes referred to as the *newly industrializing countries*. Where are they located?
   a. in East Asia
   b. in Africa
   c. in Latin America
   d. in Western Europe

6. What is the economic growth model?
   a. a model that explains trends in labor productivity
   b. a model that explains changes in real GDP per capita in the long run
   c. a model that explains how the interaction of inflation and unemployment accounts for most economic growth
   d. a model that explains why economic fluctuations and the business cycle occur

7. Which of the following are the two key factors that determine labor productivity?
   a. economic growth and real GDP per capita
   b. the amount of land and capital available in a country
   c. government policies that promote household consumption
   d. the quantity of capital per hour worked and the level of technology

8. Better machinery and equipment, increases in human capital, and better means of organizing and managing production are the three main sources of
   a. rising unemployment.
   b. increases in capital per hour worked.
   c. technological change.
   d. increases in inflation.

9. The accumulated knowledge and skills that workers acquire from education, training, and their life experiences are called
   a. labor productivity.
   b. technical knowledge.
   c. physical capital.
   d. human capital.

10. What is the name given to the relationship between real GDP per hour worked and capital per hour worked, holding the level of technology constant?
    a. the output growth function
    b. the capital-labor function
    c. the per-worker production function
    d. the production possibilities frontier

11. Along the per-worker production function, what happens to real GDP per hour worked as capital per hour worked increases?
    a. Real GDP per hour worked increases at an increasing rate.
    b. Real GDP per hour worked increases at a decreasing rate.
    c. Real GDP per hour worked decreases at an increasing rate.
    d. Real GDP per hour worked decreases at a decreasing rate.

12. The law of diminishing returns states that as we add more of one input to a fixed quantity of another input, output increases by smaller additional amounts. In the case of the per-worker production function, which input is the fixed input, and which one is the variable input?
    a. Capital is the fixed input and labor is the variable input.
    b. Capital is the variable input and labor is the fixed input.
    c. Capital is the variable input and real GDP is the fixed input.
    d. Real GDP is the variable input and capital is the fixed input.

13. The *per-worker production function* exhibits
    a. diminishing returns to labor.
    b. diminishing returns to capital.
    c. diminishing returns to real GDP per capita.
    d. all of the above

14. The per-worker production function
    a. shows that equal increases in capital per worker cause equal increases in output per hour worked.
    b. shifts up with increases in labor hours worked.
    c. shifts up with increases in technology.
    d. shifts up with increases in capital at a given level of technology.

15. A movement along the per-worker production function is *not* caused by
    a. an increase in technology.
    b. an increase in capital at a given level of technology.
    c. an increase in hours worked per worker.
    d. an increase in the number of workers.

16. What is the impact of technological change on the per-worker production function?
    a. As technological change occurs, the economy moves from one point to another along the per-worker production function.
    b. Technological change shifts the per-worker production function up.
    c. Technological change does not affect the per-worker production function.
    d. Technological change may or may not affect the per worker production function depending on how it affects the quantity of capital per worker.

17. In the long run, a country will experience an increasing standard of living only if
    a. the country's labor force increases.
    b. the country's capital stock increases.
    c. the country experiences continuing technological change.
    d. all of the above

18. In which economies is there a greater incentive for technological change?
    a. in centrally planned economies
    b. in market economies
    c. in countries with high inflation rates
    d. in countries that lack patent laws

19. Which of the following is known as the *new growth theory*?
    a. a growth model that focuses on growth in the ratio of capital to labor as the key factor in explaining long-run growth in real GDP per capita
    b. the economic growth model that was first developed in the 1950s by Robert Solow, an economist at MIT and winner of the Nobel Prize in Economics
    c. a model of long-run economic growth that emphasizes that technological change is influenced by economic incentives
    d. a model of long-run economic growth that emphasizes that increases in technology are difficult to explain

20. When are additions of knowledge capital subject to diminishing returns?
    a. when they are made at the firm level
    b. when they apply to the economy as a whole
    c. when those additions don't contribute to economic growth
    d. when the additions are due to improved education for workers

21. Which of the following is *not* a government policy that will increase the accumulation of knowledge capital?
    a. encouraging the growth of labor unions
    b. subsidizing research and development
    c. protecting intellectual property with patents and copyrights
    d. subsidizing education

22. Which of the following is nonrival and nonexcludable?
    a. labor hired by a firm
    b. a prescription drug purchased by a consumer
    c. the use of physical capital
    d. the use of knowledge capital that is not protected by a patent or copyright

23. In which case are firms more likely to try to be *free riders*?
    a. in using physical capital owned by other firms
    b. in using labor hired by other firms
    c. in using the research and development of other firms
    d. in paying taxes

24. How can government policy help increase the accumulation of knowledge capital and bring it closer to the optimal level?
    a. by protecting intellectual property with patents and copyrights
    b. by subsidizing research and development
    c. by subsidizing education
    d. all of the above

25. According to Joseph Schumpeter, which of the following provides the most important incentive for bringing the factors of production together to start new firms and to introduce new goods and services?
    a. the accumulation of knowledge capital
    b. government policies that help to increase the accumulation of physical capital
    c. the profits entrepreneurs hope to earn
    d. the existence of export markets

26. Which of the following periods in U.S. economic history had the slowest growth rate, as measured by the average annual increase in real GDP per hour worked?
    a. 1900-1950
    b. 1950-1973
    c. 1973-1995
    d. 1995-2004

27. Which of the following are explanations that have been offered for the productivity slowdown of the mid-1970s to mid-1990s?
    a. measurement problems
    b. high oil prices
    c. a decline in labor quality
    d. all of the above

28. According to economists, a major factor in the faster growth in productivity beginning in the mid-1990s was
    a. the fact that services, such as haircuts and financial advice, became a larger fraction of GDP and goods.
    b. oil price increases.
    c. the increasing skill and training of workers.
    d. the development of a "new economy" based on information technology.

29. Why has productivity growth in the United States over the last ten years been more rapid than in the other industrialized countries?
    a. because of the greater flexibility of U.S. labor markets and the greater efficiency of the U.S. financial system
    b. because the U.S. government has more restrictive regulations that make the labor and output markets more efficient
    c. because the opportunity cost of being unemployed is lower in the United States than in these other countries
    d. all of the above

30. In comparing growth rates across countries, the economic growth model predicts that
    a. richer countries will grow faster than poorer countries.
    b. poorer countries will grow faster than richer countries.
    c. richer and poorer countries will have the same growth rates.
    d. there is no consistent relationship between the level of per capita GDP and economic growth.

31. In the United States, what is a key source of funds for start-up firms bringing new technologies to market?
    a. loans from commercial banks and other financial institutions
    b. the sale of stock
    c. the sale of bonds
    d. funding from venture capital firms

32. Catch-up, or convergence, is the prediction that the level of GDP per capita (or income per person) in poor countries will
    a. grow faster than in rich countries.
    b. grow slower than in rich countries.
    c. grow at the same pace as the growth in rich countries.
    d. grow at the same rate as the growth rate of capital per hour worked.

33. Which of the following statements about catch-up is correct?
    a. The lower-income industrial countries have been catching up to the higher-income industrial countries.
    b. The developing countries as a group have been catching up to the industrial countries as a group.
    c. both a. and b.
    d. neither a. nor b.

34. Along the downward-sloping catch-up line, a country near the top of the line is
    a. a rich country growing slowly.
    b. a rich country growing rapidly.
    c. a poor country growing rapidly.
    d. a poor country growing slowly.

35. Why do many low-income countries have low growth rates?
    a. because of the failure of governments to enforce the rule of law
    b. because of wars and revolutions
    c. because of poor public education and health
    d. All of the above are reasons why some low-income countries have low growth rates.

36. Which countries grow faster?
    a. countries that have a strong rule of law, such as the Czech Republic, Tunisia, and Israel
    b. countries that have a weak rule of law, such as Haiti, Congo, and Albania
    c. countries that rely on a common law system rather than on a civil law system
    d. None of the above. There is no relationship between the rule of law and economic growth.

37. In the vicious cycle of poverty
    a. households have low incomes.
    b. households save very little.
    c. few funds are available for businesses to borrow.
    d. all of the above

38. What is the name given to the purchase or building of a facility by a corporation in a foreign country?
    a. foreign portfolio investment
    b. foreign diversification investment
    c. foreign financial investment
    d. foreign direct investment

39. Which countries have experienced faster economic growth?
    a. countries that have been generally more open to foreign trade and investment
    b. countries that have relied less on foreign trade and more on their own internal sources of saving and investment
    c. countries that focused on job preservation
    d. countries that avoided globalization

40. The migration of highly educated and successful individuals from developing countries to high-income countries is called
    a. the human portfolio drain.
    b. the brain drain.
    c. the intelligent exodus.
    d. the intellectual outsourcing.

41. One of the lessons from the economic growth model presented in this chapter is that
    a. technological change is more important than increases in physical capital in explaining long-run growth.
    b. technological change is less important than increases in physical capital in explaining long-run growth.
    c. technological change is equally important to increases in physical capital in explaining long-run growth.
    d. technological change is only possible in countries that have already attained a high level of real GDP per capita.

42. Investment tax credits allow
    a. firms to deduct from their taxes some fraction of the funds they have spent on investment.
    b. households to save for retirement by placing funds in 401(k) or 403(b) plans or in Individual Retirement Accounts (IRAs).
    c. firms to deduct from their taxes part of the wages they pay workers.
    d. the government to raise a larger amount of revenue from households.

43. As a generalization, who is opposed to economic growth?
    a. very few people, because economic growth is good for everyone, regardless of income
    b. some people who think that, at least in the high-income countries, further economic growth is not desirable
    c. many people who think that economic growth in low-income countries is undesirable
    d. most politicians in developing countries

44. Which of the following are assertions made by opponents of globalization?
    a. Globalization has undermined the distinctive cultures of many countries.
    b. Globalization has contributed to the avoidance of safety and environmental regulations by multinational firms in low-income countries that they are required to follow in the high-income countries.
    c. Economic growth and globalization may be contributing to global warming, deforestation, and other environmental problems.
    d. all of the above

Short Answer Questions

1. Why do small differences in growth rates among countries matter?

_____

_____

_____

2. Explain the effect on the per-worker production function of an increase in capital per hour worked. Now explain the effect of technological change.

_____

_____

_____

_____

_____

3. What happened to the economy of the Soviet Union? What does the experience of the Soviet economy teach us about the nature of long-run economic growth?

_____

_____

_____

_____

4. What is "catch-up"? Why would we expect catch-up to occur? Has it occurred?

_____

_____

_____

_____

5. The "brain drain" refers to highly-educated and successful individuals leaving developing countries for high-income countries, such as the United States. How does the brain drain affect growth rates in the developing countries that experience it?

_____

_____

_____

_____

True/False Questions

T F 1. Over time, economic growth rates have not significantly changed.

T F 2. The Industrial Revolution began in Japan during the seventeenth century.

T F 3. Small differences in growth rates cause significant differences in living standards in the long run.

T F 4. The standard of living in China is currently significantly higher than the standard of living in Japan.

T F 5. In New Zealand, real GDP per capita grew from $9,664 in 1950 to $18,815 in 2000. This is an average annual growth rate of 95 percent.

T F 6. Human capital is the accumulated knowledge and skills that workers acquire from education, training, and life experiences.

T F 7. An increase in capital per hour worked will shift up the per-worker production function.

T F 8. Diminishing returns to capital mean that as we add more capital to a fixed amount of labor, increases in output will become smaller and smaller.

T F 9. In the long run, a country will experience rising living standards only if it experiences continuing technological change.

T F 10. Paul Romer argues that knowledge capital is subject to increasing returns, unlike physical capital.

T F 11. A patent gives its owner the exclusive right to produce a good for two years.

T F 12. During the years 1973 to 1995, labor productivity increased at a much slower rate than during the period immediately before or immediately after.

T F 13. The catch-up hypothesis suggests that countries with lower levels of real GDP per capita will grow more slowly than countries with higher levels of real GDP per capita.

T F 14. Countries that fail to protect property rights grow at slower rates than countries that succeed in protecting property rights.

T F 15. In the 1990s, there was no difference between the growth rates of more globalized and less globalized countries.

Answers to the Self-Test

Multiple-Choice Questions

Question	Answer	Comment
1	c	Real GDP per capita is the best measure we have of a country's standard of living, because GDP measures a country's total income. Economic growth occurs when real GDP per capita increases.
2	c	Significant economic growth did not begin until the Industrial Revolution, which started in England around the year 1750.
3	d	Upholding private property rights, protecting wealth, and eliminating arbitrary increases in taxes were the institutional changes that gave entrepreneurs the incentive to make the investments necessary to use the important technological developments of the second half of the eighteenth century. Most economists accept the idea that economic growth is not likely to occur unless a country's government provides the right type of institutional framework.

4 b Compounding magnifies even small differences in interest rates or growth rates over long periods of time. The important point to keep in mind is that in the long run, small differences in economic growth rates result in big differences in living standards.

5 a In the 1980s and 1990s, a small group of countries, mostly East Asian countries such as South Korea, Taiwan, and Singapore, experienced high rates of growth and are sometimes referred to as the *newly industrializing countries.*

6 b An economic growth model is a model that explains changes in real GDP per capita in the long run.

7 d Economists believe two key factors determine labor productivity: the quantity of capital per hour worked and the level of technology. Therefore, the economic growth model will focus on technological change and changes over time in the quantity of capital per hour worked in explaining changes in real GDP per capita.

8 c Among the sources of technological change are: better machinery and equipment, increases in human capital, and better means of organizing and managing production.

9 d Human capital is the accumulated knowledge and skills that workers acquire from education, training, and their life experiences. As workers increase their human capital through education or on-the-job training, their productivity will also increase. The more educated workers are, the greater their human capital.

10 c The per-worker production function is the relationship between real GDP (output) per hour worked and capital per hour worked, holding the level of technology constant. Using the per-worker production function, we explored the effects of increases in the amount of capital per hour worked and technological change on economic growth.

11 b Holding technology constant, equal increases in the amount of capital per hour worked lead to diminishing increases in output per hour worked.

12 b As it applies to the per-worker production function, the *law of diminishing returns* states that as we add more of one input—in this case, capital—to a fixed quantity of another input—in this case, labor—output increases by smaller additional amounts.

13 b An increase in capital per hour worked increases real GDP per hour worked, but each additional increase in capital per hour worked results in progressively smaller increases in output per hour worked.

14 c In a per worker production function, changes in capital and labor cause movements along the curve, while changes in technology cause the curve to shift.

15 a In a per worker production function, changes in capital and labor cause movements along the curve, while changes in technology cause the curve to shift.

16 b Technological change shifts the per-worker production function up and allows an economy to produce more real GDP per hour worked with the same quantity of capital per hour worked.

17 c Because of diminishing returns to capital, continuing increases in real GDP per hour worked will only occur if there is technological change. Remember that a country will experience increases in its standard of living only if it experiences increases in real GDP per hour worked. Therefore, we can draw the following important conclusion: *In the long run, a country will experience an increasing standard of living only if it experiences continuing technological change.*

18 b The drive for profit provides an incentive for technological change that centrally planned economies are unable to duplicate. In market economies, decisions on which investments to make and which technologies to adopt are made by entrepreneurs and managers with their own money on the line.

19 c The *new growth theory* is a model of long-run economic growth that emphasizes that technological change is influenced by economic incentives, and, so is determined by the working of the market system.

20	a	We have seen that accumulation of physical capital is subject to diminishing returns: increases in capital per hour worked lead to increases in real GDP per hour worked, but at a decreasing rate. Paul Romer argues that the same is true of knowledge capital, at the firm level. As firms add to their stock of knowledge capital, they will increase their output, but at a decreasing rate. At the level of the economy, however, Romer argues that knowledge capital is subject to increasing returns. This is true because, once discovered, knowledge becomes available to everyone.
21	a	Labor unions do not have a role in the accumulation of knowledge capital and government policy.
22	d	The use of physical capital is rival because if one firm uses it, other firms can't, and excludable because the firm that owns the capital can keep other firms from using it. The use of knowledge capital is nonrival because one firm's use of this knowledge does not interfere with another firm's use of it. Knowledge capital is also nonexcludable because once something like a chemical formula becomes known, it becomes widely available for other firms to use.
23	c	Because knowledge capital is nonrival and nonexcludable, firms will attempt to *free-ride* on the research and development of other firms. Firms free-ride when they benefit from the results of research and development they did not pay for. (Patent law and other legal restrictions on the use of intellectual property can discourage this free riding.)
24	d	All of the above are ways the government can help to increase the accumulation of knowledge capital.
25	c	The profits an entrepreneur hopes to earn provide the incentive for bringing the factors of production—labor, capital, and raw materials—together to start new firms and to introduce new goods and services.
26	c	The growth rate in the United States increased from 1800 through the mid-1970s. Then for more than 20 years, growth slowed before increasing again in the mid-1990s.
27	d	Several explanations—including measurement problems, high oil prices, and a decline in labor quality—have been offered for the productivity slowdown of the mid-1970s to mid-1990s, but none of the explanations is completely satisfying.
28	d	Information technology industries, such as computers, semiconductors, cell phones, computer programming, and computer software, have accounted for as much as one-third of the growth in real GDP in recent years.
29	a	Many economists believe that productivity growth in the United States has been more rapid for two reasons: the greater flexibility of U.S. labor markets and the greater efficiency of the U.S. financial system.
30	b	Because the return to increasing capital and adopting new technologies is generally greater in poor countries than in rich countries, all else being equal, poor countries should grow faster than rich countries.
31	d	Many firms that start to bring new technologies to market obtain funds from *venture capital firms*. Venture capital firms raise funds from institutional investors, such as pension funds, and from wealthy individuals, to invest in startup firms. The owners of venture capital firms closely examine the business plans of startup firms, looking for those that appear most likely to succeed.
32	a	The economic growth model predicts that poor countries will grow faster than rich countries. If this prediction is correct, we should observe poor countries catching up to the rich countries in levels of GDP per capita (or income per person).
33	a	The lower-income *industrial* countries have been catching up to the higher-income industrial countries. But the developing countries as a group have not been catching up to the industrial countries as a group.

34   c   According to the economic growth model, countries that start with lower levels of GDP per capita should grow faster (points near the top of the line) than countries that start with higher levels of GDP per capita (points near the bottom of the line).

35   d   Why are many low-income countries not growing? There is no one answer, but most economists point to four key factors: failure to enforce the rule of law; wars and revolutions; poor public education and health; and low rates of saving and investment.

36   a   The *rule of law* refers to the ability of a government to enforce the laws of the country, particularly with respect to protecting private property and enforcing contracts. The 20 developing countries that have the strongest rule of law, such as the Czech Republic, Tunisia, and Israel, grew more than six times faster during the 1990s than the 20 developing countries that have the weakest rule of law, such as Haiti, Congo, and Albania.

37   d   The low savings rates in developing countries contribute to a *vicious cycle* of poverty. Because households have low incomes, they save very little. Because households save very little, few funds are available for businesses to borrow. Lacking funds, businesses do not invest in the new factories, machinery, and equipment needed for economic growth. Because the economy does not grow, household incomes remain low, as do their savings, and so on.

38   d   Foreign direct investment (FDI) occurs when corporations build or purchase facilities in foreign countries. When an individual or firm buys stock or bonds issued in another country, they are engaging in foreign portfolio investment.

39   a   As Figure 10-11 depicts, countries that were more open to foreign trade and investment grew more than six times faster during the 1980s and 1990s than countries that were less open.

40   b   The rising incomes that result from economic growth can help developing countries deal with the brain drain. The *brain drain* refers to highly educated and successful individuals leaving developing countries for high-income countries.

41   a   One of the lessons from the economic growth model is that technological change is more important than increases in capital in explaining long-run growth. For low-income countries, access to existing technologies is of paramount importance.

42   a   Investment tax credits allow firms to deduct from their taxes some fraction of the funds they have spent on investment.

43   b   It seems undeniable that increasing the growth rates of very low-income countries would help relieve the daily suffering that many people in these countries must endure. But some people are unconvinced that, at least in the high-income countries, further economic growth is not desirable.

44   d   Some people believe that globalization has undermined the distinctive cultures of many countries, as imports of food, clothing, movies, and other goods displace domestically produced goods. We have seen that allowing foreign direct investment is an important way in which low-income countries can gain access to the latest technology. Some people, however, see multinational firms that locate in low-income countries as paying very low wages, and as failing to follow the same safety and environmental regulations they are required to follow in the high-income countries.

Short Answer Responses

1. Due to the effects of compounding, small differences in growth rates when maintained for many years can lead to very large differences in real GDP per capita. The standard of living in the United States and other high-income countries is much higher than the standard of living in developing countries because the high-income countries have experienced higher growth rates than the developing countries.

2. Using the graph below, an increase in the capital stock will cause a movement along the per-worker production function. This is a movement from point A to point B. A technological change will allow the economy to produce more with the same amount of inputs (same amount of capital per hour worked). This is a shift in the per-worker production function and a movement from point B to point C.

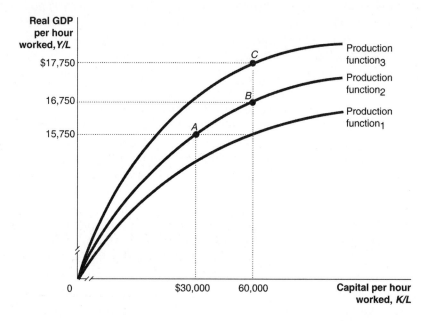

3. The Soviet economy eventually experienced very low growth rates. Although the Soviet Union was successful in increasing levels of capital per hour worked, it was unsuccessful in implementing continuing technological change. The experience of the Soviet economy shows that because of diminishing returns to capital, economic growth will persist in the long run only if an economy experiences technological change.

4. Catch-up—also known as convergence—is the prediction of the economic growth model that poor countries will grow faster than rich countries. The profitability of using additional capital or better technology is generally greater in a developing country than in a high-income country. Therefore, we would expect that developing countries would experience more rapid growth in capital per hour worked and would adopt the best technology, which would cause them to experience rapid rates of economic growth and to catch-up with the high-income countries. Among the countries that currently have high incomes, catch-up has occurred. But the developing countries as a group are not catching up with the high-income countries as a group.

5. The brain drain will cause a country to lose those individuals who can help implement and create technological change. Slower technological change means smaller upward shifts in the per-worker production function and slower rates of economic growth.

True/False Answers

1. F   See textbook Figure 10-1.
2. F   The Industrial Revolution began in England during the eighteenth century.
3. T
4. F   See the *Making the Connection* on page 313 of the textbook.
5. F   95 percent is the total percentage change rather than the average annual growth rate.
6. T
7. F   An increase in capital per hour worked results in a movement along the per-worker production function.
8. T
9. T
10. T
11. F   The life of a patent is 20 years.
12. T
13. F   Catch-up holds that countries with lower levels of real GDP per capita will have faster growth rates.
14. T
15. F   More globalized countries grew much faster than less globalized countries. See textbook Figure 10-11.

Output and Expenditure in the Short Run

Chapter Summary

Chapter 10 examined the determinants of long-run economic growth. In the short run, however, the economy experiences fluctuations in economic activity, or business cycles, around the long-run upward trend in real GDP. **Aggregate expenditure (*AE*)** is the total amount of spending in the economy. The **aggregate expenditure model** focuses on the relationship between total spending and real GDP in the short run, assuming that the price level is constant. The four components of aggregate expenditure are:

1. consumption (*C*)
2. planned investment (*I*)
3. government purchases (*G*)
4. net exports (*NX*)

When aggregate expenditure is greater than GDP, there is an unplanned decrease in **inventories**, which are goods that have been produced but not yet sold, and GDP and total employment will increase.

The five determinants of consumption are:

1. current disposable income
2. household wealth
3. expected future income
4. the price level
5. the interest rate

The **consumption function** is the relationship between consumption and disposable income. The **marginal propensity to consume (*MPC*)** is the change in consumption divided by the change in disposable income. The **marginal propensity to save (*MPS*)** is the change in saving divided by the change in disposable income. The determinants of planned investment are expectations of future profitability, the real interest rate, taxes, and **cash flow**, which is the difference between the cash revenues received by a firm and the cash spending by the firm.

The 45°-line diagram shows all the points where aggregate expenditure equals real GDP. On the 45°-line diagram, macroeconomic equilibrium occurs where the line representing the aggregate expenditure function crosses the 45° line. The economy is in recession when the aggregate expenditure line intersects the 45° line at a level of GDP that is below potential GDP.

Autonomous expenditure is expenditure that does not depend on the level of GDP. An autonomous change is a change in expenditure not caused by a change in income. An *induced change* is a change in aggregate expenditure caused by a change in income. An autonomous change in expenditure will cause rounds of induced changes in expenditure. Therefore, an autonomous change in expenditure will have a *multiplier effect* on equilibrium GDP. The **multiplier effect** is the process by which an increase in autonomous expenditure leads to a larger increase in real GDP. The **multiplier** is the ratio of the change in equilibrium GDP to the change in autonomous expenditure.

Increases in the price level cause a reduction in consumption, investment, and net exports. This causes the aggregate expenditure function to shift down on the 45°-line diagram, leading to a lower equilibrium real GDP. A decrease in the price level leads to a higher equilibrium real GDP. The **aggregate demand curve** shows the relationship between the price level and the level of aggregate expenditure, holding constant all factors that affect aggregate expenditure other than the price level.

Learning Objectives

When you finish this chapter, you should be able to:

1. **Understand how macroeconomic equilibrium is determined in the aggregate expenditure model.** The aggregate expenditure model focuses on the relationship between total spending and real GDP in the short run, assuming the price level is constant. In any particular year, the level of GDP is determined by the level of total spending, or aggregate expenditure, in the economy. The four components of aggregate expenditure are: consumption (C), planned investment (I), government purchases (G), and net exports (NX). When aggregate expenditure is greater than GDP, there is an unplanned decrease in inventories (which are goods produced but not yet sold), and GDP and total employment will increase. When aggregate expenditure is less than GDP, there is an unplanned increase in inventories, and GDP and total employment will decline. Only when aggregate expenditure is equal to GDP will businesses sell what they expected to sell, production and employment will be unchanged, and the economy will be in macroeconomic equilibrium.

2. **Discuss the determinants of the four components of aggregate expenditure and define the marginal propensity to consume and the marginal propensity to save.** The five determinants of consumption are: current disposable income, household wealth, expected future income, the price level, and the interest rate. The consumption function is the relationship between consumption and income. The marginal propensity to consume is the change in consumption divided by the change in income. The marginal propensity to save is the change in saving divided by the change in income. The determinants of planned investment are: expectations of future profitability, the real interest rate, taxes, and cash flow, which is the difference between the cash revenues received by the firm and the cash spending by the firm. Government purchases include spending by the federal government and by local and state governments for goods and services. Government purchases do not include transfer payments, such as social security payments by the federal government or pension payments by local governments to retired police officers and fire fighters. Net exports are purchases by foreign businesses and households of goods and services produced in the United States minus the purchases by U.S. businesses and households of goods and services produced in other countries. The three determinants of net exports are: the price level in the United States relative to the price levels in other countries, the growth rate of GDP in the United States relative to the growth rates of GDP in other countries, and the exchange rate between the dollar and other currencies.

3. **Use a 45°-line diagram to illustrate macroeconomic equilibrium.** The 45°-line diagram shows all the points where aggregate expenditure equals real GDP. On the 45°-line diagram, macroeconomic equilibrium occurs where the line representing the aggregate expenditure function crosses the 45° line.

4. **Define the multiplier effect and use it to calculate changes in equilibrium GDP.** An autonomous change is a change in expenditure not caused by a change in income. An induced change in expenditure is a change in expenditure caused by a change in income. An autonomous change in expenditure will cause rounds of induced changes in expenditure. Therefore, an autonomous change in expenditure will have a multiplied effect on equilibrium GDP. The multiplier is the ratio of the change in equilibrium GDP to the change in autonomous expenditure. The formula for the multiplier is $1/(1 - MPC)$, where MPC is the marginal propensity to consume.

5. **Understand the relationship between the aggregate demand curve and aggregate expenditure.** Increases in the price level cause a reduction in consumption, investment, and net exports. Price level increases cause the aggregate expenditure function to shift down on the 45°-line diagram, leading to a lower equilibrium real GDP. A decrease in the price level leads to a higher equilibrium real GDP. The aggregate demand curve shows the relationship between the price level and the level of aggregate expenditure, holding constant all factors that affect aggregate demand expenditure other than the price level.

Appendix: Apply the algebra of macroeconomic equilibrium. The chapter relies on graphs and tables to illustrate the aggregate expenditure model of short-run real GDP. The appendix uses equations to represent the aggregate expenditure model. Your instructor may cover or assign this appendix.

Chapter Review

Chapter Opener: Fluctuating Demand at Cisco Systems (pages 346-347)

In the spring of 2001, Cisco Systems, a leading seller of hardware for computer networks, discovered that a slowdown in the economy had reduced the demand for its products. This slowdown in the economy caused Cisco Systems to reduce its level of production and to reduce its level of employment (from 44,000 employees) by about 6,000 workers. In spring of 2007, Cisco announced record sales and profits with employment of more than 49,000 employees. Why the difference? In 2001, the economy was slowing down and in a period or recession. In early 2007, the economy was expanding.

📖 Helpful Study Hint

Read *An Inside Look* at the end of the chapter for a discussion of the factors that caused U.S. GDP to change during the first quarter of 2007:
1. a slowdown in residential construction
2. a decline in exports
3. slow growth of business inventories

Suppose that you work part time assembling desktop computers. Should you be worried about your job if consumer confidence falls? *Economics in YOUR Life*! at the start of this chapter poses this question. Keep the question in mind as you read the chapter. The authors will answer the question at the end of the chapter.

11.1 The Aggregate Expenditure Model (pages 348-351)

Learning Objective 1 Understand how macroeconomic equilibrium is determined in the aggregate expenditure model.

The **aggregate expenditure model** explains many aspects of business cycles. This model looks at the relationship in the short run between total planned spending and real GDP. An important assumption of the model is that the price level is constant. The main idea behind the aggregate expenditure model is that, in any year, real GDP is determined mostly by aggregate expenditure. We define **aggregate expenditure** (*AE*) as:

Aggregate expenditure = Consumption + Planned Investment + Government Purchases + Net Exports

where:

- Consumption (*C*): Spending by households on goods and services, such as automobiles and haircuts.
- Planned Investment (*I*): Spending by businesses on capital goods, such as factories, office buildings, and machine tools, and spending by households on new homes.

📖 Helpful Study Hints

Remember that investment expenditure includes the purchase of plant and equipment by firms, residential construction, and any changes in business inventories. *Planned investment* includes only planned inventory changes. Unanticipated or unplanned changes in business inventories are called unplanned investment.

- Government Purchases (*G*): Spending by local, state, and federal governments on goods and services, such as aircraft carriers, bridges, and the salaries of FBI agents.
- Net Exports (*NX*): Spending by foreign businesses and households on goods and services produced in the United States minus spending by U.S. businesses and households on goods and services produced in all other countries.

In equation form:

$$AE = C + I + G + NX$$

Planned investment in the *AE* function may differ from the actual level of investment. Actual investment will include any unplanned changes in inventories caused by differences between production and sales. If a firm produces $100 of output and only sells $80 of that output, the $20 of output produced but not sold ends up in inventories. This $20 is included in actual investment but not in planned investment.

For the economy as a whole, equilibrium occurs when aggregate expenditure equals total production or:

$$AE = \text{real GDP}.$$

In this model, equilibrium real GDP will not change unless aggregate expenditure changes.

If *AE* is less than real GDP, firms are producing more output than is being purchased and there will be an unplanned increase in inventories. Firms will respond to the increase in inventories by reducing production and employment. If *AE* is more than production, firms are producing less output than is being purchased. The only way a firm can sell more than it produces is by selling part of its inventory. Firms will respond to this unplanned decrease in inventories by increasing production and employment. In either case, the economy moves toward an equilibrium in which *AE* = real GDP. The following table—Table 11.1 in the main text—summarizes the relationship between AE and GDP:

If ...	Then ...	And
Aggregate Expenditure is **Equal** to GDP	There is no unplanned inventory change	the economy is in **Macroeconomic Equilibrium**.
Aggregate Expenditure is **Less** than GDP	There is an unplanned inventory increase	GDP and employment **decrease**.
Aggregate Expenditure is **Greater** than GDP	There is an unplanned inventory decrease	GDP and employment **increase**.

Extra Solved Problem 11-1

Chapter 11 in the textbook includes three Solved Problems. Here is an extra Solved Problem to help you build your skills solving economic problems:

Supports Learning Objective 1: Understand how macroeconomic equilibrium is determined in the aggregate expenditure model.

Unplanned Investment

To meet any unexpected increases in demand, Whirlpool would like to keep an inventory of 5,000 refrigerators. Whirlpool expects to sell 50,000 refrigerators this month, and so to keep its inventories constant, it manufactured 50,000 refrigerators this month. What will happen to Whirlpool's inventories if it sells only 49,000 refrigerators? What if it sells 52,000 refrigerators?

SOLVING THE PROBLEM

Step 1:   Review the chapter material.
This problem is about inventories and unplanned investment, so you may want to review the section "The Difference between Planned Investment and Actual Investment" on page 349 of the textbook.

Step 2:   Calculate inventory changes.
Inventories are the goods that firms have produced but have not sold. This could be intentional. For example, Whirlpool wants to keep 5,000 refrigerators on hand to meet unexpected increases in demand. A change in inventories can be planned or unplanned. For example, a firm may not have accurately forecast its sales. Unexpectedly high sales will cause an unplanned decrease in inventories and unexpectedly low sales will cause an unplanned increase in inventories. The change in inventories is calculated as production minus sales. If this difference is positive, inventories will rise. If the difference is negative, inventories will fall. Given the numbers above,

If production is 50,000 and sales are 49,000, then the change in inventories is 1,000 refrigerators, and the level of inventories will rise to 6,000.

If production is 50,000 and sales are 52,000, the change in inventories is −2,000, and the level of inventories will fall to 3,000.

11.2 Determining the Level of Aggregate Expenditure in the Economy (pages 351-363)

Learning Objective 2 Discuss the determinants of the four components of aggregate expenditure and define the marginal propensity to consume and the marginal propensity to save.

Different variables influence each of the four major parts of aggregate expenditure.

Consumption spending is determined by:

1. Current disposable income. Consumption will increase with increases in current disposable income.
2. Household wealth. Consumption will increase with increases in wealth.
3. Expected future income. If you expect your income to rise in the future, your consumption will be higher than if you do not expect your income to rise.
4. The price level. Consumption will fall with increases in the price level as a higher price level lowers the purchasing power of wealth.
5. The interest rate. Consumption will fall with increases in the real interest rate.

Planned investment is determined by:

1. Expectations of future profitability. Planned investment spending will increase if firms expect profits to rise in future years.
2. The interest rate. Planned investment will fall with increases in the real interest rate.
3. Taxes. Planned investment spending will fall with higher taxes.
4. Cash flow. Planned investment will increase with higher levels of cash flow caused by increased profits.

Government purchases are determined by:

1. The president, Congress, and state and local government decision makers.

Net exports are determined by:

1. The price level in the United States relative to the price levels in other countries. Net exports will increase if U.S. inflation is less than inflation in other countries. If U.S. prices are rising less than prices in other countries, the foreign currency price of U.S. produced goods will fall compared to the prices of similar goods made in foreign countries. Foreigners will shift their purchases away from domestic production and toward U.S. production, causing exports to rise. Similar logic explains why U.S. imports will fall. An increase in exports and a decrease in imports cause net exports to rise.

2. Growth in real GDP relative to other countries. Net exports will fall if U.S. growth rates in real GDP are greater than growth rates in real GDP in other countries. Real GDP is equivalent to real income, so higher real income means greater spending on everything, including imports. If U.S. GDP grows faster than foreign GDP, then U.S. spending will also grow faster than foreign spending. This will increase U.S. imports. U.S. exports will also rise, but our exports are determined by foreign income. Therefore, U.S. imports will rise by more than exports and net exports will fall.
3. The exchange rate. Net exports will fall as the value of the U.S. dollar increases relative to other currencies (a dollar appreciation). A dollar appreciation raises the foreign currency price of goods produced in the United States and lowers the domestic price of goods produced in other countries. The impact on net exports is the same as a change in domestic prices compared to foreign prices (but in the opposite direction).

The relationship between current real disposable income (*YD*) and real consumption spending (*C*) is called the **consumption function**. An increase in *YD* causes an increase in *C*. The change in consumption caused by a change in *YD* is called the **marginal propensity to consume** (*MPC*). Using the Greek letter delta, Δ, to represent "change in":

$$MPC = \frac{\Delta C}{\Delta YD}$$

or,

$$\Delta C = MPC \times \Delta YD.$$

Real GDP is the same as national income. National income minus net taxes equals disposable income (*YD*):

$$YD = \text{National income} - \text{Net taxes} = \text{Real GDP} - \text{Net taxes}.$$

The following table and graph show these relationships. The assumption is that the *MPC* = 0.75 and net taxes = $1,000.

National Income or Real GDP (billions of dollars)	Net Taxes (billions of dollars)	Disposable Income (billions of dollars)	Consumption (billions of dollars)	Change in National Income (billions of dollars)	Change in Disposable Income (billions of dollars)
$1,000	$1,000	$0	$750	$2,000	$2,000
3,000	1,000	2,000	2,250	2,000	2,000
5,000	1,000	4,000	3,750	2,000	2,000
7,000	1,000	6,000	5,250	2,000	2,000
9,000	1,000	8,000	6,750	2,000	2,000
11,000	1,000	10,000	8,250	2,000	2,000
13,000	1,000	12,000	9,750	2,000	2,000

If we draw a graph with real consumption spending on the vertical axis and real national income on the horizontal axis, it looks like Figure 11-3 below:

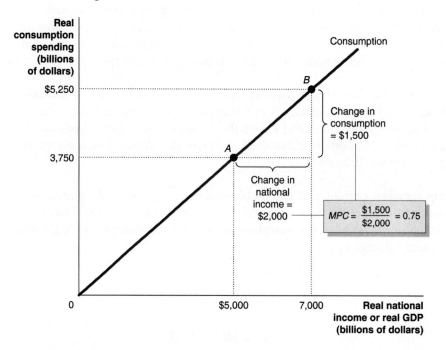

Consumers can either spend their income, save it, or use it to pay taxes. For the economy as a whole, we can write the following equation relating income (Y), consumption (C), saving (S), and taxes (T):

$$Y = C + S + T.$$

This equation implies that any change in total income must be equal to the sum of changes in consumption, saving, and taxes:

$$\Delta Y = \Delta C + \Delta S + \Delta T.$$

If we assume for simplicity that taxes are a constant amount, then $\Delta T = 0$ and

$$\Delta Y = \Delta C + \Delta S.$$

The **marginal propensity to save (MPS)** is the amount by which saving increases when disposable income increases. If we divide both sides of the last equation by ΔY, we get an equation that shows the relationship between the marginal propensity to consume and the marginal propensity to save (MPS):

$$\frac{\Delta Y}{\Delta Y} = \frac{\Delta C}{\Delta Y} + \frac{\Delta S}{\Delta Y}$$

or,

$$1 = MPC + MPS.$$

This last equation tells us that when taxes are constant, the marginal propensity to consume plus the marginal propensity to save must always equal 1. They must add up to 1 because part of any increase in income is consumed, and whatever remains must be saved.

📖 Helpful Study Hints

Work through **Solved Problem 11-2** in the main text to practice how to calculate *MPC* and *MPS*.

Making the Connection: Cisco Rides the Roller Coaster of Information Technology Spending explains how the business cycle affects firms such as Cisco.

When the economy is expanding, firms increase their levels of investment expenditures. When firms buy more information technology equipment, they often buy more products from Cisco. Cisco's sales depend on how investment expenditures are changing. As investment spending fell in 2001, Cisco's sales and profits declined. As the economy began to expand again, Cisco's profits and sales increased.

Extra Solved Problem 11-2

Chapter 11 in the textbook includes three Solved Problems. Here is an extra Solved Problem to help you build your skills solving economic problems:

Calculating the MPC and MPS

Supports Learning Objective 2: Discuss the determinants of the four components of aggregate expenditure and define the marginal propensity to consume and the marginal propensity to save.

Using the data in the table below, calculate national income, the *MPC*, and the *MPS*.

Step 1: **Review the chapter material.**
This problem is about calculating the *MPC* and *MPS*, so you may want to read the section "Determining the Level of Aggregate Expenditure in the Economy," which begins on page 351 of the textbook.

Real GDP (Y)	Net Taxes	Disposable Income	Consumption	Saving	MPC	MPS
$10,000	$1,000		$8,000			
10,500	1,000		8,350			
11,000	1,000		8,700			
11,500	1,000		9,050			
12,000	1,000		9,400			
12,500	1,000		9,750			

Step 2: **Solve the problem by filling in the values in the table.**

Disposable income is defined as real GDP less net taxes, so, for example, at a level of real GDP of $10,000 with net taxes of $1,000, disposable income is $9,000 (= $10,000 − $1,000 = $9,000). The table should then look like:

Real GDP (Y)	Net Taxes	Disposable Income	Consumption	Saving	MPC	MPS
$10,000	$1,000	$9,000	$8,000			
10,500	1,000	9,500	8,350			
11,000	1,000	10,000	8,700			
11,500	1,000	10,500	9,050			
12,000	1,000	11,000	9,400			
12,500	1,000	11,500	9,750			

Saving is the difference between disposable income and consumption (or the part of disposable income that is not consumed). At real GDP = $10,000, with net taxes of $1,000, disposable income is $9,000. If consumption is $8,000, then saving will be $1,000 (= $9,000 − $8,000 = $1,000). Using this calculation, the table will look like:

Real GDP (Y)	Net Taxes	Disposable Income	Consumption	Saving	MPC	MPS
$10,000	$1,000	$9,000	$8,000	$1,000		
10,500	1,000	9,500	8,350	1,150		
11,000	1,000	10,000	8,700	1,300		
11,500	1,000	10,500	9,050	1,450		
12,000	1,000	11,000	9,400	1,600		
12,500	1,000	11,500	9,750	1,750		

The *MPC* is defined as the change in consumption for a dollar change in disposable income; so between real GDP of $10,000 and $10,500, disposable income increased $500 (= $9,500 − $9,000 = $500). For the same change in income, consumption spending increased by $350 (= $8,350 − $8,000 = $350), which means that the *MPC* equals $350/$500 = 0.7.

The *MPS* is defined as the change in saving for a dollar change in disposable income, so between real GDP of $10,000 and $10,500, disposable income increased $500 (= $9,500 − $9,000 = $500). Saving increased by $150 (=$1,150 − $1000 = $150), so the *MPS* equals $150/$500 = 0.3.

Using these calculations, the table will look like:

Real GDP (Y)	Net Taxes	Disposable Income	Consumption	Saving	MPC	MPS
$10,000	$1,000	$9,000	$8,000	$1,000		
10,500	1,000	9,500	8,350	1,150	0.7	0.3
11,000	1,000	10,000	8,700	1,300	0.7	0.3
11,500	1,000	10,500	9,050	1,450	0.7	0.3
12,000	1,000	11,000	9,400	1,600	0.7	0.3
12,500	1,000	11,500	9,750	1,750	0.7	0.3

Notice that at all levels of real GDP, the $MPC + MPS = 1$.

11.3 Graphing Macroeconomic Equilibrium (pages 363–370)

Learning Objective 3   Use a 45°-line diagram to illustrate macroeconomic equilibrium.

The graphical view of macroeconomic equilibrium starts with a line defining all possible points of equilibrium. Because equilibrium is $AE = Y$, the line will intersect the origin at an angle of 45 degrees. This is shown in textbook Figure 11-8 below. At points below the line, AE is less than Y, and at points above the line, AE is greater than Y.

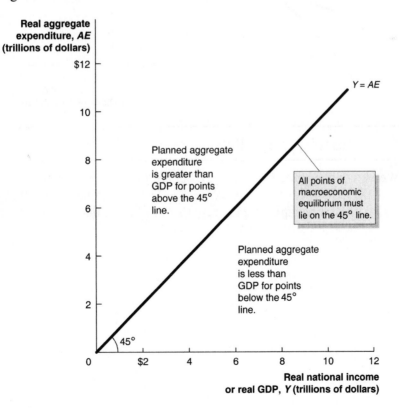

In this graph, the 45° line shows all possible points of macroeconomic equilibrium, where $Y = AE$. During any particular year, only one of these points will represent the actual level of equilibrium real GDP, given the actual level of planned expenditure. To find the macroeconomic equilibrium, we need to add a line representing the aggregate expenditure function to the graph. This is done in textbook Figure 11-9 below. Equilibrium will occur at the level of real GDP where the AE line (which is equal to $C + I + G + NX$) intersects the 45° line.

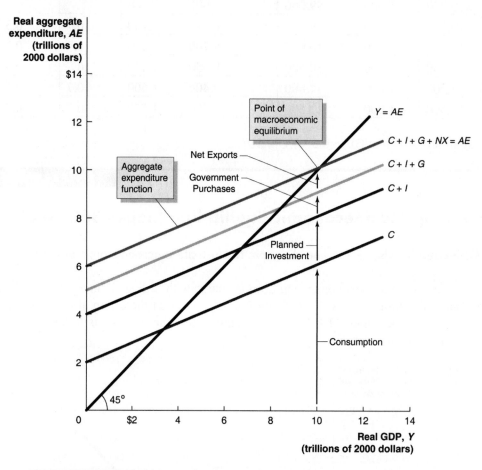

📖 Helpful Study Hints

We've assumed that net exports (NX) are positive. For over 30 years, U.S. net exports have been negative. See Figure 11-6 on page 362 of the textbook, which graphs real net exports from 1979–2006.

Equilibrium occurs at the level of real GDP that makes $AE = Y$. At production levels less than this level of real GDP, inventories will decline and firms will respond by increasing production. At production levels above the equilibrium level of real GDP, inventories will increase and firms will reduce production. This adjustment is shown in textbook Figure 11-10 below:

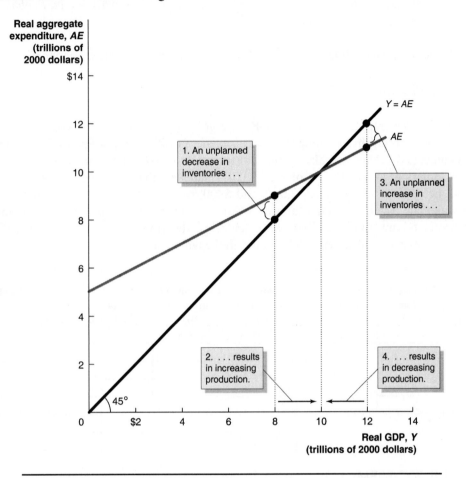

📖 Helpful Study Hints

Work through **Extra Solved Problem 11-3** in this Study Guide to practice finding equilibrium real GDP.

Extra Solved Problem 11-3

Chapter 11 in the textbook includes three Solved Problems. Here is an extra Solved Problem to help you build your skills solving economic problems:

Supports Learning Objective 3: Use a 45°-line diagram to illustrate macroeconomic equilibrium.

Calculating Equilibrium Real GDP

The table below has several values of real GDP. The goal is to determine the level of equilibrium real GDP where $Y = AE$. To do this, assume that net taxes are \$1,000 at every level of real GDP. Calculate disposable income (YD). You are also given consumption for one level of YD. If the MPC is 0.6, determine consumption at all levels of real GDP. Suppose that planned investment, government purchases, and net exports are \$2,000, \$2,000, and \$900, respectively, at all levels of real GDP. Using these values, calculate AE. Based upon these levels of AE, determine unplanned changes in inventories. From these levels of unplanned changes in inventories, determine if Y will rise or fall, or remain unchanged at each level of real GDP. Fill in values in the table below.

Real GDP (Y)	Taxes (T)	Disposable income (YD)	Consumption (C)	Planned investment (I)	Government purchases (G)	Net exports (NX)	AE = C+I+G+NX	Unplanned changes in inventories	Y will:
\$8,000	\$1,000		\$4,700	\$2,000	\$2,000	\$900			
9,000									
10,000									
11,000									
12,000									
13,000									
14,000									

SOLVING THE PROBLEM

Step 1: **Review the chapter material.**

This problem is about determining macroeconomic equilibrium, so you may want to review the section "Graphing Macroeconomic Equilibrium," which begins on page 363 of the textbook.

Step 2: **Calculate the level of disposable income.**

For this economy, net taxes are \$1,000 at each level of real GDP. The level of disposable income is calculated as real GDP – net taxes. With this information you complete the net taxes and disposable income columns.

Real GDP (Y)	Net taxes (T)	Disposable income (YD)	Consumption (C)	Planned investment (I)	Government purchases (G)	Net exports (NX)	AE = C+I+G+NX	Unplanned changes in inventories	Y will:
$8,000	$1,000	$7,000	$4,700	$2,000	$2,000	$900			
9,000	1,000	8,000							
10,000	1,000	9,000							
11,000	1,000	10,000							
12,000	1,000	11,000							
13,000	1,000	12,000							
14,000	1,000	13,000							

Step 3: **Calculate consumption.**

The *MPC* is 0.6. This means that for each $1,000 increase in disposable income, consumption will increase by $600. For example, as *YD* increases from $7,000 to $8,000, consumption will increase by $600 from $4,700 to $5,300. After calculating consumption for the remaining levels of disposable income, the table should look like:

Real GDP (Y)	Net taxes (T)	Disposable income (YD)	Consumption (C)	Planned Investment (I)	Government Purchases (G)	Net exports (NX)	AE = C+I+G+NX	Unplanned changes in inventories	Y will:
$8,000	$1,000	$7,000	$4,700	$2,000	$2,000	$900			
9,000	1,000	8,000	5,300						
10,000	1,000	9,000	5,900						
11,000	1,000	10,000	6,500						
12,000	1,000	11,000	7,100						
13,000	1,000	12,000	7,700						
14,000	1,000	13,000	8,300						

Step 4: **Fill in the values for planned investment, government purchases, and net exports.**

Planned investment, government purchases, and net exports are autonomous expenditures and are assumed to have constant values of $2,000, $2,000, and $900. Using these values, the table should look like:

Real GDP (Y)	Net taxes (T)	Disposable income (YD)	Consumption (C)	Planned investment (I)	Government purchases (G)	Net exports (NX)	AE = C+I+G+NX	Unplanned changes in inventories	Y will:
$8,000	$1,000	$7,000	$4,700	$2,000	$2,000	$900			
9,000	1,000	8,000	5,300	2,000	2,000	900			
10,000	1,000	9,000	5,900	2,000	2,000	900			
11,000	1,000	10,000	6,500	2,000	2,000	900			
12,000	1,000	11,000	7,100	2,000	2,000	900			
13,000	1,000	12,000	7,700	2,000	2,000	900			
14,000	1,000	13,000	8,300	2,000	2,000	900			

Step 5: **Calculate the values of AE.**

AE is defined as $C + I + G + NX$, so when real GDP = $8,000, the value of AE will be $4,700 + $2,000 + $2,000 + $900 = $9,600. Filling in the values for AE at every level of real GDP results in the table looking like this:

Real GDP (Y)	Net taxes (T)	Disposable income (YD)	Consumption (C)	Planned investment (I)	Government purchases (G)	Net exports (NX)	AE = C+I+G+NX	Unplanned changes in inventories	Y will:
$8,000	$1,000	$7,000	$4,700	$2,000	$2,000	$900	$9,600		
9,000	1,000	8,000	5,300	2,000	2,000	900	10,200		
10,000	1,000	9,000	5,900	2,000	2,000	900	10,800		
11,000	1,000	10,000	6,500	2,000	2,000	900	11,400		
12,000	1,000	11,000	7,100	2,000	2,000	900	12,000		
13,000	1,000	12,000	7,700	2,000	2,000	900	12,600		
14,000	1,000	13,000	8,300	2,000	2,000	900	13,200		

Step 6: **Calculate unplanned changes to inventories.**

At real GDP = $8,000 and AE = $9,600, total demand for output is $9,600, but firms are only producing $8,000. For firms to meet demand, they must sell $1,600 of products held as inventories. This $1,600 when added to real GDP will allow firms to meet the total level of demand ($8,000 + $1,600 = $9,600). Thus at real GDP = $8,000, unplanned changes in inventories are −$1,600. In general, unplanned changes in inventories equal $Y - AE$. A negative value for unplanned changes in inventories means there is an unplanned decrease in inventories. If $Y - AE$ is positive, there is an unplanned increase in inventories. Using these calculations, the table should look like:

Real GDP (Y)	Net taxes (T)	Disposable income (YD)	Consumption (C)	Planned investment (I)	Government purchases (G)	Net exports (NX)	AE = C+I+G+NX	Unplanned changes in inventories	Y will:
$8,000	$1,000	$7,000	$4,700	$2,000	$2,000	$900	$9,600	−$1,600	
9,000	1,000	8,000	5,300	2,000	2,000	900	10,200	−1,200	
10,000	1,000	9,000	5,900	2,000	2,000	900	10,800	−800	
11,000	1,000	10,000	6,500	2,000	2,000	900	11,400	−400	
12,000	1,000	11,000	7,100	2,000	2,000	900	12,000	0	
13,000	1,000	12,000	7,700	2,000	2,000	900	12,600	400	
14,000	1,000	13,000	8,300	2,000	2,000	900	13,200	800	

Step 7: **Determine if Y will rise, fall, or remain unchanged at each level of real GDP.**

If inventories are falling, then firms will increase production (real GDP). If inventories are rising, then firms will decrease production (real GDP). Knowing this, we can fill in the last column of the table:

Real GDP (Y)	Net taxes (T)	Disposable income (YD)	Consumption (C)	Planned investment (I)	Government purchases (G)	Net exports (NX)	AE = C+I+G+NX	Unplanned changes in inventories	Y will:
$8,000	$1,000	$7,000	$4,700	$2,000	$2,000	$900	$9,600	−$1,600	increase
9,000	1,000	8,000	5,300	2,000	2,000	900	10,200	−1,200	increase
10,000	1,000	9,000	5,900	2,000	2,000	900	10,800	−800	increase
11,000	1,000	10,000	6,500	2,000	2,000	900	11,400	−400	increase
12,000	1,000	11,000	7,100	2,000	2,000	900	12,000	0	not change
13,000	1,000	12,000	7,700	2,000	2,000	900	12,600	400	decrease
14,000	1,000	13,000	8,300	2,000	2,000	900	13,200	800	decrease

Equilibrium real GDP will be $12,000. At this level of real GDP, AE also equals $12,000, so $AE = Y$ and unplanned changes in inventories are zero, so production (real GDP) will not change.

📖 Helpful Study Hints

Making the Connection: Business Attempts to Control Inventories, Then…and Now explains how a firm with too high a level of inventory will have higher costs and lower profits. Today, most firms use inventory control systems to reduce costs and increase profits. Dell will not build a computer until it is ordered. Dell orders parts from its suppliers only when they are needed so that it only has a day or two of parts inventory. This tight control of inventory reduces Dell's costs and increases its profits.

Read *Don't Let This Happen to YOU!* to keep clear the difference between aggregate expenditure and consumption spending: Aggregate expenditure (AE) includes more than just consumption expenditures (which is the largest component of AE). Also included in aggregate expenditure are planned investment, government purchases, and net exports.

11.4 LEARNING OBJECTIVE

11.4 The Multiplier Effect (pages 371-377)

Learning Objective 4 Define the multiplier effect and use it to calculate changes in equilibrium GDP.

The aggregate expenditure model predicts that, in the short run, the level of real GDP is determined by the level of aggregate expenditure ($C + I + G + NX$). Changes in aggregate expenditure cause real GDP to change. This is shown in Figure 11-12:

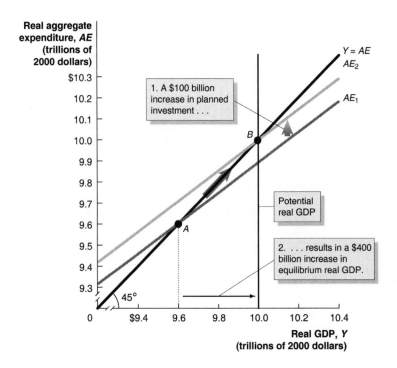

Suppose the economy is in equilibrium at point A in the figure. If AE increases to AE_2, at point A, the new level of spending, AE_2, will be greater than output ($AE > Y$). There will be an unplanned decrease in inventories. In response, firms will increase output and employment. Real GDP will therefore rise. The new equilibrium will be at point B, where $AE = Y$ again.

What can cause AE to increase? Increases in **autonomous expenditure**, spending that does not depend on the level of real GDP, cause AE to increase. In the simple model developed in this chapter, planned investment, government purchases, and net exports are autonomous.

Any rise in autonomous expenditure will cause real GDP to increase by more than the increase in autonomous expenditure. This is true because increases in expenditure lead to increases in production and income, which in turn cause increases in consumption spending as household disposable income rises. The series of induced increases in consumption spending that result from an initial increase in autonomous expenditure is called the **multiplier effect**. The multiplier effect is the process by which an increase in autonomous expenditure leads to an increase in real GDP. The size of the multiplier depends upon the size of the MPC. The formula for the simple **multiplier** is:

$$\frac{1}{1 - MPC}$$

There are several important points you should know about the multiplier effect:

- The multiplier works for both increases and decreases in autonomous expenditure.
- The multiplier effect implies that the economy is more sensitive to changes in autonomous spending than it would otherwise be.
- The larger the MPC (or smaller the MPS), the larger the multiplier.
- The multiplier derived in this chapter is based on a very simple model of the economy. There are several real world complications caused by rising real GDP and its effect on (for example) interest rates and inflation. Also, we've assumed some variables are autonomous that are not constant in the real world. For example, we expect net exports to actually fall as income rises.

But our model assumes net exports are constant. Our simple multiplier formula overstates the true value of the multiplier.

📖 Helpful Study Hints

Making the Connection: The Multiplier in Reverse: The Great Depression of the 1930s explains that while an increase in autonomous expenditure can cause an increase in real GDP, a decrease in autonomous expenditure can do the reverse, causing a decrease in real GDP. When the stock market crashed in October 1929, households and firms reduced consumption and investment. The Smoot-Hawley Tariff in June 1930 reduced net exports. As a result of these and other actions, aggregate expenditure fell, sending the economy into a downward spiral. Real GDP fell by over $225 billion between 1929 and 1933, and the unemployment rate increased from 3.2 percent to 24.9 percent.

11.5 LEARNING OBJECTIVE

11.5 The Aggregate Demand Curve (pages 377-378)

Learning Objective 5 Understand the relationship between the aggregate demand curve and aggregate expenditure.

As the price level increases, the level of autonomous expenditure will fall, and through the multiplier process, the level of aggregate expenditure and equilibrium real GDP will also fall. An increase in the price level will reduce autonomous expenditure for three reasons:

1. A higher price level will reduce the purchasing power of household wealth, reducing consumption spending.
2. A higher price level will make products produced in the United States more expensive than products produced in the rest of the world. This will reduce exports and increase imports, reducing net exports.
3. An increase in the price level will increase real interest rates, causing consumption and planned investment to fall.

In the aggregate expenditure model, a higher price level shifts the AE line down. In panel (a) of textbook Figure 11-13 below, a higher price will shift AE from AE_1 to AE_2, causing equilibrium real GDP to fall. In panel (b), a lower price level will shift AE from AE_1 to AE_2, causing equilibrium real GDP to rise.

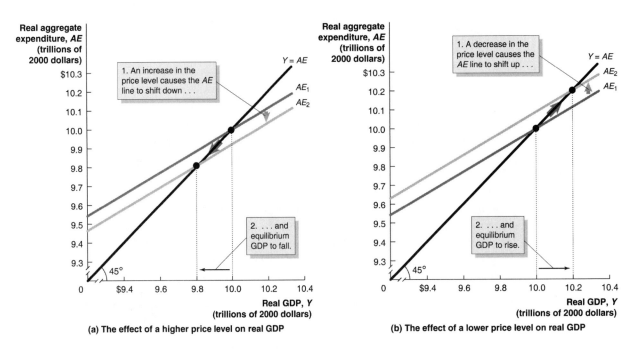

(a) The effect of a higher price level on real GDP

(b) The effect of a lower price level on real GDP

The relationship between the price level and the resulting level of real GDP is shown in an **aggregate demand curve**. The aggregate demand curve is illustrated in textbook Figure 11-14 below:

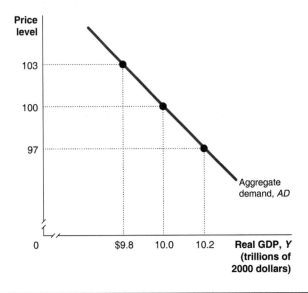

📖 Helpful Study Hints

The aggregate demand curve is different from the demand curve for a single product, like a Bic pen. The demand curve for a Bic pen shows what happens to the quantity of Bic pens that will be purchased at different prices for Bic pens, holding other prices, income, and other factors affecting demand for Bic pens constant. On the *AD* curve, the price *level* changes, not just the price of one product, so that all prices are changing at the same time. But like the microeconomic demand curves we encountered in Chapter 3, a change in the price level will cause a movement along the *AD* curve rather than a shift of the *AD* curve.

Extra Solved Problem 11-5

Chapter 11 in the textbook includes three Solved Problems. Here is an extra Solved Problem to help you build your skills solving economic problems:

Supports Learning Objective 5: Understand the relationship between the aggregate demand curve and aggregate expenditure.

The Aggregate Demand Relationship

Using the table below, determine the equilibrium level or real GDP. What is the value of the multiplier for the economy? Then suppose that because of a price level increase, net exports fall to −$1,650. What will be the new equilibrium real GDP at the new higher price level?

Real GDP (Y)	Consumption (C)	Planned investment (I)	Government purchases (G)	Net exports (NX)
$8,000	$6,050	$2,500	$2,000	−$1,350
9,000	6,750	2,500	2,000	−1,350
10,000	7,450	2,500	2,000	−1,350
11,000	8,150	2,500	2,000	−1,350
12,000	8,850	2,500	2,000	−1,350
13,000	9,550	2,500	2,000	−1,350
14,000	10,250	2,500	2,000	−1,350

SOLVING THE PROBLEM

Step 1: Review the chapter material.
This problem is about aggregate demand and aggregate expenditure, so you may want to review the section "The Aggregate Demand Curve," which begins on page 377 of the textbook.

Step 2: **Calculate equilibrium real GDP.**

Equilibrium income is where $AE = Y$. To find this level of Real GDP, calculate AE as $C + I + G + NX$. The results of this calculation are shown in the column labeled AE:

Real GDP (Y)	Consumption (C)	Planned investment (I)	Government purchases (G)	Net exports (NX)	AE = C+I+G+NX
$8,000	$6,050	$2,500	$2,000	−$1,350	$9,200
9,000	6,750	2,500	2,000	−1,350	9,900
10,000	7,450	2,500	2,000	−1,350	10,600
11,000	8,150	2,500	2,000	−1,350	11,300
12,000	8,850	2,500	2,000	−1,350	12,000
13,000	9,550	2,500	2,000	−1,350	12,700
14,000	10,250	2,500	2,000	−1,350	13,400

AE is equal to Y at a level of real GDP of $12,000.

Step 3: **Calculate the multiplier.**

The multiplier is defined as $1/MPS$ or $1/(1 - MPC)$. For this economy, a $1000 increase in real GDP increases consumption by $700. Therefore, the $MPC = 0.7$, and the $MPS = 0.3$, because the $MPC + MPS = 1$. The multiplier is $1/(1 - MPC) = 1/(1 - 0.7) = 1/0.3 = 3.33$.

Step 4: **Calculate the new equilibrium real GDP at the new level of net exports.**

With the new level of net exports, $AE = Y$ at a level of real GDP = $11,000.

Real GDP (Y)	Consumption (C)	Planned investment (I)	Government purchases (G)	Net exports (NX)	AE = C+I+G+NX	New Net Exports	AE = C+I+G+NX
$8,000	$6,050	$2,500	$2,000	−$1,350	$9,200	−$1,650	$8,900
9,000	6,750	2,500	2,000	−1,350	9,900	−1,650	9,600
10,000	7,450	2,500	2,000	−1,350	10,600	−1,650	10,300
11,000	8,150	2,500	2,000	−1,350	11,300	−1,650	11,000
12,000	8,850	2,500	2,000	−1,350	12,000	−1,650	11,700
13,000	9,550	2,500	2,000	−1,350	12,700	−1,650	12,400
14,000	10,250	2,500	2,000	−1,350	13,400	−1,650	13,100

An increase in the price level will reduce net exports and cause real GDP to fall. Notice that the fall in real GDP is the multiplier $(1/0.3)$ times the change in net exports $(-\$300)$, or $-\$1,000 = (1/0.3) \times (-\$300)$.

📖 Helpful Study Hint

At the start of the chapter, the *Economics in Your Life!* feature asked you to suppose you work part-time assembling desktop computers and you learn that because of a reduction in consumer confidence, households expect future income to fall. Should you be worried about your job? Yes, you should be somewhat concerned. As households expect lower future income, they often cut back on current consumption expenditures, which will lower aggregate demand. If your employer has to reduce production because of smaller sales, part-time jobs may be the first to go.

Appendix

The Algebra of Macroeconomic Equilibrium (pages 388-389)

LEARNING OBJECTIVE: Apply the algebra of macroeconomic equilibrium.

It is possible to view the determination of equilibrium using basic algebra. In equations, the aggregate expenditure model is:

1. $C = \overline{C + MPC(Y)}$ Consumption function

2. $I = \overline{I}$ Planned investment function

3. $G = \overline{G}$ Government spending function

4. $NX = \overline{NX}$ Net export function

5. $Y = C + I + G + NX$ Equilibrium condition

The letters with "bars" represent fixed or autonomous values. Solving for equilibrium we get

$$Y = \overline{C} + MPC(Y) + \overline{I} + \overline{G} + \overline{NX},$$

or,

$$Y - MPC(Y) = \overline{C} + \overline{I} + \overline{G} + \overline{NX},$$

or,

$$Y(1 - MPC) = \overline{C} + \overline{I} + \overline{G} + \overline{NX},$$

or,

$$Y = \frac{\overline{C} + \overline{I} + \overline{G} + \overline{NX}}{1 - MPC}.$$

Remember that $1/(1 - MPC)$ is the multiplier, and all four variables in the numerator of the last equation represent autonomous expenditure. Therefore, an alternative expression for equilibrium GDP is:

Equilibrium real GDP = Autonomous expenditure x multiplier.

Key Terms

Aggregate demand curve (*AD*). A curve showing the relationship between the price level and the level of planned aggregate expenditure in the economy, holding constant all other factors that affect aggregate expenditure.

Aggregate expenditure (*AE*). The total amount of spending in the economy: the sum of consumption, planned investment, government purchases, and net exports.

Aggregate expenditure model. A macroeconomic model that focuses on the relationship between total spending and real GDP, assuming the price level is constant.

Autonomous expenditure. Expenditure that does not depend on the level of GDP.

Cash flow. The difference between the cash revenues received by the firm and the cash spending by the firm.

Consumption function. The relationship between consumption spending and disposable income.

Inventories. Goods that have been produced but not yet sold.

Marginal propensity to consume (*MPC*). The slope of the consumption function: the amount by which consumption spending increases when disposable income increases.

Marginal propensity to save (*MPS*). The change in saving divided by the change in disposable income.

Multiplier. The increase in equilibrium real GDP divided by the increase in autonomous expenditure.

Multiplier effect. The series of induced increases in consumption spending that result from an initial increase in autonomous expenditure.

Self-Test

(Answers are provided at the end of the Self-Test.)

Multiple-Choice Questions

1. Aggregate expenditure, or the total amount of spending in the economy, equals
   a. household spending on durable goods plus household spending on nondurable goods.
   b. household spending on durable goods plus business investment spending.
   c. consumption spending plus planned investment spending plus government purchases plus net exports.
   d. total spending by households plus total spending by businesses.

2. Fluctuations in total spending in the economy may affect
   a. the level of employment in the short run.
   b. the level of production in the short run.
   c. both employment and production in the short run.
   d. neither the level of employment nor the level of production in the short run.

3. The aggregate expenditure model focuses on the relationship between total spending and
   a. nominal GDP in the short run.
   b. nominal GDP in the long run.
   c. real GDP in the short run.
   d. real GDP in the long run.

4. The key idea of the aggregate expenditure model is that in any particular year, the level of gross domestic product (GDP) is determined mainly by
   a. the economy's endowment of economic resources and the current state of technology.
   b. the level of the interest rate for the economy as a whole.
   c. the level of aggregate expenditure.
   d. the level of government expenditures.

5. Economists and business analysts usually explain fluctuations in GDP in terms of fluctuations in these four categories:
   a. interest rates, exchange rates, inflation rates, and government purchases.
   b. inflation rates, unemployment rates, interest rates, and consumer spending.
   c. investment spending, unplanned inventory changes, government transfer spending, and government purchases.
   d. consumption, planned investment, government purchases, and net exports.

6. Which of the following statements is correct?
   a. Actual investment and planned investment are always the same thing.
   b. Actual investment will equal planned investment only when inventories rise.
   c. Actual investment will equal planned investment only when there is no unplanned change in inventories.
   d. Actual investment equals planned investment only when inventories decline.

7. Macroeconomic equilibrium occurs where
    a. the unemployment rate is zero.
    b. total spending, or aggregate expenditure, equals total production, or GDP.
    c. consumption equals investment, and investment equals government expenditure.
    d. total production, or GDP, equals total planned investment.

8. Which of the following makes up the largest fraction of GDP?
    a. consumption
    b. investment
    c. government expenditures
    d. net exports

9. When aggregate expenditure is greater than GDP
    a. inventories will rise.
    b. inventories will fall.
    c. unplanned inventory adjustment will remain the same.
    d. the total amount of production in the economy is greater than the total amount of spending.

10. If aggregate expenditure is equal to GDP, then
    a. inventories are rising.
    b. GDP and employment will fall.
    c. the economy is in macroeconomic equilibrium.
    d. inventories are falling.

11. When aggregate expenditure is greater than GDP, inventories will _____ and GDP and total employment will _____.
    a. rise; increase
    b. rise; decrease
    c. fall; increase
    d. fall; decrease

12. The most important determinant of consumption is
    a. current disposable income.
    b. household wealth.
    c. the price level.
    d. the interest rate.

13. An increase in stock prices will
    a. increase the consumption component of aggregate expenditure.
    b. decrease the investment component of aggregate expenditure.
    c. increase the government purchases component of aggregate expenditure.
    d. not cause any change in the components of aggregate expenditure.

14. Which of the following causes saving to increase?
    a. an increase in consumption
    b. an increase in the interest rate
    c. an increase in unemployment
    d. an increase in the price level

15. If the marginal propensity to consume (*MPC*) is 0.9, how much additional consumption will result from an increase of $80 billion of disposable income?
    a. $88.89 billion
    b. $800 billion
    c. $72 billion
    d. $7.2 billion

16. If the *MPC* is 0.75, then a $100 increase in government expenditures will increase equilibrium GDP by
    a. $100.
    b. $75.
    c. $400.
    d. $133.

17. Which of the following equalities is correct?
    a. Disposable income is equal to national income plus government transfer payments plus taxes.
    b. Government transfer payments minus taxes equals net taxes.
    c. Disposable income is equal to national income minus net taxes.
    d. Disposable income equals national income.

18. When national income increases, there must be some combination of an increase in household
    a. consumption and saving.
    b. consumption, saving, and taxes.
    c. consumption and investment.
    d. saving and investment.

19. The amount by which consumption spending increases when disposable income increases is called
    a. marginal consumption.
    b. autonomous consumption.
    c. the marginal propensity to consume.
    d. disposable national consumption.

20. The sum of the marginal propensity to consume (*MPC*) and the marginal propensity to save (*MPS*) equals
    a. disposable income.
    b. zero.
    c. one.
    d. national income.

21. Which of the following is *not* correct?
    a. $MPS + MPC = 1$
    b. $0 < MPS < 1$
    c. $MPS = 1 - (\Delta C / \Delta YD)$
    d. $MPS = 1 - (C / YD)$

22. The behavior of consumption and investment over time can be described as follows:
    a. investment follows a smooth, upward trend, but consumption is highly volatile.
    b. consumption follows a smooth, upward trend, but investment is subject to significant fluctuations.
    c. both consumption and investment fluctuate significantly over time.
    d. neither consumption nor investment fluctuates significantly over time.

23. Which of the following statements about investment spending is correct?
    a. The optimism or pessimism of business firms is an important determinant of investment spending.
    b. A higher real interest rate results in less investment spending.
    c. When the economy moves into a recession, many firms will postpone buying investment goods even if the demand for their own product is strong.
    d. all of the above

24. Which of the following statements is correct?
    a. An increase in the corporate income tax decreases the after-tax profitability of investment spending.
    b. Changes in tax laws have no effect on investment spending.
    c. During periods of recession, the ability of firms to finance spending on new factories or machinery and equipment increases.
    d. all of the above

25. Concern about the federal budget deficit caused real government purchases to
    a. rise steadily for most of the 1979-2006 period.
    b. fall steadily for most of the 1979-2006 period.
    c. fall during the mid-1990s.
    d. rise during the mid-1990s.

26. Net exports have been _____ in most years between 1979 and 2006. Net exports have usually _____ when the U.S. economy is in recession and _____ when the U.S. economy is expanding.
    a. positive; increased; decreased
    b. positive; decreased; increased
    c. negative; increased; decreased
    d. negative; decreased; increased

27. Which of the following is among the most important determinants of the level of net exports?
    a. the price level in the United States relative to the price levels in other countries
    b. the unemployment rate in the United States relative to the unemployment rate in other countries
    c. the level of investment spending in the United States relative to the level of investment spending in other countries
    d. all of the above

28. If inflation in the United States is lower than inflation in other countries, then U.S. exports _____ and U.S. imports _____, which _____ net exports.
    a. increase; increase; decreases
    b. increase; decrease; increases
    c. decrease; increase; increases
    d. decrease; increase; decreases

29. When incomes rise faster in the United States than in other countries,
    a. U.S. net exports will rise.
    b. U.S. net exports will fall.
    c. foreign consumers' purchases of U.S. goods and services will increase faster than U.S. consumers' purchases of foreign goods and services.
    d. exports usually rise faster than imports.

30. An increase in the value of the dollar (the dollar appreciates against other currencies) will _____ exports and _____ imports, so net exports will _____.
    a. increase; decrease; rise
    b. decrease; increase; fall
    c. increase; decrease; fall
    d. increase; increase; rise

31. At points above the 45° line,
    a. aggregate expenditure is greater than GDP.
    b. aggregate expenditure is less than GDP.
    c. aggregate expenditure is equal to GDP.
    d. aggregate expenditure is in equilibrium.

32. As long as the *AE* line is above the 45° line,
    a. inventories will rise and firms will expand production.
    b. inventories will decline and firms will expand production.
    c. inventories will rise and firms will reduce production.
    d. inventories will decline and firms will reduce production.

33. Macroeconomic equilibrium in the short run
    a. must be consistent with macroeconomic equilibrium in the long run.
    b. results in a zero unemployment rate.
    c. will occur at a point on the 45° line.
    d. all of the above

34. When is the economy in a recession?
    a. when the aggregate expenditure line does not intersect the 45° line anywhere
    b. when the aggregate expenditure line intersects the 45° line at a level of GDP below potential real GDP
    c. when the aggregate expenditure line intersects the 45° line at a level of GDP above potential real GDP
    d. when the aggregate expenditure line intersects the 45° line at a level of GDP equal to potential real GDP

35. When the economy is in a recession, the shortfall in aggregate expenditure is exactly equal to
    a. the value of GDP.
    b. the shortfall in aggregate production.
    c. the unplanned increase in inventories that would occur if the economy were initially at potential GDP.
    d. all of the above

36. Which of the following statements is correct?
    a. Autonomous expenditure depends on the level of GDP.
    b. Autonomous expenditure does not depend on the level of GDP.
    c. No part of consumption spending is autonomous.
    d. No part of government purchases is autonomous.

37. What is the multiplier?
    a.   The multiplier is the amount by which investment spending increases following an initial increase in consumption spending.
    b.   The multiplier is the ratio of the unemployment rate to the inflation rate.
    c.   The multiplier is the ratio of the increase in equilibrium real GDP to the increase in autonomous expenditure.
    d.   The multiplier is the ratio of the increase in autonomous expenditure to the increase in equilibrium real GDP.

38. The multiplier works
    a.   only when autonomous expenditures rise, not when they decline.
    b.   only when autonomous expenditures decline, not when they rise.
    c.   both when autonomous expenditures rise and when they decline.
    d.   only if autonomous expenditures don't change.

39. The value of the multiplier is larger when
    a.   the value of the *MPC* is smaller.
    b.   the value of the *MPC* is larger.
    c.   the value of the *MPC* equals zero.
    d.   the value of the *MPC* is equal to the value of autonomous expenditure.

40. If we account for the impact of increasing GDP on imports, inflation, and interest rates, the simple multiplier formula would
    a.   reflect accurately the true value of the multiplier.
    b.   understate the true value of the multiplier.
    c.   overstate the true value of the multiplier.
    d.   change to $MPC/(1 - MPC)$.

41. Which of the following happens if the price level rises?
    a.   investment will rise, while consumption and net exports will fall
    b.   investment and consumption will fall, but net exports will rise
    c.   investment, consumption and net exports will all rise
    d.   investment, consumption and net exports will all fall

42. A curve showing the relationship between the price level and the level of aggregate expenditure in the economy, holding constant all other factors that affect aggregate expenditure, is called
    a.   the inflation curve.
    b.   the autonomous expenditure function.
    c.   aggregate demand.
    d.   the price-expenditure curve.

43. What is the value of *autonomous expenditure* in the following macroeconomic model?

$C = 1{,}000 + 0.75Y$	Consumption function
$I = 500$	Investment function
$G = 600$	Government spending function
$NX = -300$	Net export function
$Y = C + I + G + NX$	Equilibrium condition

   a. 800
   b. 1,800
   c. 2,400
   d. 7,200

44. Find equilibrium GDP using the following macroeconomic model:

$C = 1{,}000 + 0.75Y$	Consumption function
$I = 500$	Investment function
$G = 600$	Government spending function
$NX = -300$	Net export function
$Y = C + I + G + NX$	Equilibrium condition

   a. 800
   b. 1,800
   c. 2,400
   d. 7,200

45. Which of the following is correct concerning shifts in the aggregate demand (*AD*) curve?
   a. An increase in the price level will decrease real household wealth, which will decrease consumption and shift the *AD* curve to the left.
   b. A larger *MPS* will cause the *AD* curve to shift further to the right when there is an increase in autonomous expenditures.
   c. An increase in taxes will shift the *AD* curve to the left because the tax multiplier is negative.
   d. An increase in the price level will increase interest rates, which will reduce investment expenditures and shift the *AD* curve to the left.

Short Answer Questions

1. The *AE* curve is built up using the expenditure components as shown in Figure 11-9. How would the *AE* line and resulting macroeconomic equilibrium change if *NX* was negative?

_____

_____

2. The table below has several values of real GDP. The goal is to determine the level of equilibrium real GDP. To do this, assume that net taxes are $500 at every level of real GDP. Calculate disposable income (*YD*). Consumption is given for real GDP of $8,000. If the *MPC* is 0.7, determine consumption at the other levels of real GDP. Additionally, suppose that planned investment, government purchases, and net exports are $2,000, $2,000, and −$1,150 respectively at all levels of real GDP. Using these values, calculate *AE*. Based on these levels of *AE*, determine the unplanned changes in inventories. From the unplanned changes in inventories, determine if *Y* will rise or fall, or remain unchanged. What will be the equilibrium level of real GDP?

Real GDP (*Y*)	Net taxes (*T*)	Disposable income (*YD*)	Consumption (*C*)	Planned investment (*I*)	Government purchases (*G*)	Net exports (*NX*)	*AE* = *C+I+G+NX*	Unplanned changes in inventories	*Y* will:
$8,000	$500		$6,050	$2,000	$2,000	−$1,150			
9,000									
10,000									
11,000									
12,000									
13,000									
14,000									

3. Suppose that planned investment increases to a value of $2,300. Determine the new level of equilibrium real GDP. Use the table below.

Real GDP (*Y*)	Net taxes (*T*)	Disposable income (*YD*)	Consumption (*C*)	Planned investment (*I*)	Government purchases (*G*)	Net exports (*NX*)	*AE* = *C+I+G+NX*	Unplanned changes in inventories	*Y* will:
$8,000	$500		$6,050	$2,300	$2,000	−$1,150			
9,000									
10,000									
11,000									
12,000									
13,000									
14,000									

Explain why the level of equilibrium real GDP increases by more than the unplanned change in inventories. Calculate the value of the multiplier.

4. Suppose that the real interest rate falls. How will this fall affect the level of aggregate expenditure and the level of equilibrium real GDP? Show on a 45°-line graph.

_____

_____

5. Show how a change in government purchases will affect the *AD* curve.

_____

_____

_____

6. Suppose that current real GDP is $11,000 and potential real GDP is $12,000. If the *MPC* is 0.8, how much must autonomous spending change for the economy to move to potential GDP?

_____

_____

_____

True/False Questions

T F 1. In the aggregate expenditure model, the equilibrium level of real GDP is determined by the level of aggregate expenditure.

T F 2. Planned investment and actual investment are equal when there are no unplanned changes in inventories.

T F 3. If aggregate expenditure is greater than real GDP, then inventories will be rising.

T F 4. If aggregate expenditure is less than real GDP, then real GDP will decrease.

T F 5. Government purchases are the largest category of aggregate expenditure.

T F 6. An increase in the real interest rate will increase consumption spending.

T F 7. The marginal propensity to consume (*MPC*) is the ratio of consumption to disposable income (*C/YD*).

T F 8. If the marginal propensity to consume (*MPC*) is 0.8, then the marginal propensity to save (*MPS*) is also 0.8.

T F 9. At points above the 45° line, $AE > Y$.

T F 10. Macroeconomic equilibrium will occur when unplanned investment equals zero.

T F 11. If the $MPC = 0.8$, then the multiplier is 5.

T F 12. If the *MPS* is 0.4, then a $1,000 increase in autonomous expenditure will increase real GDP by $2,000.

T F 13. An increase in government purchases will result in an increase in autonomous expenditure.

T F 14. A decrease in the price level will increase autonomous expenditure, which will result in an increase in equilibrium real GDP.

T F 15. An increase in the price level will reduce equilibrium real GDP, shifting the *AD* curve to the right.

Answers to the Self-Test

Multiple-Choice Questions

Question	Answer	Comment
1	c	Aggregate expenditure (*AE*) is the total amount of spending in the economy: the sum of consumption, planned investment, government purchases, and net exports.
2	c	During some years, total spending in the economy, or aggregate expenditure, increases about as much as does the production of goods and services. If this happens, most firms will sell about what they expected to sell and they will probably not increase or decrease production, or the number of workers hired. During other years, total spending in the economy increases more than the production of goods and services. In these years, firms will increase production and hire more workers.
3	c	The aggregate expenditure model focuses on the relationship between total spending and real GDP in the short run.
4	c	The key idea of the aggregate expenditure model is that in any particular year, the level of gross domestic product (GDP) is determined mainly by the level of aggregate expenditure.
5	d	In 1936, the English economist John Maynard Keynes published *The General Theory of Employment, Interest, and Money*. In this book, he systematically analyzed the relationship between fluctuations in aggregate expenditure and fluctuations in GDP. Keynes identified four categories of aggregate expenditure that together equal GDP.
6	c	For the economy as a whole, we can say that actual investment spending will be greater than planned investment spending when there is an unplanned increase in inventories. Actual investment spending will be less than planned investment spending when there is an unplanned decrease in inventories. *Therefore, actual investment will only equal planned investment when there is no unplanned change in inventories.*
7	b	For the economy as a whole, macroeconomic equilibrium occurs where total spending, or aggregate expenditure, equals total production, or GDP.
8	a	Consumption is about 70 percent of GDP.
9	b	When aggregate expenditure is greater than GDP, the total amount of spending in the economy is greater than the total amount of production. The only way firms can sell more goods than they produce is to fill the excess orders from their inventories. That causes an unplanned decrease in inventories.
10	c	If aggregate expenditure is equal to real GDP, there is no reason for output to rise or fall. Therefore, the economy is in macroeconomic equilibrium.
11	c	When aggregate expenditure is greater than GDP, inventories will decline and GDP and total employment will increase.
12	a	The most important determinant of consumption is the current disposable income of households. For most households, the higher their disposable income, the more they spend, and the lower their disposable income, the less they spend.
13	a	When household wealth increases, consumption increases, and when household wealth decreases, consumption decreases. Shares of stock are an important category of household wealth. When stock prices increase, household wealth increases, and so does consumption.

14	b	When the interest rate is high, the reward for saving is increased and households are likely to save more and spend less.
15	c	We can use the *MPC* to tell us how much consumption will change as income changes. Change in consumption = change in disposable income x *MPC*. In this case: $80 billion x 0.9 = $72 billion.
16	c	The multiplier is $1/(1 - MPC)$, so with an *MPC* of 0.75 (and a multiplier of 4), a $100 increase in government purchases will increase real GDP by $400 (= 4 x $100).
17	c	Disposable income is equal to national income plus government transfer payments minus taxes. Government transfer payments minus taxes are referred to as net taxes. So, we can write:

$$\text{Disposable income} = \text{National income} - \text{Net taxes.}$$

| 18 | b | Households either spend their income, save it, or use it to pay taxes. For the economy as a whole, we can write |

$$\text{National income} = \text{Consumption} + \text{Saving} + \text{Taxes.}$$

When national income increases, there must be some combination of an increase in consumption, an increase in saving, or an increase in taxes. Therefore:

$$\text{Change in national income} = \text{Change in consumption} +$$
$$\text{Change in saving} + \text{Change in taxes.}$$

19	c	The marginal propensity to consume is also the slope of the consumption function.
20	c	The relationship between the marginal propensity to consume and the marginal propensity to save is: $1 = MPC + MPS$.
21	d	The *MPS* is defined as $\Delta S/\Delta YD$. The value of the *MPS* will be between 0 and 1, and the $MPS = 1 - MPC$ or $MPC + MPS = 1$.
22	b	Investment is subject to more fluctuations than consumption. Investment declined significantly during the recessions of 1980, 1981-82, 1990-91, and 2001. Following the recovery from the 1981-82 recession, investment increased only slowly, so that in 1992 it was at about the same level as in 1984. During the mid-to-late 1990s, investment increased very strongly; in 2000, real investment had risen to more than twice its 1992 level, before declining by more than 10 percent in 2001.
23	d	The higher the interest rate, the more expensive it becomes for firms and households to borrow. Because households and firms are interested in the cost of borrowing after taking into account the effects of inflation, investment spending will depend on the real interest rate. Therefore, holding the other factors that affect investment spending constant, there is an inverse relationship between the real interest rate and investment spending. Also, it is true that when the economy moves into a recession, many firms will postpone buying investment goods even if the demand for their own product is strong.
24	a	A reduction in the corporate income tax increases the after-tax profitability of investment spending. An increase in the corporate income tax decreases the after-tax profitability of investment spending.

25	c	Government purchases grew steadily for most of the 1979-2006 period, with the exception of the mid-1990s, when concern about the federal budget deficit caused real government purchases to fall for three years, beginning in 1992.
26	c	Net exports have been negative in most years between 1979 and 2006. Net exports rise when the U.S. economy is in recession because domestic spending falls and imports fall. Net exports decrease when the U.S. economy is expanding because domestic spending rises and imports rise.
27	a	The three most important variables that determine the level of net exports are: the price level in the United States relative to the price levels in other countries, the growth rate of GDP in the United States relative to the growth rates of GDP in other countries, and the exchange rate between the dollar and other currencies.
28	b	If inflation in the United States is lower than inflation in other countries, then prices of U.S. products increase more slowly than the prices of products of other countries. This difference in inflation rates increases the demand for U.S. products relative to the demand for foreign products. So, U.S. exports increase and U.S. imports decrease, which increases net exports.
29	b	When incomes rise faster in the United States than in other countries, American consumers' purchases of foreign goods and services will increase faster than foreign consumers' purchases of U.S. goods and services. As a result, net exports will fall.
30	b	As the value of the U.S. dollar rises, the foreign currency price of U.S. products sold in other countries rises, and the dollar price of foreign products sold in the United States falls. Therefore, an increase in the value of the dollar will reduce exports and increase imports, so net exports will fall.
31	a	At points above the line, aggregate expenditure is greater than GDP. At points below the line, aggregate expenditure is less than GDP.
32	b	As long as the *AE* line is above the 45° line, total spending is greater than total production and firms' inventories will fall. Unplanned declines in inventories lead firms to increase their production.
33	c	A key point to understand is that macroeconomic equilibrium can occur at any point on the 45° line. Ideally, we would like equilibrium to occur at potential real GDP. But in order for equilibrium to occur at the level of potential real GDP, aggregate expenditure must be high enough.
34	b	When the aggregate expenditure line intersects the 45° line at a level of GDP below potential real GDP, the economy is in recession.
35	c	When the economy is in a recession, the shortfall in aggregate expenditure can be measured as the vertical distance between the *AE* line and the 45° line at the level of potential real GDP. The shortfall in aggregate expenditure is exactly equal to the unplanned increase in inventories that would occur if the economy were initially at potential GDP. This is true because the unplanned increase in inventories measures the amount by which current aggregate expenditure is too low for the current level of production to be the equilibrium level.
36	b	Autonomous expenditure does not depend on the level of GDP. In the aggregate expenditure model that we have been using, planned investment spending, government spending, and net exports are all autonomous expenditures.
37	c	The ratio of the increase in equilibrium real GDP to the increase in autonomous expenditure is called the multiplier. The series of induced increases in consumption spending that results from an initial increase in autonomous expenditure is called the multiplier effect.

38	c	The multiplier works in forward—when increases in autonomous expenditures lead to increase in equilibrium in real GDP—but also in reverse. Many Americans became aware of this fact in the 1930s when reductions in autonomous expenditures were magnified by the multiplier into the worst economic disaster in twentieth century U.S. history.
39	b	The larger the *MPC*, the larger the value of the multiplier. With an *MPC* of 0.75, the multiplier is 4, but with an *MPC* of 0.50, the multiplier is only 2. This is because the larger the *MPC*, the greater the amount of additional consumption spending that takes place after each rise in income during the multiplier process.
40	c	Increasing GDP has an impact on imports, inflation, and interest rates that cause our simple formula to overstate the true value of the multiplier.
41	d	If the price level rises, investment, consumption and net exports will all fall, causing the *AE* line to shift down on the 45° line diagram. The *AE* line shifts down because with higher prices there will be less spending in the economy at every level of GDP or national income. Figure 11-13 shows that the downward shift of the *AE* line results in a lower level of equilibrium real GDP.
42	c	The relationship shown in Figure 11-14 between the price level and the level of aggregate expenditure is known as the aggregate demand curve (*AD*): a curve showing the relationship between the price level and the level of aggregate expenditure in the economy, holding constant all other factors that affect aggregate expenditure.
43	b	Autonomous expenditure equals $1000 + 500 + 600 - 300 = 1800$.
44	d	Equilibrium GDP = Autonomous spending x multiplier, or $1800 \times (1/(1 - 0.75)) = 1800 \times 4 = 7200$. The multiplier is 4 in this economy.
45	c	A negative tax multiplier implies that an increase in taxes will reduce real GDP. It follows that an increase in taxes will shift the *AD* curve to the left.

Short Answer Responses

1. If net exports are negative, then $C + I + G + NX$ will be less than $C + I + G$. In the 45° line graph, AE will be below $C + I + G$. Macroeconomic equilibrium still occurs at the level of Y that makes $AE = Y$.

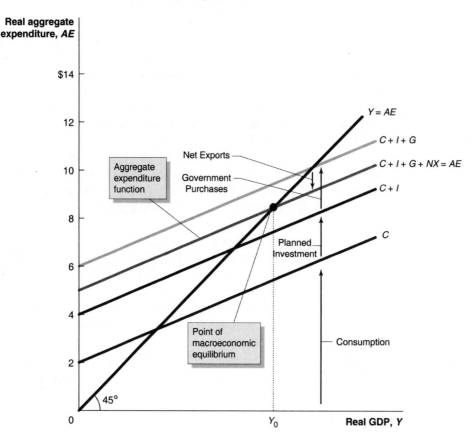

2. Filling in values for the table gives:

Real GDP (Y)	Taxes (T)	Disposable income (YD)	Consumption (C)	Planned investment (I)	Government purchases (G)	Net exports (NX)	AE = C+I+G+NX	Unplanned changes in inventories	Y will:
$8,000	$500	$7,500	$6,050	$2,000	$2,000	−$1,150	$8,900	−$900	increase
9,000	500	8,500	6,750	2,000	2,000	−1,150	9,600	−600	increase
10,000	500	9,500	7,450	2,000	2,000	−1,150	10,300	−300	increase
11,000	500	10,500	8,150	2,000	2,000	−1,150	11,000	0	no change
12,000	500	11,500	8,850	2,000	2,000	−1,150	11,700	300	decrease
13,000	500	12,500	9,550	2,000	2,000	−1,150	12,400	600	decrease
14,000	500	13,500	10,250	2,000	2,000	−1,150	13,100	900	decrease

The equilibrium level of real GDP will be at the level of real GDP where $AE = Y$ (or unplanned changes in inventories = 0). This is where real GDP = $11,000.

3. If planned investment increased to $2300, then the table would change to:

Real GDP (Y)	Net taxes (T)	Disposable income (YD)	Consumption (C)	Planned investment (I)	Government purchases (G)	Net exports (NX)	AE = C+I+G+NX	Unplanned changes in inventories	Y will:
$8,000	$500	$7,500	$6,050	$2,300	$2,000	−$1,150	$9,200	−$1,200	increase
9,000	500	8,500	6,750	2,300	2,000	−1,150	9,900	−900	increase
10,000	500	9,500	7,450	2,300	2,000	−1,150	10,600	−600	increase
11,000	500	10,500	8,150	2,300	2,000	−1,150	11,300	−300	increase
12,000	500	11,500	8,850	2,300	2,000	−1,150	12,000	0	no change
13,000	500	12,500	9,550	2,300	2,000	−1,150	12,700	300	decrease
14,000	500	13,500	10,250	2,300	2,000	−1,150	13,400	600	decrease

The new level of equilibrium real GDP equals $12,000. An increase in autonomous expenditure of $300 leads to an increase in real GDP of $1,000. This is the multiplier effect. Because $MPC = 0.7$, the multiplier $= 1/(1 − 0.7) = 3.33$, so a $300 increase in autonomous expenditure (in this case planned investment) will lead to an increase in real GDP of $1,000 ($1,000 = 3.33 x $300). You could also calculate the multiplier as

$$\Delta Y/\Delta I = (\$12,000 − \$11,000)/(\$2,300 − \$2,000) = \$1,000/\$300 = 3.33$$

4. The fall in the real interest rate will increase the level of consumption and the level of planned investment. The increase in C and I will increase AE. In the 45° line graph below, the AE curve shifts upward from AE_1 to AE_2.

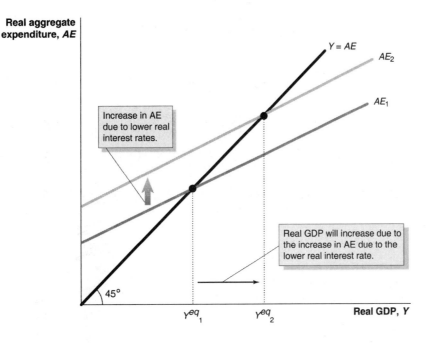

5. An increase in government spending will increase equilibrium real GDP. Because of the multiplier effect, the increase in equilibrium real GDP will be larger than the change in government purchases. This increase in equilibrium real GDP will be independent of the price level and is a shift to the right of the AD curve (from AD_0 to AD_1 in the graph below).

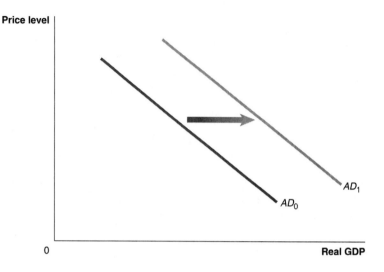

6. To increase real GDP from $11,000 to $12,000, real GDP must increase by $1,000. The simple multiplier for this economy is equal to 5 (= $1/(1 - MPC)$ = $1/(1 - 0.8)$ = $1/0.2$ = 5). For every one dollar increase in autonomous expenditure real GDP will rise by 5. The change in real GDP divided by the change in autonomous expenditure equals the multiplier, or ($1,000/Change in autonomous expenditure) = 5. Therefore, the necessary change in autonomous expenditure is $1,000/5 or $200.

True/False Answers

1. T
2. T
3. F   If aggregate expenditure is greater than real GDP, then inventories will be falling.
4. T
5. F   Consumption is the largest category of AE. See Table 11-2 in the textbook.
6. F   An increase in the real interest rate will reduce consumption spending.
7. F   The MPC is the ratio of the change in consumption to the change in disposable income, or $MPC = \Delta C/\Delta YD$.
8. F   The $MPC + MPS = 1$, so if the $MPC = 0.8$, then the $MPS = 0.2$.
9. T
10. T
11. T
12. F   If the $MPS = 0.4$, then the multiplier ($1/(1 - MPC)$ or $1/MPS$) is 2.5. With a multiplier of 2.5, an increase in autonomous expenditure of $1,000 will increase real GDP by $2,500 (($1/0.4$) x $1,000 = $2,500).
13. T
14. T
15. F   A change in the price level will cause a movement along the AD curve.

Chapter 12 (24)

Aggregate Demand and Aggregate Supply Analysis

Chapter Summary

During most years, prices rise (we have inflation) and real GDP increases (we have economic growth). The equilibrium level of real GDP and the price level are determined by aggregate demand and aggregate supply. **Aggregate demand** shows the relationship between the price level and the quantity of real GDP demanded by households, firms, and the government. **Aggregate supply** shows the relationship between the price level and the quantity of real GDP that firms are willing to produce. This chapter looks at how aggregate demand and aggregate supply determine the equilibrium level of real GDP and the price level, and how changes in aggregate demand and aggregate supply change the price level and the level of real GDP. The **aggregate demand and aggregate supply model** enables us to explain short-run fluctuations in real GDP and price level.

The **aggregate demand curve** shows the relationship between the price level and the level of planned aggregate expenditure by households, firms, and the government. The **short-run aggregate supply curve** shows the relationship in the short run between the price level and the quantity of real GDP supplied by firms. The **long-run aggregate supply curve** shows the relationship in the long run between the price level and the quantity of real GDP supplied. The four components of aggregate demand are consumption (C), investment (I), government purchases (G), and net exports (NX). **Monetary policy** involves the actions the Federal Reserve takes to manage the money supply and interest rates to pursue macroeconomic policy objectives. When the Federal Reserve takes actions to change interest rates, consumption and investment spending will change, shifting the aggregate demand curve. **Fiscal policy** involves changes in federal taxes and purchases that are intended to achieve macroeconomic policy objectives. Changes in federal taxes and purchases shift the aggregate demand curve.

The **long-run aggregate supply curve** is a vertical line because in the long run, real GDP is always at its potential level and is unaffected by the price level. The short-run aggregate supply curve slopes upward because workers and firms fail to predict accurately the future price level. A **supply shock** is an unexpected event that causes the short-run aggregate supply curve to shift. **Stagflation** is a combination of inflation and recession, usually resulting from a supply shock.

Learning Objectives

When you finish this chapter, you should be able to:

1. **Identify the determinants of aggregate demand and distinguish between a movement along the aggregate demand curve and a shift of the curve.** The **aggregate demand and aggregate supply model** enables us to explain short-run fluctuations in real GDP and the price level. The **aggregate**

demand curve *(AD)* shows the relationship between the price level and the quantity of real GDP demanded by households, firms, and the government. The **short-run aggregate supply curve (SRAS)** shows the relationship in the short run between the price level and the quantity of real GDP supplied by firms. The **long-run aggregate supply curve** shows the relationship in the long run between the price level and the quantity of real GDP supplied. The four components of aggregate demand are consumption (*C*), investment *(I)*, government purchases *(G)*, and net exports *(NX)*. The aggregate demand curve is downward sloping because a decline in the price level causes real consumption, investment and net exports to increase. If the price level changes but all else remains constant, the economy will move up or down a stationary aggregate demand curve. If any variable other than the price level changes, the aggregate demand curve will shift. The variables that cause the aggregate demand curve to shift fall into three categories: changes in government policies, changes in the expectations of households and firms, and changes in foreign variables.

2. **Identify the determinants of aggregate supply and distinguish between a movement along the short-run aggregate supply curve and a shift of the curve.** The long-run aggregate supply curve is a vertical line at full-employment GDP, because in the long run, real GDP is always at its full-employment level and is unaffected by the price level. The short-run aggregate supply curve slopes upward because workers and firms fail to predict accurately the future price level. The three main explanations why this failure results in an upward-sloping aggregate supply curve are contracts make wages and prices "sticky," businesses often adjust wages slowly, and menu costs make some prices sticky. If the price level changes but all else remains constant, the economy will move up or down a stationary aggregate supply curve. If any factor other than the price level changes, the aggregate supply curve will shift. The aggregate supply curve shifts as a result of increases in the labor force, increases in the capital stock, technological change, expected increases or decreases in the future price level, adjustments of workers and firms to errors in past expectations about the price level, and unexpected increases or decreases in the price of an important raw material.

3. **Use the aggregate demand and aggregate supply model to illustrate the difference between short-run and long-run macroeconomic equilibrium.** In long-run macroeconomic equilibrium, the aggregate demand and short-run aggregate supply curves intersect at a point *on* the long-run aggregate supply curve. In short-run macroeconomic equilibrium, the aggregate demand and short-run aggregate supply curves often intersect at a point *off* the long-run aggregate supply curve. An automatic mechanism drives the economy to long-run equilibrium. If short-run equilibrium occurs at a point below full-employment real GDP, wages and prices will fall and the short-run aggregate supply curve will shift to the right until full employment is restored. If short-run equilibrium occurs at a point beyond full-employment real GDP, wages and prices will rise and the short-run aggregate supply curve will shift to the left until full employment is restored. Real GDP can be temporarily above or below its full-employment level, either because of shifts in the aggregate demand curve or because supply shocks lead to shifts in the aggregate supply curve.

4. **Use the dynamic aggregate demand and aggregate supply model to analyze macroeconomic conditions.** To make the aggregate demand and aggregate supply model more realistic, we must make it *dynamic* by incorporating three facts that were left out of the basic model:
   a. Potential real GDP increases continually, shifting the long-run aggregate supply curve to the right.
   b. During most years, aggregate demand will be shifting to the right.
   c. Except during periods when workers and firms expect high rates of inflation, the aggregate supply curve will be shifting to the right. The dynamic aggregate demand and aggregate supply model allows us to analyze macroeconomic conditions, including the recovery from the 2001 recession.

Appendix: Understand macroeconomic schools of thought. There are three major alternative models to the aggregate demand and aggregate supply model. Monetarism emphasizes that the quantity of money should be increased at a constant rate. New classical macroeconomics emphasizes that workers and firms have rational expectations. The real business cycle model focuses on real, rather than monetary, causes of the business cycle.

Chapter Review

Chapter Opener: The Fortunes of FedEx Follow the Business Cycle (pages 390-391)

Many economists, such as former Chairman of the Federal Reserve Alan Greenspan, believe that changes in the quantity of packages shipped by FedEx are a good indicator of the overall state of the economy. FedEx was founded by Fred Smith, who in the 1960s proposed a new method of sending packages that moved away from using passenger airlines. FedEx's profits rise and fall with the quantity of packages they ship, and that quantity changes with the level of economic activity, referred to as the business cycle.

📖 Helpful Study Hint

Read *An Inside Look* at the end of the chapter to learn how a decline in the growth rate of real GDP affected freight-transportation giant United Parcel Service, Inc. (UPS).

Freight-transportation companies' earnings are dependent on the volume of shipments to retailers; in a slowing economy, retailers typically reduce their orders from manufacturers as they carry smaller planned inventories than usual.

If the economy falls into recession, will your employer cut your pay – or cut your job? *Economics in YOUR Life!* at the start of this chapter poses these questions. Keep the questions in mind as you read the chapter. The authors will answer the questions at the end of the chapter.

12.1 LEARNING OBJECTIVE

12.1 Aggregate Demand (pages 392-398)

Learning Objective 1 Identify the determinants of aggregate demand and distinguish between a movement along the aggregate demand curve and a shift of the curve.

This chapter uses the **aggregate demand and aggregate supply model** to explain fluctuations in real GDP and the price level. Real GDP and the price level are determined in the short run by the intersections of the aggregate demand curve and the aggregate supply curve. This is seen in Figure 12-1 below. Changes in real GDP and changes in the price level are caused by shifts in these two curves.

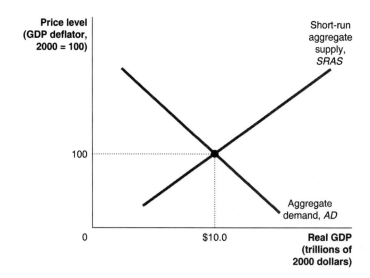

The **aggregate demand curve (AD)** shows the relationship between the price level and the level of real GDP demanded by households, firms and the government. The four components of real GDP are:

- Consumption (*C*)
- Investment (*I*)
- Government purchases (*G*)
- Net exports (*NX*)

Using *Y* for real GDP, then we can write the following:

$$Y = C + I + G + NX.$$

📖 Helpful Study Hint

The aggregate demand curve is different from the demand curve for a single product (like a Bic pen). The demand curve for a Bic pen shows what happens to the quantity of Bic pens that will be purchased at different prices for Bic pens, holding other prices, income and other factors affecting demand for Bic pens constant. On the *AD* curve, the price *level* changes, not just the price of one product, so that all prices are changing at the same time.

The aggregate demand curve is downward sloping because a decrease in the price level increases the quantity of real GDP demanded. We assume that government purchases do not change as the price level changes. There are three reasons why the other components of real GDP change as the price level changes:

- ***The wealth effect***. As the price level increases, the real value of household wealth falls, and so will consumption. In contrast, if the price level declines, real household wealth rises and so does consumption.

- ***The interest rate effect***. A higher price level will tend to increase interest rates. Higher interest rates will reduce investment spending by firms as borrowing costs rise. Additionally, higher interest rates will also reduce consumption spending.

- *The international effect*. A higher price level will make U.S. goods relatively more expensive compared to other countries' goods. This will reduce exports, increase imports, and, therefore, reduce net exports.

Price level changes cause movements along the *AD* curve. A change in any other variable that affects the willingness of households, firms, and the government to spend will cause a shift in the *AD* curve. The variables that cause *AD* to shift fall into three categories:

- *Changes in government policies*. **Monetary policy** refers to the actions the Federal Reserve takes to manage the money supply and interest rates to pursue macroeconomic policy objectives. **Fiscal policy** refers to changes in federal taxes and purchases that are intended to achieve macroeconomic policy objectives, such as high unemployment, price stability, and high rates of economic growth.
- *Changes in expectations of households and firms*. If consumers or firms are more optimistic about the future, they may purchase more goods and services, increasing consumption and investment expenditures.
- *Changes in foreign variables*. As income changes in other countries, consumers in those countries may buy more U.S. goods, causing exports to increase. Changes in exchange rates can also shift the *AD* curve; for example, if the U.S. dollar appreciates relative to other currencies, it makes imported goods less expensive and exports more expensive to foreign consumers, shifting the *AD* curve to the left.

The variables that shift the *AD* curve are summarized in textbook Table 12-1 reproduced below:

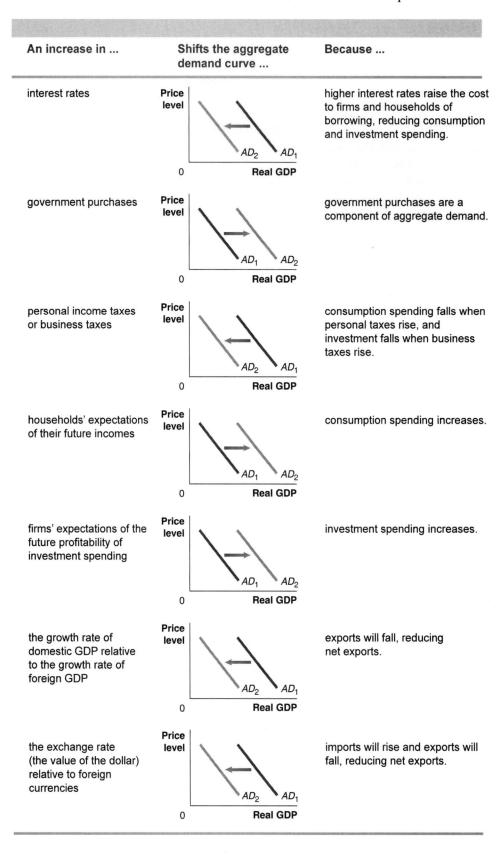

An increase in ...	Shifts the aggregate demand curve ...	Because ...
interest rates		higher interest rates raise the cost to firms and households of borrowing, reducing consumption and investment spending.
government purchases		government purchases are a component of aggregate demand.
personal income taxes or business taxes		consumption spending falls when personal taxes rise, and investment falls when business taxes rise.
households' expectations of their future incomes		consumption spending increases.
firms' expectations of the future profitability of investment spending		investment spending increases.
the growth rate of domestic GDP relative to the growth rate of foreign GDP		exports will fall, reducing net exports.
the exchange rate (the value of the dollar) relative to foreign currencies		imports will rise and exports will fall, reducing net exports.

📖Helpful Study Hint

If you own a car, do you know where the parts come from and where the car was built? Although you may own a "Japanese" car or an "American" car, you may be surprised to learn that its parts come from various countries. Read *Making the Connection: In a Global Economy, How Can You Tell the Imports from the Domestic Goods?* The level of imports and exports influence the level of aggregate demand in the United States. Some products that are produced by U.S. firms, such as the Ford Mustang, have about 35 percent of their parts from countries other than the United States or Canada. Contrast that with the Toyota Sienna, which is built in Princeton, Indiana and has about 90 percent of its contents from the United States or Canada.

It is important to understand why the *AD* curve slopes downward. Read *Don't Let This Happen to YOU!* Unlike the demand curve for an individual good where the prices of other goods are held constant, on the aggregate demand curve as the price level increases, all prices in the economy are increasing. The aggregate demand curve has a downward slope because of the wealth effect, the interest rate effect, and the international trade effect.

12.2 LEARNING OBJECTIVE

12.2 Aggregate Supply (pages 399-403)

Learning Objective 2 Identify the determinants of aggregate supply and distinguish between a movement along the short-run aggregate supply curve and a shift of the curve.

The aggregate supply curve shows the effects of price level changes on the quantity of goods and services firms are willing to supply. Because price level changes have different effects in the short run and in the long run, there is an aggregate supply curve for the long run and an aggregate supply curve for the short run.

The **long-run aggregate supply curve (*LRAS*)** is a curve showing the relationship in the long run between the price level and the level of real GDP supplied. As we saw in Chapter 10, in the long run the level of real GDP is determined by:

- the number of workers
- the capital stock
- the available technology

Because price level changes do not affect these factors, price level changes do not affect the level of real GDP in the long run. The long-run aggregate supply curve is therefore a vertical line. Increases in the number of workers, the capital stock, and the available technology will increase real GDP and shift the *LRAS* to the right. This is seen in textbook Figure 12-2:

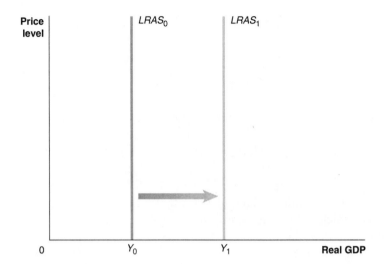

Although the *LRAS* curve is vertical, the short-run aggregate supply curve (*SRAS*) is upward sloping. In the short run, as the price level increases, the quantity of goods and services that firms are willing to supply increases. This short-run relationship between the price level and the quantity of goods and services supplied occurs because as prices of final goods and services rise, the prices of inputs, such as wages and natural resource, rise more slowly, and may even remain constant. A consequence of this is that as the prices of final goods and services rise, profits increase and firms are willing to supply more goods and services in the short run. Additionally, as the overall price level rises, some firms are slower to adjust their prices. These firms may find their sales increasing and produce more output. Economists believe that some firms adjust prices more slowly than others and wages adjust more slowly than the price level because firms and workers fail to perfectly forecast changes in the price level. If firms and workers could accurately forecast prices, the short-run and long-run aggregate supply curves would both be vertical.

The three most common explanations for the upward-sloping short run supply curve are:

- Contracts make some wages and prices sticky. For example, the labor contract between General Motors and the United Automobile Workers fixes wages by contract.
- Firms are often slow to adjust wages. Firms tend to adjust wages once or twice a year, making wages slow to change. In addition, firms are often also reluctant to cut wages.
- Menu costs make some prices sticky. Some firms are slow to change prices because of expenses associated with the price changes. These are called **menu costs**.

The short-run aggregate supply curve will shift to the right when something happens that makes firms willing to supply more goods and services at the same prices. The short-run aggregate supply curve will shift with:

- Changes in the labor force or capital stock.
- Technological change.
- Expected changes in the future price level.
- Adjustment of workers and firms to errors in past expectations about the price level.
- Unexpected changes in the price of natural resources that are important inputs to many industries (this is often referred to as a **supply shock**).

 Helpful Study Hint

Natural resource prices can rise or fall. An adverse supply shock usually refers to an increase in resource prices.

> Oil is a natural resource. When hurricane Katrina hit New Orleans in 2005, it disrupted one-quarter of U.S. oil and natural gas output. This unexpected fall in oil production caused oil prices to soar. This made it more costly for firms to operate and produce and transport their goods.

The factors that shift the *SRAS* curve are summarized in textbook Table 12-2 reproduced below:

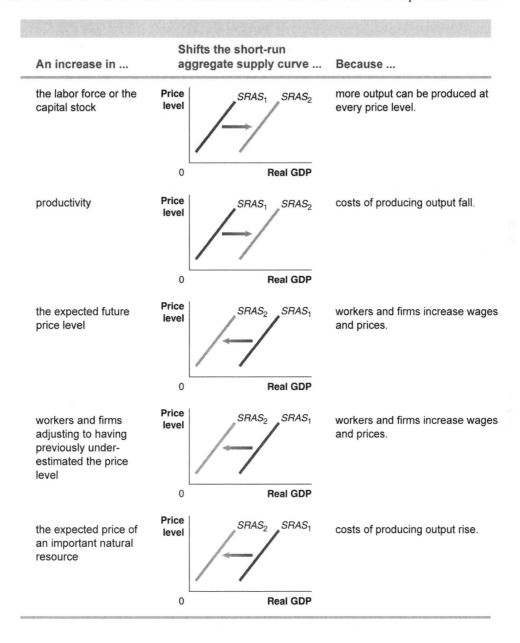

An increase in ...	Shifts the short-run aggregate supply curve ...	Because ...
the labor force or the capital stock		more output can be produced at every price level.
productivity		costs of producing output fall.
the expected future price level		workers and firms increase wages and prices.
workers and firms adjusting to having previously under-estimated the price level		workers and firms increase wages and prices.
the expected price of an important natural resource		costs of producing output rise.

Extra Solved Problem 12-2

Chapter 12 in the textbook includes two Solved Problems. Here is an extra Solved Problem to help you build your skills solving economic problems:

Shifts and Movements Along the Short-Run Aggregate Supply Curve

Supports Learning Objective 2: Identify the determinants of aggregate supply and distinguish between a movement along the short-run aggregate supply curve and a shift of the curve.

Show how an increase in wages has a different effect on the *SRAS* curve than does an increase in prices.

SOLVING THE PROBLEM

Step 1: **Review the chapter material.**
This question is about the difference in shifts and movements along the *SRAS* curve, so you may want to review the section "The Short-Run Aggregate Supply Curve," which begins on page 400 of the textbook.

Step 2: **Use a graph to show the effect on the SRAS curve of a change in the price level.**
Changes in the price level cause movements along the *SRAS* curve. This is shown in the movement from point *A* to point *B* in the graph below. The higher price level leads firms to produce more goods and services, resulting in a higher level of real GDP in the short run.

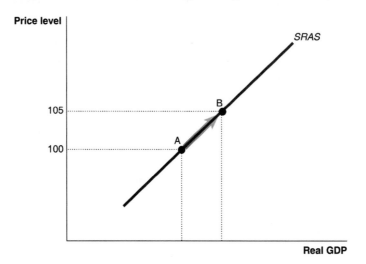

Step 3: **Use a second graph to show the effect on the SRAS curve of a change in wages.**
Wages are one of the economic variables that are held constant along a given *SRAS* curve. An increase in the overall wage rate will shift the *SRAS* curve to the left. This is seen in the movement from point *A* to point *B* in the graph below. If wages rise, the production costs of firms increase, and, in the short run, at any given price level firms are willing to supply a lower level of real GDP.

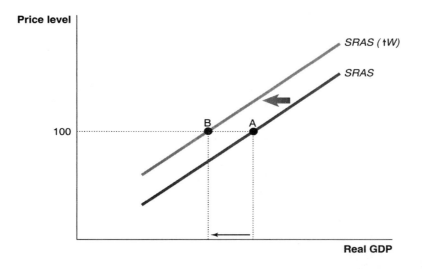

12.3 Macroeconomic Equilibrium in the Long Run and the Short Run (pages 404-407)

Learning Objective 3: Use the aggregate demand and aggregate supply model to illustrate the difference between short-run and long-run macroeconomic equilibrium.

In long-run macroeconomic equilibrium, the *AD* curve and the *SRAS* curve intersect at a point on the *LRAS* curve. This is shown in textbook Figure 12-4 below:

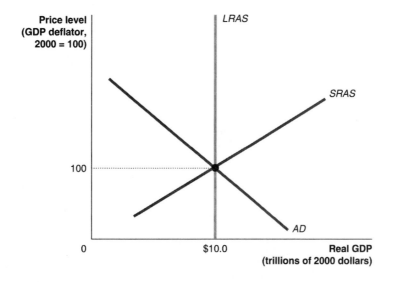

Because this point—price level of 100 and real GDP of $10.0 trillion—is on the *LRAS* curve, firms will be operating at normal levels of capacity and everyone that wants a job at the prevailing wage rate will have one (although there will still be frictional and structural unemployment).

📖 Helpful Study Hint

Remember that although in long-run macroeconomic equilibrium there is no cyclical unemployment, there will still be frictional and structural unemployment. The *LRAS* curve represents the level of real GDP that will be produced when firms are operating at their normal capacity; it does *not* represent the level of real GDP that could be produced if firms operated at their maximum capacity.

The aggregate demand and aggregate supply model can be used to examine events that move the economy away from long-run equilibrium. As a starting point, assume:

- The economy has not been experiencing inflation.
- The economy has not been experiencing long-run growth.

Recession

A decline in *AD* will cause a short-run decline in real GDP. As the *AD* curve shifts to the left, the economy will move to a new short-run equilibrium where *AD* intersects the *SRAS* curve at a level of real GDP below potential GDP. The economy will be in a recession. Because firms need fewer workers to produce the lower level of output, wages will begin to fall. As wages fall, firms' costs will decline. Over time, as costs fall, the *SRAS* curve will shift to the right and the economy will move back to long-run equilibrium at potential GDP. This is shown in textbook Figure 12-5 below:

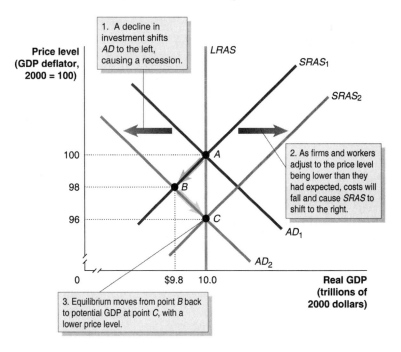

This adjustment back to long-run equilibrium will occur automatically without any form of government intervention. But it may take several years to complete this adjustment. This is usually referred to as an *automatic mechanism*.

Expansion

An increase in *AD* will cause a short-run expansion in the economy. An increase in *AD* will shift the *AD* curve to the right as spending by households, firms, or government increases. This increased spending will cause a short-run expansion as firms meet increased demand by increasing production. In expanding production, firms may hire workers who would normally be structurally or frictionally unemployed. The lower level of unemployment will eventually result in higher wages, which will raise costs to firms. These higher costs will shift the *SRAS* curve to the left and eventually return output to potential GDP. This is shown in Figure 12-6 below:

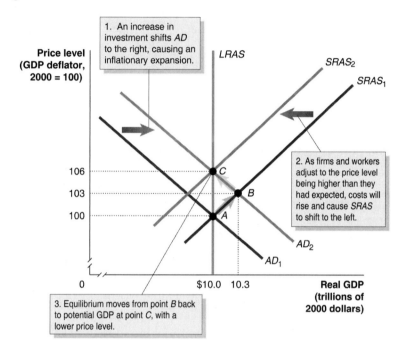

As with a recession, the return to long-run equilibrium is an automatic adjustment in the long run. The inflation caused by an expansion beyond potential GDP usually occurs fairly quickly.

Supply Shock

An adverse supply shock (such as an oil price increase) is a shift to the left of the *SRAS* curve not caused by the automatic adjustment mechanism of the economy. In the short run, this adverse supply shock will reduce real GDP and increase the price level. The higher price level and recession is often referred to as **stagflation**. The recession caused by the supply shock will result in lower wages, which will shift the *SRAS* curve to the right, returning the economy to the initial long-run equilibrium. This is shown in textbook Figure 12-7 below:

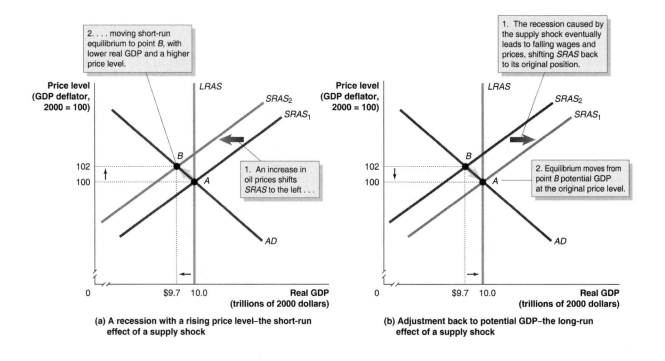

(a) A recession with a rising price level–the short-run effect of a supply shock

(b) Adjustment back to potential GDP–the long-run effect of a supply shock

Extra Solved Problem 12-3

Chapter 12 in the textbook includes two Solved Problems. Here is an extra Solved Problem to help you build your skills solving economic problems:

Determining Growth and Inflation Rates

Supports Learning Objective 3: Use the aggregate demand and aggregate supply model to illustrate the difference between short-run and long-run macroeconomic equilibrium.

Draw graphs showing how, as the *AD* and *LRAS* curves shift over time, real GDP and the price level are affected.

SOLVING THE PROBLEM

Step 1: **Review the chapter material.**
This problem is about analyzing the effects of shifts in aggregate demand and aggregate supply on the price level and real GDP, so you may want to review the section "Recessions, Expansions, and Supply Shocks," which begins on page 404 of the textbook.

Step 2: **Discuss how the price level and level of real GDP are determined in the long run.**
The price level and the level of real GDP are determined in the long run by the levels of aggregate demand and *LRAS*. Over time, *LRAS* changes due to growth in the capital stock, growth in the number of workers, and technological change. These cause the *LRAS* curve to shift to the right from $LRAS_0$ to $LRAS_1$ in the graph:

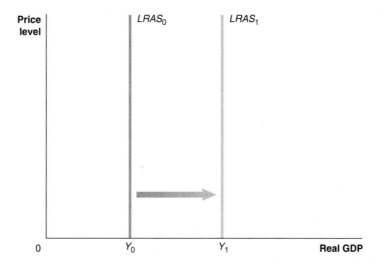

At the same time, the *AD* curve will also shift to the right as consumption, investment, and government purchases all increase. Combining the shifts of the *LRAS* and *AD* curves on one graph gives the following:

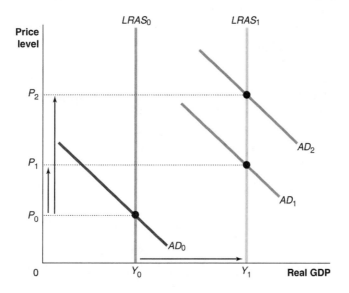

Step 3:   **Determine the amount of real GDP growth.**

The amount of real GDP growth depends on the change in *LRAS*. In the case above, real GDP will grow from Y_0 to Y_1. The shift in *AD* will not affect that long run result. How much the price level rises—in other words, how high the inflation rate is—will be affected by the shift in *AD*. The larger the change in *AD*, the higher the inflation rate. In the long run, output growth is determined by shifts in the *LRAS* curve, and inflation is determined by shifts in the *AD* curve.

12.4 A Dynamic Aggregate Demand and Aggregate Supply Model (pages 408-417)

Learning Objective 4 Use the dynamic aggregate demand and aggregate supply model to analyze macroeconomic conditions.

The dynamic model of aggregate demand and aggregate supply builds on the basic aggregate demand and aggregate supply model to account for two key macroeconomic facts: the economy experiences long-term growth as potential real GDP increases every year, and the economy experiences at least some inflation every year. Three changes are made to the basic model:

- Potential real GDP increases continually, shifting the *LRAS* curve to the right.
- During most years, the *AD* curve will also shift to the right.
- Except during periods when workers expect very high rates of inflation, the *SRAS* curve will also shift to the right.

📖 Helpful Study Hint

Spend time reviewing the acetate of Figure 12-8 on page 408 of the main text. This acetate builds the dynamic aggregate demand and aggregate supply model step by step.

An example of including these changes is shown in textbook Figure 12-9 reproduced below:

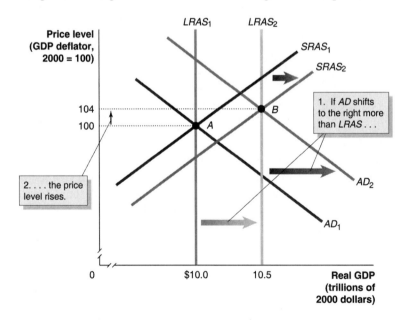

📖 Helpful Study Hint

> The dynamic aggregate demand and aggregate supply model assumes that the *LRAS* curve shifts to the right each year, which represents normal long-run growth in the economy. The *AD* curve also typically shifts to the right each year as the components of *AD* change.

If we start at point *A*, the increase in *LRAS* and *SRAS* along with the shift in the *AD* curve will move the equilibrium to point *B* where the price level and the level of real GDP are both higher. If the *AD* curve shifts to the right more than the *LRAS* curve, the economy will experience both growth and inflation. If the *AD* and *LRAS* curves had shifted to the right by the same amount, the economy would have experienced growth without inflation. If the economy had suffered an adverse supply shock during the same period (with the *SRAS* curve shifting to the left), the price level would have increased more and real GDP would have increased less.

The dynamic aggregate demand and supply model suggests that inflation is caused by increases in total spending that are larger than increases in real GDP and by the *SRAS* curve shifting to the left due to higher costs. The model can shed light on the slow recovery from the recession of 2001. This recession was due to the end of the stock market bubble. The fall in stock prices reduced consumer wealth, and reduced the increases in consumption and investment spending below what they would otherwise have been. Firms that invested to create an internet presence cut back on their investment spending due to low levels of internet sales. The terrorist attacks of September 11, 2001 increased the level of uncertainty in the economy. Corporate accounting scandals created more uncertainty. These changes are shown in Figure 12-10 below, which shows the recession and the growth of the economy in 2002.

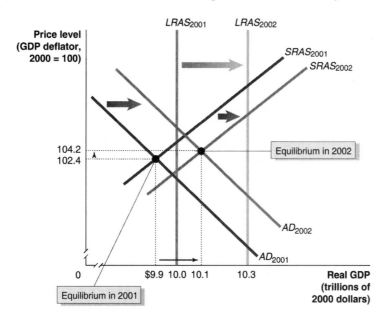

Low interest rates, tax cuts, and a rising stock market contributed to the increase in the economy in 2003-2004. This is shown in Figure 12-11 below.

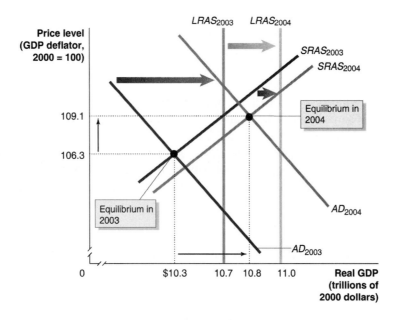

The economy in 2008 is experiencing several events that could push it into a recession. Higher oil prices, the collapse of the housing "bubble," and problems in financial markets may push the economy into a recession.

📖Helpful Study Hint

Read *Making the Connection: Does Rising Productivity Growth Reduce Employment?* Growth in labor productivity (output per worker) is a key requirement for a rising standard of living. But if firms can produce more output per worker, they are less likely to hire extra workers. This may be the cause of the slow employment growth immediately after the end of the 2001 recession. Rising productivity may have made it possible for some firms to expand production without increasing employment. This was a short-run effect, however. In the long run, employment is determined by population growth and by the fraction of the population in the labor force rather than by the rate of productivity growth.

Read *Making the Connection: Do Oil Shocks Still Cause Recessions?* An increase in oil prices will cause FedEx to increase the price of delivering packages, which will cause a reduction in the number of packages delivered. If significant cost increases resulting from higher oil prices affect enough firms, the *SRAS* curve will shift to the left, potentially moving the economy toward a recession. This happened in the recession of 1974-1975, where oil prices rose sharply from $3 per barrel to $10 per barrel. This sharp rise in the price of oil was labeled an oil price shock. Oil prices have been rising from 2004–2007, and the economy has continued to expand. This is because the economy is less vulnerable to oil price increases and because of the more gradual increase in prices. Economist Keith Sill estimates that a 10 percent increase in oil prices will result in a reduction in the annual growth rate of real GDP of about 0.5 percent.

📖 Helpful Study Hint

Economics in YOUR Life! at the start of this chapter asked if you should expect a pay cut if the economy falls into recession. Firms are not likely to cut wages because of the effect on morale and productivity and the fear that workers may leave for a competitor. Firms are very reluctant to lay off skilled workers, because they may not be able to rehire them when the recession is over.

Key Terms

Aggregate demand and aggregate supply model. A model that explains short-run fluctuations in real GDP and the price level.

Aggregate demand curve (*AD*). A curve showing the relationship between the price level and the quantity of real GDP demanded by households, firms, and the government.

Fiscal policy. These are changes in federal taxes and purchases intended to attain macroeconomic policy goals.

Long-run aggregate supply curve (*LRAS*). A curve showing the relationship in the long run between the price level and the quantity of real GDP supplied.

Menu costs. The costs to firms of changing prices.

Monetary policy. These are actions by the Federal Reserve to change the money supply and interest rates in order to achieve macroeconomic policy objectives.

Short-run aggregate supply curve (*SRAS*). A curve showing the relationship in the short run between the price level and the quantity of real GDP supplied by firms.

Stagflation. A combination of inflation and recession, usually resulting from a supply shock.

Supply shock. An unexpected event that causes the short-run aggregate supply curve to shift.

Appendix

Macroeconomic Schools of Thought (pages 426-428)

LEARNING OBJECTIVE: Understand macroeconomic schools of thought.

There are three major alternative models to the aggregate demand and aggregate supply model. **Monetarism** emphasizes that the quantity of money should be increased at a constant rate. **New classical macroeconomics** emphasizes that workers and firms have rational expectations. The **real business cycle model** focuses on real, rather than monetary, causes of the business cycle.

Key Terms – Appendix

Keynesian revolution. The name given to the widespread acceptance during the 1930s and 1940s of John Maynard Keynes's macroeconomic model.

Monetarism. The macroeconomic theories of Milton Friedman and his followers, particularly the idea that the quantity of money should be increased at a constant rate.

Monetary growth rule. A plan for increasing the quantity of money at a fixed rate that does not respond to changes in economic conditions.

New classical macroeconomics. The macroeconomic theories of Robert Lucas and others, particularly the idea that workers and firms have rational expectations.

Real business cycle model. A macroeconomic model that focuses on real, rather than monetary, causes of the business cycle.

Self-Test

(Answers are provided at the end of the Self-Test.)

Multiple-Choice Questions

1. The aggregate demand and aggregate supply model explains
   a. the effect of changes in the inflation rate on the nominal interest rate.
   b. short-run fluctuations in real GDP and the price level.
   c. the effect of long-run economic growth on the standard of living.
   d. the effect of changes in the interest rate on investment spending.

2. The aggregate demand curve shows the relationship between the price level and the quantity of real GDP demanded by
   a. households.
   b. firms.
   c. the government.
   d. all of the above

3. The *wealth effect* refers to the fact that
   a. when the price level falls, the real value of household wealth rises, and so will consumption.
   b. when income rises, consumption rises.
   c. when the price level falls, the nominal value of assets rises, while the real value of assets remains the same.
   d. all of the above

4. The *interest rate effect* refers to the fact that a higher price level results in
   a. higher interest rates and higher investment.
   b. higher interest rates and lower investment.
   c. lower interest rates and lower investment.
   d. lower interest rates and higher investment.

5. The *international-trade effect* refers to the fact that an increase in the price level will result in
   a. an increase in exports and a decrease in imports.
   b. a decrease in exports and an increase in imports.
   c. an increase in exports and an increase in imports.
   d. a decrease in exports and a decrease in imports.

6. If the price level increases, then
   a. the economy will move up and to the left along a stationary aggregate demand curve.
   b. the aggregate demand curve will shift to the right.
   c. the aggregate demand curve will shift to the left.
   d. none of the above

7. Which of the following factors *does not* cause the aggregate demand curve to shift?
   a. a change in the price level
   b. a change in government policies
   c. a change in the expectations of households and firms
   d. a change in foreign variables

8. Which of the following will *not* shift the aggregate demand curve to the right?
   a. a fall in the price level
   b. a decrease in taxes
   c. households expecting higher future income
   d. exports rising

9. Which of the following government policies affects the economy through intended changes in the money supply and interest rates?
   a. fiscal policy
   b. monetary policy
   c. both fiscal and monetary policies
   d. neither fiscal nor monetary policies

10. How can government policies shift the aggregate demand curve to the right?
    a. by increasing personal income taxes
    b. by increasing business taxes
    c. by increasing government purchases
    d. all of the above

11. Which of the following statements is correct?
    a. If households become more optimistic about their future incomes, the aggregate demand curve will shift to the right.
    b. If firms become more optimistic about the future profitability of investment spending, the aggregate demand curve will shift to the right.
    c. Both a. and b.
    d. Neither a. nor b. Optimism or pessimism do not have anything to do with shifts in the aggregate demand curve.

12. If real GDP in the United States increases faster than real GDP in other countries, U.S. imports will _____ faster than U.S. exports, and net exports will _____.
    a. increase; rise
    b. increase; fall
    c. decrease; rise
    d. decrease; fall

13. If the *exchange rate* between the dollar and foreign currencies rises (the dollar rises in value versus foreign currencies), the price in foreign currency of U.S. products will _____ and the U.S. aggregate demand curve will shift to the _____.
    a. rise; right
    b. rise; left
    c. fall; right
    d. fall; left

14. An increase in *net exports* that results from a change in the price level in the United States
    a. will shift the aggregate demand curve to the right.
    b. will shift the aggregate demand curve to the left.
    c. will not cause the aggregate demand curve to shift.
    d. will have an indeterminate effect on aggregate demand.

15. Which of the following statements is true?
    a. In the long run, increases in the price level result in an increase in real GDP.
    b. In the long run, increases in the price level result in a decrease in real GDP.
    c. In the long run, changes in the price level do not affect the level of real GDP.
    d. In the long run, changes in the price level may either increase or decrease real GDP.

16. The long-run aggregate supply curve
    a. is positively sloped.
    b. shifts to the right as technological change occurs.
    c. is negatively sloped.
    d. shifts to the left as the capital stock of the country grows.

17. Which of the following factors will cause the long-run aggregate supply curve to shift to the right?
    a. an increase in the number of workers in the economy
    b. the accumulation of more machinery and equipment
    c. technological change
    d. all of the above

18. Which of the following factors will shift the short-run aggregate supply to the right?
    a. an increase in the price level
    b. an increase in the wage rate
    c. an increase in the cost of producing output
    d. the labor force increases

19. Why does the short-run aggregate supply curve slope upward?
    a. because profits rise when the prices of the goods and services firms sell rise more rapidly than the prices they pay for inputs
    b. because an increase in market price results in an increase in quantity supplied, as stated by the *law of supply*
    c. because, as the number of workers, machinery, equipment, and technological changes increase, quantity supplied increases
    d. all of the above

20. If firms and workers could predict the future price level exactly, the short-run aggregate supply curve would be
    a. downward sloping.
    b. upward sloping.
    c. horizontal.
    d. the same as the long-run aggregate supply curve.

21. Why does the failure of workers and firms to accurately predict the price level result in an upward-sloping aggregate supply curve?
    a. because contracts make some wages and prices "sticky"
    b. because firms are often slow to adjust wages
    c. because menu costs make some prices "sticky"
    d. all of the above

22. Assume that steel is the only good produced in the economy. Which of the following would explain why the short-run aggregate supply curve for steel would be upward sloping?
    a. Steel demand and steel prices begin to rise rapidly, and the wages of steel workers rise as the demand for workers increases.
    b. Steel demand and steel prices begin to rise rapidly, but the price of coal—an input into the production of steel—remains fixed by contract.
    c. Steel demand and steel prices begin to rise rapidly, but foreign producers increase production faster than domestic producers increase production.
    d. all of the above

23. What are *menu costs*?
    a. the costs of searching for profitable opportunities
    b. the costs associated with guarding against the effects of inflation
    c. the costs to firms of changing prices
    d. the costs of a fixed list of inputs

24. What is the impact of an increase in the price level on the *short-run* aggregate supply curve?
    a. a shift of the curve to the right
    b. a shift of the curve to the left
    c. a movement up and to the right along a stationary curve
    d. a combination of a movement along the curve and a shift of the curve

25. Which of the following will cause the *short-run* aggregate supply curve to shift to the right?
    a. a higher expected future price level
    b. an increase in the actual (or current) price level
    c. a technological change
    d. all of the above

26. If workers and firms across the economy adjust to the fact that the price level is higher than they had expected it to be,
    a. there will be a movement up and to the right along a stationary aggregate supply curve.
    b. there will be a movement down and to the left along a stationary aggregate supply curve.
    c. the short-run aggregate supply curve will shift to the left.
    d. the short-run aggregate supply curve will shift to the right.

27. If oil prices rise unexpectedly,
    a. there will be a movement up and to the right along a stationary aggregate supply curve.
    b. there will be a movement down and to the left along a stationary aggregate supply curve.
    c. the short-run aggregate supply curve will shift to the left.
    d. the short-run aggregate supply curve will shift to the right.

28. An unexpected increase in the price of oil would be called _____ by economists.
    a. a demand shock
    b. an adverse supply shock
    c. disinflation
    d. an increase in menu costs

29. A supply shock will
    a. increase the real GDP in the short-run.
    b. not change real GDP in the long-run.
    c. shift the long-run aggregate supply curve to the right.
    d. decrease both the price level and real GDP in the short-run.

30. If firms reduce investment spending and the economy slumps into a recession, which of the following contributes to the adjustment that causes the economy to return to its long-run equilibrium?
    a. the eventual agreement by workers to accept lower wages
    b. the decision by firms to charge higher prices
    c. both of the above
    d. none of the above

31. If the economy adjusts through the *automatic mechanism*, then a decline in aggregate demand causes
    a. a recession in the short run, and an increase in the price level in the long run.
    b. a recession in the short run, and a decline in the price level in the long run.
    c. an expansion in the short run, and a decline in the price level in the long run.
    d. an expansion in the short run, and an increase in the price level in the long run.

32. If the economy is initially at full employment equilibrium, in the short run, an increase in aggregate demand causes _____ in real GDP, and in the long run, it causes_____ in the price level.
    a. an increase; an increase
    b. a decrease; a decrease
    c. an increase; a decrease
    d. a decrease; an increase

33. *Stagflation* is
    a. a combination of inflation and recession.
    b. a combination of stagnation and deflation.
    c. a situation of low inflation and low unemployment.
    d. stagnant employment during periods of expansion.

34. Which of the following is usually the cause of *stagflation*?
    a. reductions in government spending
    b. increases in investment
    c. a decline in net exports
    d. an adverse supply shock

35. After an adverse supply shock, what causes the short-run aggregate supply to shift to the right until the long-run level of equilibrium output is reached once again?
    a. an increase in the wages that workers earn and the prices that firms charge
    b. workers' willingness to accept lower wages and firms' willingness to accept lower prices
    c. an increase in government spending
    d. a decrease in government spending

36. How accurate is the prediction that a recession in the U.S. caused by the aggregate demand curve shifting to the left will cause the price level to fall?
    a. Very accurate. In fact, since the 1930s, this has happened every time there has been a recession in the economy.
    b. Inaccurate. This has not happened for an entire year since the 1930s.
    c. The results have been mixed. Sometimes since the 1930s this has happened, and other times it has not.
    d. Unfortunately, there is not enough data to substantiate the predictions of the model.

37. To turn the basic model of aggregate demand and aggregate supply into a dynamic model, which of the following assumptions must be made?
    a. Potential real GDP increases continually, shifting the long-run aggregate supply (*LRAS*) curve to the right.
    b. During most years, the aggregate demand (*AD*) curve will be shifting to the right.
    c. Except during periods when workers and firms expect high rates of inflation, the short-run aggregate supply (*SRAS*) curve will be shifting to the right.
    d. all of the above

38. If no other factors that affect the *SRAS* curve have changed, what impact will increases in the labor force, increases in the capital stock, and technological change have on both the short-run and the long-run aggregate supply?
    a. Over time, both the long-run aggregate supply and the short-run aggregate supply will shift to the right by the same amount.
    b. Over time, the long-run aggregate supply will shift to the right, and the short-run aggregate supply will remain stationary.
    c. Over time, the long-run aggregate supply will remain stationary, and the short-run aggregate supply will shift to the right.
    d. Both the long-run aggregate supply and the short-run aggregate supply will shift to the left by the same amount.

39. How does the dynamic model of aggregate supply and aggregate demand explain inflation?
    a. by showing that if total production in the economy grows faster than total spending, prices will rise
    b. by showing that increases in labor productivity usually lead to increases in prices
    c. by showing that if total spending in the economy grows faster than total production, prices will rise
    d. none of the above

40. In the dynamic aggregate demand and supply model, which of the following is correct?
    a. If aggregate demand increases more than aggregate supply increases, the price level will rise.
    b. If aggregate demand and aggregate supply both increase the same amount, the price level will rise.
    c. If aggregate supply increases more than aggregate demand increases, the price level will rise.
    d. If aggregate supply increases more than aggregate demand increases, the price level will not change.

41. The long economic expansion that began in March 1991 and ended in March 2001 gave way to a recession. The recession was caused by a decline in aggregate demand. Which factors contributed to this decline?
    a. the end of the stock market "bubble" and excessive investment in information technology
    b. the terrorist attacks of September 11, 2001
    c. the corporate accounting scandals
    d. all of the above

42. As productivity and real GDP rose during 2002 and 2003, economists noticed that if firms can produce more output with the same number of workers
    a. firms will be inclined to hire additional workers in the short run.
    b. firms might be less likely to hire additional workers in the short run.
    c. labor productivity will be the main determinant of output in the long run.
    d. firms will produce output using more workers and less capital.

43. The effect of productivity growth on the level of employment is as follows:
    a. Productivity growth affects the level of employment, but only in the short run.
    b. Productivity growth affects the level of employment in both the short run and the long run.
    c. There is no relationship between productivity growth and the level of employment in either the short run or the long run.
    d. Productivity growth affects the level of employment, but only in the long run.

44. The 1974-1975 recession was a clear example of
    a. the impact that a decrease in aggregate demand can have on the economy.
    b. the impact of a shift to the left in the long run aggregate supply on the economy.
    c. the impact of an adverse supply shock on the economy.
    d. none of the above

45. Which of the following are the main objectives of this chapter?
    a. to discuss the determinants of aggregate demand and aggregate supply, and distinguish between a movement along the short-run aggregate supply curve and a shift of the curve
    b. to use the aggregate demand and aggregate supply model to illustrate the difference between short-run macroeconomic equilibrium and long-run macroeconomic equilibrium
    c. to use the dynamic aggregate demand and aggregate supply model to analyze macroeconomic conditions
    d. all of the above

Short Answer Questions

1. Explain the difference between the aggregate demand curve and the demand curve for an individual product.

   _____

   _____

   _____

2. Explain the difference between a shift of the *AD* curve and a movement along the *AD* curve.

   _____

   _____

   _____

3. Over time, as the capital stock increases, the number of workers increases, and technology change occurs, what happens to the *LRAS* and *SRAS* curves?

   _____

   _____

   _____

   _____

4. Suppose the *AD* and *SRAS* curves intersect at a level of real GDP to the right of the *LRAS* curve. Show this graphically. Explain how real GDP will adjust toward potential real GDP. Show the resulting long-run equilibrium graphically.

_____

_____

_____

5. Over time, the *AD* and *LRAS* curves both shift to the right. Show that this can have three results: inflation, no price change, or deflation. Because we generally observe inflation in the U.S. economy, what does this tell us about the shifts in the *AD* and *LRAS* curves over time?

_____

_____

_____

6. Starting at potential real GDP, explain why the short-run impact of an increase in aggregate demand on output is different from the long-run impact of a change in aggregate demand on output.

_____

_____

_____

True/False Questions

T F 1. The wealth effect suggests that a fall in the price level will increase consumption spending by households.

T F 2. As the price level in the United States increases, exports from the United States will also increase.

T F 3. An increase in taxes will reduce consumption and shift the *AD* curve to the right.

T F 4. Because prices do not influence the level of the capital stock, the number of workers, or the level of technology in the long run, changes in the price level will not change the level of real GDP in the long run.

T F 5. Growth in the capital stock will shift the *LRAS* curve to the left.

T F 6. When real GDP is equal to potential real GDP, there is no unemployment.

T F 7. Generally, as prices of finished goods rise, the prices of inputs, such as labor, rise at the same pace.

T F 8. If workers expect prices to rise, the *SRAS* curve will shift to the left.

T F 9. An unexpected increase in the price of an important natural resource is called a supply shock and will shift the *SRAS* curve to the right.

T F 10. Long-run macroeconomic equilibrium occurs where the *AD* and *SRAS* curves intersect at a point on the *LRAS* curve.

T F 11. A decrease in *AD* will reduce real GDP in the short run and in the long-run.

CHAPTER 12 (24) | Aggregate Demand and Aggregate Supply Analysis   **349**

T   F   12.   If real GDP is to the left of the *LRAS* curve, there will be no cyclical unemployment.

T   F   13.   The adjustment from short-run to long-run equilibrium is due to government policy actions.

T   F   14.   A supply shock will temporarily reduce the level of real GDP.

T   F   15.   If *AD* grows faster than *LRAS*, prices will not change.

Answers to the Self-Test

Multiple-Choice Questions

Question	Answer	Comment
1	b	The aggregate demand and aggregate supply model explains short-run fluctuations in real GDP and the price level. As Figure 12-1 shows, in this model real GDP and the price level are determined in the short run by the intersection of the aggregate demand curve and the aggregate supply curve. Fluctuations in real GDP and the price level are caused by shifts in the aggregate demand curve or in the aggregate supply curve.
2	d	The aggregate demand and aggregate supply model explains short-run fluctuations in real GDP and the price level. As Figure 12-1 shows, in this model real GDP and the price level are determined in the short run by the intersection of the aggregate demand curve and the aggregate supply curve. Fluctuations in real GDP and the price level are caused by shifts in the aggregate demand curve or in the aggregate supply curve. The aggregate demand curve shows the relationship between the price level and the quantity of real GDP demanded by households, firms, and the government.
3	a	When the price level falls, the real value of household wealth rises, and so will consumption. Economists refer to this impact of the price level on consumption as the *wealth effect*.
4	b	When prices rise, businesses and households need more money to finance buying and selling. A higher interest rate raises the cost of borrowing to business firms and households. As a result, firms will borrow less to build new factories or to install new machinery and equipment, and households will borrow less to buy new houses. A lower price level will have the reverse effect, leading to an increase in investment.
5	b	If the price level in the United States rises relative to the price levels in other countries, U.S. exports will become relatively more expensive and foreign imports will become relatively less expensive. Some consumers in foreign countries will shift from buying U.S. products to buying domestic products, and some U.S. consumers will also shift from buying U.S. products to buying imported products. U.S. exports will fall and U.S. imports will rise, causing net exports to fall. A lower price level in the United States has the reverse effect, causing net exports to rise.
6	a	If the price level rises but other factors that affect the willingness of households, firms, and the government to spend are unchanged, then the economy will move up a stationary aggregate demand curve.
7	a	The factors that cause the aggregate demand curve to shift fall into three categories: changes in government policies, changes in the expectations of households and firms, and changes in foreign factors. Changes in the price level causes a movement along the aggregate demand curve, not a shift.

8	a	A price level change causes a movement along the *AD* curve rather than a shift in the curve.
9	b	The federal government uses monetary policy and fiscal policy to shift the aggregate demand curve. Monetary policy involves changes in interest rates, and fiscal policy involves changes in government purchases and taxes.
10	c	Because government purchases are one component of aggregate demand, an increase in government purchases shifts the aggregate demand curve to the right. An increase in personal income taxes reduces disposable income available to households. This reduces consumption spending and shifts the aggregate demand curve to the left. *Lower* personal income taxes shift the aggregate demand curve to the right. Increases in business taxes reduce the profitability of investment spending and shift the aggregate demand curve to the left. *Decreases* in business taxes shift the aggregate demand curve to the right.
11	c	If households become more optimistic about their future incomes, they are likely to increase their current consumption. This will shift the aggregate demand curve to the right. Similarly, if firms become more optimistic about the future profitability of investment spending, the aggregate demand curve will shift to the right.
12	b	When real GDP increases, so does the income available for consumers and businesses to spend. If real GDP in the United States increases faster than real GDP in other countries, U.S. imports will increase faster than U.S. exports, and net exports will fall. This happened in the late 1990s and early 2000s.
13	b	Net exports will fall if the exchange rate between the dollar and foreign currencies rises, because the price in foreign currency of U.S. products sold in other countries will rise, thereby lowing exports, and the dollar price of foreign products sold in the United States will fall, which increases U.S. imports. Consequently, net exports will fall. A decrease in net exports at every price level will shift the *AD* curve to the left.
14	c	A change in the U.S. domestic price level causes a movement along the U.S. aggregate demand curve, not a shift. Therefore, a change in net exports caused by a change in the price level in the United States will *not* cause the aggregate demand curve to shift.
15	c	In the long run, changes in the price level do not affect the level of real GDP. Figure 12-2 illustrates the fact that in the long run, changes in the price level do not affect real GDP by showing the long-run aggregate supply curve (*LRAS*) as a vertical line.
16	b	The long-run aggregate supply curve is vertical and shifts to the right with increases in capital, labor, and technology.
17	d	The long-run aggregate supply curve and potential real GDP increase each year as the number of workers in the economy increases, the economy accumulates more machinery and equipment, and technological improvement occurs.
18	d	A price level change will cause a movement along the short-run aggregate supply curve, while increasing costs of production and higher wages will cause the curve to shift to the left. Increases in labor force will cause the curve to shift to the right.

19	a	The short-run aggregate supply curve (*SRAS*) slopes upward because, as prices of final goods and services rise, prices of inputs—such as the wages of workers—rise more slowly. Profits rise when the prices of the goods and services firms sell rise more rapidly than the prices they pay for inputs. Therefore, a higher price level leads firms to supply more goods and services. A secondary reason the *SRAS* curve slopes upward is that as the price level rises or falls, some firms are slow to adjust their prices. A firm that is slow to raise its prices when the price level is increasing may find its sales increasing and will increase production.
20	d	It is impossible for each firm and every individual to correctly predict the future price level. If they could, the short-run aggregate supply curve would be the same as the long-run aggregate supply curve. Most economists agree that the short-run aggregate supply curve slopes upward because workers and firms cannot accurately predict the future price level.
21	d	Most economists agree that the short-run aggregate supply curve slopes upward because workers and firms fail to accurately predict the future price level. Economists are not in complete agreement on why this is true, but the three most common explanations are: contracts make some wages and prices "sticky," businesses are often slow to adjust wages, and menu costs make some prices sticky.
22	b	If steel demand and steel prices begin to rise rapidly, producing additional steel will be profitable, because coal prices will remain fixed by contract. In both of these cases, rising prices lead to higher output. If these examples are representative of enough firms in the economy, then a rising price level should lead to a greater quantity of goods and services supplied. In other words, the short-run aggregate supply curve will be upward sloping. If the workers of the coal companies had accurately predicted what would happen to prices, this would have been reflected in the contracts, and the steel mill would not have earned greater profits when prices rose. In that case, rising prices would not have led to higher output.
23	c	If demand for their products is higher or lower than they had expected, firms may want to charge prices different from the ones printed in their menus or catalogs. Changing prices would be costly, however, because it would involve printing new menus or catalogs. The costs to firms of changing prices are called *menu costs*.
24	c	If the price level changes, but other factors are unchanged, then the economy will move up or down a stationary aggregate supply curve. If any factor other than the price level changes, the aggregate supply curve will shift.
25	c	As technology improves, the productivity of workers and machinery increases, which means that firms can produce more goods and services with the same quantities of labor and capital. This reduces their costs of production and allows them to produce more output at every price level. As a result, the short-run aggregate supply curve shifts to the right.
26	c	If workers and firms across the economy are adjusting to the price level being higher than expected, the short-run aggregate supply curve will shift to the left. If they are adjusting to the price level being lower than expected, the short-run aggregate supply curve will shift to the right.

27   c   If oil prices rise unexpectedly, the costs of production will rise for many firms. Some utilities also burn oil to generate electricity, so electricity prices will rise. Rising oil prices lead to rising gasoline prices, which raise transportation costs for many firms. Oil is a key input to manufacturing plastics and artificial fibers, so costs will rise for many other products. Because many firms face rising marginal production costs, they will supply the same level of output only at higher prices, and the short-run aggregate supply curve will shift to the left.

28   b   Economists refer to an unexpected increase in the price of an important raw material as an *adverse supply shock.*

29   b   In the long run, real GDP is determined by the position of the long-run aggregate supply curve.

30   a   The decrease in aggregate demand initially leads to a short-run equilibrium with a lower price level. Workers and firms will begin to adjust to the price level being lower than they had expected it to be. Workers will be willing to accept lower wages—because each dollar of wages is able to buy more goods and services—and firms will be willing to accept lower prices. In addition, the unemployment resulting from the recession will make workers more willing to accept lower wages, and the decline in demand will make firms more willing to accept lower prices.

31   b   An important point to notice is that a decline in aggregate demand causes a recession in the short run, but in the long run it causes only a decline in the price level. Economists refer to the process of adjustment back to full employment just described as an *automatic mechanism* because it occurs without any actions by the government.

32   a   In the short run, the increase in aggregate demand causes an increase in real GDP. In the long run, it causes only an increase in the price level.

33   a   Stagflation is a combination of inflation and recession.

34   d   Stagflation is a combination of inflation and recession, usually resulting from an adverse supply shock.

35   b   The recession caused by the supply shock increases unemployment and reduces output. This eventually results in workers being forced to accept lower wages and firms being forced to accept lower prices. Lower wages cause the short-run aggregate supply curve to shift back to the long-run equilibrium output at full employment.

36   b   The basic aggregate demand and aggregate supply model gives us important insights into how short-run macroeconomic equilibrium is determined. Unfortunately, the model also gives us some misleading results: For instance, it incorrectly predicts that a recession caused by the aggregate demand curve shifting to the left will cause the price level to fall, which has not happened for an entire year since the 1930s.

37   d   The economy is not static, with an unchanging level of full-employment real GDP and no continuing inflation. Real economies are dynamic, with growing potential GDP and ongoing inflation. We can create a dynamic aggregate demand and aggregate supply model by making three changes to the basic model: 1) The full-employment level of real GDP increases continually, shifting the long-run aggregate supply (*LRAS*) curve to the right; 2) During most years the aggregate demand (*AD*) curve will be shifting to the right, and 3) Except during periods when workers and firms expect high rates of inflation, the short-run aggregate supply (*SRAS*) curve will be shifting to the right.

38	a	Increases in the labor force and the capital stock and technological change cause both the long-run aggregate supply curve and the short-run aggregate supply curve to shift. If no other factors that affect the *SRAS* curve have changed, the *LRAS* and *SRAS* curves will shift to the right by the same amount.
39	c	The dynamic aggregate demand and aggregate supply model provides a more accurate explanation than the basic model of the source of most inflation. Figure 12-9 shows that if total spending in the economy grows faster than total production, prices rise. If the *AD* curve shifts to the right by more than the *LRAS* curve, inflation will result because equilibrium will occur at a higher price level.
40	a	In a growing economy, prices rise when aggregate demand grows more than aggregate supply.
41	d	All of the factors above caused a decline in aggregate demand that ended the long expansion of the 1990s.
42	b	If firms can produce more output with the same number of workers, are they less likely to hire additional workers? Some observers argued that this was happening during 2002 and 2003 as productivity and real GDP rose, but employment grew very little.
43	a	We know that over the long run, the level of employment is determined by population growth and by factors—such as the level of retirement benefits and unemployment payments—that affect the fraction of the population in the labor force. The level of employment is not determined in the long run by the rate of productivity growth. In fact, a report from the Federal Reserve Bank of Dallas noted that between 1979 and 2003, the level of productivity in the U.S. economy increased by 67 percent, while during the same period 40 million new jobs were created. That the effect of productivity growth on employment is only temporary was demonstrated in 2004, as productivity growth remained high, but employment began to increase rapidly.
44	c	The 1974-1975 recession provides a clear example of the impact of an adverse supply shock on the economy. Following the Arab-Israeli War of 1973, the Organization of Petroleum Exporting Countries (OPEC) increased the price of a barrel of oil from less than $3 to more than $10.
45	d	We saw in Chapter 3 how powerful the microeconomic model of supply and demand is in explaining many facts about business and economics. In this chapter we have seen that the macroeconomic model of aggregate demand and aggregate supply is also very useful in explaining fluctuations in real GDP and the price level.

Short Answer Responses

1. Though the demand curve for an individual product and the *AD* curve look alike, they are very different. On the individual product demand curve, as the price changes, all other prices are held constant. On the *AD* curve, all prices are changing together.

2. A change in the price level (the GDP deflator) will cause a movement along the *AD* curve. As the price level increases, the quantity demand of real GDP falls because of the wealth effect, the interest-rate effect, and the international-trade effect. The *AD* curve shifts when something happens that changes demand for real GDP at each price level, such as a change in government purchases, investment spending, or net exports.

3. Over time as the capital stock increases, the number of workers increases, and technology change occurs, firms can produce more output. This is seen as a shift in the *LRAS* curve to the right. As this happens the *SRAS* curve also shifts out, reflecting the notion that firms can produce more with more resources. This is shown in the graph below.

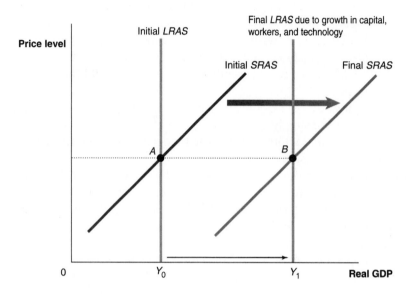

As this growth occurs, other economic variables may also change, so the shift in the *SRAS* curve could be larger or smaller than that shown above. For instance, if a supply shock occurred the new *SRAS* curve would not shift as far to the right as shown above.

4. The initial equilibrium, with the *AD* and *SRAS* curves together at an output level to the right of the *LRAS* curve, would look like:

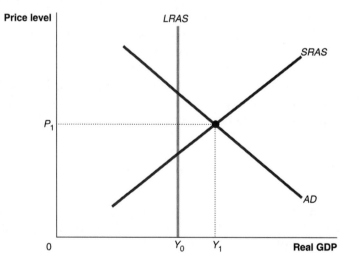

With the *SRAS* and *AD* curves above, the short-run equilibrium would be at P_1 and Y_1. Because this level of real GDP is above potential real GDP, eventually wages will start to rise. This increase in wages will shift the *SRAS* curve to the left. The *SRAS* curve will continue to shift to the left until real GDP returns to the level of potential real GDP, Y_0. This is the automatic adjustment mechanism. The final equilibrium is shown in the graph below.

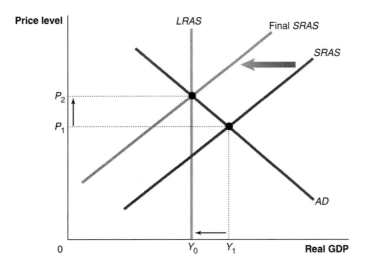

5. Over time, both the *AD* curve and the *LRAS* curve will shift to the right. What happens to the price level depends on the increase in demand relative to the increase in supply. Shown below are three possibilities. If the *AD* curve shifts to the right more than the *LRAS* curve ($AD_0 \rightarrow AD_1$), the price level will rise from P_0 to P_1, so there will be inflation. If the *AD* curve shifts the same as the *LRAS* curve ($AD_0 \rightarrow AD_2$), prices will not change. If the *AD* curve shifts to the right less than the *LRAS* curve ($AD_0 \rightarrow AD_3$), then the price level will fall from P_0 to P_2, so there will be deflation.

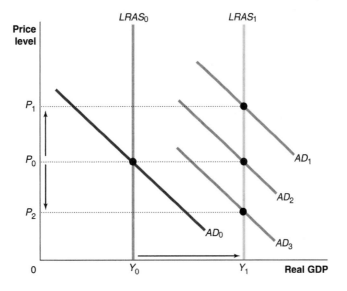

Because we observe over time that both the price level and real GDP generally increase, we can conclude that *AD* usually increases more that *LRAS*.

6. In the short run, the increase in *AD* will result in a higher price level and a higher level of output. This extra production pushes the economy above potential real GDP. At this higher level of production above potential, costs of producing will begin to rise. These higher costs will in the long run cause the *SRAS* curve to shift to the left, eventually returning the economy to potential real GDP. In the short run with costs fixed, output can rise from an increase in aggregate demand. In the long run, as costs adjust upward, the level of real GDP returns to potential GDP.

True/False Answers

1.	T	
2.	F	As U.S. prices rise, other things (prices in other countries) equal, U.S. goods get more expensive, causing exports to fall.
3.	F	Higher taxes will reduce consumption, but shift *AD* to the left.
4.	T	
5.	F	Capital growth will increase potential real GDP and shift the *LRAS* curve to the right.
6.	F	At potential real GDP there is both structural and frictional unemployment.
7.	F	The price of labor, the wage rate, rises slower than output prices. This is one of the reasons for the positively-sloped *SRAS* curve.
8.	T	
9.	F	A supply shock will shift the *SRAS* curve to the left.
10.	T	
11.	F	A change in *AD* will only change real GDP in the short run.
12.	F	At output to the left of the *LRAS* curve, there will be cyclical unemployment.
13.	F	The automatic adjustment from short-run to long-run equilibrium is due to the adjustment of input prices.
14.	T	
15.	F	If *AD* grows faster than *LRAS*, prices will rise.

Money, Banks, and the Federal Reserve System

Chapter Summary

Money plays a key role in the functioning of an economy by facilitating trade in goods and services and by making specialization possible. No advanced economy can prosper without specialization. This chapter explores the functions of money, the definitions of money, and how banks create money.

A *barter economy* is an economy that does not use money and in which people trade goods and services directly for other goods and services. Because barter is inefficient, there is strong incentive to use **money**, which is any **asset** that people are generally willing to accept in exchange for goods or services or in payment of debts. Money has four functions. It is:

1. a medium of exchange
2. a unit of account
3. a store of value
4. a standard of deferred payment

The narrowest definition of the money supply in the United States today is **M1**, which includes currency, checking account balances, and traveler's checks. A broader definition of the money supply is **M2**, which includes everything that is in M1, plus savings accounts, small-denomination time deposits (such as certificates of deposit (CDs)), money market deposit accounts in banks, and noninstitutional money market fund shares.

Reserves are deposits that the bank has retained rather than loaned out or invested. **Required reserves** are reserves that banks are legally required to hold. The fraction of deposits that banks are required to keep as reserves is called the **required reserve ratio**. Any reserves banks hold over and above the legal requirement are called **excess reserves**. When a bank accepts a deposit, it keeps only a fraction of the funds as reserves and loans out the remainder. In making a loan, a bank increases the checking account balance of the borrower. When the borrower uses a check to buy something with the funds the bank has loaned, the seller deposits the check in his bank. The seller's bank keeps part of the deposit as reserves and loans out the remainder. This process continues until no banks have excess reserves. In this way, the process of banks making new loans increases the volume of checking account balances and the money supply. The **simple deposit multiplier** is the ratio of the amount of deposits created by banks to the amount of new reserves. An expression for the simple deposit multiplier is $1/RR$.

The United States has a **fractional reserve banking system** in which banks keep less than 100 percent of deposits as reserves. In a **bank run**, many depositors decide simultaneously to withdraw money from a bank. In a **bank panic**, many banks experience runs at the same time. The **Federal Reserve System** (the Fed) is the central bank of the United States. It was originally established in 1913 to stop bank panics, but today its main role is to carry out *monetary policy*. **Monetary policy** refers to the actions the Federal Reserve takes to manage the money supply and interest rates to pursue macroeconomic policy objectives. The Fed's three monetary policy tools are open market operations, discount policy, and reserve requirements. **Open market operations** are the buying and selling of Treasury securities by the Federal Reserve. The loans the Fed makes to banks are called **discount loans**, and the interest rate the Fed charges on discount loans is the **discount rate**. The **Federal Open Market Committee (FOMC)** meets in Washington, DC, eight times per year to discuss monetary policy.

The *quantity equation* relates the money supply to the price level: $M \times V = P \times Y$, where M is the money supply, V is the *velocity of money*, P is the price level, and Y is real output. The **velocity of money** is the average number of times each dollar in the money supply is spent during the year. Economist Irving Fisher developed the **quantity theory of money**, which assumes that the velocity of money is constant.

Learning Objectives

When you finish this chapter, you should be able to:

1. **Define money and discuss its four functions.** A **barter economy** is an economy that does not use money and in which people trade goods and services directly for other goods and services. Barter trade only occurs if there is a *double coincidence of wants*, where both parties to the trade want what the other one has. Because barter is inefficient, there is strong incentive to use **money,** which is anything that people are generally willing to accept in exchange for goods or services or in payment of debts. Money has four functions: a medium of exchange, a unit of account, a store of value, and a standard of deferred payment. The *gold standard* was a monetary system under which the government produced gold coins and paper currency convertible into gold. The gold standard collapsed in the early 1930s. Today, no government in the world issues paper currency that can be redeemed for gold. Instead, paper currency is **fiat money**, which has no value except as money.

2. **Discuss the definitions of the money supply used in the United States today.** The narrowest definition of the money supply in the United States today is **M1**, which includes currency, checking account balances, and traveler's checks. A broader definition of the money supply is **M2**, which includes everything that is in M1, plus savings accounts, small-denomination time deposits (such as certificates of deposit (CDs)), and noninstitutional money market fund shares.

3. **Explain how banks create money.** On a bank's balance sheet, reserves and loans are assets, and deposits are liabilities. **Reserves** are deposits that the bank has retained, rather than loaned out or invested. **Required reserves** are reserves that banks are legally required to hold. The fraction of deposits that banks are required to keep as reserves is called the **required reserve ratio**. Any reserves banks hold over and above the legal requirement are called **excess reserves**. When a bank accepts a deposit, it keeps only a fraction of the funds as reserves and loans out the remainder. In making a loan, banks increase the checking account balance of the borrower. When the borrower uses a check to buy something with the funds the bank has loaned, the seller will deposit the check in his bank. The seller's bank will keep part of the deposit as reserves and loan out the remainder. This process will continue until no banks have excess reserves. In this way, the process of banks making new loans increases the volume of checking account balances and the money supply. This money creation process can be illustrated with T-accounts, which are stripped down versions of balance sheets that show only how a transaction changes a bank's balance sheet. The **simple deposit multiplier** is the ratio of the amount of deposits created by banks to the amount of new reserves.

4. **Discuss the three policy tools the Federal Reserve uses to manage the money supply.** The Federal Reserve System (the Fed) is the central bank of the United States and was created by Congress in 1913. It was originally established to stop banking panics, but today its main role is to control the money supply. **Monetary policy** refers to the actions the Federal Reserve takes to manage the money supply and interest rates to pursue economic objectives. The Fed's three monetary policy tools are: open market operations, discount policy, and reserve requirements. **Open market operations** are the buying and selling of Treasury securities by the Federal Reserve. The loans the Fed makes to banks are called **discount loans**, and the interest rate the Fed charges on discount loans is the **discount rate**. The **Federal Open Market Committee (FOMC)** meets in Washington, D.C. every six weeks to discuss monetary policy. Required reserves are the reserves that the Fed requires banks to hold, based on their checking account deposits.

5. **Explain the quantity theory of money and use it to explain how high rates of inflation occur.** The *quantity equation* relates the money supply to the price level: $M \times V = P \times Y$, where M is the money supply, V is the **velocity of money**, P is the price level, and Y is real output. The velocity of money is the average number of times each dollar in the money supply is spent during the year. Economist Irving Fisher developed the **quantity theory of money**, which assumes that the velocity of money is constant. If the quantity theory of money is correct, then the inflation rate should equal the rate of growth of the money supply minus the rate of growth of real output. Although the quantity theory of money is not literally correct because the velocity of money is not constant, it is true that in the long run inflation results from the money supply growing faster than real GDP. When governments attempt to raise revenue by selling large quantities of bonds to the central bank, the money supply will increase rapidly, resulting in a high rate of inflation.

Chapter Review

Chapter Opener: McDonald's Money Problems in Argentina (pages 430-431)

Money is an asset with one special feature: It can be used to purchase goods and services. Today our money has value not because of the materials used to make it, but because people have confidence that if they accept it in exchange for goods and services they will be able to use it to purchase goods and services. In Argentina recently, the public lost confidence in the official currency, the peso, and people resorted to using barter (or U.S. dollars) instead of using Argentina's official money. One Argentine province decided to issue its own money, called the patacone. McDonalds franchises in Argentina decided to accept that new currency for a meal they labeled the Patacombo: two cheeseburgers, an order of French fries, and a soft drink. When people lack confidence in money, there are serious macroeconomic consequences.

📖 Helpful Study Hint

Read *An Inside Look* at the end of the chapter to learn how China's central bank is trying to control the money supply by raising banks' reserve requirement in order to slow bank lending.

Would you like to live in a country where the purchasing power of your money rose every year? The *Economics in YOUR Life!* at the start of this chapter poses this question. Keep the question in mind as you read the chapter. The authors will answer the question at the end of the chapter.

13.1 What is Money and Why Do We Need It? (432-435)

Learning Objective 1   Define money and discuss its four functions.

Money is an asset that people are generally willing to accept in exchange for goods and services or payments of debts. Economies where goods and services are traded for other goods and services are called barter economies. Societies evolve from barter economies to economies that use money for transactions. Money serves several functions. It is a:

- *Medium of exchange*. Money is the asset that we use to buy goods and services. In the United States, we buy and sell goods and services using dollars.
- *Unit of account*. All goods and services are priced in terms of money. In the United States, goods and services are priced in dollars.
- *Store of value*. Dollars not spent on goods and services in one time period can be held for use in the future.
- *Standard for deferred payments*. In the United States, contracts involving future payments are usually written specifying payment in dollars.

For an asset to serve as a medium of exchange, it must be generally acceptable, of standardized quality, durable, valuable relative to its weight, and divisible. At one time, all money was commodity money. Commodity money has usefulness as money or as a commodity (such as a gold coin, which can be used as a coin or as jewelry). **Commodity money** can be awkward to use and inefficient, so all countries have replaced commodity money with fiat money. **Fiat money**, such as dollar bills in the United States, has no value as a commodity and is money because it has been declared money by the government and because people have confidence in it.

Extra Solved Problem 13-1

Chapter 13 of the textbook includes two Solved Problems. Here is an extra Solved Problem to help you build your skills solving economic problems:

Unit of Account and the Number of Unique Prices

Supports Learning Objective 1: Define money and discuss its four functions.

One of the functions of money is to serve as a unit of account. The prices of goods are expressed in terms of the thing we call money. This makes comparisons easier. Suppose music CDs cost $10, and DVDs cost $20. So, we can say CDs cost twice as much as DVDs. Without money, each good would have to be priced in terms of all other goods. If an economy has 100 different goods, how many prices will there be in this system?

SOLVING THE PROBLEM

Step 1: **Review the chapter material.**
This problem is about the function of money called unit of account, so you may want to review the section "The Functions of Money," which begins on page 433 in the textbook.

Step 2: **Calculate the number of prices.**
If the economy had three goods, A, B, and C, then there would be a price between A and B, between A and C, and between B and C, or three unique prices. For more than three goods, the formula we would use is $n \times [(n-1)/2]$, where n is the number of goods, so in an economy with 100 goods, the number of unique prices is $100 \times (99/2) = 4{,}950$ prices. Each good would have a price tag with 99 different prices written on it.

📖 Helpful Study Hint

Read *Making the Connection: Money Without a Government? The Strange Case of the Iraqi Dinar* for an example of how something without value can be used as money as long as people are willing to accept it in exchange for goods and services. Even after the fall of Saddam Hussein's government in 2003, the currency with his picture on it—the dinar—continued to circulate. Iraqis somewhat preferred the dinar to the U.S. dollar, because the dinar was more familiar to them. Eventually the old Saddam dinar was replaced with a new dinar printed by the new Iraqi government.

13.2 LEARNING OBJECTIVE

13.2 How Is Money Measured in the United States Today? (pages 436-440)

Learning Objective 2 Discuss the definitions of the money supply used in the United States today.

In the United States, the Federal Reserve System uses two definitions of the money supply. The two definitions of money are based on the different functions of money. The current definitions of money are:

M1, which includes:
- currency – currency is all the paper money and coins in circulation (in circulation means not held by banks or the government)
- checking account balances at banks
- the value of outstanding traveler's checks

M2, which includes:
- M1
- savings accounts and small (less than $100,000) time deposits accounts, such as certificates of deposit (CDs)
- money market deposit accounts at banks
- noninstitutional money market share funds

The M1 definition of money is more closely related to the function of money as a medium of exchange, while the M2 definition of money adds assets that are thought of as stores of value. We can write checks against M1 checking account deposits, but we can't write checks against savings accounts and CDs. Because checking accounts are a part of M1, banks play an important role in determining the supply of money and how the supply of money changes.

📖 Helpful Study Hint

Do you have pennies in your wallet? Would you bother picking up a penny if you saw it on the sidewalk? Read *Making the Connection: Do We Still Need the Penny?* to learn why some economists recommend we stop producing the penny. It now costs about 4 cents to print a $20 bill, and it costs more than 1 cent to produce a penny. In the 1980's, to reduce costs of producing pennies, the U.S. government switched from copper to zinc. There have been many suggestions to deal with the higher costs of producing pennies, such as rounding transactions to the nearest 5 cents and eliminating pennies from our currency. Some fear that this rounding will usually result in rounding up of transactions, creating a rounding tax. Evidence, however, indicates that the number of transactions that would be rounded up is about equal to the number of transactions that would be rounded down.

Read *Don't Let this Happen to YOU!* for tips on how to distinguish income from wealth. Remember that we use money to measure income and wealth. Someone that has wealth of $10 million may not have $10 million of the medium of exchange, but has assets, which when valued in money terms (for instance, they may own a house worth $500,000) add up to $10 million.

13.3 LEARNING OBJECTIVE

13.3 How Do Banks Create Money? (pages 440-448)

Learning Objective 3 Explain how banks create money.

In the United States, checking account deposit balances are about half of M1. Checking accounts at banks are owned by households, business firms, and the government. One way to look at bank operations is to look at a bank's balance sheet. The balance sheet lists what the bank owns (assets), what the bank owes (liabilities), and its stockholders' equity. The bank's net worth is the difference between the values of the bank's assets and the value of its liabilities. By definition, then:

$$\text{Assets} = \text{Liabilities} + \text{Stockholders' equity.}$$

A sample balance sheet for a bank, Andover Bank, might look as follows with assets listed on the left-hand side and liabilities and stockholders' equity on the right-hand side (values are in thousands of dollars):

Assets		Liabilities and Stockholders' Equity	
Reserves	$2,737	Deposits	$69,380
		Short-Term Borrowing	3,217
Loans and Securities	87,908	Long-Term Borrowing	12,558
		Other Liabilities	5,492
Buildings	2,142	Total Liabilities	90,647
Other Assets	7,882		
		Stockholders' Equity	10,022
Total Assets	$100,669	Total Liabilities and Stockholders' Equity	$100,669

Banks do not keep all their deposits as cash. Most banks are required by law to keep 10 percent of their deposits either physically in the bank, as vault cash, or on deposit at their regional Federal Reserve Bank. Vault cash plus deposits at the Fed are called the bank's **reserves**. Reserves are deposits that have not been loaned out or used to purchase securities. The amount of reserves a bank must keep, called **required reserves**, is determined by the **required reserve ratio** (*RR*). If a bank has more reserves than required, these reserves are called **excess reserves**.

$$\text{Excess reserves} = \text{Reserves} - \text{Required reserves}$$

We can use a T-account to look at changes in a bank's balance sheet. A T-account is a stripped down version of a balance sheet that shows only how a transaction changes a bank's balance sheet. Suppose that someone deposits $5,000 in currency in her checking account. The bank now has additional deposits and additional reserves, both equal to $5,000. The balance sheet's changes are shown in the T-account below:

Andover Bank

Assets		Liabilities	
Reserves	+$5,000	Deposits	+$5,000

📖 Helpful Study Hint

To keep the balance sheet balanced, the change in assets must be equal to the change in liabilities plus the change in stockholders' equity.

📖 Helpful Study Hint

Notice that this $5,000 deposit did not change the money supply, because the increase in deposits is matched by an equal decrease in currency held by the public.

Banks are required to keep only 10 percent of their deposits as reserves. In this case, required reserves will increase by $500 ($500 = 0.1 x $5,000). This bank now has $4,500 in excess reserves; that is, reserves over and above the level of required reserves. The bank can use these funds to grant loans or purchase securities. If the bank loans $4,500 to an individual, the bank will deposit $4,500 in the borrower's checking account. After this loan, the changes in the bank's balance sheet look like this:

Andover Bank

Assets		Liabilities	
Reserves	+$5,000	Deposits	+$5,000
Loans	+$4,500	Deposits	+$4,500

When the person who received the loan purchases goods and services using a check written against the deposits created by the loan, Andover Bank will lose reserves to another bank. Andover Bank loses these reserves because the check written by the borrower will be presented to Andover Bank for payment by the bank that receives the check. The changes in Andover Bank's balance sheet will then look like this:

Andover Bank

Assets		Liabilities	
Reserves	+ $500	Deposits	+$5,000
Loans	+$4,500		

If we assume the bank that receives the check is Bank of America, then Bank of America's balance sheet will also change:

Bank of America

Assets		Liabilities	
Reserves	+$4,500	Deposits	+$4,500

📖 Helpful Study Hint

Notice that the Andover Bank's loan caused an increase in the supply of money. After the loan, there was a new deposit account of $4,500. This deposit may leave Andover Bank, but it stays in the banking system as a whole. In our example, the check from the loan is deposited in the Bank of America. So, we started the story with $5,000 in currency, and we now have $5,000 less in currency because the currency is inside the banking system and so is not counted in the money supply. However, we have $9,500 more in checking account deposits. So, the money supply has increased by $4,500 (or, $9,500 − $5,000).

📖 Helpful Study Hint

Bank loans increase the money supply by the amount of the loan.

Bank of America now has excess reserves of $4,050, because it needs to keep only 10 percent of its new deposit of $4,500 as reserves ($4,500 − (0.01 x $4,500) = $4,050). Suppose Bank of America grants a loan for the amount of their excess reserves. Then the changes in Bank of America's balance sheet will look like this:

Bank of America

Assets		Liabilities	
Reserves	+$4,500	Deposits	+$4,500
Loans	+$4,050	Deposits	+$4,050

This loan created new deposits, and new money of $4,050. After the funds for that loan are used and a check in that amount is presented to Bank of America for payment, the changes in that bank's balance sheet will look like this:

Bank of America

Assets		Liabilities	
Reserves	+ $450	Deposits	+$4,500
Loans	+$4,050		

📖 Helpful Study Hint

Notice that at this point, Bank of America has no excess reserves.

📖 Helpful Study Hint

The newly created money at the Bank of America is not lost when it is loaned out, it just moves to another bank. The actions of individuals and firms (other than banks) do not create or destroy money; these actions can only transfer checking account balances between individuals and banks.

The $4,050 of reserves that are lost by Bank of America are gained by another bank. This bank will be able to loan (and create new money of) $3,645. This process of loans being made and new checking account deposits being created continues through many banks in the economy. We can summarize the results in the following table:

Bank	Increase in Checking Account Deposits
Andover Bank	$5,000
Bank of America	$4,500 (= 0.9 x $5,000)
The Third Bank	$4,050 (= 0.9 x $4,050)
The Fourth Bank	$3,645 (= 0.9 x $4050)
The Fifth Bank	$3280.50 (= 0.9 x $3,645)
.	.
.	.
.	.
Total Change in Checking Accounts	$50,000

The end result can be computed with the formula:

$$\Delta D = \frac{1}{RR} \Delta R,$$

where ΔD is the total change in checking account deposits, ΔR is the change in reserves, and $(1/RR)$ is the **simple deposit multiplier**. In this example, the change in reserves was $5,000, and with a required reserve ratio (RR) of 10 percent, which implies a simple deposit multiplier of 10 ($10 = 1/0.10$), the change in deposits is:

$$\Delta D = \frac{1}{0.1} \$5,000 = \$50,000.$$

📖 Helpful Study Hint

In this example, deposits increased by $50,000, but the supply of money increased by only $45,000, because the initial deposit of $5,000 resulted in a $5,000 decline in the currency component of M1.

The real world increase in the money supply as a result of an increase in bank reserves is much smaller than the increase shown by the simple deposit multiplier. This is because some reserves leave the banking system when the public takes currency from their checking accounts and because banks sometimes hold excess reserves.

The important point is that whenever banks gain reserves, they make new loans and the money supply expands. Whenever banks lose reserves, they reduce loans and the money supply contracts.

📖 Helpful Study Hint

Whenever banks gain reserves, they will make new loans and the level of deposits (and the money supply) will increase. Banks have a powerful incentive to lend excess reserves because reserves earn banks zero interest.

Read ***Don't Let This Happen to YOU!*** to learn how to distinguish between an asset and liability. Remember, your checking account is an asset to you, but a liability to your bank.

Extra Solved Problem 13-3

Chapter 13 of the textbook includes two Solved Problems. Here is an extra Solved Problem to help you build your skills solving economic problems:

Determining Actual, Excess, and Required Reserves

Supports Learning Objective 3: Explain how banks create money.

Suppose that Lehigh Bank has $500,000 in deposits and $60,000 in reserves. If the required reserve ratio for the bank is 10 percent, determine the level of actual, required, and excess reserves.

SOLVING THE PROBLEM

Step 1:   Review the chapter material.
This problem is about bank reserves, so you may want to review the section "How Do Banks Create Money?" which begins on page 440 of the textbook.

Step 2:   Determine the level of actual and required reserves.
Actual reserves represent the amount of vault cash and deposits that the bank has at the Federal Reserve. Actual reserves are determined from the bank's balance sheet. For Lehigh Bank, actual reserves are $60,000. Required reserves are calculated from the level of deposits and the required reserve ratio. The formula for required reserves is:

Required reserves = Required reserve ratio x deposits.

Given that Lehigh Bank has $500,000 in deposits:

Required reserves = 0.10 x $500,000 = $50,000.

Step 3: **Determine the level of excess reserves.**
To meet the Fed's requirements, Lehigh Bank must keep $50,000 as reserves. Any reserves that the bank has above the level of required reserves are called excess reserves. Excess reserves are calculated with the formula:

Excess reserves = Actual reserves – required reserves.

So for Lehigh Bank,

Excess reserves = $60,000 – $50,000 = $10,000.

Lehigh Bank has $10,000 in reserves above the required level. The bank can use these reserves to make loans or buy securities, allowing the bank to earn interest and increase its revenues.

13.4 LEARNING OBJECTIVE

13.4 The Federal Reserve System (pages 448-452)

Learning Objective 4 Discuss the three policy tools the Federal Reserve uses to manage the money supply.

The **Federal Reserve System** (or the Fed) is the central bank for the U.S. Congress created the Federal Reserve System in 1913. Congress divided the country into twelve Federal Reserve districts, each with a Federal Reserve Bank that provides services to banks in that district. The Board of Governors was created to oversee the system. The Board of Governors has seven members, who are appointed by the President to 14-year, nonrenewable terms. Look at Figure 13-3 on page 450 in the main text for a map showing the 12 Federal Reserve districts.

As part of **monetary policy**, the Fed has the task of managing the U.S. money supply. The Fed has three monetary policy tools: open market operations, discount policy, and reserve requirements.

Open market operations is the buying and selling of Treasury securities, such as Treasury bills. Eight times per year the **Federal Open Market Committee (FOMC)** meets in Washington, D.C. to discuss monetary policy. When the FOMC orders an open market purchase, the payment it makes for the securities puts more reserves in the banking system. When banks make new loans with these new reserves, the level of deposits and the money supply will increase. When the Fed sells securities, the payment for the securities by the public takes reserves out of the banking system and causes the money supply to fall.

📖 Helpful Study Hint

When the Fed carries out an open market purchase by buying securities from the public, the amount of bank reserves and the amount of checking account deposits (and the money supply) will increase.

Banks can borrow from the Fed. Loans from the Fed to banks are called **discount loans** and occur at an interest rate called the **discount rate**. The Fed sets the discount rate at the FOMC meetings. The Fed serves as a lender of last resort for banks and is willing to lend to banks when banks cannot borrow elsewhere. Making **discount loans** can help stop **bank runs** and **bank panics**, which occur when many depositors decide simultaneously to withdraw their deposits.

Most banking systems (including the U.S. banking system) are **fractional reserve banking systems** in which banks keep less than 100 percent of their deposits as reserves. U.S. banks keep only about 10 percent of their deposits as reserves. The Fed's reserve policy determines the fraction of deposits banks must keep. These reserves are kept in the bank as vault cash or as deposits at the Fed. The Fed changes the required reserve ratio infrequently.

Extra Solved Problem 13-4

Chapter 13 of the textbook includes two Solved Problems. Here is an extra Solved Problem to help you build your skills solving economic problems:

Open Market Operations and Changes in the Supply of Money

Supports Learning Objective 4: Discuss the three policy tools the Federal Reserve uses to manage the money supply.

Suppose that the Federal Reserve would like to increase the money supply by $500,000. How can the Fed use open market operations to bring about a $500,000 increase in the money supply? Assume the required reserve ratio is 10 percent.

SOLVING THE PROBLEM

Step 1:   Review the chapter material.
This problem is about the Fed using open market operations, so you may want to review the section "The Federal Reserve System," which begins on page 448 of the textbook.

Step 2:   Determine the level of deposits that can be created from an increase in reserves.
When the Federal Reserve uses open market operation to increase the supply of money, it buys Treasury bills from the public. When the public deposits the proceeds from these Treasury bill sales into their banks, the level of deposits and the level of reserves increase in the banking system. The level of deposits that can be created from a given amount of reserves is determined by the formula:

$$\Delta D = \frac{1}{RR} \Delta R,$$

where ΔD is the change in deposits, ΔR is the change in reserves, and RR is the required reserve ratio.

Step 3:   **Calculate the change in reserves needed.**

Using the 10 percent required reserve ratio (RR = 0.10), if the Fed would like to increase the money supply by $500,000, then the desired change in deposits is $500,000. We can use the formula in Step 2:

$$\$500,000 = \frac{1}{RR}\Delta R = \frac{1}{0.10}\Delta R.$$

Solving this formula for ΔR gives a value of ΔR = $50,000. Therefore, if the Fed buys $50,000 of Treasury bills from the public, reserves will increase by $50,000. As banks create new loans based upon these new reserves, the quantity of bank loans and deposits will increase.

Step 4:   **Determine the money supply change.**

The money supply change will be:

$$\Delta D = \frac{1}{RR}\Delta R = \frac{1}{0.10}\$50,000 = \$500,000.$$

A $50,000 Fed open market purchase will lead to a $500,000 money supply change. If the Fed wants to increase the money supply by $500,000, they must buy $50,000 of Treasury bills from the public.

📖 Helpful Study Hint

The inflation rate in the United States is usually around 2 or 3 percent. In the early 1990s, Argentina experienced an inflation rate of 2,300 percent. Read *Making the Connection: The 2001 Bank Panic in Argentina* to learn how the central bank dealt with this high inflation. In the early 1990's, the Argentine Central Bank fixed the value of the Argentine peso to the U.S. dollar, one for one. This policy helped reduce inflation, but placed the banking system in an awkward situation: Banks were encouraged to take deposits and make loans in U.S. dollars. In January 2002, the crisis was ended when the government abandoned its commitment to the one-to-one exchange rate between the peso and the dollar and decreed that dollar deposits in banks would be converted to peso deposits at a rate of 1.4 pesos to the dollar. Although some financial stability was restored, the damage to the banking system from the crisis contributed to a decline in real GDP of 11.5 percent during 2002.

13.5 The Quantity Theory of Money (pages 452-457)

Learning Objective 5 Explain the quantity theory of money and use it to explain how high rates of inflation occur.

The quantity of money in an economy plays a role in determining the inflation rate. One way of analyzing the relationship between money and prices is called the **quantity theory of money**, which can be illustrated using the quantity equation:

$$M \times V = P \times Y,$$

where M is the supply of money, P is the price level (GDP Deflator), and Y is real GDP. V is defined as the **velocity of money**, which measures the average number of times a dollar is used to purchase a final good or service, and is calculated as $V = PY/M$. From the quantity equation, it follows that:

Growth rate in M + Growth rate in V =
Growth rate in P (or the inflation rate) + Growth rate in Y (real GDP growth rate).

📖 Helpful Study Hint

The general rule is that the growth rate of two variables multiplied together equals the sum of the growth rates of each variable. So, for example, the growth rate of $M \times V$ = Growth rate of M + Growth rate of V.

Rearranging terms gives:

Inflation rate = (Growth rate in M − Growth rate in Y) + Growth rate in V.

The equation implies that if velocity is constant (which means that the growth rate in velocity = 0), then the economy will experience inflation if the growth rate in the money supply is greater than the growth rate in output. This equation suggests that in the long run, inflation results from growth in the money supply being greater than growth in output. Empirical studies show that velocity is not a constant.

Extra Solved Problem 13-5

Chapter 13 of the textbook includes two Solved Problems. Here is an extra Solved Problem to help you build your skills solving economic problems:

Calculating Velocity

Supports Learning Objective 5: Explain the quantity theory of money and use it to explain how high rates of inflation occur.

Because there are two measures of the money supply—M1 and M2—there are two measures of velocity, one based on each measure of the money supply. The table below has data on Money (M1 and M2), the

GDP deflator, and real GDP. (The values for real GDP, M1, and M2 are in billions.) Compute velocity measures using each money supply measure and also compute the growth rates in velocity with each money supply measure for each year from 2001 to 2006. Are the growth rates the same? (Remember that in the quantity equation, real GDP = Y and GDP deflator = P.)

Year	Real GDP	GDP Deflator	M1	M2
2000	$9,817	100.0	$1,087.6	$4,920.9
2001	9,891	102.4	1,182.1	5,430.3
2002	10,049	104.2	1,219.5	5,774.1
2003	10,301	106.4	1,305.5	6,062.0
2004	10,704	109.4	1,375.3	6,411.7
2005	11,049	112.7	1,373.2	6,669.4
2006	11,415	116.0	1,365.7	7,021.0

Step 1:   **Review the chapter material.**

This problem is about velocity, so you may want to review the section "The Quantity Theory of Money," which begins on page 452 of the textbook.

Step 2:   **Calculate velocity.**

Velocity is defined as $V = (P \times Y)/M$. (Note that in this calculation we need to divide the GDP deflator by 100.) The values of velocity are:

Year	Real GDP	GDP deflator	M1	M2	V(M1)	V(M2)
2000	$9,817	100.0	$1,087.6	$4,920.9	9.03	1.99
2001	9,891	102.4	1,182.1	5,430.3	8.57	1.87
2002	10,049	104.2	1,219.5	5,774.1	8.59	1.81
2003	10,301	106.4	1,305.5	6,062.0	8.40	1.81
2004	10,704	109.4	1,375.3	6,411.7	8.51	1.83
2005	11,049	112.7	1,373.2	6,669.4	9.07	1.87
2006	11,415	116.0	1,365.7	7,021.0	9.70	1.89

Step 3:   **Calculate growth rates.**

Calculate the growth rate in velocity for the velocity values based upon the different measures of the money supply.

Year	Real GDP	GDP deflator	M1	M2	V(M1)	Growth rate in V(M1)	V(M2)	Growth rate in V(M2)
2000	$9,817	100.0	$1,087.6	$4,920.9	9.03		1.99	
2001	9,891	102.4	1,182.1	5,430.3	8.57	-5.09%	1.87	-6.03%
2002	10,049	104.2	1,219.5	5,774.1	8.59	0.23	1.81	-3.21
2003	10,301	106.4	1,305.5	6,062.0	8.40	-2.21	1.81	0.00
2004	10,704	109.4	1,375.3	6,411.7	8.51	1.31	1.83	1.10
2005	11,049	112.7	1,373.2	6,669.4	9.07	6.58	1.87	2.19
2006	11,415	116.0	1,365.7	7,021.0	9.70	6.95	1.89	1.07

While the growth rates of M1 velocity and M2 velocity are different in every year, they generally move in the same direction (with the exceptions of the 2003 value, where the growth rate in M1 velocity fell while the growth rate in M2 velocity increased, and the 2006 value, where the growth rate in M1 velocity increased while the growth rate in M2 velocity fell).

📖 Helpful Study Hint

Read *Making the Connection: The German Hyperinflation of the Early 1920s* to learn how the German central bank in the 1920s addressed hyperinflation. In order to finance World War I reparation payments to the Allies, the German government sold bonds to the central bank, which resulted in large increases in the money supply. The total number of marks—the German currency—in circulation rose from 115 million in January 1922 to 1.3 billion in January 1923 and then to 497 billion billion or 497,000,000,000,000,000,000 in December 1923. Just as the quantity theory predicts, the result was a staggeringly high rate of inflation. The German price index that stood at 100 in 1914 and 1,440 in January 1922 had risen to 126,160,000,000,000 in December 1923. The German mark became worthless. The German government ended the hyperinflation by (1) negotiating a new agreement with the Allies that reduced its reparations payments, (2) reducing other government expenditures and raising taxes to balance its budget, and (3) replacing the existing mark with a new mark. Each new mark was worth 1 trillion old marks. The German central bank was also limited to issuing a total of 3.2 billion new marks.

📖 Helpful Study Hint

Economics in YOUR Life! at the end of the chapter answers the question posed at the start of the chapter: Would you like to live in a country where the purchasing power of your money rose every year? What would be the advantages or disadvantages of living in such an economy? For the purchasing power of money to be increasing, prices must be falling. If prices are falling, wages and income levels will also be falling. So, it is possible that the purchasing power of income will not be rising, even though the purchasing power of money is increasing. You are probably better off living in an economy experiencing mild inflation rather than one experiencing deflation.

Key Terms

Asset. Anything of value owned by a person or a firm.

Bank panic. Many banks experiencing runs at the same time.

Bank run. Many depositors simultaneously decide to withdraw money from a bank.

Commodity money. A good used as money that also has value independent of its use as money.

Discount loans. Loans the Federal Reserve makes to banks.

Discount rate. The interest rate the Federal Reserve charges on discount loans.

Excess reserves. Reserves that banks hold over and above the legal requirement.

Federal Open Market Committee (FOMC). The Federal Reserve committee responsible for open market operations and managing the money supply.

Federal Reserve System. The central bank of the United States.

Fiat money. Money, such as paper currency, that is authorized by a central bank or governmental body and that does not have to be exchanged by the central bank for gold or some other commodity money.

Fractional reserve banking system. A banking system in which banks keep less than 100 percent of deposits as reserves.

M1. The narrowest definition of the money supply: the sum of currency in circulation, checking account balances in banks, and holdings of traveler's checks.

M2. A broader definition of the money supply: M1 plus savings account balances, small-denomination time deposits, balances in money market deposit accounts in banks, and noninstitutional money market fund shares.

Monetary policy. The actions the Federal Reserve takes to manage the money supply and interest rates to pursue economic objectives.

Money. Assets that people are generally willing to accept in exchange for goods and services or for payment of debts.

Open market operations. The buying and selling of Treasury securities by the Federal Reserve in order to control the money supply.

Quantity theory of money. A theory of the connection between money and prices that assumes the velocity of money is constant.

Required reserve ratio. The minimum fraction of deposits banks are required by law to keep as reserves.

Required reserves. Reserves that a bank is legally required to hold, based on its checking account deposits.

Reserves. Deposits that a bank keeps as cash in its vault or on deposit with the Federal Reserve.

Simple deposit multiplier. The ratio of the amount of deposits created by banks to the amount of new reserves.

Velocity of money. The average number of times each dollar in the money supply is used to purchase goods and services included in GDP.

Self-Test

(Answers are provided at the end of the Self-Test.)

Multiple-Choice Questions

1. Assets that are generally accepted in exchange for goods and services or for payment of debts are specifically called
   a. wealth.
   b. net worth.
   c. money.
   d. capital.

2. A double coincidence of wants refers to
   a. the situation in which a good that is used as money also has value independent of its use as money.
   b. the fact that for a barter trade to take place between two people, each person must want what the other one has.
   c. the idea that a barter economy is more efficient than an economy that uses money.
   d. the situation where two parties are involved in a transaction where money is the medium of exchange.

3. By making exchange easier, money allows for
   a. a double coincidence of wants.
   b. the possible risk of inflation.
   c. specialization and higher productivity.
   d. all of the above

4. If prisoners of war use cigarettes as money, then cigarettes are
   a. token money.
   b. fiduciary money.
   c. fiat money.
   d. commodity money.

5. Money serves as a *unit of account* when
   a. sellers are willing to accept it in exchange for goods or services.
   b. it can be easily stored and used for transactions in the future.
   c. prices of goods and services are stated in the monetary unit.
   d. all of the above

6. Money serves as a standard of deferred payment when
   a. it can be easily stored today and used for transactions in the future.
   b. repayment of debts is made using money units.
   c. sellers are willing to accept it in exchange for goods or services.
   d. all of the above

7. Which of the following conditions make a good suitable for use as a medium of exchange?
   a. The good must be acceptable to (that is, usable by) most buyers and sellers.
   b. The good should be of standardized quality, so that any two units are identical.
   c. The good should be durable, valuable relative to its weight, and divisible.
   d. all of the above

8. Which of the following statements is correct?
   a. Today, most governments in the world issue paper currency that is backed by gold and can be redeemed for gold.
   b. Paper currency has no value unless it is used as money.
   c. Paper money is a commodity money.
   d. all of the above

9. What is fiat money?
   a. money that has value independent of its use as money
   b. an asset that has the ability to be easily converted into the medium of exchange
   c. money that is authorized by a central bank and that does not have to be exchanged for gold or some other commodity money
   d. money issued by financial intermediaries, such as banks and thrift institutions, not the central bank

10. To economists
    a. money is only those assets that serve as a medium of exchange.
    b. money is only currency, checking account deposits, or traveler's checks.
    c. money can be narrowly or broadly defined, depending on the types of assets included.
    d. None of the above. There is no official definition or measurement of the money supply today.

11. The sum of currency in circulation, checking account balances in banks, and holdings of traveler's checks equals
    a. M1.
    b. M2.
    c. M1 + M2.
    d. none of the above

12. Savings account balances, small-denomination time deposits, and noninstitutional money market fund shares are
    a. included only in M1.
    b. included only in M2.
    c. included in both M1 and M2.
    d. financial assets that are not included in the money supply.

13. Jill deposits $100 from her checking account into her savings account at the local bank. As a result of this transaction
    a. neither M1 nor M2 will change.
    b. M2 will increase by $100.
    c. M1 will decrease by $100.
    d. both b and c are correct

14. Which of the following statements is correct?
    a. Currency is used much more often to make payments than checking account balances.
    b. More than 80 percent of all goods and services are purchased with a check, rather than with currency.
    c. Most of the U.S. currency is held within the United States, but a small amount is actually outside the borders of the United States.
    d. all of the above

15. Which of the following statements is true?
    a. Today, U.S. law prohibits banks from paying interest on checking account deposits.
    b. Today, people are not allowed to write checks against their savings account balances.
    c. Today, the difference between checking accounts and savings accounts is greater than it was before the banking reform in 1980.
    d. all of the above

16. Which of the following are included in M2?
    a. M1
    b. savings account balances and small-denomination time deposits
    c. balances in money market deposit accounts in banks, and noninstitutional money market fund shares
    d. all of the above

17. In the definition of the money supply, where do credit cards belong?
    a. M1
    b. M2
    c. both M1 and M2
    d. Credit cards are not included in the definition of the money supply.

18. Bill Gates holds money and wealth. He also earns an annual income. Which of the three is largest?
    a. his money
    b. his income
    c. his wealth
    d. All three of the above mean the same thing and are the same size.

19. The key role that banks play in the economy is to
    a. provide a market for stocks and bonds.
    b. manage the money supply.
    c. accept deposits and make loans.
    d. serve as lenders of last resort.

20. Which of the following is an asset to a bank?
    a. reserves
    b. checking account deposits
    c. savings account deposits
    d. certificates of deposit

21. Which of the following is the largest asset of a typical bank?
    a. loans
    b. buildings
    c. vault cash
    d. checking account deposits

22. Which of the following refers to the minimum fraction of deposits banks are required by law to keep as reserves?
    a. the quantity equation
    b. the simple deposit multiplier
    c. the required reserve ratio
    d. the cash to deposit ratio

23. Which of the following is the largest liability of a typical bank?
    a. deposits
    b. loans
    c. reserves
    d. treasury bills

24. If the required reserve ratio is 10 percent, then using the simple deposit multiplier, what is the total increase in checking account deposits caused by an initial deposit of $1,000?
    a. $100
    b. $1,000
    c. $10,000
    d. $100,000

25. The simple deposit multiplier equals
    a. the inverse, or reciprocal, of the required reserve ratio.
    b. the ratio of the amount of deposits created by banks to the amount of new reserves.
    c. the formula used to calculate the total increase in checking account deposits from an increase in bank reserves.
    d. all of the above

26. A higher required reserve ratio _____ the value of the simple deposit multiplier.
    a. increases
    b. decreases
    c. leaves unchanged
    d. nullifies

27. An increase in the amount of excess reserves that banks keep _____ the value of the real-world deposit multiplier.
    a. increases
    b. decreases
    c. leaves unchanged
    d. nullifies

28. If Fenway Bank has $500 in deposits and $200 in reserves and the required reserve ratio is 10 percent, then Fenway Bank has
    a. $200 in excess reserves.
    b. $50 in required reserves.
    c. $50 in excess reserves.
    d. $200 in required reserves.

29. Whenever banks gain reserves and make new loans, the money supply _____; and whenever banks lose reserves, they reduce their loans and the money supply _____.
    a. expands; expands
    b. expands; contracts
    c. contracts; contracts
    d. contracts; expands

30. A banking system in which banks keep less than 100 percent of deposits as reserves is called
    a. the Federal Reserve System.
    b. a fractional reserve banking system.
    c. a fully-funded reserve system.
    d. wildcat banking.

31. When many depositors decide simultaneously to withdraw their money from a bank, there is
    a. an increase in bank lending.
    b. usually a decline in discount lending by the Fed.
    c. a bank run.
    d. inflation.

32. A *bank panic* occurs when
    a. there is an increase in bank lending.
    b. the central bank carries out open market purchases.
    c. many banks experience runs at the same time.
    d. many banks fail to attract depositors so their reserves increase significantly.

33. The Federal Reserve System is
    a. the central bank of the United States.
    b. the institution that regulates all state banks.
    c. the institution solely responsible for regulating the stock and bond markets.
    d. the institution also known as the Treasury of the United States.

34. There are _____ members of the Board of Governors, who are appointed by the President of the United States to _____, non-renewable terms. One of the Board members is appointed Chairman for a _____, renewable term.
    a. nine; 7-year; eight-year
    b. twelve; 4-year; four-year
    c. seven; 14-year; four-year
    d. fourteen; 4-year; four-year

35. The actions the Federal Reserve takes to manage the money supply and interest rates to pursue economic objectives is called
    a. fiscal policy.
    b. open market operations.
    c. monetary policy.
    d. financial management.

36. The Fed uses three monetary policy tools. Which of the following is *not* one of those tools?
    a. open market operations
    b. discount policy
    c. reserve requirements
    d. federal funds rate setting

37. Which of the following people vote on monetary policy at the Federal Open Market Committee (FOMC) meetings?
    a. the seven members of the Federal Reserve's Board of Governors
    b. the president of the Federal Reserve Bank of New York
    c. four presidents from Federal Reserve banks other than the president of the Federal Reserve Bank of New York (rotating basis)
    d. all of the above

38. To increase the money supply, the FOMC directs the trading desk, located at the Federal Reserve Bank of New York to
    a. buy U.S. Treasury securities from the public.
    b. sell U.S. Treasury securities to the public.
    c. print U.S. Treasury securities and put them out in circulation.
    d. buy U.S. dollars in the foreign exchange market.

39. The Fed conducts monetary policy primarily through
    a. open market operations.
    b. discount policy.
    c. reserve requirements.
    d. none of the above

40. By raising the discount rate, the Fed encourages banks to make _____ loans to households and firms, which will _____ checking account deposits and the money supply.
    a. more; increase
    b. more; decrease
    c. fewer; increase
    d. fewer; decrease

41. The theory concerning the link between the money supply and the price level that assumes the velocity of money is constant is called
    a. the quantity equation.
    b. the quantity theory of money.
    c. the constant velocity theory of money.
    d. the purchasing power parity theory of money.

42. Velocity is defined as:
    a. $V = M/(P \times Y)$.
    b. $V = M \times P \times Y$.
    c. $V = M + P + Y$.
    d. $V = (P \times Y)/M$.

43. If Irving Fisher was correct in his prediction about the value of velocity, then the quantity equation can be written to solve for the inflation rate as follows:
    a. Inflation rate = Growth rate of the money supply + Growth rate of real output.
    b. Inflation rate = Growth rate of the money supply – Growth rate of real output.
    c. Inflation rate = Growth rate of the money supply – Growth rate of velocity.
    d. Inflation rate = Growth rate of the money supply + Growth rate of velocity.

44. Which of the following predictions can be made using the growth rates associated with the quantity equation?
    a. If the money supply grows at a faster rate than real GDP, there will be inflation.
    b. If the money supply grows at a slower rate than real GDP, there will be inflation.
    c. If the money supply grows at the same rate as real GDP, the price level will fall.
    d. none of the above

Short Answer Questions

1. Suzi deposited $100 in currency in her checking account. How will that deposit affect the values of M1 and M2? Would your answer change if Suzi had deposited the money in her savings account?

   _____

   _____

   _____

   _____

   _____

2. Below are the changes in the balance sheet for Andover Bank as a result of a $10,000 deposit of currency. Suppose the required reserve ratio is 10 percent. How much can the bank safely loan?

Assets		Liabilities	
Reserves	+$10,000	Deposits	+$10,000

   Suppose the bank makes a loan for the amount you have just calculated; use the T-account below to show the changes in the bank's balance sheet after the bank grants the loan.

Assets		Liabilities	

Use the T-account below to show the change in the bank's balance sheet after the check is cashed and the bank loses reserves.

Assets	Liabilities

3. If Alice deposits $100 of currency in her bank, what will this do to the level of deposits in her bank and to the supply of money in the United States assuming the required reserve ratio is 10 percent? How would your answer change if the required reserve ratio were 20 percent?

4. When the FOMC buys Treasury bills from the public as part of open market operations, the level of reserves and the level of deposits will increase. If the Fed buys $2 million of securities from the public, reserves and deposits in the banking system will both increase by $2 million. This is reflected in the T-account below:

Assets		Liabilities	
Reserves	+$2 million	Deposits	+2 million

Assuming a 10 percent required reserve ratio, determine the potential change in deposits and change in the money supply as a result of this open market purchase by the Fed. If the Fed wished to increase the money supply by $5 million, how many dollars of securities would the Fed need to buy?

5. During 2006, the growth rate in output (real GDP) was 2.9%, and the growth rate in the money supply (M2) was 5.3%. If velocity was constant, what should the inflation rate have been? Suppose that we discover that the inflation rate during 2006 was 3.2%. What does that tell us about velocity in 2006?

_____

_____

_____

_____

6. Suppose that the required reserve ratio is 10 percent. By what amount must reserves grow for the level of deposits to rise by $500?

_____

_____

_____

True/False Questions

T F 1. Economies that trade goods and services for other goods and services are barter economies.

T F 2. Money that has value independent of its use as money is called fiat money.

T F 3. Goods and services in the U.S. are priced in dollars. This is an example of the store of value function of money.

T F 4. The U.S. government backs Federal Reserves Notes with an equal amount of gold.

T F 5. The M1 measure of money counts the currency in banks, called vault cash.

T F 6. M2 includes savings accounts but not checking accounts.

T F 7. A household checking account is an asset to the household and a liability to its bank.

T F 8. As households deposit paychecks in their banks, M1 will immediately increase.

T F 9. Excess reserves are actual reserves plus required reserves.

T F 10. If the First Bank of Boston has no excess reserves, $RR = 0.10$, and a household deposits $5,000 in currency, then that bank can now lend $4,500.

T F 11. A bank with $1,000 of excess reserves cannot safely lend more than $1,000.

T F 12. The simple deposit multiplier is $1/(1 - RR)$.

T F 13. Open market decisions are made by the FOMC.

T F 14. To expand the money supply, the Fed will buy securities from the public.

T F 15. According to the quantity theory of money, an economy will experience inflation if the money supply grows more than 2 percent per year.

Answers to the Self-Test

Multiple-Choice Questions

Question	Answer	Comment
1	c	The economic definition of money is any asset that is generally accepted in exchange for goods and services or for payment of debts.
2	b	Economies that do not use money, but instead trade goods and services directly for other goods and services, are called barter economies. For a barter trade to take place between two people, each person must want what the other one has. Economists refer to this requirement as a double coincidence of wants.
3	c	Most people in modern economies are highly specialized. The high income levels in modern economies are based on the specialization that money makes possible. By making exchange easier, money allows for specialization and higher productivity.
4	d	The usual inefficiencies of barter led the prisoners to begin using cigarettes as money. Cigarettes have a value independent of their use as money, so they are commodity money.
5	c	Instead of having to quote the price of a single good in terms of many other goods, each good has a single price quoted in terms of the medium of exchange. This function of money gives buyers and sellers a unit of account, a way of measuring value in the economy in terms of money. When the U.S. economy uses dollars as money, then each good has a price in terms of dollars.
6	b	Money is useful because of its ability to serve as a standard of deferred payment in borrowing and lending. Money can facilitate exchange at a *given point in time* by providing a medium of exchange and unit of account. It can facilitate exchange *over time* by providing a store of value and a standard of deferred payment.
7	d	What makes a good suitable to use as a medium of exchange? There are five criteria: 1) The good must be acceptable to (that is, usable by) most traders; 2) It should be of standardized quality, so that any two units are identical; 3) It should be durable, so that value is not lost by spoilage; 4) It should be valuable relative to its weight, so that amounts large enough to be useful in trade can be easily transported; and 5) Because different goods are valued differently, the medium of exchange should be divisible.
8	b	In modern economies, paper currency is generally issued by a central bank, which is a special governmental or quasi-governmental institution in the financial system (like the Federal Reserve in the United States) that regulates the money supply. Today, no government in the world issues paper currency that can be redeemed for gold. Paper currency has no value unless it is used as money and is therefore not commodity money.
9	c	Fiat money: Money, such as paper currency, that is authorized by a central bank or governmental body and that does not have to be exchanged by the central bank for gold or some other commodity money.

10	c	Economists have developed several different definitions of the money supply. Each definition includes a different group of assets. The definitions range from narrow to broad. The narrowest definition of money includes cash, checkable deposits and traveler's checks. Broader definitions include other assets that can be easily converted to cash—savings account deposits or certificates of deposit, for example.
11	a	M1 is the narrowest definition of the money supply: the sum of currency in circulation, checking account balances in banks, and holdings of traveler's checks. (Technically, M1 includes all checkable deposits, funds in commercial banks, S&Ls and credit unions that can be transferred using a check-like instrument. If the account is in an S&L, the instrument is called a negotiated order of withdrawal or NOW. If the account is in a credit union, the instrument is called a share draft.)
12	b	M2 includes M1, savings account balances, small-denomination time deposits, money market deposit accounts, and noninstitutional money market fund shares.
13	c	The reduction of checking will reduce M1 by $100, but the transfer to savings will not change M2. Only the composition of M2 changes.
14	b	Although currency and checking account balances are roughly equal in value, checking account balances are used much more often to make payments than currency. More than 80 percent of all goods and services are purchased with checks rather than with currency.
15	b	Before 1980, U.S. law prohibited banks from paying interest on checking account deposits. In 1980, the law was changed to allow banks to pay interest on certain types of checking accounts. This change reduced the difference between checking accounts and savings accounts, although people are still not allowed to write checks against their savings account balances. (But some people have checking accounts that will automatically transfer funds from their savings account if their checking account balance is not large enough to cover a specific check. However, the bank usually charges a fee for this service, meaning the savings account balance is still not as liquid as the checking account balance.)
16	d	M2 includes M1 plus savings account balances, small-denomination time deposits, balances in money market deposit accounts in banks, and noninstitutional money market fund shares.
17	d	Many people buy goods and services with credit cards, yet credit cards are not included in definitions of the money supply. The reason is that when you buy something with a credit card, you are in effect taking out a loan from the bank that issued the credit card. Only when you pay your credit card bill at the end of the month—usually with a check—is the transaction complete.
18	c	Bill Gates's wealth of $46.5 billion made him the richest person in the world in 2005. He also has a very large income, but how much money does he have? A person's *wealth* is equal to the value of his assets minus the value of any debts he has. A person's income is equal to his earnings during the year. Bill Gates's earnings as chairman of Microsoft and from his investments are very large. But his money is just equal to what he has in currency and in checking accounts.
19	c	The key role that banks play in the economy is to accept deposits and make loans. By doing this, they create checking account deposits.
20	a	The key assets on a bank's balance sheet are its reserves, its loans, and its holdings of securities, such as U.S. Treasury bills.

21	a	Loans are the largest asset of a typical bank.
22	c	Banks are required by law to keep 10 percent of their checking account deposits above a certain level as reserves. These reserves are called required reserves. The minimum fraction of deposits that banks are required to keep as reserves (currently 10 percent) is called the required reserve ratio. Any reserves banks hold over and above the legal requirement are called excess reserves.
23	a	Deposits include checking accounts, savings accounts, and certificates of deposit.
24	c	The change in deposits equals $1,000 \times (1/0.1) = \$10,000$.
25	d	The simple deposit multiplier is the ratio of the amount of deposits created by banks to the amount of new reserves. It is the formula used to calculate the total increase in checking account deposits from an increase in bank reserves. It is also the inverse of the required reserve ratio.
26	b	The simple deposit multiplier formula ($1/RR$) makes it clear that the higher the required reserve ratio, the smaller the multiplier.
27	b	The more excess reserves banks keep, the smaller the real-world deposit multiplier.
28	b	With $500 in deposits and a 10 percent required reserve ratio, required reserves are $50 = 0.10 \times \$500$. Excess reserves are actual reserves ($200) minus required reserves ($50) or $150 = \$200 - \$50$.
29	b	The most important part of the money supply is checking account balances. When banks make loans, they increase checking account balances, expanding the money supply. Banks make new loans whenever they gain reserves. The whole process can also work in reverse. If banks lose reserves, they reduce their outstanding loans and deposits, and the money supply contracts.
30	b	The United States, like nearly all other countries, has a fractional reserve banking system. In a fractional reserve banking system, banks keep less than 100 percent of deposits as reserves.
31	c	Sometimes depositors lose confidence in a bank when they question the value of the bank's underlying assets, particularly its loans. Often, the reason for a loss of confidence is bad news, whether true or false. When many depositors decide simultaneously to withdraw their money from a bank, there is a bank run.
32	c	When many depositors decide simultaneously to withdraw their money from a bank, there is a bank run. If many banks experience runs at the same time, the result is a bank panic. It is possible for one bank to handle a run by borrowing from other banks, but if many banks simultaneously experience runs, the banking system may be in trouble. In that case, the central bank should act as lender of last resort.
33	a	With the intention of putting an end to banking panics, Congress in 1913 passed the Federal Reserve Act, setting up the Federal Reserve System. The system began operation in 1914. The Federal Reserve—usually referred to as the "Fed"—is the central bank of the United States. The Fed's main job is controlling the money supply. The Fed also acts as a lender of last resort to banks and as a bankers' bank, providing services such as check clearing to banks.

34	c	There are seven members of the Board of Governors, who are appointed by the President of the United States to 14-year, non-renewable terms. Board members come from banking, business, and academic backgrounds. One of the seven Board members is appointed Chairman for a four-year, renewable term. No more than one Board member can be selected from any Federal Reserve district.
35	c	Monetary policy refers to the actions the Federal Reserve takes to manage the money supply and interest rates to pursue economic objectives.
36	d	Setting a target for the federal funds rate is not a tool of monetary policy. To manage the money supply, the Fed uses three monetary policy tools: 1) Open market operations, 2) Discount policy, and 3) Reserve requirements. Remember that the most important component of the money supply is checking account balances. (The federal funds rate is, however, the main operating target of U.S. monetary policy.)
37	d	The Federal Open Market Committee is responsible for open market operations and managing the money supply. The FOMC has 12 members: the seven members of the Federal Reserve's Board of Governors, the president of the Federal Reserve Bank of New York, and four presidents from the other 11 Federal Reserve banks. These four presidents serve one-year rotating terms.
38	a	To increase the money supply, the FOMC directs the trading desk, located at the Federal Reserve Bank of New York, to buy U.S. Treasury securities—most frequently bills, but sometimes notes or bonds—from the public. When the sellers of the Treasury securities deposit the funds in their banks, the reserves of banks will rise. This increase in reserves will start the process of increasing loans and checking account deposits, increasing the money supply.
39	a	The Fed conducts monetary policy principally through open market operations for three reasons. First, because the Fed initiates open market operations, it completely controls their volume. Second, the Fed can make both large and small open market operations. Third, the Fed can implement its open market operations quickly, with no administrative delay or required changes in regulations. Many other central banks, including the European Central Bank and the Bank of Japan, use open market operations in conducting monetary policy.
40	d	By lowering the discount rate, the Fed can encourage banks to increase the volume of their borrowing from the Fed. When banks borrow from the Fed, they are borrowing reserves. With more reserves, banks will make more loans to households and firms, which will increase checking account deposits and the money supply. Raising the discount rate will have the opposite effect.
41	d	Irving Fisher turned the quantity equation into the quantity theory of money, by asserting that velocity was constant. He asserted that the average number of times a dollar is spent depends on how often people get paid, how often they do their grocery shopping, how often businesses mail bills, and other factors that do not change very often. Because this assertion may be true or false, the quantity theory of money is, in fact, a theory.
42	b	$M \times V = P \times Y$, so $V = (P \times Y)/M$.
43	b	If Irving Fisher was correct that velocity is constant, then the growth rate of velocity will be zero. That is, if velocity is, say, always 8.6, then its percentage change from one year to the next will always be zero. This allows us to rewrite the equation as: Inflation rate = Growth rate of the money supply – Growth rate of real output.

44   a   The growth rate version of the quantity equation leads to the following predictions (recall that deflation is a decline in the price level): 1) If the money supply grows at a faster rate than real GDP, there will be inflation; 2) If the money supply grows at a slower rate than real GDP, there will be deflation, and 3) If the money supply grows at the same rate as real GDP, the price level will be stable. There will be neither inflation nor deflation.

Short Answer Responses

1. Because M1 includes both currency and checking accounts, the deposit of $100 currency in her checking account will change the composition of M1 (less currency and more checking deposits), not the level of M1. Because M2 includes M1 plus savings accounts, then the deposits of $100 in her checking account will also not change M2. If she had deposited the $100 currency in her savings account, then M1 would decrease by $100 (less currency) and M2 would not change (less currency and more savings accounts).

2. As a result of the currency deposit, Andover Bank's required reserves will increase by $1,000 (10 percent of the increase in deposits, or 0.10 x $10,000). The bank can now create a loan for $9,000, the amount of excess reserves ($10,000 – $1,000). After that loan the balance sheet will be:

Assets		Liabilities	
Reserves	+$10,000	Deposits	+$10,000
Loans	+$9,000		+$9,000

When the person that receives the loan uses it to write checks, the level of deposits at the bank will fall, and the bank will lose reserves to other banks. The bank balance sheet will then look like:

Assets		Liabilities	
Reserves	+$1,000	Deposits	+$10,000
Loans	+$9,000		

3. If Alice deposits $100 in her checking account, the supply of money will not change, but the level of bank deposits and the level of excess reserves in the bank will change. This is shown in the T-account below:

Assets		Liabilities and Net Worth	
Reserves	+$100	Deposits	+$100

With $RR = 0.10$ (or 10%), Alice's bank has $90 of excess reserves that it can use to make a new loan, which will create $90 of new deposits and $90 of new money. The banking system can create deposits according to the formula:

$$\Delta D = \frac{1}{RR} \Delta \text{Reserves} = \frac{1}{0.1} \$100 = \$1,000$$

The level of deposits will increase by $1,000 and the money supply will increase by $900. If $RR = 0.20$ (or 20%), then the same $100 deposit by Alice will increase the level of deposits by $500 (1/0.20) x $100) and the money supply will increase $400.

4. If the Fed buys $2 million of securities from the public as part of open market operations, the level of bank reserves will increase by $2 million. Assuming a 10 percent required reserve ratio, the new level of deposits is determined with the formula:

$$\Delta D = \frac{1}{RR}\Delta Reserves = \frac{1}{0.1}\$2 \text{ million} = \$20 \text{ million.}$$

In this case, since the deposit did not start with a deposit of currency by the public, the supply of money will also increase $20 million.

If the Fed wanted to increase the money supply by $5 million, then using the formula:

$$\Delta D = \frac{1}{RR}\Delta Reserves \quad \text{or} \quad \$5 \text{ million} = \frac{1}{0.1}\Delta Reserves, \quad \text{or} \quad \Delta Reserves = \$0.5 \text{ million.}$$

Because the simple deposit = 10, a $0.5 million security purchase will result in a $5 million deposit and money supply change.

5. If velocity was constant (which means the growth rate in velocity is zero) then using the equation:

Inflation rate = (Growth rate in M – Growth rate in Y) + Growth rate in V

we would predict an inflation rate of 2.4% (5.3% – 2.9% = 2.4%). However, if we observe that inflation was 3.2%, then that would imply from the equation that the velocity growth rate was 0.8%, meaning velocity increased in 2006.

6. The simple deposit expansion formula is:

$$\Delta Deposits = \frac{1}{RR}\Delta Reserves = \frac{1}{.1}\Delta Reserves = 10\Delta Reserves.$$

So if we want deposits to increase by $500, then reserves must grow by $50 ($500 = 10 x ΔReserves, or ΔReserves = $50).

True/False Answers

1.	T	
2.	F	Money that has value other than as money is called a commodity money.
3.	F	This is the unit of the account function of money.
4.	F	Federal Reserve Notes are not backed by any commodity. They are an example of fiat money.
5.	F	M1 only counts currency outside banks or the government.
6.	F	M2 includes both savings accounts and checking accounts.
7.	T	
8.	F	When the household's checking account increases from the deposit, the firm's checking account decreases the same amount so that M1 will not change.
9.	F	Excess reserves are actual reserves minus required reserves.
10.	T	
11.	T	

12.   F   The simple deposit multiplier is $1/RR$.

13.   T

14.   T

15.   F   According to the quantity theory, an economy will experience inflation if money growth exceeds output growth.

Monetary Policy

Chapter Summary

In Chapter 13, you learned that banks play an important role in creating the money supply and in how the Fed manages the money supply. In Chapter 14, you will learn about **monetary policy**, the actions the Fed takes to manage the money supply and interest rates to pursue its macroeconomic policy objectives. The Fed has set four *monetary policy goals* that are intended to promote a well-functioning economy:

1. Price stability
2. High employment
3. Economic growth
4. Stability of financial markets and institutions

The Fed's *monetary policy targets* are economic variables that it can affect directly and that in turn affect variables such as real GDP and the price level that are closely related to the Fed's policy goals. The Federal Open Market Committee announces a target for the **federal funds rate** after each meeting. The federal funds rate is the interest rate banks charge each other for overnight loans.

To fight a recession, the Fed conducts **expansionary monetary policy**, which lowers interest rates to increase consumption, investment, and net exports. To reduce the inflation rate, the Fed conducts **contractionary monetary policy**, which raises interest rates to decrease consumption, investment, and net exports. Over the past decade, many economists and central bankers have expressed significant interest in using **inflation targeting**, under which monetary policy is conducted to commit the central bank to achieving a publicly announced inflation target. A number of foreign central banks have adopted inflation targeting, but the Fed has not.

Learning Objectives

When you finish this chapter, you should be able to:

1. **Define monetary policy and describe the Federal Reserve's monetary policy goals. Monetary policy** is the Federal Reserve's use of changes in the money supply and interest rates to pursue its policy objectives. The Fed has set four *monetary policy goals* that are intended to promote a well-functioning economy: price stability, high employment, economic growth, and stability of financial markets and institutions. The Fed's *monetary policy targets* are economic variables that it can affect directly. In turn, the targets affect variables such as real GDP and the price level that are closely related to the Fed's policy goals. The two main monetary policy targets are the money supply and the interest rate. The Fed has most often chosen to use the interest rate as its monetary policy target. The Federal Open Market Committee announces a target for the **federal funds rate** after each meeting. The federal funds rate is the interest rate banks charge each other for overnight loans.

2. **Describe the Federal Reserve's monetary policy targets and explain how expansionary and contractionary monetary policies affect the interest rate.** A macroeconomic policy that successfully reduces the severity of the business cycle is called a *countercyclical policy*. To fight a recession, the Fed conducts an *expansionary policy* by increasing the money supply. The increase in the money supply lowers the interest rate. To reduce the inflation rate, the Fed conducts a *contractionary policy* by increasing the money supply. The decrease in the money supply raises the interest rate. In a graphical analysis of the money market, an expansionary policy shifts the money supply curve to the right, causing a movement down the money demand curve, and a new equilibrium at a lower interest rate. A contractionary policy shifts the money supply curve to the left, causing a movement up the money demand curve, and a new equilibrium at a higher interest rate.

3. **Use aggregate demand and aggregate supply graphs to show the effects of monetary policy on real GDP and the price level.** An **expansionary monetary** policy lowers interest rates to increase consumption, investment, and net exports. This increased spending causes the aggregate demand curve (*AD*) to shift to the right more than it otherwise would, raising the level of real GDP and the price level. A **contractionary monetary policy** raises interest rates in order to decrease consumption, investment, and net exports. This decreased spending causes the aggregate demand curve to shift to the right less than it otherwise would, reducing the level of real GDP and the price level.

4. **Discuss the Fed's setting of monetary policy targets.** Some economists have argued that the Fed should use the money supply as its monetary target, rather than an interest rate. Milton Friedman and other monetarists argue that the Fed should adopt a monetary growth rule of increasing the money supply every year at a fixed rate. Support for this proposal declined after 1980 because the relationship between movements in the money supply and movements in real GDP and the price level has weakened. John Taylor has analyzed the factors involved in Fed decision making and developed the *Taylor rule* for federal funds targeting. The Taylor rule links the Fed's target for the federal funds rate to economic variables. Over the past decade, many economists and central bankers have expressed significant interest in using *inflation targeting*. Under inflation targeting, monetary policy is conducted so as to commit the central bank to achieving a publicly announced inflation target. A number of foreign central banks have adopted inflation targeting, but the Fed has not. The Fed's performance in the 1980s, 1990s, and early 2000s has generally received high marks from economists, even without formal inflation targeting.

5. **Assess the arguments for and against the independence of the Federal Reserve.** The Fed conducts monetary policy without input from the Congress or the president. The Fed's entire operating budget is the interest it earns from purchasing U.S. Treasury bills. That means the Fed does not depend on Congress for its operating funds. But the Fed's independence is not absolute, because Congress and the president can pass legislation at any time to reorganize (or even abolish) the Fed. Advocates of Fed independence argue that isolating it from political pressure allows it to choose policies in the best interest of the economy. Internationally, countries with more independent central banks tend to have lower inflation rates. Opponents of Fed independence argue that concentrating so much power in the hands of unelected officials is inconsistent with democratic principles.

Chapter Review

Chapter Opener: Monetary Policy, Toll Brothers, and the Housing Market (pages 466-467)

Usually, recessions hit the homebuilding industry very hard as new home sales fall due to increases in unemployment and falling income. The recession of 2001 was very different. Residential construction increased by 5 percent during this recession. The profits of Toll Brothers, a residential construction company, increased to record levels. This unusual behavior was a direct result of the Fed's decision in early 2001 to begin to implement an expansionary monetary policy to keep the recession as short and mild as possible. By lowering interest rates sharply, the Fed was able to head off what was predicted to be a prolonged and severe recession. By 2005, however, the housing market had turned into a housing "bubble." Prices rose to levels that are not sustainable and then began to fall. With lower levels of construction, Toll Brothers' profits fell. Initially, the Fed did not lower interest rates because it believed that doing so might make inflation worse. By late 2007, Toll Brothers and most other home builders were suffering significant losses, and the Fed had begun to cut interest rates.

📖 Helpful Study Hint

Read *An Inside Look* at the end of the chapter to learn the macroeconomic effects of housing market slowdowns in the United States and Europe. Although the prices of houses are increasing more slowly in both economies, only the U.S. economy has slowed as a result of this weakness. While home-equity loans are readily available to U.S. homeowners, they are not readily available to euro-zone homeowners. This is important because a home-equity loan allows a homeowner to borrow against—and, in effect, spend—the difference between the value of a home and the amount of the mortgage loan on the home. Therefore, in an economy in which home equity loans are prevalent, consumption spending may rise and fall with house prices; however, in an economy where home equity loans are not prevalent, consumption spending may not be much affected by changes in house prices. According to the article, the weak housing market slowed consumption spending in the United States, but had relatively little effect on consumption spending in the euro-zone economy.

Imagine that you have graduated and are working full time. You've built up enough money for a down payment on a house. Now, imagine that the economy dips into a recession. Would you buy a house during a recession? The *Economics in YOUR Life!* at the start of this chapter poses this question. Keep the question in mind as you read the chapter. The authors will answer the question at the end of the chapter.

14.1 What Is Monetary Policy? (pages 468–469)

Learning Objective 1   Define monetary policy and describe the Federal Reserve's monetary policy goals.

Monetary policy refers to actions taken by the Federal Reserve System (the Fed, which is the central bank of the United States) to manage the money supply and interest rates in order to influence the level of economic activity. The Fed's conduct of monetary policy is driven by four goals:

- *Price stability*. Low inflation is one of the Fed's important goals. Low inflation over the long run gives the Fed the flexibility to lessen the impact of recessions.
- *High employment*. Low employment (or high unemployment) causes the level or real GDP to be below potential.
- *Economic growth*. Growth is important to the economy to increase standards of living.
- *Stability of financial markets and institutions*. A stable economy, without wide swings in prices and employment rates, will grow faster than an unstable economy.

Extra Solved Problem 14-1

Chapter 14 of the textbook includes two Solved Problems. Here is an extra Solved Problem to help you build your skills solving economic problems:

Monetary Policy and Economic Growth

Supports Learning Objective 1: Define monetary policy and describe the Federal Reserve's monetary policy goals.

Monetary policy refers to the Federal Reserve System's actions to control the money supply and interest rates in order to pursue its economic objectives. The textbook lists the Federal Reserve's four monetary policy goals: (1) price stability (2) high employment (3) economic growth (4) stability of financial markets and institutions. The control the Fed has over the supply of money and interest rates is the source of its influence over goals (1) and (4), but how much control does the Fed have over real variables such as employment and economic growth? In chapter 10, the textbook argues that increases in per-capita real GDP are the result of the growth of labor productivity. In turn, increases in labor productivity are caused by increases in the quantity of capital per hour worked and the level of technology, not changes in the money supply. Laurence H. Meyer made the following comments in a speech while he served as a member of the Federal Reserve's Board of Governors.

> "…monetary policy cannot influence real variables – such as output and employment…This is often referred to as the principle of the neutrality of money. One of the most important disciplines for policymakers is understanding what they can and what they cannot accomplish. The Fed, for example, cannot raise the long-run rate of economic growth. It should not try."

Source: Lawrence H. Meyer. "Come with Me to the FOMC." The Federal Reserve Board. April 2, 1998. http://www.federalreserve.gov/boarddocs/Speeches/1998/199804022.htm

Is Lawrence Meyer correct in stating that the Federal Reserve cannot affect output (or economic growth) and employment?

SOLVING THE PROBLEM:

Step 1: **Review the chapter material.**

This problem concerns monetary policy, so you may want to review the section "What is Monetary Policy?" which begins on page 468 of the textbook.

Step 2: **Is Lawrence Meyer correct in stating that the Federal Reserve cannot affect output (or economic growth) and employment?**

An important phrase was left out of Meyer's comments. The full quotation is "…monetary policy cannot influence real variables—such as output and employment—in the long run (except via the contribution of price stability to living standards)." Meyer also states "…because prices in many markets are slow to react to changes in supply and demand, shocks to the economy can lead to persistent departures of the economy from full employment…This…offers at least the potential for monetary policy to play a role in smoothing out business cycles." In other words, monetary policy can affect output and employment, but only in the short run. In the long run, a nation's economic growth is determined by real factors such as investment in capital and the level of technology, not by monetary policy. We saw that this was true in Chapter 12, where we indicated that potential real GDP was not affected by the level of aggregate demand.

14.2 LEARNING OBJECTIVE

14.2 The Money Market and the Fed's Choice of Monetary Policy Targets (pages 470-476)

Learning Objective 2   Describe the Federal Reserve's monetary policy targets and explain how expansionary and contractionary monetary policies affect the interest rate.

The Fed tries to keep both the unemployment rate and the inflation rate low, but it cannot affect either of these economic variables directly. Using its tools of open market operations, changing the required reserve ratio, and changing the discount rate, the Fed can only directly affect interest rates or the money supply. The Fed uses monetary policy targets that it can affect directly. These targets then affect the goal variables. The Fed chooses between money supply targets and interest rate targets. In practice, the Fed has typically chosen interest rate targets.

Money supply and interest rate targets are linked by the money market and the demand and supply of money. The demand for money curve is shown in a graph by a downward-sloping line, with the interest rate on the vertical axis and the quantity of money on the horizontal axis. As the interest rate rises, the opportunity cost of holding money increases. With high interest rates, financial assets such as bonds earn more interest income, and the public chooses to hold less money and hold more bonds. This is shown in textbook Figure 14-2 on the following page.

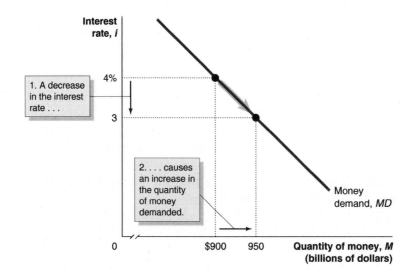

A change in the interest rate causes a movement up or down a stationary money demand curve. If other factors that affect the willingness of households and firms to hold money change, then the money demand curve will shift. A shift to the right in the demand for money curve is caused by:

- An increase in real GDP
- An increase in the price level (the GDP deflator)

A shift in the money demand curve is shown in textbook Figure 14-3 reproduced below:

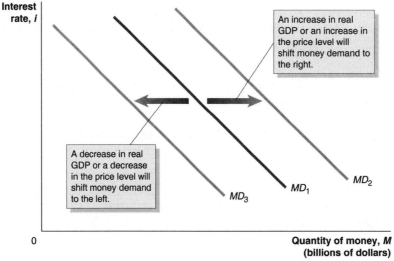

The supply of money is determined by the Fed. The Fed can use open market operations (buying and selling Treasury bills) to change the supply of money.

📖 Helpful Study Hint

Recall from the last chapter, when the Fed buys Treasury bills from the public, the supply of money will increase and interest rates will usually fall. When the Fed sells Treasury bills to the public, the money supply will decrease and interest rates will usually rise.

Money market equilibrium occurs when the quantity of money supplied is equal to the quantity of money demanded. This equilibrium is shown in textbook Figure 14-4:

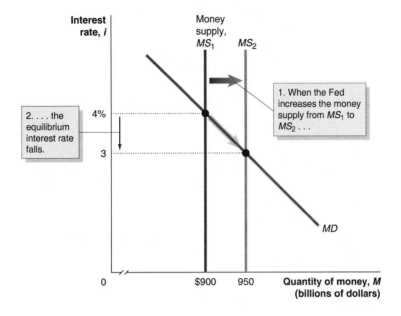

Figure 14-4 above shows that the Fed can change both the money supply and the interest rate. Equilibrium occurs where the money supply curve and the money demand curve intersect. As the Fed increases the supply of money, the public will use these new dollars to buy financial assets. This purchase of financial assets, such as Treasury bills or other short-term bonds, will increase bond prices and lower interest rates. So, the result of the Fed increasing the money supply will be a new equilibrium with a lower interest rate. Thus, the Fed can change both the money supply and the interest rate.

When the Fed chooses an interest rate target, it must change the money supply to keep the interest rate at the target level as money demand changes. If the Fed chooses a money supply target, the interest rate will change with changes in money demand.

The Fed's primary monetary policy target is the interest rate known as the federal funds rate. The **federal funds rate** (or fed funds rate) is the interest rate banks charge each other for overnight loans of bank reserves. Changes in the federal funds rate usually cause changes in other interest rates, such as the interest rate on Treasury bills, corporate bond rates, and home mortgage rates.

The Federal Open Market Committee (FOMC) picks a target federal funds interest rate and announces that rate at the end of the FOMC meeting. The actual federal funds rate is usually very close to the target rate. Because the Fed can control the supply of bank reserves, it has a great deal of control over the fed funds rate.

14.3 Monetary Policy and Economic Activity (pages 477-489)

Learning Objective 3   Use aggregate demand and aggregate supply graphs to show the effects of monetary policy on real GDP and the price level.

As the Fed changes the target federal funds rate, other interest rates change, which will influence the level of aggregate demand. Other things equal, increases in the interest rate will tend to:

- Decrease consumption spending as the financing costs of consumer durables increase.
- Decrease investment as the financing costs of new capital goods purchased by firms increase and as mortgage interest rates rise (recall that spending on residential construction is included as part of investment spending).
- Decrease exports as the value of the dollar increases. Higher interest rates in the United States increase the demand for dollars as foreign investors increase their purchases of U.S. financial assets. A higher value for the dollar makes U.S. goods more expensive in foreign markets.

If the current level of real GDP is below potential real GDP, to reach the goal of high employment the Fed needs to carry out an **expansionary monetary policy** by increasing the money supply and decreasing interest rates. This is shown in the left panel in the graph below (textbook Figure 14-7). If the short-run equilibrium is at a level of real GDP to the right of the *LRAS* supply curve, to reach the goal of price stability, the Fed needs to carry out a contractionary monetary policy by decreasing the money supply and increasing interest rates. This is shown in the graph below (textbook Figure 14-7) in the right panel.

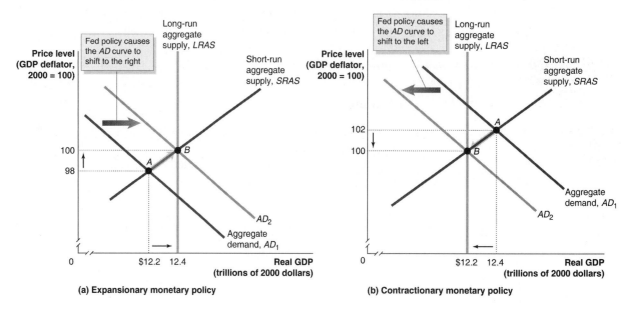

(a) Expansionary monetary policy   (b) Contractionary monetary policy

The Fed can use monetary policy to affect the price level, and the level of real GDP in the short-run. The effect of monetary policy on short-run real GDP and the price level allows the Fed to attain the goals of price stability and high employment.

In a growing economy, expansionary monetary policy is used if increases in aggregate demand are not great enough to bring the economy to equilibrium at potential GDP. This slow growth in aggregate demand could be due to weak consumption or investment growth, a cut back in government purchases, or a fall in exports. The Fed can use monetary policy to increase aggregate demand to the desired level. The effects of monetary policy can be shown using the dynamic aggregate demand and supply model that was developed in Chapter 12. Textbook Figure 14-8 reproduced below illustrates an expansionary monetary policy using the dynamic aggregate demand and aggregate supply model:

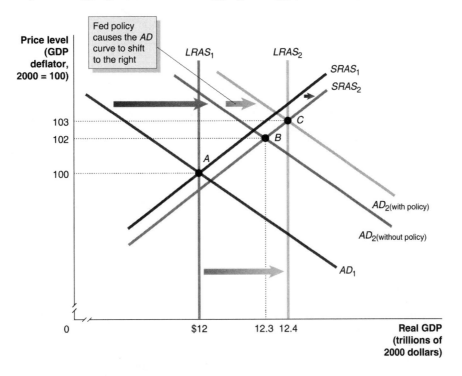

In this example, the Fed uses monetary policy to eliminate a recession by bringing the economy to equilibrium at potential GDP of $12.4 trillion. In practice, however, the Fed has discovered that it is able to use monetary policy to reduce the severity of recession but not eliminate recessions. This was shown in the 2001 recession. The Fed's lower interest rates helped increase spending on housing, as we saw in the chapter opener from the experience of Toll Brothers, but was not able to entirely eliminate the recession.

The Fed can also use a contractionary monetary policy if aggregate demand is increasing too rapidly and causing inflation to increase. This is shown in textbook Figure 14-9, where the contractionary monetary policy reduces the size of the aggregate demand growth, resulting in a lower inflation rate.

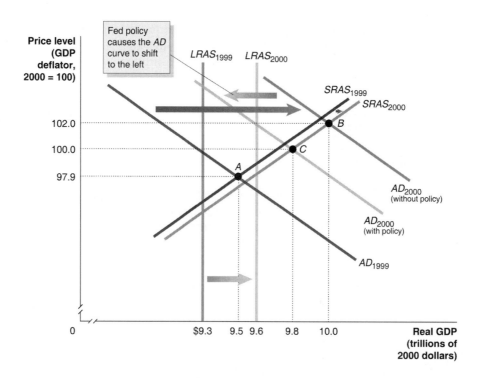

During 1999-2000, the FOMC raised the target for the federal funds rate to slow the growth of aggregate demand and reduce the inflation rate. The Fed was able to slow but not stop inflation during this period.

Textbook Table 14-1 below summarizes how expansionary and contractionary monetary policy work, relative to what would have happened without the policy. Note that sometimes expansionary monetary policy is called *loose* or *easy policy*, and contractionary monetary policy is called *tight policy*.

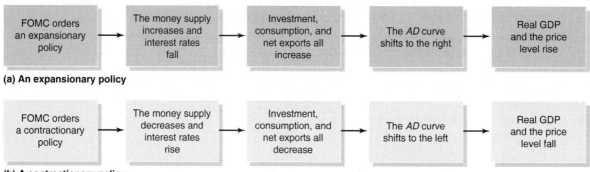

The Fed's ability to recognize the need for a change in policy is very important. If the Fed is late in recognizing that a recession has begun or that inflation is increasing, its policy response may be too late to correct the problem, and potentially may actually make the problem worse. This is shown in textbook Figure 14-10 reproduced below, where the Fed moves too late to implement monetary policy to bring the economy out of a recession and increases aggregate demand too much, thereby increasing the inflation rate. In this case, the delay in the response to the recession has a procyclical effect, which means that it increases the fluctuations of the business cycle, rather than reducing them.

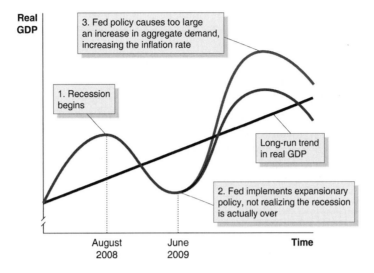

📖 Helpful Study Hint

Read *Making the Connection: The Inflation and Deflation of the Housing Market "Bubble."* Low interest rates during the 2001 recession helped boost the demand for housing. Continuing low interest rates through the early 2000s contributed to a housing market bubble. A bubble occurs when the price of housing increases beyond the value of the services offered by the housing. The increase in prices was also fueled by sub-prime and exotic mortgages that allowed many first-time homeowners to enter the market for housing. During 2006 and 2007, when the bubble burst, sales of homes and housing prices started to fall in many local markets. This decline in home sales and construction caused a reduction in demand for construction materials and home appliances. The Fed's dilemma was whether to (1) reduce target interest rates to help increase spending on new houses, thereby reducing the probability of a recession or (2) hold interest rates constant to help achieve the goal of price stability. By late 2007, the threat of recession led the Fed to dramatically decrease the target for the federal funds rate. By early 2008, it was unclear whether the economy would be able to avoid a recession.

To learn how the Fed helped prevent a financial panic, read *Making the Connection: The Fed Responds to the Terrorist Attacks of September 11, 2001.* Following the terrorist attacks on September 11, 2001, the Fed made discount loans to banks to help eliminate the possibility of bank runs where depositors withdraw large amounts of deposits from banks. Discount loans after September 11 rose to about 500 times the usual level.

Read *Making the Connection: Why Does Wall Street Care About Monetary Policy?* Before each FOMC meeting, Fed watchers try to predict the results of the meeting. Changes in the federal funds rate influence the stock market. Falling federal funds rates tend to increase real GDP, increasing the profitability of many stocks. When interest rates fall, investments in stocks are more profitable because of the lower returns on other assets, such as saving accounts or bonds.

📖 Helpful Study Hint

Test your understanding of the effects of monetary policy by reviewing main text *Solved Problem 14-3*.

Also read the *Don't Let this Happen to YOU!* feature, which explains how monetary policy works. It is only when the interest rate falls due to a money supply increase that spending changes. It is the lower interest rate that stimulates the economy, not the extra dollars in circulation.

14.4 LEARNING OBJECTIVE

14.4 A Closer Look at the Fed's Setting of Monetary Policy Targets (pages 490-494)

Learning Objective 4 Discuss the Fed's setting of monetary policy targets.

Monetarist economists have argued that the Fed should adopt a money supply growth rule that would set the growth rate of the money supply at about 3.5 percent per year. These economists argue that a money supply growth rule would reduce fluctuations in real GDP and keep the inflation rate low. Most economists, however, believe that using an interest rate target is better than adopting a money supply growth rule.

The Fed cannot have a money supply target and an interest rate target at the same time. To see why, suppose money demand increases because of rising real GDP. If the Fed targets the money supply by keeping the current level of the money supply constant, the increase in money demand will cause the interest rate to rise. If the Fed targets the interest rate by keeping it constant, the increase in money demand will force the Fed to increase the money supply in order to keep the interest rate at the target level. This is shown in textbook Figure 14-11 below:

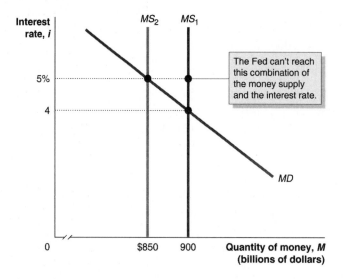

John Taylor, an economist at Stanford University, has developed an equation to predict the target federal funds rate. His equation, known as the **Taylor Rule**, is as follows:

Federal funds target rate = Current inflation rate + Real equilibrium federal funds rate +
(1/2) x Inflation gap + (1/2) x Output gap

The inflation gap is the difference between current inflation and the target inflation rate (about 2 percent), and the output gap is the percentage difference between actual and potential real GDP. The equilibrium real federal funds rate (about 2 percent) is the federal funds rate – adjusted for inflation – that would be consistent with real GDP being equal to potential real GDP in the long run. The Taylor Rule equation predicts that

- as inflation increases, the Fed will raise the target for the federal funds rate, and
- as real GDP rises above potential real GDP, the Fed will also raise the target for the federal funds rate.

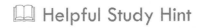 Helpful Study Hint

The Taylor Rule is not a rigid rule the FOMC uses to set target interest rates. It is a formula that is helpful in explaining FOMC actions.

An alternative way of conducting monetary policy is for the Fed to have an explicit target for the inflation rate. This is called **inflation targeting**, and is the framework that many countries use to conduct monetary policy. The reasons to move to an inflation-targeting approach to monetary policy are:
- In the long run, real GDP returns to potential, and potential real GDP is not influenced by monetary policy.
- An announced target makes it easier to form accurate expectations about inflation.
- Monetary policy would not change as policymakers change.
- An announced target will promote accountability for the Fed, giving a measure of its performance.

Extra Solved Problem 14-4

Chapter 14 of the textbook includes two Solved Problems. Here is an extra Solved Problem to help you build your skills solving economic problems:

Targeting Inflation

Supports Learning Objective 4: Discuss the Fed's setting of monetary policy targets.

On February 1, 2006, Ben S. Bernanke was sworn in as chairman of the Federal Reserve Board. Although Bernanke is a respected macroeconomist, he succeeded a chairman, Alan Greenspan, who was given high marks for his leadership of the Fed during a period (1987-2006) of remarkable prosperity and low inflation. In the months leading up to the end of Greenspan's tenure, much speculation surrounded how the Reserve Board would operate under its new chairman. Long before his appointment as chairman, Bernanke proposed that the Fed engage in "inflation targeting." In a 2004 interview, Bernanke was asked if the Fed's prior commitment to price stability was not a de facto inflation targeting policy. Bernanke gave the following response.

"It's true that the Federal Reserve is already practicing something close to de facto inflation targeting, and I think we've seen many benefits from that. My main suggestion is to take the natural next step and give an explicit objective…to provide the public with a working definition of price stability in the form of a number or a numerical range for inflation…First, such a step would increase the coherence of policy…I think the…[Federal Reserve's] decision-making process would be improved if members shared a collective view of where we want the inflation rate to be once the economy is on a steady expansion path. Second, there's…evidence now that tightly anchored public expectations of inflation are very beneficial not only for stabilizing inflation but also in reducing the volatility of output…Third, from a communications viewpoint, financial markets would be well served by knowing the…inflation objective of the Fed…[it] would help market participants accurately price long-term assets…"

Source: Interview with Ben S. Bernanke. *The Region*. Federal Reserve Bank of Minneapolis. June 2004. http://minneapolisfed.org/pubs/region/04-06/bernanke.cfm

Given that rates of inflation were low during the tenure of Alan Greenspan, what purpose would be served by setting a target for inflation?

SOLVING THE PROBLEM

Step 1: **Review the chapter material.**
This problem concerns the monetary policy targets of the Federal Reserve System, so you may want to review the section "A Closer Look at the Fed's Setting of Monetary Policy Targets," which begins on page 490 of the textbook.

Step 2: **Explain why setting a target for inflation might still be a good idea even though rates of inflation were low during the tenure of Alan Greenspan.**
The main reason for establishing an inflation rate target is that it strengthens the commitment of the Federal Reserve to price stability. In the article cited above, Bernanke stated, "I think that announcing a target would strengthen our commitment to…price stability…and…give more emphasis to long-run considerations… Having a medium-to long-term objective would force us to keep in view where we want the economy to be in the longer run." Central banks can come under political pressure to engage in expansionary monetary policy in order to increase output and employment in the short run, even though the result of the policy may also be an increase in inflation. An explicit target for inflation can help a central bank to resist this political pressure. An explicit inflation target also makes it easier for the public to evaluate a central bank's performance.

📖 Helpful Study Hint

Read *Making the Connection: How Does the Fed Measure Inflation?* There are several measures of inflation available to the Fed. The CPI is biased upward because of measurement issues. The GDP deflator is not a measure of the average price of goods purchased by consumers because it includes industrial goods. The personal consumption expenditure (PCE) price index is a better measure because it concentrates on consumer goods. In 2002, the Fed began to look more at the PCE that the CPI. In 2004, the Fed began to look at a sub-category of the PCE, called core PCE which excludes food and energy prices. Core PCE has been more stable than CPI or PCE.

14.5 Is the Independence of the Federal Reserve a Good Idea? (pages 494-497)

Learning Objective 5   Assess the arguments for and against the independence of the Federal Reserve.

The Federal Reserve System makes monetary policy decisions independently. Monetary policy decisions in the United States are made by the Federal Reserve System independently of Congress or the president. Although the Fed is financially independent because it earns interest on Treasury securities, this independence is not absolute because Congress could pass new laws that could reorganize the Fed, or even eliminate it. Is the independence of the Fed a good idea?

A key argument in favor of the independence of the Fed is that an independent Fed can concentrate on keeping inflation low. Without independence, the Fed might be required to help finance government budget deficits by buying government issued bonds. The result could be rapid increases in the money supply, which can cause high inflation. The Fed might also be required to increase the money supply before elections as the government tries to increase its popularity by increasing employment and GDP. In the long run, though, these increases in the money supply might also lead to higher inflation rates. However, some economists and policymakers argue that the Fed should be less independent. In democracies, elected representatives usually decide important policy matters. In the United States, on the other hand, the unelected members of the Federal Open Market Committee make the key monetary policy decisions. Despite this argument, at this point it appears unlikely that Congress would consider legislation to reduce the independence of the Fed.

📖 Helpful Study Hint

Textbook Figure 14-12 shows that countries with more independent central banks tend to have lower inflation. For example, during the period 1955–1988, Germany's central bank had a high index of independence of 4 and Germany had a low average inflation rate of just over 3 percent. New Zealand's central bank had a low index of independence of 1 and New Zealand had a high average inflation rate of over 7 percent.

📖 Helpful Study Hint

Economics in YOUR Life! at the end of the chapter answers the question posed at the start of the chapter: Should you buy a home during a recession? Two things to consider: How safe is your job? During recessions, unemployment increases. Is it possible that you might lose your job? The second thing to consider is that during recessions the Fed often lowers interest rates to stimulate the economy (which is an expansionary monetary policy). This will lower the payments on a mortgage loan, which would make buying a home more affordable.

Key Terms

Contractionary monetary policy. The Fed's adjusting the money supply to increase interest rates to reduce inflation.

Expansionary monetary policy. The Federal Reserve's increasing the money supply and decreasing interest rates to increase real GDP.

Federal funds rate. The interest rate banks charge each other for overnight loans.

Inflation targeting. Conducting monetary policy so as to commit the central bank to achieving a publicly announced level of inflation.

Monetary policy. The actions the Federal Reserve takes to manage the money supply and interest rates to pursue its economic objectives.

Taylor rule. A rule developed by John Taylor that links the Fed's target for the federal funds rate to economic variables.

Self-Test

(Answers are provided at the end of the Self-Test.)

Multiple-Choice Questions

1. In early 2001, the members of the Federal Open Market Committee (FOMC) concluded that a recession was about to begin. To keep the recession as short and mild as possible, they implemented a
   a. fiscal policy that increased government spending and reduced taxes.
   b. fiscal policy that decreased government spending and increased taxes.
   c. monetary policy that lowered interest rates.
   d. monetary policy that raised interest rates.

2. Which of the following are monetary policy goals of the Federal Reserve?
   a. price stability
   b. high employment and economic growth
   c. stability of financial markets
   d. all of the above

3. *Monetary policy* refers to the actions the Fed takes to
   a. regulate business activity.
   b. manage the money supply and interest rates.
   c. manage government spending and taxation.
   d. all of the above

4. Which of the following periods had the highest inflation rate?
   a. the 1950s and 1960s
   b. the 1970s
   c. the 1990s
   d. All of the periods above experienced similar inflation rates.

5. Attempts to ensure that there will be an efficient flow of funds from savers to borrowers is the objective of which monetary policy goal?
   a. price stability
   b. high employment
   c. economic growth
   d. stability of financial markets

6. Which two policy goals can be pursued simultaneously without being at odds with each other?
   a. high employment and inflation reduction
   b. economic growth and inflation reduction
   c. high employment and economic growth
   d. Any of the combinations above can be pursued simultaneously without being at odds with each other.

7. Which of these two variables are the main *monetary policy targets* of the Fed?
   a. real GDP and the price level
   b. the money supply and the interest rate
   c. the inflation rate and the unemployment rate
   d. economic growth and productivity

8. Which of the following is not a goal of monetary policy?
   a. price stability
   b. high employment
   c. economic growth
   d. low interest rates

9. When is the opportunity cost of holding money higher?
   a. when interest rates are high
   b. when interest rates are low
   c. when the inflation rate is lower
   d. when the money supply increases

10. When the interest rate decreases,
    a. the money demand curve shifts to the right.
    b. the money demand curve shifts to the left.
    c. there is a movement down along a stationary money demand curve.
    d. there is a movement up along a stationary money demand curve.

11. When interest rates on Treasury bills and other financial assets are low, the opportunity cost of holding money is _____, so the quantity of money demanded will be _____.
    a. low; low
    b. high; high
    c. low; high
    d. high; high

12. If real GDP increases,
    a. the money demand curve shifts to the right.
    b. the money demand curve shifts to the left.
    c. there is a movement down along a stationary money demand curve.
    d. there is a movement up along a stationary money demand curve.

13. If the price level increases,
    a. the money demand curve shifts to the right.
    b. the money demand curve shifts to the left.
    c. there is a movement down along a stationary money demand curve.
    d. there is a movement up along a stationary money demand curve.

14. If the FOMC decides to increase the money supply, it orders the trading desk at the Federal Reserve Bank of New York to
    a. buy stocks.
    b. sell stocks.
    c. buy U.S. Treasury securities.
    d. sell U.S. Treasury securities.

15. If the FOMC orders the trading desk to sell Treasury securities,
    a. the money supply curve will shift to the left, and the equilibrium interest rate will fall.
    b. the money supply curve will shift to the left, and the equilibrium interest rate will rise.
    c. the money supply curve will shift to the right, and the equilibrium interest rate will rise.
    d. the money supply curve will shift to the right, and the equilibrium interest rate will fall.

16. The prices of financial assets and the interest rates on these assets
    a. move in the same direction.
    b. move in opposite directions.
    c. are identical.
    d. are unrelated.

17. Suppose you buy for $950 a U.S. Treasury bill that matures in one year, at which time the Treasury will pay you $1,000. How much interest will you earn on your investment of $950?
    a. 4.75%
    b. 5.26%
    c. 19%
    d. 5%

18. Suppose that when the Fed decreases the money supply, households and firms initially hold less money than they want to, relative to other financial assets. Households and firms will then _____ Treasury bills and other financial assets, thereby _____ their prices, and _____ their interest rates.
    a. buy; increasing; increasing
    b. sell; increasing; reducing
    c. buy; reducing; reducing
    d. sell; reducing; increasing

19. Which of the following will shift the money demand curve to the right?
    a. an increase in the interest rate
    b. an increase in real GDP
    c. a decrease in the interest rate
    d. an increase in the money supply

20. The interest rate that banks charge each other for overnight loans is called the
    a. Treasury bill rate.
    b. prime lending rate.
    c. discount rate.
    d. federal funds rate.

21. Which of the following statements is correct?
    a. Changes in the federal funds rate usually will result in changes in both short-term and long-term interest rates on financial assets.
    b. The effect of a change in the federal funds rate on long-term interest rates is usually smaller than it is on short-term interest rates.
    c. A majority of economists support the Fed's choice of the interest rate as its monetary policy target, but some economists believe the Fed should concentrate on the money supply instead.
    d. all of the above

22. As interest rates decline, stocks become a _____ attractive investment relative to bonds, and this causes the demand for stocks and their prices to _____.
    a. more; rise
    b. more; fall
    c. less; rise
    d. less; fall

23. If interest rates in the United States rise relative to interest rates in other countries, the demand for dollars will _____, which will _____ the value of the dollar and cause net exports to _____.
    a. fall; lower; fall
    b. rise; increase; rise
    c. fall; lower; rise
    d. rise; increase; fall

24. An increase in the money supply will
    a. shift the money demand curve to the right and reduce the interest rate.
    b. shift the money supply curve to the right and increase the interest rate.
    c. shift the money demand curve to the left and increase the interest rate.
    d. shift the money supply curve to the right and reduce the interest rate.

25. The Fed's strategy of increasing the money supply and lowering interest rates in order to increase real GDP is called
    a. reactionary monetary policy.
    b. contractionary monetary policy.
    c. expansionary monetary policy.
    d. contractionary fiscal policy.

26. Suppose that the FOMC meets and learns that real GDP will fall short of potential real GDP by $200 billion. If the FOMC tries to correct this situation, it will enact which type of policy?
    a. expansionary monetary policy to decrease short-run aggregate supply
    b. expansionary monetary policy to increase aggregate demand
    c. expansionary monetary policy to increase short-run aggregate supply
    d. contractionary monetary policy to decrease long-run aggregate supply

27. How did the FOMC react to the recession that began in March 2001?
    a. The FOMC increased the target for the federal funds rate steadily throughout 2001.
    b. The FOMC reduced the target for the federal funds rate steadily throughout 2001.
    c. The FOMC decided to leave interest rates unchanged for the remainder of 2001.
    d. The FOMC did not react because it failed to recognize that a recession was taking place.

28. The actions of the Fed during the 2001 recession demonstrated that
    a. the ability of the Fed to head off a severe recession is almost nonexistent.
    b. the Fed is able to "fine tune" the economy, practically eliminating the business cycle, and achieving absolute price stability.
    c. the Fed is able to reduce the severity of a recession, but unable to eliminate it entirely.
    d. the Fed prefers to allow the economy to correct its problems on its own, without active monetary policy.

29. Which of the following is a consequence of deflation?
    a. an increase in real interest rates
    b. an increase in the real value of debts
    c. consumers may postpone their purchases in the hope of experiencing even lower prices in the future
    d. all of the above

30. When the Fed acts as it did during 2000, decreasing the money supply and increasing interest rates in order to reduce inflation, it is engaging in
    a. contractionary fiscal policy.
    b. expansionary monetary policy.
    c. contractionary monetary policy.
    d. discretionary fiscal policy.

31. A *procyclical policy* is one that
    a. is used to stabilize the economy.
    b. inadvertently increases the severity of the business cycle.
    c. minimizes the cost of economic recessions.
    d. enhances the benefits of economic expansions.

32. A countercyclical policy is one that
    a. is used to attempt to stabilize the economy.
    b. inadvertently increases the severity of the business cycle.
    c. follows the fluctuations in the business cycle.
    d. enhances the benefits of economic expansions.

33. *Monetarism* is a school of economic thought that favors
    a. a plan for increasing the money supply at a constant rate that does not change in response to economic conditions.
    b. a monetary growth rule.
    c. increasing the money supply every year at a rate equal to the long-run growth rate of real GDP.
    d. all of the above

34. If the economy moves into recession, monetarists argue that the Fed should
    a. increase the money supply.
    b. decrease the money supply.
    c. keep the money supply growing at a constant rate.
    d. keep the money supply fixed.

35. Which of the following statements is true?
    a. The only monetary policy target the Fed can choose is the money supply.
    b. The only monetary policy target the Fed can choose is the interest rate.
    c. The Fed could simultaneously choose an interest rate and the money supply as its monetary policy targets.
    d. The Fed is forced to choose between the interest rate and the money supply as its monetary policy target.

36. The Taylor rule for federal funds rate targeting does which of the following?
    a. It links the Fed's target for the federal funds rate to economic variables.
    b. It sets the target for the federal funds rate so that it is equal to the sum of the inflation rate and the unemployment rate.
    c. It multiplies the inflation gap by the output gap to obtain a target of the federal funds rate.
    d. all of the above

37. The federal funds rate target predicted by the Taylor Rule is_____ than the actual target used by the Fed during the period of the late 1970s and early 1980s when Paul Volcker was Federal Reserve Chairman, and _____ than the actual federal funds target used by the Fed when Arthur Burns was chairman from 1970 to 1978.
    a. higher; higher
    b. lower; lower
    c. higher; lower
    d. lower; higher

38. According to the Taylor Rule, if the Fed reduces its target for the inflation rate, this will result in
    a. a higher target federal funds rate.
    b. no change in the target federal funds rate.
    c. a lower target federal funds rate.
    d. a higher target output growth rate.

39. When the central bank commits to conducting policy in a manner that achieves a publicly announced inflation target, it is using
    a. inflation targeting.
    b. the Taylor rule.
    c. contractionary monetary policy.
    d. monetary policy independence.

40. Which of the following can be affected by monetary policy?
    a.   the level of real GDP in the long run
    b.   inflation in the long run
    c.   both the level of real GDP and inflation in the long run
    d.   neither the level of real GDP nor inflation in the long run

41. The Fed's performance in the 1980s, 1990s, and early 2000s received high marks from economists. Which of the following contributed to the Fed's good performance during those years?
    a.   inflation targeting
    b.   a strategy of keeping inflation low and stable in the long run, but without inflation targeting
    c.   the ability of the Fed to conduct monetary policy in close coordination with Congress and the president
    d.   the pursuit of effective fiscal policy

42. The main reason to keep the Fed – or any country's central bank – independent of the rest of the government is to avoid
    a.   inflation.
    b.   unusually low interest rates.
    c.   high taxes.
    d.   all of the above

43. The more bonds the central bank buys, the _____ the money supply grows, and the _____ the inflation rate will be.
    a.   slower; lower
    b.   slower; higher
    c.   faster; lower
    d.   faster; higher

44. The Federal Reserve System is
    a.   less independent than others agencies of the federal government.
    b.   required to ask Congress for the funds it needs to operate.
    c.   an institution where the chairman has only one vote in seven on the Board of Governors but plays an outsized role in policy setting.
    d.   all of the above

Short Answer Questions

1. Using a money demand and money supply graph, show the effect on the interest rate of an increase in real GDP.

_____

_____

_____

_____

_____

2. A U.S. Treasury bill that matures in one year has a face value of $1,000 and a current price of $900. What will be the interest rate on the bond? What if the current price is $890?

_____

_____

_____

3. Using a money demand and money supply graph, show how the Fed can keep the interest rate at a predetermined rate (i_0) as money demand increases.

_____

_____

_____

_____

_____

4. Suppose that the economy experiences weak *AD* growth and a supply shock at the same time. Discuss the monetary policy options using the dynamic *AD-AS* model.

_____

_____

_____

_____

_____

5. During the third quarter of 2005, potential real GDP was $11,503 billion in constant year 2000 dollars and actual real GDP was $11,202 billion in year 2000 dollars. The inflation rate (annual percentage change GDP deflator) was 2.7%. What does the Taylor rule predict for the target federal funds rate?

_____

_____

_____

_____

_____

_____

True/False Questions

T F 1. The only economic goal of the Fed is sustained economic growth with high levels of employment.

T F 2. The stability of financial markets helps to efficiently transfer funds between savers and borrowers.

T F 3. The opportunity cost of holding money is measured by the nominal interest rate.

T F 4. As bond prices increase, the interest rates on the bonds also increase.

T F 5. An increase in the price level will cause the money demand curve to shift to the right, resulting in a lower interest rate.

T F 6. The federal funds rate is the interest rate banks charge each other for overnight loans.

T F 7. Increases in interest rates tend to increase the level of investment purchases.

T F 8. A reduction in the Fed's interest rate target will tend to increase the level of aggregate demand.

T F 9. An expansionary monetary policy will tend to generate higher real GDP growth and higher inflation.

T F 10. Using interest rate targets, the Fed has been able to eliminate recessions.

T F 11. Interest rate targets are chosen by the Monetary Policy Committee of Congress.

T F 12. If the Fed implements an expansionary or contractionary policy too late in the business cycle, the policy change will still work.

T F 13. If the Fed targets the interest rate, then money supply growth is determined by growth in money demand.

T F 14. According to the Taylor rule calculations, an increase in the inflation rate will lead to both an increase in nominal and real interest rates.

T F 15. The Federal Reserve System is an agency of the Treasury Department.

Answers to the Self-Test

Multiple-Choice Questions

Question	Answer	Comment
1	c	In early 2001, the members of the FOMC concluded that a recession was about to begin and implemented a strongly expansionary monetary policy to keep the recession as short and mild as possible. By driving down interest rates, the Fed succeeded in heading off what some economists had predicted would be a prolonged and severe recession.
2	d	The Fed has four policy goals: (1) price stability, (2) high employment, (3) economic growth, and (4) stability of financial markets.
3	b	Monetary policy refers to any action the Fed takes to manage the money supply and interest rates.
4	b	For most of the 1950s and 1960s the inflation rate in the United States was 4 percent or less. During the 1970s, the inflation rate increased, peaking during 1979-1981, when it averaged more than 11 percent. Since 1992, the inflation rate has been less than 4 percent.
5	d	The Fed has four policy goals: (1) price stability, (2) high employment, (3) economic growth, and (4) stability of financial markets. The Fed attempts to promote the stability of financial markets and institutions so that there will be an efficient flow of funds from savers to borrowers.

6	c	The Fed can sometimes be successful in pursuing multiple goals at the same time. For example, it can spur both high employment and economic growth because steady economic growth contributes to high employment. At other times, however, the Fed encounters conflicts between its policy goals. For example, to reduce the inflation rate, the Fed may have to raise interest rates.
7	b	The Fed uses variables, called *monetary policy targets*, that it can affect directly and that in turn affect variables such as real GDP and the price level that are closely related to the Fed's policy goals. The two main monetary policy targets are the money supply and the interest rate. The Fed typically uses an interest rate as its policy target.
8	d	Low interest rates are not a Fed goal, although in certain circumstances low interest rates may help the Fed achieve its goals.
9	a	When interest rates on financial assets such as U.S. Treasury bills are high, the amount of interest that households and firms lose by holding money is also high. When interest rates are low, the amount of interest households and businesses lose by holding money is low. Remember that opportunity cost is what you have to forego in order to engage in an activity. The interest rate is the opportunity cost of holding money.
10	c	The money demand curve slopes downward because lower interest rates cause households and firms to switch from financial assets such as Treasury bills to money. An increase in the interest rate will decrease the quantity of money demanded.
11	c	When interest rates on Treasury bills and other financial assets are low, the opportunity cost of holding money is low, so the quantity of money demanded will be high; when interest rates are high, the opportunity cost of holding money will be high, so the quantity of money demanded will be low. This explains why the money demand curve slopes downward.
12	a	An increase in real GDP means that the amount of buying and selling of goods and services will increase. This additional buying and selling increases the demand for money as a medium of exchange, so the quantity of money households and firms want to hold increases at each interest rate.
13	a	An increase in the price level increases the quantity of money demanded at each interest rate, shifting the money demand curve to the right. A decrease in the price level decreases the quantity of money demanded at each interest rate, shifting the money demand curve to the left.
14	c	If the FOMC decides to increase the money supply, it orders the trading desk at the Federal Reserve Bank of New York to purchase U.S. Treasury securities. The sellers of these Treasury securities deposit the funds they receive from the Fed in banks, which increases the banks' reserves. The banks loan out most of these reserves, which creates new checking account deposits and expands the money supply. If the FOMC decides to decrease the money supply, it orders the trading desk to sell Treasury securities, which decreases banks' reserves, and contracts the money supply.
15	b	If the Fed sells Treasury securities, the money supply will decrease, the money supply curve will shift to the left, and the equilibrium interest rate will rise. This is the opposite case to the one shown in Figure 14-4.
16	b	The prices of financial assets and their interest rates move in opposite directions.
17	b	The interest rate on the Treasury bill is: ($50/$950) x 100 = 5.26%.

18	d	When the Fed decreases the money supply, households and firms will initially hold less money than they want to, relative to other financial assets. Households and firms will sell Treasury bills and other financial assets, reducing their prices, and increasing their interest rates.
19	b	Interest rate changes cause movements along the money demand curve. Increases in real GDP cause the money demand curve to shift to the right.
20	d	The interest rate banks charge each other for overnight loans is called the *federal funds rate*.
21	d	Changes in the federal funds rate usually will result in changes in both interest rates on other short-term financial assets, such as Treasury bills, and interest rates on long-term financial assets, such as corporate bonds and mortgages. The effect of a change in the federal funds rate on long-term interest rates is usually smaller than it is on short-term interest rates. Although a majority of economists support the Fed's choice of the interest rate as its monetary policy target, some economists believe the Fed should concentrate on the money supply instead.
22	a	As interest rates decline, stocks become a more attractive investment relative to bonds. The increase in demand for stocks raises their prices. An increase in stock prices signals firms that the future profitability of investment projects has increased. Firms often issue new shares of stocks and use the proceeds to buy new plants and equipment, thereby increasing investment.
23	d	If interest rates in the United States rise relative to interest rates in other countries, the desirability of investing in U.S. financial assets will increase, causing foreign investors to increase their demand for dollars, and this will increase the value of the dollar. As the value of the dollar increases, net exports will fall.
24	d	An increase in the money supply will shift the money supply curve to the right, causing it to intersect the money demand curve at a lower interest rate. So, the equilibrium interest rate will be lower.
25	c	When the Fed increases the money supply and decreases interest rates to increase real GDP, it is engaging in expansionary monetary policy.
26	b	The FOMC may then decide to take action to lower interest rates in order to stimulate aggregate demand.
27	b	In January 2001, the FOMC decided to reduce the target for the federal funds rate from 6½ percent to 6 percent. The committee continued to reduce the federal funds target at subsequent meetings. By December 2001 they had reduced the rate to 1¾ percent. Further decreases brought it to 1 percent in June 2003, the lowest it had been in more than 40 years.
28	c	Although the Fed was able to successfully use expansionary monetary policy to reduce the severity of the 2001 recession, it was unable to entirely eliminate it. The Fed has no realistic hope of "fine tuning" the economy to eliminate the business cycle and achieve absolute price stability.
29	d	Deflation can contribute to slow growth by raising real interest rates, increasing the real value of debts, and causing consumers to postpone purchases in the hope of experiencing even lower prices in the future.
30	c	When the Fed acts as it did during 2000, decreasing the money supply and increasing interest rates in order to reduce inflation, it is engaging in contractionary monetary policy.
31	b	A procyclical policy is one that inadvertently increases the severity of the business cycle, while a countercyclical policy—which is what the Fed intends to use—would stabilize the economy.

32	a	A countercyclical policy involves the Fed attempting to stabilize the economy.
33	d	Monetarists favor replacing current monetary policy with a monetary growth rule. Ordinarily we expect monetary policy to respond to changing economic conditions: When the economy is in recession, the Fed reduces interest rates, and when inflation is increasing, the Fed raises interest rates. A monetary growth rule, in contrast, is a plan for increasing the money supply at a constant rate that does not change in response to economic conditions. Monetarists have proposed a monetary growth rule of increasing the money supply every year at a rate equal to the long-run growth rate of real GDP, which has been 3.5 percent.
34	c	The Fed should stick to the monetary growth rule even during recessions. Monetarists believe active monetary policy destabilizes the economy, increasing the number of recessions and their severity. By keeping the money supply growing at a constant rate, Friedman argues, the Fed would greatly increase economic stability.
35	d	The Fed is forced to choose between using either an interest rate or the money supply as its monetary policy target.
36	a	According to the Taylor rule, the federal funds target rate = Current inflation rate + Real equilibrium federal funds rate + (1/2) x Inflation gap + (1/2) x Output gap.
37	d	The Taylor rule predicts a federal funds rate target lower than the actual target used by the Fed during the period when Paul Volcker was chairman. This indicates that Chairman Volcker kept the federal funds rate at an unusually high level in order to rapidly bring down the very high inflation rates plaguing the economy in the late 1970s and early 1980s. In contrast, using data from the chairmanship of Arthur Burns from 1970 to 1978, the Taylor rule predicts a federal funds rate target higher than the actual target. This indicates that Chairman Burns kept the federal funds rate at an unusually low level during these years, which can help explain why the inflation rate grew worse.
38	a	A reduction in the target inflation rate requires the Fed to carry out a contractionary monetary policy. This will be done by raising the target for the federal funds rate.
39	a	With *inflation targeting*, the central bank commits to conducting policy so as to achieve a publicly announced inflation target of, for example, 2 percent.
40	b	In the long run, real GDP returns to its potential level, and potential real GDP is not affected by monetary policy. Therefore, in the long run, the Fed can have an impact on inflation, but not on real GDP.
41	b	Although not stated explicitly, the Fed's strategy has been to keep inflation low and stable in the long run. In addition, in recent years the Fed has acted to head off the threat of future inflation before it can become established. The Fed has successfully built public support for the idea that low inflation is important to the efficient performance of the economy.
42	a	The main reason to keep the Fed – or any country's central bank – independent of the rest of the government is to avoid inflation. There is also the fear that if the government controls the central bank, it may use that control to further its political interests.
43	d	Many developing countries have difficulty finding anyone other than their central bank to buy their bonds. The more bonds the central bank buys, the faster the money supply grows, and the higher the inflation rate will be. Even in developed countries, governments that control their central banks will be tempted to sell bonds to the central bank, rather than to the public.

44   c   The chairman has only one vote in seven on the Board of Governors and only one vote in twelve on the FOMC. Nevertheless, the very strong tradition at the Fed is that the chairman plays an outsized role in policy setting.

Short Answer Responses

1. Beginning in equilibrium, the increase in the real GDP will increase money demand and shift the M_d curve to the right. With the money supply unchanged, the increased demand for money will result in the public selling bonds to try to increase the quantity of money they hold. The sale of the bonds will lower bond prices and increase the interest rate. Graphically we have:

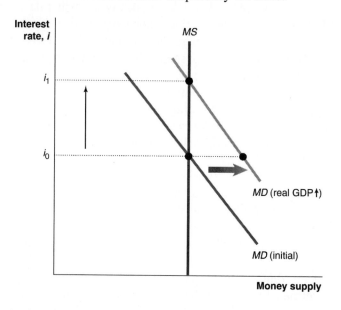

2. If the current price of a $1000 face value U.S. Treasury bill is $900, then the interest rate on the bond will be:

$$(\$1000 - \$900)/\$900 = 11.11\%$$

If the price of the bond falls to $890, then the interest rate will rise to:

$$(\$1000 - \$890)/\$890 = 12.36\%$$

Notice that the fall in the price of a bond increases the interest rate on the bond.

3.

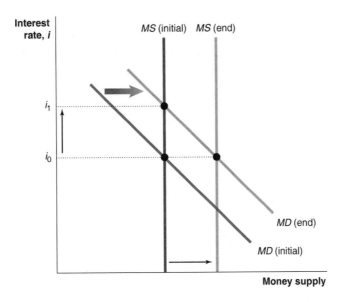

As money demand grows from *MD* (initial) to *MD* (end), the money demand curve shifts out. If the Fed had kept the money supply constant (targeted the money supply), the interest rate would have increased from i_0 to i_1. If the Fed targets the interest rate, then the Fed must increase the money supply from *MS* (initial) to *MS* (end) to keep the interest rate constant at i_0.

4. Weak *AD* growth and a supply shock can be seen in the following graph. The adverse supply shock will cause the ultimate shift in *SRAS* to be smaller than the shift in *SRAS* without the supply shock. Because of the weak growth, the Fed decides to follow an expansionary monetary policy and reduce target interest rates.

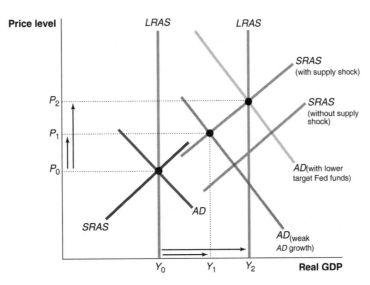

As a result of the initial changes, prices increase from P_0 to P_1 and real GDP increases from Y_0 to Y_1. Because of the low growth, the Fed reduces the target Fed funds rate, and begins a more expansionary monetary policy. This is done to increase real GDP, and as a result of the policy, real GDP increases to Y_2. Notice that as a result of this policy decision, inflation will be higher, because price rises to P_2.

Alternatively, the Fed might decide to follow a contractionary monetary policy and fight the inflation caused by the supply shock. In this case, the Fed would increase target Fed funds rates in order to restrict aggregate demand growth. This is seen in the following graph.

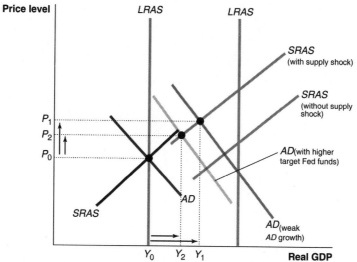

Again, as a result of the initial changes, prices increase from P_0 to P_1 and real GDP increases from Y_0 to Y_1. This time the Fed follows a contractionary monetary policy to fight the inflation effects of the supply shock. As a result of this, AD declines (or does not grow as much), and inflation will be lower as prices only rise to P_2 instead of P_1. However, the consequence of the policy is that real GDP will grow even less than before $Y_0 \rightarrow Y_1$.

5. The output gap is calculated as 100 x (Actual – Potential)/Actual = –2.7%, so the predicted target federal fund rate is:

Target federal funds rate = 2.7% + 2% + (1/2) x (2.7) + (1/2) x (–2.7) = 4.7%.

The actual target was 3.75% at the end of third quarter 2005.

True/False Answers

1.	F	The Fed has goals of low inflation, strong economic growth with high employment, and financial market stability.
2.	T	
3.	T	
4.	F	Bond prices and interest rates move in opposite directions.
5.	F	The shift to the right in money demand will result in increases in the interest rate.
6.	T	
7.	F	Interest rate increases tend to reduce investment purchases.
8.	T	
9.	T	
10.	F	The Fed cannot "fine tune" the economy to the degree necessary to eliminate recessions.

11.   F   Target interest rate decisions are made by the FOMC.
12.   F   If the Fed implements a policy too late, it can destabilize the economy.
13.   T
14.   T
15.   F   The Federal Reserve System is independent of the Treasury Department.

Fiscal Policy

Chapter Summary

In Chapter 14, you learned how the Federal Reserve uses monetary policy to pursue macroeconomic policy goals. In this chapter, you will learn how the government uses fiscal policy to achieve similar goals. **Fiscal policy** involves changes in federal taxes and purchases that are intended to achieve macroeconomic policy objectives. **Automatic stabilizers** are government spending and taxes that automatically increase or decrease along with the business cycle.

To fight recessions, Congress and the president can increase government purchases or cut taxes. This expansionary policy causes the aggregate demand curve to shift to the right more than it otherwise would, raising the level of real GDP and the price level. To fight rising inflation, Congress and the president can decrease government purchases or raise taxes. This contractionary policy causes the aggregate demand curve to shift to the right less than it otherwise would, reducing the increase in real GDP and the price level.

Because of the **multiplier effect**, an increase in government purchases or a cut in taxes will have a multiplied effect on equilibrium real GDP. The *government purchases multiplier* is equal to the change in equilibrium real GDP divided by the change in government purchases. The *tax multiplier* is equal to the change in equilibrium real GDP divided by the change in taxes. Increases in government purchases and cuts in taxes have a positive multiplier effect on equilibrium real GDP. Decreases in government purchases and increases in taxes have a negative multiplier effect on equilibrium real GDP. Poorly timed fiscal policy can do more harm than good by increasing, rather than reducing, fluctuations in real GDP and the inflation rate. Because an increase in government purchases may lead to a higher interest rate, it may result in a decline in consumption, investment, and net exports. A decline in private expenditures as a result of an increase in government purchases is called **crowding out**. Crowding out may cause an expansionary fiscal policy to fail to meet its goal of keeping the economy at potential GDP.

A **budget deficit** occurs when the federal government's expenditures are greater than its tax revenues. A **budget surplus** occurs when the federal government's expenditures are less than its tax revenues. The **cyclically adjusted budget deficit or surplus** is the deficit or surplus in the federal government's budget if the economy were at potential GDP. The federal government debt is the value of outstanding bonds issued by the U.S. Treasury. More than half of the national debt is actually owned by other federal agencies. The national debt is a problem if interest payments on it require taxes to be raised substantially or require other federal expenditures to be cut.

The difference between the pretax and posttax return to an economic activity is known as the **tax wedge**. Economists believe that the smaller the tax wedge for any economic activity—such as working, saving, investing, or starting a business—the more of that economic activity will occur. Economists debate the size of the supply-side effects of tax changes.

Learning Objectives

When you finish this chapter, you should be able to:

1. **Define fiscal policy. Fiscal policy** refers to changes in federal taxes and purchases that are intended to affect production, employment, or inflation. The federal government's share of total government expenditures has been falling since World War II. Federal government *expenditures* have been around 20 percent of GDP since the early 1970s, while federal government *purchases* have declined as a percentage of GDP since the end of the Korean War in the early 1950s. The largest component of federal expenditures is transfer payments. The largest source of federal government revenue is individual income taxes. The second largest source is social insurance taxes, which are used to fund the Social Security and Medicare systems.

2. **Explain how fiscal policy affects aggregate demand and how the government can use fiscal policy to stabilize the economy.** To fight recessions, Congress and the president can increase government spending or cut taxes. This expansionary policy causes the aggregate demand curve (*AD*) to shift to the right more than it otherwise would, raising the level of real GDP and the price level. To fight rising inflation, Congress and the president can decrease government spending or raise taxes. This contractionary policy causes the aggregate demand curve to shift to the right less than it otherwise would, reducing the increase in real GDP and the price level.

3. **Explain how the government purchases and tax multipliers work.** Because of the **multiplier effect**, an increase in government purchases or a cut in taxes will have a multiplied effect on equilibrium real GDP. The government purchases multiplier is equal to the change in equilibrium real GDP divided by the change in government purchases. The tax multiplier is equal to the change in equilibrium real GDP divided by the change in taxes. Increases in government purchases and cuts in taxes have a positive multiplier effect on equilibrium real GDP. Decreases in government purchases and increases in taxes have a negative multiplier effect on equilibrium real GDP.

4. **Discuss the difficulties that can arise in implementing fiscal policy.** Poorly timed fiscal policy can do more harm than good. Getting the timing right with fiscal policy can be difficult because getting a new fiscal policy approved can be a very long process and because after Congress approves an increase in spending, it can take months for the spending to actually take place. Because an increase in government purchases may lead to a higher interest rate, it may result in a decline in consumption, investment, and net exports. A decline in private expenditures as a result of an increase in government purchases is called **crowding out.** Crowding out may cause an expansionary fiscal policy to fail to meet its goal of keeping the economy at potential GDP.

5. **Define federal budget deficit and federal government debt and explain how the federal budget can serve as an automatic stabilizer.** A **budget deficit** occurs when the federal government's expenditures are greater than its tax revenues. A **budget surplus** occurs when the federal government's expenditures are less than its tax revenues. The budget deficit automatically increases during recessions and decreases during expansions. The automatic movements in the federal budget help to stabilize the economy by cushioning the fall in spending during recessions and restraining the increase in spending during expansions. The federal government debt, frequently referred to as the national debt, is the value of outstanding bonds issued by the U.S. Treasury. More than half of the national debt is actually owned by other federal agencies. The national debt is a problem if interest payments on it require the government to raise taxes substantially or to cut other federal expenditures.

6. **Discuss the effects of fiscal policy in the long run.** Some fiscal policy actions are intended to have long-run effects by expanding the productive capacity of the economy and increasing the rate of economic growth. Because these policy actions primarily affect aggregate supply rather than aggregate demand, they are sometimes referred to as *supply-side economics.* The difference between the pre-tax and post-tax return to an economic activity is known as the **tax wedge.** Economists believe that the smaller the tax wedge for any economic activity – such as working, saving, investing, or starting a business – the more of that economic activity will occur. Economists debate the size of the supply-side effects of tax changes.

Appendix: Apply the multiplier formula. In the chapter, you will see that changes in government purchases and changes in taxes have a multiplied effect on equilibrium real GDP. In the appendix, you will build a simple economic model of the multiplier effect. Your instructor may cover the appendix in class or assign it for reading.

Chapter Review

Chapter Opener: A Boon for H&R Block (pages 508-509)

H&R Block employs about 80,000 tax preparers to prepare about 19.5 million tax returns a year. The complicated nature of the U.S. tax code has generated a need for companies to help in the tax preparation process. The tax codes are complicated because Congress and the president change them repeatedly to achieve economic and social goals. Some changes in tax law are the result of discretionary fiscal policy and are intended to achieve the macroeconomic goals of high employment, economic growth, and price stability.

📖 Helpful Study Hint

Read *An Inside Look* at the end of the chapter for a news article from the *Wall Street Journal* that presents the debate in Congress about the alternative minimum tax (AMT), which was originally intended to ensure that wealthy individuals pay a minimum amount of income tax, but may soon be applied to individuals with middle class incomes.

If you are eligible for a $500 tax rebate, what would you do with that rebate? Spend it? Save it? Pay down credit card debt? What if you expect your taxes to be $500 lower in future years as well? The ***Economics in YOUR Life!*** at the start of this chapter poses these questions. Keep the questions in mind as you read the chapter. The authors will answer the questions at the end of the chapter.

15.1 LEARNING OBJECTIVE

15.1 Fiscal Policy (pages 510-514)

Learning Objective 1 Define fiscal policy.

Fiscal policy refers to changes in federal taxes and spending that are intended to achieve macroeconomic policy objectives, such as high levels of employment, price stability, and economic growth. Fiscal policy is restricted to tax and spending decisions by the federal government and does not include spending decisions not intended to achieve macroeconomic policy goals, such as military spending or spending to aid people with low incomes.

Some types of government spending and taxes are automatic stabilizers, while other types are discretionary fiscal policy. **Automatic stabilizers** are spending and tax changes that increase or decrease over the business cycle without actions by the government. An example is unemployment insurance payments, which rise because of layoffs in a recession and fall as employment increases in the expansion phase of the business cycle. Discretionary fiscal policy requires the government to take action to change spending or taxes.

Federal government purchases include all purchases of goods, as well as the wage costs of providing services. Federal government expenditures include purchases plus:

- interest on the national debt
- grants to state and local governments
- transfer payments

About 42 percent of federal government revenue comes from individual income taxes and about 36 percent from social insurance taxes. Corporate profit taxes contribute about 15 percent of tax revenues, and the remainder comes from sales taxes and import fees.

Extra Solved Problem 15-1

Chapter 15 of the textbook includes two Solved Problems. Here is an extra Solved Problem to help you build your skills solving economic problems:

Growth in Government Purchases and Taxes

Supports Learning Objective 1: Define fiscal policy.

Generally, over time, federal government purchases and taxes have risen. Below are data on federal government tax receipts and expenditures from 2001 to 2006 (all values are in billions of dollars). Calculate receipts and expenditures as a percentage of GDP. While the level of receipts and expenditures is generally rising, are receipts and expenditures also rising as a percentage of GDP?

Year	Nominal GDP	Federal government tax receipts	Federal government expenditures
2001	$10,128.0	$2,016.2	$1,969.5
2002	10,469.6	1,853.2	2,101.1
2003	10,960.8	1,879.9	2,252.1
2004	11,685.9	2,008.9	2,379.5
2005	12,433.9	2,243.4	2,561.6
2006	13,194.7	2,495.8	2,715.8

SOLVING THE PROBLEM

Step 1: **Review the chapter material.**

This problem refers to the definition of fiscal policy, so you may want to review the section "What Fiscal Policy Is and What It Isn't," which begins on page 510 of the textbook.

Step 2: **Calculate receipts and expenditures as a percentage of GDP.**

Receipts and expenditures as a percentage of GDP are calculated as the value of the year's receipts divided by GDP. Notice that since receipts and expenditures are nominal, we are also using nominal GDP. These percentages are shown in the table below.

Year	Nominal GDP	Federal government tax receipts	Federal government expenditures	Federal government tax receipts as a percentage of GDP	Federal government expenditures as a percentage of GDP
2001	$10,128.0	$2,016.2	$1,969.5	19.9%	19.4%
2002	10,469.6	1,853.2	2,101.1	17.7	20.1
2003	10,960.8	1,879.9	2,252.1	17.2	20.5
2004	11,685.9	2,008.9	2,379.5	17.2	20.4
2005	12,433.9	2,243.4	2,561.6	18.0	20.6
2006	13,194.7	2,495.8	2,715.8	18.9	20.6

Notice that while the dollar value of tax receipts has increased over this period, tax receipts as a percentage of GDP were lower in 2006 than in 2001. On the other hand, federal government expenditures as a percentage of GDP have increased slightly. Because federal expenditures as a percentage of GDP have been larger than receipts for each year since 2002, the federal budget has been in deficit. To eliminate the deficit, receipts would have to rise or expenditures would have to be cut.

📖 Helpful Study Hint

You've probably heard about problems with the Social Security program for retired workers. To learn more about this problem, read *Making the Connection: Is Spending on Social Security and Medicare a Fiscal Time Bomb?* The Social Security and Medicare programs have taken up an increasing fraction of federal expenditures. Although for many years the Social Security and Medicare programs have been a great success in reducing poverty among elderly Americans, they have begun to encounter problems as birth rates have fallen from the high levels of the baby boom. There are currently about three workers per retired worker, but this ratio will fall to about two workers per retired worker in the coming decades. Congress has attempted to deal with this problem by increasing the retirement age and increasing payroll taxes. Under the Medicare program, the federal government provides health care to people over 65. Expenditures on Medicare are increasing because of longer lives, more expensive medical procedures, and a rapidly increasing population of people over age 65. Over the coming decades, the gap between spending on Medicare and the revenues raised from Medicare taxes will grow larger. The choices are to either increase taxes, reduce benefits, or a combination of the two. Workers may decide that if benefits are reduced, they must save more to cover future health-care costs.

15.2 LEARNING OBJECTIVE

15.2 The Effects of Fiscal Policy on Real GDP and the Price Level (pages 514–518)

Learning Objective 2 Explain how fiscal policy affects aggregate demand and how the government can use fiscal policy to stabilize the economy.

Like monetary policy, fiscal policy can be used by the president and Congress to influence the level of aggregate demand, and consequently influence the level of real GDP and the inflation rate. Expansionary fiscal policy is shown in the left panel of textbook Figure 15-5 below. Expansionary fiscal policy involves increases in government purchases or decreases in taxes. Increases in government purchases directly increase aggregate demand, while decreases in taxes have indirect effects on aggregate demand. Tax cuts increase household disposable income and bring about higher levels of consumption spending and, therefore, higher levels of aggregate demand. Expansionary fiscal policy can reduce the impact of weak aggregate demand growth. Increasing government purchases or decreasing taxes will shift the aggregate demand curve to the right. Contractionary fiscal policy involves decreases in government purchases or increases in taxes. Contractionary fiscal policy will cause aggregate demand to increase less than it otherwise would. The *AD* will be to the left of where it would have been without the contractionary policy. Contractionary fiscal policy is generally used when aggregate demand is growing too rapidly, which may worsen the inflation rate. This is shown in the right panel of textbook Figure 15-5 below:

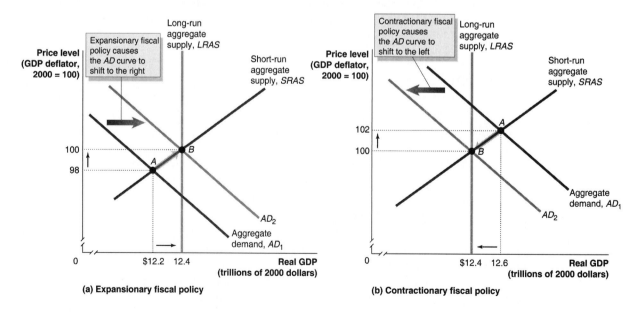

(a) Expansionary fiscal policy

(b) Contractionary fiscal policy

In the dynamic aggregate demand and supply model, expansionary fiscal policy adds to the growth in aggregate demand. In textbook Figure 15-6 below, the growth in aggregate demand without fiscal policy results in equilibrium at less than potential GDP (point *A* to *B*). Fiscal policy adds to aggregate demand and pushes the economy to potential GDP at point *C*.

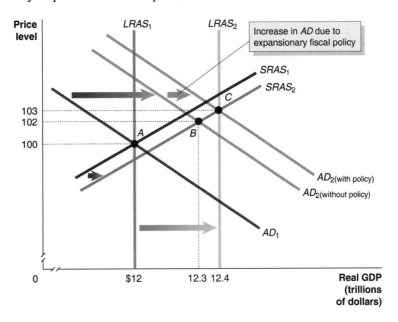

Contractionary fiscal policy involves fiscal policy changes to reduce the growth in aggregate demand. This is shown in textbook Figure 15-7 below. The expansion in aggregate demand without policy (from point *A* to *B*) will result in inflation. With the contractionary fiscal policy, demand will not increase as much and the economy will move instead to point *C* with less inflation.

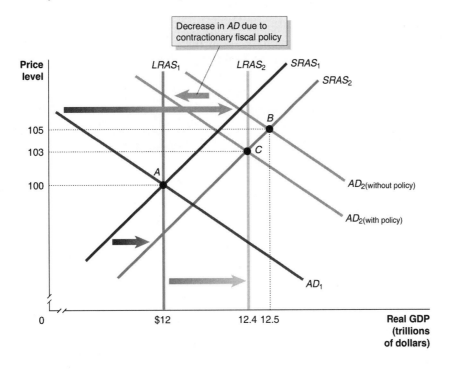

The table below summarizes the use of fiscal policy:

PROBLEM	TYPE OF POLICY	ACTIONS BY CONGRESS AND THE PRESIDENT	RESULT
Recession	Expansionary	Increase government spending or cut taxes	Real GDP and the price level rise
Rising inflation	Contractionary	Decrease government spending or raise taxes	Real GDP and the price level fall

Extra Solved Problem 15-2

Chapter 15 of the textbook includes two Solved Problems. Here is an extra Solved Problem to help you build your skills solving economic problems:

Expansionary Fiscal Policy

Supports Learning Objective 2: Explain how fiscal policy affects aggregate demand and how the government can use fiscal policy to stabilize the economy.

Suppose that the economy is at a level of real GDP below potential real GDP. Show this graphically, and show how expansionary fiscal policy can be used to move the economy to the potential real GDP level.

SOLVING THE PROBLEM

Step 1:   Review the chapter material.
This problem refers to expansionary fiscal policy, so you may want to review the section "Expansionary and Contractionary Fiscal Policy: An Initial Look," which begins on page 515 of the textbook.

Step 2:   Draw the initial equilibrium with output below potential real GDP.
If output ($Y_0 = \$10,000$) is below potential real GDP($Y_{potential} = \$11,000$), *AD* will intersect the *SRAS* below the LRAS. This is shown in the following graph.

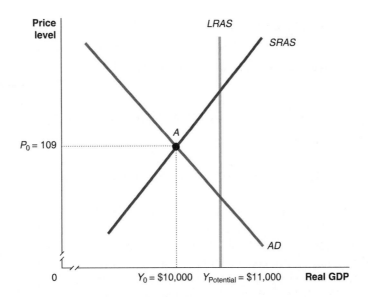

Step 3: **Draw the equilibrium with the expansionary fiscal policy.**

If output is below potential real GDP, expansionary fiscal policy can add to the existing level of aggregate demand. This will shift *AD* to the right, resulting in equilibrium at a higher level of real GDP. This is shown in the graph below. Fiscal policy causes a movement from point *A* to point *B*, and output grows from $10,000 to $11,000. This implies that fiscal policy can be used to push the economy to potential GDP, though expansionary fiscal policy will also cause an increase in the price level (from 109 to 112 in the graph).

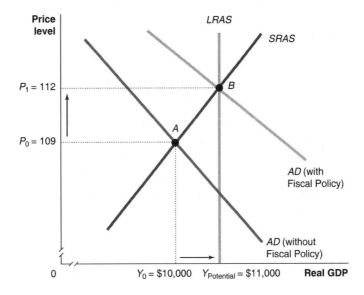

📖 Helpful Study Hint

Read ***Don't Let This Happen to YOU! Don't Confuse Fiscal Policy and Monetary Policy.*** The purpose of expansionary monetary policy is to lower interest rates, which will increase aggregate demand. The purpose of expansionary fiscal policy is to increase aggregate demand by adding to the level of government purchases or to induce consumers to spend more by lowering taxes. Fiscal and monetary policies have the same goals, but have different ways of reaching the goals.

15.3 The Government Purchases and Tax Multipliers (pages 518–523)

Learning Objective 3 Explain how the government purchases and tax multipliers work.

Fiscal policy changes have a **multiplier effect** on the level of aggregate demand. Increases in government purchases lead to further increases in spending. The initial increase in government spending will lead to increases in income, which will generate additional spending by households and firms, which will lead to additional increases in aggregate demand. It may take several time periods for the multiplier process to complete itself. Economists refer to the initial change as *autonomous* because it does not depend on the level of real GDP. The changes in real GDP in other rounds are referred to as *induced* because they are changes caused by the initial change in autonomous spending. An increase in government spending causes the aggregate demand curve to shift to the right because the level of equilibrium real GDP will be higher at each price level. There are then two outward shifts in *AD* due to an expansionary fiscal policy, one for the autonomous change and one for the induced changes. This is shown in textbook Figure 15-8 below.

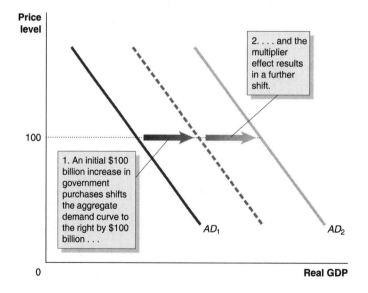

The ratio of the change in equilibrium real GDP to the change in government purchases is known as the government purchases multiplier:

$$\text{Government purchases multiplier} = \frac{\text{Change in equilibrium real GDP}}{\text{Change in government purchases}}$$

Economists have estimated that the government purchases multiplier is about 2, so that a \$100 billion increase in autonomous government purchases will increase *AD* by about \$200 billion, other things equal.

Taxes also have a multiplier effect. The tax multiplier is:

$$\text{Tax multiplier} = \frac{\text{Change in equilibrium real GDP}}{\text{Change in taxes}}$$

The tax multiplier will be negative, because an increase in taxes will result in a reduction in spending. These spending reductions will cause decreases in income, which will cause further decreases in spending, resulting in additional decreases in aggregate demand. If the tax multiplier is −1.6, then a $100 million increase in taxes will result in a $160 million decrease in *AD*, other things equal. The tax multiplier is negative because an increase in taxes lowers spending, causing real GDP to fall.

📖 Helpful Study Hint

In absolute value, the tax multiplier should be smaller than the government purchases multiplier. A $1 increase in government purchases will increase autonomous spending by $1. A $1 decrease in taxes will increase disposable income by $1, but consumption spending will fall by less than $1 because some of the increase in income will be saved.

The multiplier effect results in an additional shift of the *AD* curve. Because the *SRAS* curve is upward sloping, an expansionary fiscal policy results in a higher price level as well as a higher level of real GDP. Textbook Figure 15-10 shown below illustrates the multiplier effect:

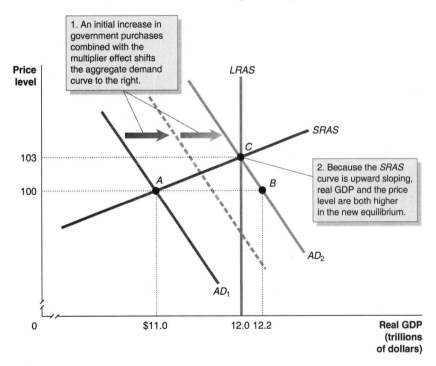

It is important to note that the multiplier works in both directions. A decrease in government purchases will cause a fall in *AD* greater than the fall in government purchases. An increase in taxes will cause a fall in *AD* greater than the increase in taxes.

Extra Solved Problem 15-3

Chapter 15 of the textbook includes two Solved Problems. Here is an extra Solved Problem to help you build your skills solving economic problems:

The Multiplier and Shifts in the Aggregate Demand Curve

Supports Learning Objective 3: Explain how the government purchases and tax multipliers work.

Using the basic aggregate demand-aggregate supply model with potential real GDP constant, show that the short-run effect of an increase in government purchases on real GDP depends upon the size of the multiplier, but the long-run effects are independent of the size of the multiplier.

SOLVING THE PROBLEM

Step 1:   **Review the chapter material.**
This problem is about understanding the multiplier effect, so you may want to review the section "The Government Purchases and Tax Multipliers," which begins on page 518 of the textbook.

Step 2:   **Illustrate the shift in aggregate demand with a larger and smaller multiplier.**
The change in equilibrium real GDP will depend on the size of the multiplier, as we can see from the following formula:

Change in equilibrium real GDP = multiplier × change in government purchases.

It makes sense that the larger the multiplier, the larger the change in real GDP. In the aggregate demand-aggregate supply model, the larger the multiplier, the larger the shift in *AD* from a given change in government purchases.

Consider an increase in government purchases with a larger multiplier and a smaller multiplier. These shifts are shown in the graph below:

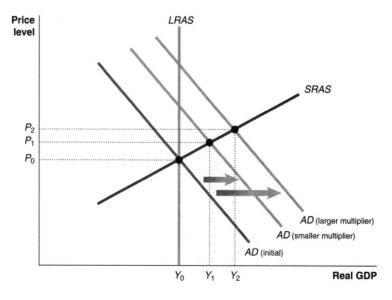

Step 3:   Analyze the results in the short run.

In the short run, the increase in government purchases will increase real GDP from Y_0 to Y_1 with the smaller multiplier, and from Y_0 to Y_2 with the larger multiplier. A larger multiplier will cause a larger short-run change in real GDP.

Step 4:   Analyze the results in the long run.

In the long run, the increase in aggregate demand will eventually cause wages and other costs to increase. This will cause the *SRAS* curve to shift to the left. The *SRAS* curve will continue to shift until real GDP returns to potential real GDP at Y_0. The long run is shown in the graph below:

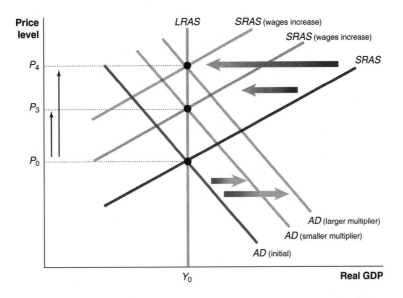

In the long run, real GDP will return to potential real GDP at Y_0. Consequently, the smaller and larger multiplier both have the same long-run effect on real GDP: zero. In the long run, *AD* changes do not change the level of real GDP. However, in the long run, multipliers of different sizes do have different effects on the price level. The larger the multiplier, the greater the increase in the price level.

15.4 LEARNING OBJECTIVE

15.4 The Limits of Using Fiscal Policy to Stabilize the Economy (pages 523-527)

Learning Objective 4   Discuss the difficulties that can arise in implementing fiscal policy.

Proper timing is an important part of a stabilization policy. Implementing a policy too late may not help the economy and may destabilize it instead. Fiscal policy decisions are made by Congress and the president. Because it generally takes considerable time for Congress and the president to agree on a change in policy, fiscal policy changes will generally not be quickly implemented. The Federal Open Market Committee, which meets eight times per year, can change monetary policy quickly.

In addition to problems with timing, **crowding out** also limits the effectiveness of fiscal policy. In the short run, expansionary fiscal policy will increase real GDP and the price level. Increases in real GDP and the price level will increase money demand, which will result in a higher interest rate. This is shown in textbook Figure 15-11 below:

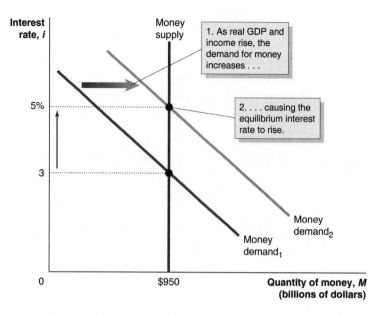

This higher interest rate will reduce the level of aggregate demand by reducing investment and consumption spending. So, crowding out will slow the growth in aggregate demand. The effects of crowding out are illustrated in textbook Figure 15-12 below:

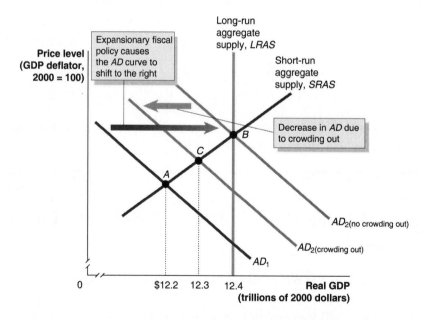

Most economists believe that, in the short run, increases in government purchases cause partial but not complete crowding out. Most economists also believe that, in the long run, there is complete crowding out. This is true because in the long run the economy returns to potential real GDP. Therefore, in the long run, an increase in government purchases must cause some other component of GDP—consumption, investment, or net exports—to fall by an equal amount. In the short run, if the economy is below potential real GDP, it is possible for both government purchases and private purchases to increase.

📖 Helpful Study Hint

While crowding out may be complete in the long run, it may take several—possibly many—years to arrive at that outcome.

📖 Helpful Study Hint

Have you ever lost a job or know someone who has? Although losing a job can be stressful, it can also be beneficial. Read *Making the Connection: Is Losing Your Job Good for Your Health?* Christopher Ruhm, an economist at the University of North Carolina, Greensboro, recently found evidence that during recessions the unemployed, on average, experience improving health. The unemployed tend to smoke less, drink less alcohol, eat a healthier diet, lose weight, and exercise more. The unemployed person has more time to exercise, prepare healthier food, and visit the doctor. Additionally, he or she has less workplace stress. Ruhm estimates that, during a business cycle expansion, a one-percent decline in the unemployment rate is associated with 3,900 additional deaths. Ruhm found that long developing diseases like cancer are not affected by the business cycle. Also, mental health problems do tend to increase during recessions and decline during expansions. Over the longer run, rising income tends to lead to higher levels of health.

15.5 LEARNING OBJECTIVE

15.5 Deficits, Surpluses, and Federal Government Debt (pages 527-532)

Learning Objective 5 Define federal budget and federal government debt and explain how the federal budget can serve as an automatic stabilizer.

If the federal government spends less than its revenues, there is a **budget surplus**. If the federal government spends more than its revenues, there is a **budget deficit**. Deficits tend to increase during recessions. Deficits also increase during wars and other periods when extra government purchases are not offset by additional taxes.

📖 Helpful Study Hint

The United States had four years of budget surpluses from 1998-2001. The recession of 2001, along with tax cuts and additional spending on homeland security and spending on the wars in Afghanistan and Iraq, converted the budget surplus into a budget deficit.

The federal budget serves as an automatic stabilizer for the economy. During a recession, deficits occur automatically for two reasons: Lower tax revenues and higher levels of transfer payments (such as unemployment insurance payments). During an expansion, the budget moves toward a surplus as tax revenues increase and transfer payments fall as more workers are employed. The **cyclically adjusted**

budget deficit or surplus removes the effect of the business cycle on the budget by evaluating the budget at potential GDP, not the current level of GDP.

Although many economists believe it is a good idea for the federal government to have a balanced budget, few economists think the budget needs to be balanced each year. In certain circumstances, the changes in government spending or taxes necessary to achieve a balanced budget may push the economy away from potential GDP.

When the federal government runs a budget deficit, the Treasury borrows from the public by selling Treasury bonds. In years of budget surpluses, the Treasury pays off some of the existing bonds. Because the federal budget has been in deficit during many more years than it has been in surplus, the stock of outstanding Treasury bonds has grown over time. The value of these bonds is known as the federal government debt. In the long run, this debt can create a problem due to the crowding out of investment spending as the government borrows funds that would otherwise have been borrowed by firms.

📖 Helpful Study Hint

Read *Making the Connection: Did Fiscal Policy Fail During the Great Depression?* Modern macroeconomics began in the 1930s with the publication of *The General Theory of Employment, Interest and Money* by John Maynard Keynes. A conclusion from Keynes's writing was that expansionary fiscal policy could reduce the severity of a recession. In spite of deficit spending, the economy recovered very slowly during the Great Depression and did not reach potential GDP until World War II in 1941. Does this imply that fiscal policy did not work to pull the economy out of the depression? Economists E. Cary Brown and Larry Pepper have shown that even though there was a budget deficit, the cyclically adjusted budget was in surplus. This implies that expansionary fiscal policy was really not tried.

Extra Solved Problem 15-5

Chapter 15 of the textbook includes two Solved Problems. Here is an extra Solved Problem to help you build your skills solving economic problems:

The Ownership of the U.S. Government Debt

Supports Learning Objective 5: Define federal budget deficit and federal government debt and explain how the federal budget can serve as an automatic stabilizer.

The federal government debt (also referred to as the "national debt" or the "public debt") grows as a result of budget deficits. Determine the percentages of the debt owned by:

a. U.S. government agencies (including the Federal Reserve)
b. U.S. citizens (individuals and firms)
c. Individuals, firms, and governments outside the United States

Use data for the fiscal years 2002-2006, which are shown below (in billions of dollars):

Year	Total public debt	Held by Federal Reserve and government accounts	Held by foreign and international investors	Held by domestic investors
2002	$6,228.2	$3,303.5	$1,200.8	$1,723.9
2003	6,783.2	3,515.3	1,454.2	1,813.7
2004	7,379.1	3,772.0	1,836.6	1,770.5
2005	7,932.7	4,067.8	2,069.0	1,795.9
2006	8,507.0	4,432.8	2,133.6	1,940.6

SOLVING THE PROBLEM

Step 1:   Review the chapter material.

This problem is about the federal government debt, so you may want to review the section "Deficits, Surpluses, and Federal Government Debt," which begins on page 527 of the textbook.

Step 2:   Calculate the percentages of the debt owned by the different groups.

The percentages owned by the different groups are calculated as the group value divided by the total public debt. These numbers are in the table below:

Year	Total public debt	Held by Federal Reserve and government accounts (percent)	Held by foreign and international investors (percent)	Held by domestic investors (percent)
2002	$6,228.2	53.0%	19.3%	27.7%
2003	6,783.2	51.8	21.4	26.7
2004	7,379.1	51.1	24.9	24.0
2005	7,932.7	51.3	26.1	22.6
2006	8,507.0	52.1	25.1	22.8

Step 3:   Determine the percentage owned within the United States and the percentage owned outside of the United States.

The percentages indicate that about half of the U.S. debt is owned internally by the U.S. government. Currently the portion owned by those outside the United States is larger than the domestic ownership and that portion is higher than in 2002. This implies that the interest payments on the debt owned externally will become income to residents of countries other than the United States. Economists debate the significance of a large percentage of federal government debt being held by foreign investors.

15.6 The Effects of Fiscal Policy in the Long Run (pages 532-537)

Learning Objective 6   Discuss the effects of fiscal policy in the long run.

Some fiscal policy changes are designed to have long-run effects by expanding the productive capacity of the economy and encouraging economic growth. These fiscal policy changes are usually done through taxes and have their effect by changing aggregate supply. Because these policy changes primarily affect aggregate demand rather than aggregate supply, they are sometimes referred to as *supply-side economics*.

Tax changes influence the **tax wedge**. The tax wedge is the difference between pretax and posttax returns to economic activity. Cutting tax rates can affect aggregate supply in several ways:

- A lower individual tax rate will increase posttax wages and increase the quantity of labor supplied. Additionally, lower individual tax rates will increase the return to saving, increasing the level of saving in the economy.
- Reducing the corporate tax rate will encourage investment spending and can increase the rate of technological innovation.
- Lowering the tax rate on dividends and capital gains can increase the supply of loanable funds, which lowers real interest rates. The lower interest rates cause increases in investment spending by firms, which will increase the growth rate of the capital stock.

In addition to gains from cutting taxes, there are gains from tax simplification. A simpler tax code means that resources that are currently being used to comply with the tax laws can be used more productively.

The economic effects of tax simplification and tax reduction can increase the growth rate of long-run aggregate supply. This is shown in textbook Figure 15-15 reproduced below. Tax reduction and simplification can result in more economic growth and lower inflation.

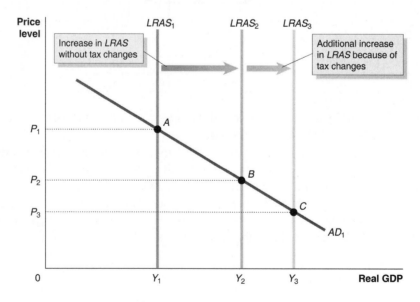

While economists agree that the effects of tax reduction and simplification exist, there is not agreement on the size of the effects. There is also disagreement on the magnitude of the effects of tax changes on aggregated supply compared to the effects on aggregate demand.

Extra Solved Problem 15-6

Long-Run Effects of a Tax Increase

Supports Learning Objective 6: Discuss the effects of fiscal policy in the long run.

Show what will happen to the long-run aggregate supply curve when there is an increase in the individual income tax rate.

SOLVING THE PROBLEM

Step 1:   **Review the chapter material.**
           This problem is about the effects on the long run aggregate supply curve of an increase in the tax rate, so you may want to review the section "The Economic Effect of Tax Reform," which begins on page 535 of the textbook.

Step 2:   **Show the change in the long-run aggregate supply curve in the absence of a tax increase.**
           Potential real GDP grows each year as the labor force and the capital stock increase and technological change occurs. This growth is seen in the graph below as LRAS shifts out from LRAS1 to LRAS2. This growth will move the economy from point A to point B and real GDP will increase from Y0 (= $10,000) to Y1 (= $11,000).

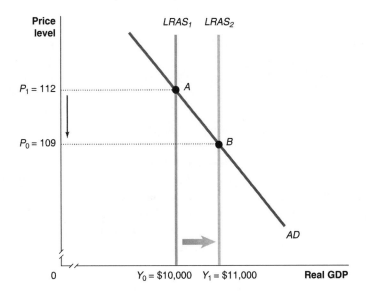

Step 3: **Now show the effects on the long-run aggregate supply curve of the tax increase.**

An increase in the individual income tax rate will reduce the posttax wage and reduce the increase that would otherwise occur in the labor supply. Fewer workers means a lower level of potential real GDP. This can be shown as a reduction in the shift of the $LRAS_1$ to $LRAS_3$ instead of $LRAS_2$ as in the graph below.

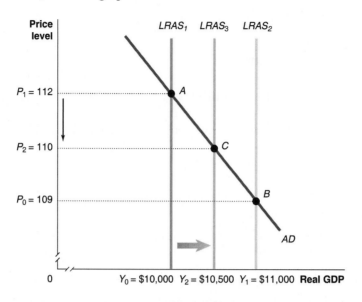

So, as a result of the tax increase, real GDP only increases to Y_2 (= $10,500) and the price level only falls to P_2 (= 110). The tax increase will consequently slow growth in real GDP (from $10,000 to $10,500, instead of from $10,000 to $11,000) and reduce the decline in the price level (the price level falls from 112 to 110, instead of 112 to 109).

📖 Helpful Study Hint

Read *Making the Connection: Should the United States Adopt the "Flat Tax"?* During the 2000 presidential campaign, candidate Steve Forbes proposed a "flat tax." Under Forbes's flat tax proposal, the first $36,000 of income would be exempt from taxes and all income above that would be taxed at 17 percent, as would all corporate income. Several Eastern European countries have instituted a flat tax system. These countries have found that it is easier to administer and results in more income being reported. In the United States and Western Europe, proponents of a flat tax argue it would be simpler and easier to understand. Opponents argue that it would remove the ability of the government to use tax policy to influence the economy (for example, by using tax rebates to encourage consumers to buy hybrid cars) and would create more inequity in income distribution by reducing taxes for higher-income taxpayers.

📖 Helpful Study Hint

Economics in YOUR Life! at the end of the chapter answers the question posed at the start of the chapter: Suppose you received a $500 tax rebate and in future years your taxes will be $500 less per year. How would you respond to this increase in your disposable income? Evidence suggests that you will respond to this permanent increase in disposable income by increasing your spending. Evidence also shows that this will have a multiplier effect on the economy: If output is currently less than potential real GDP, the rebate will increase output in the short run.

Key Terms

Automatic stabilizers. Government spending and taxes that automatically increase or decrease along with the business cycle.

Budget deficit. The situation in which the government's spending is greater than its tax revenue.

Budget surplus. The situation in which the government's expenditures are less than its tax revenue.

Crowding out. A decline in private expenditures as a result of an increase in government purchases.

Cyclically adjusted budget deficit or surplus. The deficit or surplus in the federal government's budget if the economy was at potential GDP.

Fiscal policy. Changes in federal taxes and purchases that are intended to achieve macroeconomic policy objectives, such as high employment, price stability, and high rates of economic growth.

Multiplier effect. The series of induced increases in consumption spending that results from an initial increase in autonomous expenditures.

Tax wedge. The difference between the pretax and posttax return to an economic activity.

Self-Test

(Answers are provided at the end of the Self-Test.)

Multiple-Choice Questions

1. *Fiscal policy* refers to
   a. changes in the money supply and interest rates to pursue macroeconomic policy goals, including price stability and high employment.
   b. changes in federal taxes and spending that are intended to achieve macroeconomic policy objectives.
   c. the manipulation of the price level, the level of real GDP, and total employment by the Federal Reserve.
   d. the use of economic policies to improve the functioning of the public sector.

2. Economists use the term fiscal policy to refer to changes in taxing and spending policies by
   a. only state and local governments.
   b. only the federal government.
   c. all levels of government, federal, state, and local.
   d. none of the above

3. The U.S. government increased spending for defense and homeland security after 2001 to fund the war on terrorism and the invasion of Iraq. These spending increases are considered
   a. strictly monetary policy.
   b. strictly fiscal policy.
   c. part of defense and homeland security policy, but not fiscal policy.
   d. both fiscal and monetary policy.

4. Changes in taxes and spending that happen without actions by the government are called
   a. discretionary fiscal policy changes.
   b. automatic stabilizers.
   c. transfer payments.
   d. autonomous fiscal expenditures.

5. Which of the following fiscal policy actions will increase real GDP in the short run?
   a. an increase in government expenditures
   b. an increase in the individual income tax
   c. an increase in the money supply
   d. an increase in the Social Security tax

6. When the government takes actions to change taxes and spending, the type of policy involved is called
   a. discretionary fiscal policy.
   b. automatic stabilizers.
   c. transfer payments.
   d. autonomous fiscal expenditures.

7. What is the relationship between government purchases and government expenditures?
   a. Government purchases include government expenditures.
   b. Government expenditures include government purchases.
   c. Government purchases and government expenditures are the same thing.
   d. Government purchases include all government spending, while government expenditures do not.

8. Which of the following are categories of federal government expenditures?
   a. transfer payments
   b. interest on the national debt
   c. grants to state and local governments
   d. all of the above

9. The largest and fastest growing category of federal expenditures is
   a. interest on the national debt.
   b. grants to state and local governments.
   c. transfer payments.
   d. defense spending.

10. Spending on most of the federal government's day-to-day activities – including running federal agencies like the Environmental Protection Agency, the FBI, the National Park Service, and the Immigration and Naturalization Service – make up
    a. about 85 percent of federal government expenditures.
    b. about 45 percent of federal government expenditures.
    c. less than 10 percent of federal government expenditures.
    d. less than 1 percent of federal government expenditures.

11. Which of the following is the main reason for the long-run funding problems of Social Security?
    a. The health of the typical American is declining.
    b. Too many workers are delaying their retirement until after age 65.
    c. The number of workers per retiree continues to decline.
    d. Increasing levels of immigration will eventually lead to larger numbers of retirees.

12. Which of the following are the largest sources of federal government revenues?
    a. corporate income taxes and sales taxes
    b. revenue from tariffs on imports and other fees
    c. individual income taxes and social insurance taxes
    d. property taxes and excise taxes

13. When the economy is in a recession, the government can
    a. reduce expenditures and leave taxes constant in order to stimulate aggregate demand.
    b. increase government purchases or decrease taxes in order to increase aggregate demand.
    c. decrease government purchases or increase taxes in order to decrease aggregate supply.
    d. change spending and taxation but not aggregate demand or aggregate supply.

14. Which of the following will reduce the inflation rate?
    a. increasing the money supply
    b. increasing government purchases
    c. reducing government purchases or increasing taxes
    d. none of the above

15. The goal of expansionary fiscal policy is
    a. to decrease short-run aggregate supply.
    b. to decrease long-run aggregate supply.
    c. to increase aggregate demand.
    d. all of the above

16. An attempt to reduce inflation requires _____ fiscal policy, which causes real GDP to _____ and the price level to _____.
    a. expansionary; rise; rise
    b. expansionary; rise; fall
    c. contractionary; rise; fall
    d. contractionary; fall; fall

17. Which of the following statements is *incorrect*?
    a. Just as increasing or decreasing the money supply does not have any direct effect on government spending or taxes, increasing or decreasing government spending or taxes will not have any direct effect on the money supply.
    b. Fiscal policy and monetary policy may have the same goals, but they have different effects on the economy.
    c. The only difference between fiscal policy and monetary policy in fighting recessions and stimulating spending is where the money comes from.
    d. All of the above statements are correct.

18. By how much will equilibrium real GDP increase as a result of a $100 billion increase in government purchases?
    a. by more than $100 billion
    b. by less than $100 billion
    c. by exactly $100 billion
    d. None of the above; equilibrium real GDP will not change as a result of an increase in government purchases.

19. The *multiplier effect* consists of
    a. a series of autonomous expenditures that result from an initial increase in government expenditures.
    b. a series of autonomous expenditure increases that result from an initial increase in induced expenditures.
    c. a series of induced increases in consumption spending that result from an initial increase in autonomous expenditures.
    d. a change in government spending resulting from a change in equilibrium income.

20. How would you decompose the total effect of an increase in government purchases on the aggregate demand curve? (Note: the magnitudes of the shifts don't have to be the same.)
    a. The aggregate demand curve shifts once to the right and then back to the left.
    b. The aggregate demand curve shifts as a result of two distinct effects, twice to the right.
    c. The aggregate demand curve shifts as a result of two distinct effects, twice to the left.
    d. The aggregate demand curve does not shift, but there are two movements, one downward and one upward, along the curve.

21. The *tax multiplier* equals
    a. the change in taxes divided by the change in equilibrium GDP.
    b. the change in equilibrium GDP multiplied by the change in taxes.
    c. the change in equilibrium GDP divided by the change in taxes.
    d. the change in taxes multiplied by the resulting change in consumption.

22. We would expect the tax multiplier to be _____ in absolute value than the government purchases multiplier.
    a. smaller
    b. larger
    c. the same
    d. either smaller or larger, depending on the current tax rate

23. When the tax rate increases, the size of the multiplier effect _____.
    a. increases
    b. decreases
    c. remains the same
    d. increases for small increases in the tax rate and decreases for large increases in the tax rate

24. Increases in government purchases and decreases in taxes have a _____ multiplier effect on equilibrium real GDP, and decreases in government purchases and increases in taxes have a _____ multiplier effect on equilibrium real GDP.
    a. positive; negative
    b. negative; positive
    c. positive; positive
    d. negative; negative

25. Getting the timing right can be more difficult with one of these policies. Which one?
    a. fiscal policy
    b. monetary policy
    c. environmental policy
    d. all of the above

26. Because they can quickly change policy in response to changing economic conditions,
    a. the Fed plays a larger role in stabilizing the economy than the president and Congress.
    b. the president and Congress play a larger role than the Fed in stabilizing the economy.
    c. the U.S. Treasury plays a larger role in stabilizing the economy than do the treasuries of other countries.
    d. the U.S. tax commission plays a larger role in stabilizing the economy than do either the Fed or the president and Congress.

27. *Crowding out* refers to
    a. the problem arising from having to consult with a large number of people in order to get fiscal policy approved in time to help the economy.
    b. the decline in private expenditures that result from an increase in government purchases.
    c. the ever-decreasing amount of induced expenditures that eventually stop the government purchases multiplier.
    d. the reduction in government expenditures following an increase in consumption or investment expenditures.

28. According to the crowding out effect, if the federal government increases spending, the demand for money and the equilibrium interest rate will _____, which will cause some consumption, investment, and net exports to _____.
    a. increase; increase
    b. increase; decrease
    c. decrease; decrease
    d. decrease; increase

29. Higher interest rates in the United States will attract foreign investors. This will cause _____ in the exchange rate between the dollar and other currencies, and _____ in net exports.
    a. an increase; an increase
    b. an increase; a decrease
    c. a decrease; an increase
    d. a decrease; a decrease

30. What is the long-run effect of a permanent increase in government spending?
    a. a decline in investment, consumption, and net exports that is smaller than the increase in government purchases, therefore, aggregate demand increases
    b. a decline in investment, consumption, and net exports that is larger than the increase in government purchases, therefore, aggregate demand decreases
    c. a decline in investment, consumption, and net exports that exactly offsets the increase in government purchases, therefore, aggregate demand remains unchanged
    d. no change in investment, consumption, or net exports, therefore, no change in aggregate demand

31. Which of the following is true of any permanent increase in government purchases in the long run?
    a. Any permanent increase in government purchases can be accommodated by the economy in the long run so as to maintain a steady level of private expenditures.
    b. In the long run, any permanent increase in government purchases must come at the expense of private expenditures.
    c. In the long run, a permanent increase in government purchases does not affect private expenditures in any way.
    d. In the long run, any permanent increase in government purchases is usually accompanied by an increase in private expenditures of the same amount.

32. If the federal government's expenditures are greater than its revenue, there is a
    a. budget deficit.
    b. budget surplus.
    c. balanced budget.
    d. declining federal government debt.

33. Which of the following was a period of federal budget surpluses?
    a. from 1970 through 1997
    b. from 1998 through 2001
    c. from 2002 through 2006
    d. None of the above; the federal government has experienced budget deficits every year since 1970.

34. Budget deficits automatically _____ during recessions and _____ during expansions.
    a. increase; increase
    b. increase; decrease
    c. decrease; increase
    d. decrease; decrease

35. The cyclically adjusted budget deficit,
    a. is never negative.
    b. is measured as if the economy were at potential real GDP.
    c. moves up and down as the economy moves around potential real GDP.
    d. is always in balance.

36. To obtain a more accurate measure of the effects on the economy of the government's spending and tax policies, economists prefer to look at
    a. the actual budget deficit or surplus.
    b. the cyclically adjusted budget deficit or surplus.
    c. changes in the federal government debt.
    d. changes in the inflation rate.

37. Every time the federal government runs a budget deficit, the Treasury must
    a. buy securities from the Fed in order to increase its reserves.
    b. print money in order to finance the excess expenditures.
    c. borrow funds from savers by selling Treasury securities.
    d. supply funds in the federal funds market.

38. At the end of June 2007, the federal government debt was $8.9 trillion. More than half of this debt was held by
    a. households.
    b. business firms.
    c. agencies of the federal government.
    d. foreigners.

39. Which of the following statements about the federal debt is correct?
    a. The federal government is in danger of defaulting on its debt.
    b. Given the current interest payments as a percent of total federal expenditures, there is a great need for tax increases or significant cutbacks in other types of federal spending.
    c. If the debt becomes very large relative to the economy, then the government may have to raise taxes to high levels, or cut back on other types of spending to make the interest payments on the debt.
    d. Interest payments are currently about 60 percent of total federal expenditures.

40. If a tax cut has supply-side effects, then
    a. it will affect only aggregate demand.
    b. it will affect only aggregate supply.
    c. it will affect both aggregate demand and aggregate supply.
    d. it will definitely not increase the federal budget deficit.

41. Economists believe that the smaller the *tax wedge* for any economic activity, such as working, saving, investing, or starting a business,
    a. the lower the equilibrium interest rate.
    b. the greater the difference between the pretax and posttax return to those activities.
    c. the more of that economic activity that will occur.
    d. the greater the marginal tax rate.

42. The effect on the economy of tax reduction and simplification is
    a. a change in the costs and expectations of producers, as shown by an upward shift in the short-run aggregate supply curve.
    b. an increase in consumption and investment spending, and a rightward shift of the aggregate demand curve.
    c. an increase in the quantity of real GDP supplied at every price level, or a shift in the long-run aggregate supply curve.
    d. higher employment and real GDP but also a higher price level.

43. Tax simplification and reductions in tax rates will result in
    a. additional shifts to the right in *LRAS* leading to a higher price level and lower real GDP.
    b. additional shifts to the right in *LRAS* leading to a lower price level and lower real GDP.
    c. additional shifts to the right in *LRAS* leading to a lower price level and higher real GDP.
    d. additional shifts to the right in *LRAS* leading to a higher price level and higher real GDP.

Short Answer Questions

1. Give an example of government spending that is not fiscal policy and an example of government spending that is fiscal policy.

    _____

    _____

    _____

    _____

2. Show how expansionary fiscal policy can be used to lessen the impact of weak *AD* growth on the economy.

    _____

    _____

    _____

    _____

    _____

3. Determine the government purchases multiplier if an increase in government purchases of $10 billion increases equilibrium real GDP by $25 billion. Suppose the tax multiplier is −2. How much must taxes change to change equilibrium real GDP by $10 million?

    _____

    _____

    _____

    _____

    _____

4. Why is crowding out from an increase in government purchases complete in the long run but not in the short run?

    _____

    _____

    _____

    _____

5. Explain how the federal government debt grows over time.

_____

_____

_____

_____

_____

6. Suppose at the beginning of the current year, the federal government debt is at $9,000 billion, and that during the year federal expenditures are $2,900 billion and receipts are $2,600 billion. Determine the value of the surplus or deficit during the year and the value of the federal government debt at the end of the year.

_____

_____

_____

_____

_____

True/False Questions

T F 1. Fiscal policy refers to the level of spending by the states and the federal government.

T F 2. Fiscal policy actions are those that are designed to achieve macroeconomic policy goals.

T F 3. Falling federal government tax collections as the level of economic activity slows down is an example of an automatic stabilizer.

T F 4. Defense spending is the difference between federal government purchases and federal government expenditures.

T F 5. Increases in government spending will tend to shift the aggregate demand curve to the right.

T F 6. The larger the government purchases multiplier, the further to the right the aggregate demand curve will shift.

T F 7. A reduction in taxes will tend to, in the short run, increase the level of real GDP and reduce the price level.

T F 8. The tax multiplier is always positive.

T F 9. The larger the change in equilibrium real GDP from a given change in government spending, the larger the government purchases multiplier.

T F 10. Fiscal policy changes in spending can be quickly implemented by Congress.

T F 11. Other things equal, an increase in government spending will not change the interest rate.

T F 12. In the long run, an increase in government purchases will reduce private spending by the same amount.

T F 13. If federal government spending is larger than tax revenues, there will be a budget deficit and the federal government debt will fall.

T F 14. When there is a budget deficit, the Treasury department will borrow from the public by selling bonds.

T F 15. A lower individual income tax rate will increase labor supply and shift the *LRAS* to the right.

Answers to the Self-Test

Multiple-Choice Questions

Question	Answer	Comment
1	b	Changes in federal taxes and spending that are intended to achieve macroeconomic policy objectives are called fiscal policy.
2	b	Economists restrict the term fiscal policy only to the actions of the federal government. State and local governments will sometimes change their taxing and spending policies to aid their local economies, but these are not fiscal policy actions because they are not intended to affect the national economy.
3	c	The defense and homeland security spending increases in the years after 2001 to fund the war on terrorism and the invasion of Iraq were part of defense and homeland security policy, not fiscal policy. These decisions are not part of fiscal policy actions because they are not intended to achieve macroeconomic policy goals. Nevertheless, the increased spending had an impact on the economy.
4	b	Automatic stabilizers are government spending and taxes that automatically increase or decrease along with the business cycle. The word "automatic" refers to the fact that changes in these types of spending and taxes happen without actions by the government.
5	a	An increase in government expenditures will shift *AD* to the right, and increase real GDP in the short run.
6	a	With discretionary fiscal policy, the government takes actions to change spending or taxes. For example, the tax cuts passed by Congress in 2001 are an example of a discretionary fiscal policy action.
7	b	There is a difference between federal government purchases and federal government expenditures. When the federal government purchases an aircraft carrier or the services of an FBI agent, it receives a good or service in return. Federal government expenditures include purchases plus all other federal government spending. One large expenditure not included in purchases is transfer payments such as Social Security.
8	d	In addition to purchases, there are three categories of federal government expenditures: transfer payments, interest on the national debt, and grants to state and local governments.
9	c	The largest and fastest growing category of federal expenditures is transfer payments. Some of these programs, such as Social Security and unemployment insurance, began in the 1930s. Others, such as Medicare, which provides health care to the elderly, or the Food Stamps and Temporary Assistance for Needy Families programs that are intended to aid the poor, began in the 1960s or later.

10	c	Spending on most of the federal government's day-to-day activities – including running federal agencies like the Environmental Protection Agency, the FBI, the National Park Service, and the Immigration and Naturalization Service – make up less than 10 percent of federal government expenditures.
11	c	Falling birth rates after 1965 will mean long-run problems for the Social Security system, as the number of workers per retiree will continue to decline. Currently there are only about three workers per retiree and that ratio will decline to two workers per retiree in the coming decades.
12	c	In 2006, the individual income tax raised about 42 percent of the federal government's revenues. The corporate income tax raised about 15 percent of the revenue. Payroll taxes to fund the Social Security and Medicare programs have risen from less than 10 percent of federal government revenues in 1950 to more than 36 percent in 2006. The remaining 7 percent of revenues were raised from sales taxes, tariffs on imports, and other fees.
13	b	Because changes in government purchases and taxes lead to changes in aggregate demand, they can affect the level of real GDP, employment, and the price level. When the economy is in a recession, increases in government purchases or decreases in taxes will increase aggregate demand.
14	c	The inflation rate may increase when aggregate demand is increasing faster than aggregate supply. Decreasing government purchases or raising taxes can slow the growth of aggregate demand, and reduce the inflation rate.
15	c	The goal of both expansionary monetary policy and expansionary fiscal policy is to increase aggregate demand relative to what it would have been without the policy.
16	d	Reducing inflation requires contractionary fiscal policy, or a decrease in government spending and/or higher taxes, which causes real GDP and the price level to fall.
17	c	If the government wants to spend more than its tax revenue, it must issue bonds. Only the Federal Reserve can issue money. Just as increasing or decreasing the money supply does not have any direct effect on government spending or taxes, increasing or decreasing government spending or taxes will not have any direct effect on the money supply. Fiscal policy and monetary policy have the same goals, but they have different effects on the economy.
18	a	We know that the answer is greater than $100 billion because we know the initial increase in aggregate demand will lead to additional increases in income and spending.
19	c	Economists refer to the series of induced increases in consumption spending that result from an initial increase in autonomous expenditures as the *multiplier effect*.
20	b	An initial increase in government purchases causes the aggregate demand to shift to the right from the impact of the initial increase in government purchases. Because this initial increase raises incomes and leads to further increases in consumption spending, the aggregate demand curve will shift further to the right.
21	c	The *tax multiplier* equals the change in equilibrium GDP divided by the change in taxes.

22	a	We would expect the tax multiplier to be smaller in absolute value than the government purchases multiplier. The entire amount of an increase in government purchases results in an increase in aggregate demand. But some portion of a decrease in taxes will be saved by households and not spent, and some portion will be spent on imported goods. The fractions of the tax cut that are saved and/or spent on imports will not increase aggregate demand.
23	b	The higher the tax rate, the smaller the amount of any increase in income households have available to spend, which reduces the size of the multiplier effect.
24	a	Increases in government purchases and cuts in taxes have a positive multiplier effect on equilibrium real GDP. Decreases in government purchases and increases in taxes also have a multiplier effect on equilibrium real GDP, only in this case the effect is negative.
25	a	Getting the timing right can be more difficult with fiscal policy than with monetary policy because fewer people are involved in making decisions about monetary policy, while the president and a majority of the 535 members of Congress have to agree on changes in fiscal policy.
26	a	Congress and the president use fiscal policy relatively infrequently because they are well aware of the timing problem. The Fed plays a larger role in stabilizing the economy because they can quickly change monetary policy in response to changing economic conditions.
27	b	A decline in private expenditures as a result of an increase in government purchases is called crowding out.
28	b	If the federal government increases spending, the demand for money will increase as real GDP and income rise. With the supply of money constant, the result is an increase in the equilibrium interest rate, which crowds out some consumption, investment, and net exports.
29	b	Higher interest rates in the United States will attract foreign investors. German, Japanese, and Canadian investors will want to exchange the currencies of their countries for U.S. dollars in order to invest in U.S. Treasury bills and other U.S. financial assets. This increased demand for U.S. dollars will cause an increase in the exchange rate between the dollar and other currencies. When the dollar increases in value, the prices of U.S. products in foreign countries rise – causing a reduction in U.S. exports – and the prices of foreign products in the U.S. fall – causing an increase in U.S. imports. Falling exports and rising imports mean that net exports are falling.
30	c	Most economists agree that the long-run effect of a permanent increase in government spending is complete crowding out. In the long run, the decline in investment, consumption, and net exports exactly offsets the increase in government purchases and aggregate demand remains unchanged.
31	b	An expansionary fiscal policy does not have to cause complete crowding out in the short run. If the economy is below potential real GDP, it is possible for both government purchases and private expenditures to increase. But in the long run, any permanent increase in government purchases must come at the expense of private expenditures.
32	a	The federal government's budget shows the relationship between its expenditures and its tax revenue. If the federal government's expenditures are greater than its revenue, there is a budget deficit. If the federal government's expenditures are less than its revenue, there is a budget surplus.

33	b	The federal government entered into a long period of continuous budget deficits in 1970. From 1970 through 1997, the federal government's budget was in deficit every year. From 1998 through 2001, there were four years of budget surpluses. The recession of 2001, tax cuts, and increased government spending on homeland security and the war in Iraq kept the budget in deficit in the years after 2001.
34	b	Deficits occur automatically during recessions for two reasons: First, during a recession, wages and profits fall, which cause government tax revenues to fall. Second, the government automatically increases its spending on transfer payments when the economy moves into recession.
35	b	By definition, the cyclically adjusted budget deficit or surplus is measured at potential GDP.
36	b	Because budget deficits automatically increase during recessions and fall during expansions, economists often look at the cyclically adjusted budget deficit or surplus, which can provide a more accurate measure of the effects on the economy of the government's spending and tax policies than does the actual budget deficit or surplus.
37	c	Every time the federal government runs a budget deficit, the Treasury must borrow funds from savers by selling Treasury securities. These securities are bills, notes, and bonds. When the federal government runs a budget surplus, the Treasury pays off some existing bonds. The total value of U.S. Treasury bonds outstanding is referred to as the federal government debt (or, sometimes, as the national debt). Each year the federal budget is in deficit, the federal government debt grows. Each year the federal budget is in surplus, the debt shrinks.
38	c	At the end of June 2007, the federal government debt was $8.9 trillion, but more than half of this debt was actually held by agencies of the federal government, including the Federal Reserve. In effect, the Treasury had borrowed more than half the debt from agencies of the federal government.
39	c	The federal government is in no danger of defaulting on its debt. Ultimately, the government can raise the funds it needs through taxes to make the interest payments on the debt. But if the debt becomes very large relative to the economy, then the government may have to raise taxes to high levels, or cut back on other types of spending to make the interest payments on the debt. Interest payments are currently about 10 percent of total federal expenditures. At this level, tax increases or significant cutbacks in other types of federal spending are not required.
40	c	Proponents of supply side theory argue that a tax cut can increase aggregate supply by increasing the quantity of labor supplied, and the quantities of saving and investment. It is also true that a tax cut can affect aggregate demand by increasing disposable income and, therefore, consumption spending.
41	c	In general, economists believe that the smaller the tax wedge for any economic activity—such as working, saving, investing, or starting a business—the more of that economic activity that will occur.
42	c	If tax reduction and simplification is effective, it should result in a larger quantity of labor supplied, an increase in saving, investment, the formation of new firms, and an increase in economic efficiency. The result would be an increase in the quantity of real GDP supplied at every price level. We show the effects of the tax changes by a shift in long-run aggregate supply. In effect, this is a beneficial supply shock.

43   c   Tax simplifications and reductions can increase employment, which will increase *LRAS*. The shift to the right in *LRAS* will result in a lower price level and higher real GDP.

Short Answer Responses

1. Suppose that because of a cold winter, it is necessary for the federal government to spend more to heat government offices in Washington D.C. This change in government purchases is not fiscal policy because it was not undertaken to influence the level of economic activity. Fiscal policy changes are done to achieve macroeconomic policy objectives. A reduction in taxes designed to increase consumer spending to help pull the economy out of (or prevent) a recession is an example of fiscal policy.

2. In the graph below, the weak *AD* growth, along with growth in aggregate supply ($LRAS_0 \rightarrow LRAS_1$ and $SRAS_0 \rightarrow SRAS_1$) has moved the economy from P_0, Y_0 to P_1, Y_1 so that real GDP (Y_1) is now below the new potential real GDP (Y_2).

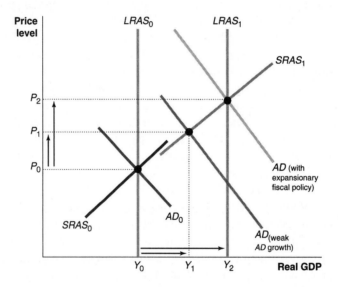

Expansionary fiscal policy can shift the *AD* curve out by increasing government purchases or by reducing taxes. As *AD* shifts to the right, real GDP will increase to its potential level at Y_2. This increase in aggregate demand also increases the price level to P_2.

3. Using the government purchases multiplier equation, the government purchases multiplier implied by a $10 billion increase in government purchases is:

$$\text{Government purchases multiplier} = \frac{\text{Change in equilibrium real GDP}}{\text{Change in government purchases}} = \frac{\$25\,\text{billion}}{\$10\,\text{billion}} = 2.5$$

Using the tax multiplier equation,

$$\text{Tax multiplier} = \frac{\text{Change in equilibrium real GDP}}{\text{Change in taxes}}$$

Then to increase real GDP by $10 billion, the needed change in taxes is:

$$-2 = \frac{\$10 \text{ billion}}{\text{Change in taxes}}$$

Solving this equation for the change in taxes yields the needed tax change of −$5 billion. The negative sign implies that taxes must fall by $5 billion. In other words, cutting taxes by $5 billion will increase disposable personal income by $5 billion, causing equilibrium real GDP to rise by $10 billion.

4. In the short run, the shift in the *AD* curve will increase real GDP. Because real GDP is larger, government purchases can increase without other components of real GDP decreasing. In the long run, however, output returns to potential real GDP. Because the amount of output is the same, if one component of GDP increases, one or more of the other components must decrease.

5. The federal budget deficit is the difference between government expenditures and federal tax receipts, or:

Federal budget deficit = Federal government expenditures − Federal tax receipts.

When the deficit is positive, the government borrows, increasing the federal government debt. When there is a federal budget surplus the government can repay some debt, lowering the federal government debt. It follows that:

Federal government debt (end of year) = federal budget deficit (during year)
+ federal government debt (beginning of year).

Therefore, the federal government debt will increase when there is a budget deficit, and fall when there is a federal budget surplus.

6. In any year, the value of the federal government's budget surplus is the difference between government receipts and expenditures. If this is positive, there is a budget surplus. If the difference is negative, there is a budget deficit. For this year, the difference is −$300 billion (= $2,600 − $2,900 = −$300). The federal government debt at the end of the year is the federal government debt at the beginning of the year minus the value of the surplus. So, in this case, the end of year federal government debt is $9,300 (= $9,000 − (−$300)).

True/False Answers

1.	F	Fiscal policy refers to spending only at the federal government level.
2.	T	
3.	T	
4.	F	The differences between expenditures and purchases are interest on the national debt, grants to state and local governments, and transfer payments.
5.	T	
6.	T	
7.	F	It will increase equilibrium real GDP and *increase* the price level.
8.	F	The tax multiplier is negative. Higher taxes reduce *AD*.
9.	T	
10.	F	Fiscal policy changes are generally very slow to implement.

11.   F   An increase in government spending will tend to increase real GDP and the price index. Both of these changes will increase money demand and tend to increase interest rates.

12.   T

13.   F   During periods of budget deficits, the federal government debt will increase.

14.   T

15.   T

Inflation, Unemployment, and Federal Reserve Policy

Chapter Summary

Inflation and unemployment are two very important macroeconomic issues. The **Phillips curve** illustrates the short-run trade-off between the unemployment rate and the inflation rate. The inverse relationship between unemployment and inflation shown by the Phillips curve is consistent with the aggregate demand and aggregate supply (*AD-AS*) analysis we developed in Chapter 12. The *AD-AS* model indicates that slow growth in aggregate demand leads to both higher unemployment and lower inflation, and rapid growth in aggregate demand leads to both lower unemployment and higher inflation. This relationship explains why there is a short-run trade-off between unemployment and inflation. In the 1960s, many economists believed that the Phillips curve was a **structural relationship** that depended on the basic behavior of consumers and firms and that remained unchanged over time. If the Phillips curve was a stable relationship, it would present policymakers with a menu of combinations of unemployment and inflation from which they could choose. Nobel laureate Milton Friedman argued that there is a **natural rate of unemployment**, which is the unemployment rate that exists when the economy is at potential GDP and to which the economy always returns. As a result, there is no trade-off between unemployment and inflation in the long run, and the long-run Phillips curve is a vertical line at the natural rate of unemployment. There is a short-run trade-off between unemployment and inflation only if the actual inflation rate differs from the inflation rate that workers and firms had expected.

During the high and unstable inflation rates of the mid-to-late 1970s, Robert Lucas and Thomas Sargent argued that workers and firms would have *rational expectations*. Consumers and firms form **rational expectations** by using all the available information about an economic variable, including the effect of the policy the Federal Reserve is using. Lucas and Sargent argued that if people have rational expectations, expansionary monetary policy will not work. If workers and firms know that an expansionary monetary policy is going to raise the inflation rate, the actual inflation rate will be the same as the expected inflation rate. Therefore, the unemployment rate won't fall. Many economists remain skeptical of Lucas and Sargent's argument in its strictest form. **Real business cycle models** focus on "real" factors—technology shocks—rather than changes in the money supply to explain fluctuations in real GDP.

Inflation worsened through the 1970s. Paul Volcker became Fed chairman in 1979, and, under his leadership, the Fed used contractionary monetary policy to reduce inflation. A significant reduction in the inflation rate is called **disinflation**. This contractionary monetary policy pushed the economy down the short-run Phillips curve. As workers and firms lowered their expectations of future inflation, the short-run Phillips curve shifted down, improving the short-run trade-off between unemployment and inflation. This change in expectations allowed the Fed to switch to an expansionary monetary policy to bring the economy back to the natural rate of unemployment. During Alan Greenspan's terms as Fed chairman, inflation remained low, and the credibility of the Fed increased. During late 2007 and early 2008, Fed chairman Ben Bernanke was faced with the policy dilemma of dealing with slowing rates of real GDP growth without causing an acceleration in the rate of inflation.

Learning Objectives

When you finish this chapter, you should be able to:

1. **Describe the Phillips curve and the nature of the short-run trade-off between unemployment and inflation.** The **Phillips curve** illustrates the short-run tradeoff between the unemployment rate and the inflation rate. The Phillips curve's inverse relationship between unemployment and inflation is consistent with the aggregate demand and aggregate supply analysis developed in Chapter 12. The *AD-AS* model indicates that slow growth in aggregate demand leads to both higher unemployment and lower inflation, and rapid growth in aggregate demand leads to both lower unemployment and higher inflation. This relationship explains why there is a short-run tradeoff between unemployment and inflation. Many economists initially believed that the Phillips curve was a **structural relationship** that depended on the basic behavior of consumers and firms and that remained unchanged over time. If the Phillips curve was a stable relationship, then it would present policymakers with a menu of combinations of unemployment and inflation from which they could choose.

2. **Explain the relationship between the short-run and long-run Phillips curves.** Nobel laureate Milton Friedman has argued that there is a **natural rate of unemployment** to which the economy always returns. As a result, there is no tradeoff between unemployment and inflation in the long run, and the long-run Phillips curve is a vertical line at the natural rate of unemployment. There is a short-run tradeoff between unemployment and inflation only if the actual inflation rate turns out to be different from the inflation rate that had been expected by workers and firms. There is a different short-run Phillips curve for every expected inflation rate. Each short-run Phillips curve intersects the long-run Phillips curve at the expected inflation rate. With a vertical long-run Phillips curve, it is not possible to buy a permanently lower unemployment rate at the cost of a permanently higher inflation rate. If the Federal Reserve attempts to keep the economy below the natural rate of unemployment, the inflation rate will increase. Eventually, the expected inflation rate will also increase, which causes the short-run Phillips curve to shift up and pushes the economy back to the natural rate of unemployment. The reverse happens if the Fed attempts to keep the economy above the natural rate of unemployment. In the long run, the Federal Reserve can affect the inflation rate, but not the unemployment rate.

3. **Discuss how expectations of the inflation rate affect monetary policy.** When the inflation rate is moderate and stable, workers and firms tend to have *adaptive expectations*. That is, they form their expectations under the assumption that future inflation rates will be about the same as past inflation rates. During the high and unstable inflation rates of the mid-to-late 1970s, Nobel laureates Robert Lucas and Thomas Sargent argued that workers and firms would have **rational expectations.** People form rational expectations by using all available information about an economic variable, including the effect of the policy the Federal Reserve is using. Lucas and Sargent argued that if people have rational expectations, expansionary monetary policy will not work. If workers and firms know that an expansionary monetary policy is going to raise the inflation rate, the actual inflation rate will be the same as the expected inflation rate. Therefore, the unemployment rate won't fall. Many economists remain skeptical of Lucas' and Sargent's argument in its strictest form. Real business cycle models focus on "real" factors—technology shocks—rather than changes in the money supply to explain fluctuations in real GDP.

4. **Use a Phillips curve graph to show how the Federal Reserve can permanently lower the inflation rate.** Inflation worsened through the 1970s. Paul Volcker became Fed chairman in 1979, and under his leadership the Fed used contractionary monetary policy to reduce inflation. This contractionary monetary policy pushed the economy down the short-run Phillips curve. As workers and firms lowered their expectations of future inflation, the short-run Phillips curve shifted down, improving the short-run tradeoff between unemployment and inflation. This change in expectations allowed the Fed to switch to an expansionary monetary policy in order to bring the economy back to full employment at the natural rate. During Alan Greenspan's term as Fed chairman, inflation remained low and the credibility of the Fed increased. Some economists and policymakers (including Fed chairman Ben Bernanke) believe a central bank's credibility is increased if it follows a *rules strategy* for monetary policy, which involves the central bank's following specific and publicly-announced guidelines for policy. Other economists and policymakers support a *discretion strategy* for monetary policy, under which the central bank adjusts monetary policy as it sees fit to achieve its policy goals, such as price stability and high employment.

Chapter Review

Chapter Opener: Why Does Whirlpool Care About Monetary Policy? (pages 552–553)

How does inflation affect monetary policy and how does monetary policy affect inflation? Ben Bernanke, testifying before Congress in March 2007, noted that the Fed was going to continue with a relatively high federal funds rate target because the inflation rate was considered higher than levels consistent with price stability. In 2001, Whirlpool Corporation benefited from the Fed's expansionary monetary policy that lowered interest rates. Low interest rates encouraged housing demand, which increased the demand for home appliances. The higher interest rates of early 2007, resulting from higher inflation, reduced the demand for home appliances, and Whirlpool's profits declined.

📖 Helpful Study Hint

Read *An Inside Look* at the end of the chapter for a news article from the *Wall Street Journal* that discusses new economic research from the Federal Reserve showing that inflation is influenced to a large extent by:

1. The public's expectation of future inflation.
2. Changes in oil prices.
3. Changes in housing rents.

When you start to work full time, you will probably receive annual pay raises. How big a raise should you ask for if it has just been announced that the Fed is going to try to maintain the unemployment rate at 3 percent? The *Economics in YOUR Life!* at the start of this chapter poses this question. Keep the question in mind as you read the chapter. The authors will answer the question at the end of the chapter.

16.1 The Discovery of the Short-Run Trade-off between Unemployment and Inflation (pages 554-559)

Learning Objective 1   Describe the Phillips curve and the nature of the short-run trade-off between unemployment and inflation.

Inflation and unemployment are two important macroeconomic problems that the Fed must deal with in the short run. Increases in aggregate demand often lead to higher inflation and lower unemployment, while decreases in aggregate demand often lead to lower inflation and higher unemployment. The inverse relationship between unemployment and inflation is often shown as a negatively sloped graph known as the **Phillips curve**. A Phillips curve is shown in textbook Figure 16.1, which is reproduced below:

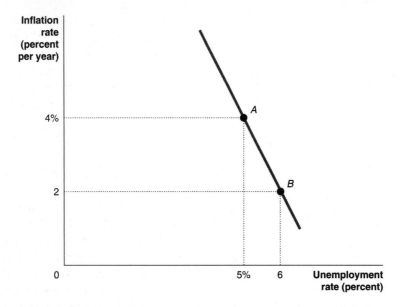

During years when inflation is relatively high, unemployment tends to be relatively low (point *A*). During years when inflation is relatively low, unemployment tends to be relatively high (point *B*).

📖 Helpful Study Hint

Remember that even when the inflation rate is low, the price level is still rising. The price level is just rising at a slower rate when inflation is low than when inflation is high.

We can use the *AD-AS* model to explain the Phillips curve. In textbook Figure 16-2 reproduced below, the economy in 2011 is in macroeconomic equilibrium at potential real GDP of $14 trillion. The unemployment rate for the year is 5 percent and the inflation rate is 4 percent. In panel (a), point *A* at the intersection of *AD* and *SRAS* marks this initial equilibrium, which corresponds to point *C* on the Phillips curve in panel (b). Suppose that in 2012 there is strong growth in aggregate demand. In panel (a), macroeconomic equilibrium in 2012 occurs at real GDP of $14.5 trillion. The price level rises from 100 to 104, so the inflation rate remains 4 percent. The new macroeconomic equilibrium corresponds to point *C* on the Phillips curve. If growth in aggregate demand is weak, however, macroeconomic equilibrium in panel (a) occurs at $14.3 trillion, at point *B*. The unemployment rate rises from 5 percent to 6 percent. At the same time, the price level rises only from 100 to 102, so the inflation rate has fallen from 4 percent in the previous year to 2 percent. The short-run equilibrium has moved down the Phillips curve from point *C,* with an unemployment rate of 5 percent and an inflation rate of 4 percent, to point *B,* with an unemployment rate of 6 percent and an inflation rate of 2 percent.

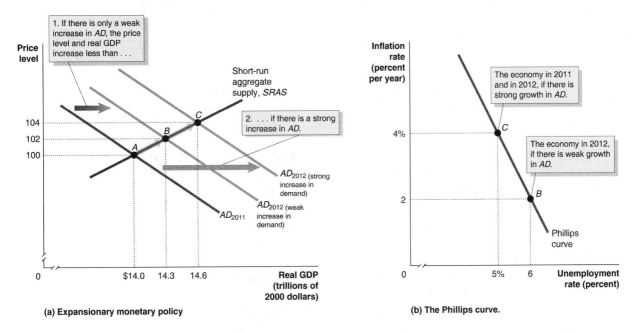

(a) Expansionary monetary policy

(b) The Phillips curve.

A **structural relationship** depends on the basic behavior of consumers and firms and remains unchanged over long periods. In the 1960s, many economists and policymakers believed the Phillips curve was a structural relationship and represented a permanent trade-off between unemployment and inflation. Today, most economists believe the Phillips curve is not a structural relationship and they view the trade-off between inflation and unemployment as temporary, rather than permanent. A short-run tradeoff exists only because workers and firms sometimes expect the inflation rate to be either higher or lower than it turns out to be. For example, if workers and firms both expect an inflation rate of 5 percent, and the actual inflation rate is 5 percent, wages will rise by 5 percent, so that the real cost of hiring workers will not change (for more on this point, see Short Answer Question 2 in the "Self-Test" section). Because the real cost of hiring workers is the same, the unemployment rate will not change. If, however, workers and firms believe that inflation will be 3 percent, and wages adjust based upon that belief, but actual inflation is 5 percent, then real wages will fall (for more on this point, see Short Answer Question 3 in the "Self-Test" section). Lower real wages will cause firms to hire more workers, and the unemployment rate will decrease. The short-run trade-off between inflation and unemployment comes from unanticipated inflation, not inflation itself. Because there is no trade-off between unemployment and inflation in the long run, economists believe that the long-run Phillips curve is vertical at the natural rate of unemployment. We saw in Chapter 12 that because the *LRAS* curve is vertical at potential GDP, in the long run, higher prices will not affect the level of real GDP or the level of employment. Similarly, the vertical long-run Phillips curve tells us that higher inflation rates will not lower unemployment in the long run. The level of unemployment that corresponds with potential real GDP is known as the natural rate of unemployment. The long-run Phillips curve is shown below in the graph on the right from textbook Figure 16-3 along with the *LRAS* curve in the graph on the left.

📖 Helpful Study Hint

Remember that at potential real GDP, although there will be no cyclical unemployment there will be frictional and structural unemployment, so the unemployment rate will not be zero.

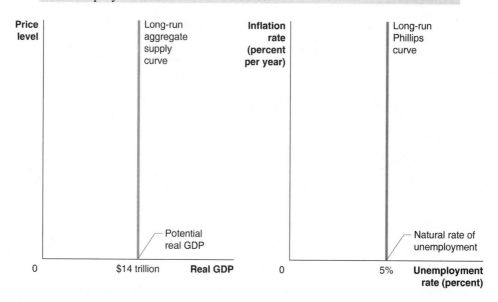

A long-run vertical Phillips curve indicates that there is no trade-off between inflation and unemployment in the long run. This conclusion is different from the experience of the 1950s and 1960s.

There is a trade-off between unemployment and inflation in the short run because workers often expect inflation to be higher or lower than it turns out to be. Differences between the actual inflation rate and the expected inflation rate can cause the unemployment rate to be higher or lower than the natural rate (and real GDP to be higher or lower than potential real GDP).

Textbook Table 16-1 reproduced below shows how differences between actual and expected inflation cause differences between actual and expected real wages.

NOMINAL WAGE	EXPECTED REAL WAGE	ACTUAL REAL WAGE	
	Expected P_{2009} = 105	Actual P_{2009} = 102	Actual P_{2009} = 108
	Expected inflation = 5%	Actual inflation = 2%	Actual inflation = 8%
$31.50	$\dfrac{\$31.50}{105} \times 100 = \$30$	$\dfrac{\$31.50}{102} \times 100 = \$30.88$	$\dfrac{\$31.50}{108} \times 100 = \$29.17$

Milton Friedman argued that inflation will increase employment only if inflation is unexpected; that is, if the actual inflation rate is greater than the expected inflation rate. These higher levels of employment are temporary and will disappear when the inaccurate expectations are changed. This short-run trade-off is shown in textbook Table 16-2 below:

IF . . .	THEN . . .	AND . . .
actual inflation is greater than expected inflation,	the actual real wage is less than the expected real wage,	the unemployment rate falls.
actual inflation is less than expected inflation,	the actual real wage is greater than the expected real wage,	the unemployment rate rises.

📖 Helpful Study Hint

Understanding the effects of inflation can be difficult—especially if you're not an economist. Read *Making the Connection: Do Workers Understand Inflation?* A higher inflation rate can lead to lower unemployment if both workers and firms mistakenly expect inflation to be lower than it turns out to be. Firms generally have more accurate information about inflation than do workers. Workers often fail to realize that wages will typically rise as prices rise.

16.2 LEARNING OBJECTIVE

16.2 The Short-Run and Long-Run Phillips Curves (pages 559–563)

Learning Objective 2 Explain the relationship between the short-run and long-run Phillips curves.

The short-run Phillips curve is drawn with the expected rate of inflation held constant. When the expected inflation rate and the actual inflation rate are equal, unemployment will be at the natural rate of unemployment. Textbook Figure 16.4 shows an example of a short-run and a long-run Phillips curve.

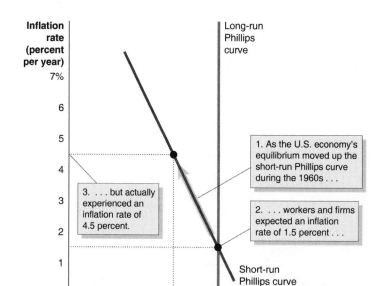

In this graph, the short-run and long-run Phillips curves intersect at an inflation rate of 1.5 percent. At the point where the short-run and long-run Phillips curves intersect, we know that the expected inflation rate is equal to the actual inflation rate. Changes in expectations cause shifts in the short-run Phillips curve. Increases in expected inflation cause upward shifts in the short-run Phillips curve, as seen in Figure 16-5 below, which illustrates the impact of the expected inflation rate rising from 1.5 percent to 4.5 percent:

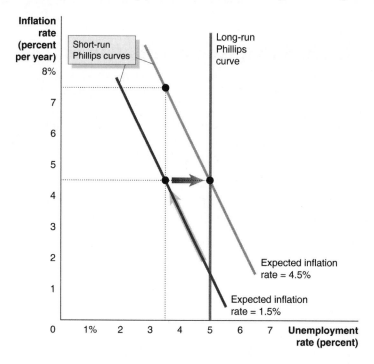

Increases in inflation will cause unemployment to fall, *as long as expected inflation does not change.* This is a movement along the short-run Phillips curve. When workers and firms begin to adjust their expectations to the actual inflation rate being higher than they had expected, the short-run Phillips curve will shift up to reflect the higher expected inflation rate. Therefore, there is a short-run Phillips curve for every expected inflation rate. Each short-run Phillips curve intersects the long-run Phillips curve at the expected inflation rate. This is shown in textbook Figure 16-6 below:

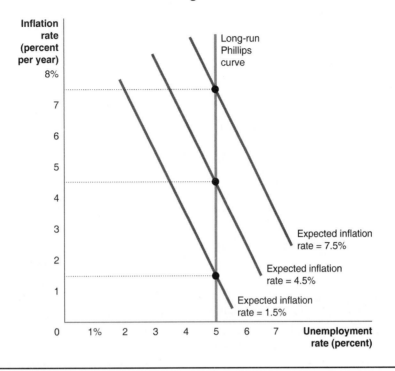

📖 Helpful Study Hint

The expected inflation rate is held constant along any single short-run Phillips curve. When expected inflation changes, the short-run Phillips curve shifts.

The short-run and long-run Phillips curves have important implications for the conduct of monetary policy. If the Fed tries to use an expansionary monetary policy to lower unemployment by increasing inflation, this can be successful only in the short run. As workers and firms begin to expect higher inflation, the short-run Phillips curve will shift and unemployment will eventually return to the natural rate of unemployment. Thus to keep unemployment below the natural rate of unemployment, the actual inflation rate must constantly increase to stay higher than the upward adjustment of the expected inflation rate. This acceleration of inflation is seen in the following Figure 16-7.

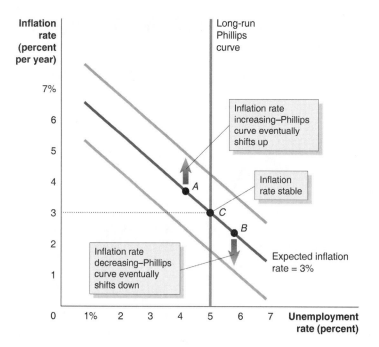

At point *C*, the current inflation rate will not change because expected inflation equals actual inflation. At point *A*, the inflation rate will increase because actual inflation is greater than expected inflation and the short-run Phillips curve shifts up. At point *B*, the inflation rate will decrease because actual inflation is less than expected inflation and the short-run Phillips curve shifts down. The unchanging unemployment rate along the long-run Phillips curve is called the **nonaccelerating inflation rate of unemployment (NAIRU)**.

📖 Helpful Study Hint

In the long run, expansionary and contractionary monetary policies will only change the inflation rate. Monetary policy cannot affect the level of real GDP or the unemployment rate in the long run.

The natural rate of unemployment will change over time as a result of changes in demographics, changes in labor market institutions, and the effects of high past levels of unemployment.

📖 Helpful Study Hint

Read *Making the Connection: Does the Natural Rate of Unemployment Ever Change?* At the natural rate of unemployment, only structural and frictional unemployment remain. The amount of frictional and structural unemployment can change over time, however, particularly as demographic changes occur. To give two examples of demographic changes resulting in changes in the natural rate of unemployment:

- As baby boom workers first hit the labor market in large numbers during the 1970s and 1980s, because these workers initially had lower job skills, the natural rate of unemployment increased.

> ■ As the number of young unskilled workers declined in the 1990s, the natural rate fell.

16.3 Expectations of the Inflation Rate and Monetary Policy (pages 564–566)

Learning Objective 3 Discuss how expectations of the inflation rate affect monetary policy.

How long the economy can remain at a point that is not on the long-run Phillips curve depends on how long it takes workers and firms to adjust their expectations of inflation to the actual inflation rate. People are said to have adaptive expectations if they assume that future rates of inflation will follow the pattern of rates of inflation in the recent past. Experience indicates that how fast workers adjust their expectations depends upon how high the inflation rate is. There are three possibilities:

- ■ *Low inflation*. When inflation is low, workers and firms tend to ignore it.
- ■ *Moderate but stable inflation*. With stable inflation, individuals and firms tend to expect inflation to be what it was last period. This is called adaptive expectations.
- ■ *High and unstable inflation*. With higher inflation rates and less stable inflation rates, workers attempt to estimate inflation rates more accurately. **Rational expectations** says that workers will use all available information to try to accurately forecast the inflation rate.

Lucas and Sargent argued that if workers and firms have rational expectations and if they expect an expansionary monetary policy will raise the inflation rate, they will use this information in their forecasts of the inflation rate. Consequently, the increase in the inflation rate would *not* be unanticipated, and the expansionary policy would not cause a decline in unemployment, even in the short run. If Lucas and Sargent are correct, an expansionary policy will cause only a movement along the long-run Phillips curve. This is shown in the following textbook Figure 16-8. In the graph, if workers and firms have adaptive expectations, and expansionary monetary policy will move the economy up the short-run Phillips curve and the unemployment rate will fall. But if workers and firms have rational expectations, the inflation rate will increase, while the unemployment rate will not change.

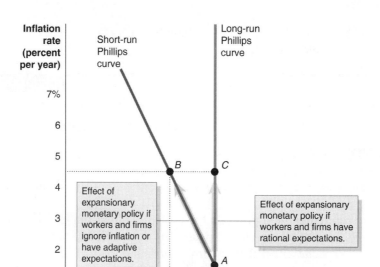

The logic of Lucas and Sargent's argument is that the Phillips curve is vertical, even in the short run. With a vertical short-run Phillips curve, expansionary monetary policy cannot reduce the unemployment rate below the natural rate of unemployment. Many economists do not agree that the Phillips curve is vertical in the short run either because they do not believe that workers and firms have rational expectations or because they believe that wages and prices adjust only slowly to changes in aggregate demand.

Other economists believe that workers and firms have rational expectations, but argue that fluctuations in unemployment are due to changes in real factors rather than mistakes about the actual inflation rate. These real factors are often referred to as technology shocks, which make it possible to produce more or less output with the same level of employment. Models that focus on real rather than monetary explanations of fluctuations in real GDP and employment are referred to as **real business cycle models**. Some economists are skeptical of these models because they explain recessions as caused by negative technology shocks, which are uncommon (apart from oil price shocks).

Extra Solved Problem 16-3

Chapter 16 of the textbook includes two Solved Problems. Here is an extra Solved Problem to help you build your skills solving economic problems:

Expectation Errors and Unemployment

Supports Learning Objective 3: Discuss how expectations of the inflation rate affect monetary policy.

Suppose that workers and firms expect that the inflation rate is going to increase from 3 percent to 5 percent. Suppose, though, the inflation rate actually rises only to 4 percent. What would you predict would be the effect on the unemployment rate of the actual inflation rate being less than the expected inflation rate?

SOLVING THE PROBLEM

Step 1:   Review the chapter material.
This problem is about expectations of inflation and monetary policy, so you may want to review the section "Expectations of the Inflation Rate and Monetary Policy," which begins on page 564 of the textbook.

Step 2:   Use a graph to show the effect of workers and firms expecting the inflation rate to increase from 3 percent to 5 percent.
The increase in the expected inflation rate will shift the short-run Phillips curve upward.

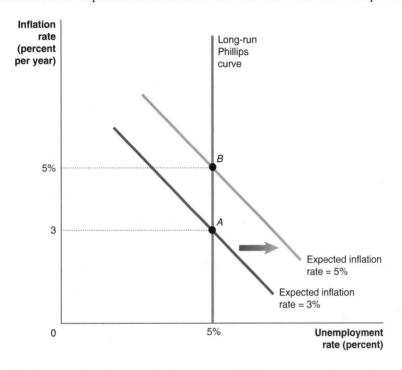

If the inflation rate had increased as workers and firms expected, macroeconomic equilibrium would move from point *A* to point *B* and the unemployment rate would not change.

Step 3:   Draw a second graph showing the effect of the actual inflation rate being less than the expected inflation rate.
If, however, inflation did not increase as much as workers and firms expected, the real wage is likely to have increased as nominal wages increased faster than the price level. Higher real wages will result in a higher unemployment rate. So, the new short-run macroeconomic equilibrium will be at point *C* in the graph, rather than point *B*. In the short-run macroeconomic equilibrium at point *C* the inflation rate is lower, but the unemployment rate is higher, than at point *B*.

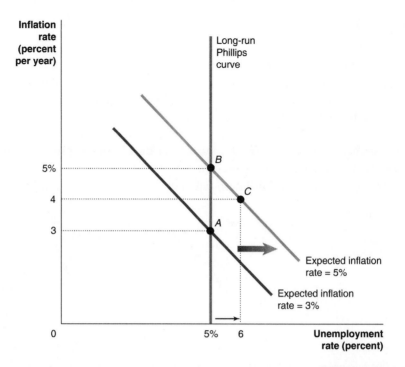

16.4 How the Fed Fights Inflation (pages 567–574)

Learning Objective 4 Use a Phillips curve graph to show how the Federal Reserve can permanently lower the inflation rate.

The high inflation rates of the late 1960s and early 1970s was in part due to the Fed's attempts to keep the unemployment rate below the natural rate. A supply shock in the 1970s due to higher oil prices made inflation worse.

A supply shock will cause the short-run Phillips curve to shift. A supply shock will shift the *SRAS* to the left. This shift will lower real GDP and increase the price level. On a Phillips curve graph, the Phillips curve will shift up to indicate that both inflation and unemployment have increased. The effect of a supply shock on short-run aggregate supply and the Phillips curve is shown in the following textbook Figure 16-9.

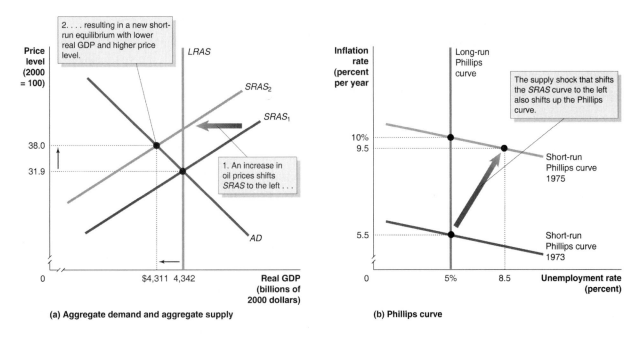

(a) Aggregate demand and aggregate supply

(b) Phillips curve

If the Fed uses contractionary monetary policy to fight the inflation resulting from a supply shock, it can lower the inflation rate, but only at the cost of higher unemployment in the short run. If the Fed decides to use expansionary monetary policy to fight the unemployment increases, this will cause more inflation as the economy moves up the short-run Phillips curve. When confronted with this situation in the 1970s, the Fed chose to fight high unemployment with an expansionary monetary policy, even though this decision worsened the inflation rate.

Paul Volcker was appointed Fed chairman in August 1979. Under Volcker, the Fed was able to reduce inflation from 10 percent to 5 percent. This **disinflation**—or significant reduction in the inflation rate—is shown in textbook Figure 16-10 below, where each dot represents the inflation and unemployment rates in a particular year, beginning with 1979:

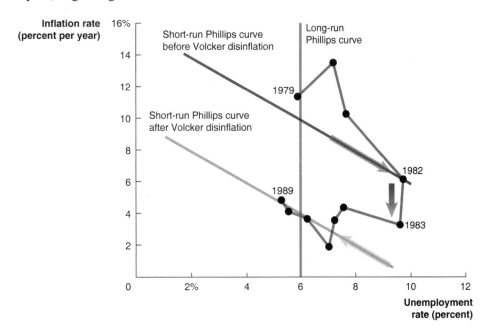

Alan Greenspan, who followed Volcker as Fed Chairman in 1987, was able to keep the inflation rate low. Greenspan de-emphasized the money supply as a policy target in favor of the federal funds rate. The Federal Open Market Committee has continued to target the federal funds rate in the years since. The fed has also been successful at increasing its credibility by publicly announcing its target for the federal funds rate and by demonstrating a strong commitment to fighting inflation.

To increase Fed credibility, some economists have suggested that the Fed follow a rules strategy, where the Fed announces a rule for monetary policy and follows it. Such a rule might be that the money supply should grow at some fixed percentage each year, regardless of economic conditions. Economists who oppose rules support discretionary monetary policy, a policy approach in which the Fed adjusts monetary policy as it sees fit, based on current economic conditions. A middle course is a rule based on economic conditions, such as the Taylor rule, where monetary policy is based on inflation gaps and output gaps. Rules add to the Fed's credibility by removing flexibility, but rules may not be appropriate in all settings. Some economists suggest that the Fed be more transparent in its inflation goals and announce inflation targets.

The Bank of Japan faced credibility problems through the 1990s because the country's economy experienced falling prices (or deflation). By 1999, the bank lowered its target interest rate (equivalent to the federal funds rate) to zero. Other interest rates remained high as the Japanese public doubted the willingness of the Bank of Japan to continue expansionary monetary policy. The Bank was not willing to state an explicit inflation target, which might have caused workers to increase the rate of inflation they expected and caused the deflation to end.

Extra Solved Problem 16-4

Chapter 16 of the textbook includes two Solved Problems. Here is an extra Solved Problem to help you build your skills solving economic problems:

Stagflation and the Short-Run Phillips Curve

Learning Objective 4   Use a Phillips curve graph to show how the Federal Reserve can permanently lower the inflation rate.

Stagflation is the simultaneous increase in inflation and unemployment. Given the negative slope of the short-run Phillips curve, how is it possible for there to be simultaneous increases in inflation and unemployment?

SOLVING THE PROBLEM

Step 1:   **Review the chapter material.**
This problem is about supply shocks, so you may want to review the section "The Effect of a Supply Shock on the Phillips Curve," which begins on page 567 of the textbook.

Step 2:   **Illustrate the short-run trade-off between inflation and unemployment.**
The short-run Phillips curve shows the short-run trade-off between inflation and unemployment. Along any short-run Philips curve, an increase in inflation will be accompanied by a decrease in unemployment. The graph illustrates this point by showing that a movement from point *A* to point *B* results in lower unemployment and higher inflation.

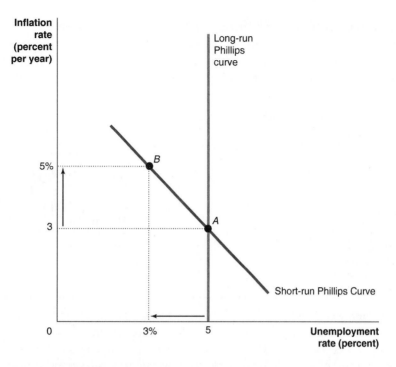

Step 3: **Illustrate the effect of an adverse supply shock.**

Periods of stagflation are often caused by adverse supply shocks, such as a rapid increase in oil prices. We saw in Chapter 12 that a supply shock causes the short-run aggregate supply curve (*SRAS*) to shift to the left. In this chapter, we learned that an adverse supply shock that shifts the *SRAS* curve to the left will also shift the short-run Phillips curve upward. We show the shift in the short-run Phillips curve caused by a supply shock in the graph below:

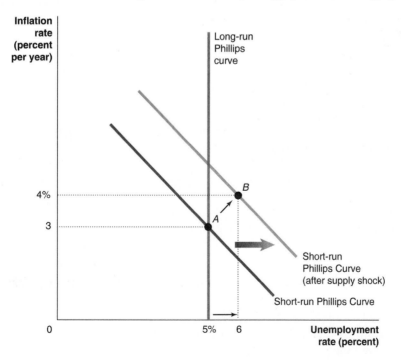

Step 4:   **Analyze the effect of a shift in the short-run Phillips curve.**

A shift in the short-run Phillips curve creates the possibility of a simultaneous increase in inflation and unemployment. Stagflation is shown as a movement from point *A* to point *B* in the graph above. At point *B*, both the unemployment rate and the inflation rate are higher than at point *A*.

📖 Helpful Study Hint

Read *Don't Let This Happen to YOU! Don't Confuse Disinflation with Deflation*. Remember disinflation means the inflation rate is falling. As long as the inflation rate is still positive, prices are rising, just not as fast as at the higher inflation rate. Deflation means that the inflation rate is negative and the price level is falling.

📖 Helpful Study Hint

Economics in YOUR Life! at the end of the chapter answers the question posed at the start of the chapter: How do you know how much of a raise you can ask for at work if it has just been announced that the Fed is going to try to maintain the unemployment rate at 3 percent? Because the long–run Phillips curve is at about 5 percent, the 3 percent unemployment rate will be below the NAIRU and we would expect the inflation rate to begin to increase. You should ask for a large raise to preserve you future purchasing power.

Key Terms

Disinflation. A significant reduction in the inflation rate.

Natural rate of unemployment. The normal unemployment rate that exists when the economy is at potential GDP.

Nonaccelerating inflation rate of unemployment (NAIRU). The unemployment rate where the inflation rate has no tendency to increase or decrease.

Phillips curve. A curve showing the short-run relationship between the unemployment rate and the inflation rate.

Rational expectations. Expectations formed by using all available information about an economic variable.

Real business cycle models. Models that focus on real rather than monetary explanations of fluctuations in real GDP.

Structural relationship. A relationship that depends on the basic behavior of consumers and firms and remains unchanged over long periods.

Self-Test

(Answers are provided at the end of the Self-Test.)

Multiple-Choice Questions

1. A trade-off between inflation and unemployment exists
    a. only in the short run.
    b. only in the long run.
    c. in both the short run and the long run.
    d. in neither the short run nor the long run.

2. When aggregate demand increases, unemployment will usually _____ and inflation will _____.
    a. rise; rise
    b. rise; fall
    c. fall; fall
    d. fall; rise

3. A Phillips curve is
    a. a curve showing the relationship between the inflation rate and the money supply.
    b. a curve showing the short-run relationship between the unemployment rate and the inflation rate.
    c. a curve showing the relationship between the inflation rate and the exchange rate.
    d. a curve showing the relationship between the size of the federal budget deficit and the size of the federal debt.

4. The long-run Phillips curve
    a. has a negative slope.
    b. is vertical at the natural rate of unemployment.
    c. shifts to the right with an increase in inflation.
    d. shifts to the right as cyclical unemployment decreases.

5. A point near the top left segment of the short-run Phillips curve represents
    a. a combination of high unemployment and high inflation.
    b. a combination of high unemployment and low inflation.
    c. a combination of low unemployment and low inflation.
    d. a combination of low unemployment and high inflation.

6. Slow growth in aggregate demand leads to
    a. higher unemployment and higher inflation.
    b. higher unemployment and lower inflation.
    c. lower unemployment and lower inflation.
    d. lower unemployment and higher inflation.

7. Which of the following statements concerning the Phillips curve is correct?
   a. Most economists in the 1960s and 1970s believed the Phillips curve was vertical in the long run.
   b. Many economists and policymakers in the 1960s and 1970s viewed the Phillips curve as a structural relationship.
   c. Economists have always recognized that there is a permanent trade-off between inflation and unemployment.
   d. The only economist who ever viewed the Phillips curve as a structural relationship was A.W. Phillips.

8. If the long-run aggregate supply curve is vertical, then
   a. the Phillips curve must be horizontal in the short run.
   b. the Phillips curve must be vertical in the short run.
   c. the Phillips curve cannot be downward sloping in the long run.
   d. the Phillips curve must be downward sloping in the long run.

9. Which of the following statements is *correct*?
   a. In the long run, a higher or lower price level has no effect on real GDP.
   b. In the long run, a higher or lower inflation rate has no effect on the unemployment rate.
   c. In the long run, the Phillips curve is a vertical line at the natural rate of unemployment.
   d. all of the above

10. The natural rate of unemployment is
    a. the prevailing rate of unemployment in the economy in the short run.
    b. the unemployment rate that results when the economy produces the potential level of real GDP.
    c. the rate of unemployment when the inflation rate equals zero.
    d. the lowest unemployment rate on the short-run Phillips curve.

11. According to Milton Friedman, differences between the actual and expected inflation rates could lead the actual unemployment rate to
    a. rise above or fall below the natural rate.
    b. rise above the natural rate, but not fall below it.
    c. fall below the natural rate, but not rise above it.
    d. remain equal to the natural rate for a long time.

12. If expected inflation is higher than actual inflation, actual real wages in the economy will turn out to be _____ than expected real wages; consequently, firms will hire _____ workers than they had planned.
    a. higher; more
    b. higher; fewer
    c. lower; more
    d. lower; fewer

13. An increase in expected inflation will
    a. shift the short run Phillips curve up.
    b. shift the long run Phillips curve to the right.
    c. shift the short run Phillips curve down.
    d. shift the short run Phillips curve up and the long run Phillips curve to the right.

14. Which change in the inflation rate is more likely to affect the trade-off between inflation and unemployment?
    a. a change in the inflation rate that is expected
    b. a change in the inflation rate that is unexpected
    c. a change in the inflation rate that is exactly equal to the percentage change in the unemployment rate
    d. a change in the inflation rate when the unemployment rate equals the natural rate of unemployment

15. If the annual inflation rate is 3 percent, which of the following will increase real wages?
    a. an increase in nominal wages of less than 3 percent
    b. an increase in nominal wages of more than 3 percent
    c. an increase in nominal wages equal to 3 percent
    d. a decrease in nominal wages of more than 3 percent

16. If the wage rate is $15.00 and the price level is 125, then the real wage rate is
    a. $15.00.
    b. $12.00.
    c. $1.20.
    d. $1.25.

17. If banks need to receive a 4 percent real interest rate on home mortgage loans, what nominal interest rate must they charge if they expect the inflation rate to be 1.5 percent?
    a. 2.5%
    b. 5.5%
    c. 1.5%
    d. 4%

18. If workers and firms revise their expectations of inflation upward
    a. there will be a movement downward along the short-run Phillips curve.
    b. there will be a movement upward along the short-run Phillips curve.
    c. the short-run Phillips curve will shift up.
    d. the short-run Phillips curve will shift down.

19. There is a different short-run Phillips curve for every level of the _____ inflation rate. The inflation rate at which the short-run Phillips curve intersects the long-run Phillips curve equals the _____ inflation rate.
    a. actual; expected
    b. expected; actual
    c. actual; actual
    d. expected; expected

20. If the unemployment rate is below the natural rate, the inflation rate tends to _____ and, eventually, the short-run Phillips curve will shift _____.
    a. increase; up
    b. increase; down
    c. decrease; up
    d. decrease; down

21. The concept of a nonaccelerating inflation rate of unemployment (NAIRU) helps us to understand why
    a. in the long run, the Federal Reserve can affect both the inflation rate and the unemployment rate.
    b. in the long run, the Federal Reserve cannot affect either the inflation rate or the unemployment rate.
    c. in the long run, the Federal Reserve can affect the unemployment rate but not the inflation rate.
    d. in the long run, the Federal Reserve can affect the inflation rate but not the unemployment rate.

22. There are three types of unemployment. Changes in two of the types will cause a change in the natural rate of unemployment. Which two?
    a. frictional and cyclical unemployment
    b. structural and cyclical unemployment
    c. frictional and structural unemployment
    d. seasonal and cyclical unemployment

23. When do workers and firms tend to ignore inflation?
    a. when inflation is low
    b. when inflation is moderate
    c. when inflation is high
    d. never

24. If people assume that future rates of inflation will be about the same as past rates of inflation, they are said to have
    a. naïve expectations.
    b. adaptive expectations.
    c. rational expectations.
    d. consistent expectations.

25. Expectations formed by using all available information about an economic variable are called
    a. naïve expectations.
    b. adaptive expectations.
    c. rational expectations.
    d. consistent expectations.

26. If workers and firms have rational expectations and wages and prices adjust quickly, an expansionary monetary policy will
    a. increase the inflation rate, but lower the unemployment rate.
    b. increase the inflation rate, but not change the unemployment rate.
    c. increase both the inflation and unemployment rates.
    d. change neither the inflation nor the unemployment rates.

27. If workers and firms have adaptive expectations or if they ignore inflation, what is the effect of an expansionary monetary policy?
    a. a move upward along the short-run Phillips curve
    b. a move downward along the short-run Phillips curve
    c. a move upward along the long-run Phillips curve
    d. a move downward along the long-run Phillips curve

28. In a real business cycle model, which of the following best explains an increase in real GDP above the full-employment level?
    a. adaptive expectations
    b. an increase in the money supply
    c. a positive technology shock
    d. all of the above

29. The monetary explanations of Lucas and Sargent and the real business cycle models are sometimes grouped together under the label of
    a. monetarism.
    b. the new classical macroeconomics.
    c. the new Keynesian macroeconomics.
    d. the new growth theory.

30. Like the classical economists, the new classical macroeconomists believe that
    a. the economy cannot correct itself, but requires government intervention in order to remain stable.
    b. the short-run Phillips curve is horizontal.
    c. the economy will normally be at its potential level.
    d. all of the above

31. A supply shock will
    a. shift the short-run Phillips curve up.
    b. shift the long-run Phillips curve to the right.
    c. shift the long-run Phillips curve down.
    d. shift the short-run Phillips curve up and the long-run Phillips curve to the right.

32. A negative supply shock, such as the OPEC oil price increases of the early 1970s, can be illustrated by a(n) _____ shift of the short-run aggregate supply curve and a _____ shift of the short-run Phillips curve.
    a. leftward; upward
    b. leftward; downward
    c. rightward; upward
    d. rightward; downward

33. How can the Fed fight a combination of rising unemployment and rising inflation?
    a. By applying expansionary monetary policy, the Fed can solve both problems simultaneously.
    b. By applying contractionary monetary policy, the Fed can solve both problems simultaneously.
    c. Not easily. Neither expansionary nor contractionary monetary policy can solve both problems simultaneously.
    d. By resorting to the use of fiscal policy instead of monetary policy.

34. In August 1979, President Jimmy Carter appointed Paul Volcker as Chairman of the Board of Governors of the Federal Reserve System. Which of the following statements is true about the state of the economy or the monetary policy chosen by the new Chairman?
    a. High inflation rates were inflicting significant damage on the economy.
    b. Paul Volcker chose to reduce the growth rate of the money supply.
    c. Paul Volcker adopted contractionary monetary policy that caused interest rates to rise and aggregate demand to decline.
    d. all of the above

35. After Fed Chairman Paul Volcker decided to fight inflation in 1979, the Fed's monetary policy resulted in
    a. lower interest rates.
    b. a lower unemployment rate.
    c. lower expectations of future inflation by firms and workers.
    d. all of the above

36. After Fed Chairman Paul Volcker began fighting inflation in 1979, workers and firms eventually _____ their expectations of future inflation; consequently, the short-run Phillips curve shifted _____.
    a. raised; up
    b. raised; down
    c. lowered; up
    d. lowered; down

37. A significant reduction in the inflation rate is called
    a. deflation.
    b. disinflation.
    c. stagflation.
    d. cost-push inflation.

38. Paul Volcker's monetary policy caused the Phillips curve to shift down, but only after several years of high unemployment. This means that, apparently, workers and firms had
    a. rational expectations, that is, they used all available information to form their expectations of future inflation.
    b. adaptive expectations, that is, they changed their expectations of future inflation after the current inflation rate had fallen.
    c. naïve expectations, that is, they expected inflation today to be exactly what it was yesterday.
    d. no expectations at all of future inflation.

39. Disinflation refers to a decline in the _____ _____, while deflation refers to a decline in the _____ _____.
    a. inflation rate; price level
    b. price level; inflation rate
    c. market prices; economy-wide prices
    d. money supply; price level

40. In order to drive down the inflation rate, the unemployment rate will have to rise more if the short-run Phillips curve is
    a. flatter.
    b. steeper.
    c. vertical.
    d. upward sloping.

41. During the 1980s and 1990s, the relationship between growth in the money supply and inflation
    a. broke down, and the Fed announced that it would no longer set targets for M1 and M2.
    b. strengthened significantly, renewing the Fed's confidence in using monetary targets for M1 and M2.
    c. involved higher inflation rates leading to higher rates of growth of the money supply.
    d. caused inflation to soar to its highest levels since World War II.

42. A rules strategy refers to
    a. the central bank's rules for overseeing the banking system.
    b. the central bank's following specific and publicly announced guidelines for policy.
    c. the Fed's policy of keeping secret the target for the federal funds rate.
    d. all of the above

43. A discretion strategy consists of
    a. adopting the monetarist's monetary growth rule.
    b. adjusting monetary policy as the central bank sees fit to achieve its policy goals, such as price stability and high employment.
    c. following specific and publicly announced guidelines for policy.
    d. maintaining a particular monetary policy goal, regardless of the state of the economy.

44. Which of the following is a monetary policy rule where the Fed sets a target for the federal funds rate according to an equation that includes the inflation rate, the equilibrium real federal funds rate, the "inflation gap," and the "output gap?"
    a. the growth rule
    b. the Taylor rule
    c. the Friedman rule
    d. the Bernanke rule

45. Which of the following is a problem with deflation?
    a. Deflation causes real interest rates to fall.
    b. Deflation causes the value of debts to increase.
    c. Deflation can cause consumers to consume now rather than postpone purchases.
    d. all of the above

Short Answer Questions

1. Why does the short-run Phillips curve have a negative slope?

_____

_____

_____

_____

_____

2. In 2006, average hourly earning in manufacturing was $16.80 and the price level (measured by the GDP deflator) was 116.6. Suppose that in 2007, the inflation rate was 3 percent. How much would average hourly earnings needed to have changed to keep the real wage constant?

_____

_____

_____

_____

_____

3. Suppose that workers and firms both expect prices to increase by 3 percent. The current average wage rate is $16.80. The price level is 116.6. Show what will happen to the real wage if the actual inflation rate is 5 percent but expected inflation remains at 3 percent.

_____

_____

_____

_____

_____

4. Why does a vertical long-run aggregate supply curve imply a vertical long-run Phillips curve?

_____

_____

_____

_____

5. If the Fed tries to reduce the inflation rate using contractionary monetary policy, the impact the policy will have on the unemployment rate depends on how expectations of inflation are formed. Explain.

_____

_____

_____

_____

_____

6. Explain the different effects expansionary monetary policy will have on unemployment with adaptive expectations compared to rational expectations.

_____

_____

_____

_____

_____

True/False Questions

T   F   1.   A trade-off between inflation and unemployment means that lower unemployment rates imply higher inflation rates.

T   F   2.   Milton Friedman was the first economist to draw a Phillips curve.

T   F   3.   The short-run Phillips curve has a positive slope.

T   F   4.   The long-run Phillips curve has a negative slope.

T   F   5.   The natural rate of unemployment is zero.

T   F   6.   If nominal wages increase at the same rate as inflation, the real wage will not change.

T   F   7.   If prices rise more than expected, the real wage rate will also rise.

T   F   8.   Unanticipated inflation is the difference between the actual and expected inflation rates.

T   F   9.   An increase in the expected inflation rate will shift the short-run Phillips curve up.

T   F   10. At points where the short-run Phillips curve crosses the long-run Phillips curve, the public's expectations of inflation are accurate.

T   F   11. In the long run, the Federal Reserve system can affect the inflation rate but not the unemployment rate.

T   F   12. The natural rate of unemployment is fixed and does not change.

T   F   13. If expectations of inflation are rational, then they are based only on past inflation rates.

T   F   14. A supply shock will shift the _SRAS_ curve to the left and the short-run Phillips curve up.

T   F   15. Paul Volcker's contractionary monetary policy reduced inflation without changing the unemployment rate.

Answers to the Self-Test

Multiple-Choice Questions

Question	Answer	Comment
1	a	An important consideration for the Fed is that in the short run there can be a trade-off between unemployment and inflation: Lower unemployment rates can result in higher inflation rates. In the long run, however, this tradeoff disappears and the unemployment rate is independent of the inflation rate.
2	d	When aggregate demand increases, unemployment will usually fall and inflation will rise. When aggregate demand decreases, unemployment will usually rise and inflation will fall. As a result, there is a short-run tradeoff between unemployment and inflation.
3	b	The Phillips curve is a curve showing the short-run relationship between the unemployment rate and the inflation rate.
4	b	The long-run Phillips curve shows the unemployment rate at different inflation rates assuming people's expectations of inflation are accurate. If expectations are correct, there will be no adjustment in unemployment, and the curve is vertical at the natural rate of unemployment.
5	d	Figure 16-1 shows a typical short-run Phillips curve.
6	b	The *AD-AS* model indicates that slow growth in aggregate demand leads to both higher unemployment and lower inflation. This relationship explains why there is a short-run trade-off between unemployment and inflation, as shown by the downward-sloping Phillips curve.
7	b	Because many economists and policymakers in the 1960s and 1970s viewed the Phillips curve as a structural relationship, they believed it represented a permanent trade-off between unemployment and inflation. As long as policymakers were willing to accept a permanently higher inflation rate, they would be able to keep the unemployment rate permanently lower.
8	c	Friedman and Phelps noted that economists had come to agree that the long-run aggregate supply curve was vertical. If this was true, then the Phillips curve could not be downward sloping in the long run. There was a critical inconsistency between a vertical long-run aggregate supply curve and a long-run Phillips curve that is downward sloping. Friedman and Phelps argued, in essence, that there is no trade-off between unemployment and inflation in the long run.
9	d	In the long run, a higher or lower price level has no effect on real GDP, because real GDP is always at its potential level in the long run. In the same way, in the long run, a higher or lower inflation rate will have no effect on the unemployment rate, because the unemployment rate is always equal to the natural rate in the long run. Figure 16-3 illustrates Friedman's conclusion that the long-run aggregate supply curve is a vertical line at the potential real GDP and the long-run Phillips curve is a vertical line at the natural rate of unemployment.
10	b	At potential real GDP, firms will operate at their normal level of capacity and everyone who wants a job will have one, except the structurally and frictionally unemployed. Milton Friedman defined the natural rate of unemployment as the unemployment rate that exists when the economy is at potential GDP.

11	a	Friedman argued that the short-run trade-off between unemployment and inflation exists only because workers and firms sometimes expect the inflation rate to be either higher or lower than it turned out to be. Differences between the expected inflation rate and the actual inflation rate could lead the unemployment rate to rise above or dip below the natural rate.
12	b	If expected inflation is higher than actual inflation, actual real wages in the economy will turn out to be higher than expected real wages and firms will hire fewer workers than they had planned.
13	a	If the public expects higher inflation, it will be necessary for the inflation rate to rise to keep unemployment at the same level. This is an upward shift in the short-run curve.
14	b	Milton Friedman and Edmund Phelps concluded that an increase in the inflation rate increases employment (and decreases unemployment) only if it is unexpected: There is always a temporary trade-off between inflation and unemployment; there is no permanent trade-off. The temporary trade-off comes not from inflation as such, but from unanticipated inflation.
15	b	Firms know that only nominal wage increases of more than 3 percent will increase real wages. Workers realize that unless they receive a nominal wage increase of at least 3 percent, their real wage will be falling.
16	b	The real wage rate is defined as the nominal wage divided by the price level and multiplied by 100, or ($15.00/125) x 100 = $12.00.
17	b	The real interest rate is the nominal interest rate minus the expected inflation rate. If banks need to receive a 4 percent real interest rate on home mortgage loans, they will charge a nominal interest rate of 5.5 percent if they expect the inflation rate to be 1.5 percent.
18	c	If workers and firms revise their expectations of inflation upward, the short-run Phillips curve will shift up, which will make the short-run trade-off between unemployment and inflation worse.
19	d	There is a different short-run Phillips curve for every expected inflation rate. Each short-run Phillips curve intersects the long-run Phillips curve at the expected inflation rate.
20	a	As shown in Figure 16-7, the inflation rate is only stable if the unemployment rate equals the natural rate. If the unemployment rate is below the natural rate, the inflation rate increases and, eventually, the short-run Phillips curve shifts up. If the unemployment rate is above the natural rate, the inflation rate decreases, and, eventually, the short-run Phillips curve shifts down.
21	d	As discussed in the chapter, in the long run the economy always returns to the natural rate of unemployment, which is sometimes called the nonaccelerating inflation rate of unemployment, or NAIRU. We can conclude that: In the long run, the Federal Reserve can affect the inflation rate, but not the unemployment rate.
22	c	Remember that at the natural rate of unemployment, only frictional and structural unemployment remain. Frictional or structural unemployment can change if there are demographic changes, changes in labor market institutions, or evidence of persistently high past rates of unemployment.
23	a	When the inflation rate is low, as it was during most of the 1950s, the early 1960s, the 1990s, and the early 2000s, workers and firms tend to ignore it. For instance, if the inflation rate is low, a restaurant may not want to pay for printing new menus that would show slightly higher prices.
24	b	People are said to have adaptive expectations of inflation if they assume that future rates of inflation will be about the same as past rates of inflation.

25	c	Expectations formed by using all available information about an economic variable are called rational expectations.
26	b	If workers have rational expectations, they will adjust their expectations about inflation following an expansionary monetary policy. As a result, the inflation rate will increase, but the unemployment rate will not change.
27	a	If workers and firms ignore inflation, or if they have adaptive expectations, an expansionary monetary policy will cause the short-run equilibrium to move upward along the short-run Phillips curve; inflation will rise and unemployment will fall. If workers and firms have rational expectations, an expansionary monetary policy will cause the short-run equilibrium to move up the long-run Phillips curve. Inflation will still rise, but there will be no change in unemployment.
28	c	Real GDP will be above its previous potential level following a positive technology shock and below its previous potential level following a negative technology shock. Real business cycle models focus on real factors, rather than changes in the money supply, to explain fluctuations in real GDP. This is why they are known as real business cycle models.
29	b	The approach of Lucas and Sargent and the real business cycle models are sometimes grouped together under the label of new classical macroeconomics, because these approaches share the assumptions that people have rational expectations and that wages and prices adjust rapidly. These assumptions are similar to those held by "classical economists."
30	c	John Maynard Keynes, in his book *The General Theory of Employment, Interest, and Money*, published in 1936, referred to economists before the Great Depression as "classical economists." Like the classical economists, the new classical macroeconomists believe that the economy will normally be at its potential level.
31	a	A supply shock increases the cost of production. At a given expected inflation rate, increased production costs will reduce real GDP, increasing unemployment, and shifting the short-run Phillips curve up.
32	a	As shown in Figure 16-9, when OPEC increased the price of a barrel of oil from less than $3 to more than $10, the *SRAS* curve shifted to the left. Between 1973 and 1975, real GDP declined from $4,342 billion to $4,311 billion and the price level rose from 31.9 to 38.0. Also, the supply shock shifted the Phillips curve up. In 1973, the U.S. economy had an inflation rate of about 5.5 percent and an unemployment rate of about 5 percent. By 1975, the inflation rate had risen to about 9.5 percent and the unemployment rate to about 8.5 percent.
33	c	A combination of rising unemployment and rising inflation places the Federal Reserve in a difficult position. If the Fed uses an expansionary monetary policy to fight the high unemployment rate, the *AD* curve would shift to the right and the economy's equilibrium would move up the short-run Phillips curve. Real GDP would increase and the unemployment rate would fall, but at the cost of higher inflation. If the Fed used a contractionary monetary policy to fight the high inflation rate, the *AD* curve would shift to the left and the economy would move down the short-run Phillips curve. This would cause real GDP to fall and reduce the inflation rate, but at the cost of higher unemployment.

34	d	In August 1979, President Jimmy Carter appointed Paul Volcker as Chairman of the Board of Governors of the Federal Reserve System. Along with most economists, Volcker was convinced that high inflation rates were inflicting significant damage on the economy and needed to be reduced. To reduce inflation, he decided to reduce the annual growth rate of the money supply. This contractionary monetary policy raised interest rates, causing a decline in aggregate demand.
35	c	As it became clear the Fed was determined to lower the inflation rate, workers and firms lowered their expectations of future inflation.
36	d	Fed Chairman Paul Volcker began fighting inflation in 1979 by reducing the growth of the money supply, thereby raising interest rates. By 1982, the unemployment rate had risen to almost 10 percent and the inflation rate had fallen to 6 percent. As workers and firms lowered their expectations of future inflation, the short-run Phillips curve shifted down, improving the short-run trade-off between unemployment and inflation.
37	b	Under Paul Volcker's leadership, the Fed had reduced the inflation rate from more than 10 percent to less than 5 percent. The inflation rate has generally remained below 5 percent ever since. A significant reduction in the inflation rate is called disinflation.
38	b	Volcker's announcement in October 1979 that he planned to use a contractionary monetary policy to bring down the inflation rate was widely publicized. If workers and firms had rational expectations, we might have expected them to quickly reduce their expectations of future inflation. The economy should have moved smoothly down the long-run Phillips curve. However, the economy moved down the existing short-run Phillips curve and only after several years of high unemployment did the Phillips curve shift down. Apparently, workers and firms had adaptive expectations – only changing their expectations of future inflation after the current inflation rate had fallen.
39	a	Disinflation refers to a decline in the inflation rate. Deflation refers to a decline in the price level.
40	a	How much the unemployment rate would need to rise in order to drive down the inflation rate depends on the steepness of the short-run Phillips curve. The flatter the Phillips curve, the more the unemployment rate will need to rise in order to reduce the inflation rate.
41	a	During the 1980s and 1990s, there was a breakdown in the close relationship between growth in the money supply and inflation. Before 1987, the Fed would announce annual targets for how much M1 and M2 would increase during the year. In February 1987, near the end of Paul Volcker's term, the Fed announced that it would no longer set targets for M1. In July 1993, Alan Greenspan announced that the Fed would also no longer set targets for M2. Instead, the Federal Open Market Committee (FOMC) has relied on setting targets for the federal funds rate to meet its goals of price stability and high employment.
42	b	A rules strategy for monetary policy involves the central bank's following specific and publicly announced guidelines for policy. When the central bank chooses a rule, this strategy requires that it follow the rule, whatever the state of the economy.

43	b	Economists and policymakers who oppose the rules strategy support a discretion strategy for monetary policy. With a discretion strategy, the central bank should adjust monetary policy as it sees fit to achieve its policy goals, such as price stability and high employment.
44	b	According to the Taylor rule, the Fed should set the target for the federal funds rate according to an equation that includes the inflation rate, the equilibrium real federal funds rate, the "inflation gap," and the "output gap," as discussed in Chapter 14.
45	b	Deflation can contribute to slow growth by raising real interest rates, increasing the real value of debts, and causing consumers to postpone purchases in the hope of experiencing even lower prices in the future.

Short Answer Responses

1. Increases in inflation, if unanticipated, will cause reductions in real wages. Because wages usually keep pace with expected inflation, an unexpected increase in inflation will cause the real wage rate to fall. As the real wage rate falls, firms will try to hire more workers to take advantage of the lower cost of resources. This will result in output above potential real GDP and increases in employment, and consequently, a reduction in unemployment. Higher inflation (if unanticipated) will result in lower unemployment, so the short-run Phillips curve has a negative slope.

2. If the nominal wage is $16.80 and the price level is 116.6, then the real wage is:

$$\text{Real Wage} = \frac{\$16.80}{116.6} \times 100 = \$14.41$$

If inflation is 3 percent, the price level will increase to 120.10 (116.6 x 1.03), so to keep the real wage the same, the new nominal wage will need to increase to $17.30, or

$$\$14.41 = \frac{\text{New Wage}}{120.1} \times 100 = \frac{\$17.30}{120.1} \times 100$$

Notice that the percentage increase in the wage rate is 3 percent (3.0 = 100 x ($17.30 – $16.80)/ $16.80), which is the same as the inflation rate.

3. If wages rise as much as workers and firms expect prices to rise, wages will also increase 3 percent, so that wages will rise to $17.30 ($16.80 x 1.03 = $17.30). If prices rise 5 percent, then the new price level will be 122.4 (116.6 x 1.05 = 122.4). The real wage will then be:

$$\text{Real Wage} = \frac{\$17.30}{122.4} \times 100 = \$14.13$$

Because the real wage in 2006 was $14.41 (see Question 2), the unanticipated inflation reduced the real wage rate by 2 percent.

4. The vertical long-run aggregate supply curve implies that, regardless of the level of aggregate demand and the resulting price level, the level of output will in the long-run move toward potential real GDP. Consequently, whatever the inflation rate (the rate of change in the price level), in the long run, output will be at potential real GDP. If output is always at potential real GDP, unemployment will always be at the natural rate of unemployment. Therefore, in the long run at each inflation rate, the

resulting unemployment rate will be the natural rate, which means the long-run Phillips curve will be vertical.

5. If the Fed is successful in using a contractionary monetary policy to reduce inflation, the impact this will have on the unemployment rate will depend on how expectations are formed. If expectations are formed adaptively, then inflation expectations are based on past inflation. In this case, the lower inflation will cause a movement along a short-run Phillips curve, so that the lower inflation will be accompanied by higher unemployment. This is shown in a movement from point *A* to point *B* in the graph below. If expectations of inflation are formed rationally, then because the public is able to predict the reduction in inflation, expected inflation will fall as the inflation rate falls. This implies that the short-run Phillips curve will shift to the left as the inflation rate falls. In this case, the reduction in inflation will not be accompanied by higher unemployment. This is shown in the movement from point *A* to point *C* in the graph below.

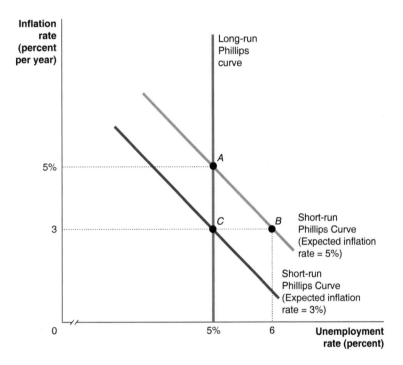

6. If expectations of inflation are formed adaptively, then an expansionary monetary policy will not be anticipated by workers or firms, and the inflation caused by the policy will be a surprise. In this case, the higher inflation rate will result in a decrease in the unemployment rate. This is the movement from point *A* to point *B* in the graph below. If however, the expansionary monetary policy is anticipated by workers and firms—as would be the case with rational expectations—the resulting inflation will be anticipated and workers and firms will not be surprised by the price increases. In this case, the unemployment rate will not change, and the economy will move from point *A* to point *C* as in the following graph.

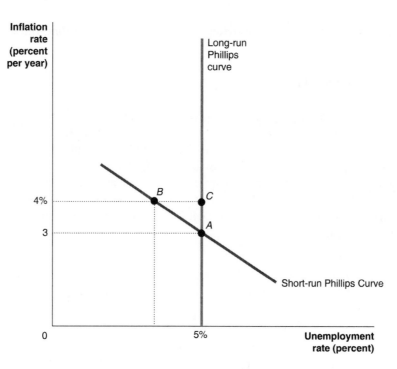

True/False Answers

1.	T	
2.	F	A.W. Phillips drew the graph that indicated the trade-off between inflation and unemployment.
3.	F	The short-run Phillips curve has a negative slope, indicating the trade-off between inflation and unemployment.
4.	F	The long-run Phillips curve is vertical.
5.	F	The natural rate of unemployment is the unemployment rate consistent with potential real GDP. At this point there is no cyclical unemployment, but there will be frictional and structural unemployment.
6.	T	
7.	F	If prices rise more than expected, the real wage will fall.
8.	T	
9.	T	
10.	T	
11.	T	
12.	F	The natural rate of unemployment may change if there are demographic changes, changes in labor market institutions, or if the unemployment rate remains high for an extended period.
13.	F	Rational expectations of inflation are based on all available information about inflation, including expected monetary policy changes.
14.	T	
15.	F	During the Volcker time period, as inflation fell, the unemployment rate rose. See Figure 16-10 in the textbook.

Macroeconomics in an Open Economy

Chapter Summary

Nearly all economies are **open economies** that trade with and invest in other economies. A **closed economy** has no interactions in trade or finance with other economies. The **balance of payments** is the record of a country's trade with other countries in goods, services, and assets. The **nominal exchange rate** is the value of one country's currency in terms of another country's currency. The exchange rate is determined in the foreign exchange market by the demand for and supply of a country's currency. **Currency appreciation** occurs when a currency's market value increases relative to another currency. **Currency depreciation** occurs when a currency's market value decreases relative to another currency.

When the government runs a budget deficit, national saving will decline unless private saving increases by the full amount of the budget deficit, which is unlikely. As the saving and investment equation ($S = I + NFI$) shows, the result of a decline in national saving must be a decline in either domestic investment or net foreign investment.

When the Federal Reserve engages in an expansionary monetary policy, it buys government bonds to lower interest rates and increase aggregate demand. When the Fed wants to slow the rate of economic growth to reduce inflation, it engages in a contractionary monetary policy. With a contractionary policy, the Fed sells government bonds to increase interest rates and reduce aggregate demand. Monetary policy has a greater impact on aggregate demand in an open economy than in a closed economy. To engage in an expansionary fiscal policy, the government increases government spending or cuts taxes. An expansionary fiscal policy can lead to higher interest rates. A contractionary fiscal policy will reduce the budget deficit and may lower interest rates. Fiscal policy has a smaller impact on aggregate demand in an open economy than in a closed economy.

Learning Objectives

When you finish this chapter, you should be able to:

1. **Explain how the balance of payments is calculated.** Nearly all economies are **open economies** that trade with and invest in other economies. The **balance of payments** is the record of a country's trade with other countries in goods, services, and assets. The **current account** shows a country's exports and imports of goods and services. The **financial account** shows the purchases of assets a country has made abroad and foreign purchases of assets in the country. The **balance of trade** is the difference between the value of the goods a country exports and the value of the goods a country imports. Apart from measurement errors, the sum of the current account and the financial account must equal zero. Therefore, the balance of payments must also equal zero.

2. **Explain how exchange rates are determined and how changes in exchange rates affect the prices of imports and exports.** The **nominal exchange rate** is the value of one country's currency in terms of another country's currency. The exchange rate is determined in the foreign exchange market by the demand for and supply of a country's currency. Changes in the exchange rate are caused by shifts in demand or supply. The three main sets of factors that cause the supply and demand curves in the foreign exchange market to shift are:

   a. Changes in the demand for U.S. produced goods and services and changes in the demand for foreign produced goods and services.
   b. Changes in the desire to invest in the United States and changes in the desire to invest in foreign countries.
   c. Changes in the expectations of currency traders – particularly *speculators* – concerning the likely future value of the dollar and the likely future values of foreign currencies.

3. A currency **appreciates** when its market value rises relative to another currency. A currency **depreciates** when its market value falls relative to another currency. The **real exchange rate** is the price of domestic goods in terms of foreign goods. The real exchange rate is calculated by multiplying the nominal exchange rate by the ratio of the domestic price level to the foreign price level.

4. **Explain the saving and investment equation.** A current account deficit must be exactly offset by a financial account surplus. The financial account is equal to net capital flows, which is equal to net foreign investment, but with the opposite sign. Because the current account balance is roughly equal to net exports, we can conclude that net exports will equal net foreign investment. National saving is equal to private saving plus government saving. Private saving is equal to national income minus consumption and minus taxes. Government saving is the difference between taxes and government spending. As we saw in previous chapters, GDP (or national income) is equal to the sum of investment, consumption, government spending, and net exports. We can use this fact, our definitions of private and government saving, and the fact that net exports equal net foreign investment, to arrive at an important relationship known as the **saving and investment equation**: $S = I + NFI$.

5. **Explain the effect of a government budget deficit on investment in an open economy.** When the government runs a budget deficit, national saving will decline unless private saving increases by the amount of the budget deficit, which is unlikely. As the saving and investment equation, $S = I + NFI$, shows, the result of a decline in national saving must be a decline in either domestic investment or net foreign investment.

6. **Discuss the difference between the effectiveness of monetary and fiscal policy in an open economy and in a closed economy.** When the Federal Reserve engages in an expansionary monetary policy, it buys government bonds to lower interest rates and increase aggregate demand. In a closed economy, the main effect of lower interest rates is on domestic investment spending and purchases of consumer durables. In an open economy, lower interest rates will also cause an increase in net exports. When the Fed wants to slow the rate of economic growth to reduce inflation, it engages in a contractionary monetary policy. With a contractionary monetary policy, the Fed sells government bonds to increase interest rates and reduce aggregate demand. In a closed economy, the main effect is once again on domestic investment and purchases of consumer durables. In an open economy, higher interest rates will also reduce net exports. We can conclude that monetary policy has a greater impact on aggregate demand in an open economy than in a closed economy. To engage in an expansionary fiscal policy, the government increases government spending or cuts taxes. An expansionary fiscal policy can lead to higher interest rates. In a closed economy, the main effect of higher interest rates is on domestic investment spending and spending on consumer durables. In an open economy, higher interest rates will also reduce net exports. A contractionary fiscal policy will reduce the budget deficit

and may lower interest rates. In a closed economy, lower interest rates increase domestic investment and spending on consumer durables. In an open economy, lower interest rates also increase net exports. We can conclude that fiscal policy has a smaller impact on aggregate demand in an open economy than in a closed economy.

Chapter Review

Chapter Opener: NewPage Paper versus China (pages 584-585)

NewPage, a paper manufacturing firm in Dayton, Ohio, produces glossy paper used in catalogs and magazines. In recent years, the company's strongest competition is from Chinese paper firms. Chinese firms have advantages selling in the United States because they pay their workers about one tenth of what U.S. firms pay their workers. In addition to this, NewPage thought it was at a disadvantage because the Chinese government was giving Chinese paper firms special tax breaks. Because of the Chinese tax breaks, the U.S. Department of Commerce imposed a 10 percent to 20 percent tariff on imports of glossy paper from China. While paper firms like NewPage applauded this action, U.S. publishing firms that use the paper products complained that the action would increase their costs and the prices of their products would rise.

Countries with a high level of net exports must also have a high level of net foreign investment. If the net foreign investment takes the form of stocks and bonds, it causes little political friction. If the net foreign investment comes in the form of purchasing foreign firms, it may cause political difficulties as occurred, for example, when Chinese firms attempted to buy U.S. oil company Unocal and U.S. appliance maker Maytag.

📖 Helpful Study Hint

Read *An Inside Look* at the end of the chapter for an article from the *Economist* about the U.S. current account deficit. In 2006, the current account deficit was $857 billion – 6.5 percent of U.S. GDP. Even though economists have argued that a country can't indefinitely sustain a large current account deficit, they believe that the United States may be the exception to that rule. Why? One explanation is that many investors in developing countries can't buy stocks and bonds issued by domestic firms because of weak property rights and court systems in those countries. Those investors invest abroad – particularly in the United States.

📖 Helpful Study Hint

Imagine that you are about to take out a bank loan to purchase a car. If a foreign country, such as South Korea, sells its holdings of U.S. Treasury bonds, would that action affect the interest rate on your car loan? *Economics in YOUR Life!* at the start of this chapter poses this question. Keep the question in mind as you read the chapter. The authors will answer the question at the end of the chapter.

17.1 The Balance of Payments: Linking the United States to the International Economy (pages 586-590)

Learning Objective 1   Explain how the balance of payments is calculated.

Most economies in the world today are open economies. An **open economy** has interactions with other economies through the trading of goods and services and financial assets. A **closed economy** has no interactions or trade with other countries. The best way to look at a country's financial interactions with other countries is to look at its balance of payments. The **balance of payments** is the record of a country's trade with other countries in goods, services and assets. The balance of payments includes three accounts: the current account, the financial account, and the capital account.

The **current account** measures current flows of funds into and out of a country. The current account includes:

- Net exports (Exports – Imports).
- Net investment income (the difference between investment income earned by U.S. residents in other countries and investment income on U.S. investments paid to residents in all other countries).
- Net transfers (the difference between transfers received by U.S. residents and transfers made to individuals in other countries by U.S. residents).

Note that these terms are defined from the perspective of the United States. We could also calculate net investment income or net transfers for France or any other country.

The **balance of trade**, which is the difference between goods exported and imported, is the largest component of the current account. If exports are greater than imports, there is a balance of trade surplus. If exports are less than imports, there is a balance of trade deficit.

📖 Helpful Study Hint

Net exports are the sum of the balance of trade and the balance of services. The balance of services is the difference between the value of a country's exports of services and the value of its imports of services.

The **financial account** records the purchases of assets a country has made abroad and foreign purchases of assets in the country. A capital outflow occurs when an individual or firm in the United States buys a financial asset issued by a foreign company or government or builds a factory in another country. A capital inflow occurs when a foreign individual or firm buys a bond issued by a U.S. firm or the U.S. government or builds a factory in the United States. The financial account is a measure of net capital flows, or the difference between capital inflows and capital outflows. **Net foreign investment** is the opposite of net capital flows and is capital outflows minus capital inflows.

The **capital account** is less important than the financial account or the current account. It measures the net flow of funds for things like migrants' transfers and the purchase and sale of nonproduced, nonfinancial assets (such as trademarks, patents, or copyrights). In the discussion that follows, we will not focus on the capital account because it is very small.

The sum of the current account, the financial account, and the capital account is the balance of payments. The balance of payments must always be zero because if the current account is negative (the typical situation for the United States), more dollars flowed out of the United States as a result of U.S. households and firms buying foreign goods and services than flowed back into the United States as a result of the United States selling goods and services to foreign households and firms. These extra dollars were either used to buy U.S. financial assets or to buy physical assets, such as office buildings or factories, in the United States, or were added to foreign dollar holdings. Changes in foreign holding of U.S. dollars are called official reserve transactions. Foreign investment in the United States and additions to foreign holdings of dollars are positive entries in the financial account. The positive entries in the financial account exactly equal the negative entries in the current account. As a result, the current account plus the financial account will sum to zero.

📖 Helpful Study Hint

Remember, we are ignoring the capital account. If the current account and the financial account do not sum to zero, as they should, there has been some form of measurement error. An entry in the balance of payments called the "statistical discrepancy" accounts for the measurement error.

Spend some time reviewing Table 17-1, "The Balance of Payments of the United States, 2006," on page 587 of the main text. The table shows the current account, financial account, and balance on capital account for the United States in 2006. The balance of payments is zero.

Read *Don't Let This Happen to YOU! Don't Confuse the Balance of Trade, the Current Account Balance, and the Balance of Payments*. Remember, the balance of trade includes the flow of goods between countries – but it does not include services.

The current account balance includes:
1. The balance of trade.
2. The balance of services.
3. Net investment income.
4. Net transfers.

The balance of payments is the sum of the current account and the financial account balances and must always equal zero. When the phrase "balance of payments surplus" or "balance of payments deficit" is used, it usually is a mistaken reference to the balance of trade, or the phrase is addressing the balance of payments without including changes in currency holdings, or official reserve transactions in the financial account.

17.2 LEARNING OBJECTIVE

17.2 The Foreign Exchange Market and Exchange Rates (pages 590-597)

Learning Objective 2 Explain how exchange rates are determined and how changes in exchange rates affect the prices of imports and exports.

The exchange rate is the price of one currency in terms of another currency. For example, the **nominal exchange rate** between the dollar and the yen (¥) can be expressed as ¥120 = $1. (This exchange rate means that the price of 1 U.S. dollar in the market for foreign exchange is 120 yen. Instead of stating the exchange rate as the number of yen per dollar, we could state it as number of dollars per yen: ¥1 = $0.0083 (which we can calculate as $1/¥120). The exchange rate is determined by the demand for and supply of dollars in the foreign exchange market. In a graph with the exchange rate plotted on the vertical axis, the demand curve for dollars is downward sloping. The demand for dollars comes from three sources:

- Consumers and firms in other countries that would like to buy goods and services made in the United States.
- Consumers and firms in other countries that would like to buy U.S. assets, such as buildings, bonds, and stocks.
- Currency traders that believe the value of the dollar will increase over time.

The supply of dollars in exchange for yen is upward sloping. When the value of the dollar is high, the demand for Japanese goods is high and U.S. households and firms supply a larger quantity of dollars in exchange for the yen necessary to buy these Japanese goods. When the value of the dollar is low, Japanese goods are expensive, so U.S. households and firms want to buy a smaller quantity of Japanese goods and consequently need a smaller quantity of yen. This results in an upward-sloping supply curve for dollars in international exchange markets.

Textbook Figure 17-2, reproduced below, shows the demand for and supply of U.S. dollars in exchange for Japanese yen.

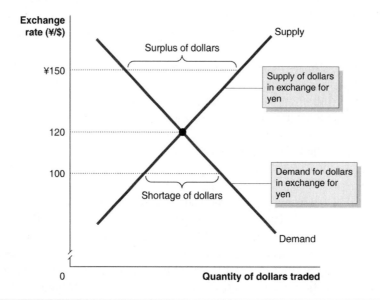

📖 Helpful Study Hint

The supply of dollars is the result of the desire of U.S. households and firms to buy Japanese goods, services, and assets. To obtain the yen necessary to buy Japanese goods, services, and assets, U.S. residents supply dollars.

As the exchange rate increases in the graph (from ¥100 = $1, to ¥120 = $1, to ¥150 = $1), U.S. goods, services, and financial assets are more expensive to households and firms in Japan. As U.S. goods become more expensive, Japanese households and firms will buy fewer U.S. goods and need fewer dollars. This explains why the demand curve for dollars is downward sloping. As the exchange rate increases, Japanese goods, services, and assets become cheaper to households and firms in the United States. As Japanese goods get cheaper, U.S. consumers and firms will want to buy more Japanese goods. To buy more, they will need more yen, and to get those yen they will supply more dollars. This explains why the supply curve for dollars is upward sloping.

📖 Helpful Study Hint

At an exchange rate of ¥150 = $1, a ¥5,000 shirt will cost $33.33.
At an exchange rate of ¥120 = $1, the same ¥5,000 shirt will cost $41.67.
At an exchange rate of ¥150 = $1, a $50 shirt will cost ¥7,500.
At an exchange rate of ¥120 = $1, the same $50 shirt will cost ¥6,000.

Equilibrium occurs where the quantity of dollars supplied equals the quantity of dollars demanded in the foreign exchange market. In the graph, equilibrium occurs at an exchange rate of ¥120 = $1. A **currency appreciates** when it rises in value compared to other currencies, and a **currency depreciates** when its value falls compared to other currencies.

The equilibrium exchange rate changes due to changes in the demand for and supply of dollars. The three main factors that cause the demand and supply curves in the foreign exchange market to shift are:

- Changes in the demand for U.S. produced goods and services and changes in the demand for foreign produced goods and services.
- Changes in foreigners' desire to buy assets in the United States and changes in U.S. residents' desire to buy assets in foreign countries.
- Changes in currency traders' expectations about the future value of the dollar and the future value of other currencies.

The demand curve for dollars will shift to the right when households and firms in Japan want to buy more U.S. goods and services or more U.S. assets. This will happen as incomes rise in Japan, or U.S. interest rates rise. The demand curve for dollars will also shift to the right when speculators decide that the value of the dollar will rise relative to the yen. The supply of dollars will shift to the right when U.S. consumers and firms want to buy more Japanese goods and services or more Japanese assets. This will happen as U.S. incomes rise, or interest rates rise in Japan, or **speculators** believe the yen will rise in value relative to the dollar.

The change in the exchange rate over time depends on changes in the supply of and demand for a currency. The following textbook Figure 17-3 shows the exchange rate increasing when the demand curve shifts out more than the supply curve.

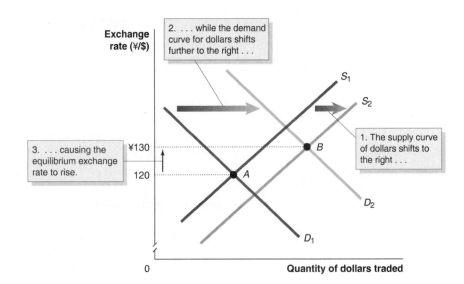

While this model works well for major currencies, such as the dollar, euro, pound and yen, not all exchange rates are determined by demand and supply. For example, the Chinese yuan-dollar exchange rate is set by the Chinese government.

Exchange rate changes will affect the quantities of exports and imports. As a country's currency appreciates, other countries' goods and services become cheaper, and its goods and services become more expensive when sold in other countries. Consequently, as a country's currency appreciates, its exports should fall and its imports should rise, causing net exports to decline. Similarly, as a country's currency depreciates, its net exports should increase.

The **real exchange rate** measures the price of domestic goods in terms of foreign goods. The relative prices between two countries' goods and services are based on two variables, the relative price levels and the nominal exchange rate. The real exchange rate is calculated as:

$$\text{Real exchange rate} = \text{Nominal exchange rate} \times \frac{\text{Domestic price level}}{\text{Foreign price level}}.$$

Changes in nominal exchange rates or changes in relative prices cause the real exchange rate to change. Real exchange rates are reported as index numbers, with one year chosen as the base year. The main value of real exchange rates is to track changes over time.

Extra Solved Problem 17-2

Chapter 17 of the textbook includes three Solved Problems. Here is an extra Solved Problem to help you build your skills solving economic problems:

Using Exchange Rates

Supports Learning Objective 2: Explain how exchange rates are determined and how changes in exchange rates affect the prices of imports and exports.

Suppose that the exchange rate between the euro and the dollar is now $1.21 = €1. How much will a $20.00 bottle of California wine cost in the euro area (ignoring transportation costs)? How much will a €30 bottle of French wine cost in the United States (ignoring transportation costs)?

SOLVING THE PROBLEM

Step 1:   Review the chapter material.
This problem is about understanding exchange rates, so you may want to review the section "The Foreign Exchange Market and Exchange Rates," which begins on page 590 of the textbook.

Step 2:   Calculate the price of the bottle of California wine in the euro area using the current exchange rate.
At the current exchange rate of $1.21 = €1, we can calculate the price using the formula:

Price in the United States = Exchange rate ($/€) x Price in the euro area.

$20.00 = $1.21/€ x Price in the euro area.

Price in the euro area = $20.00/$1.21/€ = €16.53.

Step 3:   Calculate the price of the bottle of French wine in the United States using the current exchange rate.
At the current exchange rate of $1.21 = €1, we can calculate the price using the formula:

Price in the United States = Exchange rate ($/€) x Price in the euro area.

Price in the United States = $1.21/€ x €30 = $36.30.

📖 Helpful Study Hint

Read *Making the Connection: Exchange Rates in the Financial Pages*. The business pages in most newspapers list exchange rates between the dollar and most other major currencies. The exchange rate (using the dollar – euro [€] exchange rate as an example) is usually listed both as dollars per unit of foreign currency (for example, $1.330/€) and as units of foreign currency per dollar (€0.752/$). When individuals buy foreign currency, they usually buy it from banks, which charge a fee for the transaction, so the price paid by individual currency purchasers is not what is listed in newspapers.

📖 Helpful Study Hint

Read ***Don't Let This Happen to YOU! Don't Confuse What Happens When a Currency Appreciates with What Happens When it Depreciates.*** Exchange rates can be expressed in two ways. For example, as dollars per yen or yen per dollar. If the yen per dollar number increases (from ¥100/dollar to ¥120/dollar), we say that the dollar has appreciated and the yen has depreciated. Dollars are more expensive when purchased in exchange for yen. If the dollar per yen number increases (from $0.01/yen to $0.105/yen), the dollar has depreciated and the yen has appreciated. Yen are more expensive when purchased in exchange for dollars.

17.3 LEARNING OBJECTIVE

17.3 The International Sector and National Saving and Investment (pages 597-601)

Learning Objective 3 Explain the saving and investment equation.

When a household spends more than it earns, it must sell assets – such as stocks or bonds – or borrow. The same is true for a country. When a country has an excess of imports over exports, it must sell assets or borrow. In balance of payment terms, a country's current account deficit must be offset by a financial account surplus (or net foreign investment). In equation form, this is:

Current Account Balance + Financial Account Balance = 0

or,

Current Account Balance = – Financial Account Balance

or,

Net Exports = Net Foreign Investment.

📖 Helpful Study Hint

The relationship between net exports and net foreign investment given in this equation tells us that countries such as the United States that import more than they export must borrow more from abroad than they lend abroad. If net exports are negative – as they usually are for the United States – then net foreign investment will also be negative.

In Chapter 9, we saw the following

$$\text{National Saving} = \text{Private saving} + \text{Public saving}$$

or,

$$S = S_{\text{private}} + S_{\text{public.}}$$

And, by definition:

$$S_{\text{private}} = \text{National Income} - \text{Consumption} - \text{Taxes}$$

or,

$$S_{\text{private}} = Y - C - T.$$

And,

$$S_{\text{public}} = \text{Taxes} - \text{Government Spending}$$

or,

$$S_{\text{public}} = T - G.$$

And, since $Y = C + I + G + NX$, then

$$S = I + NX.$$

Because net exports equal net foreign investment, we can now state the **saving and investment equation**:

$$\text{National Saving} = \text{Domestic Investment} + \text{Net Foreign Investment}$$

or,

$$S = I + NFI$$

or,

$$S\text{-}I = NFI.$$

📖 Helpful Study Hint

The saving and investment equation tells us that a country's saving is either invested domestically (I) or abroad (NFI).

For the United States, where NX is typically negative and NFI is typically positive, the amount of domestic investment is greater than the level of national saving. The level of investment over and above the level of national saving is financed by borrowing from abroad (which means NFI is negative).

In countries like Japan, where saving is typically greater than domestic investment, net foreign investment is positive, and has taken the form, to give one example, of building automobile factories in the United States.

17.4 The Effect of a Government Budget Deficit on Investment (pages 601-603)

Learning Objective 4 Explain the effect of a government budget deficit on investment in an open economy.

The saving and investment equation also helps us understand the role of government budget deficits. When the government runs a budget deficit ($T < G$, or $S_{\text{public}} < 0$), national saving will decline unless private saving increases by the amount of the budget deficit, which is unlikely. This decrease in national saving will lead to a decrease in domestic investment or net foreign investment. The bonds the U.S. Treasury sells to finance the deficit may increase interest rates, which will discourage domestic investment. In addition, the higher interest rates will also increase the demand for U.S. financial assets, which will increase the demand for dollars foreigners need to buy these assets. This will increase the exchange rate, which will lead to lower exports from the United States and higher imports to the United States. Net exports, and therefore net foreign investment, will fall. When a budget deficit leads to a decline in net exports, the result is sometimes referred to as the twin deficits. The experience of the United States and other countries shows, however, that a budget deficit is not always accompanied by a current account deficit as indicated by the twin deficits idea.

Extra Solved Problem 17-4

Chapter 17 of the textbook includes three Solved Problems. Here is an extra Solved Problem to help you build your skills solving economic problems:

U.S. Budget Deficits and Investment

Supports Learning Objective 4: Explain the effect of a government budget deficit on investment in an open economy.

Figure 17-5 on page 602 in the textbook shows that the United States had large federal budget deficits and large current account deficits in the early 1980s, but not in the 1990s. Federal Reserve chairman Ben Bernanke offered an explanation for these changes in the federal budget and current account.

> "...over the past decade a combination of diverse forces has created a significant increase in the global supply of saving...which helps to explain both the increase in the U.S. current account deficit and the relatively low level of long-term interest rates in the world today...All investment in new capital goods must be financed in some manner. In a closed economy...the funding for investment would be provided entirely by the country's national saving...but...virtually all economies today are open economies, and well-developed international capital markets allow savers to lend to those who wish to make capital investments in any country...In the United States, national saving...falls considerably short of U.S. capital investment...this shortfall is made up by net foreign borrowing...[one reason for] the emergence of a global saving glut...is

the strong saving motive of rich countries with aging populations…With slowly growing…workforces, as well as high capital-labor ratios, many advanced economies outside the United States also face an apparent dearth of domestic opportunities…a possibly more important source of the rise in the global supply of saving is the recent metamorphosis of the developing world from a net user to a net supplier of funds to international capital markets."

Global Account Balances
(billions of U.S. dollars)

Countries	1996	2000	2004
Industrial	$41.5	−$331.5	−$400.3
United States	−120.2	−413.4	−665.9
Japan	65.7	119.6	171.8
Euro Area	78.5	−71.7	53.0
Developing	−90.4	131.2	326.4

"The increase in the U.S. current account deficit from 1996 to 2004 was matched by a shift toward surplus of equal magnitude in other countries. Most of this swing did not occur in industrial countries as a whole, but in developing countries. A key reason for this was a series of financial crises those countries experienced in the past decade. These crises caused rapid capital outflows, currency depreciation, declines in asset prices, weakened banking systems and recession. Some of these countries built up their foreign-exchange reserves as a buffer against potential future capital outflows. These countries issued debt to their citizens and used the proceeds to buy U.S. securities and other assets…The development… of new technologies and rising productivity …with the country's long-standing advantages such as lower political risk…made the U.S. economy exceptionally attractive to international investors…capital flowed rapidly into the United States, helping to fuel large appreciations in stock prices and the value of the dollar…Thus the rapid increase in the U.S. current account deficit between 1996 and 2000 was fueled to a significant extent both by increased global saving and the greater interest on the part of foreigners in investing in the United States."

Source: Ben S. Bernanke. "The Global Savings Glut and the U.S. Current Account Deficit." The Federal Reserve Board. April 14, 2005. http://www.federalreserve.gov/boarddocs/speeches/2005/20050414/default.htm

Bernanke argues that the pattern of international capital flows he describes—the developing world lending large amounts of saving to developed countries—has some benefits but could prove counterproductive if it persists. Briefly explain why it might be better for the United States and developing countries if the pattern of capital flows Bernanke describes is eventually reversed.

SOLVING THE PROBLEM

Step 1:   Review the chapter material.
This problem is about the impact of a government budget deficit, so you may want to review the section "The Effect of a Government Budget Deficit on Investment," which begins on page 601 of the textbook.

Step 2: **Explain whether it would be better for the United States and developing countries if the pattern of capital flows Bernanke describes is eventually reversed.**

In the United States and other developed countries, workers have large quantities of capital to work with. Population is growing slowly and workforces are aging. These countries have very good reasons to save to support their future retirees. In contrast, developing countries have younger and more rapidly growing populations and offer relatively high returns to capital. Therefore, in the long run it would probably be better for developed countries to run current account surpluses and lend some of their savings to the developing world.

📖 Helpful Study Hint

Read *Making the Connection: Why is the United States Called the "World's Largest Debtor"?* Since 1982, the United States has had a current account deficit in every year except 1991. During the 1980s, the U.S. budget deficits pushed up interest rates which attracted foreign investors to U.S. bonds. These deficits increased the exchange rate, which made U.S. products more expensive to the rest of the world and made the rest of the world's goods cheaper in the United States. The result was a drop in exports and a rise in imports, producing a current account deficit. In the 1990s, when U.S. budget deficits were getting smaller and disappearing, the exchange rate remained high and current account deficits continued because foreign investors continued to purchase U.S. assets. In what is called a flight to quality, investors sold assets in other countries and purchased U.S. investments. Current account deficits imply net foreign investment is negative, or foreign investors are accumulating more U.S. assets than U.S. investors are accumulating foreign assets. At the end of 2006, foreign investors owned about $2.7 trillion more of U.S. assets, such as stocks, bonds, and factories, than U.S. investors owned of foreign assets. This is why the United States is called the "world's largest debtor." With lower U.S. savings rates, this flow of funds into the U.S. has allowed the United States to maintain the high levels of domestic investment required for economic growth.

17.5 LEARNING OBJECTIVE

17.5 Monetary Policy and Fiscal Policy in an Open Economy (pages 604-605)

Learning Objective 5 Discuss the difference between the effectiveness of monetary and fiscal policy in an open economy and in a closed economy.

In a closed economy, an expansionary monetary policy lowers interest rates, which will increase aggregate demand by increasing demand for investment goods and consumer durables. In an open economy, the lower interest rates from the expansionary monetary policy will also affect the exchange rate. Lower U.S. interest rates will increase the demand by U.S. and foreign investors for foreign assets. This will lower the demand for the dollar relative to other currencies and cause the value of the dollar to fall, which will result in an increase in U.S. net exports. We can conclude that monetary policy has a greater impact on aggregate demand in an open economy than in a closed economy.

An expansionary fiscal policy will result in higher interest rates. In an open economy, these higher interest rates will lead to an increase in the foreign exchange value of the dollar, which will reduce net exports. So, in an open economy an expansionary fiscal policy may crowd out both investment spending and net exports. We can conclude that fiscal policy has a smaller impact on aggregate demand in an open economy than in a closed economy.

Extra Solved Problem 17-5

Chapter 17 of the textbook includes three Solved Problems. Here is an extra Solved Problem to help you build your skills solving economic problems:

Monetary and Fiscal Policy in a Recession

Supports Learning Objective 5: Discuss the difference between the effectiveness of monetary and fiscal policy in an open economy and a closed economy.

Assume that the United States, an open economy, has slipped into a recession. Policymakers consider two different strategies for increasing aggregate demand. First, the Federal Reserve can use open market operations to lower the federal funds rate by one percentage point. Second, Congress and the president can pass legislation to cut income taxes.

a. If the United States were a closed economy, would the Federal Reserve have to lower the federal funds rate by more or less than one percentage point to have the same impact on aggregate demand as in an open economy? Briefly explain your answer.

b. In an open economy, as national income or GDP increases, so will spending on imports. Let's define the marginal propensity to import (MPI) as the increase in imports divided by the increase in GDP. Assume two different values for the MPI for the United States: MPI = 0.10 and MPI = 0.20. For which value of the MPI would an income tax cut have a greater impact on aggregate demand? Explain your answer.

SOLVING THE PROBLEM

Step 1:   Review the chapter material.
This problem concerns the impact of fiscal policy and monetary policy, so you may want to review the section "Monetary Policy and Fiscal Policy in an Open Economy," which begins on page 604 of the textbook.

Step 2:   Answer question (a) by explaining whether an expansionary monetary policy has a greater impact in a closed economy or in an open economy.
Because the United States has an open economy, open market operations that reduce the federal funds rate will cause some investors to switch from investing in U.S. financial assets to investing in foreign assets that have higher yields. As investors sell dollars to buy foreign currencies, the value of the dollar will fall relative to other currencies. The depreciation of the dollar will eventually cause U.S. exports to rise. If the United States was a closed economy, lowering the federal funds rate would have no effect on the exchange rate or exports. Therefore, the Federal Reserve would have to lower the federal funds rate by more than one percentage point to have the same impact on aggregate demand.

Step 3: **Answer question (b) by explaining for which value of the MPI an income tax cut would have the greater impact on aggregate demand.**

The multiplier effect of a given change in taxes or government spending would be greater in a closed economy than in an open economy. The *MPI* in a closed economy would equal zero because there would no increase in imports as GDP increases. In an open economy, the larger the value of the *MPI*, the larger the increase in imports as GDP increases, and, therefore, the larger the decline in net exports and aggregate demand. We can conclude that a given size tax cut will have a larger impact on aggregate demand when the *MPI* equals 0.10 than when the *MPI* equals 0.20, because with the smaller *MPI* there will be a smaller decrease in net exports.

📖 Helpful Study Hint

Economics in YOUR Life! at the end of the chapter answers the question posed at the start of the chapter: Suppose you are getting ready to borrow money for a new car and you hear that the Bank of Korea is going to sell a large quantity of U.S. Treasury bonds. How does this action affect your loan? The increased supply of bonds will cause their prices to fall and the interest rates on them to rise. Other interest rates in the U.S. economy, including rates on car loans, are also likely to rise. This will make your car loan (and the payments on the car you intend to buy) more expensive. Economies are interdependent, and interest rates in the United States are influenced by the actions of other countries.

Key Terms

Balance of payments. The record of a country's trade with other countries in goods, services, and assets.

Balance of trade. The difference between the value of the goods a country exports and the value of the goods a country imports.

Capital account. The part of the balance of payments that records relatively minor transactions, such as migrants' transfers, and sales and purchases of nonproduced, nonfinancial assets.

Closed economy. An economy that has no interactions in trade or finance with other economies.

Currency appreciation. Occurs when the market value of a currency rises relative to another currency.

Currency depreciation. Occurs when the market value of a currency falls relative to another currency.

Current account. The part of the balance of payments that records a country's net exports, net investment income, and net transfers.

Financial account. The part of the balance of payments that records purchases of assets a country has made abroad and foreign purchases of assets in the country.

Net foreign investment. The difference between capital outflows from a country and capital inflows, also equal to net foreign direct investment plus net foreign portfolio investment.

Nominal exchange rate. The value of one country's currency in terms of another country's currency.

Open economy. An economy that has interactions in trade or finance with other economies.

Real exchange rate. The price of domestic goods in terms of foreign goods.

Saving and investment equation. An equation showing that national saving is equal to domestic investment plus net foreign investment.

Speculators. Currency traders who buy and sell foreign exchange in an attempt to profit by changes in exchange rates.

Self-Test

(Answers are provided at the end of the Self-Test.)

Multiple-Choice Questions

1. Nearly all economies in the world are
   a. open economies.
   b. closed economies.
   c. able to trade in goods, but not services.
   d. open to trade, but closed to investment and financial interactions with other economies.

2. The balance of payments is
   a. a record of the assets and liabilities of one country relative to the assets and liabilities of other countries.
   b. a record of a country's trade with other countries in goods, services, and assets.
   c. a record of the payments made to other countries when a country engages in trade.
   d. the difference between a country's exports and its imports.

3. The part of the balance of payments that records a country's exports and imports of goods and services is
   a. the financial account.
   b. the capital account.
   c. the current account.
   d. the international account.

4. In the balance of payments, the current account records
   a. imports and exports of goods and services.
   b. income received and income paid for investments between U.S. residents and foreigners.
   c. the difference between transfers made to residents of other countries and transfers received by U.S. residents from other countries.
   d. all of the above

5. In the balance of payments, the difference between the value of the goods a country exports and the value of the goods a country imports is called
   a. the current account balance.
   b. the balance of trade.
   c. the balance of net exports.
   d. the net export position.

6. The balance of trade
   a. is equal to net exports.
   b. is equal to the difference between exports of goods and imports of goods.
   c. is always zero.
   d. can never be negative.

7. In 2006, the United States ran a _____ _____ with all of its major trading partners and with every region of the world.
   a. trade surplus
   b. trade deficit
   c. trade balance
   d. favorable surplus

8. In relation to the balance of payments, the net exports component of aggregate expenditures can be obtained by
   a. subtracting the balance of trade from the balance of services.
   b. adding together exports and imports.
   c. subtracting exports from imports.
   d. adding together the balance of trade and the balance of services.

9. From a balance of payments point of view, the net exports component of aggregate expenditures equals
   a. the current account balance.
   b. net income on investments.
   c. net transfers.
   d. none of the above

10. Purchases of assets a country has made abroad and foreign purchases of assets in the country are recorded in
    a. the current account.
    b. the financial account.
    c. the capital account.
    d. all of the above

11. In the financial account
    a. there is a capital outflow from the United States when an investor in the United States buys a foreign bond.
    b. there is a capital inflow into the United States when a U.S. firm builds a factory abroad.
    c. foreign direct investment is always equal to the government budget deficit.
    d. capital inflows and outflows are always equal.

12. When a foreign investor buys a bond issued by either a U.S. firm or the federal government, or when a foreign firm builds a factory in the United States, the transaction is recorded in the balance of payments as
    a. only a capital inflow.
    b. only a capital outflow.
    c. both a capital outflow and a capital inflow.
    d. neither a capital outflow nor a capital inflow.

13. When firms build or buy facilities in foreign countries, they are engaging in foreign _____ _____. When investors buy stocks or bonds issued in foreign countries, they are engaging in foreign _____ _____.
    a. venture capital; venture investment
    b. direct finance; indirect finance
    c. direct investment; portfolio investment
    d. capital investment; financial investment

14. Which of the following measures is closely associated with the concept of *net foreign investment*?
    a. net capital flows
    b. capital outflows and capital inflows
    c. net foreign direct investment and net foreign portfolio investment
    d. all of the above

15. Which of the following is the least important component of the balance of payments?
    a. the current account
    b. the financial account
    c. the capital account
    d. None of the above. All three components are equally important.

16. Which of the following statements about the balance of payments is correct?
    a. Foreign investment in the United States shows up as positive entry in the U.S. financial account.
    b. Additions to foreign holdings of dollars show up as positive entries in the U.S. financial account.
    c. A current account deficit must be exactly offset by a financial account surplus, leaving the balance of payments equal to zero.
    d. All of the above statements are correct.

17. Which of the following statements is correct?
    a. A country that runs a current account surplus must also run a financial account surplus.
    b. A country that runs a current account surplus must run a financial account deficit.
    c. A country that runs a current account surplus may run a financial account surplus or deficit.
    d. None of the above statements are correct.

18. The United States usually imports more goods than it exports, but it usually exports more services than it imports. As a result, the U.S. trade deficit is almost always
    a. smaller than the current account deficit.
    b. larger than the current account deficit.
    c. equal to the current account deficit.
    d. equal to zero.

19. Which of the following determines how many units of a foreign currency you can purchase with one dollar?
    a. the real exchange rate
    b. the nominal exchange rate
    c. the inflation rate
    d. the purchasing power parity of one dollar

20. Which of the following are sources of foreign demand for U.S. dollars?
    a. foreign firms and consumers who want to buy goods and services produced in the United States
    b. foreign firms and consumers who want to invest in the United States
    c. currency traders who believe that the value of the dollar in the future will be greater than its value today
    d. all of the above

21. When the exchange rate is above the equilibrium exchange rate, there is a _____ of dollars, and consequently _____ pressure on the exchange rate.
    a. surplus; upward
    b. surplus; downward
    c. shortage; upward
    d. shortage; downward

22. Currency _____ occurs when the market value of a country's currency rises relative to the value of another country's currency, while currency _____ occurs when the market value of a country's currency declines relative to value of another country's currency.
    a. appreciation; depreciation
    b. depreciation; appreciation
    c. valuation; devaluation
    d. devaluation; valuation

23. If the exchange rate changes from ¥100 = $1 to ¥120 = $1, the dollar has _____ and the yen has _____.
    a. appreciated; depreciated
    b. depreciated; appreciated
    c. revalued; devalued
    d. devalued; revalued

24. Which of the following factors cause both the demand curve and the supply curve for dollars in the foreign exchange market to shift?
    a. changes in the demand for U.S.-produced goods and services and changes in the demand for foreign produced goods and services
    b. changes in the desire to invest in the United States and changes in the desire to invest in foreign countries
    c. changes in the expectations of currency traders concerning the likely future value of the dollar and the likely future value of foreign currencies
    d. all of the above

25. Currency traders who buy and sell foreign exchange in an attempt to profit from changes in exchange rates are
    a. hedgers.
    b. speculators.
    c. arbitrageurs.
    d. risk takers.

26. When will the demand curve for dollars shift to the right?
    a. when incomes in Japan fall
    b. when interest rates in the United States fall
    c. when speculators decide that the value of the dollar will rise relative to the value of the yen
    d. all of the above

27. An increase in interest rates in Japan will
    a. leave the supply curve of dollars unchanged.
    b. shift the supply curve of dollars to the right.
    c. shift the supply curve of dollars to the left.
    d. shift the demand curve for dollars to the right.

28. A recession in the United States will
    a. leave the supply curve of dollars unchanged.
    b. shift the supply curve of dollars to the right.
    c. shift the supply curve of dollars to the left.
    d. shift the demand curve for dollars to the right.

29. In the foreign exchange market for dollars, which of the following will cause the equilibrium exchange rate to rise?
    a. an increase in supply that is greater than an increase in demand
    b. a decrease in demand that is greater than an increase in supply
    c. a decrease in supply that is greater than a decrease in demand
    d. a decrease in demand accompanied by an increase in supply

30. A depreciation in the domestic currency will
    a. increase exports and decrease imports, thereby increasing net exports.
    b. increase exports and imports, thereby increasing net exports.
    c. decrease exports and increase imports, thereby decreasing net exports.
    d. decrease exports and imports, thereby decreasing net exports.

31. Which two factors do economists combine to establish the real exchange rate between two countries?
    a. the balance of payments and whether or not the currency of either country faces a shortage or surplus in the foreign exchange market
    b. the money supply in each country and the fixed exchange rate between the two countries
    c. the relative price levels and the nominal exchange rate between the two countries' currencies
    d. net exports and whether there is currency appreciation or depreciation between the two countries

32. If the exchange rate between the U.S. dollar and the yen is $1 = ¥100, the price level in the United States is 110 and the price level in Japan is 100, what is the real exchange rate?
    a. 90.90
    b. 110
    c. 121
    d. 1.10

33. If the dollar price of a euro is $1.45, then the euro price of a dollar is
    a. €1.45.
    b. €1.00.
    c. €0.69.
    d. €0.45.

34. In which of the following situations does a country experience a net capital inflow and a financial account surplus?
    a. when the country sells more assets to foreigners than it buys from foreigners
    b. when the country borrows more from foreigners than it lends to foreigners
    c. when the country runs a current account deficit
    d. all of the above

35. Which of the following statements is correct?
    a. Net exports is roughly equal to the current account balance.
    b. The financial account balance is roughly equal to net capital flows.
    c. Net capital flows are roughly equal to net foreign investment, but with the opposite sign.
    d. all of the above

36. When imports are greater than exports, as is usually the case for the United States, which of the following must be true?
    a. There will be a net capital inflow as people in the United States sell assets and borrow to pay for the surplus of imports over exports.
    b. The United States must be a net borrower from abroad.
    c. U.S. net foreign investment must be negative.
    d. all of the above

37. An increase in income in both the United States and the United Kingdom income will
    a. increase both the demand and supply for pounds and cause the dollar to appreciate.
    b. increase the demand for pounds and cause the dollar to appreciate.
    c. increase the supply of pounds and cause the dollar to appreciate.
    d. increase the supply and demand for pounds and have an uncertain effect on the exchange rate.

38. Which of the following is the saving-investment equation?
    a. Private Saving = National Income – Consumption – Taxes
    b. National Saving = Domestic Investment + Net Foreign Investment
    c. Public Saving = Taxes – Government Spending
    d. Domestic Investment = Private Saving + Public Saving

39. The savings and investment equation shows that
    a. the government budget's must always be balanced.
    b. $S = I$ at all times.
    c. $S = I + NFI$.
    d. net exports are always positive.

40. Given the definition of net foreign investment, a country such as the United States that has negative net foreign investment must be
    a. investing less than it is saving domestically.
    b. saving less than it is investing domestically.
    c. experiencing positive net exports.
    d. a net lender, not a borrower.

41. Budget deficits may reduce
    a. domestic investment but not net foreign investment.
    b. net foreign investment but not domestic investment.
    c. both domestic investment and net foreign investment.
    d. neither domestic investment nor net foreign investment.

42. A country experiences twin deficits when a government budget deficit causes
    a. a capital account deficit.
    b. a service exports deficit.
    c. a current account deficit.
    d. a financial account deficit.

43. What impact does the additional policy channel available in an open economy have?
    a. It increases the ability of an expansionary monetary policy to affect aggregate demand.
    b. It decreases the ability of an expansionary monetary policy to affect aggregate demand.
    c. It does not have any impact on the ability of an expansionary monetary policy to affect aggregate demand.
    d. It has an indeterminate effect, sometimes increasing and sometimes decreasing the ability of an expansionary monetary policy to affect aggregate demand.

44. In an open economy, an expansionary fiscal policy may be _____ effective because the crowding out effect could be _____.
    a. more; larger
    b. more; smaller
    c. less; larger
    d. less; smaller

45. In an open economy, a contractionary fiscal policy will have a _____ impact on aggregate demand, and therefore will be _____ effective in slowing down an economy.
    a. larger; more
    b. larger; less
    c. smaller; more
    d. smaller; less

Short Answer Questions

1. Explain why a current account surplus implies a financial account deficit.

_____

_____

_____

_____

_____

2. Suppose that the exchange rate between the dollar and the British pound is £0.58 = $1, or $1.72 = £1. In dollars, what will be the price of a £40 West End London theater ticket? How much will a $60 Broadway play ticket cost in pounds?

_____

_____

_____

3. Suppose that real GDP is rising in both the United States and Japan. Using a graph showing the demand for and supply of dollars in the foreign exchange market, predict what will happen to the exchange rate.

_____

_____

_____

_____

_____

4. Suppose that the government runs a budget deficit. Under what circumstances will this lead to a current account deficit?

_____

_____

_____

_____

_____

5. Why is the ability of monetary and fiscal policy to influence aggregate demand different in an open economy than in a closed economy?

_____

_____

_____

_____

_____

6. Suppose *The Appeal* by John Grisham has a price of $19.97 at a U.S. bookstore, and *Harry Potter and the Deathly Hallows* by J. K. Rowling has a price of £9.95 at a U.K. bookstore. If the exchange rate is $2.08 = £1, then what will be the price of *Harry Potter* in the United States (ignoring transportation charges) and what will be the price of *The Appeal* in the United Kingdom (ignoring transportation costs)?

_____

_____

_____

True/False Questions

T F   1. If a country's exports of goods exceed its imports of goods, there will be a balance of trade surplus.

T F   2. Net investment income measures the difference between income received by U.S. residents from investments abroad and income paid on investments in the United States to residents of other countries.

T F   3. The purchase of a bond issued by a German corporation by a U.S. resident represents a capital inflow.

T F   4. Net capital flows is the same as net foreign investment.

T F   5. The balance of payments will have the same value as the balance of trade.

T F   6. Suppose the dollar/euro exchange rate is $1.18 = €1.00. The price of a dollar, in terms of euros, is €0.95 = $1.00.

T F   7. If the price of a euro increases from $1.18 to $1.20, then the dollar has appreciated.

T F   8. An increase in the U.S. interest rate will increase the demand for dollars in the foreign exchange market and shift the demand for dollars to the right.

T F   9. An increase in the supply of dollars lowers the exchange rate and causes the value of the dollar to appreciate.

T F 10. As the dollar appreciates, net exports will rise, increasing aggregate demand.

T F 11. Public saving is always positive.

T F 12. If domestic investment is larger than national saving, then net foreign investment must be positive.

T F 13. An increase in the federal budget deficit always causes an increase in the current account deficit.

T F 14. An expansionary monetary policy will tend to cause the domestic currency to depreciate.

T F 15. Fiscal policy will cause smaller changes in aggregate demand in an open economy than in a closed economy.

Answers to the Self-Test

Multiple-Choice Questions

Question	Answer	Comment
1	a	Nearly all economies are open economies and have extensive interactions in trade or finance with other countries.
2	b	The best way to understand the interactions between one economy and other economies is through the balance of payments. The balance of payments provides a record of a country's trade with other countries in goods, services, and assets.
3	c	The current account records a country's exports and imports of goods and services. The current account represents current, or short-term, flows of funds into and out of a country.
4	d	The current account for the United States includes imports and exports of goods and services, income received by U.S. residents from investments in other countries, income paid on investments in the United States owned by residents of other countries, and the difference between transfers made to residents of other countries and transfers received by U.S. residents from other countries.
5	b	The difference between the value of the goods a country exports and the value of the goods a country imports is called the balance of trade.
6	b	The balance of trade is defined as exports of goods minus imports of goods.
7	b	As Figure 17-1 shows, in 2006, the United States ran a trade deficit with all of its major trading partners and with every region of the world.
8	d	Net exports is a component of aggregate expenditures. Net exports can be calculated by adding together the balance of trade and the balance of services.
9	d	Net exports is a component of aggregate expenditures. Net exports can be calculated by adding together the balance of trade and the balance of services. Technically, net exports is not equal to the current account balance, because the current account balance also includes net income on investments and net transfers.
10	b	The financial account records purchases of assets a country has made abroad and foreign purchases of assets in the country. The financial account records long-term flows of funds into and out of a country.
11	a	When a U.S. investor buys a foreign bond, dollars flow out of the United States to the other country. This is a capital outflow.
12	a	When an investor in the United States buys a bond issued by a foreign company or government, or when a U.S. firm builds a factory in another country, there is a *capital outflow* from the United States. There is a *capital inflow* into the United States when a foreign investor buys a bond issued by a U.S. firm or by the federal government or when a foreign firm builds a factory in the United States.
13	c	When firms build or buy facilities in foreign countries, they are engaging in foreign direct investment. When investors buy stocks or bonds issued in another country, they are engaging in foreign portfolio investment.

14   d   A closely related concept to net capital flows is net foreign investment, which is equal to capital outflows minus capital inflows. Net foreign investment is the difference between capital outflows from a country and capital inflows, and also equal to net foreign direct investment plus net foreign portfolio investment. Net capital flows and net foreign investment are always equal, but have opposite signs: When net capital flows are positive, net foreign investment is negative, and when net capital flows are negative, net foreign investment is positive.

15   c   A less important part of the balance of payments is called the capital account. The capital account records relatively minor transactions such as migrants' transfers and sales and purchases of nonproduced, nonfinancial assets.

16   d   Changes in foreign holdings of dollars are known as official reserve transactions. Foreign investment in the United States or additions to foreign holdings of dollars both show up as positive entries in the U.S. financial account. Therefore, a current account deficit must be exactly offset by a financial account surplus, leaving the balance of payments equal to zero. Similarly, a country such as China or Japan, that runs a current account surplus, must run a financial account deficit of exactly the same size.

17   b   It is impossible to run a current surplus *and* a financial account surplus simultaneously. A country that runs a current account surplus *must* run a financial account deficit, and vice versa.

18   b   The balance of trade includes only trade in goods; it does not include services. This observation is important because the United States usually imports more goods than it exports, but it usually exports more services than it imports. As a result, the U.S. trade deficit is almost always larger than the current account deficit. The current account balance includes the balance of trade, the balance of services, net income on investments, and net transfers. Net income on investments and net transfers are much smaller than the balance of trade and the balance on services.

19   b   The nominal exchange rate determines how many units of a foreign currency you can purchase with one dollar.

20   d   There are three sources of foreign currency demand for the U.S. dollar: 1) Foreign firms and consumers who want to buy goods and services produced in the United States; 2) Foreign firms and consumers who want to invest in the United States either through foreign direct investment—buying or building factories or other facilities in the United States—or through foreign portfolio investment—buying stocks and bonds issued in the United States; and, 3) Currency traders who believe that the value of the dollar in the future will be greater than its value today.

21   b   As Figure 17-2 shows, at exchange rates above the equilibrium exchange rate, there will be a surplus of dollars and downward pressure on the exchange rate. The surplus and the downward pressure will not be eliminated until the exchange rate falls to equilibrium.

22   a   Currency appreciation occurs when the market value of a country's currency rises relative to the value of another country's currency. Currency depreciation occurs when the market value of a country's currency declines relative to the value of another country's currency.

23   a   When a currency appreciates, it increases in value relative to another currency. When it depreciates, it decreases in value relative to another currency. More precisely, currency A appreciates relative to currency B if, after a change in the exchange rate, one unit of currency A will buy more units of currency B. Currency X depreciates relative to currency Y if, after a change in the exchange rate, one unit of currency X will buy fewer units of currency X. If the exchange rate changes from ¥100 = $1 to ¥120 = $1, the dollar has appreciated and the yen has depreciated, because it now takes more yen to buy one dollar.

24   d   The supply and demand curves for dollars in the foreign exchange market shift with changes in the demand for U.S.-produced goods and services and changes in the demand for foreign-produced goods and services, changes in the desire to invest in the United States and changes in the desire to invest in foreign countries, and changes in the expectations of currency traders concerning the likely future value of the dollar and the likely future value of foreign currencies.

25   b   Speculators buy and sell foreign exchange in an attempt to profit from changes in exchange rates. If a speculator becomes convinced that the value of the dollar is going to rise in the future relative to the value of the yen, the speculator will sell yen and buy dollars now. A speculator is anyone who buys or sells a good today because they expect the price to change in the future.

26   c   When incomes in Japan rise, when interest rates in the United States rise, or when speculators decide that the value of the dollar will rise relative to the value of the yen, the demand curve for dollars shifts to the right.

27   b   An increase in interest rates in Japan will make financial instruments in Japan more attractive to U.S. savers. This will cause the supply of dollars to shift to the right, as U.S. savers use their dollars to purchase yen.

28   c   A recession in the United States will decrease the demand for Japanese products and cause the supply curve for dollars to shift to the left. Similarly, a decrease in interest rates in Japan will make financial instruments in Japan less attractive and cause the supply curve of dollars to shift to the left. And if traders become convinced that the future value of the yen will be lower relative to the dollar, the supply curve will also shift to the left.

29   c   A decrease in the supply of dollars will increase the equilibrium exchange rate, holding other factors constant. A decrease in the demand for dollars will decrease the equilibrium exchange rate, holding other factors constant. In this case, the demand curve and the supply curve have both shifted, but because the supply curve has shifted to the left by more than the demand curve, the equilibrium exchange rate will increase.

30   a   Depreciation in the domestic currency will increase exports and decrease imports, thereby increasing net exports. An appreciation in the domestic currency should have the opposite effect: Exports should fall and imports should rise, which will reduce net exports, aggregate demand, and real GDP.

31   c   An important factor in determining the level of a country's exports to and imports from another country is the relative prices of each country's goods. The relative prices of two countries' goods are determined by two factors: the relative price levels in the two countries and the nominal exchange rate between the two countries' currencies. Economists combine these two factors in the real exchange rate.

32	b	The real exchange rate is computed as follows: real exchange rate = nominal exchange rate x (domestic price level/foreign price level). In this case, 100 x (110/100) = 100 x 1.1 = 110. This means that the prices of U.S. goods and services are 10 percent higher relative to the prices of Japanese goods and services.
33	c	1/$1.45/€ = €0.69/$.
34	d	When a country sells more assets to foreigners than it buys from foreigners, or borrows more from foreigners than it lends to foreigners – as it must if it is running a current account deficit – the country experiences a net capital inflow and a financial account surplus.
35	d	Net exports are roughly equal to the current account balance. Also, the financial account balance is roughly equal to net capital flows, which are in turn equal to net foreign investment, but with the opposite sign.
36	d	When imports are greater than exports, net exports are negative and there will be a net capital inflow as people in the United States sell assets and borrow to pay for the surplus of imports over exports. Therefore, net capital flows will be equal to net exports (but with the opposite sign), and net foreign investment will also be equal to net exports (and with the same sign). Because net exports are usually negative for the United States, in most years, the United States must be a net borrower from abroad and U.S. net foreign investment will be negative.
37	d	The increase in income will increase purchases in the other country, increasing the demand for that country's currency. This will increase both the supply and demand for pounds. Because both curves are shifting to the right, and because we do not know the size of each shift, the impact on the exchange rate is uncertain.
38	b	National Saving = Private Saving + Public Saving, and net exports equal net foreign investment. From these equalities we deduct the saving-investment equation, which can be written as: National Saving = Domestic Investment + Net Foreign Investment. The saving and investment equation tells us that a country's saving will be invested either domestically or overseas.
39	c	By definition, $S = I + NFI$. This is true by definition.
40	b	A country such as the United States, that has negative net foreign investment, must be saving less than it is investing domestically. To see this, rewrite the saving and investment equation by moving domestic investment to the left-hand side: $S - I = NFI$. If net foreign investment is negative – as it is for the United States nearly every year – domestic investment (I) must be greater than national saving (S).
41	c	Higher interest rates will discourage some businesses from borrowing funds to build new factories or to buy new equipment or computers. Also, higher interest rates on financial assets in the United States will attract foreign investors. Investors in Great Britain, Canada, or Japan will have to buy U.S. dollars in order to purchase bonds in the United States. This greater demand for dollars will increase their value relative to foreign currencies. As the value of the dollar rises, exports from the United States will fall and imports to the United States will rise. Net exports and, therefore, net foreign investment will fall.

42	c	When a government budget deficit leads to a decline in net exports, the result is sometimes referred to as the *twin deficits*. The twin deficits refers to the possibility that a government budget deficit will also lead to a current account deficit. The twin deficits first became widely discussed in the United States during the early 1980s when the federal government ran a large budget deficit that resulted in high interest rates, a high exchange value of the dollar, and a large current account deficit.
43	a	In a closed economy, the main effect of lower interest rates is on domestic investment spending and purchases of consumer durables. In an open economy, lower interest rates will also affect the exchange rate between the dollar and other economies. Lower interest rates will cause some investors in the United States and abroad to switch from investing in U.S. financial assets to investing in foreign financial assets. This switch will lower the demand for the dollar relative to foreign currencies and cause its value to decline. A lower exchange rate will decrease the price of U.S. products in foreign markets and increase the price of foreign products in the United States. As a result, net exports will increase. This additional policy channel will increase the ability of an expansionary monetary policy to affect aggregate demand.
44	c	An expansionary fiscal policy may result in higher interest rates. In a closed economy, the main effect of higher interest rates is to reduce domestic investment spending and purchases of consumer durables. In an open economy, higher interest rates will also lead to an increase in the foreign exchange value of the dollar and a decrease in net exports. Therefore, in an open economy, an expansionary fiscal policy may be less effective because the crowding out effect may be larger. In a closed economy, only consumption and investment are crowded out by an expansionary fiscal policy. In an open economy, net exports may also be crowded out.
45	d	A contractionary fiscal policy cuts government spending or raises taxes to reduce household disposable income and consumption spending. But a contractionary fiscal policy also reduces the federal budget deficit (or increases the budget surplus), which may lower interest rates. Lower interest rates will increase domestic investment and purchases of consumer durables, thereby offsetting some of the reduction in government spending and increases in taxes. In an open economy, lower interest rates will also reduce the foreign exchange value of the dollar and increase net exports. Therefore, in an open economy, a contractionary fiscal policy will have a smaller impact on aggregate demand, and therefore will be less effective in slowing down an economy. In summary: Fiscal policy has a smaller impact on aggregate demand in an open economy than in a closed economy.

Short Answer Responses

1. When the current account is positive (net exports are positive), a country is selling more goods abroad than it is buying from abroad. This means that more of other currencies are coming into the country from the sale of goods than are leaving the country from the purchase of goods. These foreign currencies are used either to purchase financial assets or physical assets in the other country (these transactions are not part of net exports) or held as additional units of foreign currency. Both of those options are considered capital outflows and are negative entries in the balance of payments. The financial account balance should then be the same size as the current account balance but with the opposite sign.

2. The West End London theater ticket that costs £40 will cost $68.80 (£40 x $1.72/£ = $68.80). The Broadway theater ticket that costs $60.00 will cost £34.80 ($60.00 x £.058/$ = £34.80). Note that 1/1.72 = 0.58.

3. An increase in U.S. real GDP will increase spending in the United States. Consumers and firms in the United States will buy more U.S. goods and also more Japanese goods. As U.S. consumers and firms buy more Japanese goods, they must buy more yen, which implies that they must supply more dollars in the foreign exchange market. Rising U.S. real GDP will increase the supply of dollars. This is shown in the graph below:

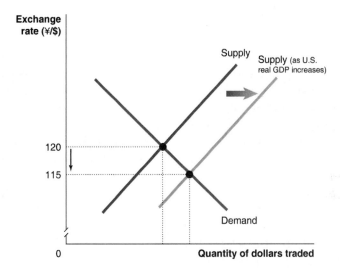

An increase in Japanese real GDP will increase spending in Japan. Consumers and firms in Japan will buy more Japanese goods and also more U.S. goods. As Japanese consumers and firms buy more U.S. goods, they must buy more dollars, which implies an increase in the demand for dollars in the foreign exchange market. Rising Japanese real GDP will increase the demand for dollars. This is shown in the graph below:

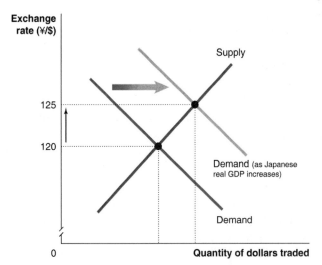

The increase in U.S. real GDP increases the supply of dollars. This lowers the (¥/$) exchange rate and causes the value of the dollar to depreciate. The increase in Japanese real GDP increases the demand for dollars. This increases the (¥/$) exchange rate and causes the value of the dollar to appreciate. If both of these events happen at the same time, then the impact on the exchange rate is uncertain. It is not possible to tell if the size of the increase in demand will be larger, smaller, or the same size as the size of the increase in supply.

4. According to the saving and investment equation,

$$S = S_{\text{private}} + S_{\text{public}} = I + NFI.$$

A budget deficit enters the equation as a negative value for S_{public}, and because the current account balance = – financial account balance or net current account balance = net foreign investment, an increase in the budget deficit (S_{public} falls) will lower NFI or the current account if domestic saving does not increase or domestic investment does not fall. Therefore, we can conclude that a budget deficit may lead to a current account deficit but there is no guarantee that it will do so.

5. Because monetary and fiscal policy affect the interest rate, these policies also affect the exchange rate in an open economy. Expansionary monetary policy tends to lower the interest rate; in an open economy the lower U.S. interest rate makes foreign financial assets more attractive (and U.S. financial assets less attractive to investors outside the United States). This will result in an increase in the supply of dollars and a decrease in the demand for dollars in the foreign exchange market. This will cause the dollar to depreciate. The lower value of the dollar will increase exports and lower imports. This will increase net exports and provide additional increases in aggregate demand compared with the effects of monetary policy in a closed economy. The expansionary fiscal policy will lead to a higher interest rate. In an open economy, the higher interest rate will make U.S. financial assets more attractive to consumers and firms outside the United States (and make foreign assets less attractive to U.S. investors). This will increase the demand for dollars and reduce the supply of dollars in the foreign exchange market. This will cause the dollar to appreciate. The higher value of the dollar will cause exports to decrease and imports to increase. This will reduce net exports and reduce the level of aggregate demand (this is an added form of crowding out) compared with the effects of fiscal policy in a closed economy.

6. With the exchange rate of $2.08 = £1, *Harry Potter* will have a price in the United States of $20.70 (£9.95 x $2.08/£ = $20.70). *The Appeal* will have a price of £9.60 (=$19.97/$2.08/£) in the United Kingdom.

True/False Answers

1. T
2. T
3. F   The purchase of a bond of a corporation or government of another country by a U.S. resident represents a capital outflow.
4. F   Net capital flows and net foreign investment (NFI) are equal but of opposite signs (if one is positive, the other is negative).
5. F   The balance of payments is the sum of the current account balance (the sum of the balance of trade and balance of services), the financial account balance, and the capital account balance. The balance of trade can be positive, negative, or zero. The balance of payments will always be zero.
6. F   The price of a dollar, in terms of the euro, will be €0.85 = $1.00 (0.85 = 1/1.18).
7. F   If the price of a euro increases from $1.18 to $1.20, then the euro has gotten more expensive to U.S. citizens, or the dollar has fallen in value. So, the dollar has depreciated.
8. T
9. F   An increase in the supply of dollars will lower the exchange rate and cause the value of the dollar to depreciate.

10. F   As the dollar appreciates, net exports will fall, which will cause a reduction in the level of aggregate demand.
11. F   Public saving is equal to taxes minus government purchases. Public saving will be positive if there is a budget surplus, and negative if there is a budget deficit.
12. F   Because $S = I + NFI$, if $I > S$, then NFI must be negative.
13. F   An increase in the federal budget deficit will increase the current account deficit only if private saving and domestic investment do not change.
14. T
15. T

The International Financial System

Chapter Summary

When countries agree on how exchange rates should be determined, economists say that there is an **exchange rate system**. A **floating currency** is the outcome of a country allowing its currency's exchange rate to be determined by demand and supply. The current exchange rate system is a **managed float exchange rate system** under which the value of most currencies is determined by demand and supply, with occasional government intervention. A **fixed exchange rate system** is a system under which countries agree to keep the exchange rates among their currencies fixed.

The theory of **purchasing power parity** states that in the long run, exchange rates move to equalize the purchasing power of different currencies. This theory helps to explain some of the long-run movements in the value of the U.S. dollar relative to other currencies. Purchasing power parity does not provide a complete explanation of movements in exchange rates for several reasons, including the existence of **tariffs,** taxes imposed by a government on imports, and **quotas,** government-imposed limits on the quantity of a good that can be imported. When a country keeps its currency's exchange rate fixed against another country's currency, it is **pegging** its currency.

Learning Objectives

When you finish this chapter, you should be able to:

1. **Understand how different exchange rate systems operate.** When countries agree on how exchange rates should be determined, economists say that there is an **exchange rate system**. A currency floats when its exchange rate is determined by demand and supply. The current exchange rate system is a **managed float exchange rate system** under which the value of most currencies is determined by demand and supply, with occasional government intervention. A **fixed exchange rate system** is a system under which countries agree to keep the exchange rates among their currencies fixed. Under the gold standard, the exchange rate between two currencies was automatically determined by the quantity of gold in each currency. By the end of the Great Depression of the 1930s, every country had abandoned the gold standard. Under the Bretton Woods System, which was in place between 1944 and the early 1970s, the United States agreed to exchange dollars for gold at a price of $35 per ounce. The central banks of all other members of the system pledged to buy and sell their currencies at a fixed rate against the dollar.

2. **Discuss the three key features of the current exchange rate system.** The three key aspects of the current exchange rate system are:

   a. The U.S. dollar floats against other major currencies.
   b. Most countries in Western Europe have adopted the euro as their common currency.
   c. Some developing countries have fixed their currency's exchange rate against the dollar or against another major currency.

Since 1973, the value of the U.S. dollar has fluctuated widely against other major currencies. The theory of **purchasing power parity** states that, in the long run, exchange rates move to equalize the purchasing power of different currencies. This theory helps to explain some of the long-run movements in the value of the U.S. dollar relative to other currencies. Currently 13 countries of the European Union use a common currency, known as the **euro**. The experience of the countries using the euro will provide economists with information on the costs and benefits to countries from using the same currency. When a country keeps its currency's exchange rate fixed against another country's currency, it is pegging its currency. Pegging can result in problems similar to the problems countries encountered with fixed exchange rates under the Bretton Woods system. If investors become convinced that a country pegging its exchange rate will eventually allow the exchange rate to decline to a lower level, the demand curve for the currency will shift to the left, which makes it more difficult for the country's central bank to maintain the pegged exchange rate. The tendency for investors to sell a currency whose value they expect to decline is referred to as destabilizing speculation.

3. **Discuss the growth of international capital markets.** A key reason that exchange rates fluctuate is that investors seek out the best investments they can find anywhere in the world. Since 1980, the markets for stocks and bonds have become global. Foreign purchases of U.S. corporate bonds and stocks and U.S. government bonds have increased greatly just in the period since 1995. As a result, firms around the world are no longer forced to rely on only the savings of domestic households for funds.

Appendix: Explain the gold standard and the Bretton Woods System. While the chapter covers the current exchange rate system, the appendix covers two earlier systems: the gold standard and the Bretton Woods system. Together, these systems lasted from the early nineteenth century through the early 1970s. Your instructor may assign this appendix.

Chapter Review

Chapter Opener: Molson Coors Deals with Fluctuating Exchange Rates (pages 614-615)

Molson Coors Brewing Company faces exchange rate risk. The company sells beer in many different international markets. The company must convert revenues earned in Canada, the United Kingdom, and the United States back into U.S. dollars, the home currency. Changes in the exchange rate make the value of these conversions uncertain. Before its merger with Coors, Molson Breweries purchased the Montreal Canadiens hockey team in 1957. In 2001, Molson decided to sell the team, partly because of exchange rate problems. Molson was required to pay salaries and other operating expenses in U.S. dollars. Most of the team's revenues were from sales of tickets and radio and TV broadcasting, which were received in Canadian dollars. During the 1990's, as the Canadian dollar fell in value against the U.S. dollar, the team's costs rose more than its revenues.

📖 Helpful Study Hint

Read *An Inside Look* at the end of the chapter for a news article from the *Wall Street Journal* that explains government-imposed capital controls in Asia that restrict foreign investors' ability to speculate in these countries' currencies. Most investors believe that capital controls are bad for the international system because, they contend, markets allocate capital more efficiently than do governments.

Would you like to spend part of your career working overseas? Imagine that you accept a job in Spain and plan to work and live there for 10 years. Also imagine that the average productivity of Spanish firms is expected to grow faster than that of U.S. firms. What will your accumulated savings in euros be worth in U.S. dollars ten years from now? The *Economics in YOUR Life!* at the start of this chapter poses this question. Keep the question in mind as you read the chapter. The authors will answer the question at the end of the chapter.

18.1 LEARNING OBJECTIVE

18.1 Exchange Rate Systems (pages 616-617)

Learning Objective 1 Understand how different exchange rate systems operate.

An **exchange rate system** is the method that countries use to determine the exchange rates among their currencies. Some countries use a **floating currency system**, where the exchange rate is determined by the demand and supply of the currency in foreign exchange markets. Other countries, including the United States, occasionally intervene to buy and sell their currencies or other currencies to affect exchange rates. This is called a **managed float exchange rate system**. Until 1971, exchange rates were determined by a **fixed exchange rate system**, where the exchange rates remained constant for long periods of time. The gold standard was a fixed exchange rate system that lasted from the nineteenth century until the 1930s. The Bretton Woods system was also a fixed exchange rate system and lasted from 1944 to 1971.

Extra Solved Problem 18-1

Chapter 18 of the textbook includes two Solved Problems. Here is an extra Solved Problem to help you build your skills solving economic problems:

A Tale of Two Currencies

Supports Learning Objective 1: Understand how different exchange rate systems operate.

From 1994 to July 2005, China maintained a fixed exchange rate between its currency – called the renminbi (which means "people's currency" in Chinese) or yuan – and the U.S. dollar. The exchange rate was 8.28 yuan per dollar. Pegging the yuan to the dollar reduced the risk of losses from changes in the exchange rate for anyone doing business in China. Assume that Apple, a firm with headquarters in the United States, establishes a manufacturing plant in Beijing. If Apple earns a profit of 1 million yuan in June 2005 this is equivalent to $120,773. If the exchange rate had changed to 10 yuan per dollar, Apple's profit would only equal $100,000. Unlike China, Canada has a floating exchange rate. A floating exchange rate increases the risk faced by those engaging in international trade and investment. The *Making the Connection* on page 618 of the textbook provides an example of the impact of exchange rate fluctuations on the owners of the Toronto Blue Jays, whose revenue is primarily in Canadian dollars but whose player salaries and some other expenses are paid in U.S. dollars. A fixed exchange rate creates other problems when the exchange rate differs greatly from the fundamental value of the currency. One way to measure the fundamental value of a currency is by computing its purchasing power parity. In the long run, floating exchange rates should adjust to reflect equivalent purchasing power. (Other factors can keep purchasing power parity from completely explaining exchange rates. See the section "What Determines Exchange Rates in the Long Run?" beginning on page 619 of the textbook). The World Bank compared the actual exchange rates of China and Canada to their purchasing power parity (PPP) conversion factors (the number of units of a country's currency required to buy the same amount of goods and services in the domestic market as a U.S. dollar would buy in the United States) for 2003.

	Actual Exchange Rate	PPP Exchange Rate
China	8.28	1.8
Canada	1.4	1.2

Source: 2005 World Development Indicators. Table 5.7, Relative Prices and Exchange Rates.
http://devdata.worldbank.org/wdi2005/Table5_7.htm

Critics of the Chinese exchange rate policy, including U.S. government officials, claimed that the yuan was undervalued. Assume that the purchasing power parity exchange rate accurately measures the relative purchasing power of the dollar and yuan in 2003.

a. Explain how the undervalued yuan affected trade between the United States and China.

b. Based on its purchasing power parity, was the Canadian dollar overvalued or undervalued relative to the U.S. dollar in 2003?

c. On July 21, 2005 the Chinese government changed the exchange rate between the yuan and the dollar to a new fixed rate of 8.11 yuan to the dollar. Did this action cause the yuan to appreciate or depreciate relative to the U.S. dollar?

SOLVING THE PROBLEM

Step 1:   Review the chapter material.
This problem concerns foreign exchange rates, so you may want to review the section "Exchange Rate Systems," which begins on page 616 of the textbook.

Step 2:   Answer question (a) by explaining how the undervalued yuan affected trade between the United States and China.
If the purchasing power parity exchange rate is accurate, it implies that $100 had the same purchasing power as 180 yuan in 2003. But if someone had exchanged dollars at the fixed exchange rate, she would have received 828 yuan (ignoring transactions costs). If similar goods could be purchased in both countries, it would be much cheaper to buy them in China – by first exchanging dollars for yuan – than it would be to buy them in the United States. The overvalued yuan resulted in greater U.S. imports from China and a lower level of U.S. exports to China than if the exchange rate equaled the purchasing power parity exchange rate.

Step 3:   **Answer question (b) by explaining whether, based on its purchasing power parity, the Canadian dollar was overvalued or undervalued relative to the U.S. dollar in 2003.**

The actual exchange rate was 1.4. This means that 100 U.S. dollars would buy 140 Canadian dollars. Because the purchasing power parity exchange rate was 1.2, 100 U.S. dollars should have exchanged for only 120 Canadian dollars. So, the U.S. dollar was overvalued or the Canadian dollar was undervalued. But remember that the purchasing power parity is only an approximation of the fundamental value of the Canadian and U.S. dollars.

Step 4:   **Answer question (c) by explaining whether the yuan appreciated or depreciated relative to the U.S. dollar when on July 21, 2005 the Chinese government changed the fixed exchange rate to 8.11 yuan per dollar.**

Because fewer yuan were required to buy one dollar, the dollar depreciated as the exchange rate fell. This meant that the yuan appreciated or increased in value relative to the dollar. Some U.S. government officials expressed their preference for an even larger appreciation.

📖 Helpful Study Hint

Read *Don't Let this Happen to YOU! Remember that Modern Currencies are Fiat Money.* Even though the United States owns a large amount of gold, held in Fort Knox, Kentucky and the basement of the Federal Reserve Bank of New York, this gold does not back U.S. currency. The U.S. dollar is an example of fiat money that does not have to be exchanged by the central bank for gold or some other commodity money. U.S. currency is money mainly because the government says it is money and people are willing to accept it in exchange for goods and services.

18.2 LEARNING OBJECTIVE

18.2 The Current Exchange Rate System (pages 617-631)

Learning Objective 2   Discuss the three key features of the current exchange rate system.

The current world exchange rate system has three important features:

1.   The United States allows the dollar to float against other major currencies.
2.   Most countries in Western Europe have adopted a single currency, the **euro**.
3.   Some developing countries have tried to keep their currencies fixed against the dollar or other major currencies.

Over time, the value of the dollar fluctuates against other major currencies, increasing in value against some, and decreasing in value against others. In the short run, the two most important causes of exchange rate movements are interest rate changes and changes in investors' expectations about the future value of currencies.

In the long run, exchange rates move to the point where it is possible to buy the same amount of goods and services with an equivalent amount of currencies. This is the principle of **purchasing power parity**. If a good or service is cheaper in one country than in another country, consumers and firms will try to buy that good from the country with the lower price. That action will drive up the price of the cheaper country's currency, increasing the price of the good to the rest of the world. This will continue until there is no longer an advantage to buying the good in one country or another.

📖 Helpful Study Hint

Purchasing power parity should imply that:
The price of a good in Japan = exchange rate (¥/$) x the price of the good in the United States.
Or,
The price of a good in the United States = (1/exchange rate (¥/$)) x the price of the good in Japan, where (1/exchange rate (¥/$)) = exchange rate ($/¥).

Several complications may keep purchasing power parity from exactly holding, even in the long run:

- Not all goods are traded internationally. If the services of a plumber are more expensive in the United States than in the United Kingdom, after adjusting for exchange rates, homeowners will not go to the United Kingdom to hire a plumber to fix a clogged drain.
- Consumer preferences for products are different across countries.
- Countries impose barriers to trade. **Tariffs** and **quotas** limit the price adjustments of some goods.
- Shipping, storage, and insurance costs will also affect the foreign price of domestic goods. Consider goods that must be handled carefully (wine) or that must be kept refrigerated (frozen orange juice).

📖 Helpful Study Hint

A quota limits the amount of a good that can be imported.
A tariff is a tax imposed by the government on imports.

There are four main determinants of exchange rates in the long run:

- *Relative price levels*. Purchasing power parity is the most powerful long-run determinant of exchange rates.
- *Relative rates of productivity growth*. If Japanese productivity grows faster than U.S. productivity, then Japan should have relatively lower prices, causing the value of the yen to rise relative to the dollar.
- *Preference for domestic and foreign goods*. If consumers and firms in Japan prefer U.S. products to Japanese products, the demand for U.S. products will increase, which will increase the value of the U.S. dollar.
- *Tariffs and quotas*. A tariff or quota forces domestic manufacturers to buy more expensive domestic goods. Tariffs and quotas lead toward higher exchange rates.

A second aspect of the current exchange rate system is the introduction of a common currency, the **euro**, in most Western European countries. See Figure 18-2 on page 623 of the main text for a map showing the countries that have adopted the Euro. The European Central Bank (ECB) controls the quantity of euros. The ECB operates very similarly to the Federal Reserve System. A common currency can make it easier for consumers and firms to buy and sell goods across country borders. The increased ease of cross-border trade can aid in growth of the countries using the common currency. Potential drawbacks of using a common currency are that:

1. The participating countries can no longer undertake independent monetary policies.
2. An individual country's currency cannot change in value during a recession to stimulate aggregate demand.

A third important feature of the current exchange rate system is that some countries have attempted to keep their exchange rates fixed against the dollar or other major currencies. When a country keeps its exchange rate fixed compared to another country's currency, its currency is **pegged** to the other currency. With the exchange rate between countries fixed, business planning is much easier.

📖 Helpful Study Hint

> For instance, if the exchange rate is fixed, the interest on a loan from a U.S. bank to a business in Thailand that is repayable in dollars will always be a constant number of units of Thai currency (the baht). If the exchange rate changes, the loan payment will also change.

Because there is no guarantee that the market exchange rate will be the same as the pegged exchange rate, the government must be willing to buy its currency with dollars or buy dollars with its currency to maintain the exchange rate at the pegged rate. If a currency is pegged at a value above the market exchange rate, the currency is said to be overvalued. If the currency is pegged at a value below the exchange rate, the currency is said to be undervalued. The recent trend is for pegged exchange rate systems to be replaced with managed floating exchange rate systems. The textbook uses the case of Thai baht in the late 1990s to illustrate the problems that countries may encounter when they attempt to peg the value of their currencies. In textbook Figure 18-3, Thailand must buy their currency (the baht) to maintain the pegged exchange rate at $0.04.

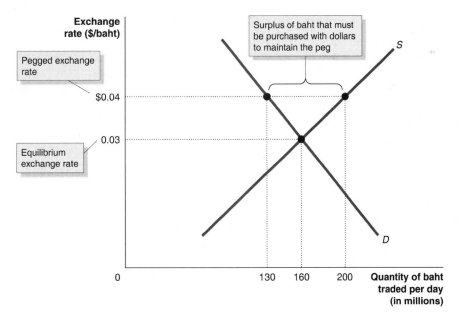

Pegging made it easier for Thai firms to export products to the United States and protected Thai firms that had taken out dollar loans. The Thai government ran into problems in 1997 when they had used up their dollar reserves buying their currency on the exchange market. The Thai government increased domestic interest rates in hopes of attracting dollars to increase the government's dollar reserves. The Thai government was afraid of the negative consequences of abandoning the peg even though it had led to the baht being overvalued.

The higher interest rates made it difficult for Thai firms and households to borrow, and domestic consumption and investment fell, pushing the economy into a recession. The high interest rates caused speculators to sell the baht in exchange for dollars in anticipation of a future lower exchange rate due to the Thai government's problems with maintaining the pegged rate. This destabilizing speculation is shown in textbook Figure 18-4 reproduced below.

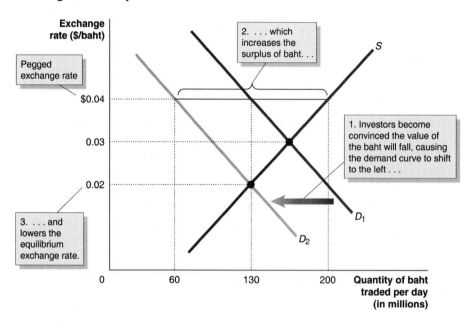

Foreign investors also began to sell off their investments and exchange baht for dollars. This capital flight forced the Bank of Thailand to run through its dollar reserves. In 1997 when the Thai government abandoned the peg and let the currency float, Thai firms that had to make loan payments in dollars discovered that the value of these payments in baht had increased. Many firms declared bankruptcy, which pushed the Thai economy deeper into recession. The fear that they might experience the same problems as Thailand caused other countries also to abandon their pegged currencies. As a result of these events, the number of pegged exchange rates has fallen dramatically. Most countries that have pegged exchange rates are small and trade only with one big country. Several Caribbean countries peg their currency to the dollar, and several African countries, because of their French background, peg their currency to the euro.

The Chinese yuan was pegged against the dollar in 1994 at 8.28 yuan to the dollar. The pegging against the dollar ensured Chinese exporters a stable dollar price for what they sell in the United States. For the Chinese government to maintain this pegged rate, it had to buy dollars with yuan. By 2005, the Chinese government had accumulated about $700 billion in U.S. dollars which were used to purchase U.S. Treasury Bonds. The Chinese government began to allow the yuan to float in 2005. By mid-2007, the exchange rate was about 7.62 yuan per dollar.

📖 Helpful Study Hint

There are four *Making the Connection* features in section 18.2. Here is a summary of each:

The Toronto Blue Jays Gain from the Rising Value of the Canadian Dollar

The Toronto Blue Jays must pay their baseball players in U.S. dollars. In addition, most of their away game expenses are in U.S. dollars. Because of the increasing value of the Canadian dollar, the currency in which the team generates revenues, the team has found that its expenses have been falling. Instead of having to make payroll payments of 125 million in Canadian dollars, the team had to only pay $90 million in Canadian dollars. In addition, because of the stronger Canadian dollar, attendance at spring training games increased 33 percent as more Canadians traveled to Florida to attend these games.

The Big Mac Theory of Exchange Rates

The *Economist* magazine has been using the price of a Big Mac to examine purchasing power parity. Under purchasing power parity, the price of a Big Mac should be the same in all countries after converting the price to a single currency using the exchange rate. So if Big Macs sell for an average of $3.22 in the United States and ¥280 in Japan, for purchasing power parity to hold, the exchange rate should be ¥280/$3.22 or ¥87 = $1.00. The actual exchange rate in early 2007 was ¥121 = $1.00, so in terms of Big Mac purchasing power, the yen was undervalued. It should have taken 28 percent fewer yen to buy a dollar than it actually did.

Was the Euro Undervalued or Overvalued in 2007?

It is difficult to determine if a currency is undervalued or overvalued. Stephen Jen of the investment firm Morgan Stanley tried to determine if the euro was undervalued or overvalued. The dollar has declined in value from 1.13 euros per dollar in 2002 to 0.74 euros per dollar in 2007. Jen studied economic variables that have been correlated with exchange rate movements in the past. He then used current values of these variables to determine if the euro was undervalued or overvalued. He concluded that the euro was overvalued.

Crisis and Recovery in South Korea

The South Korean government pegged the value of its currency, the won, in terms of U.S. dollars to make it easier for South Korean firms (like Hyundai) to trade with the United States and to protect firms that had taken out loans in dollars. Following the Thai government's decision to abandon the peg of its currency against the dollar, the South Korean government allowed the won to float in October 1997. South Korea had attempted to maintain the peg by increasing interest rates. This increase in interest rates reduced aggregate demand and pushed the economy into a severe recession. Unlike other East Asian countries, South Korea bounced back quickly. This is because of:

1.   A $21 billion loan from the International Monetary Fund that helped stabilize the won.
2.   The ability of South Korean firms to obtain financing through the stock and bond markets.
3.   The flexibility of its labor market that allowed wages to fall to offset the effects of the falling value of the won on profits.

Extra Solved Problem 18-2

Chapter 18 of the textbook includes two Solved Problems. Here is an extra Solved Problem to help you build your skills solving economic problems:

Purchasing Power Parity Exchange Rates

Supports Learning Objective 2: Discuss the three key features of the current exchange rate system.

At a leading U.S. Internet bookstore, *Harry Potter and the Half-Blood Prince* by J.K. Rowling sells for $16.99. The same book sells for £9.95 at a leading U.K. Internet bookstore. What is the implied purchasing power parity exchange rate? If the current exchange rate is £0.56 = $1, is the dollar overvalued or undervalued?

SOLVING THE PROBLEM

Step 1:   Review the chapter material.
This problem requires an understanding of exchange rates, so you may want to review the section "The Current Exchange Rate System," which begins on page 617 of the textbook.

Step 2:   Calculate the purchasing power parity exchange rate.
The purchasing power parity exchange rate is the exchange rate such that the good sells for an equivalent price in each country. We can calculate it from the equation:

Price in the United States = Exchange Rate ($/£) x price in the United Kingdom.

Using the U.S. price of $16.99 and the U.K. price of £9.95, the purchasing power parity exchange rate is calculated as:

Exchange rate (£/$) = Price in the United Kingdom/Price in the United States

$$= £9.95/$16.99 = £0.59/\$.$$

This implies that if the exchange rate were £0.59 = $1, then the Harry Potter book would sell for an equivalent price in both countries.

Step 3:   **Determine if the dollar is overvalued or undervalued at the current exchange rate of £0.56 = $1.**

The dollar is overvalued if the actual exchange rate (£/$) is greater than the implied purchasing power parity exchange rate. The dollar is undervalued if the actual exchange rate is less than the implied purchasing power parity exchange rate. Since the actual exchange rate of £0.56 = $1 is less than the implied exchange rate of £0.59 = $1, we would say the dollar is currently undervalued.

18.3 International Capital Markets (pages 631-632)

Learning Objective 3   Discuss the growth of international capital markets.

One important reason for exchange rate fluctuations is savers seeking the highest rate of return they can find anywhere in the world. To purchase foreign financial assets, savers must first purchase foreign currency, and when they sell foreign assets, they must purchase their home currency with the foreign currency in which the asset is denominated. Shares of stocks and long-term debt, both corporate and government, are bought and sold in capital markets. The largest capital markets are in the United States, Europe, and Japan. The three most important financial centers are in New York, London, and Tokyo. The use of world capital markets has helped increase growth in the world economy. Firms are no longer limited to domestic savings to help finance investment spending, and household savings can be used to purchase assets anywhere in the world.

In the 1990s, the flow of foreign funds into U.S. stocks and bonds – which is called portfolio investment – increased substantially. Investors in the United Kingdom accounted for more than 40 percent of all foreign purchases of U.S. stocks and bonds. Investors in China accounted for 10 percent, and investors in Japan accounted for 5 percent. Globalization of financial markets has helped increase growth and efficiency in the world economy. It is now possible for savings from around the world to move to the highest possible return anywhere.

Extra Solved Problem 18-3

Chapter 18 of the textbook includes two Solved Problems. Here is an extra Solved Problem to help you build your skills solving economic problems:

Buying a Foreign Bond

Supports Learning Objective 3: Discuss the growth of international capital markets.

The globalization of capital markets means that for individuals and firms the opportunities for purchasing foreign financial assets have significantly increased. Not only can someone save by buying domestic government bonds or stocks, but he or she can save by buying bonds and stocks issued by foreign corporations or foreign governments.

In December 2004, the exchange rate between the dollar and the pound was $1.93 = £1. In December 2005, the exchange rate between the dollar and the pound was $1.74 = £1. Suppose that in December 2004, a U.K resident paid $1,000 for a bond paying 5 percent interest issued by a U.S. corporation.

Assume that the bond will mature in one year, at which time the U.K. resident will be paid back the $1,000 value of the bond. What would the rate of return on this investment be for this year, taking into account the change in the dollar-pound exchange rate during 2005?

SOLVING THE PROBLEM

Step 1: **Review the chapter material.**

This problem requires an understanding of the current exchange rate system, so you may want to review the section "International Capital Markets," which begins on page 631 of the textbook.

Step 2: **Determine the price of the bond in the U.S.**

To buy the U.S. bond, the U.K. resident must first buy U.S. dollars. The cost of $1,000 at the December 2004 exchange rate would be

£518.13 ($1,000/ $1.93/£ = £518.13).

Step 3: **Determine the interest earned from holding the bond.**

Because the bond was issued by a U.S. corporation, it will pay interest in dollars. With a 5 percent interest rate, the interest income will be

0.05 x $1,000 = $50.

Step 4: **Determine the rate of return earned on the investment by the U.K. resident.**

After one year, the bond holder will receive the interest payment of $50 and the value of the bond of $1,000, or a total of $1,050. The U.K. resident can then convert this back to pounds at the December 2005 exchange rate of $1.74 = £1. This conversion will result in the investor receiving

$1,050/$1.74/£ = £603.45.

Thus, the rate of return the U.K. resident receives from investing in the bond is 16.5 percent:

(£603.45 − £518.13)/£518.13 = 0.165 or 16.5 percent).

The U.K. resident not only earned interest income from investing in the bond, but also gained from the increasing value of the dollar over that time period.

📖 Helpful Study Hint

Economics in YOUR Life! at the end of the chapter answers the question posed at the start of the chapter. If you were to work in Spain instead of the United States, and if Spain's productivity increases faster that the U.S.'s productivity, what would happen to the value of the money you had saved in euros in Spain? In this chapter, we see that if the productivity of firms in one country increases faster than the productivity of firms in another country, the value of the faster growing country's currency should, other things equal, increase against the slower growing country's currency. However, because Spain is only one of the 13 countries using the euro, the value of productivity increases in Spain on the value of the euro may not be large.

Key Terms

Bretton Woods System. An exchange rate system that lasted from 1944 to 1971, under which countries pledged to buy and sell their currencies at a fixed rate against the dollar.

Capital controls. Limits on the flow of foreign exchange and financial investment across countries.

Devaluation. A reduction in a fixed exchange rate.

Euro. The common currency of many European countries.

Exchange rate system. An agreement among countries on how exchange rates should be determined.

Fixed exchange rate system. A system under which countries agree to keep the exchange rates among their currencies fixed.

Floating currency. The outcome of a country allowing its currency's exchange rate to be determined by demand and supply.

International Monetary Fund (IMF). An international organization that provides foreign currency loans to central banks and oversees the operation of the international monetary system.

Managed float exchange rate system. The current exchange rate system under which the value of most currencies is determined by demand and supply, with occasional government intervention.

Pegging. The decision by a country to keep the exchange rate fixed between its currency and another currency.

Purchasing power parity. The theory that, in the long run, exchange rates move to equalize the purchasing power of different currencies.

Revaluation. An increase in a fixed exchange rate.

Quota. A limit on the quantity of a good that can be imported.

Tariff. A tax imposed by a government on imports.

Appendix

The Gold Standard and the Bretton Woods System (pages 639-645)

LEARNING OBJECTIVE: Explain the gold standard and the Bretton Woods system.

The Gold Standard (pages 641-642)

The gold standard was the basis of the exchange rate system from the early nineteenth century to the 1930s. Under the gold standard, each country's currency could be redeemed for a given quantity of gold. Therefore, exchange rates were determined by the relative amounts of gold in each country's currency. If there was one-fifth of an ounce of gold in a U.S. dollar and one ounce of gold in a British pound, the exchange rate would be $5.00 = £1.00. Under the gold standard, the quantity of money depended on the quantity of gold a country owned. Many countries abandoned the gold standard during the 1930s because under that system monetary expansion was limited by the quantity of gold and countries could not follow independent monetary policies. During the Great Depression of the 1930s, countries on the gold standard experienced larger declines in real GDP than did countries not on the gold standard.

The Bretton Woods System (pages 642-643)

After the collapse of the gold standard, a conference held in Bretton Woods, New Hampshire created an exchange rate system in which the United States agreed to buy and sell gold at a fixed price of $35 per ounce. The central banks of other countries agreed to buy and sell their currencies at a fixed rate against the dollar. Under this system, central banks were required to sell dollar reserves in exchange for domestic currency. If a central bank ran out of dollar reserves, it could borrow dollars from the newly created **International Monetary Fund**, which was designed to oversee the operations of the exchange rate system and approve adjustments to the agreed-on exchange rates.

Under the **Bretton Woods system**, a fixed exchange rate was called the par exchange rate. If the market exchange rate was different from the par exchange rate, the central bank would intervene in the market and buy or sell its country's currency in exchange for dollars. A persistent surplus or shortage of domestic currency was evidence of a fundamental disequilibrium (the par exchange rate was not equal to the equilibrium exchange rate) and required an adjustment in the par exchange rate. A reduction in the fixed exchange rate was referred to as a **devaluation** and an increase in the fixed exchange rate was a **revaluation**. A surplus of currency is shown in textbook Figure 18A-1 reproduced below. The graph shows that the par exchange rate of the pound against the dollar is higher than the equilibrium exchange rate. As a result, the Bank of England has to purchase pounds in exchange for dollars to maintain the exchange rate at the agreed upon level.

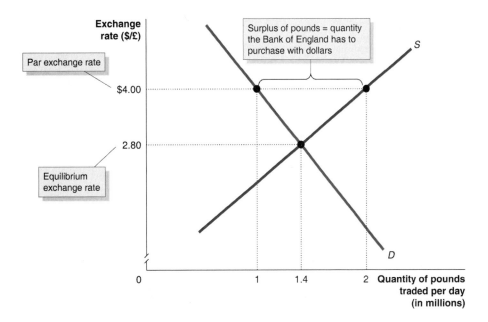

Textbook Figure 18A-2 reproduced below shows that the par exchange rate of the German deutsche mark against the dollar is lower than the equilibrium exchange, resulting in a surplus of U.S. dollars that the West German central bank must buy in exchange for marks to maintain the exchange rate.

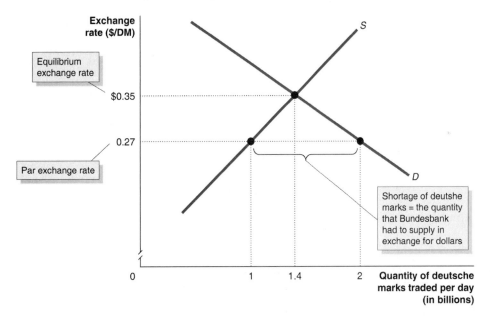

The Bretton Woods system began to collapse in the late 1960s when the dollar value of reserves held in other countries exceeded the value of the U.S. stock of gold, so that the United States would not be able to redeem dollars at the agreed on $35 per ounce price. In addition, some countries, particularly West Germany, were reluctant to devalue their currencies when faced with a fundamental disequilibrium. In August 1971, President Nixon decided to abandon the U.S. commitment to redeem dollars for gold. By 1973, the Bretton Woods system was effectively finished and was replaced by the current exchange rate system of floating rates.

Key Terms – Appendix

Bretton Woods System. An exchange rate system that lasted from 1944 to 1971, under which countries pledged to buy and sell their currencies at a fixed rate against the dollar.

Capital controls. Limits on the flow of foreign exchange and financial investment across countries.

Devaluation. A reduction in a fixed exchange rate.

International Monetary Fund (IMF). An international organization that provides foreign currency loans to central banks and oversees the operation of the international monetary system.

Revaluation. An increase in a fixed exchange rate.

Self-Test

(Answers are provided at the end of the Self-Test.)

Multiple-Choice Questions

1. A country that allows demand and supply to determine the value of its currency is said to have
   a. a pegged exchange rate.
   b. a fixed exchange rate system.
   c. a managed float exchange rate system.
   d. a floating currency.

2. An agreement among countries on how exchange rates should be determined is called
   a. an exchange rate system.
   b. a fixed exchange rate mechanism.
   c. an integrated exchange rate approach.
   d. a Bretton Woods solution.

3. Which of the following happens in a managed float exchange rate system?
   a. Countries agree to keep the value of their currencies constant.
   b. Countries agree not to intervene in foreign exchange markets.
   c. Countries will occasionally intervene to buy and sell their currency or other currencies in order to affect exchange rates.
   d. Countries allow their currencies' exchange rates to be determined solely by demand and supply.

4. When countries agree to keep the value of their currencies constant, there is
   a. a fixed exchange rate system.
   b. a managed float exchange rate system.
   c. no exchange rate system.
   d. exchange rate integration.

5. The theory of purchasing power parity states that, in the long run
   a. exchange rates move to equalize the purchasing power of different currencies.
   b. exchange rates are determined by movements in interest rates.
   c. exchange rates are determined by changes in investors' expectations about the future values of currencies.
   d. all of the above

6. According to purchasing power parity
   a. inflation rates should be the same in all countries.
   b. exchange rates move to equalize the purchasing power of different currencies.
   c. exchange rates will not change.
   d. countries can gain from trading.

7. Which of the following is *not* a reason why purchasing power parity is not a complete explanation of exchange rates?
   a. Not all products can be traded internationally.
   b. Products and consumer preferences are different across countries.
   c. Countries have different wage rates.
   d. Countries impose barriers to trade.

8. Which of the following facts keeps purchasing power parity from being a complete explanation of exchange rates?
   a. The fact that all products are traded internationally.
   b. The fact that products and consumer preferences are different across countries.
   c. The fact that most countries don't have any barriers to trade.
   d. All of the above

9. A quota is
   a. a limit on the quantity of a good that can be imported.
   b. an agreement to voluntarily restrain the quantity of goods that a country may import into another country.
   c. a tax on imported goods.
   d. a tax on exported goods.

10. In June 2005, a Big Mac sold for 6,000 pesos in Colombia and $3.00 in the United States. The exchange rate in June 2005 was 2,300 pesos per dollar. So, on Big Mac purchasing power parity grounds, the Colombian peso was
    a. undervalued against the dollar.
    b. overvalued against the dollar.
    c. neither overvalued nor undervalued. Purchasing power parity between the Colombian peso and the dollar held.
    d. devalued against the dollar.

11. If prices in Colombia have risen faster on average than prices in the United States, while prices in Japan have risen more slowly, it must be true that in the long run the U.S. dollar has _____ value against the Colombian peso, and _____ value against the Japanese yen.
    a. gained; lost
    b. lost; gained
    c. maintained; gained
    d. gained; maintained

12. If the average productivity of Colombian firms increases faster than the average productivity of U.S. firms, then
    a. Colombian products will become relatively more expensive than U.S. products.
    b. the demand for Colombian products will fall relative to U.S. products.
    c. the value of the Colombian peso should rise against the dollar.
    d. All of the above

13. If consumers in the United States increase their demand for Colombian coffee, the result will be to
    a. decrease the value of the Colombian peso relative to the dollar.
    b. increase the value of the Colombian peso relative to the dollar.
    c. have no effect on the value of the Colombian peso relative to the dollar.
    d. increase the demand for dollars.

14. The euro
    a. is the currency of all European countries.
    b. is used only in France, Italy, Spain, and Germany.
    c. has the same dollar value as a British pound.
    d. is controlled by the European Central bank (ECB).

15. Which of the following statements is *not* correct about the creation of the euro?
    a. The euro will help economic growth in the EU countries by making it easier for consumers and firms to buy and sell across borders.
    b. The euro will reduce costs and increase competition.
    c. The euro will increase the ability of participating countries to run independent monetary policies.
    d. The euro is used as currency in Germany, France, and Italy among other countries.

16. When the value of a currency falls, the prices of imports _____. If imports are a significant fraction of the goods consumers buy, this fall in the value of the currency may significantly _____ the inflation rate.
    a. rise; increase
    b. rise; decrease
    c. fall; increase
    d. fall; decrease

17. Pegging refers to the decision by a country to
    a. share the same currency with another country, such as the decision of EU countries to adopt the euro.
    b. allow two currencies to circulate simultaneously within the country.
    c. keep the exchange rate fixed between its currency and another currency.
    d. share the same fiscal policy with one or more countries.

18. When currency traders become convinced that countries will have to abandon their pegged exchange rates, a wave of selling of these countries' currencies may occur. These waves of selling are sometimes referred to as
    a. speculative attacks.
    b. arbitrage.
    c. hedging.
    d. currency blitzes.

19. The trend in pegging has been toward
    a. replacing fixed exchange rates with pegged exchange rates.
    b. replacing managed floating exchange rates with pegged exchange rates.
    c. replacing pegged exchange rates with managed floating exchange rates.
    d. replacing pegged exchange rates with fixed exchange rates.

20. China has pegged its exchange rate with the U.S. dollar at a rate (in terms of yuan per dollar) above the equilibrium exchange rate. We can conclude that
    a. the Chinese Central bank must sell dollars to maintain this rate.
    b. the yuan is undervalued.
    c. Chinese exports to the United States and imports from the United States will be equal.
    d. the Chinese Central bank must buy yuan to maintain this rate.

21. Like other countries that underwent an exchange rate crisis, South Korea had attempted to maintain the value of the won by _____ domestic interest rates. The result was a sharp _____ in aggregate demand and a severe _____.
    a. lowering; increase; inflation
    b. raising; decline; recession
    c. lowering; decrease; deflation
    d. raising; increase; recession

22. If Chinese savers increase their demand for U.S. Treasury bills, the demand for dollars will _____, and the value of the dollar will _____.
    a. increase; rise
    b. increase; fall
    c. decrease; rise
    d. decrease; fall

23. Shares of stock and long-term debt, including corporate and government bonds and bank loans, are bought and sold in
    a. capital markets.
    b. money markets.
    c. investment markets.
    d. foreign exchange markets.

24. In the 1980s and 1990s, European governments _____ many restrictions on foreign investments in financial markets. Then, U.S. and other foreign investors _____ investments in Europe and European investors _____ investments in foreign markets.
    a. removed; increased; increased
    b. imposed; decreased; decreased
    c. removed; increased; decreased
    d. imposed; decreased; increased

25. Today, the U.S. capital market is
    a. larger than all of the foreign capital markets combined.
    b. smaller than any of the capital markets operating in Europe and Japan.
    c. smaller than the markets operating in Europe and Japan but larger than the markets operating in Latin America and East Asia.
    d. large, but there are also large capital markets operating in Europe and Japan and somewhat smaller markets operating in Latin America and East Asia.

26. The three most important international financial centers today are
    a. Zurich, Paris, and Montreal.
    b. New York, London, and Tokyo.
    c. Seoul, Moscow, and Buenos Aires.
    d. Los Angeles, London, and Shanghai.

27. By 2007, corporations, banks, and governments had raised more than _____ in funds on global financial markets.
    a. $1 billion
    b. $10 billion
    c. $100 billion
    d. $1 trillion

28. During the 1990s, the flow of foreign funds into U.S. stocks and bonds
    a. increased dramatically.
    b. decreased substantially.
    c. remained fairly stable.
    d. was practically nonexistent.

29. Which of the following statements about foreign purchases of U.S. stocks and bonds is correct?
    a. Since 1995, there has been a large rise in foreign purchases of bonds issued by U.S. corporations and by the federal government.
    b. Falling stock prices in the United States caused a fall in foreign ownership of corporate stocks between 2001 and 2006.
    c. Foreign investment in stocks and bonds in 2006 was more than twice as great as it was in 1995.
    d. All of the above

30. Which of the following reflects the distribution of foreign purchases of U.S. stocks and bonds?
    a. Investors in the United Kingdom accounted for more than 40 percent of all foreign purchases of U.S. stocks and bonds.
    b. Investors in Japan, China, and other Asian countries accounted for 25 percent of all foreign purchases of U.S. stocks and bonds.
    c. Investors from European countries other than the United Kingdom accounted for 11 percent of all foreign purchases of U.S. stocks and bonds.
    d. All of the above

31. The globalization of financial markets has helped to
    a. increase growth and efficiency in the world economy.
    b. allow for the savings of investors around the world to be channeled to the best investments available.
    c. allow firms in nearly every country to tap into the savings of investors around the world in order to find the funds needed for expansion.
    d. All of the above

32. Under the gold standard, the central bank
    a. has substantial control over the money supply and a highly effective way of conducting monetary policy.
    b. lacks the control of the money supply necessary to pursue an active monetary policy.
    c. has control of monetary policy, but not of fiscal policy.
    d. can manipulate the economy in precise ways by adjusting its supply of gold.

33. Which of the following periods marks the collapse of the gold standard?
    a. The 1930s
    b. The 1920s
    c. The 1940s
    d. The 1970s

34. A tariff is
    a. a limit on the quantity of goods that a country may import into another country.
    b. an agreement to voluntarily restrain the quantity of goods that a country may import into another country.
    c. a tax on imported goods.
    d. a tax on exported goods.

35. The Bretton Woods System was
    a. an agreement between participating countries to reduce trade barriers.
    b. an agreement in which central banks pledged to buy and sell their currencies at a fixed rate against the dollar.
    c. an agreement in which the exchange rate between two currencies was automatically determined by the quantity of gold in each currency.
    d. an agreement by countries to go off the gold standard to allow their central banks to expand the money supply and pay for war expenditures.

36. The International Monetary Fund (IMF) is an organization that
    a. provides foreign currency loans to central banks.
    b. oversees the operation of the international monetary system.
    c. approves adjustments to agreements regarding fixed exchange rates.
    d. All of the above

37. Under the Bretton Woods System, if the par exchange rate was above equilibrium, the result would be
    a. a shortage of domestic currency in the foreign exchange market.
    b. a surplus of domestic currency in the foreign exchange market.
    c. a shift to the left of the demand curve for domestic currency.
    d. a shift to the right of the demand curve for domestic currency.

38. Which of the following is *not* a determinant of the exchange rate in the long run?
    a. relative price levels
    b. rates of productivity growth
    c. tariffs and quotas
    d. population growth rates

39. In a fixed exchange rate system, when the par exchange rate is above the equilibrium exchange rate, the central bank must
    a. use its own currency to buy foreign currency.
    b. use foreign currency to buy its own currency.
    c. expand the domestic money supply to drive down interest rates.
    d. be willing in the short run to accept a lower unemployment rate at the expense of a higher inflation rate.

40. A reduction of a fixed exchange rate is a(n) _____, and an increase in a fixed exchange rate is a(n) _____.
    a. appreciation; depreciation
    b. depreciation; appreciation
    c. revaluation; devaluation
    d. devaluation; revaluation

41. Which of the following factors contributed to the collapse of the Bretton Woods system?
    a. After 1963, the total number of dollars held by foreign central banks was larger than the gold reserves of the United States.
    b. The credibility of the U.S. promise to redeem dollars for gold was called into question.
    c. Some countries with undervalued currencies, particularly West Germany, were unwilling to revalue their currencies.
    d. All of the above

42. Refer to the market for Deutsche marks in a fixed exchange rate system. Suppose that the par exchange rate is below the equilibrium exchange rate. In this situation, the quantity of Deutsche marks demanded is _____ than the quantity of Deutsche marks supplied. To maintain the exchange rate at par, the Bundesbank would have to _____ dollars and _____ Deutsche marks.
    a. greater; buy; sell
    b. greater; sell; buy
    c. less; buy; sell
    d. less; sell; buy

43. Capital controls are
    a. requirements that force countries with undervalued currencies to revalue their currencies.
    b. limits on the flow of foreign exchange and financial wealth across countries.
    c. measures that allow countries to adjust their exchange rates when evidence of a fundamental disequilibrium in that country's exchange rate exists.
    d. All of the above.

44. Actions by investors that make it more difficult for a central bank to maintain a fixed exchange rate are referred to as
    a. a fundamental disequilibrium.
    b. a panic run.
    c. an exchange rate market bubble.
    d. destabilizing speculation.

45. Among the important aspects of the exchange rate system today is that
    a. the United States allows the dollar to float against other major currencies (with some intervention by central banks).
    b. many countries in Western Europe have adopted a single currency, the euro.
    c. some developing countries have attempted to keep their currency's exchange rate fixed against the dollar, or against another major currency.
    d. All of the above

Short Answer Questions

1. What is the difference between a floating and managed exchange rate system?

   _____

   _____

   _____

   _____

   _____

2. Based on purchasing power parity, how much should a Bob Dylan DVD, which costs $18.99 in the United States, cost in London if the pound exchange rate is £0.56 = $1?

   _____

   _____

   _____

3. Ignoring transportation costs, suppose that we discover that the price of the Bob Dylan DVD (in Question 2) is £8.97. How is it possible to earn a profit buying and selling the DVD? How will this action lead to the elimination of the profits? How would the answer be different if we did not ignore transportation costs? (Prices from amazon.com and amazon.com.uk)

   _____

   _____

   _____

   _____

4. Suppose that in 2008, the U.S. inflation rate was 2.7 percent and the Canadian inflation rate was 1.8 percent. Based upon this, other things equal, would we expect the dollar to appreciate or depreciate relative to the Canadian dollar?

   _____

   _____

   _____

   _____

5. The interest payment of a business loan from a U.S. bank to a firm in Thailand is $100,000 per year. How will the interest rate payments change if the exchange rate changes from 25 baht = $1 to 30 baht = $1?

_____

_____

_____

_____

6. When we buy bonds in other countries, it is necessary to think not only about the exchange rate now, because we need to buy foreign currency in order to purchase the bond, but also the exchange rate when the bond matures, when we would want to convert the end value back into our currency. Suppose the current price of a U.K. bond is £960, and the bond has a face value of £1,000. Suppose that the exchange rate is $2.08 = £1, and we expect the exchange rate to change to $2.10 = £1 at the time the bond matures in one year. Based upon this, what would be the interest rate on the bond?

_____

_____

_____

_____

True/False Questions

T F 1. A floating currency's exchange rate is determined by the demand and supply of the currency.

T F 2. In a managed float exchange rate system, the exchange rate is determined by the demand and supply of the currency.

T F 3. The gold standard is a fixed exchange rate system.

T F 4. The value of the U.S. dollar is fixed against most other major currencies.

T F 5. Purchasing power parity implies that a good that costs $5 will cost ¥5 in Japan.

T F 6. Purchasing power parity implies that in the long run, exchange rates are determined by relative real GDP growth.

T F 7. Because some goods are not traded internationally, purchasing power parity may not hold for those goods.

T F 8. Tariffs and quotas may keep purchasing power parity from holding for all goods.

T F 9. Suppose that based upon Big Mac prices, the implied exchange rate between the yen and the dollar is ¥85 = $1, and the actual exchange rate is ¥120 = $1. We can conclude that the yen is undervalued against the dollar.

T F 10. If people in Japan increase their preferences for U.S. goods, this will increase the demand for dollars and cause the yen to increase in value.

T F 11. The euro exchange rate is determined by the European Central Bank.

T F 12. The euro makes it easier for consumers and firms to buy and sell goods between countries that use the euro.

T F 13. A fixed exchange rate makes business planning more difficult.

T F 14. To peg a country's exchange rate, the country's government must buy or sell its currency to keep its price (the exchange rate) at the pegged rate.

T F 15. In international capital markets, savers buy and sell bonds and stocks only from their own country.

Answers to the Self-Test

Multiple-Choice Questions

Question	Answer	Comment
1	d	A country that allows demand and supply to determine the value of its currency is said to have a floating currency.
2	a	When countries can agree on how exchange rates should be determined, economists say that there is an exchange rate system.
3	c	In a managed float exchange rate system, countries will occasionally intervene to buy and sell their currencies or other currencies in order to affect exchange rates.
4	a	When countries agree to keep the value of their currencies constant, they are using a fixed exchange rate system.
5	a	It seems reasonable that, in the long run, exchange rates should be at a level that makes it possible to buy the same amount of goods and services with the equivalent amount of any country's currency. In other words, the purchasing power of every country's currency should be the same. The idea that, in the long run, exchange rates move to equalize the purchasing power of different currencies is referred to as the theory of purchasing power parity.
6	b	Purchasing power parity says that exchange rates should adjust so that goods cost the same amount in different currencies. If this is not true, people will purchase the cheaper good, and that extra demand will drive the prices to similar levels.
7	c	Exchange rates adjust for differences in wages, so differences in wages will not affect purchasing power parity.
8	b	The three factors that keep purchasing power parity from being a complete explanation of exchange rates are: 1) the fact that most products are not traded internationally, 2) products and consumer preferences are different across countries, and 3) countries impose barriers to trade.
9	a	A quota is a limit on the quantity of a good that can be imported. For instance, the United States has a quota on imports of sugar. As a result, the price of sugar in the United States is much higher than the price of sugar in other countries. Economists have estimated that the price of sugar in the U.S. is about three times what it would be without the quota.

10	a	If a Big Mac sold for 6,000 pesos in Colombia and $3.00 in the United States, for purchasing power parity to hold, the exchange rate should have been 6,000/$3.00, or 2,000 pesos = $1. The actual exchange rate in June 2005 was 2,300 pesos = $1. So, on Big Mac purchasing power parity grounds, the Colombian peso was *undervalued* against the dollar by 13 percent (((2,300 − 2,000)/2,300) x 100 = 13 percent).
11	a	If prices in Colombia have risen faster on average than prices in the United States, while prices in Japan have risen more slowly, this difference in inflation rates is a key reason why the U.S. dollar would have gained value against the Colombian peso, while losing value against the Japanese yen.
12	c	If the average productivity of Colombian firms increases faster than the average productivity of U.S. firms, Colombian products will become relatively less expensive than U.S. products, which increases the demand for Colombian products relative to U.S. products. The value of the Colombian peso should rise against the dollar.
13	b	If consumers in the U.S. increase their preferences for Colombian products, the demand for pesos will increase relative to the demand for dollars, and the Colombian peso will increase in value relative to the U.S. dollar.
14	d	Not all European countries use the euro. The euro is issued and controlled by the European Central Bank.
15	c	The statement is incorrect. The creation of the euro will help growth in the EU countries. Having a common currency makes it easier for consumers and firms to buy and sell across borders. This change should reduce costs and increase competition. However, the participating countries are no longer able to run independent monetary policies. And with fixed exchange rates, the value of one country's currency cannot fall during a recession, thereby expanding net exports to help revive aggregate demand.
16	a	When the value of a currency falls, the prices of imports rise. If imports are a significant fraction of the goods consumers buy, a fall in the value of the currency may significantly increase the inflation rate.
17	c	Pegging is the decision by a country to keep the exchange rate fixed between its currency and another currency.
18	a	As the textbook describes the destabilizing speculation against the Thai baht, many currency traders became convinced that East Asian countries, such as South Korea, Indonesia, and Malaysia, would have to follow Thailand and abandon their pegged exchange rates. The result was a wave of speculative selling of these countries' currencies. These waves of selling are sometimes referred to as speculative attacks.
19	c	Following the disastrous experience of the East Asian countries, the number of countries with pegged exchange rates declined sharply. Overall, the trend has been toward replacing pegged exchange rates with managed floating exchange rates.
20	b	Because the Chinese central bank is keeping the exchange rate too high, the yuan is considered to be undervalued.
21	b	Like other countries that underwent an exchange rate crisis, South Korea had attempted to maintain the value of the won by raising domestic interest rates. The result was a sharp decline in aggregate demand and a severe recession. However, unlike other East Asian countries—particularly Thailand and Indonesia—that made only slow progress in recovering from exchange rate crises, South Korea bounced back rapidly.

22	a	We have seen that a key reason that exchange rates fluctuate is that in the current economy, investors seek out the best investments they can find anywhere in the world. For instance, if Chinese investors increase their demand for U.S. Treasury bills, the demand for dollars will increase, and the value of the dollar will rise.
23	a	Shares of stock and long-term debt, including corporate and government bonds and bank loans, are bought and sold in *capital markets*.
24	a	In the 1980s and 1990s, European governments removed many restrictions on foreign investments in financial markets. It became possible for U.S. and other foreign investors to freely invest in Europe and for European investors to freely invest in foreign markets.
25	d	At one time, the U.S. capital market was larger than all foreign capital markets combined, but this is no longer true. Today, there are large capital markets operating in Europe and Japan and somewhat smaller markets operating in Latin America and East Asia.
26	b	The three most important international financial centers today are New York, London, and Tokyo. Each day the front page of the on-line version of the Wall Street Journal displays not just the Dow Jones Industrial Average and the Standard and Poor's 500 stock indexes of U.S. stocks, but also the Nikkei 225 average of Japanese stocks and the Euro STOXX 50 index of European stocks.
27	d	By 2007, corporations, banks, and governments raised more than $1 trillion in funds on global financial markets.
28	a	During the 1990s, the flow of foreign funds into U.S. stocks and bonds – or portfolio investments – increased dramatically. As Figure 18-5 shows, since 1995, there has been a dramatic increase in foreign purchases of bonds issued by corporations and by the federal government.
29	d	Since 1995, there has been a large rise in foreign purchases of bonds issued by U.S. corporations and by the federal government. Even though falling stock prices in the United States caused a fall in foreign ownership of corporate stocks between 2001 and 2006, foreign investment in these securities was still more than twice as great as it was in 1995.
30	d	As shown in Figure 18-6 on page 632 of the textbook, the percentages given in a., b., and c. are all correct.
31	d	The globalization of financial markets has helped increase growth and efficiency in the world economy. It is now possible for the savings of investors around the world to be channeled to the best investments available. It also possible for firms in nearly every country to tap the savings of investors around the world to gain the funds needed for expansion. Firms no longer are forced to rely only on the savings of domestic investors to finance investment.
32	b	Under the gold standard, the central bank cannot determine how much gold will be discovered. It therefore lacks the control of the money supply necessary to pursue an active monetary policy. If the gold standard is adhered to in foreign exchange markets with a fixed exchange rate, the problem becomes worse as pressures on the exchange rate can cause gold inflows and outflows, further weakening the central bank's control of the money supply.
33	a	In 1931, Great Britain became the first major country to abandon the gold standard. A number of other countries also went off the gold standard that year. The United States remained on the gold standard until 1933, and a few countries, including France, Italy, and Belgium, stayed on even longer. By the late 1930s, the gold standard had collapsed.

34	c	A tariff is a tax on imported goods. The United States started the tariff wars in June 1930 by enacting the Smoot-Hawley Tariff, which raised the average U.S. tariff rate to more than 50 percent. Many other countries raised tariffs during the next few years, leading to a collapse in world trade and contributing to the severity of the Great Depression.
35	b	A conference held in Bretton Woods, New Hampshire in 1944 set up a system in which the United States pledged to buy or sell gold at a fixed price of $35 per ounce. The central banks of all other members of the new Bretton Woods System pledged to buy and sell their currencies at a fixed rate against the dollar.
36	d	Under the Bretton Woods System, central banks were committed to selling dollars in exchange for their own currencies. This commitment required them to hold dollar reserves. If a central bank ran out of dollar reserves, it could borrow them from the newly created International Monetary Fund (IMF). The IMF is an international organization that provides foreign currency loans to central banks and oversees the operation of the international monetary system. In addition to providing loans to central banks that were short of dollar reserves, the IMF would oversee the operation of the system and approve adjustments to the agreed on fixed exchange rates.
37	b	Under the Bretton Woods System, central banks were obligated to defend par exchange rates by buying and selling their countries' currencies at fixed rates against the dollar. If the par exchange rate was above equilibrium, the result would be a surplus of domestic currency in the foreign exchange market. If the par exchange rate was below equilibrium, the result would be a shortage of domestic currency.
38	d	Population growth rates will influence output growth, but will have no direct effect on exchange rates in the long run.
39	b	In the textbook example, the quantity of pounds demanded by people wanting to buy British goods and services or wanting to purchase British assets is smaller than the quantity of pounds supplied by people who would like to exchange them for dollars. As a result, the Bank of England must use dollars to buy the surplus of £1 million per day.
40	d	In the early years of the Bretton Woods System, many countries found that their currencies were *overvalued* versus the dollar, meaning that their par exchange rates were too high. A reduction of a fixed exchange rate is a devaluation; and an increase in a fixed exchange rate is a revaluation. In 1949, there was a devaluation of several currencies, including the British pound, reflecting the fact that those currencies had been overvalued against the dollar.
41	d	All of the factors above contributed to the collapse of the Bretton Woods system.

42	a	Under the Bretton Woods System, the Bundesbank, the German central bank, was required to buy and sell Deutsche marks for dollars at a rate of $0.27 per Deutsche mark. The equilibrium that would have prevailed in the foreign exchange market if the Bundesbank did not intervene was about $0.35 per Deutsche mark. Because the par exchange rate was below the equilibrium exchange rate, the quantity of Deutsche marks demanded by people wanting to buy German goods and services, or wanting to invest in German assets, was greater than the quantity of Deutsche marks supplied by people who wanted to exchange them for dollars. To maintain the exchange rate at a par of $0.27 per Deutsche mark, the Bundesbank had to buy dollars and sell Deutsche marks. The amount of Deutsche marks supplied by the Bundesbank was equal to the shortage of Deutsche marks at the par exchange rate.
43	b	During the 1960s, most European countries, including Germany, relaxed their capital controls. Capital controls are limits on the flow of foreign exchange and financial investment across countries. The loosening of capital controls made it easier for investors to speculate on changes in exchange rates.
44	d	In the Bretton Woods System, an increased demand for a given currency by investors hoping to make a profit from an expected revaluation will increase demand for the currency. Because of this expectation, the central bank has to increase the quantity it supplies in exchange for dollars, raising the risk of inflation. Because these actions by investors make it more difficult to maintain a fixed exchange rate, they are referred to as *destabilizing speculation*.
45	d	All of the above are important aspects of the exchange rate system today.

Short Answer Responses

1. A floating exchange rate is determined by the demand and supply of one currency compared to another currency. A change in supply and/or demand, caused by such events as interest rate changes or price changes, will change the exchange rate. In a managed floating exchange rate system, the government may decide that the exchange rate change is not in the country's best interests, and decide to offset the change in the exchange rate. To do this, the government must intervene in the foreign exchange market. For instance, if the ¥/$ exchange rate rose from ¥120/$ to ¥130/$ and the Bank of Japan wanted to return the rate to the ¥120/$ level, they might do so by reducing the demand for dollars (by tariffs or quotas) or by increasing the supply of dollars by buying yen with U.S. dollars.

2. According to purchasing power parity, adjusted for exchange rates, traded goods should cost the same in all countries. Therefore the Bob Dylan DVD which costs $18.99 in the U.S. should cost $18.99 x £0.56/$ = £10.63.

3. You could take $16.02 and exchange that dollar amount for £8.97, which is enough to buy the DVD in London. You could then sell the DVD in the United States for $18.99, giving you a profit of $2.97. If you exchanged enough dollars for pounds to buy one million DVDs in London, you would make a profit of $2.97 million. Unfortunately, as you continued to exchange dollars for pounds, you would drive up the value of the pound until the exchange rate reached the point where you would no longer make a profit. Transportation costs will also eat up part, or maybe all, of your profit. For instance, if it costs $3.00 to ship the British DVD to the United States, all of your potential profit would be eliminated.

4. Because prices are rising relatively slower in Canada, goods and services should be increasing in price relatively slower in Canada, which will increase the demand for Canadian goods relative to the (more expensive) U.S. goods. As a result, there will be an increase in the supply of U.S. dollars in

exchange for Canadian dollars and a decrease in demand for U.S. dollars (by Canadians who will not be buying as many of the more expensive U.S. goods). This will cause the U.S. dollar to depreciate (the Canadian dollar will appreciate).

5. Exchange rate changes can provide considerable uncertainty in day-to-day business operations. If a firm in Thailand borrows from a U.S. bank and has a $100,000 per year interest payment, that payment is fixed in dollars. The price to the firm depends upon the exchange rate. If the exchange rate is 25 baht = $1, then the interest payment will be 2,500,000 baht, but if the exchange rate were to rise to 30 baht = $1, then the same fixed dollar interest payment would rise to 3,000,000 baht. Note that if the Thai firm sells products in the U.S., the exchange rate change will also change the firm's revenues. This will not happen if the firm sells products only in Thailand.

6. If the exchange rate is $2.08 = £1, to purchase the U.K. bond, the U.S. price would be $1,996.80 (= $2.08/£ x £960 = $1,996.80). When the bond matured in one year the £1,000 be worth $2,080 (= £1,000 x $2.08/£ = $2,080). Based on this, the interest rate on the bond would be 4.17 percent (= 100 x ($2,080 − $1,996.80)/$1,996.80 = 4.17 percent). Now if the exchange rate was $2.10 = £1 when the bond matured, the £1,000 would be worth $2,100 (= $2.10/£ x £1,000 = $2,100) and the interest rate would be 5.17 percent (= 100 x ($2,100 − $1,996.80)/$1,996.80 = 5.17 percent).

True/False Answers

1.	T	
2.	F	The managed float exchange rate system's exchange rate is determined by demand and supply but with occasional government intervention.
3.	T	
4.	F	The dollar is a floating currency.
5.	F	The good will cost $5 x (exchange rate (¥/$)), so if the exchange rate were ¥120 = $1, then the good should cost ¥600.
6.	F	Actually, purchasing power parity implies that exchange rates will change to equalize purchasing power across countries.
7.	T	
8.	T	
9.	T	
10.	F	If people in Japan increase their preferences for U.S. goods, this will increase the demand for dollars and cause the yen to decrease in value (or the dollar to increase in value).
11.	F	The euro is a floating currency.
12.	T	
13.	F	A fixed exchange rate eliminates a source of uncertainty. See Short Answer Question 5. above.
14.	T	
15.	F	In international capital markets, savers may buy and sell bonds and stocks from many different countries.